Payroll Accounting 2024

Payroll Accounting 2024

Tenth Edition

Jeanette M. Landin, Ed.D., M.B.A.
Landmark College

Paulette Schirmer, D.B.A., M.B.A.
University of Alaska Southeast

PAYROLL ACCOUNTING 2024, TENTH EDITION

Published by McGraw Hill LLC, 1325 Avenue of the Americas, New York, NY 10019. Copyright ©2024 by McGraw Hill LLC. All rights reserved. Printed in the United States of America. Previous editions ©2023, 2022, and 2021. No part of this publication may be reproduced or distributed in any form or by any means, or stored in a database or retrieval system, without the prior written consent of McGraw Hill LLC, including, but not limited to, in any network or other electronic storage or transmission, or broadcast for distance learning.

Some ancillaries, including electronic and print components, may not be available to customers outside the United States.

This book is printed on acid-free paper.

1 2 3 4 5 6 7 8 9 LWI 27 26 25 24 23

ISBN 978-1-264-44346-8 (bound edition)
MHID 1-264-44346-3 (bound edition)
ISBN 978-1-266-84437-9 (loose-leaf edition)
MHID 1-266-84437-6 (loose-leaf edition)
ISSN 2373-2644

Portfolio Manager: *Steve Schuetz*
Product Developer: *Amanda Lam*
Marketing Manager: *Lindsay Wolfsmith*
Content Project Managers: *Jill Eccher; Brian Nacik*
Manufacturing Project Manager: *Laura Fuller*
Content Licensing Specialist: *Sarah Flynn*
Cover Image: *Chombosan/Shutterstock*
Compositor: *Straive*

All credits appearing on page or at the end of the book are considered to be an extension of the copyright page.

The Internet addresses listed in the text were accurate at the time of publication. The inclusion of a website does not indicate an endorsement by the authors or McGraw Hill LLC, and McGraw Hill LLC does not guarantee the accuracy of the information presented at these sites.

mheducation.com/highered

About the Authors

©Tom Raffelt

Jeanette Landin
Landmark College

Jeanette Landin is an associate professor of professional studies at Landmark College in Putney, Vermont, where she teaches undergraduate accounting and business courses to an at-risk student population. She is a baccalaureate student advisor and is the program coordinator for both associate's and bachelor's level degrees offered by the school of Professional Studies. Dr. Landin earned her B.A. degree from the University of California at Irvine before receiving her M.B.A. and Ed.D. from the University of Phoenix, where she researched college success strategies for at-risk students. She has earned master's certificates in accounting and autism spectrum disorders.

Dr. Landin is an active member of the Institute for Management Accountants (IMA), the American Accounting Association, Teachers of Accounting at Two-Year Colleges (TACTYC), the Society for Human Resource Management (SHRM), Association of Certified Fraud Examiners (ACFE), and Vermont Women in Higher Education (VWHE) and a Fellow with the International Society for Development and Sustainability. She previously served as an active member of the California Business Educators Association and the Western Business Educators Association. Dr. Landin has served as the IMA's Committee for Academic Relations chair and as a peer reviewer for the American Accounting Association. She is a peer reviewer for the *Transnational Journal of Business* and the associate editor for accounting with the Multimedia Educational Resource for Learning and Online Teaching (MERLOT).

©Ryan Kauzlarich

Paulette Schirmer
University of Alaska Southeast

Paulette Schirmer is an assistant professor of accounting with the University of Alaska Southeast for its accounting courses. She received her B.S. in accounting from Metropolitan State College of Denver (now Metropolitan State University of Denver), her M.B.A. from Regis University, and her D.B.A. from the University of Phoenix, where she researched globalization strategies for small businesses.

Dr. Schirmer was also recently an accountant with the Division of Finance for the State of Alaska. She worked as the statewide training coordinator and assisted with developing and troubleshooting the accounting program's reporting system. Dr. Schirmer was active in preparing Alaska's Annual Comprehensive Financial Report, Annual Compensation and Travel Report, assisted with budgetary implementation, departmental accounting, and structure training. Dr. Schirmer is an active member of the Institute for Management Accountants (IMA), Teachers of Accounting at Two-Year Colleges (TACTYC), the Society for Human Resource Management (SHRM), American Payroll Association, and Quality Matters.

Dedications

The authors dedicate this book to the following individuals:

For Chris, Kira, and Meg, who remind me to relax,
and for Mom and Dad, who believed in me until the very end.

—Jeanette Landin

For Royce and Elizabeth, who kept me grounded and reminded me to have fun. For Christina, who reminds me to stop and breathe.

—Paulette Schirmer

A Note from the Authors

We are excited to share the new edition of *Payroll Accounting 2024* with you. Payroll accounting is detailed, deadline-driven, and of utmost importance for the successful functioning of a business. The changing, detailed nature of payroll accounting involves legal challenges, economic changes, technological advances, and—above all—governmental obligations. Our text takes a modern approach to payroll accounting, incorporating coverage of real-world issues that many students will face in their careers, such as cybersecurity, payroll fraud, labor planning, artificial intelligence, and labor costs. We believe that this textbook's information and ancillary materials contribute to a comprehensive understanding of payroll accounting in the 21st century and will make accounting students more valuable to the organizations they work for in their careers.

But as educators, we understand that providing the content is not enough, so we provide multiple opportunities for students to practice in Connect. Whether you are teaching face-to-face, hybrid, or online, *Payroll Accounting 2024* is flexible enough to be used in courses as short as 3 weeks and as long as 15 weeks. We are proud of what we have accomplished with this text, and we thank the faculty and students who have provided feedback to refine the content in this edition. We strongly believe that we have taken payroll accounting education to a higher level of rigor.

Our payroll accounting approach differs from other texts because of our perspective on payroll's role in business. To us, payroll is more than pressing buttons, writing checks, and submitting forms—payroll is the story of **people.** These people include the ones within the business who make decisions about the company's directions and the people who work for the business and depend on their paychecks to support their livelihoods. We wrote this text because we wanted students to understand how business directly affects employees' lives and vice versa.

In light of the COVID-19 pandemic and changes to payroll practices that started in 2020, we have included information specific to employees' and employers' governmental provisions, many of which are sunsetting soon. We wanted to make the information available for students who may encounter workplace issues related to the pandemic in the future.

To foster the connection between business and people, each chapter's introductory story contains recent events involving payroll accounting that highlight the connections among payroll, legislation, business decisions, and people affected by all the decisions made. In Chapter 1, we highlighted a shift in workers' attitudes to work that emanated from the changes to the work environment during COVID-19 shutdowns: the demand for a better work-life balance supported by employers. For Chapter 2, we discussed the current movement of refugees into the workplace and highlighted the difference between H-1B and refugee work visas. In Chapter 3, we explored the challenges of new pay transparency laws that have been enacted in many places. Chapter 4 explores the need for flexible benefits that suit both traditional and remote workers and the "out of sight, out of mind" challenges that remote workers face. In Chapter 5, we focused on the demand for flexible pay or on-demand pay that is gaining popularity. In Chapter 6, we discussed the challenge of rising labor costs that employers face, many of which have resulted in layoffs. Finally, our Chapter 7 introduction considers the effects of artificial intelligence, the Great Resignation, and COVID-19, all of which have led to a shortage of accountants.

What makes this text a modern approach is that we believe that payroll is the connection between financial and managerial accounting. It has everyday connections to businesses, people, and the greater economy in a myriad of ways. Our approach is to encourage students to know the **how** of computing payroll and the **why** inherent to its logic because we believe strongly that the future of the accounting profession involves people with higher-order knowledge of both the process and the purpose within the broader scheme of business. We have included materials to demonstrate the integration of payroll in other aspects of both managerial and financial accounting and business operations. Within Appendixes D and E, we have provided information that allows readers to connect their learning about payroll within the context of their own state's legal framework and links to each state's revenue department to facilitate specific learning. We are passionate about the connections students make between college education and their lives because we understand their importance, and we bring a wealth of experience in accounting, education, industry, and governmental settings that informs our writing.

Our text features many interesting real-world connections. We have drawn examples from many disciplines to help make payroll accounting come alive for teachers and students alike. We want to call specific attention to two discussions that are unique to our text: (1) the content in Chapter 6 explores labor planning for employers (Learning Objectives 6-5 and 6-6), and (2) the discussion in Chapter 7 about the function of labor costs in business and employee benefits reports as strategic tools (Learning Objectives 7-5 and 7-6). We believe this information contributes to a comprehensive understanding of payroll accounting as it evolves in the 21st century. It will make accounting students more valuable as emerging accountants embark upon their careers.

We strongly believe that payroll accounting needs to be applied, so we provide both a continuing problem, located at the end of each chapter, and a comprehensive problem, located in Appendix A, that may be presented in either three-month or one-month versions. Technological integration of the continuing problem and Appendix A within Connect provides an excellent tool for student learning and faculty assessment of course learning objectives. To facilitate student assessment, we included formative assessments in our comprehensive problem in Appendix A in the form of Stop & Check questions. SmartBook 2.0 and guided example videos of tax-form completion reinforce integral concepts and key terminology. We are excited to produce this work through McGraw-Hill because of its top-quality teaching and learning resources available through Connect. Teaching traditional payroll accounting and Internet-based financial accounting via McGraw-Hill's Connect platform for several years has been a wonderful experience for our students and ourselves.

The AACSB guidelines encourage achieving the highest possible standards in business education. We believe that students should understand both how payroll should be completed and how it can be manipulated for personal gain. Payroll fraud continues to be a major source of loss for companies, and it is surprising to find how common it is. We have included examples of the frauds that employees have perpetrated in recent years. According to the Association of Certified Fraud Examiners, payroll fraud of all types, including misclassification of workers, costs businesses $62,000 per instance and approximately $130 billion annually. We hope that these stories enliven and enrich your class discussions. We have updated the payroll processing options in Chapter 1 to reflect an accurate representation of the current state of the available technology used by businesses of any size (Learning Objective 1-5). In Chapter 2, we explored situations where an individual may have multiple employers and how to report new employees per legal requirements (Learning Objective 2-2). We believe that this information about multiple employers and multistate employees is a growing issue that will challenge employers, especially as payroll employees have been working from remote locations. As such, we explored cybersecurity and payroll in more depth in Learning Objective 2-5 to attenuate students to this growing concern.

We have updated our section about cryptocurrency as a means of transmitting payroll amounts due in Learning Objective 5-6. It is important to understand that cryptocurrency as a means of paying employees, while being considered, is a complicated issue because of its connection to the stock market, as opposed to a central bank, as a basis for its value. This topic is evolving. We are certain that we will witness the evolution of payment methods involving cryptocurrency in the future regarding regulating its use and protecting employee pay and employer tax remittance.

We continue to rely on our colleagues' guidance, instructor feedback, and student suggestions to keep us grounded and push us to deliver the best possible content. We hope you enjoy reading this book as much as we enjoy writing it!

Jeanette Landin
Paulette Schirmer

Changes to the Tenth Edition

We have included additional content in this tenth edition of *Payroll Accounting* based on our reviewers' and users' feedback. While updating the tenth edition content, we updated many laws in Chapter 1. In Chapter 2, we added clarity to the pros and cons of Internet-based payroll apps. In Chapter 3, we explored a trend toward repealing the subminimum wage laws in some states. For Chapter 4, we added a summary of pre- and post-tax deductions with the note that some can be either. Chapter 5 contains information about pay on demand and its implications for employers. We added a year-end payroll checklist to Chapter 6, and information about the integration of artificial intelligence into the payroll industry in Chapter 7.

We have maintained our content about the available payroll certification exams. A correlation guide is included in Appendix F that aligns the learning objectives in the text with the topics included on payroll certification examinations offered by the National Association of Certified Professional Bookkeepers (NACPB), the American Institute of Professional Bookkeepers (AIPB), and the American Payroll Association (APA).

We appreciate all feedback and user recommendations we have received because they have helped us create a stronger, more complete text. The changes we have made have added clarity, updated information, and additional opportunities for students to demonstrate their understanding of the concepts presented.

The following are specific changes to each chapter.

Chapter 1

Chapter 1 contained the biggest changes of the year. It involved the enactment of the SECURE 2.0 and Respect for Marriage Acts. These two acts changed many pieces affecting payroll, especially the treatment of retirement accounts and student loan payments and the treatment of spouses. Another important piece of legislation is the burgeoning amount of pay transparency laws. We updated payroll-related legislation to reflect as many changes as possible before publication. We updated the U.S. Bureau of Labor Statistics' employment and salary information and updated COVID-19 pandemic changes regarding payroll and OSHA penalties. We updated ERISA guidelines about retirement funds that are sensitive to environmental, sustainability, and governance risks. We updated right-to-work laws and paid family leave. We included industry best practices for cybersecurity.

Chapter 2

Chapter 2 contains a table of state payday requirements to facilitate an understanding of statewide pay frequency laws. We updated the list of required employee data and updated data about paycard use and the rationale for the expansion of its use. We discussed the growing practice of flexible workplaces, which started during COVID-19 and has started becoming a norm in many companies.

Chapter 3

Chapter 3 contains an updated the Department of Labor ruling about gig economy workers. We clarified travel time with multiple stops per workday and added an example. We updated guidance about the use of subminimum wages, which has seen a legislative reduction in its use. We have clarified pay practices for on-call time and have included holiday and vacation pay examples using the payroll register. We continued to update the minimum wage tables and tipped minimum wage tables.

Chapter 4

We continue to expand the discussion of fringe benefits in Chapter 4. We explored specific fringe benefits that employers have offered during the pandemic. We added information on new benefits requested by employees. We added contribution limits for SIMPLE 401(k) and updated amounts for 2023. We also added guidance from the IRS about household employees.

Chapter 5

Chapter 5 expanded our explanation about using pages 3 and 4 of the 2020 (and later) Form W-4. We added clarification to the computation of Social Security tax for employees whose wages approach the annual wage base, which increased significantly for 2023. We discussed how employees who work from home might be subject to different state and local taxes because of the change in their primary work location. We added tables to explain garnishment maximums by category. We updated information on the number of people who use online banking.

Chapter 6

In Chapter 6, we explained how the CARES Act provisions affect employer tax due dates. We discussed the changes to tax forms in 2023. We explored exclusions to FUTA for U.S. citizens who work for foreign employers. We updated the required periodic employer reporting forms.

Chapter 7

Chapter 7 explores the declining number of accountants and efforts to bring more people into the profession. We explored the use of artificial intelligence and how it could affect the payroll profession. We highlighted the need for payroll accountants as a vital part of business operations.

Appendix A: Comprehensive Payroll Project

In Appendix A, we continued to emphasize the completion of the payroll register and data transfer to both employees' earnings records and accounting entries. We included the New Hire Report form for Nevada and updated the payroll register to reflect current practices. We included Stop & Checks in the Appendix to provide formative assessment opportunities.

Appendix C: Federal Income Tax Tables

We updated the percentage and the wage-bracket methods of determining federal income tax withholding to reflect the most current tax rates available. We have included Publication 15-T in this appendix.

Appendix D: State Income Tax Information

We updated the tax rates for each state in Appendix D.

Appendix F: Payroll Certification Information

We continued to correlate the learning objectives in this text with the topics included in payroll certification examinations offered by the National Association of Certified Professional Bookkeepers (NACPB), the American Institute of Professional Bookkeepers (AIPB), and the American Payroll Association (APA). We included the certification exam requirements and contact information for each certification organization.

Text Features

Chapter Opener

Each chapter opens by focusing on a payroll accounting topic related to real-world companies to set the stage for the chapter's topic.

Healthy Work-Life Policies Are the New Norm

The "Now Hiring" signs remain, but the unemployment rate in the United States is at a historic low. Employers seek employees, but the most recent crop of workers no longer wants to work for low wages or in demeaning work environments. They seek fulfilling jobs, both monetarily and culturally, and want bosses who respect their skills and future potential. This shift may seem like worker entitlement; however, it reflects the aftereffects of the COVID pandemic and a new breed of employees who know what they want, know who they are, and demand healthy work-life boundaries.

In response to employee demands, employers such as Nintendo and Microsoft, among many others, have included work–life balance offerings demonstrating respect for their employees. Nintendo explicitly expresses an attitude of partnership with its employees, an example of which is the acceptance of diversity and equality issues, which may not be a societal norm in some places in the world but is how the company chooses to treat its employees. Microsoft, Netflix, and Salesforce offer unlimited paid time off to salaried employees.

While some companies have experienced issues with staffing shortages, it is increasingly important to understand why the shortage is occurring and what can be done to balance employer needs and employee desires while following legal mandates and corporate mission and vision statements. Employees' demands for respectful, livable working conditions have also extended to pay transparency laws, flexible pay dates, and expanded benefit offerings, which have driven changes in contemporary workplaces. Employers are responding by offering higher pay and remote work opportunities. Other hiring tactics have included emphasizing professional development and career progression, promoting company culture, and benchmarking salary offers to similar jobs in the industry.

(Sources: Nintendo, Paychex, SHRM)

Stop & Check

Which Law?

1. Requires employers to verify the employee's legal right to work in the United States.
2. Protects the rights of disabled workers.
3. Governs the management of retirement plans.
4. Protects workers over age 40 from employment discrimination.
5. Creates safe work environments for employees.
6. Mandates equal pay for equal work.
7. Extends medical benefits for terminated employees.
8. Ensures that child support obligations will be paid.
9. Protects workers and families with preexisting medical conditions.
10. Enforces payment of monetary damages because of discrimination.
11. Requires int... on payroll practices of public...

a. COBRA
b. ERISA
c. Civil Rights Act of 1991
d. PRWOR
e. SOX
f. ADEA
g. HIPAA
h. ADA
i. OSHA
j. Equal Pay Act of 1963
k. IRCA
l. SECURE 2.0

The Stop & Check feature allows students to review their understanding of the content just read. It also enables instructors to conduct formative assessments at multiple points throughout each chapter, testing the students' understanding informally and offering opportunities to expand on the material.

Trends to Watch

Each chapter contains a feature box that connects payroll-related recent events with industry trends that shape the future of the profession. These trends offer instructors more opportunities to expand upon chapter topics, fostering discussion and application.

Trends to Watch

LEGAL ENVIRONMENT

To say that the legal environment of payroll is continually evolving is an understatement. Since 2018, we have witnessed the following legal challenges:

- Increasing numbers of private employers and localities raise the minimum wage significantly to close the gap between the minimum wage and the living wage.
- Supplemental wage rate changes for payments of bonuses.
- State enforcement of predictive scheduling and fair/flexible scheduling laws on changing employees' schedules.
- Reframing the federal income tax structure, treatment for nonresident aliens, supplemental wage withholding rates, and inflation adjustments.
- An increase in the need for centralized and fully communicated company policies to meet remote workers' and companies' needs.

Future trends to watch include:

- A shift to complete digitalization of payroll processes, including partial or complete remote work options.
- Increased guidance about payroll tax impacts involving Indian tribal employees and student loan deferrals.
- A focus on employee retention could include unlimited paid time off without specific tracking of hours used.
- Increases in employees with multiple part-time jobs could lead to legislative changes involving "gig" employee classification and re... benefits.

End-of-Chapter Assessments

Students can demonstrate their understanding through assessments that complement the chapter's learning objectives. Each chapter has review questions, exercises, and problems, with the exercises and problems having two sets in each chapter (Set A and Set B). Each type of assessment is designed to measure student learning as follows:

- Questions for review are designed to check for students' remembrance of concepts.
- Exercises check for understanding and application of chapter concepts.
- Problems allow students to apply and analyze payroll accounting principles.

Exercises Set A

E1-1A. LO 1-1, 1-2 Lupore Fabrics obtained a contract in Watts Mills, South Carolina, that involves the production of materials for military uniforms, a project contracted with the federal government for $2,800,000. What laws govern the wages Lupore Fabrics pays its workers for this project? (Select all that apply.)
1. Davis–Bacon Act
2. Sarbanes–Oxley Act
3. Walsh–Healey Act
4. FLSA

E1-2A. LO 1-1, 1-2 Dylan Piccirillo works as the payroll clerk for Centinix, a security company that hires many part-time and temporary workers who are paid hourly. What law(s) govern(s) the hiring or documenting of these workers?
1. ADEA
2. FLSA
3. IRCA
4. USERRA

E1-3A. London Franco was dismissed from employment at Precision Dynamics

Critical Thinking Exercises

Critical Thinking

CT1-1. You have been hired as a Dynozz Medical Software consultant, facing an IRS of its accounting records. During your review, you notice anomalies in the pay system involving overpayments for labor and payments to terminated employe What should you do?

CT1-2. You are the accountant for Cryologic, a local nonprofit organization. You h been tasked with managing the payroll costs so that staffing levels can remain same even if funding levels change. One consideration is outsourcing the pay functions to a payroll processing company. What are some factors that should

Want to challenge your students further? The Critical Thinking exercises require students to consider complex real-world situations that build confidence and turn learning into mastery. These exercises offer possibilities for team presentations or class debates.

In the Real World: Scenario for Discussion

Each chapter contains a discussion scenario that is drawn from real-world events. These scenarios encourage the expansion of chapter content and allow students to apply their learning to real situations.

In the Real World: Scenario for Discussion

Domino's Pizza franchises in New York were sued by the state of New York for wage at 10 stores. Under New York law, a corporation and a franchiser are joint employ they meet certain employee control criteria. The state found that Domino's met the

Internet Activities

The Internet Activities at the end of each chapter offer students the chance to use their online navigation skills to expand their learning. These exercises attract tech-savvy learners, allowing them to form their understanding of payroll concepts on their terms.

> **Internet Activities**
>
> 1-1. Using the website www.jstor.org, search for articles about payroll-related laws or relevant employment legislation. Once you find an article, summarize the article and explain how the legislation influenced contemporary payroll practices.
>
> 1-2. Visit the website of the American Payroll Association at www.americanpayroll.org. On the right side of the home page, you will find articles about recent developments in payroll practices and legislation. Choose an article and create a presentation to your class about how its content affects payroll practice.
>
> 1-3. Want to know more about the specifics of some of the concepts in this chapter? Check out these websites:

Continuing Payroll Project: Prevosti Farms and Sugarhouse

Starting with Chapter 1, each chapter has an integrated, continuing payroll project—about fictional company Prevosti Farms and Sugarhouse—that matches the chapter content and affords students a macro-level understanding of how each piece of payroll fits together.

> **Continuing Payroll Project: Prevosti Farms and Sugarhouse**
>
> Toni Prevosti is opening a new business, Prevosti Farms and Sugarhouse, a small company that will harvest, refine, and sell maple syrup products. In subsequent chapters, students will have the opportunity to establish payroll records and complete payroll information for Prevosti Farms and Sugarhouse.
>
> Toni has decided that she needs to hire employees for the business to grow. Complete the application for Prevosti Farms and Sugarhouse's Employer Identification Number (Form SS-4) with the following information:

sianc/Shutterstock

Comprehensive Payroll Project: Wayland Custom Woodworking

The Comprehensive Payroll Project (Appendix A) allows students to track a quarter's worth of payroll transactions for a company. This Comprehensive Payroll Project offers instructors increased flexibility in teaching and assessment by offering a simulation equivalent to a full quarter of a fictitious company's payroll activities, including payroll transactions, pay processing, and tax form completion. The Comprehensive Payroll Project may be presented in different lengths—as short as one month or in its three-month entirety—to meet curricular needs. Instructors may assign this in connection with many book chapters or use it as a final project for their courses.

> **Appendix A**
>
> # Comprehensive Payroll Project: Wayland Custom Woodworking
>
> Wayland Custom Woodworking is a firm that manufactures custom cabinets and woodwork for business and residential customers. Students will have the opportunity to establish payroll records and complete a month of payroll information for Wayland.
>
> Wayland Custom Woodworking is located at 12850 Old Highway 50, Glenbrook, Nevada, 89413, phone number 775-555-9877. The owner is Mark Wayland. Wayland's EIN is 91-7444533, and the Nevada Employer Account Number is E6462582020-6. Wayland has determined it will pay its employees on a semimonthly basis. Federal income tax should be computed using the **percentage** method for manual payrolls with Forms W-4 from 2020 or later.
>
> Students will complete the payroll for the final quarter of 2023 and will file the fourth quarter and annual tax reports on the appropriate dates. At the instructor's discretion, students may complete a short version, which contains the payroll transactions beginning December 1. Directions for completion of the short version follow the November 30 transactions.
>
> Rounding can create a challenge. For these exercises, the rate for the individuals is not rounded. Take the employee's salary and divide it by 2,080 (52 weeks at 40 hours per week) for full-time, nonexempt employees. Note: Leave the hourly rate rounded to five decimal places as shown in the next example. Once the gross pay has been calculated, then...

Connect for *Payroll Accounting 2024*

- **SmartBook® 2.0** A personalized and adaptive learning tool used to maximize the learning experience by helping students study more efficiently and effectively. SmartBook 2.0 highlights where in the chapter to focus, asks review questions on the materials covered, and tracks the most challenging content for later review. SmartBook 2.0 is available both online and offline.
- **End-of-chapter content** is a robust offering of review and question material designed to aid and assess the student's retention of chapter content. The end-of-chapter content is composed of both static and algorithmic exercises, problems, critical thinking exercises, and continuing payroll projects, which are designed to challenge students using McGraw Hill Education's state-of-the-art online homework technology. Guided example videos are also provided with select end-of-chapter problems, which help walk students through complex payroll processes. Instructors can also assign test bank questions to students in static and algorithmic versions.
- **Auto-graded payroll and tax forms** are integrated into Connect and are assignable. Students can complete the forms in these problems to gain a better understanding of how payroll forms are prepared in today's digital world.
- **Guided example videos** are also provided with select end-of-chapter problems, which help walk students through complex payroll processes. Instructors can also assign test bank questions to students in static and algorithmic versions.
- **Lecture videos** are new to this edition! There are three- to five-minute videos that accompany each learning objective per chapter. There is also an introduction/overview video for Appendix A and a continuing project at the end of each chapter.
- The **comprehensive payroll project** from Appendix A is available on Connect in an auto-graded format. Students will apply skills, such as preparing tax forms and payroll registers, to complete the payroll process for a company from start to finish. Instructors can choose from the full three-month version or the shorter one-month version for their Connect assignment.
- The **test bank** for each chapter has been updated for the ninth edition to stay current with new and revised chapter material, with all questions available for assignment through Connect. Newly available within Connect, Test Builder is a cloud-based tool that enables instructors to format tests that can be printed or administered within an LMS. Test Builder offers a modern, streamlined interface for easy content configuration that matches course needs without requiring a download. Test Builder provides a secure interface for better content protection and allows just-in-time updates to flow directly into assessments.

Auto-Graded Forms

Comprehensive Payroll Project

Tools to enhance your unique voice
The Power of Connections

A complete course platform

Connect enables you to build deeper connections with your students through cohesive digital content and tools, creating engaging learning experiences. We are committed to providing you with the right resources and tools to support all your students along their personal learning journeys.

65%
Less Time Grading

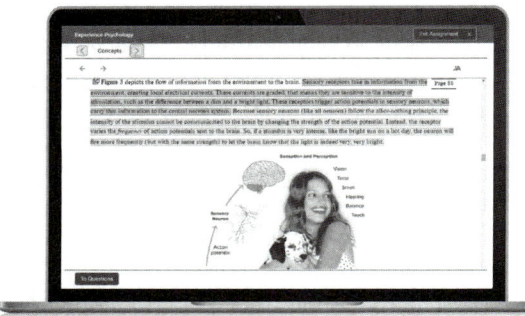

Laptop: Getty Images; Woman/dog: George Doyle/Getty Images

Every learner is unique

In Connect, instructors can assign an adaptive reading experience with SmartBook® 2.0. Rooted in advanced learning science principles, SmartBook 2.0 delivers each student a personalized experience, focusing students on their learning gaps, ensuring that the time they spend studying is time well-spent.
mheducation.com/highered/connect/smartbook

Affordable solutions, added value

Make technology work for you with LMS integration for single sign-on access, mobile access to the digital textbook, and reports to quickly show you how each of your students is doing. And with our Inclusive Access program, you can provide all these tools at the lowest available market price to your students. Ask your McGraw Hill representative for more information.

Solutions for your challenges

A product isn't a solution. Real solutions are affordable, reliable, and come with training and ongoing support when you need it and how you want it. Visit **supportateverystep.com** for videos and resources both you and your students can use throughout the term.

Students
Get Learning that Fits You

Effective tools for efficient studying

Connect is designed to help you be more productive with simple, flexible, intuitive tools that maximize your study time and meet your individual learning needs. Get learning that works for you with Connect.

Study anytime, anywhere

Download the free ReadAnywhere® app and access your online eBook, SmartBook® 2.0, or Adaptive Learning Assignments when it's convenient, even if you're offline. And since the app automatically syncs with your Connect account, all of your work is available every time you open it. Find out more at **mheducation.com/readanywhere**

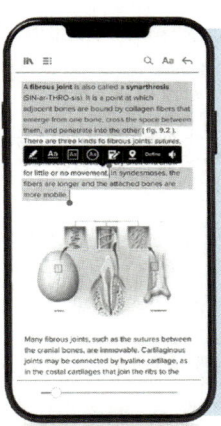

"I really liked this app—it made it easy to study when you don't have your textbook in front of you."

- Jordan Cunningham, Eastern Washington University

iPhone: Getty Images

Everything you need in one place

Your Connect course has everything you need—whether reading your digital eBook or completing assignments for class—Connect makes it easy to get your work done.

Learning for everyone

McGraw Hill works directly with Accessibility Services Departments and faculty to meet the learning needs of all students. Please contact your Accessibility Services Office and ask them to email accessibility@mheducation.com, or visit **mheducation.com/about/accessibility** for more information.

Acknowledgments

This tenth edition of *Payroll Accounting* would not have been possible without the patience, guidance, and encouragement of Steve Schuetz, executive portfolio manager; the support and leadership of Jill Eccher and Brian Nacik, content project managers; and Amanda Lam, product coordinator, who handled every formatting request with professionalism. Special thanks to M. Jeff Quinlan, Madison Area Technical College, for his contributions to verifying the accuracy of our content.

Countless other colleagues have offered their feedback, insights, and inspiration during various stages of this project. We want to extend sincere thanks to the reviewers who helped us shape the tenth edition:

Kim Anderson
Elgin Community College

Kathleen Bent
Cape Cod Community College

Gerald Childs
Waukesha County Technical College

Crystal Cleary
Terra State Community College

Arnold L. Cristobal
Kapiolani Community College and UH Maui College

Clint Doyle
Lehigh-Carbon County Community College

Corey Frad
Eastern Iowa Community College

Marina Grau
Houston Community College

Tanya Haddad
Southwestern College

James Halstead
Neosho County Community College

Jessica Hazel
McLennan Community College

Sophia Ju
Edmonds College

Melody Kamerer
Butler County Community College

Gary Laycock
Ivy Tech Community College

Christy M. Lefevers
Catawba Valley Community College

William Gregory Luszcz
South Piedmont Community College

Richard Mandau
Piedmont Technical College

Gerald T. McFadden
Lorain County Community College

Kelly Westphal Murphy
Des Moines Area Community College

Joseph Malino Nicassio
Westmoreland County Community College

Matthew Njoku
Central Piedmont Community College

Roshelle Overton
Central New Mexico Community College

Denice Pardee
Arapahoe Community College

Paige Paulsen
Salt Lake Community College

Theresa Powell
Central Community College

Suzette Reagan, CPP
Florida State College at Jacksonville

Morgan Rockett
Moberly Area Community College

Erynn Stainback
Central Carolina Community College

Stephanie Swaim
Dallas College North Lake Campus

Pamela Watkins
Durham Technical Community College

Cammy Wayne
Harper College

Our heartfelt thanks go to all who have helped us continue to develop this text throughout the ever-changing world of payroll accounting.

Jeanette Landin
Paulette Schirmer

Brief Contents

1. Payroll Practices and System Fundamentals 2
2. Payroll System Procedures 46
3. Gross Pay Computation 118
4. Fringe Benefits and Voluntary Deductions 176
5. Employee Net Pay and Pay Methods 216
6. Employer Payroll Taxes and Labor Planning 278
7. The Payroll Register, Employees' Earnings Records, and Accounting System Entries 360

APPENDIXES

- A. Comprehensive Payroll Project: Wayland Custom Woodworking 404
- B. Special Classes of Federal Tax Withholding 448
- C. Federal Income Tax Tables 455
- D. State Income Tax Information 513
- E. State Revenue Department or Labor Information 518
- F. Payroll Certification Information 523

GLOSSARY 527

INDEX 533

Contents

About the Authors v

Text Features x

Chapter 1
Payroll Practices and System Fundamentals 2

1-1 Identify Legislation That Pertains to Payroll and Business 4
1-2 Discuss the Legal Framework Specific to Payroll Accounting 11
1-3 Discuss the Ethical Guidelines for Payroll Accounting 19
    Confidentiality 20
    Professionalism 20
    Integrity 20
    Objectivity and Independence 21
    Professional Competence and Due Care 21
1-4 Identify Contemporary Payroll Practices 22
    Payroll Preparation Options 23
    Privacy Protection 25
1-5 Compare Payroll Processing Options for Different Businesses 28
    Large Businesses 28
    Small Businesses 29
    Computer-Based Systems 30
    Internet-Based Systems 31
    Manual Systems 32
    Outsourced Payroll Systems 32
    Certified Payroll 33
Trends to Watch: Legal Environment 34
Summary of Payroll Practices and System Fundamentals 35
Key Points 35
Vocabulary 36
Review Questions 36
Exercises Set A 37
Problems Set A 38
Exercises Set B 39
Problems Set B 40
Critical Thinking 41
In the Real World:
Scenario for Discussion 41
Internet Activities 42
Continuing Payroll Project: Prevosti Farms and Sugarhouse 42
Answers to Stop & Check Exercises 44

Chapter 2
Payroll System Procedures 46

2-1 Identify Important Payroll Procedures and Pay Cycles 48
    Pay Cycles 49
2-2 Prepare Required Employee Documentation 51
    Employees versus Independent Contractors 51
    Reporting New Employees 54
    Entering New Employees into the Database 64
2-3 Differentiate between Exempt and Nonexempt Workers 65
    Leased and Temporary Employees 67
2-4 Explain Pay Records and Employee File Maintenance 68
    Pay Records 68
    Pay Rate 69
    Entering Hours 71
    Calculations of Weekly Regular Time and Overtime 72
2-5 Describe Internal Controls and Record Retention for a Payroll System 73
    Review of Time Collected 75
    Overtime Approval 75
    Approval for Leave of Absence or Other Unpaid Time Off 76
    File Security 76
    Cybersecurity and Payroll 77
    Alternating Duties and Cross-Training 78
    Best Practices Involved in Employee File Maintenance 79
    Electronic Records 79
    Payroll as a Non-Solo Effort 80
    Document Retention Requirements 81
2-6 Discuss Employment Termination and Document Destruction Procedures 84
    Employee Termination 84
    Document Destruction 85
    Electronic Records 87
Trends to Watch: Payroll Procedures 88
Summary of Payroll System Procedures 88
Key Points 89
Vocabulary 89
Review Questions 89
Exercises Set A 90
Problems Set A 92
Exercises Set B 98

Problems Set B 99
Critical Thinking 105
In the Real World:
Scenario for Discussion 105
Internet Activities 105
Continuing Payroll Project: Prevosti Farms and Sugarhouse 105
Answers to Stop & Check Exercises 115

Chapter 3
Gross Pay Computation 118

- 3-1 Analyze Minimum Wage Pay for Nonexempt Workers 120
  - *Minimum Wage* 120
  - *Tipped Employees* 123
- 3-2 Compute Gross Pay for Different Pay Bases 127
  - *Salaried Workers* 127
  - *Hourly Workers* 130
  - *Hourly Workers in More Than One Job Classification* 130
  - *Commission Work* 131
  - *Piece-Rate Work* 133
- 3-3 Calculate Pay Based on Hours and Fractions of Hours 136
  - *Hourly Calculations* 137
  - *Quarter-Hour System* 137
  - *Hundredth-Hour System* 138
- 3-4 Calculate Overtime in Various Situations 140
  - *Standard Overtime Pay* 140
  - *Overtime for Employees of Hospitals and Residential Care Facilities* 141
  - *Tipped Employee Overtime* 142
  - *Piece-Rate Employee Overtime* 143
  - *Salaried Nonexempt Overtime* 144
  - *Overtime for Employees Who Work in Two or More Separate Functions* 144
- 3-5 Create a Payroll Register 145
  - *Payroll Register Data* 145
  - *Track Employee Compensation Using a Payroll Register* 147
- 3-6 Apply Combination Pay Methods 149
  - *Base Salary Plus Commission* 149
  - *Payroll Draw* 150
  - *Salary Plus Commission and Draw* 151
  - *Incentive Stock Options (ISOs)* 152
- 3-7 Explain Special Pay Situations 153
  - *Compensatory Time* 153
  - *On-Call Time* 153
  - *Sleep Time, Travel Time, and Wait Time* 154
  - *Jury Duty* 155
  - *Vacation and Holiday Hours* 155
  - *Subminimum Wage Situations* 156
  - *Nonqualified Deferred Compensation* 158

Pension Payments 158
Retroactive Pay 158
Wages for Deceased Employees 159
Trends to Watch: Employee Compensation 159
Summary of Gross Pay Computation 160
Key Points 160
Vocabulary 161
Review Questions 161
Exercises Set A 162
Problems Set A 163
Exercises Set B 166
Problems Set B 168
Critical Thinking 171
In the Real World:
Scenario for Discussion 171
Internet Activities 171
Continuing Payroll Project: Prevosti Farms and Sugarhouse 172
Answers to Stop & Check Exercises 173

Chapter 4
Fringe Benefits and Voluntary Deductions 176

- 4-1 Define Fringe Benefits within the Context of Payroll 178
  - *Purpose of Fringe Benefits* 178
  - *Including Benefits in Pay* 179
  - *Fringe Benefits and Payroll Taxes* 179
- 4-2 Interpret Cafeteria Plan Types 182
  - *Premium-Only Plan (POP)* 182
  - *Flexible Spending Arrangement (FSA)* 183
  - *Health Savings Account (HSA)* 185
  - *FSA vs. HSA* 185
- 4-3 Describe Fringe Benefit Exclusion Rules 187
  - *Prizes and Awards* 187
  - *Gym Memberships* 187
  - *Personal Use of Company Vehicle* 188
  - *Gift Cards* 188
  - *Employer-Provided Snacks and Meals* 188
- 4-4 Explain Fringe Benefit Valuation Rules 189
  - *General Valuation Rule* 189
  - *Unsafe Conditions* 191
  - *Other Transportation Benefits* 192
- 4-5 Differentiate between Pre-Tax and Post-Tax Deductions 193
  - *Insurance* 193
  - *Supplemental Health and Disability Insurance* 194
  - *Retirement Plans* 195
  - *Post-Tax Deductions* 196
- 4-6 Apply Rules for Withholding, Depositing, and Reporting Benefits 198
  - *Rules for Withholding Amounts Related to Benefits* 198

Treatment of Taxable Benefit Withholdings 199
Rules for Depositing Amounts Related to Benefits 199
Rules for Reporting Benefits 200
Trends to Watch: Employee Benefits 201
Summary of Fringe Benefits and Voluntary Deductions 202
Key Points 202
Vocabulary 203
Review Questions 203
Exercises Set A 203
Problems Set A 205
Exercises Set B 206
Problems Set B 208
Critical Thinking 209
In the Real World:
Scenario for Discussion 210
Internet Activities 210
Continuing Payroll Project: Prevosti Farms and Sugarhouse 211
Answers to Stop & Check Exercises 214

Chapter 5
Employee Net Pay and Pay Methods 216

5-1 Compute Employee Net Pay 218
   Pay Computation Steps 218
5-2 Determine Federal Income Tax Withholding Amounts 220
   Federal Income Taxes 220
   Federal Income Pre-Tax Computation Examples 221
   Wage-Bracket Method 225
   Percentage Method 227
5-3 Compute Social Security and Medicare Tax Withholding 233
   Social Security Tax 234
   Examples of Social Security Tax Computations 235
   Medicare Tax 235
   Examples of Medicare Tax Computations 236
5-4 Calculate State and Local Income Taxes 238
   State-Specific Taxes 239
   Local Income Taxes 240
5-5 Apply Post-Tax Deductions 241
   Charitable Contributions 241
   Garnishments 242
   Consumer Credit 244
   Union Dues 245
   Employee Advances and Overpayments 245
5-6 Discuss Employee Pay Methods 246
   Cash 246
   Check 247
   Direct Deposit 249
   Paycards 250
   Cryptocurrency 251
Trends to Watch: Taxes and Payment Methods 252

Summary of Employee Net Pay and Pay Methods 253
Key Points 253
Vocabulary 254
Review Questions 254
Exercises Set A 254
Problems Set A 256
Exercises Set B 262
Problems Set B 264
Critical Thinking 268
In the Real World:
Scenario for Discussion 269
Internet Activities 269
Continuing Payroll Project: Prevosti Farms and Sugarhouse 269
Answers to Stop & Check Exercises 276

Chapter 6
Employer Payroll Taxes and Labor Planning 278

6-1 List Employer-Paid and Employee-Paid Obligations 280
   Social Security and Medicare Taxes 280
   Federal and State Unemployment Taxes 282
   FUTA Credit Reduction 285
   State Unemployment Taxes 285
   Other State and Local Employer-Only Payroll Taxes 288
   Workers' Compensation Insurance 288
6-2 Discuss Reporting Periods and Requirements for Employer Tax Deposits 290
   Lookback Period 290
   Deposit Frequencies 291
6-3 Prepare Mid-Year and Year-End Employer Tax Reporting and Deposits 293
   Form 941 293
   Schedule B 293
   State Tax Remittance 295
   Form 944 295
   Unemployment Tax Reporting 305
   Matching Final Annual Pay to Form W-2 307
6-4 Describe Payroll within the Context of Business Expenses 315
   Taxes and Other Deductions Remittance 315
   Tax Penalties 316
   Employees and Company Framework 318
6-5 Relate Labor Expenses to Company Profitability 318
   The Labor Distribution Report 319
6-6 Complete Benefit Analysis as a Function of Payroll 320
   Annual Total Compensation Report 321
Trends to Watch: Employer Taxes and Benefit Analysis 324

Summary of Employer Payroll Taxes and Labor Planning 324
Key Points 325
Vocabulary 325
Review Questions 326
Exercises Set A 326
Problems Set A 328
Exercises Set B 339
Problems Set B 340
Critical Thinking 351
In the Real World:
Scenario for Discussion 352
Internet Activities 352
Continuing Payroll Project: Prevosti Farms and Sugarhouse 352
Answers to Stop & Check Exercises 357

Chapter 7
The Payroll Register, Employees' Earnings Records, and Accounting System Entries 360

7-1 Connect the Payroll Register to the Employees' Earnings Records 362
The Employees' Earnings Records and Periodic Tax Reports 363

7-2 Describe Financial Accounting Concepts 364
Debits and Credits 365
The General Journal 365
The General Ledger 366

7-3 Complete Payroll-Related General Journal Entries 367
Employee Pay-Related Journal Entries 368
Employer Payroll-Related Journal Entries 368
Other Payroll-Related Journal Entries 369
Payroll Accruals and Reversals 369

7-4 Generate Payroll-Related General Ledger Entries 371
General Ledger Posting Practices 374
Payroll Account Reconciliation 374

7-5 Describe Payroll Effects on the Accounting System 375
Payroll-Related Business Expenses 375
Payroll-Related Liabilities 376

7-6 Explain Payroll Entries in Accounting Reports 377
Labor Reports 379
Trends to Watch: Economic Effects of Payroll 381
Summary of the Payroll Register, Employees' Earnings Records, and Accounting System Entries 381
Key Points 381
Vocabulary 382
Review Questions 382
Exercises Set A 383
Problems Set A 384
Exercises Set B 389
Problems Set B 390
Critical Thinking 396
In the Real World:
Scenario for Discussion 397
Internet Activities 397
Continuing Payroll Project: Prevosti Farms and Sugarhouse 398
Answers to Stop & Check Exercises 401

Appendixes

Appendix A: Comprehensive Payroll Project: Wayland Custom Woodworking 404

Appendix B: Special Classes of Federal Tax Withholding 448

Appendix C: Federal Income Tax Tables 455

Appendix D: State Income Tax Information 513

Appendix E: State Revenue Department or Labor Information 518

Appendix F: Payroll Certification Information 523

Glossary 527

Index 533

Payroll Accounting 2024

Chapter One

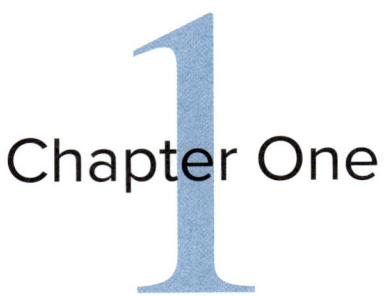

Payroll Practices and System Fundamentals

Payroll systems are essential for job planning and strategic human resource management, cost management for products and services, and benefits analysis. A company's payroll system has historically connected human resources and accounting departments. In contemporary businesses, payroll has taken on a strategic role in company direction and plans. The continual evolution of technological tools to manage company resources, including monetary and human, provides opportunities and challenges to employers regarding employee access and private information protection. A well-designed payroll system is a critical element in company management. For this reason, an understanding of payroll foundations is imperative. This chapter will explore the need for a payroll system, legal requirements, ethical guidelines, best practices, and variations in payroll practices among different-sized companies.

LEARNING OBJECTIVES

After studying Chapter 1, you should be able to:

- **LO 1-1** Identify Legislation That Pertains to Payroll and Business
- **LO 1-2** Discuss the Legal Framework Specific to Payroll Accounting
- **LO 1-3** Discuss the Ethical Guidelines for Payroll Accounting
- **LO 1-4** Identify Contemporary Payroll Practices
- **LO 1-5** Compare Payroll Processing Options for Different Businesses

Andrey_Popov/Shutterstock

Healthy Work-Life Policies Are the New Norm

The "Now Hiring" signs remain, but the unemployment rate in the United States is at a historic low. Employers seek employees, but the most recent crop of workers no longer wants to work for low wages or in demeaning work environments. They seek fulfilling jobs, both monetarily and culturally, and want bosses who respect their skills and future potential. This shift may seem like worker entitlement; however, it reflects the aftereffects of the COVID-19 pandemic and a new breed of employees who know what they want, know who they are, and demand healthy work-life boundaries.

In response to employee demands, employers such as Nintendo and Microsoft, among many others, have included work–life balance offerings demonstrating respect for their employees. Nintendo explicitly expresses an attitude of partnership with its employees, an example of which is the acceptance of diversity and equality issues, which may not be a societal norm in some places in the world but is how the company chooses to treat its employees. Microsoft, Netflix, and Salesforce offer unlimited paid time off to salaried employees.

While some companies have experienced issues with staffing shortages, it is increasingly important to understand why the shortage is occurring and what can be done to balance employer needs and employee desires while following legal mandates and corporate mission and vision statements. Employees' demands for respectful, livable working conditions have also extended to pay transparency laws, flexible pay dates, and expanded benefit offerings, which have driven changes in contemporary workplaces. Employers are responding by offering higher pay and remote work opportunities. Other hiring tactics have included emphasizing professional development and career progression, promoting company culture, and benchmarking salary offers to similar jobs in the industry.

(Sources: Nintendo, Paychex, SHRM)

> Employment legislation is highly complex and dynamic. Large or small, employers must abide by the law and know when it changes. In Chapter 1, we will explore the basics of payroll systems, including legal and ethical issues involved with employee pay.

LO 1-1 Identify Legislation That Pertains to Payroll and Business

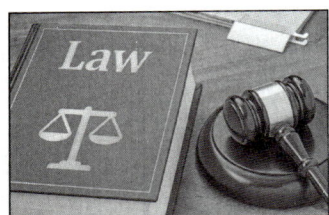
Zerbor/Shutterstock

Unlike many other types of accounting, payroll affects everyone in an organization. Payroll errors can lead to serious internal and external problems. Internal errors may cause a company to pay excessive wages for unneeded overtime, underpay employees, forego profits, employ the wrong number or types of workers during seasonal or workflow changes, or misclassify employees. To ensure operational effectiveness, managers use internal reports about labor usage, staffing levels, and employee compensation trends. Organizational decision-makers use these reports to control labor costs, hire additional employees to meet surge demands, and manage the cost of goods sold. Payroll errors can result in governmental fines, taxes, or legal charges related to labor law violations. Employers provide external reports to the Internal Revenue Service (IRS), state government tax departments, and many more agencies, depending upon the company's nature.

> Compliance with payroll regulations is a complex, multifaceted process. The type and location of the company are the starting point, and a comprehensive view is vital to payroll compliance. The integration of automated technology assists payroll personnel by ensuring legal compliance, reducing human error, and facilitating business growth.
>
> (Source: ADP)

According to the **U.S. Bureau of Labor Statistics**, as of 2021, employment in accounting jobs was expected to increase by 6 percent through 2031, which is the average growth for business professions. Salaries average $47,459 for entry-level payroll clerks, $91,842 for payroll supervisors, and $112,988 for payroll managers, according to the 2023 salary guides available via www.salary.com.

The legislative framework governing employers' payroll systems is complex. Although several fundamental laws still exist, payroll and human resource laws reflect societal evolution. Note how some of these laws have been challenged or changed since their inception.

The **Equal Pay Act of 1963**, which extended the provisions of the **Fair Labor Standards Act (FLSA)**, mandated that males and females be paid equally for equal work. As of 2023, all 50 states have enacted legislation that clarifies and/or extends the original 1963 act. As of the end of 2022, pay transparency laws have been implemented in 17 states with the intent of promoting equal pay for equal work. Any employees who feel they have been paid unequally based on sex have legal options to rectify the situation:

- First, they should gather documentation regarding the differential and determine if other employees can substantiate the difference.
- Second, they should speak with their supervisor to question the pay differential.
- Should the supervisor be unwilling to discuss or adjust the pay discrepancy, an attorney may become a necessary third step.

This act was modified by the **Lilly Ledbetter Fair Pay Act of 2009**, which removed the 180-day statute of limitations on unequal treatment claims.

> In 1979, Lilly Ledbetter, an employee of Goodyear Tire and Rubber Company, started at the same pay rate as males in the same position. Over time, management declined her raises based on negative reviews that Ms. Ledbetter later claimed were discriminatory. Under the provisions of the 1963 Equal Pay Act, the claimant had 180 days to file a complaint. Although the U.S. Supreme Court agreed with her discrimination claims, it ruled in favor of Goodyear because of the lack of timeliness of Ms. Ledbetter's filing. This ruling ultimately led to the Lilly Ledbetter Fair Pay Act of 2009.
>
> In June 2022, Google, LLC, agreed to pay $118 million in a class-action suit started in 2017 and involving 15,500 female employees. In *Ellis v. Google, LLC,* the company was required to submit to external verification of equality in hiring and pay practices for three years.
>
> (Sources: U.S. EEOC; CNET)

Ground Picture/Shutterstock

The ***Civil Rights Act of 1964*** prohibited discrimination based on race, creed, color, sex, and national origin. Since 1964, this act has been extended by Executive Order 11478 to protect people with AIDS, pregnant workers, people with different sexual orientations, and people with disabilities. In 2022, the ***Respect for Marriage Act*** legislated that all marriage, including same-sex and interracial, was legal and could not be banned in any state. This extension of the 1964 Civil Rights Act represented another step toward the legal protection of worker dignity.

The ***Age Discrimination in Employment Act of 1967 (ADEA)*** prevents mandatory retirement of older employees (older than age 40) and prohibits age-based discrimination in hiring.

> An American Association for Retired Persons (AARP) survey conducted in 2022 reported that two out of three workers over age 50 have experienced age discrimination in their workplaces. Examples of age discrimination reported in this survey were unprofessional comments about age and being passed over for deserved promotions. Of the survey respondents, 93 percent reported that age discrimination was commonplace in their work environment.
>
> In 2022, the **U.S. Equal Employment Opportunity Commission (EEOC)** sued Eli Lilly and Co. for illegally refusing the employment of older-age sales workers. The pharmaceutical company claimed its "40 percent early career" policy of hiring millennials for its sales force promoted increased sales and allowed people to obtain a good start to their careers. The EEOC sought to end this discriminatory practice. As of this writing, the case is in progress.
>
> (Source: AARP, Reuters)

The ***Occupational Safety and Health Act of 1970 (OSHA)*** defined and enforced rules for healthy and safe working environments for employees. Employee safety programs and personal protective equipment represent an additional cost to the employer. Still, fines for noncompliance and payments made following workplace injuries are often far more costly: fines range from $15,625 per violation (serious and other-than-serious) to $156,259 per willful or repeated violation (2023 figures).

> Serious OSHA violations often occur, with an average of approximately a dozen cases per month. Numerous COVID-19 related violations occurred during 2022 and resulted in employer fines for worker safety and health. OSHA published workplace COVID-19 regulations, summarized as follows:
>
> *(continued)*

(concluded)

1. OSHA required employers to provide appropriate personal protective equipment (PPE) for employees, including protection for eyes, hands, and face. Special provisions of this requirement included a respiratory protection plan when respirators were required.

2. OSHA amended the general duty clause to require that employers provide a safe workplace that protects employees from physical harm to the greatest possible extent.

3. Controversy:
    A. Mandatory COVID-19 vaccination policy with testing alternative
    B. Monitoring of vaccination status
    C. Maintaining documentation of vaccination
    D. Written notice to employees regarding COVID-19
    E. Enforcing masking and quarantine/isolation periods for exposed and infected employees per CDC guidelines

(Sources: OSHA; Porzio, Bromberg & Newman)

The ***Employee Retirement Income Security Act of 1974 (ERISA)*** regulates retirement and pension plans. ERISA has been extended by the ***Consolidated Omnibus Budget Reformation Act of 1985 (COBRA)***. During 2007–2009, some employee retirement funds' values decreased, causing employees to postpone retirement. The Internal Revenue Service imposes limitations on retirement plan contributions, and those limits have shifted to reflect the need for employees to recoup losses sustained during a recession. Since that time, employee retirement benefits have shifted from being a financial burden to becoming an employee hiring and retention strategy. As of late 2022, ERISA-governed retirement plan participants could focus their investments on environmental, social, and corporate governance funds at their discretion, which reflected a change to prior rules.

In 2019, the ***Setting Every Community Up for Retirement Enhancement (SECURE) Act*** granted small employers tax incentives to implement an automatic retirement plan enrollment for their employees. Alternatively, the act allows small employers to form a group that would allow each business's employees to have better access to retirement plans than the employer could offer by itself. Legislation in 2022 passed as part of the Consolidated Appropriations Act extended provisions of the SECURE Act, known as the ***SECURE 2.0*** Act.

The SECURE 2.0 Act had 92 new provisions that can be summarized in a few categories, many of which will be mandatory as of 2025 for employers with 10 or more employees. The list of provisions includes, but is not limited to, the following:

1. Automatic enrollment in retirement plans at a rate between 3 and 10 percent of their annual pay. Employees can opt out of this benefit, which differs from the current opt-in model, and may withdraw funds within 90 days of their first contribution at no penalty.

2. Automatic escalation of contributions at a rate of 1 percent per year up to a maximum of 10 to 15 percent of annual wages.

3. Employees 50 years of age and older may make post-tax "catch-up" contributions of up to $7,500 in 2023 and up to $10,000 as of 2025.

4. Starting in 2023, employees may elect to make contributions post-tax to avoid later taxation on retirement funds.

5. Effective in 2023, nonunion part-time employees who work a minimum of 500 hours for three consecutive years must be allowed to participate in their employer's retirement plan.

6. Starting in 2024, employee student loan payments may be treated as contributions to the employee's retirement plan.

7. Employees may make emergency savings plan contributions to their retirement plan and may elect to withdraw such contributions without penalty or need for emergency documentation.

8. As of 2027, low-income employees may be eligible for up to $2,000 annual retirement savings match from the federal government. The federal matching contribution would be 50 percent of the employee's contribution and is phased out as employee income increases.

(Source: ADP)

Ground Picture/Shutterstock

COBRA extended medical benefits for terminated employees at the employee's expense for up to 18 months post-employment by qualified employers. It should be noted that not all companies are subject to COBRA provisions and that states may offer "mini-COBRA" plans for companies with fewer than 20 employees. The repeal of the Defense of Marriage Act (DOMA) in 2013 forced employers to offer COBRA coverage to same-sex spouses, which has now been strengthened by the Respect for Marriage Act. As of 2021, terminated employees who opt not to enroll in COBRA plans could enroll in *Marketplace* plans or Medicaid for up to 60 days post-termination. If employees choose not to use the COBRA plan immediately, they may enroll at the company's next enrollment period.

COBRA benefits currently extend to beneficiaries, including employees, dependent spouses, and children. Benefits are paid to beneficiaries in the event of reduced hours or separation of employment for any reason, excluding gross misconduct and upon the employee's death. If the company offers retiree benefits, COBRA coverage also extends to beneficiaries in Chapter 11 bankruptcy.

The *Immigration Reform and Control Act of 1986 (IRCA)* requires employers to verify that employees are legally able to work in the United States. Form I-9 is the most common payroll-related application of this law. Immigration and citizenship laws require collecting information within an I-9, and retention is three years from the date of hire or one year from the date of termination, whichever is longer.

Information collected on Form I-9 is monitored closely to ensure that the employee is legally authorized to work in the United States. Employers may also use the *E-Verify* system to confirm legal employment eligibility. Note that the E-Verify system does not replace the completion of the I-9 but does offer employers the opportunity to check legal employment eligibility rapidly via the Internet. The Department of Homeland Security issued guidance on extensions and flexibility with I-9 requirements in January 2022 due to the continued effects of COVID-19.

(Source: U.S. Citizenship and Immigration Services)

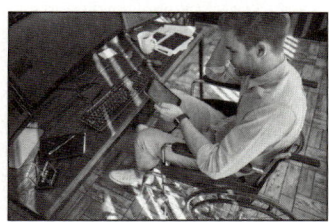
BAZA Production/Shutterstock

The *Americans with Disabilities Act of 1990 (ADA)* extended the provisions of the Civil Rights Act of 1964 by ensuring that people with disabilities have the same opportunities as those without mental or physical impairment. This law applies to employers with 15 or more employees on the payroll, including full-time and part-time workers. The enactment of the *Americans with Disabilities Act Amendments Act (ADAAA)* in 2008 extended the definition of disability to include many disabilities. Final regulations on the ADAAA in 2011 clarified the definitions of disability and the required accommodations to include the following:

- The expansion of the definition of disability includes a lower standard of the definition of impairment.

- The determination of impairments requires the employee to be assessed individually.
- Except for corrective lenses, the determination of disability does not include devices that provide relief or mitigation of the condition, such as hearing aids.
- Impairments that occur periodically or episodically or that are in remission are still considered impairments.
- Any disability determination must not require extensive analysis.

The *Civil Rights Act of 1991* granted employees who have been discriminated against the chance to be paid monetary damages through legal proceedings. This act applies to American employers and American-controlled employers with international-based operations.

> Workplace diversity and inclusion have become an increasing priority at workplaces during the last decade. As of 2022, Diversity for Social Impact posted its listing of the best workplaces for diversity and inclusion, sourced from the diversity and inclusion policies of thousands of companies worldwide. In the United States, the top three companies for diversity and inclusion were:
>
> 1. Disney
> 2. CarMax
> 3. Novartis
>
> (Source: Diversity for Social Impact)

TommyStockProject/Shutterstock

The *Family and Medical Leave Act of 1993 (FMLA)* granted employees the right to take medical leave under reasonable circumstances without fear of job loss. The employee may take unpaid leave, but medical benefits must continue under FMLA provisions. Upon returning from family leave, the employer must provide an equivalent position with equivalent pay, benefits, and employment terms. The employer has many responsibilities under the FMLA that involves employee notification of benefits and processes while on leave.

As of 2023, 11 states have enacted paid family leave legislation: California, Colorado, Connecticut, Delaware, Maryland, Massachusetts, New Jersey, New York, Oregon, Rhode Island, Washington, and Washington, DC. Other states have voluntary opt-in insurance programs to provide an option for paid family leave. Hawaii provides temporary disability insurance, which is similar to paid family leave.

In 2017, legislators passed the *Tax Cuts and Jobs Act* in Washington, DC. This provided a tax credit to employers offering paid leave under the FMLA. Employers may be eligible for a credit of 12.5 percent up to 25 percent, whereas the employee's rate of payment is 50 percent or more of what the employee would normally be paid during the normal course of work for the company. Eligibility limits of the type of employer and employee exist under regulations (see Sec. §13403).

> The Tax Cuts and Jobs Act (TCJA) has led to specific focus areas for employers. These areas of focus include:
>
> - Controversy: When the TCJA provisions expire at the end of 2025, companies may need to refile tax returns, making record-keeping and changes made due to the TCJA enactment a critical function in payroll.
> - International tax: For companies with an international presence, including employees, the TCJA may result in new tax liabilities.

- Compensation for executives: TCJA affected highly compensated employees' tax treatment and fringe benefits offered to workers. This has led to scrutiny of compensation plans and their legal compliance.
- State taxes: Because of TCJA provisions, taxes have increased for employees in some states. Since each state has different tax laws, and not all states have chosen to comply with TCJA provisions, state taxation has become increasingly complex.

(Source: AICPA)

The *Uniformed Services Employment and Reemployment Rights Act of 1994 (USERRA)* governs military service members' rights regarding the length of military service, return to work, and accommodations for injured veterans. USERRA was amended to further address service members' rights in 2005. In 2011, USERRA was further amended by the Veterans Opportunity to Work Act, which allowed USERRA to recognize claims of a hostile work environment resulting from an individual's military status.

The U.S. Department of Labor investigates many cases involving service members' rights. Army veteran Lisa Slater returned to her job as a security officer, which she held for 13 years with her company, after deployment on active duty. However, upon her return to her employment, she found that she was classified as a new employee, which was a violation of USERRA. She received approximately $20,000 in back wages, and her seniority was restored following arbitration.

(Source: U.S. DOL)

The *Personal Responsibility and Work Opportunity Reconciliation Act of 1996 (PRWOR)* mandated that employers file a new hire reporting form within 20 days after an employee initially commences work. This act protects children and needy families by enforcing child support obligations. The child support provisions of PRWOR were strengthened by the passage of the *Personal Responsibility, Work and Family Promotion Act of 2002*, which reauthorized PRWOR when it expired. PRWOR is still federally mandated as of 2023.

According to the Office of Child Support Enforcement (OSCE), collections supported approximately 18 percent of all children under age 18 in the United States and collected over $29.5 billion for families as of the end of 2022. OSCE reported that employers collect approximately 63 percent of child and medical support through payroll deductions.

(Sources: Office of Child Support Enforcement)

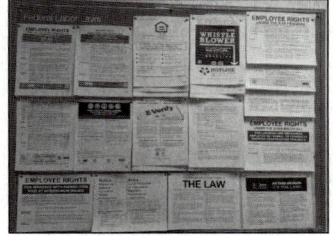

Jeanette Landin

The *Health Insurance Portability and Accountability Act of 1996 (HIPAA)* protects workers and their families with preexisting medical conditions from discrimination based on those conditions. The Ebola outbreak in 2014 and the COVID-19 pandemic led to additional guidance about HIPAA rights and notifications to interested parties, including employers, during emergencies.

> HIPAA protections continue even after a business ceases operations. Filefax Inc. of Illinois was ordered to pay approximately $100,000 in fines because of HIPAA violations, although the company was no longer in business. The issue leading to the fines involved a lack of secure storage of employee health records following an investigation by the Office of Civil Rights.
>
> (Source: U.S. HHS)

The *Defense of Marriage Act of 1996 (DOMA)* restricted payroll-related taxes and benefits to include only traditionally married couples, denying married status to people in same-sex unions. The U.S. Supreme Court overturned DOMA's ruling in *U.S. v. Windsor* on September 6, 2013. The Internal Revenue Service subsequently mandated that all married same-sex couples must be treated as married for all tax purposes. The repeal of DOMA had a ripple effect throughout all payroll phases because of the need to amend business and personal tax return filings back to 2011, owing to the three-year amendment rule. The repeal of DOMA provoked the need to clarify the term "family member." Following the U.S. Supreme Court decision in *Obergefell v. Hodges (2015)*, the U.S. Department of Labor updated the definition of a spouse to include same-sex marriages, regardless of where they live. *Obergefell v. Hodges* was codified by the *Respect for Marriage Act* in 2022.

Maskot/Getty Images

> In *U.S. v. Windsor,* Ms. Windsor and her wife were recognized as a married couple by the state of New York, and her compensation was taxed accordingly. However, the IRS sued Windsor for unpaid taxes because her same-sex marriage violated DOMA. The U.S. Supreme Court found that DOMA violated Windsor's Fifth Amendment right to liberty and overturned DOMA. The IRS subsequently dropped its lawsuit.
>
> (Source: U.S. Supreme Court)

The *Sarbanes–Oxley Act of 2002 (SOX)* provided criminal penalties for violations of ERISA. SOX provides protections for whistleblowers (Sec. § 806) and mandates auditors' rotation among publicly owned companies (Sec. § 203). SOX Section 302 mandates that corporate officers attest to the accuracy and completeness of the contents of the financial statements. An additional consideration for SOX public companies regarding payroll is that the internal controls of a payroll system must be reported under the law's guidelines (Sec. § 404). Costs of SOX compliance have sparked discussion about the act's effectiveness.

> In 2020, SOX and the Dodd–Frank Act, which involved consumer protection and oversight of trading via the New York Stock Exchange, intersected to strengthen consumer protections (known as *qui tam* rewards). The intersection led to a bill introduced in Congress to create an independent board to oversee auditor conduct in publicly held companies, thus limiting conflicts of interest and protecting individuals who invest in companies traded on the stock market.
>
> (Source: National Law Review)

The *American Recovery and Reinvestment Act of 2009 (ARRA)* provided tax credits for employers and employees through the Making Work Pay provisions. Although ARRA's provisions have expired, parts of it were reinstated through the *American Taxpayer Relief Act of 2012 (ATRA)*. Many of the ATRA provisions were extended through 2015 by

Which Law?

Stop & Check

1. Requires employers to verify the employee's legal right to work in the United States.
2. Protects the rights of disabled workers.
3. Governs the management of retirement plans.
4. Protects workers over age 40 from employment discrimination.
5. Creates safe work environments for employees.
6. Mandates equal pay for equal work.
7. Extends medical benefits for terminated employees.
8. Ensures that child support obligations will be paid.
9. Protects workers and families with preexisting medical conditions.
10. Enforces payment of monetary damages because of discrimination.
11. Requires internal controls on payroll practices of public companies.
12. Gives employees incentives to participate in retirement plans.

a. COBRA
b. ERISA
c. Civil Rights Act of 1991
d. PRWOR
e. SOX
f. ADEA
g. HIPAA
h. ADA
i. OSHA
j. Equal Pay Act of 1963
k. IRCA
l. SECURE 2.0

extending the Work Opportunity Tax Credit, which has been authorized until the end of 2025. The *Protecting Americans from Tax Hikes (PATH) Act* of 2015, which also prevented certain tax fraud schemes, extended the ATRA provisions by offering employers tax credits for hiring qualified veterans and individuals who have endured long-term unemployment.

As times change, new legislation will be enacted, and existing laws are sometimes repealed and amended. An example of evolving legislation includes new local laws regarding fairness in scheduling employees' shift work schedules. Right-to-work laws are another example of employment-related legislation. As of 2023, 28 U.S. states and Guam have enacted right-to-work legislation that promotes an employee's right to opt out of union membership. At the time of this writing, the notion of the right to work without forcing union participation is being considered by the U.S. Congress.

The payroll accountant's job requires continual learning and research to ensure that the company complies with all current regulations and reporting requirements. Many states, but not all, have additional payroll tax laws. Federally mandated payroll laws will be addressed in the next section.

(Source: WagePoint)

LO 1-2 Discuss the Legal Framework Specific to Payroll Accounting

Federal income tax withholding was temporarily instituted in 1861 to recover from the Civil War's high costs; however, this tax was repealed in 1872. Throughout the 19th century, cities were growing in the wake of the Industrial Revolution, as factories and companies increased automation and institutionalized mass production. In unprecedented numbers, people moved from rural to urban areas, and the need for infrastructure and civil

Create jobs 51/Shutterstock

services grew. Roads needed to be built, more law enforcement personnel needed to be hired, and disease outbreaks prompted the development of sanitation systems. Therefore, the U.S. Congress formalized the permanent continuation of the federal income tax instituted during the Civil War as a means to fund the infrastructure improvements of the booming cities. After many failed attempts to reinstate a federal income tax, Congress passed the *Sixteenth Amendment to the U.S. Constitution* in 1909, ratified by states in 1913. This version incorporated a tiered income tax, including exemptions and deductions, to limit the tax on wages earned; it was the harbinger of many employment-related laws (see Figure 1-1).

During the Great Depression of the 1930s, the stock market collapsed, financial institutions went bankrupt, and companies released workers or ceased business operations. The government needed money to fund programs that would stimulate economic recovery. Additionally, the need for a social welfare system emerged as the number of displaced workers increased. The 1930s became a decade of landmark employment legislation that defined the legal environment for employers and employees, most of which remains in effect in 2023.

In 1931, Congress passed the *Davis–Bacon Act*, creating a standard of wages for governmental contracts totaling more than $2,000. The increased standard wages created under the Davis–Bacon Act brought additional revenue to small businesses and the communities where the contract workers lived, bought groceries, and purchased other services or goods. The Davis–Bacon Act comprised more than 60 federal statutes, providing a prevailing wage and wage classification strategy to guide employers and contractors. The minimum contract rate for all employees affected by the Davis–Bacon Act increased in 2022 to reflect economic changes. Per the minimum contract rate effective for 2023 is $16.20 per hour. Additionally, tipped employees working in connection with contracts covered by Executive Order 14026 have a minimum cash wage of $13.75 per hour. Both of these will be adjusted if the local prevailing minimum wage rate is higher.

> The determination of wages paid to workers affected by the Davis–Bacon Act varies by geographic area, contract, and type of work performed. The U.S. Department of Labor maintains a website (https://sam.gov/). Employers may access the specific contract in question and research the contract provisions to ensure that employees are paid appropriately.

The *Walsh–Healey Public Contracts Act* of 1936 affected governmental contractors providing goods or services exceeding $10,000. The act required companies to pay workers a minimum wage for all 40 or fewer hours worked per week. Additionally, employers must pay a premium (regular pay times 1.5) for work over 40 hours per week. The Walsh–Healey

FIGURE 1-1
Timeline of Payroll Legislation

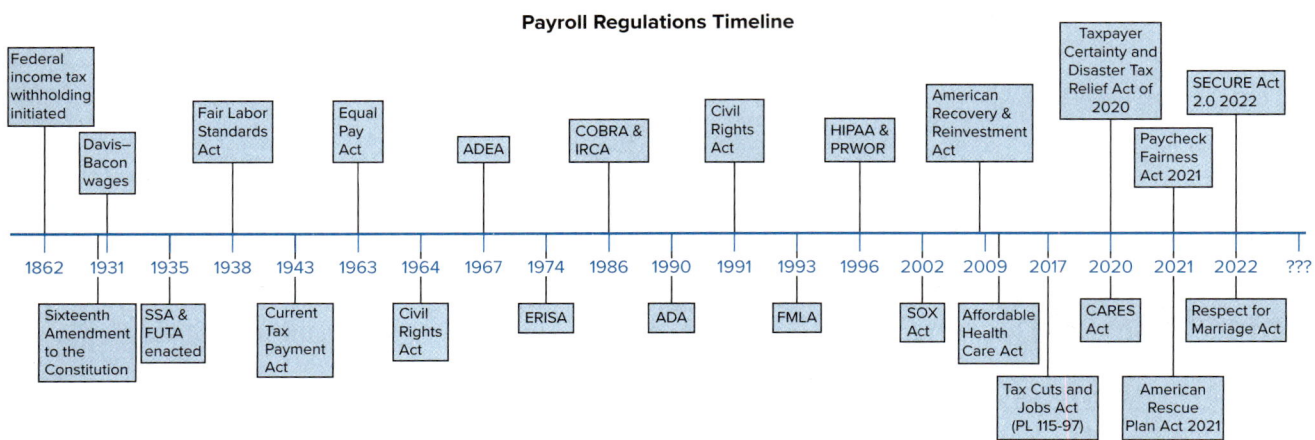

Public Contracts Act also prohibited the employment of individuals younger than 16 years of age. Compliance with this act is enforced through the Employment Standards Administration Wage and Hour Division of the Department of Labor. These standards also apply to workers within the District of Columbia.

In 1935, the *Social Security Act (SSA)*, also known as the *Federal Insurance Contributions Act (FICA)*, established a contribution-driven fund to help the average U.S. worker respond to the social and financial distress caused by the Great Depression. Originally, the Social Security tax was designed such that younger workers supported retired, disabled workers, and surviving families of deceased workers, and was known as *Old-Age, Survivors, and Disability Insurance (OASDI)*. It is important to note that the worker does not need to die or become disabled to receive Social Security benefits; the truth is that age and disability are components in the decision but are not the only factors considered when awarding Social Security benefits.

B Christopher/Alamy Stock Photo

As a contribution-based fund, employees and employers pay a set percentage of earnings into the Social Security fund. Originally, the fund was designed to be earmarked for a specific individual upon retirement. Still, the fund currently assists families who experience diminished wages and working situations because of the worker's infirmity or the illness of a family member that prevents their entry into the workforce, and it provides monetary benefits to dependents of retired or deceased workers. Social Security is synonymous with Old-Age, Survivors, and Disability Insurance (OASDI). *Medicare*, a government-mandated health insurance program for individuals, was instituted to amend the Social Security Act under the *Medicare and Medicaid Act of 1965* to fund medical services needed by older adults, disabled people, and low-income persons. As of 2023, the age at which one may receive full retirement benefits is 67 years for people born after 1960. The full retirement age will increase from 65 years by two months each year for people born before 1960 until it reaches the full retirement age of 67. Individuals may begin receiving permanently reduced benefits as early as age 62, but their Social Security payments will be reduced incrementally. As a side note, workers may continue to work past their full retirement age to increase their Social Security benefit payment.

(Source: Social Security Administration)

> As of 2023, approximately 20 percent of all Americans receive payments from Social Security. This figure includes 47 million retirees and dependents, 6 million survivors of deceased workers, and 10 million disabled workers and dependents. The 2023 cost of living increase in Social Security payments, combined with the increased number of recipients, reflects the largest increase in Social Security payments in 40 years.
>
> Furthermore, SSA estimated that approximately 62 percent of American retirees depended on their Social Security checks for basic food and shelter needs. The funds received from Social Security reduce the poverty rate among senior citizens. Social Security payouts vary based on age, years of work, and the highest wages earned.
>
> (Source: Motley Fool, MSN)

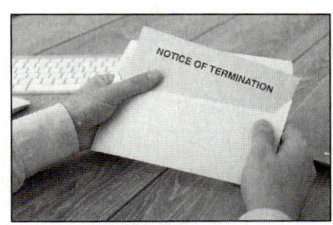

Tommaso79/Shutterstock

As another part of its social welfare legislation, the U.S. Congress passed the *Federal Unemployment Tax Act (FUTA)* to help displaced workers, individuals from the workforce who find themselves unemployed and meet certain state or federal qualifications. FUTA and its state counterpart, the *State Unemployment Tax Act (SUTA)*, are based on the employees' wages. Unlike Social Security taxes, only employers pay FUTA. Some states require both employers and employees to contribute to SUTA. For example, Alaskan employees contribute up to an annual amount of $240.21 (2023 figure) to SUTA, which is collected at a rate of 0.51 percent of wages; employers contribute between 1 and 5.4 percent of employee wages until they reach $47,100 in annual gross earnings (2023 figure). Should an employee have more than one employer, the employee can request a return for the amounts over the annual earnings maximum in the following year. The COVID-19 pandemic strained states' unemployment funds in 2020 and 2021, and increases in SUTA rates and policies may be significant in future years.

The Fair Labor Standards Act (FLSA) of 1938 required more detailed record-keeping and worker protection. Before FLSA's enactment, employers determined employee pay rates and hours. Low wages, long hours, and child labor were commonplace. This act regulates the minimum wage, which most workers are familiar with, stated as the lowest an individual under certain classifications can be paid. It stipulates the maximum hours per workweek at 40. It also set the minimum age of 16 years for the workplace, although exceptions apply for family-run businesses and farms. Less commonly known, the minimum wage applies only to workers at businesses that meet certain conditions defined by either enterprise or individual coverage. Additionally, tipped employees, such as restaurant servers, are exempt from minimum wage standards under FLSA. In the contemporary business world, a business that does not conduct interstate commerce is rare, but the provision in FLSA remains in effect.

FLSA: Enterprise vs. Individual Coverage

Under FLSA, two types of coverage prevail: Enterprise coverage and Individual coverage.

Enterprise Coverage:

- The company must have a minimum of two employees.
- The volume of sales or business performed annually must exceed $500,000.
- Firms such as hospitals, schools, government agencies, and residential care facilities are always considered under enterprise coverage.

Individual Coverage:

- Firms that regularly conduct interstate business, such as companies that produce goods for shipment to a different state, have employees who travel to other states or otherwise conduct business with firms or people in other states.

(Source: DOL)

An important fact about FLSA wage guidelines is that no maximum wage cap exists. Securities and Exchanges Commission (SEC) regulations stipulate that high-ranking public companies' employees' compensation packages must be published with the company's mandatory annual report.

The Department of Health and Human Services determined in 2023 that the poverty level for a single-person household was $14,580, which translates to a wage of approximately $7.00 per hour, assuming a 40-hour workweek. In other words, the minimum wage for a person to live comfortably (a *living wage*) varies by state and ranges from $14.85 to $23.13 per hour, depending on the state and city. As of this publication date, the federal *minimum wage* is $7.25 per hour, although many states and municipalities mandate a higher minimum wage.

(Source: The Assistant Secretary for Planning and Evaluation, World Population Review)

FLSA guidelines define maximum hours, minimum age, pay rates, and mandatory break times. This part of the FLSA was an outgrowth of the early 20th century's industrial environment when no such guidelines existed. Horror stories about working conditions and children working 12- to 14-hour days abounded during the 1930s. The FLSA created the classifications of exempt and nonexempt workers. Exempt workers are salaried workers who are not subject to certain wage and overtime provisions of FLSA. Nonexempt workers are protected by the provisions of the FLSA and are subject to wage and overtime provisions.

Additionally, FLSA regulation does not apply to pay periods or the amount of paid time off given to employees. Those two items are at the discretion of the employer. Mandatory paid time off has become a topic of discussion since 2010. McDonald's began offering it to nonexempt employees in 2015 as a regular part of employee benefit packages in response to pressure from labor leaders. Fifteen states and more than 30 municipalities have instituted paid sick leave for employees as of 2023. The paid sick leave laws vary widely among the states.

The third class of workers, independent contractors, is not subject to the payment provisions of the FLSA. *Independent contractors* are typically treated as vendors of a business. Independent contractors are not company employees and are not reflected in payroll records. The IRS uses *Form SS-8* to help determine employee or independent contractor status. The Department of Labor ruled that improper classification of workers diminished workers' legal protections under the FLSA and declared that the following items must be considered when classifying a worker as an employee or an independent contractor:

1. The extent to which a worker is an integral element of the employer's business.
2. Whether the worker's managerial skills affect his or her opportunity for profit or loss.
3. Relative investments in facilities and equipment by *both* the employee and the employer.
4. The extent to which the worker exercises independent business judgment.
5. The permanent nature of the working relationship between the employer and employee.
6. The type and extent of the control that the employer has over the employee.

(Source: U.S. Department of Labor)

> Penalties for the misclassification of employees as independent contractors can be high. If the misclassification is intentional on the employer's part, the monetary amount of the penalty is higher. In the case of *Fair v. Communications Unlimited Inc.*, the U.S. District in Missouri found that the employer had deliberately miscategorized workers in 10 states as independent contractors to avoid paying overtime wages required under the FLSA. The employer was ordered to provide the names and other contact information to the court to determine appropriate overtime compensation awards.
>
> (Source: Google Scholar)

To obtain the remittance of employers' withholding taxes, the federal government needed a way to standardize the collection of taxes from employers. Before the *Current Tax Payment Act (CTPA) of 1943*, no formalized guidelines for the remittance of taxes existed. Before the CTPA, employers' remittance was inconsistent and unreliable as a funding source for governmental projects. The CTPA was passed during World War II to guarantee funds to support the country's involvement in the war. The CTPA created the requirement to submit estimated taxes on wages earned during the year of earning instead of after the end of the year as previously required.

Another employer obligation is *workers' compensation*, commonly known as *workers' comp*. Unlike other payroll-specific laws, state laws govern workers' compensation laws. Employer requirements for providing workers' comp coverage vary from state to state. They are not required in certain states if the employer has fewer than a certain minimum number of employees. Because workers' compensation is an insurance program, it is not considered a tax. However, it is a state-mandated employer payroll expense.

Workers' compensation is an insurance policy employers carry to provide wage continuation and pay for medical services for workers injured while doing business. The amounts assigned to the policy vary by work

Fertnig/Getty Images

performed and associated risks for various professions. For example, heavy equipment operators would have a higher workers' comp rate than office workers because their injury exposure is deemed to be higher by the insurance industry. The COVID-19 pandemic's impact on certain businesses, such as meat-packing plants, could lead to changes in workers' compensation insurance procedures in future years.

Workers' compensation plans are subject to annual audits and are based upon payroll wages less any employees exempted from the coverage, typically working owners. Employers must report all employee wages; however, only one-third of overtime hours have historically been reported to the workers' compensation auditor. Each state has different requirements for coverage and eligibility. The number of employees over which workers' compensation insurance is required varies per state, as shown in Table 1-1.

The *Affordable Care Act (ACA)* of 2010 was one of the most significant payroll accounting changes in recent years. Although the act's primary focus was to ensure healthcare coverage for all Americans, employers have several reporting responsibilities related to the act. One of the responsibilities included in Section 1003 is the disclosure and justification for rates of plans and any increases in premiums. Another reporting requirement is the number of full-time equivalent (*FTE*) employees, the cost of insurance coverage provided to employees, and the elimination of a waiting period for health insurance coverage. The Affordable Care Act legislation comprises 974 pages and contains many provisions and contingencies, including a requirement for continuing premium review. In 2017, the provision of the Affordable Care Act mandating financial penalties on individuals who elected not to have medical insurance was overturned by Executive Order 13765. In 2018, a judge in Texas ruled that Executive Order 13765 caused the ACA to be unconstitutional. In 2021, the U.S. Supreme Court vacated the lower court's ruling in Texas, which means the ACA is consistent with the U.S. Constitution and remains a current law.

According to the Internal Revenue Service, employers must report whether they provide Minimum Essential Coverage as part of their company-sponsored benefits, including any group health plans, COBRA plans, or preexisting insurance coverage. Health insurance coverage is reported on IRS Form 1095 A, B, or C as follows:

- Form 1095-A is for individuals who have purchased insurance from the Healthcare Marketplace, not through an employer. The Marketplace issues this form.

- Form 1095-B reports information to the IRS for individuals with minimum essential coverage through group insurance plans provided by governmental and qualified private-sector employers. Additionally, employers who are not applicable large employers but who sponsor self-insured group health plans must report information about employees (and their spouses and dependents) who enroll in the coverage to their employees, even though the employers are not subject to the employer shared-responsibility provisions or the information reporting requirements for applicable large employers.

- Form 1095-C applies to large employers who provide health insurance where the employer is responsible for the act's shared responsibility provision. This form is issued by employers who offer coverage but are not self-insured and have 50 or more full-time and/or full-time equivalent employees.

The employer must file IRS form 1095-B or 1095-C and furnish a copy to the insured if the insured received medical insurance benefits for as few as one day of one month during a calendar year. The transmittal form, which contains a summary of all Form 1095s issued, required by the IRS is Form 1094-A, B, or C, depending on the type of 1095 issued.

(Source: IRS)

TABLE 1-1
Workers' Compensation Laws by State

STATE	MINIMUM NUMBER OF EMPLOYEES
Alabama	5
Alaska	1 (could be self-insured)
Arizona	1
Arkansas	3
California	1
Colorado	1
Connecticut	1 (including uninsured subcontractors)
Delaware	1
District of Columbia	1 (Homeowners with domestic workers must have coverage if they work more than 240 hours in a quarter during a previous year)
Florida	4 (except noted industries), 1 (construction), 6 (agricultural), 12 (seasonal)
Georgia	3
Hawaii	1 (LLC members must also be covered)
Idaho	1 (including part-time workers)
Illinois	1 (including part-time workers)
Indiana	1
Iowa	1
Kansas	1 (exempt if annual gross payroll is less than $20,000 or agricultural employer; sole proprietors and LLC members are exempt from coverage)
Kentucky	1
Louisiana	1 (including part-time, either employees or subcontractors, with exceptions for agriculture-only employers)
Maine	1 (subcontractors must also be covered)
Maryland	1 (agricultural employers must have at least 3 employees or a payroll of less than $15,000 annually)
Massachusetts	1 (domestic workers must be covered if they work more than 16 hours per week)
Michigan	1 (certain family members who are employees may be exempt, certain very small employers are exempt), 3 (private employers)
Minnesota	1
Mississippi	5 (certain subcontractors' employees are covered, excludes domestic, farm, nonprofit fraternal, charitable, religious, or cultural organizations)
Missouri	5 (includes full and part-time, seasonal, temporary, corporate officers), 1 (construction), except farm laborers, domestic servants, certain real estate agents, direct sales, commercial motor-carrier owner-operators
Montana	1
Nebraska	1 (including part-time workers)
Nevada	1 (excluding independent enterprises)
New Hampshire	1 (including part-time workers)
New Jersey	1
New Mexico	3 (construction employers must cover any employees)
New York	1
North Carolina	3 (only 1 employee for businesses that involve radiation exposure)
North Dakota	1 (including part-time, seasonal, and temporary workers)
Ohio	1
Oklahoma	1 (when a business has 5 or fewer family members as employees, the family members are exempt from coverage)
Oregon	1
Pennsylvania	1
Rhode Island	4
South Carolina	4 (some occupations exempt if <$3,000 in annual payroll), (including part-time workers)
South Dakota	1
Tennessee	5 (construction, subcontractors, and coal businesses must always have it)
Texas	No mandatory coverage except for government contractors
Utah	1
Vermont	1 (agricultural/farming employers with annual payroll <$10,000 are exempt) (including part-time workers)
Virginia	2 (including part-time workers)
Washington	1
West Virginia	1 (independent contractors, agricultural employers with <3 employees, and casual employers are exempt)
Wisconsin	3 (including part-time workers, compliance time requirement varies by industry)
Wyoming	1

(Sources: NFIB; WCC)

The 2017 Tax Cuts and Jobs Act represented sweeping changes to the tax code. This law profoundly affected payroll taxes, especially employee federal income tax liability, and required a comprehensive reframing of employee income tax computation. Specific changes to payroll included a change to the Social Security wage base, adjustments to nonresident alien withholding, adjustments for inflation, and decreases in supplemental wage withholding rates. The Internal Revenue Service issued new mid-year tax withholding tables and forms in response to the changes mandated in this act. It introduced a new Employee's Withholding Certificate (Form W-4) and tax guide (Publication 15-T) starting in 2020.

The *Consolidated Appropriations Act of 2018* increased funding for the E-Verify program, an Internet-based system that offers employers instant verification of an employee's eligibility to work in the United States. It is important to note that the E-Verify program does not replace the need to complete Form I-9 upon employee hire because it is a voluntary service. The following table from the USCIS compares the E-Verify program against the I-9 requirement.

Form I-9	E-Verify
Mandatory	Voluntary for most businesses
Requires a Social Security number	Requires a Social Security number
No photo is required on identity documents	A photo is required on identity documents
MUST be used to re-verify expired employment authorization	MAY NOT be used to re-verify expired employment authorization

(Source: USCIS)

Another important part of the 2018 Consolidated Appropriations Act included monetary penalties of $1,000 per instance (plus damages) for employers who withhold employee tip earnings inappropriately. This section of the act repealed a 2017 Department of Labor regulation that prevented employers from requiring that all tips be placed into a pool for tipped and nontipped employees. Although the act did not remove tip pools, it prevented managers and supervisors from participating in the tip pools.

The *Coronavirus Aid, Relief, and Economic Stimulus (CARES) Act of 2020* was enacted to provide economic relief for individuals and businesses. It included an individual economic stimulus and encouragement for businesses to keep their employees. A tax credit of 50 percent of employees' wages (up to $10,000 in wages per employee) promoted employee retention for firms that sustained economic hardship during the pandemic and offered loans, funded by the Small Business Administration, to employers.

The *Taxpayer Certainty and Disaster Tax Relief Act (TCDRA) of 2020* made adjustments to the CARES Act by extending the employee retention credits (ERC) through June 30, 2021, and increasing the amount of the credit per employee to $14,000. This legislation also allowed employers to take a refundable credit against their share of Social Security taxes up to 70 percent of qualified wages paid to the employees between December 31, 2020, and June 30, 2021. The qualified wages were limited to $10,000 per employee per calendar quarter.

The *American Rescue Plan Act (ARPA) of 2021* extended the ERC for COVID-19–related closures to include periods after June 30, 2021, and allowed companies to claim the credits for the entire calendar year. This extension also included changes to the employee sick and family leave credits by extending the time period to September 30, 2021, increasing the maximum amount of the family leave credit to $12,000, and eliminating the 10-day waiting period.

> Pay transparency laws became enshrined in state law in Rhode Island, California, and Washington and were effective as of January 2023. These pay transparency laws required employers to post pay ranges on company pages and third-party websites like Glassdoor. Other states and cities are considering similar legislation, and certain companies have posted their wages voluntarily. The intent is to give applicants accurate pay information when choosing potential employers.
>
> (Source: CNBC)

Stop & Check

Which Payroll Law?

1. Established requirements for employer record-keeping.
2. Provided government assistance for workers who are too old or infirm to work.
3. Established protection for displaced workers.
4. Required employers to file taxes collected promptly.
5. Set aside funds for health insurance.
6. Regulated wages for employees whose employer engaged in governmental contracts.
7. Is governed on a state-by-state basis and protects employees injured during the course of work activities.
8. Is responsible for reporting requirements of essential health coverage for full-time equivalent employees.
9. Restructured payroll tax calculations, supplemental withholding allowances, and the Social Security wage base.
10. Funded E-Verify programs for employee eligibility to work.

a. Social Security Act
b. Workers' compensation
c. Current Tax Payment Act
d. Fair Labor Standards Act
e. Tax Cuts and Jobs Act
f. Federal Unemployment Tax Act
g. Medicare
h. Consolidated Appropriations Act
i. Affordable Care Act
j. Davis–Bacon Act

Stuart Miles/Shutterstock

FIGURE 1-2
Basic Guidelines for a Code of Ethics

- Confidentiality
- Professional Competence and Due Care
- Professionalism
- Objectivity and Independence
- Integrity

LO 1-3 Discuss the Ethical Guidelines for Payroll Accounting

Professional *ethics* is critical in any accounting context, especially in payroll accounting. After the Enron accounting scandal and the subsequent passage of the Sarbanes–Oxley Act of 2002 (SOX), ethics became a focus of the accounting profession. Even with the SOX framework, the payroll industry is rife with ethical violations, including fraud and theft. The payroll accountant is entrusted to handle money belonging to the firm and rightfully owed to the government and company employees. Payment of these monies becomes a moral contract between the company and the recipients; therefore, ethics are vital in payroll accounting. Several accounting organizations, including the American Institute of Certified Public Accountants (AICPA), the Institute of Management Accountants (IMA), and the International Federation of Accountants (IFAC), have delineated codes of ethics that are applied in the accounting profession. The basic guidelines of an ethics code include the tenets shown in Figure 1-2.

> Ethisphere maintains an annual list of the most ethical companies in the world. In 2023, the list included many companies based in the United States, such as Best Buy, Hasbro, Salesforce, TIAA, and others. Although the companies on the list are in various industries, certain ethical principles are common: integrity, social responsibility, care for all stakeholders, and honesty and transparency in all business dealings. An interesting fact is that Ethisphere found that large-cap companies that were on the list of most ethical companies outperformed similar unlisted companies by about 25 percent over a five-year period. It pays to be ethical.
>
> (Source: Ethisphere)

Confidentiality

An accountant is responsible for protecting confidential information and exercising moral judgment. A payroll accountant deals with sensitive personnel information that must remain confidential. Social Security numbers, employee legal obligations, and an employer's tax liabilities are a few examples of information that a payroll accountant must protect.

> New Jersey enacted the Diane B. Allen Equal Pay Act, strengthening existing antidiscrimination laws by preventing pay differences based on traits protected under other civil rights laws. It also protected employees who discussed pay with other employees. However, it should be noted that the payroll accountant is still responsible for maintaining the confidentiality of employee records for this law to function in the way it was intended.
>
> (Source: State of New Jersey 2018 Legislature)

Professionalism

Accountants must uphold *professionalism* by maintaining confidentiality, upholding the public's trust, and upholding professionalism in their practice. In terms of payroll accounting, professionalism includes honoring the firm's needs, its employees, and associated governmental entities. A payroll accountant must complete all tasks and adhere to deadlines despite personal issues. Personal honesty and transparency of transactions are the core of acting professionally.

fizkes/Shuttestock

> Bechtel, a company that focuses on sustainable energy, company planning, and other location-based issues, has a code of conduct that has evolved over 100 years and in multiple countries. Their ethical code requires employees to become educated and aware of potential ethical and legal conflicts in the United States and other countries where they operate.
>
> (Source: Bechtel)

Integrity

Integrity is the most important asset a professional can possess in the workplace. *Integrity* involves doing the right thing despite external pressure, personal temptations, or conflicts of interest. When weighing the integrity of a decision, the main question is: Am I doing what is right and just for everyone concerned? Any course of action that lacks integrity potentially restricts the rights of interested parties and compromises the company's best interests. The AICPA's code of ethics includes explicit direction about not covering up mistakes as part of an accountant's integrity.

> Payroll fraud can happen where pressures, opportunities, and rationalizations exist. A payroll specialist for a District of Columbia consulting firm was indicted on embezzlement charges involving fictitious employees. The payroll specialist stole over $250,000, including amounts deposited for payroll taxes, by changing the pay disbursement details of terminated employees. Instead of leaving the employees' files in a "terminated" status, the altered detail allowed automatic salary payments to continue but deposited to the payroll specialist's personal account. The payroll specialist, who pled guilty to wire fraud, was ordered to repay the employer $250,000 and was sentenced to 21 months in prison.
>
> (Source: U.S. Department of Justice)

Objectivity and Independence

Accountants must take care to be independent of any pressures that would compromise the integrity of their work. These pressures can come from business or personal relationships that may affect a payroll accountant's judgment concerning the best interests of all concerned in a given situation. *Objectivity* in accounting means that the accountant considers only facts relevant to the task at hand, independent of all other pressures. The Public Company Accounting Oversight Board (PCAOB) specifies that *independence* may be compromised if any of the following situations occur:

- Commitment to a future purchase of a financial interest in a client's business.
- Personal or family ownership is over 5 percent of a client's business.
- Professional engagement with a client's firm in which the payroll professional had a personal interest, such as partial ownership.

> Social obligations may compromise a payroll accountant's objectivity. The AICPA Code of Ethics Section 17 specifically addresses social club membership as a factor in losing an accountant's independence or objectivity. Such club membership could create a social debt that may cause an accountant to commit payroll fraud.
>
> (Source: AICPA)

Professional Competence and Due Care

Professional competence and *due care* revolve around an accountant's competence and assume that the accounting professional is equally as competent as others in a similar role. In payroll accounting, due care is an ongoing process that involves education, training, and experience. According to the AICPA, an accountant must remain current with accounting practices and legal developments to comply with due care requirements. Payroll laws and tax guidelines change regularly. As a payroll accountant, it is essential to remain aware of annual changes that the IRS and other accounting bodies publish through participation in professional accounting organizations, subscriptions to accounting industry publications, and discussions at accounting conferences.

Olivier Le Moal/Shutterstock

> Staying current with payroll changes is an ongoing task. Some sources for this information include:
>
> - IRS (www.irs.gov).
> - AICPA (www.aicpa.org).
> - Financial Accounting Standards Board (FASB) (www.fasb.org).
> - American Payroll Association (www.americanpayroll.org).
> - U.S. Department of Labor (www.dol.gov).
> - Compliance Tools for HR Professionals (www.hr.blr.com).

What's Ethical?

Stop & Check

1. Stevie is the payroll accountant for Alpha Printworks. The boss informs Stevie that the company is considering switching payroll systems and asks for input. What are some ethical concerns involved in changing accounting software?
2. Karsyn, the payroll manager, is in a sorority. At a social event, she discovers that one of her sorority sisters works for the same company. Her sorority sister asks Karsyn for confidential information about one of her department employees, claiming that the sorority oath requires Karsyn's compliance. What should Karsyn do?

LO 1-4 Identify Contemporary Payroll Practices

Jirsak/Shutterstock

Contemporary accounting practices reflect the effects of technology and electronic communications on business. Payroll practices have adapted to include modern tools that facilitate data transmission, and new challenges such as the following have emerged:

- Direct deposit regulations for employee pay and tax remittances.
- Electronic filing requirements.
- New timekeeping methods.
- The availability of paycards as a method of wage and salary disbursement.
- Government contract influences on payroll.
- International employees.
- Simultaneous in-house and outsourced payroll personnel.
- Integration of payroll into other company functions.
- Security of confidential, electronic personnel information.
- Cloud-based software designed for the security, accessibility, and portability of data.

Payroll is not a stand-alone department. Integrated software packages offered by mainstream accounting software providers, such as QuickBooks and Sage 100, allow business owners to view data across departments and synthesize the information to make large-scale decisions. Contemporary payroll systems serve as a tool for strategic planning, performance measurement, customer/vendor relations using mobile, and cloud-based platforms that may be accessed through Internet-connected devices. Payroll accountants are a key element in the decision-making process. They must remain educated about legal and compliance issues and remain current in their knowledge of software applications and relevant technological concerns.

The payroll accountant plays a vital role in a company's structure, whether large or small. Payroll and other employee benefits often represent the largest category of a company's expenses. Chipotle Mexican Grill Inc. (CMG) originally started as a subsidiary of McDonald's. Now a separate entity, CMG reported over $1.9 billion in labor expenses in its stores during the fiscal year 2022, which represented a 14.6 percent increase over 2011. As an innovative company in the fast-food market, CMG has integrated technology and sustainability measures to engage customers and promote locally sourced ingredients to support local farmers. Notice in the following table how, despite technology integration, CMG's labor expenses are nearly as large as its product-related expenses.

CHIPOTLE MEXICAN GRILL INC.			
OPERATING COSTS AND EXPENSES (in thousands, selected data)			
Company-operated restaurant expenses	**2022**	2021	2020
Food, beverage, and packaging	2,602.2	2,308.6	1,932.8
Labor	2,198.0	1,917.8	1,593.0
Occupancy	460.4	416.6	387.8
Other operating costs	1,311.9	1,197.1	1,030.0
General and administrative expenses	564.2	606.9	466.3
Total operating expenses	7,474.2	6,742.1	5,694.5
Operating income	1,160.4	804.9	290.2

(Source: SEC)

Payroll Preparation Options

Several options exist for payroll preparation. The most frequently used methods for contemporary payroll preparation are electronic accounting programs. Other options available are the manual calculation of payroll using spreadsheets and charts prepared by the Internal Revenue Service and payroll preparation by outsourcing the process to a third party such as **ADP**, **Paychex®**, or **myPay Solutions**. A hybrid solution that allows the company to outsource certain payroll functions to an external provider exists with online accounting software provided by companies such as Intuit and Sage, creators of **QuickBooks** and **Sage 100**, respectively.

Online banks are starting to enter the payroll industry to facilitate smartphone access to payroll. **Wells Fargo** and **Capital One 360** advertise access to directly deposited funds up to two days before the employer's payment date, based on the employer's funds availability. Another option targeted for small employers includes **U.S. Bank**, which offers payroll processing, reporting, and banking services that simplify the payroll process for employers and their employees.

Regardless of the payroll preparation method, the payroll accountant must understand how the process should work. In the event of hardware failure, legislative actions, or tax changes, the accountant must ensure accurate payroll preparation. Companies can lose credibility due to flawed payroll computations and be subject to substantial fines, IRS audits, and civil litigation. Cases in which companies have paid fines for improper payroll practices abound.

> A class-action lawsuit was filed against poultry producers for unfair worker practices. The companies named in the lawsuit (Cargill, Sanderson Farms, and Wayne Farms, who employ approximately 90 percent of all workers in the poultry industry) engaged in price fixing of their products that included the exchange of information among the involved companies about employee compensation to reduce the number of employees changing employers to earn a better salary and benefits. As of early January 2023, most firms named in the lawsuit have settled with plaintiffs.
>
> (Sources: PBS, Law360)

Some companies have seriously shortchanged employees' paychecks, paying fines in addition to the standard payroll expenditures. Other tales of employee overpayment highlight payroll systems problems, such as computer glitches that have delayed payment of the company's wages. Because the computer glitches are ultimately the responsibility of a company's president or CEO and represent a potential for ethical breaches, the volume of legislation and stories of problems involving payroll administration point to the need for a well-established payroll system. Despite the numerous federal and state legislative actions concerning payroll practices, none delineate the format and design of a payroll system.

The information contained in the personnel records is highly sensitive and must be protected against intrusion from unnecessary parties. The *Privacy Act of 1974* guarantees the safeguarding of information in private personnel records and mandates information safekeeping and due process rights to individuals. Consider the implications of the legal requirements of information safekeeping:

- Personnel records contain information about an individual's marital status, children, other dependents, and legal residence—sensitive information that must be protected under the Privacy Act of 1974.
- Payroll records generally contain each employee's hourly rate and salary information. Access to these records is protected by provisions of the Equal Employment Opportunity Commission (EEOC) and could provoke or inhibit discrimination lawsuits.
- The information contained in payroll records influences the accuracy and integrity of a company's accounting records. The recording of payroll expenses and liabilities affects a company's profitability, which influences investor and customer relations.
- Companies engaging in business with the federal government must comply with the Davis–Bacon Act (for federal contracts) and potentially the *Copeland Anti-Kickback Act* of 1934 (or construction projects, protecting taxpayers from unethical pay practices).
- The number of hours an employee works must comply with the Fair Labor Standards Act provisions.
- Payroll deductions, especially for retirement plan contributions, must be documented and verified per the Sarbanes–Oxley Act of 2002.

Employers must file tax deposits for employee withholding, Social Security, Medicare, FUTA, and SUTA taxes according to an identified timeline depending upon the size of the company's payroll. Taxes may be remitted via telephone, Internet, mail, or the company's payroll software. Additional reports are required from the employer on either a quarterly or an annual basis. A company has many responsibilities within its payroll system:

Dilok Klaisataporn/Shutterstock

- Tax withholding must be done consistently, reflecting the requirements of federal, state, and local authorities.
- Employers must match amounts withheld from employee paychecks for certain payroll taxes.
- Withholding of deductions that the employee voluntarily elects, such as health care, insurance, and investments, must be correctly recorded and reported.
- Timely and accurate payment must be made to the employee, government agencies, and companies for which the employee has designated the voluntary deductions.
- Tax and other liabilities must be reported to governmental agencies per established deadlines.

An accurate payroll system allows managers to focus on the firm's business, not payroll administration. A well-designed system benefits the employees, governmental agencies, and the firm. The timely forwarding of any monies withheld from employees, either by governmental regulation or voluntary election, is critical to a firm's success.

> According to the accounting firm Ernst & Young, full-time employees spend a tremendous amount of time and money each year correcting payroll errors. The average payroll error costs a company approximately $291 per employee. The errors were classified into the following categories:
>
> - Missing or incorrect time recording
> - Missing expense documentation
> - Miscalculations in paid time off
> - Employee availability to work a shift
> - Incorrectly computed accruals for paid time off

> These errors, which are costly for employers, conceal the other parts of the expenses: Legal costs, negotiated settlements, and fines. For these and other reasons, companies need dedicated, trained payroll specialists.
>
> (Source: Paycom)

Besides administrating employee pay, a well-designed and accurately maintained payroll system is necessary during inevitable governmental audits or potential business operation interruptions, as seen during the COVID-19 pandemic. An audit is a process by which a third-party organization, either a public accounting firm or a government agency, inspects the accounting records for accuracy, integrity, and compliance with federal rules and regulations. During a payroll audit, the auditor inspects the company's employee pay records, tax remittance, and voluntary deduction maintenance. The thought of audits instills fear into the hearts of even the most seasoned accounting professionals. Their salvation, however, is to establish and maintain an accurate payroll system.

Consider the growth of selected companies:

- Tom's of Maine started in 1968 as a local organic personal care product company and is now a nationally recognized leader in environmental stewardship and sustainability. (Source: www.tomsofmaine.com)
- Ben and Jerry's, which started with a $5 correspondence course in ice-cream making and a $12,000 investment in 1978, has become an icon of premium ice cream and environmental causes. Ben and Jerry's has since been purchased by the Unilever Corporation and maintains an independent board of directors and the rights to product formulas. (Source: www.benjerry.com)
- McDonald's Corporation was started in 1955 by the McDonald brothers, who sold their hamburger business to Ray Kroc. The brand is now an international icon for fast food, serving approximately 68 million customers in 120 countries daily.

These companies share similar beginnings: one location, a few employees, and a simple payroll. As each company has grown, so has the payroll complexity, including multiple departments and facilities in many states and countries. At each company's heart are a well-run business model and a sound payroll system that has evolved with it.

Tracking and monitoring employee hours, locations, and applicable governmental requirements within various nations require knowledgeable payroll staff willing to remain current with accounting trends and international regulations. Sophisticated payroll systems enable companies to create, populate, and file many documents using current software and Internet technology.

Privacy Protection

A company must make every reasonable effort to protect personnel information contained in payroll records. This is a critical part of any payroll accountant's job. Several federal privacy acts exist to protect the information contained in payroll and personnel records. Additionally, many states have enacted or expanded specific data privacy legislation. Each state's privacy law refers to "reasonable" steps companies must take to protect customers' information.

PopTika/Shutterstock

Privacy acts include (but are certainly not limited to):

- U.S. Department of Health and Human Services Privacy Act 09-40-0006 pertains to public employees' eligibility for pay, entitlements, raises, and benefits.
- Common-Law Privacy Act, which pertains to freedom from misuse or abuse of one's private affairs.
- Privacy Act of 1974, about the use of information about private citizens.
- Computer Fraud and Abuse Act (CFAA) of 1986 addresses cybercrime, an issue that has grown in importance in recent years.

The following image contains best practices as of 2023 to strengthen payroll system security:

Payroll security audit	Employee payroll training	Continual payroll software updates	Regularly scheduled changes to user login credentials
Payroll access restriction	Limit access to paper check information	Security when an employee leaves the company	Consider outsourcing payroll
Maintain separate bank accounts	Strong computer security	Physical payroll data protection	Separation of payroll duties

(Source: Forbes)

The General Accounting Office of the federal government has been working on revising guidelines about the privacy of records and releasing information as the Internet and e-business evolve. The U.S. Congress has sought ways to address contemporary computer-based cyber threats but has not passed legislation at the federal level. States have enacted privacy laws, especially regarding social media use, to protect employees against cyber hacks.

The common element among these laws is protecting sensitive employee information such as addresses, dependents, compensation amounts, and payroll deductions. The payroll accountant is also responsible for discretion in discussing pay rates, bonuses, or other compensation-related topics with employees and management. Sensitive topics should never be discussed with anyone other than the employee or appropriate managers. All employment-related items may be viewed during an audit of payroll records, and auditors must treat the information with absolute confidentiality.

One way the federal government keeps track of employers is with *Employer Identification Numbers (EINs)*. The EIN allows the IRS to know which companies may have employees, generating employment tax revenue for the government and creating tax liabilities for employers. Form SS-4 (see Figure 1-3) is used to apply for an EIN by providing the personal Social Security number, type of business, and the existence of any prior EINs for a business owner. The EIN is required for all tax deposits, tax returns, and informational returns. It will appear on the company's Forms W-2, 940, and 941, state tax forms, and the company's annual tax return. Form SS-4 may be completed either on paper or through an IRS online request portal that contains the same information as the paper form.

Confidential Records

Stop & Check

You are the payroll clerk of a company. A group of students approaches you to work on a class project and asks to see confidential personnel and payroll records. What would you do? What are the laws regarding the situation?

FIGURE 1-3
Example of Form SS-4

Form SS-4 (Rev. December 2019)
Department of the Treasury
Internal Revenue Service

Application for Employer Identification Number
(For use by employers, corporations, partnerships, trusts, estates, churches, government agencies, Indian tribal entities, certain individuals, and others.)
▶ Go to *www.irs.gov/FormSS4* for instructions and the latest information.
▶ See separate instructions for each line. ▶ Keep a copy for your records.

OMB No. 1545-0003
EIN

Type or print clearly.

1 Legal name of entity (or individual) for whom the EIN is being requested
Thomas Braden

2 Trade name of business (if different from name on line 1)
Braden Fisheries

3 Executor, administrator, trustee, "care of" name

4a Mailing address (room, apt., suite no. and street, or P.O. box)
1234 Coastal Highway

4b City, state, and ZIP code (if foreign, see instructions)
Anchorage, AK 99509

5a Street address (if different) (Don't enter a P.O. box)

5b City, state, and ZIP code (if foreign, see instructions)

6 County and state where principal business is located
Anchorage, Alaska

7a Name of responsible party
Thomas Braden

7b SSN, ITIN, or EIN
445-54-4554

8a Is this application for a limited liability company (LLC) (or a foreign equivalent)? ☑ Yes ☐ No

8b If 8a is "Yes," enter the number of LLC members ▶ 3

8c If 8a is "Yes," was the LLC organized in the United States? ☑ Yes ☐ No

9a Type of entity (check only one box). **Caution:** If 8a is "Yes," see the instructions for the correct box to check.
- ☐ Sole proprietor (SSN) _____
- ☐ Partnership
- ☐ Corporation (enter form number to be filed) ▶ _____
- ☐ Personal service corporation
- ☐ Church or church-controlled organization
- ☐ Other nonprofit organization (specify) ▶ _____
- ☑ Other (specify) ▶ Disregarded Entity
- ☐ Estate (SSN of decedent) _____
- ☐ Plan administrator (TIN) _____
- ☐ Trust (TIN of grantor) _____
- ☐ Military/National Guard ☐ State/local government
- ☐ Farmers' cooperative ☐ Federal government
- ☐ REMIC ☐ Indian tribal governments/enterprises

Group Exemption Number (GEN) if any ▶

9b If a corporation, name the state or foreign country (if applicable) where incorporated | State | Foreign country

10 Reason for applying (check only one box)
- ☑ Started new business (specify type) ▶ Commercial Fishing
- ☐ Hired employees (Check the box and see line 13.)
- ☐ Compliance with IRS withholding regulations
- ☐ Other (specify) ▶
- ☐ Banking purpose (specify purpose) ▶
- ☐ Changed type of organization (specify new type) ▶
- ☐ Purchased going business
- ☐ Created a trust (specify type) ▶
- ☐ Created a pension plan (specify type) ▶

11 Date business started or acquired (month, day, year). See instructions.
05/01/2023

12 Closing month of accounting year December

13 Highest number of employees expected in the next 12 months (enter -0- if none). If no employees expected, skip line 14.

Agricultural	Household	Other
		15

14 If you expect your employment tax liability to be $1,000 or less in a full calendar year **and** want to file Form 944 annually instead of Forms 941 quarterly, check here. (Your employment tax liability generally will be $1,000 or less if you expect to pay $5,000 or less in total wages.) If you don't check this box, you must file Form 941 for every quarter. ☐

15 First date wages or annuities were paid (month, day, year). **Note:** If applicant is a withholding agent, enter date income will first be paid to nonresident alien (month, day, year) ▶ 05/15/2023

16 Check **one** box that best describes the principal activity of your business.
- ☐ Construction ☐ Rental & leasing ☐ Transportation & warehousing ☐ Accommodation & food service ☐ Wholesale-agent/broker
- ☐ Real estate ☐ Manufacturing ☐ Finance & insurance ☑ Other (specify) ▶ Commercial Fishing ☐ Wholesale-other ☐ Retail
- ☐ Health care & social assistance

17 Indicate principal line of merchandise sold, specific construction work done, products produced, or services provided.
Fish and Seafood

18 Has the applicant entity shown on line 1 ever applied for and received an EIN? ☐ Yes ☑ No
If "Yes," write previous EIN here ▶

Third Party Designee
Complete this section **only** if you want to authorize the named individual to receive the entity's EIN and answer questions about the completion of this form.

Designee's name	Designee's telephone number (include area code)
Address and ZIP code	Designee's fax number (include area code)

Under penalties of perjury, I declare that I have examined this application, and to the best of my knowledge and belief, it is true, correct, and complete.

Name and title (type or print clearly) ▶ Thomas Braden, President

Applicant's telephone number (include area code)
907-555-1346

Signature ▶ *Thomas Braden* Date ▶ 5/1/2023

Applicant's fax number (include area code)
907-555-9876

For Privacy Act and Paperwork Reduction Act Notice, see separate instructions. Cat. No. 16055N Form **SS-4** (Rev. 12-2019)

(Source: Internal Revenue Service)

LO 1-5 Compare Payroll Processing Options for Different Businesses

Companies have several options for payroll processing. The option a company chooses depends on the business's size, complexity in terms of geographic placement and business model, the capital available for payroll processing, and the availability of trained personnel.

During the middle of the 20th century, employers measured workers' time using punch clocks and handwritten time sheets, and some employers continue to use this method. Contemporary time collection devices serve as more than simple time clocks. Companies have integrated different time-collection systems in their office security and computer access procedures. Time clocks are part of a security system to log in people as they enter a building for work, yielding analysis of simple on-site versus working-hour time.

Jeanette Landin

Practices relating to time collection are a vital element in payroll accuracy. Many companies now use biometric devices such as fingerprint readers to collect time for their hourly employees. Systems such as **UKG** (formerly Kronos) and **Paychex Flex** offer biometric badges and time-collection devices that connect with office telephones and employee smartphones. Using computer access as another collection device serves a similar function and can offer specific task tracking and precise timekeeping functionality. With mobile connectivity growth, companies now have many smartphone apps to track employee attendance and productivity, such as **WhenIWork** and **ExakTime**. These apps are particularly useful for tracking the attendance and working hours of remote employees.

The basic elements of a payroll system are similar for all companies, but this is when size does matter. However, it is the company's size and the complexity of the federal, state, and local laws that affect payroll procedures. Let's examine the differences between large and small company payrolls and then explore certified payroll issues.

Large Businesses

Large companies present intricate problems for payroll accountants. Companies such as **Apple**, **Alphabet**, and **Microsoft** have multiple divisions, many of which exist in dispersed geographical locations. **General Electric (GE)** has different companies that operate as separate entities. Payroll procedures reflect the intricacy of the company's structure and may take many forms.

One of the major challenges in larger organizations is the existence of multiple departments in which an individual employee may work on any given day. Some companies can have shared employees who allocate time to more than one department. For example, one employee may work for both the marketing and the production departments. When this occurs, the payroll accountant will have to record the time worked for each department and apply the appropriate pay rates based on the tasks that the employee performs for each department.

A common payroll procedure with large companies involves employee portals on company websites. On the company's payroll website, employees may enter vacation time, overtime, and other payroll data issues. Through the same website, employees may change withholding allowances and voluntary deductions and maintain certain aspects of their human resources files. Such web-based portals contain highly sensitive information, and the security of the information is an obvious concern for the companies who use them. Multiple identity checks and security measures are in place to ensure employee data privacy, such as SSL (secure sockets layer) encryption, *VPN* (a virtual private network), and CAPTCHA programs designed to differentiate between humans and other computer programs.

> Providing employees with Internet-based access to their personnel files is a challenging issue. Federal laws do not grant employees the right to access their personnel files, and companies must be aware of state laws before providing access. Questions of assigning access to other parties (such as union representatives), access to file artifacts, and the employee's right to challenge items in their file are issues that a firm should address when creating a web portal through which employees may access payroll records. Most importantly, issues of cybersecurity and online privacy must be addressed.
>
> (Source: SHRM)

To overcome some of the issues with payroll processing, large companies may rely heavily on payroll service vendors to assist with payroll preparation and human resources integration. Providers such as **MyPaySolutions** and **ADP** work with the company's security needs to offer websites that are secure and integrate multiple personnel functions seamlessly. Some larger firms will work with software engineers to develop independent systems tailored to unique company needs.

Large companies face other issues related to accurate timekeeping, such as the volume of employee records. Companies with computerized time-measurement systems may link employees' computer logins, telephone logins, or building access with the payroll system. Companies working with radio frequency time cards and electronic payroll monitoring can properly allocate employee time to specific machines or production lines. With the currently available computer software and services, large companies have many options to maintain their payroll systems' accuracy and integrity.

stockasso/123RF

Small Businesses

One apparent difference between large and small businesses is the volume and handling of payroll records. A small number of employees generally leads to fewer payroll-related transactions. Manual payroll systems may be maintained in small businesses, including handwritten time cards. Outsourcing payroll activities may not be as prominent due to the cost of the service versus its benefits. With a small company, the amount of time to complete payroll-related tasks may be less than in a large company. For a small company, the task can be performed without disrupting the revenue-producing tasks of the business.

Mavo/Shutterstock

While small companies have the option of processing payroll in-house with a minimum of difficulty, they may lack specifically trained payroll personnel, which may place employee pay and benefits on other personnel and increase the risk of pay or tax inaccuracies. The human resource director, office manager, and payroll professional may be the same employee. Using payroll software and a properly designed payroll system, the task of payroll for a small company is generally manageable by minimal company staff. Small companies may choose to explore outsourcing as the company grows. Outsourcing payroll may be a viable option if the task becomes unwieldy or legal obligations become unmanageable.

> Small companies have the option to use hosting services as a way to access cloud storage, subscription-based services that possess security comparable to on-site accounting software. Hosted payroll accounting software can change in scale without additional software licensing, update issues, or specific hardware.

(continued)

(concluded)

For more information about hosted payroll, check out these top-rated services:

- Paychex
- Intuit Payroll
- Gusto
- OnPay
- SurePayroll

(Source: Business News Daily)

Depending on the size of the company, the number of employees, and the complexity of the payroll process, the company may choose to purchase a computer- or cloud-based accounting system, it may continue to prepare worksheets and manual payroll checks, or it can decide to use an *outsourced vendor* for payroll preparation and associated tasks. Contemporary best practices often include cloud-based software due to the frequency and necessity of software updates and the file size. Whichever decisions the company makes as it grows, understanding the mechanics of the payroll process is paramount. Whether a company performs the payroll process in-house or outsources it, it is liable for payroll filing compliance. The next section provides an overview of the various computer-based systems available.

Common payroll mistakes made by small firms include:

- Misclassifying employees as independent contractors.
- Paying payroll late.
- Omitting the value of gift cards awarded to employees as part of their taxable income.
- Failure to make timely and/or accurate payroll tax deposits.
- Improper treatment of expense reimbursements made to employees.
- Incorrect treatment of taxable fringe benefits.

(Source: *Accounting Today*)

Large vs. Small

Stop & Check

1. What are three potential payroll processing issues faced by large companies?
2. How does payroll processing differ between large and small companies?

Computer-Based Systems

Various accounting software packages exist to facilitate payroll-related accounting tasks, including QuickBooks, Sage 100, and Microsoft Dynamics 365 GP. Using computerized payroll systems eliminates approximately 80 percent of payroll processing time and errors, but the company is still responsible for the payroll data's accuracy. Computerized accounting

FIGURE 1-4
Form W-2 Wage and Tax Statement

[Form W-2 Wage and Tax Statement, 2023, Copy 1—For State, City, or Local Tax Department]

(Source: Internal Revenue Service)

systems foster the integration of payroll data with other company financial functions through Enterprise Resource Planning (ERP), allowing decision-makers to develop a comprehensive understanding of the company's operational needs. Although payroll professionals must verify employee data and update the software at regular intervals, computerized systems reduce the burdens of manual pay calculations, pay disbursement, and report compilation from the payroll accountant.

When used properly, small companies may benefit from a computerized payroll system. Although concerns about the confidentiality of personnel records exist, electronic access to records may streamline certain tasks, such as employee information updates and overtime reporting. Additionally, as the year-end approaches, companies can deliver the employees' W-2 (see Figure 1-4) tax forms electronically, ensuring employees' rapid access to their tax documents.

A trend in payroll processing involves the issuance of electronic paycards, much like preloaded credit cards, instead of paper checks. Paycards allow employees to wait for their paychecks to be deposited at a bank. Companies that offer direct deposit as a payment option must offer paycards to employees who do not have bank accounts. However, a paycard can be lost or stolen and, with it, the employee's paycheck. Additionally, employers may be charged fees for loading a paycard. When companies consider paycards as an option, it is important to communicate to employees an understanding that there may be costs assessed by the card issuer.

Internet-Based Systems

Internet-based accounting software is an option for a company that does not need (or has the resources to purchase) a computer-based accounting system. Computer-based accounting systems such as **QuickBooks**, **Microsoft Dynamics 365 GP**, and **Sage 100** offer both desktop and Internet-based services for businesses. Companies such as **Wave** have developed Internet-only accounting packages accessible for a monthly fee. The advantages of using Internet-based services include easy access for accounting personnel, employees, and managers and automatic software updates. A potential disadvantage of relying on Internet-based software for a company's accounting is information security issues.

> *Accounting Today* conducted case studies with firms that had used Internet-based accounting software and highlighted the following:
>
> | Positive Aspects | Challenges |
> | --- | --- |
> | Timely identification of financial issues because of the ease of access to company records | Users cannot usually customize certain information layouts to suit specific company needs |
> | Low price for software access and "real-time" knowledge of business information | Not suitable for highly complex businesses such as large manufacturing operations |
> | Increased opportunity for collaboration in the business planning and monitoring process | Employee resistance to learning about new software and company accounting process |
> | Continual software updates for changes in tax rates or other related practices | More options available than company personnel knew how to use |
>
> It is estimated that advances in predictive software and artificial intelligence-based systems will make accounting software more useful for small businesses, enabling companies to engage in real-time business analysis previously out of their reach. Additionally, software advances will enable business owners to be more flexible in conducting business regarding work location, information demands, and data transmittal.
>
> (Source: *Accounting Today*)

Manual Systems

With manual payroll systems, the payroll employee relies on deduction percentages presented in publications from the Internal Revenue Service. *Publication 15* (also known as *Circular E*) and *Publication 15-T* are the payroll accountant's best friends, along with periodic updates and supplemental publications.

The largest challenges the manual payroll preparer faces are time constraints and updated tax tables. Companies can determine the time between the end of the payroll period and the employee payments. However, employers must make every reasonable effort to pay their employees in a timely and accurate manner to avoid ethical breaches and potentially costly litigation.

Manual payroll accountants may use spreadsheet programs, such as Microsoft Excel. The accountant can create lookup formulas or other connecting formulas to facilitate the accurate completion of the payroll process. Spreadsheets with formulas or macros should be used only if the accountant understands the formulas and can verify the linkage before finalizing payroll to ensure that calculations are correct.

> Approximately 40 percent of all small businesses make payroll errors, averaging $845 in annual fines. Additionally, one-third of all employers make payroll errors. The most common errors include mathematical computations, missed payments, or late payments. When employees work during paid time off, make errors due to fatigue, or engage in time theft, the employer is vulnerable to payroll errors.
>
> (Source: Business2Community)

Outsourced Payroll Systems

Outsourced payroll processing has become rather popular to ensure compliance with the changing legal structure and withholding requirements. When a company chooses to use an outsourcing firm to complete the payroll processes, there are several considerations: records retention, confidentiality, compliance, timeliness, and thoroughness. Managers should review the cost/benefits of outsourcing a firm's payroll processes before committing.

External payroll providers offer flexibility and advanced data analysis that might be challenging for smaller internal departments. During a survey of over 2,000 accounting professionals, an overwhelming margin stated they would prefer to outsource payroll functions because of the time involved. External payroll management providers such as ADP and Paychex® assist company owners and managers with strategic planning and related human resources issues. However, outsourcing is not a wise decision for all companies. For a small company, outsourcing may not be cost-effective. For large or international companies, outsourcing may be the only option to manage payroll complexity and maintain legal compliance.

A trend in payroll accounting involves cloud-based computing, meaning that the data is housed on a server external to the firm and accessible via an Internet connection. Companies such as ADP offer cloud-based payroll and human resource functions for businesses. These services reduce costs by allowing a company to avoid hardware and software costs associated with payroll. However, issues have arisen with payroll vendor stability and information security.

> Payroll processing company Kronos was the victim of a ransomware attack in late 2021. Although Kronos was operating again as of January 2022, the company was the defendant in multiple lawsuits from companies such as PepsiCo and Marriott International. By the end of March 2022, Kronos was subject to nearly two dozen lawsuits alleging FLSA violations. As of this writing, Kronos no longer exists as an option for outsourced payroll, and its tribulations have become a cautionary tale for businesses that use similar outsourced vendors.
>
> (Source: Bloomberg Law)

Certified Payroll

Companies who do business with the federal government under the Davis–Bacon Act must file a report (see Figure 1-5 for Form WH-347) delineating the payroll paid as part of the government contract with each payroll. *Certified payroll* is how the federal government keeps track of the money spent on government contracts. Davis–Bacon Act–related wages and the state versions of those regulations require special handling and knowledge. Certified payroll facilitates governmental internal accountability and verifies that Davis–Bacon Act requirements are met.

Information needed to complete a Certified Payroll report includes:

- Company-specific identifying information.
- The job being worked on and its duration.
- Employee information that includes a Social Security number and address.
- Hours worked on each job and the pay rate associated with it.
- Gross pay earned for the week.
- Taxes, withholdings, and fringe benefits.
- Net pay earned per employee.

FIGURE 1-5
Form WH-347 Certified Payroll

(Source: U.S. Department of Labor)

Choosing payroll technology can be a complex task for employees charged with finding appropriate technological solutions. Some of the considerations include:

- Flexibility in employee pay options.
- Time collection procedures.
- Tax reporting.
- Geotagging of employee work locations.
- Software affordability.
- Software update schedules.

Stop & Check

What Is the Difference?

In a few words, compare the following:

a. Manual payroll systems
b. Computerized payroll systems
c. Outsourced payroll systems
d. Certified payroll

Trends to Watch

LEGAL ENVIRONMENT

To say that the legal environment of payroll is continually evolving is an understatement. Since 2018, we have witnessed the following legal challenges:

- Increasing numbers of private employers and localities raise the minimum wage significantly to close the gap between the minimum wage and the living wage.
- Supplemental wage rate changes for payments of bonuses.
- State enforcement of predictive scheduling and fair/flexible scheduling laws on changing employees' schedules.
- Reframing the federal income tax structure, treatment for nonresident aliens, supplemental wage withholding rates, and inflation adjustments.
- An increase in the need for centralized and fully communicated company policies to meet remote workers' and companies' needs.

Future trends to watch include:

- A shift to complete digitalization of payroll processes, including partial or complete remote work options.
- Increased guidance about payroll tax impacts involving Indian tribal employees and student loan deferrals.
- A focus on employee retention could include unlimited paid time off without specific tracking of hours used.
- Increases in employees with multiple part-time jobs could lead to legislative changes involving "gig" employee classification and related benefits.
- Changes in worker attitudes about the minimum pay for which they are willing to work, as opposed to the legislated minimum wage.

Summary of Payroll Practices and System Fundamentals

Accounting practices have existed for centuries, and a need continually exists for employers to compensate employees for the work they have performed. Payroll processing became increasingly complex once the United States began taxing personal income. During the 20th century, payroll practices evolved to include withholding taxes from employees, remitting payroll taxes to government agencies, maintaining accurate and confidential records, and incorporating civil rights-related legislation. Payroll accounting is a field that requires precision and attention to minute details due to its changing nature. Additionally, payroll accountants must adhere to ethical guidelines, including due care, objectivity, independence, professional competence, integrity, and confidentiality because of the nature of their work.

The establishment of a 21st-century payroll system involves careful, deliberate planning. The framework used for the payroll system must have ample room for company growth, structure to ensure system stability, and trained payroll personnel to ensure that company and government deadlines are met. Using the best practices outlined in this chapter may help a company implement a robust payroll system, whether the system is maintained by company personnel, outsourced, completed manually, or accomplished using specifically designed software. A resilient payroll system design may reduce or prevent problems with employees and governmental entities.

Key Points

- Legislation that has affected employees' working conditions has mandated many aspects of the workplace, including civil rights, retirement and health benefits, and reinvestment in American workers.
- Payroll-specific legislation has influenced working hours and employee wages and was updated in 2020 and later years to address contemporary employer concerns.
- Employer and employee tax laws have been enacted, and the remittance of tax obligations has been mandated.
- Payroll accountants must adhere to ethical guidelines because of the nature of the work performed.
- The ethical principles of confidentiality, integrity, objectivity, independence, professional competence, and due care guide the payroll accounting profession.
- Payroll practices include the electronic transmission of employee pay and tax obligations.
- Employee information security is an ongoing concern for companies, especially with the electronic transmission of sensitive data.
- Payroll may be processed at a central corporate site or through an outsourced payroll processing company.
- Many small companies use payroll accounting software, such as QuickBooks and Sage 100.
- Cloud-based payroll processing has offered many resources for companies, including partial or total payroll preparation services.
- Payroll security and privacy are critical to ensure employer legal compliance and to protect employees.
- Outsourced payroll security has been vulnerable to cyberattacks, resulting in industry guidance regarding payroll security.

Vocabulary

- ACA
- ADA
- ADAAA
- ADEA
- ARRA
- ARPA
- ATRA
- CARES Act
- Certified payroll
- Circular E
- Civil Rights Act of 1964
- Civil Rights Act of 1991
- COBRA
- Consolidated Appropriations Act of 2018
- Copeland Anti-Kickback Act
- Coronavirus Aid, Relief and Economic Stimulus (CARES) Act of 2020
- Current Tax Payment Act (CTPA) of 1943
- Davis–Bacon Act of 1931
- DOMA
- Due care
- EEOC
- Employer Identification Number (EIN)
- Enterprise coverage
- Equal Pay Act of 1963
- ERISA
- Ethics
- E-Verify
- FICA
- FLSA
- FMLA
- FUTA
- FTE
- HIPAA
- Independence
- Independent contractor
- Individual coverage
- Integrity
- IRCA
- Lilly Ledbetter Fair Pay Act of 2009
- Living wage
- Marketplace
- Medicare tax
- Minimum wage
- OASDI
- Objectivity
- OSHA
- Outsourced vendor
- Personal Responsibility, Work and Family Promotion Act of 2002
- Privacy Act of 1974
- Protecting Americans from Tax Hikes (PATH) Act
- Professional competence
- Professionalism
- PRWOR
- Publication 15
- Publication 15-T
- Respect for Marriage Act
- Sarbanes–Oxley Act of 2002 (SOX)
- SECURE Act
- SECURE 2.0 Act
- Sixteenth Amendment to the U.S. Constitution
- Social Security Act (SSA)
- SOX
- SUTA
- Tax Cuts and Jobs Act
- TCDRA
- USERRA
- VPN
- Walsh–Healey Public Contracts Act
- Workers' compensation

Review Questions

1. What is the purpose of a payroll system?
2. What are two of the differences between large- and small-company payroll practices?
3. What is certified payroll? Which entities must use it?
4. Why might it be a good idea to let employees manage their payroll records? What are some of the pitfalls?
5. What are two ways a payroll system may protect a company in the event of a visit from a government auditor?
6. What is payroll outsourcing? When might a company consider outsourcing its payroll?
7. What are three examples of federal laws that are essential to ensure legal, fair hiring practices?
8. What are the major types of payroll processing methods?
9. What are two laws governing the taxes that employers must withhold from employees?
10. What are the guidelines for FLSA in terms of overtime and pay rate?
11. Why was the Social Security Act of 1935 created? What were its provisions?
12. How did the Medicare and Medicaid Act of 1965 modify the Social Security Act of 1935?
13. What are two of the advantages of a computerized payroll system over a manual system?

14. Which act created the term "full-time equivalents"?
15. How has cloud-based payroll processing affected contemporary payroll practices?
16. What are two of the differences between the completion of the I-9 and the use of E-Verify systems?
17. What were three provisions of the SECURE 2.0 Act?
18. What are two of the challenges that arise from the use of outsourced payroll systems?
19. What distinguishes a "living wage" from the minimum wage?
20. How does the Equal Pay Act of 1963 differ from the Lilly Ledbetter Fair Pay Act of 2009?
21. What are the differences between ARPA and TCDRA?
22. What did ARPA and TCDRA do to the CARES Act?

Exercises Set A

E1-1A.
LO 1-1, 1-2

Lupore Fabrics obtained a contract in Watts Mills, South Carolina, that involves the production of materials for military uniforms, a project contracted with the federal government for $2,800,000. What laws govern the wages Lupore Fabrics pays its workers for this project? (Select all that apply.)
1. Davis–Bacon Act
2. Sarbanes–Oxley Act
3. Walsh–Healey Act
4. FLSA

E1-2A.
LO 1-1, 1-2

Dylan Piccirillo works as the payroll clerk for Centinix, a security company that hires many part-time and temporary workers who are paid hourly. What law(s) govern(s) the hiring or documenting of these workers?
1. ADEA
2. FLSA
3. IRCA
4. USERRA

E1-3A.
LO 1-1, 1-2

London Franco was dismissed from employment at Precision Dynamics because of a race-related incident. London sued Precision Dynamics for $150,000 because of the discrimination. Which of the following laws provides for monetary awards during discrimination lawsuits?
1. FLSA
2. ADEA
3. ADA
4. Civil Rights Act of 1991

E1-4A.
LO 1-1, 1-2

Ines, Inc., is a qualified private-sector company that provides health insurance to its employees. The company is self-insured. Which of the following forms should the company provide its employees to comply with the Affordable Care Act?
1. 1095-A
2. 1095-B
3. 1095-C

E1-5A.
LO 1-3

Addison Roy is a payroll accountant who works for a private firm. Their most recent professional development course was completed in 2010. Which of the following ethical issues has Addison violated?
1. Confidentiality
2. Objectivity and independence
3. Professional competence and due care
4. Integrity

E1-6A. Max Anson owns Uninix Computers, a company with five employees. As a small business owner, Max has several options for payroll processing. What factors should be considered when deciding which payroll processing option is best for Uninix Computers? (Select all that apply.)
LO 1-4, LO 1-5
1. The number of independent contractors.
2. The physical size of the office facility.
3. The amount of money Max has to spend on payroll processing.
4. The computer technology used by the business.

Match the following terms with their definitions:

E1-7A.	Manual payroll	a.	A preloaded credit card is used to pay employees.
E1-8A.	Time card	b.	The process of gathering information about hours worked for one or more employees.
E1-9A.	Paycard	c.	A web-based application wherein employees can modify certain payroll-related information.
E1-10A.	Employee Internet portal	d.	Governs accounting for firms with federal government contracts in excess of $2,000.
E1-11A.	Certified payroll	e.	A record of the time worked during a period for an individual employee.
E1-12A.	Outsourced payroll	f.	Examples of companies used for outsourcing payroll processing.
E1-13A.	Auditor	g.	Provided funding for the E-Verify program.
E1-14A.	ADP and Paychex®	h.	Payroll administration using a paper payroll register.
E1-15A.	Time collection	i.	The use of an external company to track time and benefits and pay employees.
E1-16A.	Davis–Bacon Act	j.	A person or group who examines a company's accounting records for accuracy.
E1-17A.	Consolidated Appropriations Act	k.	A way for governmental agencies to track the payroll associated with a government contract.

Problems Set A

P1-1A. Ash Accardi is the accounting manager for a small local firm with full- and part-time staff. How do FLSA guidelines regarding working hours apply to Ash's employees?
LO 1-2

P1-2A. Micah Sherman works in the payroll department at Radiance Windows. The employer has determined that the payroll functions should be moved to a cloud-based platform that can support its 500 employees, be used remotely, and has requested recommendations. What options could Micah propose?
LO 1-4, 1-5

P1-3A. Eden Motta is the office manager and payroll clerk for his company, composed of 12 employees. An employee, Xai Gladwin, stops by Eden's office and wants to view their payroll record. What privacy regulations must Eden consider before granting coworker access?
LO 1-1, 1-2

P1-4A. A group of employees who read on a website that income tax collection is illegal approach Jules Furst, the controller for a large company. They ask that the company stop withholding income taxes from their pay without an explanation of what laws govern income tax collection. What should Jules tell them?
LO 1-3

P1-5A. Callen Germain is a warehouse worker for a small grocery market. While some merchandise was being moved, the loading dock door unexpectedly fell and injured Callen. How does OSHA apply to Callen for this type of injury?
LO 1-1, 1-2

P1-6A.
LO 1-4
Quinn Magnus is a payroll accountant for Mama Bear Trading Co. A coworker from the packaging department contacts Quinn via electronic communication and asks to see all employees' payroll records for a specific payroll date. How should Quinn respond?

P1-7A.
LO 1-3
Parker Alberighi and Val van Peij are friends who work for the same company. Parker manages a manufacturing department, and Val supervises the payroll clerks. Which ethical guidelines or rules would these friends need to remember when discussing work?

P1-8A.
LO 1-1, 1-2
At Denniston Industries, employees have the option of choosing employer-sponsored health insurance. According to COBRA, what responsibilities does the employer have upon the termination of an employee?

P1-9A.
LO 1-3
Xan Preston is a new manager at Resterra, Inc. Xan is looking at using the E-Verify process for new hires. What recommendations can you give regarding the differences between having employees complete the I-9 and the E-Verify process?

P1-10A.
LO 1-4
Landry Russell is a new employee in the payroll department for Palermo Industries. Landry has had several employees approaching with questions but is unsure how privacy regulations could affect the responses. What advice would you give Landry about privacy laws and payroll?

Exercises Set B

E1-1B.
LO 1-1, 1-2
Emery Devi is a military veteran who requires many absences for medical reasons. The supervisor at Baytery Farms has demanded Emery either reduce the number of sick days used or provide a medical history to support the absences. Which law(s) protect Emery? (Select all that apply.)
1. ADA
2. FLSA
3. USERRA
4. HIPAA

E1-2B.
LO 1-1, 1-2
Galen Rana is a production worker at Gexo Manufacturing, which produces air-conditioning systems. After working there for 10 years, she discovers through conversations with a colleague with the same title and similar seniority that her wage is 20 percent lower than his wage. She feels that she has been a victim of discrimination. Which law(s) govern her situation?
1. FLSA
2. Civil Rights Act of 1964
3. ADEA
4. Lilly Ledbetter Fair Pay Act of 2009

E1-3B.
LO 1-4, 1-5
Lyric Tesfaye is the new bookkeeper for Birch Online Enterprises, a small business consulting firm, and was hired to replace a long-time employee who retired. Lyric notices that the previous bookkeeper used a manual system. The company owner has said that Lyric may update the payroll system. What options are available?

E1-4B.
LO 1-2
Zyon Deng is a payroll accountant at Sucre Foods. Zyon works remotely from home, communicates with colleagues via Zoom, and has a VPN to prevent hackers from accessing the computer data. Which privacy law(s) require Zyon to protect the information on the computer, even from family members? (Select all that apply.)
1. HHS Privacy Act 09-40-0006
2. Common-Law Privacy Act
3. Privacy Act of 1974
4. CFAA of 1986

E1-5B.
LO 1-3

Regan Marrioni is in the payroll department at Seven Wonders International Foods. Regan is part of a social organization, along with several of his coworkers. Which of the following ethical standards could become compromised in social situations?
1. Integrity
2. Professionalism
3. Professional competence and due care
4. Confidentiality

E1-6B.
LO 1-5

Kennedy Watson is the payroll accountant for Antizio Electronics, a company that engages in federal contracts. Kennedy wants to ensure that the company is compliant with the provisions of the Davis–Bacon Act. What is the process used to monitor payroll compliance in this situation?
1. Contracted payroll
2. Davis–Bacon verification
3. Certified payroll
4. Outsourced payroll

Match the following items with their definitions:

E1-7B.	USERRA	a.	A provision of the Sarbanes–Oxley Act.
E1-8B.	Respect for Marriage Act	b.	Instituted a tiered income tax on workers.
E1-9B.	Internal controls documentation	c.	Prohibited employment of individuals younger than 16 years of age.
E1-10B.	HIPAA	d.	Strengthened the child support provisions of PRWOR.
E1-11B.	Lilly Ledbetter Fair Pay Act	e.	Legislation that governs the treatment of military service personnel.
E1-12B.	Sixteenth Amendment	f.	A worker who is not subject to a company's direction or its payroll laws.
E1-13B.	Walsh–Healey Public Contracts Act	g.	Repealed the 180-day statute of limitations on equal pay complaints.
E1-14B.	Independent contractor	h.	Reframing federal employee income tax computations.
E1-15B.	Personal Responsibility, Work and Family Promotion Act of 2002	i.	The law guaranteeing marriage equality under any circumstances.
E1-16B.	IRCA	j.	Protects the confidentiality of employee medical records.
E1-17B.	Tax Cuts and Jobs Act	k.	Mandates completion of Form I-9.

Problems Set B

P1-1B.
LO 1-4, 1-5

Peyton Hatton is a payroll accountant with Embotelladora Traders, Inc. One of the employees poses a question about the legality of the deduction for Social Security tax from their pay. What should Peyton tell the colleague?

P1-2B.
LO 1-1, 1-2

Jaylin Thomas is the payroll clerk for Telemba Communications. One of the company's employees, Dakota Boon, informs Jaylin that he feels that he was the victim of unequal pay three years prior. What law(s) guide Dakota's complaint?

P1-3B.
LO 1-3

Blake Hudnall is Conosis Incorporated's payroll accountant. During a casual conversation with coworkers, Blake learns that Teagan Vinkovic, a coworker, is deliberately overstating the number of hours worked during each pay period because of a personal economic situation. Which ethical guidelines pertain to this situation? What should Blake do with this knowledge?

P1-4B.
LO 1-4

Amari Meyers works in the payroll department for Racine Traders. The company has experienced a decline in revenue over the past six months. The company president asks Amari to delay the remittance of payroll taxes to make more cash available to the company. Which act would be violated if Amari complies with the company president's request?

P1-5B.
LO 1-1, 1-2, 1-3

During a review of payroll records, Ocean Morena notices that a female employee in Department A receives a significantly lower salary than similarly skilled male employees in the same department. What actions should Ocean take in this situation?

P1-6B.
LO 1-3

Sawyer Alescio is an accountant for Diado, a multinational firm. Sawyer notices that the new state payroll tax updates have not been installed during payroll processing in the firm's software. What ethical guidelines govern Sawyer's behavior in this situation?

P1-7B.
LO 1-2

Nyx Croce is an employee of Autonder, a contractor that provides governmental construction services in Washington, DC. The current contract is for $250,000. Nyx is 22 and is paid $9.50 per hour. How does the Walsh–Healey Public Contracts Act affect Nyx?

P1-8B.
LO 1-4

Marlon Moyo works as a payroll clerk at Semiconductor, Inc. Marlon shares an office with three other coworkers and must examine documents containing personal information as a regular part of the duties. Based on the provisions of the Privacy Act of 1974, what responsibilities does Marlon have regarding handling the payroll records?

P1-9B.
LO 1-5

West is a senior payroll administrator for Falcive Landscape Design. The company has 15 employees and annual revenues of $10 million. The company has been using and maintaining manual payroll records for the last 20 years. The president of Falcive Landscape Design wants to explore options for computerized payroll processing. Which payroll option is the most suitable for both West and Falcive Landscape Design? Why?

P1-10B.
LO 1-2

Angel Bellini is the payroll accountant for Pyrondo Fireworks, and has been asked for information about employees and independent contractors. What are three of the key differences between employees and independent contractors?

Critical Thinking

CT1-1. You have been hired as a Dynozz Medical Software consultant, facing an IRS audit of its accounting records. During your review, you notice anomalies in the payroll system involving overpayments for labor and payments to terminated employees. What should you do?

CT1-2. You are the accountant for Cryologic, a local nonprofit organization. You have been tasked with managing the payroll costs so that staffing levels can remain the same even if funding levels change. One consideration is outsourcing the payroll functions to a payroll processing company. What are some factors that should be considered in this decision? Why are these factors important?

In the Real World: Scenario for Discussion

Domino's Pizza franchises in New York were sued by the state of New York for wage theft at 10 stores. Under New York law, a corporation and a franchiser are joint employers if they meet certain employee control criteria. The state found that Domino's met the criteria for being a joint employer because it mandates many policies with which franchisers must comply. The problem arose when Domino's mandated the use of PULSE payroll software, which the pizza company knew to be flawed and did not attempt to remedy. The flawed software led to employees being paid at rates below the legal minimum wage, failing to pay overtime, not reimbursing employees for vehicle use, and abusing tip credit guidelines.

Food for Thought:

1. Should the franchisees be held liable as joint employers with Domino's? Why or why not?
2. Which laws pertain to employee wages? How would they apply in this situation?
3. What could be done to ensure future legal compliance?

Internet Activities

1-1. Using the website www.jstor.org, search for articles about payroll-related laws or relevant employment legislation. Once you find an article, summarize the article and explain how the legislation influenced contemporary payroll practices.

1-2. Visit the website of the American Payroll Association at www.americanpayroll.org. On the right side of the home page, you will find articles about recent developments in payroll practices and legislation. Choose an article and create a presentation to your class about how its content affects payroll practice.

1-3. Want to know more about the specifics of some of the concepts in this chapter? Check out these websites:

   www.dol.gov/whd/

   www.taxhistory.com/1943.html

   www.workerscompensationinsurance.com

   connecteam.com/employee-time-clock-app/

   www.adp.com

   www.paychex.com

1-4. Would it help to see a video explanation of FLSA coverage? Go to the following link and select Topic 1: Coverage. https://www.dol.gov/whd/flsa/videos.htm

1-5. Check out www.employer.gov to see the Department of Labor's Office of Compliance site. This site contains guidelines for employers about their specific responsibilities to employees, compliance deadlines, posters, and other resources. Its employee-focused website, www.worker.gov, contains worker-focused resources geared to foster an understanding of employee rights under the law.

1-6. Using the website www.ncsea.org, search for research about child support statistics, collections per year, and payroll professionals' role in the process.

Continuing Payroll Project: Prevosti Farms and Sugarhouse

sianc/Shutterstock

Toni Prevosti is opening a new business, Prevosti Farms and Sugarhouse, a small company that will harvest, refine, and sell maple syrup products. In subsequent chapters, students will have the opportunity to establish payroll records and complete payroll information for Prevosti Farms and Sugarhouse.

Toni has decided that she needs to hire employees for the business to grow. Complete the application for Prevosti Farms and Sugarhouse's Employer Identification Number (Form SS-4) with the following information:

Form SS-4 — **Application for Employer Identification Number**
(Rev. December 2019)
(For use by employers, corporations, partnerships, trusts, estates, churches, government agencies, Indian tribal entities, certain individuals, and others.)
Department of the Treasury
Internal Revenue Service
▶ Go to *www.irs.gov/FormSS4* for instructions and the latest information.
▶ See separate instructions for each line. ▶ Keep a copy for your records.

OMB No. 1545-0003
EIN

Type or print clearly.

1 Legal name of entity (or individual) for whom the EIN is being requested

2 Trade name of business (if different from name on line 1)

3 Executor, administrator, trustee, "care of" name

4a Mailing address (room, apt., suite no. and street, or P.O. box)

5a Street address (if different) (Don't enter a P.O. box.)

4b City, state, and ZIP code (if foreign, see instructions)

5b City, state, and ZIP code (if foreign, see instructions)

6 County and state where principal business is located

7a Name of responsible party

7b SSN, ITIN, or EIN

8a Is this application for a limited liability company (LLC) (or a foreign equivalent)? . . . . [✓] Yes [ ] No

8b If 8a is "Yes," enter the number of LLC members . . . . . . ▶

8c If 8a is "Yes," was the LLC organized in the United States? . . . . [✓] Yes [ ] No

9a **Type of entity** (check only one box). **Caution:** If 8a is "Yes," see the instructions for the correct box to check.
[ ] Sole proprietor (SSN) _____
[ ] Partnership
[ ] Corporation (enter form number to be filed) ▶ _____
[ ] Personal service corporation
[ ] Church or church-controlled organization
[ ] Other nonprofit organization (specify) ▶ _____
[✓] Other (specify) ▶ _____
[ ] Estate (SSN of decedent) _____
[ ] Plan administrator (TIN) _____
[ ] Trust (TIN of grantor) _____
[ ] Military/National Guard   [ ] State/local government
[ ] Farmers' cooperative   [ ] Federal government
[ ] REMIC   [ ] Indian tribal governments/enterprises
Group Exemption Number (GEN) if any ▶ _____

9b If a corporation, name the state or foreign country (if applicable) where incorporated
State: _____   Foreign country: _____

10 **Reason for applying** (check only one box)
[✓] Started new business (specify type) ▶ _____
[ ] Hired employees (Check the box and see line 13.)
[ ] Compliance with IRS withholding regulations
[ ] Other (specify) ▶
[ ] Banking purpose (specify purpose) ▶ _____
[ ] Changed type of organization (specify new type) ▶ _____
[ ] Purchased going business
[ ] Created a trust (specify type) ▶ _____
[ ] Created a pension plan (specify type) ▶ _____

11 Date business started or acquired (month, day, year). See instructions.

12 Closing month of accounting year

13 Highest number of employees expected in the next 12 months (enter -0- if none). If no employees expected, skip line 14.
| Agricultural | Household | Other |

14 If you expect your employment tax liability to be $1,000 or less in a full calendar year **and** want to file Form 944 annually instead of Forms 941 quarterly, check here. (Your employment tax liability generally will be $1,000 or less if you expect to pay $5,000 or less in total wages.) If you don't check this box, you must file Form 941 for every quarter. [ ]

15 First date wages or annuities were paid (month, day, year). **Note:** If applicant is a withholding agent, enter date income will first be paid to nonresident alien (month, day, year) . . .

16 Check **one** box that best describes the principal activity of your business.
[ ] Construction [ ] Rental & leasing [ ] Transportation & warehousing [ ] Health care & social assistance [ ] Wholesale-agent/broker
[ ] Real estate [ ] Manufacturing [ ] Finance & insurance [ ] Accommodation & food service [ ] Wholesale-other [ ] Retail
[✓] Other (specify) ▶

17 Indicate principal line of merchandise sold, specific construction work done, products produced, or services provided.

18 Has the applicant entity shown on line 1 ever applied for and received an EIN? [ ] Yes [✓] No
If "Yes," write previous EIN here ▶

Third Party Designee
Complete this section **only** if you want to authorize the named individual to receive the entity's EIN and answer questions about the completion of this form.
Designee's name | Designee's telephone number (include area code)
Address and ZIP code | Designee's fax number (include area code)

Under penalties of perjury, I declare that I have examined this application, and to the best of my knowledge and belief, it is true, correct, and complete.
Name and title (type or print clearly) ▶
Applicant's telephone number (include area code)
Applicant's fax number (include area code)

Signature ▶ *Thomas Braden*   Date ▶ 5/1/2023

For Privacy Act and Paperwork Reduction Act Notice, see separate instructions.   Cat. No. 16055N   Form **SS-4** (Rev. 12-2019)

(Source: Internal Revenue Service)

Prevosti Farms and Sugarhouse is located at 820 Westminster Road, Bridgewater, Vermont, 05520 (which is also Ms. Prevosti's home address), with phone number 802-555-3456. Bridgewater is in Windsor County, Vermont. Toni, the responsible party for a limited liability corporation created in the United States with one member (disregarded entity), has decided that Prevosti Farms and Sugarhouse will pay its employees biweekly. Toni's Social Security number is 055-22-0443. The beginning date of the business is February 1, 2023. Prevosti Farms and Sugarhouse will use the calendar year as its accounting year. Toni anticipates that she will need to hire six employees initially for the business, three of whom will be agricultural and three who will be office workers. The first pay period ends on February 10, 2023, and the first wage disbursement to employees will be on February 14, 2023. Toni has not had a prior EIN. The reason for filling out the SS-4 is the establishment of the new business.

Answers to Stop & Check Exercises

Which Law?

1. k
2. h
3. b
4. f
5. i
6. j
7. a
8. d
9. g
10. c
11. e
12. l

Which Payroll Law?

1. d
2. a
3. f
4. c
5. g
6. j
7. b
8. i
9. e
10. h

What's Ethical?

1. Answers will vary. Some concerns include data privacy and integrity in the software switchover, tax and employee pay integrity on the new software, and employee pay methods.
2. Answers will vary. Karsyn could choose to ignore her sorority sister's request, claiming confidentiality. She could also discontinue active participation in the sorority. In any case, Karsyn must not consent to her sorority sister's request for confidential information.

Confidential Records

As a payroll clerk, your task is to protect the privacy and confidentiality of the information you maintain for the company. If a student group—or any personnel aside from the company's payroll employees and officers—wishes to review confidential records, you should deny their request. If needed, you should refer the group to your department's manager to discuss the matter in more depth. The laws that apply to this situation are the Privacy Act of 1974, the U.S. Department of Health and Human Services Privacy Act 09-40-0006, the Common-Law Privacy Act, the Computer Fraud and Abuse Act, and potentially HIPAA.

Large vs. Small

1. Large companies face issues with multiple departments, employee access to online personnel portals, employee data security, and timekeeping accuracy.
2. For small companies, payroll processing will involve fewer employees than for larger companies. Smaller companies could maintain their payroll needs using company personnel because of the lower volume of transactions. Larger companies need to consider their available trained payroll accountants and other staff to determine if they can reliably handle the volume of payroll needs in a timely and accurate manner.

What Is the Difference?

a. Manual payroll systems involve paper-and-pencil record-keeping or a spreadsheet program, such as Microsoft Excel. This is most appropriate for very small firms.
b. Computerized payroll systems can be used by any company, regardless of size. Examples of computerized systems include QuickBooks, Sage 100, and Microsoft Dynamics 365 GP. These computer packages range in price, depending on the company size and operational scope.
c. Outsourced payroll involves the engagement of a third party to manage a company's payroll data, issue employee compensation, and prepare tax forms.
d. Certified payroll pertains to companies with employees who work on federal government contracts. Certified payroll ensures that a company reports payroll expenditures of contractually allocated money.

Chapter Two

Payroll System Procedures

Payroll procedures have a dual focus: (1) governmental rules and (2) the company's needs. The company must abide by the applicable governmental and industrial regulations or face potential fines, sanctions, or closure. To comply with regulations, a company must make several decisions: pay frequency, pay types (e.g., direct deposit, paycards, or paper checks), employee benefits, and handling of pay advances. The payroll accountant must prepare for the integration of new hires, transfer of employees among departments, and terminations that occur during the normal course of business. Employee benefits and government-required payroll deductions complicate the employee payment process.

Accountants handle documents that have varying levels of confidentiality. Some items include receipts for expenses, invoices from vendors, and other business-related documents that are not confidential. Payroll accountants handle employee-related documents that are usually private and often contain highly sensitive personal information. Various regulations regarding the length of retention and storage procedures apply to payroll documents. An important note about financial or personnel documentation is that any documents connected with fraudulent activity have no time limit for retention purposes. In the event of suspected fraud, investigators may request relevant fraud-related documents at any time.

LEARNING OBJECTIVES

After studying Chapter 2, you should be able to:

LO 2-1   Identify Important Payroll Procedures and Pay Cycles
LO 2-2   Prepare Required Employee Documentation
LO 2-3   Differentiate between Exempt and Nonexempt Workers
LO 2-4   Explain Pay Records and Employee File Maintenance
LO 2-5   Describe Internal Controls and Record Retention for a Payroll System
LO 2-6   Discuss Employee Termination and Document Destruction Procedures

Jasmin Merdan/Moment/Getty Images

Refugees Enter the Workforce

Immigrant labor is nothing new in the United States. The use of H-1B visas is common but is generally restricted in terms of the time allowed to work in the United States and the number of visas allowed. H-1B visas are generally issued to people with special skills, mostly with a bachelor's degree or higher. The specialty skills include doctors, architects, educators, and accountants, among other professions. H-1B visa costs are usually paid by the employer and generally permit the worker to stay in the United States for up to three years.

The United States has experienced an influx of asylum seekers from many countries, including Afghanistan, Syria, and Ukraine, among others. Those seeking asylum must prove the need to leave their country of origin because of war or other violence that threatens them or their family. Asylum seekers receive a special employment authorization document (EAD) that replaces the need for an H-1B visa and does not have a time limit attached. To become employed, refugees must present their EAD, the Social Security card received upon admission to the United States, and a document from list B on the I-9 to prove identity. Employers do not pay the fee for refugee workers. The maximum number of refugees permitted into the United States each year remains at 125,000 persons as of 2023.

(Sources: USCIS, SHRM, Forbes)

> **Personnel and payroll files are closely related. In Chapter 2, we will explore payroll system procedures, including information about file security, legally required documents, and internal controls.**

LO 2-1 Identify Important Payroll Procedures and Pay Cycles

The documentation required for paying employees starts before the first employee is hired. The Employer Identification Number (EIN), obtained online from the IRS, is the first step in employer documentation, closely followed by the employee information files. Under the Fair Labor Standards Act (FLSA), certain information is required in every employee file. According to the U.S. Department of Labor, the required information to be maintained in the employee file includes:

1. Employee's full name as used for Social Security purposes, and the employee's identifying symbol or number, if used in place of the employee's name on any time, work, or payroll records.
2. Address, including zip code.
3. Birthdate, if younger than 19.
4. Sex and occupation.
5. Time and day of the week when the employee's workweek begins.
6. Hours worked each day and total hours worked each workweek.
7. The basis on which employee's wages are paid.
8. Regular hourly pay rate.
9. Total daily or weekly straight-time earnings.
10. Total overtime earnings for the workweek.
11. All additions to or deductions from the employee's wages.
12. Total wages paid each *pay period*.
13. Date of payment and the pay period covered by the payment.

Payroll documentation regulations protect employees by ensuring that they receive accurate paychecks. These regulations also keep employers in compliance with tax regulations and provide an audit trail for government bodies. *New-hire reporting* requirements ensure that employees pay legal obligations such as child support and garnishments.

Figure 2-1 shows a sample Employee Information Form, which contains elements of the employee file's information. Note that the firm's human resources department maintains the employee file. The payroll department maintains the employee information form shown in Figure 2-1, so some FLSA elements may not appear on the form.

FIGURE 2-1
Sample Employee Information Form

EMPLOYEE EARNING RECORD

NAME	Jonathan A. Doe	Hire Date	1/3/2023	Dependent child<17	1
ADDRESS	100 Main Street	Date of Birth	4/16/2002	Dependent other	1
CITY/STATE/ZIP	Anytown, MD 21220	Position	Sales PT/(FT)	Step 4a W-4 Inf	none
TELEPHONE	202-555-4009	Filing Status	Married/Joint	Step 4b W-4 Inf	none-standard
SOCIAL SECURITY NUMBER	987-65-4321	Pay Rate	$15 (HR)/WK/MO	Step 4c W-4 Inf HR/Wk/Mo	none

Period Ended	Hrs Worked	Reg Pay	OT Pay	Gross Pay	401(k)	Fed Inc. Tax	Social Sec. Tax	Medicare	State Inc. Tax	Total Deduct	Net Pay	YTD
1/13/2023	80.00	1,200.00		1,200.00	25.00	12.28	74.40	17.40	49.94	179.02	1,020.98	1,020.98

The Equal Employment Opportunity Commission's protection of employee rights, especially when it leads to a lawsuit, involves the firm's personnel documentation. Accurate and correctly maintained payroll records are vital because they reflect employees' treatment. In certain states, such as Illinois, employees can inspect their personnel files and issue rebuttals for incorrect items.

When a company develops or reviews its payroll system, the payroll accountant faces myriad tasks. The employer must answer several questions, including:

- How will the company handle new hires?
- What information will be maintained in employee personnel files?
- Where will files be stored, and who is responsible for file security?
- What will the procedure be when an employee transfers from one department to another?
- What is the procedure to follow upon employee termination?
- What processes should the company establish to ensure government compliance?
- How will employee time and attendance be tracked?
- How long do employee files need to be retained after an employee leaves the company?
- Do employees have the legal right to inspect their files, and what procedures should be in place when employees ask to see their files?
- Where will the mandatory FLSA Minimum Wage Poster (Figure 2-2) be displayed?

Pay Cycles

Let's start with a basic question: How often should the company pay its employees? Regardless of which accounting system the company uses, determining the pay cycle, or pay periods, is the first thing a new company needs to establish. Options for payroll cycles include the following:

Daily payroll is typically paid at the end of the day or by the next business day. This payroll processing method is typical in day labor situations; however, it should be noted that day labor could be treated as independent contractor work and thus not be subject to payroll, payroll taxes, or a W-2. Due to a leap year, daily payroll could potentially have 365 or 366 pay periods.

Weekly payroll is typically used in a five-day workweek. The employees receive their paychecks the following Friday. Several types of companies use a weekly payroll system, including grocery stores, construction, and professional offices. This pay frequency may lead to 52 pay periods per year.

Biweekly payroll is typically processed based on a two-week period, and employees receive their paychecks approximately a week after the end of the pay period. Pay dates may be any weekday. This pay frequency generally has 26 pay periods per year. There may be 27 pay periods in a biweekly payroll; however, this is rare, and typical calculations will use 26.

Semimonthly payroll is paid twice a month. Examples of semimonthly payroll pay dates include (1) the 1st and 15th of the month and (2) the 15th and last day of the month. This is not the same as biweekly payroll, and taxation and hours paid are different. Employees receive 24 pay disbursements per year when using a semimonthly payroll system.

Monthly payroll is less frequently used than other methods. Some companies process payroll once per month and may allow a semimonthly draw to the employees. When employees are allowed to draw their wages at mid-month, the employer may or may not take payroll taxes out of the draw. If the mid-month draw does not have payroll taxes withheld, the month-end payroll will need to recover all taxes and withholdings for the month from the employee.

Figure 2-3 shows the different types of pay cycles a company can offer its employees.

FIGURE 2-2
FLSA Minimum Wage Poster

EMPLOYEE RIGHTS
UNDER THE FAIR LABOR STANDARDS ACT

FEDERAL MINIMUM WAGE
$7.25 PER HOUR
BEGINNING JULY 24, 2009

The law requires employers to display this poster where employees can readily see it.

OVERTIME PAY — At least 1½ times the regular rate of pay for all hours worked over 40 in a workweek.

CHILD LABOR — An employee must be at least 16 years old to work in most non-farm jobs and at least 18 to work in non-farm jobs declared hazardous by the Secretary of Labor. Youths 14 and 15 years old may work outside school hours in various non-manufacturing, non-mining, non-hazardous jobs with certain work hours restrictions. Different rules apply in agricultural employment.

TIP CREDIT — Employers of "tipped employees" who meet certain conditions may claim a partial wage credit based on tips received by their employees. Employers must pay tipped employees a cash wage of at least $2.13 per hour if they claim a tip credit against their minimum wage obligation. If an employee's tips combined with the employer's cash wage of at least $2.13 per hour do not equal the minimum hourly wage, the employer must make up the difference.

NURSING MOTHERS — The FLSA requires employers to provide reasonable break time for a nursing mother employee who is subject to the FLSA's overtime requirements in order for the employee to express breast milk for her nursing child for one year after the child's birth each time such employee has a need to express breast milk. Employers are also required to provide a place, other than a bathroom, that is shielded from view and free from intrusion from coworkers and the public, which may be used by the employee to express breast milk.

ENFORCEMENT — The Department has authority to recover back wages and an equal amount in liquidated damages in instances of minimum wage, overtime, and other violations. The Department may litigate and/or recommend criminal prosecution. Employers may be assessed civil money penalties for each willful or repeated violation of the minimum wage or overtime pay provisions of the law. Civil money penalties may also be assessed for violations of the FLSA's child labor provisions. Heightened civil money penalties may be assessed for each child labor violation that results in the death or serious injury of any minor employee, and such assessments may be doubled when the violations are determined to be willful or repeated. The law also prohibits retaliating against or discharging workers who file a complaint or participate in any proceeding under the FLSA.

ADDITIONAL INFORMATION
- Certain occupations and establishments are exempt from the minimum wage, and/or overtime pay provisions.
- Special provisions apply to workers in American Samoa, the Commonwealth of the Northern Mariana Islands, and the Commonwealth of Puerto Rico.
- Some state laws provide greater employee protections; employers must comply with both.
- Some employers incorrectly classify workers as "independent contractors" when they are actually employees under the FLSA. It is important to know the difference between the two because employees (unless exempt) are entitled to the FLSA's minimum wage and overtime pay protections and correctly classified independent contractors are not.
- Certain full-time students, student learners, apprentices, and workers with disabilities may be paid less than the minimum wage under special certificates issued by the Department of Labor.

WAGE AND HOUR DIVISION
UNITED STATES DEPARTMENT OF LABOR
1-866-487-9243
TTY: 1-877-889-5627
www.dol.gov/whd

WH1088 REV 07/16

(Source: U.S. Department of Labor)

FIGURE 2-3
Pay Periods

Frequency	Periods
Daily	365 or 366 periods
Weekly	52 periods
Biweekly	26 periods
Semimonthly	24 periods
Monthly	12 periods

What's in the File?

Stop & Check

1. Which of the following artifacts must be included in the employee file?
   a. Full name and address
   b. Occupation
   c. Mother's maiden name
   d. Pay rate
   e. Date of payment
   f. Spouse's name

Match the pay frequencies:
2. Monthly
3. Semimonthly
4. Biweekly
5. Weekly

The number of pay periods:
a. 26 or 27
b. 12
c. 52
d. 24

LO 2-2 Prepare Required Employee Documentation

Employees versus Independent Contractors

Maria Vonotna/Shutterstock

People who work for a company may be classified as either employees or independent contractors, depending on the nature of the work and withholding payroll-related taxes from the worker's compensation. According to the Internal Revenue Service (IRS), millions of workers have been misclassified, which has led to employers not depositing the full amount of taxes. Employees miss out on benefits. The use of IRS **Form SS-8**, the Determination of Worker Status for Purposes of Employment Taxes and Income Tax Withholding, is a way that employers may receive official guidance about worker classification. This form is available from the IRS and elicits information about behavioral control, financial control, and the worker's relationship to the firm as ways to determine the correct status of the worker as an employee or an independent contractor. When the employer submits this form, the IRS makes the final determination of employee status.

Employees

The determination of a worker as an employee has two primary criteria according to labor laws. The first is *work direction,* meaning the employer substantially directs the worker's performance. The employer provides the primary tools an employee uses; for example, the employee may be given a desk, computer, company car, or other items needed to complete the assigned work. The other criterion is *material contribution,* which means that the work that the employee completes must involve substantial effort. An employer withholds payroll taxes from an employee's compensation, provides company-specific benefits, and includes the worker on governmental reports.

Independent Contractors

Classification of a worker as an independent contractor (IC) means that the employer does not direct the worker's specific actions or provide the tools needed to complete the work. For example, if a worker performed accounting services for a company but used a privately owned computer and printer and determined the number and timing of the hours worked for the company, the worker could be classified as an independent contractor. An independent contractor may or may not perform work that constitutes a material contribution to the employer.

Another identifier of an independent contractor is the duration of the relationship with the employer. Independent contractors tend to have shorter-term relationships with the business than employees do. Furthermore, an independent contractor will not share in the profits or losses of the company in the same manner as employees. Finally, independent contractors are not subject to FLSA provisions for minimum wage and overtime pay.

Payment records for independent contractors, although maintained separately from payroll records, are instances in which payroll accountants must be aware of employee classification and record-keeping requirements to avoid fraudulent activity. Independent contractors generally work for specified fees that they bill to the company, which typically pays them through their accounts payable department, not payroll. Independent contractors are also responsible for their own payroll taxes. The topic of worker classification as an employee or independent contractor has become increasingly important in the past decade. Many employers have sought to reduce governmental fines and other liabilities stemming from the incorrect classification of workers.

The IRS uses three common-law tests to clarify whether a worker is an employee or an independent contractor:

1. **Behavioral Control:** To what extent does the employer have the right to control and direct the worker's actions?
2. **Financial Control:** This guideline pertains to the worker's unreimbursed expenses, investment in job-related tools, availability of the worker's services to other entities outside the company, and how the worker is paid.
3. **Relationship of the Parties:** This includes details related to any work-related contracts between the employer and the worker, benefits offered, the permanency of the relationship, and the relationship between the worker's services and the firm's normal business operations.

As of 2020, the U.S. Department of Labor issued a final rule to clarify independent contractor status determination. The Department of Labor withdrew this rule in 2021, returning to its earlier guidelines in **Fact Sheet #13**:

1. The worker's contribution of equipment to perform the job
2. The permanence of the working relationship between the individual and the business
3. The importance of the individual's work within the scope of the firm's operations
4. Control of the worker's activities by the employer

5. The amount of the worker's judgment necessary for the company to remain competitive in its industry
6. The extent to which the worker is an independent organization (i.e., how much the worker performs tasks for one company versus several)

For additional clarification, the employer should review the new **Independent Contractor Status** final rule, which may be obtained via the Department of Labor.

The gig economy, where individuals engage in part-time, self-directed work, has evolved since the term was introduced over the last decade. One part of this evolution is governmental regulation, which has lacked clarity because of the independent nature of workers' duties and needs. Another issue is the power of workers engaged in the gig economy. These workers have not formed unions, which would cloud the distinction between an employee and an independent contractor. Furthermore, workers who rely on gig work to meet financial needs do not have long-term benefits such as company-sponsored medical and retirement assistance, leading to economic issues in the years to come.

McKinsey and Company researched the shift from workers having one employer to those with a traditional job and a second source of income, or "side hustle." Based on their research, depicted below, the American workforce comprises 100 million workers, and approximately 69 million workers engage in freelance ("gig") work either as a side hustle or as their primary income source.

Freelance workforce distribution in the United States as of 2022 (in millions)

Category	Number of workers (millions)
Gig and contract, freelance, and temporary workers	25
Contract, freelance, and temporary only	29
Gig only	14
Unemployed	6
Permanent workers	100

(Source: McKinsey & Company via Statista)

Further clarification about determining employment status may be located in IRS **Publication 1779**. Upon request, the firm may request official guidance from the IRS by submitting **Form SS-8**. Penalties are levied on employers who deliberately misclassify employees to cut payroll costs; in addition to penalties, employers may have to provide unpaid wages to misclassified employees. As of 2022, the **Wage and Hour Division** of the Department of Labor had recovered more than $91 million in back wages due to approximately 1,600 workers. Starting with the tax year 2020, the IRS switched from using form 1099-MISC to 1099-NEC for reporting independent contractor earnings over $600 when they have performed a service in line with the business. In 2022, the IRS removed the last two digits of the date, making this form useful going into future years without needing to update.

Reporting New Employees

Reporting newly hired employees is considered important by governmental bodies. Why is this so?

- First, reporting employees creates a registry to monitor people who owe child support or other court-ordered garnishments.
- Second, it helps immigration agencies track immigrants to ensure that they are still legally able to work in the United States.
- Third, for certain professions such as teaching, the new-hire reporting system can be used to communicate issues such as ethical violations for which governmental or accrediting bodies have censured the professional.
- Finally, the new-hire reporting system assists with administering COBRA medical benefits.

All newly hired employees must provide specific documentation. For legal purposes, the minimum amount of documentation allowed is Form *W-4* (see Figure 2-4) and the *I-9* (see Figure 2-5). Form W-4 is a publication of the Internal Revenue Service. The main purpose behind the W-4 is to help the employer determine the correct amount of federal income taxes to withhold from the employee's payroll. Employees may change the information on Form W-4 at any time during the year. A best practice concerning Form W-4 is to request that employees file a new form each January. States may have similar withholding forms, which should similarly be completed. Since Form W-4 was significantly changed in 2020, it is worth noting that employees hired before 2020 do not need to complete a new Form W-4. Anyone hired in the current year must complete the new form. When providing employees with Form W-4, it is important to give them all four pages because there is information to help them complete it. If an employee is truly exempt from taxes, they only need to fill out Steps 1 and 5, writing "EXEMPT" in Step 4. One interesting thing to note is that employers are not responsible for verifying the exempt status or information claimed on the W-4 except for Steps 1 and 5.

> Notice that the Form W-4 for 2020 and future years is significantly different from prior years:
>
> - Step 1: Personal information, including full name, address, Social Security number, and marital status.
> - Steps 2–4: These are used only for employees with additional income through a spouse's job, deductions for dependents, and additional income tax adjustments based on worksheets contained in the full form. An employee will list "EXEMPT" in Step 4 if they do not owe, or expect to owe, any federal income taxes.
> - Step 5: Employee's and employer's signature and date.

Chapter 2 Payroll System Procedures 55

FIGURE 2-4
Form W-4 Employee Withholding Certificate (Completed Example)

Form **W-4**	**Employee's Withholding Certificate**	OMB No. 1545-0074
Department of the Treasury Internal Revenue Service	Complete Form W-4 so that your employer can withhold the correct federal income tax from your pay. Give Form W-4 to your employer. Your withholding is subject to review by the IRS.	**2023**

Step 1: Enter Personal Information

(a) First name and middle initial: **Jonathan W.**   Last name: **Doe**
(b) Social security number:

Address: **123 Main Street**
City or town, state, and ZIP code: **Anytown, KS 54932**

Does your name match the name on your social security card? If not, to ensure you get credit for your earnings, contact SSA at 800-772-1213 or go to www.ssa.gov.

(c) [✓] Single or Married filing separately
    [ ] Married filing jointly or Qualifying surviving spouse
    [ ] Head of household (Check only if you're unmarried and pay more than half the costs of keeping up a home for yourself and a qualifying individual.)

Complete Steps 2–4 ONLY if they apply to you; otherwise, skip to Step 5. See page 2 for more information on each step, who can claim exemption from withholding, other details, and privacy.

Step 2: Multiple Jobs or Spouse Works

Complete this step if you (1) hold more than one job at a time, or (2) are married filing jointly and your spouse also works. The correct amount of withholding depends on income earned from all of these jobs.

Do **only one** of the following.

(a) Reserved for future use.
(b) Use the Multiple Jobs Worksheet on page 3 and enter the result in Step 4(c) below; **or**
(c) If there are only two jobs total, you may check this box. Do the same on Form W-4 for the other job. This option is generally more accurate than (b) if pay at the lower paying job is more than half of the pay at the higher paying job. Otherwise, (b) is more accurate . . . . [ ]

TIP: If you have self-employment income, see page 2.

Complete Steps 3–4(b) on Form W-4 for only ONE of these jobs. Leave those steps blank for the other jobs. (Your withholding will be most accurate if you complete Steps 3–4(b) on the Form W-4 for the highest paying job.)

Step 3: Claim Dependent and Other Credits

If your total income will be $200,000 or less ($400,000 or less if married filing jointly):

Multiply the number of qualifying children under age 17 by $2,000 $ **2000**

Multiply the number of other dependents by $500 . . . . . $

Add the amounts above for qualifying children and other dependents. You may add to this the amount of any other credits. Enter the total here . . . .   3 $ **2000**

Step 4 (optional): Other Adjustments

(a) **Other income (not from jobs).** If you want tax withheld for other income you expect this year that won't have withholding, enter the amount of other income here. This may include interest, dividends, and retirement income . . . .   4(a) $

(b) **Deductions.** If you expect to claim deductions other than the standard deduction and want to reduce your withholding, use the Deductions Worksheet on page 3 and enter the result here . . . .   4(b) $

(c) **Extra withholding.** Enter any additional tax you want withheld each **pay period** . .   4(c) $

Step 5: Sign Here

Under penalties of perjury, I declare that this certificate, to the best of my knowledge and belief, is true, correct, and complete.

Jonathan W. Doe   **5/2/2023**
Employee's signature (This form is not valid unless you sign it.)   Date

Employers Only

Employer's name and address: **Homestead Retreat, 9010 Old Manhattan Highway, Olathe, KS 59384**
First date of employment: **May 2, 2023**
Employer identification number (EIN): **92-1117654**

For Privacy Act and Paperwork Reduction Act Notice, see page 3.   Cat. No. 10220Q   Form **W-4** (2023)

(Source: irs.gov)

FIGURE 2-5
I-9 Employment Eligibility Verification Form

Employment Eligibility Verification
Department of Homeland Security
U.S. Citizenship and Immigration Services

USCIS Form I-9
OMB No. 1615-0047
Expires 10/31/2022

▶ **START HERE:** Read instructions carefully before completing this form. The instructions must be available, either in paper or electronically, during completion of this form. Employers are liable for errors in the completion of this form.

ANTI-DISCRIMINATION NOTICE: It is illegal to discriminate against work-authorized individuals. Employers **CANNOT** specify which document(s) an employee may present to establish employment authorization and identity. The refusal to hire or continue to employ an individual because the documentation presented has a future expiration date may also constitute illegal discrimination.

Section 1. Employee Information and Attestation
*(Employees must complete and sign Section 1 of Form I-9 no later than the **first day of employment**, but not before accepting a job offer.)*

Last Name (Family Name)	First Name (Given Name)	Middle Initial	Other Last Names Used (if any)
Doe	Jonathan	W	

Address (Street Number and Name)	Apt. Number	City or Town	State	ZIP Code
123 Main Street		Anytown	KS	54932

Date of Birth (mm/dd/yyyy)	U.S. Social Security Number	Employee's E-mail Address	Employee's Telephone Number
5/17/1991	987-65-4321	jonathandoe@anymail.com	(620) 555-2299

I am aware that federal law provides for imprisonment and/or fines for false statements or use of false documents in connection with the completion of this form.

I attest, under penalty of perjury, that I am (check one of the following boxes):

- [x] 1. A citizen of the United States
- [ ] 2. A noncitizen national of the United States *(See instructions)*
- [ ] 3. A lawful permanent resident (Alien Registration Number/USCIS Number): _____
- [ ] 4. An alien authorized to work until (expiration date, if applicable, mm/dd/yyyy): _____
      Some aliens may write "N/A" in the expiration date field. *(See instructions)*

Aliens authorized to work must provide only one of the following document numbers to complete Form I-9: An Alien Registration Number/USCIS Number OR Form I-94 Admission Number OR Foreign Passport Number.

1. Alien Registration Number/USCIS Number: _____
   OR
2. Form I-94 Admission Number: _____
   OR
3. Foreign Passport Number: _____
   Country of Issuance: _____

QR Code - Section 1
Do Not Write In This Space

Signature of Employee	Today's Date (mm/dd/yyyy)
Jonathan W. Doe	5/2/2023

Preparer and/or Translator Certification (check one):

- [x] I did not use a preparer or translator.
- [ ] A preparer(s) and/or translator(s) assisted the employee in completing Section 1.

(Fields below must be completed and signed when preparers and/or translators assist an employee in completing Section 1.)

I attest, under penalty of perjury, that I have assisted in the completion of Section 1 of this form and that to the best of my knowledge the information is true and correct.

Signature of Preparer or Translator	Today's Date (mm/dd/yyyy)

Last Name (Family Name)	First Name (Given Name)

Address (Street Number and Name)	City or Town	State	ZIP Code

STOP *Employer Completes Next Page* **STOP**

Form I-9 10/21/2019

LISTS OF ACCEPTABLE DOCUMENTS
All documents must be UNEXPIRED

Employees may present one selection from List A
or a combination of one selection from List B and one selection from List C.

LIST A Documents that Establish Both Identity and Employment Authorization	LIST B Documents that Establish Identity	LIST C Documents that Establish Employment Authorization
1. U.S. Passport or U.S. Passport Card	1. Driver's license or ID card issued by a State or outlying possession of the United States provided it contains a photograph or information such as name, date of birth, gender, height, eye color, and address	1. A Social Security Account Number card, unless the card includes one of the following restrictions: (1) NOT VALID FOR EMPLOYMENT (2) VALID FOR WORK ONLY WITH INS AUTHORIZATION (3) VALID FOR WORK ONLY WITH DHS AUTHORIZATION
2. Permanent Resident Card or Alien Registration Receipt Card (Form I-551)		
3. Foreign passport that contains a temporary I-551 stamp or temporary I-551 printed notation on a machine-readable immigrant visa	2. ID card issued by federal, state or local government agencies or entities, provided it contains a photograph or information such as name, date of birth, gender, height, eye color, and address	2. Certification of report of birth issued by the Department of State (Forms DS-1350, FS-545, FS-240)
4. Employment Authorization Document that contains a photograph (Form I-766)	3. School ID card with a photograph	3. Original or certified copy of birth certificate issued by a State, county, municipal authority, or territory of the United States bearing an official seal
5. For a nonimmigrant alien authorized to work for a specific employer because of his or her status: a. Foreign passport; and b. Form I-94 or Form I-94A that has the following: (1) The same name as the passport; and (2) An endorsement of the alien's nonimmigrant status as long as that period of endorsement has not yet expired and the proposed employment is not in conflict with any restrictions or limitations identified on the form.	4. Voter's registration card	
	5. U.S. Military card or draft record	
	6. Military dependent's ID card	4. Native American tribal document
	7. U.S. Coast Guard Merchant Mariner Card	5. U.S. Citizen ID Card (Form I-197)
	8. Native American tribal document	6. Identification Card for Use of Resident Citizen in the United States (Form I-179)
	9. Driver's license issued by a Canadian government authority	
	For persons under age 18 who are unable to present a document listed above:	7. Employment authorization document issued by the Department of Homeland Security
6. Passport from the Federated States of Micronesia (FSM) or the Republic of the Marshall Islands (RMI) with Form I-94 or Form I-94A indicating nonimmigrant admission under the Compact of Free Association Between the United States and the FSM or RMI	10. School record or report card	
	11. Clinic, doctor, or hospital record	
	12. Day-care or nursery school record	

Examples of many of these documents appear in the Handbook for Employers (M-274).

Refer to the instructions for more information about acceptable receipts.

Form I-9 10/21/2019

(Source: USCIS)

In the following example, Jonathan W. Doe was born on 5/17/1991 and lives at 123 Main Street, Anytown, Kansas 54932. He is single and claims one withholding under 17. His Social Security number is 987-65-4321. His employer is Homestead Retreat at 9010 Old Manhattan Highway, Olathe, Kansas 59384, with an Employer Identification Number of 92-1117654. His email address is jonathandoe@anymail.com, and his phone number is (620) 555-2299. When he filled out his new-hire paperwork on May 2, 2023, Omin Sop in Human Resources for Homestead Retreat verified his identity with both his Social Security card and his driver's license (G93847562), which expires on his birthday in 2025.

Additional Withholding

If an employee has more than one job or a spouse who works, an option to avoid paying taxes at the end of the year is to withhold additional federal income taxes from each check. Additional withholdings are requested within the employee's Form W-4. This can be either a straight dollar value or an additional percentage. These amounts are withheld from the employee and submitted with the employer's normal federal payroll tax deposits. Employees may elect to include backup withholding amounts in Step 4 of Form W-4, which directs the employer to withhold additional tax amounts. Backup withholding may occur when the employee received additional, nontaxable income (such as dividends, royalties, or interest payments) or when the IRS notified the employee of underreported income issues.

The I-9 form is published by the Department of Homeland Security, which stipulates that this form must be completed within three business days of the employee's start date. Registration of employees using the I-9 form minimizes negative implications associated with monitoring legally authorized workers in the United States and tracking people with legal obligations such as child support and other garnishments.

The final page of the I-9 form contains the documents the employee provides to verify identity and eligibility to work in the United States. Employees must provide either one item from List A *or* one item from both List B *and* List C.

> The U.S. Citizen and Immigration Service (USCIS) implemented new changes in 2020:
> - A fillable PDF version of the form with drop-downs for dates and prefilled lists
> - A new citizenship/immigration status section
> - Form availability in Spanish
>
> The E-Verify system was implemented in 2017 to provide employers with a fast, free way to verify an employee's legal eligibility to work in the United States. It should be noted that participation in E-Verify is *voluntary,* and that completion of the I-9 is *mandatory.*
>
> (Source: USCIS)

The payroll accountant should retain a copy of the Employment Eligibility Verification Form (I-9) and a current Employee Withholding Allowance Certificate (W-4) in every employee's permanent file, although no legislation mandates that practice. The employer should request a new Form W-4 from employees annually in January to ensure that all addresses, life situations, and other information remain current. Because of the timing constraints on releasing annual tax documents such as Forms W-2 and W-3, employers should verify employees' Form W-4 information as close as possible to January 1 each year.

Hiring Packet Contents

Many companies' **hiring packets** may be as basic as completing the Forms W-4 and I-9 or could be incredibly complex if foreign workers and multiple types of voluntary or mandated deductions are involved. Common items in a hiring packet are the aforementioned federal forms, state and local withholding allowance forms, elections for voluntary deductions, insurance paperwork, and an offer letter that specifies the pay rate and start date. Not all companies have the same items in the hiring packet, and no federal legislative guidelines exist. After reviewing the company's needs and the legal requirements for the position, the firm's management determines the hiring packet contents. Many companies also include diversity self-declaration paperwork to ensure compliance with equal opportunity legislation, requirements under federal contracts, and other special requirements in the event of a payroll audit.

Notification of New Hires to State Offices

The Immigration Reform and Control Act mandates that employers notify state offices within 20 days of an employee's start date. State forms for fulfilling this requirement vary, and states offer online registration for new hires. One purpose of registering new hires with states is to maintain databases for child support enforcement. Fines for nonreporting of new hires vary, both on the number of unreported new hires and incomplete information. The penalty for noncompliance is strictly enforced and ranges from $25 per unreported employee to $500 for intentional nonreporting. An example of a new-hire reporting form is in Figure 2-6.

Reporting new hires is a complex task with a high potential for errors when companies have employees in multiple states. The Office of Management and Budget (OMB) has designed a form (see excerpt in Figure 2-7) for multistate employers to register and designate one state as the primary place to which they will send new-hire reports. They can designate on the form the other states in which they have employees. The use of the multistate registry helps employers ensure they remain in compliance with the law.

Another issue to consider is the multiple employer rule. For workers with multiple, and sometimes joint, employers, the issue of withholding appropriate taxes arises. According to the **U.S. Department of Labor**, the joint employer test involves four factors:

1. Who hires/fires the employee
2. Which employer substantially controls the employee's work
3. Which employer determines the employee's pay rate and method
4. Who maintains the employee's employment records

Foreign Workers

Employers who hire foreign citizens face additional challenges. The employer must verify that the employee is legally allowed to work in the United States. Generally, the I-9 form serves this purpose, but there may be occasions when the prospective employee does not have an appropriate government-issued visa for working in the United States. If no visa exists, the employer may file a petition with the U.S. Citizenship and Immigration Services office to gain permission for the foreign employee to work in the United States through an H-1B visa. The *H-1B* visa is authorized for employers to hire foreign workers who have specialized university-level expertise to benefit the company. As of 2023, the maximum number of regular H-1B visas permitted by USCIS was 65,000 employees. An additional 20,000 H-1B visas were available for foreign workers with advanced degrees. The fees for permanent workers not in the protected classes range from $500 to $5,000, depending on the classification of the worker's preference, the size of the employer, and the employee's nonimmigrant status. In the case of foreign workers, the employer must file Form 1042 for any payments made. For information about the Permanent Worker Visa Preference Categories, please visit the U.S. Citizenship and Immigration Services website (www.uscis.gov).

FIGURE 2-6
Sample New-Hire Reporting Form

Michigan Department of Treasury
3281(Rev. 9-12)

State of Michigan New Hire Reporting Form

Michigan New Hire Operations Center
P.O. Box 85010
Lansing, MI 48908-5010
Phone: (800) 524-9846
Fax: (877) 318-1659

Federal law requires public (State and local) and private employers to report all newly hired or rehired employees who are working in Michigan to the State of Michigan.[1] This form is recommended for use by all employers who do not report electronically.

- A newly hired employee is an individual not previously employed by you, and a rehired employee is an individual who was previously employed by you but separated from employment for at least 60 consecutive days.
- Reports must be submitted within 20 days of hire date (i.e., the date services are first performed for pay).
- This form may be photocopied as necessary. Many employers preprint employer information on the form and have the employee complete the necessary information during the hiring process.
- When reporting new hires with special exemptions, please use the MI-W4 form.
- Online and other electronic reporting options are available at: www.mi-newhire.com.

- Employers who report electronically and have employees working in two or more states may register as a multi-state employer and designate a single state to which new hire reports will be transmitted. Information regarding multi-state registration is available online at: http://www.acf.hhs.gov/programs/cse/newhire/employer/private/newhire.htm#multi or call (410) 277-9470.
- Reports will not be processed if mandatory information is missing. Such reports willl be rejected and you must correct and resubmit them.
- For optimum accuracy, please print neatly in all capital letters and avoid contact with the edge of the box. See sample below.

| A | B | C | 1 | 2 | 3 |

EMPLOYEE Information (Mandatory)

Social Security Number: 987 65 4321

First Name: Isabelle
Middle Initial: I
Last Name: Libertie
Address: 2022 Watson Way
City: Charlevoix
State: MI
Zip Code: 49720
Hire Date: 03 01 2023

OPTIONAL
Date of Birth: 08 28 1999
Driver's License No: J 253 647 896 864

EMPLOYER Information (Mandatory)

Federal Employer Identification Number (FEIN): 12 3456789

Employer Name: Charlevoix Ski and Sports
Address: 5632 State Street
City: Charlevoix
State: MI
Zip Code: 49720

OPTIONAL
Contact Name: Gerald Morris
Contact Phone: 231 555 6445
Contact Fax: 231 555 6488
Contact Email:

[1] Ref: Social Security Act section 453A and the Personal Responsibility and Work Opportunity Reconciliation Act (PRWORA) of 1996 (P.L. 104-193), effective October 1, 1997.

FIGURE 2-7
Multistate Employer Registration Form

OMB Control No: 0970-0166
OMB Expiration Date: 07/31/2025

Multistate Employer Registration Form for New Hire Reporting

Employers who have employees working in two or more states may use this form to register to submit their new hire reports to one state or make changes to a previous registration. Multistate employers may register online at https://ocsp.acf.hhs.gov/OCSE/.

Note: If you are a third-party provider, your clients must have employees in two or more states to register as a multistate employer.

Federal law (42 U.S.C. § 653A(b)(1)(A)) requires employers to supply the following information about newly hired employees to the State Directory of New Hires in the state where the employee works:

- Employee's name, address, Social Security number, and the date of hire (the date services for remuneration were first performed by the employee)
- Employer's name, address, and Federal Employer Identification Number (FEIN)

If you are an employer with employees working in two or more states, and you will transmit the required information or reports magnetically or electronically, you can use this form to designate one state where any employee works to transmit all new hire reports to the State Directory of New Hires.

If you are no longer a multistate employer or you are a multistate employer but no longer report to a single state, select the **No Longer a Multistate Employer** check box below.

☐ **No Longer a Multistate Employer** (If selected, complete items 1–4 and 7) and return the form to the email address msedb@acf.hhs.gov or mail it to the address located on page 3.

If you need help completing this form, contact the Multistate Employer Help Desk at 800-258-2736 (8 a.m. – 5 p.m. ET, Monday through Friday).

Note: All required fields are followed by a red asterisk *.

1. Enter your company's FEIN without a hyphen. This is the nine-digit number used by the IRS to identify your company.
   FEIN *:

2. Enter today's date in MM/DD/YYYY format.
   Date *:

3. Enter your company's legal name used for child support documents. This is the name associated with the FEIN in item 1.
   Employer Name *:

Enter your company's address, including city, state, and ZIP code. This is the address associated with the FEIN in item 1. If your company's FEIN address is a foreign address, enter the country's name and postal code.

Employer Address *:

City *:   **State *:**

ZIP Code *:

(For foreign addresses only) **Country Name:**   **Country Postal Code:**

Subsidiary Information: Please go to www.acf.hhs.gov/css/resource/multiple-fein-spreadsheet to access the Multiple FEIN Spreadsheet, enter information about all your company's subsidiaries, and submit it with this form. Subsidiaries are companies wholly controlled by your company.

We need the below information about your company's subsidiaries.

FEIN	Organization Name	Address Line1	Address Line2	Address Line3	City	State	Province	Country	ZIP/ Postal Code	Address Delivery Type (Optional)
										■ Payroll/Income Withholding Order ■ National Medical Support Notice ■ Verification of Employment ■ Workers Compensation

4. Enter the name of the state or U.S. territory your company designated to report new hire information to.

    NOTE: The state you choose must be a state in which you have one or more employees. Refer to the state listing shown in item 5.

5. Check the box next to the additional states or U.S. territories where your company has employees working. Do not put a check next to the state or territory you selected in item 4. You must select at least one state or territory in this list to register as a multistate employer.

☐ Alabama	☐ Alaska	☐ Arizona	☐ Arkansas	☐ California	☐ Colorado
☐ Connecticut	☐ Delaware	☐ Dist. of Col	☐ Florida	☐ Georgia	☐ Guam
☐ Hawaii	☐ Idaho	☐ Illinois	☐ Indiana	☐ Iowa	☐ Kansas
☐ Kentucky	☐ Louisiana	☐ Maine	☐ Maryland	☐ Massachusetts	☐ Michigan
☐ Minnesota	☐ Mississippi	☐ Missouri	☐ Montana	☐ Nebraska	☐ Nevada
☐ New Hampshire	☐ New Jersey	☐ New Mexico	☐ New York	☐ North Carolina	☐ North Dakota
☐ Ohio	☐ Oklahoma	☐ Oregon	☐ Pennsylvania	☐ Puerto Rico	☐ Rhode Island
☐ South Carolina	☐ South Dakota	☐ Tennessee	☐ Texas	☐ Utah	☐ Vermont
☐ Virgin Islands	☐ Virginia	☐ Washington	☐ West Virginia	☐ Wisconsin	☐ Wyoming
☐ All States and Territories					

6. Enter your name, title, work phone number, work email address (do not use Gmail, Yahoo, MSN, or Hotmail email addresses), and work fax number.

    Company's Business Contact Name: _____

    Phone: _____   Fax (optional): _____

    Email: _____

7. **BE SURE TO SIGN THIS FORM.** By completing this form, I certify that the information provided is accurate and that I am authorized to complete this form on my company's behalf.

    Signature of the person completing this form: _____

(Source: U.S. Department of Health and Human Services)

> An H-1B visa's purpose is to facilitate the employment of foreign workers who possess specialized skills, as defined by U.S. statute 20 CFR § 655.700. "Specialty occupation" is defined as possessing specialized knowledge, with the minimum educational requirement being a bachelor's degree or commensurate experience, or a distinguished fashion model.
>
> (Source: Cornell Law School)

U.S. Workers in Foreign Subsidiaries

Many companies have foreign subsidiaries and divisions that employ U.S. expatriate workers. The **Foreign Account Tax Compliance Act (FATCA)** of 2010 requires employers to report to the IRS the wages of permanent U.S. citizens working in foreign locations to facilitate the appropriate taxation of such workers. Under the IRS Foreign Earned Income Exclusion, expatriate workers must file **Form 673** with their employer to exclude the first $120,000 of annual wages (2023 figure) from U.S. taxation. Still, they must pay income tax on income over that amount and declare foreign assets.

> Payroll for companies that operate in multiple countries requires additional considerations in the payroll process. After establishing a legal business presence in another country, the firm must consider the country's payroll laws. For example, some countries require employers to issue meal vouchers to employees, and employment contracts' legal content varies.
>
> Another significant area of difference between the United States and other countries is data privacy. While many privacy laws exist in the United States, the General Data Protection Regulation (GDPR) in the European Union delineates stringent guidelines for personal information handling. Under GDPR, even Microsoft Excel spreadsheets must have privacy protection to meet regulatory guidelines.
>
> Other significant issues involve continual awareness of currency exchange rates and money transfers to ensure accurate and timely pay for employees. Finally, global companies should maintain consistent calendars to remain consistent in payments among the countries in which they operate, and they should issue receipts for amounts paid to employees.
>
> (Source: Global Payroll Management Institute)

Statutory Employees

Some personnel, normally classified as independent contractors, must be treated as employees for tax purposes. The IRS classifies *statutory employees* as workers who meet any of the following guidelines:

Ahmet Misirligul/Shutterstock

- A driver who distributes beverages (other than milk) or meat, vegetable, fruit, or bakery products or picks up and delivers laundry or dry cleaning, if the driver is a single company's agent or is paid on commission.
- A full-time life insurance sales agent whose principal business activity is selling life insurance or annuity contracts, or both, primarily for one life insurance company.
- An individual who works at home on materials or goods that a company supplies and that must be returned to that company or a designated agent in accordance with furnished specifications for the work to be done.

- A full-time traveling or city salesperson who works on a single company's behalf and turns in orders from wholesalers, retailers, contractors, or operators of hotels, restaurants, or other similar establishments. The goods sold must be merchandise for resale or supplies for use in the buyer's business operation. The work performed for that single company must be the salesperson's principal business activity.

Recall that the primary differences between an employee and an independent contractor are that the independent contractor sets his or her own hours and provides the tools necessary to complete the task. A statutory employee is a hybrid of an employee and an independent contractor. To ensure proper and timely remittance of employment taxes, the IRS has mandated that the employer withhold FICA taxes from statutory employees in the same manner as other company personnel; however, federal income taxes are not withheld from statutory employees' pay.

> The term *statutory employee* may be applied to other types of workers on occasion. In 2019, Slawomir Fiedziuszko, an aerospace engineer who was semi-retired at the time, performed consulting work for a contractor of Space Systems Loral (now called Maxam). He contested the withholding of employment taxes, claiming that he was a consultant, not an employee. In the case, the judge upheld the decision to classify Mr. Fiedziuszko as an employee because he worked from home doing work designed specifically to meet Maxam's specifications. Under the definition of a statutory employee, Mr. Fiedziuszko met the third criterion to be considered a statutory employee because his work was completed using Maxam's proprietary software in accordance with established specifications.
>
> (Source: *Forbes*)

Entering New Employees into the Database

The method of entering a new employee into the payroll system depends on the employer's system. A manual system would require tasks such as adding the employee to the federal, state, and local lists for taxes withheld and adding the new hire to the list of employees to pay. Manual systems should have a checklist of all employees to ensure that no one is missed in the process.

Setting up a new employee in an automated system involves many more steps. The payroll employee enters in the pertinent data (see Figure 2-8). Employee number, name, address, Social Security number, wage, pay frequency, withholding information from W-4, department, and contact information are typically included. The payroll employee must designate a worker's compensation classification, state of employment, and local jurisdiction (when local taxes are applicable). Depending on state requirements and employer preferences, additional location codes, job classification codes, and other identifying characteristics may also be required.

FIGURE 2-8
Employee Database Information Sample

Employee Details   **Bibitor LLC**

PERSONAL INFO	PAY INFO		TAX INFO	
	Regular Pay:	$14.00/hr	SSN:	122-13-1231
	Pay By:		Fed:	Single / 1
Jackson L. Mann	Deductions:	Vanguard 3.0%	VT:	Single/ 0
19 River Road South	Contributions:	Vanguard 1.0%		
Putney VT 05346		Vacation: 40 hours/year (accrued at start of year)		
Hired: 01/01/2021				
Born: 08/24/1996	Time Off	Paid time off: 40 hours/year (accrued at start of year)		
		Sick: 40 hours/year (accrued at start of year)		

Who Are You?

Stop & Check

1. Go to the U.S. Citizenship and Immigration Services website, located at www.uscis.gov, and type I-9 into the search box on the website. Click on the link for the PDF version of the I-9 form to obtain a digital copy. What are two different ways that you would be able to prove your eligibility for work in the United States?
2. Go to the IRS website, located at www.irs.gov, and type W-4 into the website's search box. Click on the link for the PDF version of the W-4 to obtain a digital copy. Assume you have more than one job, and estimate the amount to include as income from other jobs. Complete the multiple job worksheet. Was your estimate close? Explain.
3. What are three examples of statutory employees?

LO 2-3 Differentiate between Exempt and Nonexempt Workers

Kimberly P. Mitchell/Detroit Free Press/TNS/Alamy Stock Photo

Company employees may be classified as either exempt or nonexempt workers. The distinction between the two terms is how the wage and hour provisions of FLSA apply to the worker. *Exempt* workers are not subject to (i.e., are exempt from) the FLSA wage and hour provisions; wage and hour laws usually apply to *nonexempt* workers. The details of the worker's classification as exempt or nonexempt are always maintained in payroll records. Still, the inclusion of this information in other personnel records is at the employer's discretion.

Different types of employees are automatically classified as exempt from FLSA provisions, including certain computer professionals and outside salespersons. Companies will typically classify highly skilled workers such as accountants, general managers, human resource managers, and upper management as exempt, salaried employees. Because job titles alone are not a basis for the classification of employees as exempt from FLSA provisions, the U.S. Department of Labor has issued guidelines for the most common types of employees. Note that for workers to be classified as exempt, they must meet *all* elements in the following tests to achieve exempt status.

- Executive Exemption
  - Salary compensation must be no less than $684 per week.
  - Managing the firm must be the primary duty of the employee.
  - The employee must supervise and otherwise direct at least two other full-time employees (or an equivalent).
  - The employee must have the authority to hire and fire other employees.
- Administrative Exemption
  - Salary compensation must be no less than $684 per week.
  - The primary duty must include office performance or other nonmanual labor related directly to the management of the firm's operations.
  - The employee must exercise independent judgment in the performance of normal duties.
- Professional Exemption
  - Learned Professional
    - Salary compensation must be no less than $684 per week.

- This employee must perform work characterized by advanced learning, primarily academic in nature, and requires consistent discretion and judgment.
- The employee's advanced knowledge must be in a field that involves science or learning.
- The employee must have acquired that knowledge through specialized intellectual education.
- Creative Professional
  - Salary compensation must be no less than $684 per week.
  - This employee's primary work duty must involve invention, imagination, or originality, requiring judgment and discretion.

(Source: DOL)

When workers are employed on a salary basis, they are paid to perform a specific job regardless of the number of hours worked to accomplish that job. A primary difference bet exempt and nonexempt salaried workers is that nonexempt salaried workers receive overtime pay for any hours exceeding 40 per week. The difference between salaried and hourly workers regarding overtime calculation is that salaried workers will receive their normal shift hours of pay, even when not working the full shift, and do not receive overtime when they work more than 40 hours per week.

Hourly nonexempt employees receive a predetermined amount per hour of work performed (or a fraction thereof). Some employers may make an election that permits four 10-hour shifts; should the election be made, the employee would be subject to overtime rates only after the 40 hours have been performed. It should be noted that certain states and employers have a company policy stating that they pay overtime for employees who work more than 8 hours per day (or 10 hours, if that is the normal work shift); however, paid overtime is only mandated by the FLSA weekly. According to the Bureau of Labor Statistics (BLS), the average number of hours worked per week was 34.3 hours in 2022 (see Figure 2-9) and fluctuated monthly. The BLS noted the number of hours worked per week varied by industry.

Classifying employee wages as salary versus hourly is a basic determination linked to the type of work performed and its position. Salaried *exempt* employees are not subject to overtime, are paid to do a specific job, and fulfill the FLSA requirement of self-direction; however,

FIGURE 2-9
Average Working Hours of All Employees

Monthly length of the average working week of all employees in the United States from December 2021 to December 2022

Month	Hours of Work
Dec '21	34.8
Jan '22	34.6
Feb '22	34.7
Mar '22	34.6
Apr '22	34.6
May '22	34.6
Jun '22	34.5
Jul '22	34.6
Aug '22	34.5
Sep '22	34.5
Oct '22	34.5
Nov '22*	34.4
Dec '22*	34.3

(Source: Bureau of Labor Statistics, Statista, 2023)

not all salaried employees are classified as exempt. Certain jobs such as nurses, police officers, and upper-level administrators may earn a fixed salary but are classified as *nonexempt* because of the nature of management direction in their function. Nonexempt workers do not generally supervise other employees and generally work under the direction of a supervisor.

Leased and Temporary Employees

Employers occasionally experience a need to have an additional employee but do not have the time to use a traditional hiring process. In this event, employers may either lease an employee or contact a temporary employment agency. Although these terms may sound similar, the difference between the leased and temporary employees involves determining employer intent and liability for worker injuries and errors.

Under IRS code section **414(n)**, an employee is classified as a *leased employee* if all the following conditions exist:

1. A formal agreement exists between the employer and the employee leasing organization.
2. The employee works on a full-time basis.
3. Employee actions are directed by the recipient company (i.e., the lessee).

Leased employees are considered common-law employees and are eligible for the same benefits as regular employees, including compensation practices, employer contributions, and so forth. The IRS stipulates that no more than 20 percent of a company's workers may be leased.

> The Tax Cuts and Jobs Act of 2017 included a provision in which employers who leased employees from Professional Employer Organizations (PEOs) could qualify for a 20 percent profit deduction under section 199A of the Act. PEOs serve companies by acting as the hiring body and human resource managers for workers. In January 2019, the IRS clarified under §1.199A-2(b)(2)(ii) that employers who use third-party employees through a PEO could consider those leased employees as common-law employees and would qualify for the profit deduction and subsequent decrease in tax liability.
>
> (Source: JDSupra)

A temporary employee differs from a leased employee in the direction of the employee's actions. The *temporary employee* is an employee of the employment agency, which directs them to fill specific short-term needs of various employers. Temporary employees may work either full-time or part-time, depending on the employer's needs, and are only eligible for the benefits made available by the temporary agency.

Stop & Check

Exempt vs. Nonexempt

1. What is the difference between exempt and nonexempt workers?
2. What is the threshold after which an employee must be paid overtime, according to FLSA?
   a. 30 hours
   b. 35 hours
   c. 40 hours
   d. 45 hours
3. What is the difference between a leased employee and a temporary employee?

LO 2-4 Explain Pay Records and Employee File Maintenance

One of the most important parts of any payroll system is maintaining employee pay records, especially considering the classification of exempt versus nonexempt employees and the legislation that pertains to overtime pay. The maintenance of accurate and detailed records that reflect the pay period, pay date, pay rate, and deductions is critical not only because it is a legal requirement for delivering accurate pay but also for positive employee relations. Employers retain physical copies of employees' time records, pay advice, and any other documentation processed with the paycheck. Other types of documentation include:

- Request for paid time off.
- Reports of tardiness or absenteeism.
- Detailed records of work completed during that day's shift.
- Records of overtime worked.
- Performance appraisals.
- Training records.
- Awards or recognitions (especially if cash is involved).
- Resignation letter or termination notice.

Technological advances allow employers to scan and save this information digitally, such as using a digital file within the payroll accounting system or human resources information system. The trend toward remote work implies that employee records could become increasingly digital. Transitioning to digitized employee records has the advantage of being accessible through encrypted sites. They are also more vulnerable to hacking.

Mert Toker/Shutterstock

> Many payroll apps allow for multiple payment methods and payment of employees, independent contractors, and part-time workers by scanning images directly into the software. These apps often include Human Resources integration. The following apps are examples of the increasing digitization of payroll functions:
>
> - Square Payroll
> - eFileCabinet
> - TriNet

The availability of digital copies facilitates managerial, auditor, or authorized executives' review, approval, or commentary on the documentation attached to payroll-related documents. Digital copies also permit transparency of records between the employer and employee, reducing miscommunication and payroll discrepancies, and facilitating Internet employee record portals.

Pay Records

Employee wages involve far more than simple hourly rates or periodic salary payments. The first payroll decision should be the company's pay frequency (daily, weekly, biweekly, semimonthly, monthly). The choice of payment frequency affects the applicable amounts for employee income tax withholding. Separate schedules for federal income taxes are provided in IRS Publication 15-T (available at www.irs.gov), which is released in November for the following year (i.e., 2023 tax information would normally be released during November 2022). Once the employer determines the pay frequency, the payroll accountant can establish the payroll record submission and pay disbursement schedule for company employees.

Department of the Treasury
Internal Revenue Service

Publication 15-T
Cat. No. 32112B

Federal Income Tax Withholding Methods

For use in **2023**

Contents

Introduction	2
1. Percentage Method Tables for Automated Payroll Systems and Withholding on Periodic Payments of Pensions and Annuities	9
2. Wage Bracket Method Tables for Manual Payroll Systems With Forms W-4 From 2020 or Later	12
3. Wage Bracket Method Tables for Manual Payroll Systems With Forms W-4 From 2019 or Earlier	27
4. Percentage Method Tables for Manual Payroll Systems With Forms W-4 From 2020 or Later	56
5. Percentage Method Tables for Manual Payroll Systems With Forms W-4 From 2019 or Earlier	62
6. Alternative Methods for Figuring Withholding	65
7. Tables for Withholding on Distributions of Indian Gaming Profits to Tribal Members	66
How To Get Tax Help	67

One aspect of pay dates a company must recognize is the minimum pay frequency mandated by state laws. The purpose of the requirement is to ensure that workers are paid on a predictable basis, and some states have limits on the time between paydays. Not every state has a pay frequency requirement. For the states that do, employers may pay their employees more often than required, but they cannot pay their employees less often. Table 2-1 has the requirements for each state. States without payday requirements have not been included in the table.

Pay Rate

The pay rate is the amount per hour that employees receive for their labor. The company determines the amount an employee should be compensated. The determination of pay rate depends upon many employee variables: experience, education, certifications, governmental regulations (e.g., minimum wage, Davis–Bacon wages), hours worked, or a combination of all of the above. Employers may also pay specific rates for jobs performed. For example, employees working in a manufacturing environment may be subject to a different pay scale when cross-trained and working in a sales capacity. Minimum wage rates vary per state, and different parts of the same state may have different wages and may increase minimum wage amounts at various times during the year. Salaried workers receive a fixed amount per pay period, no matter the number of hours worked.

There is a lot of attention being brought to the minimum wage and the concept of a living wage. Given the cost of living in some communities, the minimum wage can be far below the poverty level. Part of the push toward a $15 per hour minimum wage comes from the related concept of a living wage.

EXAMPLE: PAY PERIOD COMPUTATION, BIWEEKLY EMPLOYEE

Juan de la Cruz is a manager for a textile firm. He earns $52,000 per year, is classified as an exempt employee, and is paid biweekly. He normally works 40 hours per week.
  During June, the following occurred:
  Pay period ending June 15: Juan worked 85 hours.
  Pay period ending June 29: Juan worked 78 hours.
  Salary for the June 15 pay period = $52,000/26 periods per year = $2,000
  Salary for the June 29 pay period = $52,000/26 periods per year = $2,000
  Juan's salary for each pay period would be a fixed amount no matter how many hours he worked because he is classified as an exempt employee.

TABLE 2-1
State Payday Requirements

State	Weekly	Biweekly	Semimonthly	Monthly
Alaska			XX	XX
Arizona			XX	
Arkansas			XX	
California	XX	XX	XX	XX
Colorado				XX
Connecticut	XX			
Delaware				XX
D.C.			XX	
Georgia			XX	
Hawaii			XX	XX
Idaho				XX
Illinois			XX	XX
Indiana		XX	XX	
Iowa	XX	XX	XX	XX
Kansas				XX
Kentucky			XX	
Louisiana		XX	XX	
Maine			XX	
Maryland		XX	XX	
Massachusetts	XX	XX		
Michigan	XX	XX	XX	XX
Minnesota			XX	XX
Missouri			XX	
Nevada			XX	XX
New Hampshire	XX	XX	XX	XX
New Jersey			XX	XX
New Mexico			XX	XX
New York	XX		XX	
North Dakota				XX
Ohio			XX	
Oklahoma			XX	
Oregon				XX
Rhode Island	XX	XX	XX	
South Dakota				XX
Tennessee			XX	
Texas		XX	XX	XX
Utah			XX	XX
Vermont	XX	XX	XX	
Virginia	XX	XX	XX	XX
Washington				XX
West Virginia		XX		
Wisconsin				XX
Wyoming			XX	

(Source: U.S. DOL)

Hourly employees are protected by the FLSA and are eligible for overtime pay. When overtime pay is applied, hourly employees may earn more than their salaried counterparts. The FLSA determines overtime rules and rates; however, some states may have additional requirements for overtime pay. Overtime is calculated at one-and-a-half times the employee's hourly rate. For FLSA, overtime applies only to hours worked exceeding 40 in a week (with some exceptions). Some states, such as California, may also require that employees receive overtime pay for any hours worked exceeding 8 per day in addition to the 40 hours per week, making it possible for an hourly employee to earn overtime pay without reaching 40 hours in the week.

Note: In this textbook, nonexempt employees receive overtime pay for hours worked more than 40 hours per week, unless otherwise noted.

> The concept of a fluctuating workweek for salaried nonexempt employees has been a source of confusion for employers. Some salaried nonexempt employees work in industries that require them to be available at different times based on company needs. Employees who are nonexempt and salaried but have hours that are changeable due to the nature of the job may receive overtime during periods when they work more than 40 hours in a given week.

Commissions and piece-rate compensation offer employees incentives for specific jobs. A *commission* is a percentage of sales or services performed by an individual. An example of a commission would be a sales representative receiving 1 percent of all sales he or she initiates. *Piece rate* connects employee compensation with the production of a good or service. Piece rate compensation was widely used in the United States before industrialization and automated manufacturing. For example, when a shoe was being made, the person preparing the sole would receive a set rate per item.

emin kuliyev/Shutterstock

> The State of California enacted enhanced pay transparency legislation under **SB 1162**. As of January 1, 2023, employers with 15 or more employees, one of whom must work in California, must publish pay rates when advertising jobs. For piece-rate and commission work, the employer must post a reasonable range the employee could expect to earn in the course of work.
>
> (Source: Mondaq)

Compensation structures can become complex if the employee is compensated using multiple payment types. A sales representative may receive a salary and commissions while working on the sales floor but receive hourly and piece rates if filling in on the manufacturing floor. Proper classification of the various aspects of the employee's workday becomes exceptionally important for the payroll to be processed correctly.

Entering Hours

When it is time to prepare the payroll, an automated system will provide the payroll employee with a simple form to complete, typically including wage type and hours worked. An additional classification of job location may be required in complex organizations if the employee works in multiple departments or locations. The automated systems will complete mathematics to obtain gross pay. Most automated systems will calculate overtime and shift differentials (i.e., higher pay for working during times not considered "normal business hours") when entered into the system by the payroll accountant.

> Many web-based applications exist to track employee attendance and calculate pay. **TimeStation**, **ClockShark**, and **TimeDock** use quick response (QR) codes, employee PINs, and GPS location tagging to verify employee work. These apps may be useful tools for companies with employees at remote locations. Apps such as **CalculateHours** allow employees to calculate their hours worked and email the time sheet to a supervisor. Other apps, such as the **iTookOff** paid leave tracker, allow employees to manage their paid time off through a synchronized app. With the shift to flexible work locations, the market for payroll time-tracking applications has expanded to include many niche companies.
>
> vinnstock/Shutterstock

Calculations of Weekly Regular Time and Overtime

Even with automated systems, the payroll accountant must determine the breakdown of each employee's regular and overtime hours. Recall the discussion regarding the FLSA standard of 40 hours in a week. This is where the calculation of overtime becomes important. The employee's hours are added up. The pay period's total is computed to determine if the employee worked more than 40 hours total for any given week, and overtime is separated from regular hours worked for wage calculations. If the employee did not work more than 40 hours, the total regular hours are noted on the time card. If the employee did work more than 40 hours, the hours worked will be divided between the 40 regular hours and the overtime pay computation.

Employers' definitions of workweek hours vary, although 40 is the standard length because of FLSA. According to **IRS Fact Sheet 23**, employers who define their standard workweek as greater than 40 hours must pay nonexempt employees overtime pay for any hours worked in excess of 40.

> Seb is a nonexempt employee at PMJ Plastics, where the standard workweek is 45 hours. Seb earns $15 per hour and is paid weekly. The pay would be computed as follows:
>
> | | Number of Hours | Pay Rate | Total |
> | --- | --- | --- | --- |
> | **Standard hours** | 45 | $15.00 | $675.00 |
> | **Overtime hours** | 5 | $7.50 | 37.50 |
> | **Total pay** | | | $712.50 |
>
> Notice that Seb will receive overtime pay for the hours. In the above example, the overtime hours are computed as an extra 0.5 times the regular rate. The computation method could be different. It is important to follow FLSA guidelines and pay the employee appropriately to avoid legal issues.

Depending upon company policy, the existence of paid holidays or sick days may alter payroll calculations. However, holiday hours, sick time used, and vacation days are not usually included in the worked hours to determine overtime. Figure 2-10 shows a few examples of states and locations that offer mandatory paid sick leave.

According to the FLSA, employers are not required to pay for employee sick time; however, many states have either passed legislation or have pending bills that would mandate employer-paid sick time. More than 30 separate locations, including cities and entire states, have passed paid sick time legislation. This is a partial list of areas that have legislated paid sick leave.

FIGURE 2-10
Locations with Mandatory Paid Sick Leave

States/Districts	Counties	States/Districts	Counties
Washington, DC	Orange County, FL	Michigan	
Arizona	Montgomery County, MD	Nevada	
California	Cook County, IL	New Jersey	
Colorado	Westchester County, NY	New Mexico	
Connecticut		Oregon	
Maine		Rhode Island	
Maryland		Vermont	
Massachusetts		Washington	

(Source: **SHRM**)
Note: States that have passed mandatory sick-time laws may have cities whose sick-time laws differ. City regulations may change frequently and are not represented individually.

Worker Facts

Stop & Check

1. Which classification of workers is subject to the wage and hour provisions for overtime in the Fair Labor Standards Act?
2. What is the difference between exempt and nonexempt employees in overtime pay requirements?
3. What is the difference between commission and piece-rate pay as the basis for compensation?
4. How do electronic time recording apps differ from manual time reporting?

LO 2-5 Describe Internal Controls and Record Retention for a Payroll System

Vitalii Vodolazskyi/Shutterstock

The confidentiality of payroll information is one of the most important controls in establishing a payroll system, and internal controls are critical. Pay records such as time sheets are considered confidential documents, and personnel who handle or maintain such files, either paper or computerized, must ensure the privacy of the information they contain. Small firms may maintain the confidentiality of handwritten time sheets; however, multifacility companies may need to use more secure time-collection methods to ensure information privacy.

Strategic planning of the payroll system prior to implementation can prevent data errors and losses related to inadequate *internal controls*. Most importantly, the payroll system design should be reviewed regularly to determine its effectiveness and appropriateness for the company size and to correct errors before they become magnified.

> Internal controls are a necessity, especially for small companies. The need for internal controls increases as a company engages more fully with Internet portals such as time-tracking and payroll processing sites. Technological changes introduce a new level of vulnerability to a company's data, so robust internal control practices are vital. The shift to remote and flexible workplaces highlighted unexpected risks in the payroll audit process, including:
>
> - Increased opportunity for fraud
> - Compromised internal controls
> - Increased potential for legal noncompliance
> - Time tracking through apps linked to the company's payroll department
> - Increased working from home
>
> At a time when businesses are experiencing employee shortages, cybercrime companies seem to have an abundance of employees who are highly skilled at their trade. Companies must be diligent and ensure that internal controls are in place. In small companies, separation of duties or internal verification is essential to prevent fraud.

A company with many departments and many employees will generally have a more complex *review process* than a small company. In an organization with one office and a dozen or fewer employees, certain steps of the verification process may be omitted, and fewer people are required to conduct it. Conversely, a large organization with several departments and many employees could have several verification levels in the *payroll review* process. Even outsourced payroll requires levels of the review process. The payroll executed by an external company is only as accurate as the data provided. For instance, a company could have a payroll review process like the one shown in Figure 2-11.

A critical issue for internal controls is the determination of authorized signers. A best practice is to have more than one designated signatory for payroll checks. Often, these signers are different people than those involved in the review process. The extra time it takes to review and obtain the necessary signatures is time well spent, as long as it prevents costly errors.

> In Brattleboro, Vermont, an assistant judge was found to have received over $8,500 in wages by reporting hundreds of hours she did not work. This is not the first occurrence of misreporting from assistant judges. In Chittenden County, two assistant judges self-approved $2,000 bonuses for personal use. These cases highlight a weakness in the payroll system for judges at different levels in the state.
>
> (Source: VT Digger)

FIGURE 2-11
Payroll Review Process: Steps to Ensure Accurate Payroll

Employee completes time card. → Manager verifies the employee's time card. → Payroll clerk computes the period wages for the employee. → Payroll supervisor verifies the payroll clerk's math. → Employee's check is presented with payroll register for verification and signatures.

TABLE 2-2
Documentation Controls

Procedure	Example of Internal Control Activities	Could Be Performed By
Review and approval of time data from time cards or other time-collection devices	Completion of the time-collection procedure Review of time collection for accuracy and approval	Employee's supervisor
Overtime approval	Approve the amount and type of overtime to be paid	Employee's supervisor
Approval for leave of absence or other unpaid time off	Obtain all prior approvals for unpaid time away due to FMLA or other reasons	Employee's supervisor
Timely entering of payroll data	Enter the payroll data into the payroll system on time, and check for data integrity and accuracy	Payroll clerk
Payroll system security	Make sure that only designated employees or payroll vendors have access to payroll data	Payroll supervisor
Approval of the payroll before issuance	Obtain approval from the signatory before issuing checks	An authorized signer(s)
Maintenance of paid time off (e.g., vacation, sick)	Ensure that employees receive the exact amount agreed upon	Payroll clerk, employee, supervisor, other designees
Access to payroll data	Ensure that payroll data is confidential and secure	Payroll supervisor
Separation of duties	Make sure that different people verify data, enter data, verify checks	Payroll supervisor
Training of payroll staff	Ensure that payroll department employees and other department supervisors are aware of and follow company payroll policies	Payroll supervisor

Documentation of the payroll process is vital. As should be clear by now, the execution of payroll is not merely writing checks to employees. Proper documentation of payroll entails a well-delineated procedure and properly trained personnel. Table 2-2 contains examples of different documentation controls, the activities involved in each, and the employees required to participate in internal controls.

Review of Time Collected

All workers' hours reported manually on time cards or electronically through other methods must be verified for accuracy before completing any payroll. Simple issues in employee underpayment (which can cause federal penalties) or overpayment (which can erode the company's available cash) can occur even with sophisticated systems. Time collection and employee payment errors can lead to reduced employee morale, lawsuits, and fines.

> One of the largest payroll fraud schemes involved $70 million in payroll deposits made to MyPayrollHR, a New York–based company engaged in cloud-based payroll processing. Although the clients had done everything correctly, the owner of MyPayrollHR abruptly stopped operating after collecting employer funds and not disbursing payroll amounts due to employees for two consecutive pay periods.
>
> (Source: KrebsonSecurity)

Overtime Approval

Hourly employees are subject to federal overtime provisions, commonly known as time-and-a-half, but may include other pay bases such as double-time and so forth. FLSA guarantees nonexempt employees' rights to appropriate pay for the hours worked; however, employees can misreport the overtime they work, costing the company money in the process. Therefore, the best practice is to obtain supervisor approval on all employee-reported overtime. Computerized systems can also affect the reported overtime. The data is subject to the accuracy of the person who entered it.

One of the authors worked at a company that once paid her for 75 hours of overtime in one pay period—when she should have had only 7.5. This kind of error can cause chaos for both the employee, who must return the money, and the employer, who should not have paid it in the first place. Once again, improper pay can erode the morale of the employees. Overpayment on hours can create many other overpayments, including (but not limited to) federal withholding taxes, Medicare, Social Security taxes, and pension or 401(k) contributions that are driven by gross wages.

> A significant percentage of corporate fraud involves payroll tampering or embezzlement. In Atlanta, Georgia, a payroll and accounting manager pleaded guilty to wire fraud after investigators discovered that she had embezzled $1.5 million over a six-year period through improper payroll deposits. The employee had created a fake employee and instructed the outsourced payroll company to direct deposit that employee's pay into her own personal bank account. The employee had a file for the fictitious worker. A multiperson payroll verification process could have shortened the duration and reduced the amount of the embezzlement.
>
> (Source: Accounting Today)

Approval for Leave of Absence or Other Unpaid Time Off

The employee's supervisor is one level of oversight to ensure that the payroll data reaches the payroll department accurately and quickly. Supervisors work closely with their employees and should approve overtime and paid time off. Supervisors review individual time sheets for accuracy before delivery to the payroll department. Control of time away from work is the responsibility of the employee's supervisor, at the very minimum. The department supervisor should approve the time off. This approval must be tracked and maintained by the payroll department to ensure the integrity of the payroll records. A suggested best practice is to keep requests for time away attached to the payroll stub for the affected pay period. The use of leave forms provides companies with a paper trail used to clarify perceived discrepancies in pay.

> Web-based services facilitate requests, approvals, and tracking for paid time off. Apps such as *Paychex Flex* and *Zenefits* allow managers to adjust paid time off, approve and track employee requests, synchronize calendars, and download reports detailing employee time away from work.

File Security

Based on the amount of legislation regarding the privacy and security of personnel information, it is important to understand that all files about payroll, whether paper or electronic, must be kept secure from tampering. Another reason for *file security*, or restriction of personnel file access, is the firm's governmental payroll obligations. The tax information contained in the payroll records is required to prepare timely and accurate payment of payroll taxes, which is nearly as important as paying the employees. Examples of secure payroll records include multiple passwords for system access, the locking of file cabinets with controlled key disbursement, and encryption programs.

Because payroll data contains highly personal and private information, the security of the data is important. To maintain file security, access to payroll records is restricted to a relatively small number of people. Paper-based payroll data is stored in a secure location; similarly, electronic payroll data is securely backed up and encrypted.

Rawpixel.com/Shutterstock

Data privacy and fund protection are a high priority for companies and legislators. Preventing breaches of payroll record security is a high priority and an evolving issue. The Electronic Fund Transfer Act of 1978, created to prevent problems with newly created ATM cards, has been expanded to address fraud and theft issues with *paycards*, a preloaded credit card that allows an employee to access funds without needing a bank account. Paycard use for payroll disbursement was estimated to be nearly $57 billion in 2015. It continues to be the fastest-growing payroll method in the United States, with 5.9 million active paycards being used as of 2017, 8.4 million in 2022, and continued expected growth to accommodate workers' pay disbursement needs. With the gig economy's expansion and the number of unbanked employees, paycards are a relatively secure method of disbursing immediately accessible pay. Interestingly, in 2019, 18 percent of users of paycards earned more than $200,000; 13 percent earned between $150,000 and $200,000; and 18 percent earned between $100,000 and $150,000 per year.

(Source: Creditcards.com)

In *Jessie Chavez v. PVH Corporation* (2013), the defendant had to pay $1.85 million to Chavez because of fees deducted from the plaintiff's payroll card, which meant that the full amount of the wages was reduced; additionally, the plaintiff had not agreed to paycard use in advance. State laws vary regarding employment authorization for disbursing pay in the form of a paycard. As of 2021, at least 10 percent of all employees are unbanked, meaning that they do not have a bank account and rely on paycards to receive their earnings.

The Consumer Financial Protection Bureau (CFPB) proposed legislation in 2014 to include specific language on paycards, informing employees of their right to request another form of payroll disbursement. As of October 2016, the CFPB issued a rule that regulated the posting of accounting, disclosures, and overdraft credit that became effective in October 2017. This rule was updated and finalized in 2019.

The Electronic Funds Transfer Act, of which **Regulation E** is the most pertinent to payroll cards, implemented specific protections for employees who use paycards to receive their pay. This ruling, which was effective in 2019, added **Regulation Z** that mandated the disclosure of all paycard-related fees and other paycard-related information to employees.

(Sources: American Payroll Association; Law360)

Cybersecurity and Payroll

Gorodenkoff/Shutterstock

More than 70 percent of targeted companies for cybercriminals have been small businesses. This is a high risk for a small entity and can cause them to go out of business. Some firms reported losses of up to $308,000, and many businesses reported repeated attacks. When discussing cybersecurity in the context of payroll, the accountant needs to understand the defense of computers, servers, mobile devices, systems, and some home networks from attacks by individuals with a desire to get personal information or to hold the company hostage.

Once into the company's servers, the cybercriminal can have access to personnel data and bank accounts, and can even lock companies out of their own computers using ransomware. This makes the protection against cybercriminals something that companies should put at the forefront of their technology planning. The information taken from the company can cause the employees distress and can create distrust of the company as their personal information is spread and opens them up to personal identity theft exposure.

Payroll accountants could play a vital role in preventing cybersecurity breaches. By working with IT professionals, they can identify possible security gaps and use tools to avoid them, such as multifactor authentication. An example of this is the use of an authenticator that can only be unlocked through another computer (e.g., a smartphone or tablet) enabled with biometric security measures, such as the Google Authenticator app. Companies can strengthen their existing cybersecurity programs by encouraging longer, more complex passwords, training employees as part of their employment on common security breach techniques, keeping the most current versions of anti-spyware and antivirus software on exposed equipment, and using secured connections to the servers. Another method to promote cybersecurity could be the use of IP lockdowns paired with a VPN if the payroll personnel worked from home. This method allows only people with a specific IP address and access to the VPN to access payroll records.

Once a company has been the target of a cybersecurity breach, there can be revenue losses, reputational damage, and regulatory costs, as well as loss of employees or customers. With the rising number of cyberattacks, many states, municipalities, and the federal government are looking at adopting regulations to encourage companies to protect themselves against this threat. Humans are the ultimate tool against company exposure in many cases, and education goes a long way toward preventing cyberattacks.

> At Ultimate Kronos Group, the parent company of Kronos payroll software, a cyberattack that began on December 11, 2021, created payroll nightmares for the company and its customers. What started as a ransomware attack led to a system outage for weeks, forcing employers to use manual payroll methods to remain current with their payroll obligations. The timing of the attack disrupted end-of-period tax filings and left Kronos vulnerable to lawsuits and loss of customers. It was estimated that approximately 8 million employees of both public and private entities were affected by the payroll software outage, resulting in missed paychecks and compromised personally identifying information. Kronos no longer exists as a result of these attacks.
>
> (Source: NPR)

Alternating Duties and Cross-Training

The cross-training of payroll professionals can act as a safeguard of payroll information. One of the goals of the Sarbanes–Oxley Act of 2002 was to protect the integrity of accounting data by legislating document retention requirements, corporate officer responsibility for financial accuracy, and the rotation of duties by auditors. The same principle applies to payroll system workers. Cross-training and alternating the people's duties in the payroll process may avoid or minimize errors and potential issues stemming from corruption. Cross-training and rotation of duties foster professional development and proficiency with multiple tasks. This rotation of payroll duties refers only to personnel within the payroll department, not opening the payroll processing to non-accounting departments. Furthermore, cross-training can be highly effective in preventing cybersecurity breaches by restricting the information that each person could modify.

> Cross-training employees has more benefits than fraud deterrence. Offering employees the chance to learn other duties empowers them in their professional development, fostering a sense of fulfillment among employees. Cross-training also grants employees the opportunity to consider different perspectives and gain a broader understanding of the company's operations. Finally, cross-training is linked to better problem-solving ability because employees understand diverse tasks.
>
> (Source: Forbes)

Who Does Which Job?

Stop & Check

Imagine that you have been approached to assist a business owner concerned about the security of his or her company's payroll. In a team of three or four people, decide how you would distribute payroll responsibilities to implement excellent internal control procedures. How did you divide the responsibilities? Explain.

Best Practices Involved in Employee File Maintenance

Maintenance of employee files is as important as the protection of employee information. IRS Regulation 26 CFR 1.6001 clearly states that the method of *file maintenance* is the employer's responsibility. The Internal Revenue Code recommends record labeling, the creation of backup copies, and secure record storage. An important note is that despite the choice of record maintenance, the employer retains all liability for auditor access to the information upon demand. Items such as time and work records, including time cards and electronic work records, must be maintained to be available for auditors because these items are vital components of a payroll system audit.

---

26 CFR 1.6001–1 Records.

(a) *In general.* Except as provided in paragraph (b) of this section, any person subject to tax under subtitle A of the Code (including a qualified State individual income tax which is treated according to section 6361(a) as if it was imposed by chapter 1 of subtitle A), or any person required to file a return of information concerning income, shall keep such permanent books of account or records, including inventories, as are sufficient to establish the amount of gross income, deductions, credits, or other matters required to be shown by such person in any return of such tax or information.

(Source: GPO)

Modella/Shutterstock

Payroll record maintenance is important for employees at all levels of the organization. IRS Revenue Procedure 98-25, 1998-1 CB 689, was enacted in 1998 to govern the maintenance procedures and duration of record-keeping for companies with employees. Provisions of the law include payroll transaction details such as time worked, pay dates, employee status, record reconciliation, and correlation of IRS reports and employee records. Concerning executive-level pay, the company must keep records of how the executive's pay was derived, including benchmarks from similar companies, payout periods, and scheduled increases. All pay disbursed must be justified according to the amount and type of work performed, regardless of employee level or classification. A company's payroll and legal department should work closely to determine and implement a maintenance and record destruction program that complies with IRS requirements but avoids the inaccessibility of data that occurs with information overload.

Electronic Records

Many companies have moved to electronic scanned copies of payroll records that allow immediate access to employee files from a password-protected format. In remote locations, payroll accountants can send the managers and employees Adobe Acrobat files requiring a password to access pay records or use a secure web portal. Several data encryption programs are currently on the market, allowing payroll managers to select the best fit for their individual companies. All hard copies (i.e., paper versions) of payroll information must be in a locked file cabinet with limited access.

Computers have become a necessary part of a business and offer significant benefits to the accounting department. Most accounting software for the preparation of payroll includes password requirements that the company can control, limiting access to electronic information about employees, pay, and personal information. Many regulatory agencies have addressed record security and safeguarding procedures; for example, the Food and Drug Administration enacted 21 CFR Part 11, which delineates electronic record security and safeguarding procedures.

Payroll accounting, according to the definition by the Internal Revenue Code, is a closed system because only certain employees are granted access to the information contained in the electronic records. All aspects of information security are the employer's responsibility, including access to, creating, and maintaining electronic personnel and pay records. Record identifiers log who had accessed an electronic file, when, and from what location. Record logging provides an additional measure of security and protection against hacking, as well as tracking whether unauthorized changes occur on records.

Andrey_Popov/Shutterstock

> According to the FBI, more than $1 billion per year has been lost to hackers using ransomware. Ransomware is malicious code placed into a computer system by hackers to obtain a monetary fee to release access to a company's computerized information. The city of Atlanta, Georgia, encountered ransomware that was downloaded onto the city's computer system during a city-related Internet search. As a result of the attack, the city's daily operations were halted because workers could not access their computers.
>
> (Sources: ArsTechnica; TrendMicro)

Like other payroll records, electronic records, especially those accessible over the Internet, must be safeguarded to prevent fraudulent activity and data corruption. Employers can access information via a company's intranet (inside the organization) or the Internet using encryption programs, passwords, and secured website locations. It is important to note that once a company has allowed Internet access to its payroll files, it is opening itself up to additional risks from hacking or wrongful use of the payroll information. It is the payroll accountant's responsibility to report any suspicious activity to company managers or the company's information security department.

Payroll as a Non-Solo Effort

One best practice is to have more than one person involved in generating and maintaining payroll records. Many errors can occur when the total payroll responsibility rests with one person. Errors that occur may result from a complex hacking effort or a simple failure to remove the system access from a former employee.

James Lauritz/Getty Images

> - Nonexistent or "ghost" employees could be created and paid via the payroll system. The person committing the fraud could circumvent the payroll system and divert the funds to himself or an accomplice.
> - Terminated employees could continue to be paid via the payroll system, or the funds could be subverted to someone else perpetrating the fraud.

- Sales commission plans, employee bonus plans, incentive programs, and other arrangements intended to induce particular behaviors are subject to the employee's and management's manipulation.
- The payroll checks distributed to employees could be stolen individually or *en masse* before their distribution. Also, check fraud could be perpetrated using actual checks or just the account information.
- The company's payroll system or payroll service provider could suffer a breach of the security protocols protecting the computer systems, allowing any combination of fraud or theft to be perpetrated.

Other instances of payroll fraud could have been avoided with a *separation of duties*, which involves the division of related tasks to prevent fraud. Internal controls promote improved accuracy when more than one person is involved in payroll preparation and disbursement. A division of record maintenance, employee verification, and the spread of pay disbursement responsibilities among different employees, depending upon the company's size, would prevent many of the preceding problems. This protects the employer from complaints and potential legal issues stemming from payroll anomalies and provides a level of protection and verification to employees. Auditors look for well-defined internal controls within organizations to ensure legal compliance and file integrity.

- A payroll worker, disgruntled with his job, stole almost $300,000 from different companies by transferring the organizations' money into different bank accounts that he owned.
- A former bookkeeper forged $80,000 in payroll checks before the company owner discovered the discrepancy.
- In the Los Angeles Unified School District, internal inspectors found that the pay system was issuing paychecks to deceased employees.
- In an audit of the Department of Transportation records in Florida, the auditors found that the paper files supporting the payroll system had been discarded to make room in the office. The audit revealed overpayments to employees caused by incorrect calculations and a lack of payroll verification. Of the employees who were overpaid, only one returned the money.

In the event of a data breach, the company must act quickly to contain the damage and prevent additional issues. The American Payroll Association offered the following action steps that companies should take when they experience a breach in their accounting data software:

Step 1   Prevent the spread of the data breach by taking payroll systems to an offline state and restricting access to records.

Step 2   Determine the scale of the threat or breach. Gather all related data and facts involving the breach and assess any vulnerabilities in the system.

Step 3   Contact the appropriate law enforcement officials to notify them of the crime and to open an investigation. Notify the Federation of Tax Administrators at www.taxadmin.org to engage their service in the investigation.

Step 4   Review the company's data storage, retention, and authorization policies to identify ways to prevent future occurrences.

Document Retention Requirements

According to IRS Regulation 26 CFR 1.6001, records about any financial transaction must remain available for *payroll audit*, the inspection by regulating bodies, at all times. The purpose of the tax code is to maintain records for legal purposes in the suspicion of fraudulent activity. IRS Regulation 26 CFR 1.6001 pertains to manual and computerized records, including payroll records prepared by third-party sources. Both manual and electronic documents must be maintained so that they maintain accessibility for the duration, similar to tax record retention.

When a company institutes a retention schedule, the requirements of legislation and the IRS must be considered. The retention period does not begin until the disbursement of pay occurs or the employee terminates employment, whichever occurs last. Remember: In the event of fraudulent activity, retention requirements no longer apply, and the courts can request all company records.

Companies must abide by both state and federal law regarding document retention. Employee payroll records, consisting of all forms and payroll compensation statements, must be retained following *termination* or separation. Although no regulations exist for the retention and archiving of internal payroll documents (e.g., a *payroll register*), a general guideline is that the internal documents should be stored with the other payroll accounting records and destroyed per accounting record guidelines.

According to the FLSA, the following records must be maintained for a minimum of **three** years:

- Payroll and other related records.
- Union contracts.
- Contacts involving exclusions from the regular pay rate.
- Any agreements about overtime rates.
- Any certificates about workers who would receive sub-minimum wages.
- Records referring to sales that would form the basis for employee commissions.

Similarly, the following records must be retained for a minimum of **two** years under FLSA:

- Employment and earnings records.
- Any tables used to compute company wage rates.
- Worker schedules to support time worked.
- Any other records that contain information about wage additions or deductions.

Note that no guidelines exist for any particular order of these documents, but any copies of these records must be clear if copied or otherwise transmitted.

When an employee is terminated, records for the employee and reason for termination must be retained for a period of one year. If an employee qualifies under ADEA, all payroll records must be retained for a period of three years. The Lilly Ledbetter Fair Pay Act created a record retention requirement of an additional three years for primary records (pay records or bargaining agreements) and two years for supplementary data (time cards, wage rate tables, and piece-rate records).

Note: As a suggested practice to meet the various requirements, many businesses will set document retention at three years for all files.

The Zeller Law Group, PC, posted guidelines for document retention for California employers. Although the retention guidelines are specific to California law, they are worth considering for all employers. The guidelines are as follows:

1. Maintenance of employee time records for four years.
2. Computer maintenance and backup of electronic employee paystubs to avoid loss due to technological or cybersecurity issues.
3. Protection of confidential employee records for at least four years.
4. Retrievability of I-9 forms for a long enough period.
5. Assurance that managers and supervisors are appropriately trained about payroll documentation procedures.

(Source: Zeller Law Group)

Agencies that have the right to audit payroll records include:

- The Internal Revenue Service (IRS)
- Federal and state Departments of Labor
- Department of Homeland Security
- Other state and local agencies
- Labor unions

The following is a chart that explains federal record retention requirements, including relevant laws and types of documents:

Document Type	Retention Requirements
Payroll Records (time sheets, electronic records, etc.)	• Three-year retention period • An additional five-year post-termination retention is recommended due to Lilly Ledbetter Act • Includes employee data, any pay records, and all compensation, financial and nonfinancial
Employee Federal, State, and Local Tax Records	• Four years from date the tax is due or paid • Includes all W-4s, state and local tax withholding forms, requests for additional tax withholding, and tax remittances
Form I-9 and Accompanying Employment Eligibility Documents	• Three years after hire OR • One year after termination, whichever is longer
Employee Benefits and Contributions	• Six years • All retirement plan contributions, plan changes, records pertaining to any other employee voluntary deductions
Health Plan Documentation	• No written guidelines, but a minimum of six years is recommended • All written notices about changes in health coverage, especially for health coverage after termination of employment

Even if your company outsources payroll activities, it is still accountable for all records and the information transmitted to the payroll service companies. The third-party payroll service provider attends only to the processing of company payroll but is not responsible for payroll tax payments. Tax remittance remains the liability of the company. Instances in which companies have diverted payroll tax liabilities for personal purposes have resulted in sizable fines and corporate sanctions.

> In 2017, the IRS levied a $1 million lien against the property of CCH Oncology of Buffalo, New York. The company failed to remit or file returns for income, Social Security, and Medicare taxes for both the employees' and the employer's shares starting approximately July 2016. The lien amount included failure to pay and failure to file penalties as well as interest.
>
> (Source: *The Buffalo News*)

Internal Controls and Audits

Stop & Check

1. Which of these is *not* a payroll internal control procedure?
   a. Overtime approval
   b. Removal of payroll oversight
   c. Cross-training
   d. File security
2. Which of these records should be retained in the event of a payroll audit?
   a. Employee medical records
   b. Employee reviews
   c. Employee time and work records
   d. Employee nonpayroll correspondence
3. Which of the following represents protections against cyberattacks?
   a. Complex passwords
   b. Open networks
   c. Employee training on common techniques of cyber criminals
   d. Antivirus and anti-spyware software

LO 2-6 Discuss Employment Termination and Document Destruction Procedures

When employees are terminated, either voluntarily or involuntarily, the employer has payroll issues unique to the situation. The common element to each termination is the paperwork needed. When an employer terminates a worker's employment involuntarily, the burden of proof for the termination is on the employer, should the case ever require legal scrutiny.

> In *Graziadio v. Culinary Institute of America* (2016), the plaintiff was terminated involuntarily after taking two consecutive three-week leaves to care for her children. The Culinary Institute of America claimed that Graziadio had not filed the required paperwork for leave under the FMLA. At first, the court ruled in favor of the Culinary Institute of America because the proper paperwork was not on file. However, further investigation found that the Culinary Institute of America's human resources director, who refused to allow Graziadio to return to work, had not responded to Graziadio's numerous email requests for FMLA paperwork to justify her absence and to return to work.
>
> (Source: FindLaw)

Steve Debenport/Getty Images

Employee Termination

There are two different methods of separation of an employee from the company: *termination* and *resignation*. Termination is generally initiated by the employer; resignation is usually requested by the employee. When an employee leaves a company, the payroll accountant must complete several steps concerning the employee's and the firm's records. The employee's final paycheck will reflect a culmination of hours worked and, depending on company policies, vacation earned and not taken and sick time earned and not taken. Depending on the company's policies, if the employee's compensation is commission-based, there should be an agreement between management and the employee regarding their sales and the final paycheck's timing to ensure the payment of all earned commissions.

Final hours are calculated the same as for any normal pay period. The employee's daily hours are calculated to determine regular and overtime, and the worked hours are added together to determine weekly hours and weekly overtime. If the employee earned any vacation or sick time, those hours might also need to be paid out on the final paycheck. Vacation and sick time are not included in the worked hours for the determination of overtime.

A limited amount of legislation exists about the payment of a severance package upon termination. In general, two situations exist in which severance packages may be required by legislation: The closure of a company facility and many employee layoffs. If a large number of employees is laid off, a severance package may be required if any promise, written or oral, of a severance package exists or if the company has a history of paying severance packages to laid-off employees. For specific guidelines, the state's employment department would be the primary resource for official guidance (see **Appendix E** for state contact information).

In terms of payroll accounting, a major difference between the termination and the resignation of an employee, besides the circumstances surrounding the employee's separation from the company (layoff, termination for cause, resignation, etc.), is the timing of the delivery of the final pay disbursement. When an employee quits, any compensation due will be processed and disbursed on the company's next scheduled pay date. However, when the employee is terminated, the company may be mandated to immediately issue the final paycheck or within a short time frame to comply with state labor laws. There is no federal regulation for the timing of the issuance of the employee's final pay, although the Department of Labor explicitly mandates back pay owed to former employees. Table 2-3 contains information about states' employee termination pay guidelines.

> United Furniture Industries Inc. operated from its headquarters in Mississippi since 1983 and was an industry leader in home furnishings. In November 2022, 2,700 employees received emails and texts during overnight hours, informing them that they should not report to work and that their employment was terminated immediately. All compensation and other benefits were terminated immediately. Mississippi currently has no termination pay guidelines. The employees had no access to retrieve personal items and no information about when they would receive any earned wages. United Furniture filed for bankruptcy in January 2023, and investigations commenced into that company's demise and plans for former employees.
>
> (Sources: Daily Mail, New York Post)

Document Destruction

Although many state and federal laws delineate the time requirement for document retention, there are also several methods for regulated *document destruction* of sensitive payroll data. How must confidential payroll-related documents be destroyed? It is not as simple as throwing old payroll documents in the trash. Preferred destruction methods of confidential payroll documents include incineration, confidential shredding services, or paper records pulping. Electronic records must be purged from the server. Although specific destruction procedures and regulations vary among states and localities, the basic guidelines for confidential destruction after the required retention period are common in most areas. From small-scale record destruction using in-office paper shredders to large-scale operations such as **ProShred**, **Iron Mountain**, and many other companies, the secure storage and destruction of confidential business documents is a serious concern because of the federal privacy laws governing payroll documents.

Ingram Publishing/SuperStock

TABLE 2-3
States' Termination and Resignation Pay Guidelines

State	Guideline	State	Guideline
AK	Within three working days upon termination; at the next regular pay date that is at least more than three days upon resignation.	MS	No termination pay guidelines.
		MT	Immediately upon termination unless the employer's written policy extends the time to the next regular payday; the next regular pay date, or 15 days, whichever is earlier, for resignation.
AL	No termination pay guidelines.		
AR	Within seven days of discharge; next scheduled pay date upon resignation.	NC	Next regularly scheduled payday for both termination and resignation.
AZ	Within seven working days or the end of the next pay period, whichever is sooner.	ND	Next regularly scheduled payday for both termination and resignation.
CA	Immediately upon discharge for termination; within 72 hours upon resignation.	NE	Next regular payday or within two weeks, whichever is sooner, for both termination and resignation.
CO	Immediately upon discharge (i.e., within six hours of the next business day or 24 hours if payroll is processed off-site) for termination; next scheduled pay date upon resignation.	NH	Within 72 hours upon termination; the next pay date in the event of a layoff.
		NJ	Next regularly scheduled payday for both termination and resignation.
CT	No later than the next business day upon termination; next scheduled pay date upon resignation.	NM	Within five days upon termination; next scheduled pay date upon resignation. Task, commission, and piece rate are due within 10 days.
DC	No later than the next business day following termination; the next scheduled pay date or within seven days upon resignation.	NV	Within three days upon termination; the next scheduled pay date or seven days, whichever is sooner, upon resignation.
DE	Next regularly scheduled payday for termination and resignation.		
FL	No termination pay guidelines.	NY	Next regularly scheduled payday for both termination and resignation.
GA	No termination pay guidelines.		
HI	At the time of termination unless conditions render pay impossible, otherwise the next business day. Next scheduled payday if resignation without notice or immediately if resignation with notice.	OH	Next scheduled pay date or within 15 days for both termination and resignation.
		OK	Next regularly scheduled payday for both termination and resignation.
IA	Next regularly scheduled payday for both termination and resignation.	OR	By the end of the next business day upon termination; immediately if the employee gave 48-hour notice or within five days without 48-hour notice.
ID	Next regular payday or within 10 days, excluding weekends and holidays, whichever occurs first; within 48 hours upon employee's written request for both termination and resignation.	PA	Next regularly scheduled payday for both termination and resignation.
		RI	Next regularly scheduled payday for both termination and resignation.
IL	Immediately when possible or the next regularly scheduled payday for both termination and resignation.	SC	Within 48 hours or the next scheduled payday, not to exceed 30 days, upon both termination and resignation.
IN	Next regularly scheduled payday for both termination and resignation.	SD	Next regularly scheduled payday or whenever the terminated employee returns all the employer's property for both termination and resignation.
KS	Next regularly scheduled payday for both termination and resignation.		
KY	Next regular payday or 14 days, whichever is later, for both termination and resignation.	TN	Next regularly scheduled payday or 21 days, whichever comes later, for both termination and resignation.
LA	Next regular payday or 15 days, whichever is sooner, for both termination and resignation.	TX	No later than six days after termination; by the next scheduled pay date upon resignation.
MA	Immediately upon termination; next scheduled pay date or the following Saturday upon resignation.	UT	Within 24 hours upon termination; next scheduled pay date upon resignation.
MD	Next regularly scheduled payday for both termination and resignation.	VA	Next regularly scheduled payday for both termination and resignation.
ME	Next scheduled payday or within two weeks after a demand from the employee, whichever is sooner, for both termination and resignation.	VT	Within 72 hours upon termination; the next scheduled pay date or the following Friday (if not pay date) upon resignation.
MI	Next regularly scheduled payday for both termination and resignation. Some industry-specific rules for termination timing.	WA	Next regularly scheduled payday for both termination and resignation.
		WI	Next regularly scheduled payday for both termination and resignation.
MN	Immediately upon termination; the next regular pay date upon resignation, unless there are less than 5 days until payday, then 20 days after the last day of work under resignation.	WV	Next regularly scheduled payday for both termination and resignation.
MO	Immediately upon termination; no law for resignation.	WY	Next regularly scheduled payday for both termination and resignation.

(Source: Paycor)

A best practice in document destruction is creating a policy regarding document retention and destruction schedules. An employee in charge of these schedules would be tasked with ensuring that all paper records are stored appropriately and retained for the proper legal time. Another best practice is to separate payroll-related documentation into the following categories:

- Private personnel information such as Forms W-4 and I-9, court-ordered garnishments, wage information, and direct deposit instructions.
- Employee benefits paperwork, including benefit elections, FMLA documentation, workers' compensation evidence, and flexible spending account information.
- Any investigative information is maintained separately because of the absence of a statute of limitations on employee fraud.

By separating the employee paper files into these categories, document retention and destruction guidelines may be observed more efficiently.

Electronic Records

As the use of electronic payroll records has grown, the need to define appropriate destruction procedures has become increasingly apparent. Simply deleting a website or a portion of the data does not guarantee the security of confidential information. Details of the website's design and system change documentation must be maintained to facilitate record disposal. Guidelines for electronic records disposition include:

- Data disposition instructions, including dates and authorized administrators.
- Record destruction schedules involving security encryption.
- Technical documentation for each record system.
- Identifying information for file indexes and unique records.
- If a website is involved, technical documentation of the site architecture should be maintained.

> The proliferation of electronic accounting records, especially payroll-related data, has led to the Department of Defense Data Wipe Method's adoption, commonly referred to as DoD 5220.22-M (the National Industrial Security Program Operating Manual), which sanitizes electronic records by forcing the user to verify multiple passes of the electronic document destruction process to prevent accidental document destruction. Various data wiping tools have this software tool, including DBAN, CBL Data Shredder, and ErAse.
>
> (Source: Lifewire)

Destroy and Terminate

Stop & Check

1. How should paper payroll records be destroyed? How about electronic records?
2. Apollo, a resident of Hawaii, is terminated without cause from his job on October 11. He is terminated at the end of the day after the payroll manager has left. When must he receive his final pay? Is the employer required to pay a severance package? Explain.

Trends to Watch

PAYROLL PROCEDURES

As we move further into the digital age, payroll procedures are changing to meet employer needs, technological availability, and employee accessibility. Some procedures that have changed since 2018 include:

- Affordable Care Act employer reporting requirement clarifications
- An increase in the use of Internet-based employee files, which requires increasingly sophisticated security software and company protocols
- Changes to limitations on the number of and fees related to visas for foreign workers
- More mobile-friendly workplaces and payroll management
- Increased use of cloud-based payroll processing
- Remote workers in the same and other states than the company

Future trends to watch include:

- An increase in the "virtual marketplace," in which employers and employees will telecommute or otherwise perform work from geographically dispersed locations
- Changes to paid time off demands from workers
- Increases in the accuracy of worked hours using technology to track work hours and locations
- Digitization of employee records becoming the norm, not the exception
- Security breaches increasing in number and frequency, requiring stronger, more vigilant record-keeping controls
- Increased desire for earned wage pay

Summary of Payroll System Procedures

The establishment of a payroll system involves careful planning and deliberation. The framework used for the payroll system needs to have enough room for company growth and enough structure to make sure that company and governmental deadlines are met. Using the best practices outlined in this chapter can help a company implement a robust payroll system, whether the system is maintained by company personnel or outsourced, completed manually or electronically using specifically designed software. Adequate payroll system design can save a company from problems with employees and governmental entities and prevent data breaches and fraud.

Although pay processes and methods vary among companies, the framework of internal review and the necessity for accuracy remains the fundamental aspects of any payroll system. Documentation of an employee's eligibility to work in the United States and the compensation method, rates, tax liabilities, and voluntary withholdings are critical elements of employee files that the payroll accountant needs to produce accurate payroll disbursements. The process of entering items into a payroll system varies, depending on the type of work done and the compensation rates, for which the payroll accountant must have documentation. Depending on the company's preferences, anything from manual records to computerized records to external payroll vendors may be used to track the payroll. At employee termination, a final payment must be issued, but the final payment's timing depends on state legislation.

Payroll record-keeping and maintenance are complex issues and are subject to several federal and state regulations. Employee personal information must be safeguarded at all times, and information privacy is paramount. Now that many companies are resorting to electronic pay records, information safeguarding is essential, and encryption efforts are multidimensional, involving the accounting, legal, and information systems departments of an organization. Many electronic records and remote workers have created additional opportunities for cybercriminals to breach company defenses, and cybersecurity measures have evolved to counteract those breaches. Destruction of payroll-related documents after the required retention period is a serious concern, and an entire industry focuses on document retention and destruction.

Key Points

- Communication protocol varies among companies and departments within companies.
- Upon employment, company personnel must ensure Form W-4 and the I-9 to determine accurate taxes and legal eligibility to work in the United States.
- States have a variety of required pay periods to protect workers and promote predictable paychecks.
- Ethical payroll practices require the protection of information and dissemination only to the employee or specifically relevant supervisory staff.
- Employees are classified as either exempt or nonexempt from FLSA provisions.
- To be classified as an exempt employee requires an examination of job duties.
- Control of the payroll system involves regular system design review and delineation of specific tasks.
- Whether completed internally or by an outsourced vendor, payroll is only as accurate as the information provided.
- Pay periods are at the discretion of the company.
- File security is of utmost importance, especially when files are stored electronically and accessed via an Internet portal.
- Documentation for payroll exceptions such as time away from work should be maintained separately from regular work time documentation.
- Calculations of pay can involve many variables and require reviewing each employee's information before pay issuance.
- Final pay needs to reflect all earned compensation, paid time off, and deductions up to the termination date.
- The timing of final pay disbursement when an employee is terminated depends on state law.
- Document retention and destruction procedures are important for data security and audit purposes.

Vocabulary

Biweekly payroll
Commission
Daily payroll
Document destruction
Exempt
File maintenance
File security
Foreign Account Tax Compliance Act (FATCA)
Form SS-8
H-1B visa
Hiring packet
I-9
Independent Contractor
Internal control
Leased employee
Monthly payroll
New-hire reporting
Nonexempt
Pay period
Paycard
Payroll audit
Payroll register
Payroll review
Piece rate
Resignation
Remit
Review process
Semimonthly payroll
Separation of duties
Statutory employee
Temporary employee
Termination
W-4
Weekly payroll

Review Questions

1. What are three necessary elements of internal control for a payroll department?
2. Why should more than one person prepare and verify payroll processing?
3. What documents should be included in all new-hire packets?

4. Why are new hires required to be reported to the state's employment department?
5. When must a terminated employee be paid his or her final paycheck for the state in which you live?
6. What are the five main pay period frequencies?
7. How would you distinguish between exempt and nonexempt workers?
8. What are two of the best practices for establishing a payroll system?
9. What are the important considerations in setting up a payroll system?
10. What are two different tasks involved in payroll accounting?
11. What agencies or organizations can audit a company's payroll records?
12. How can a company protect itself from cybersecurity breaches?
13. How long should employee records be retained?
14. Why are independent contractors not paid through a company's payroll system?
15. What is the difference between termination and resignation?
16. Explain some of the differences in termination and resignation pay regulations.
17. What are the differences among daily, weekly, biweekly, semimonthly, and monthly pay periods?
18. What differentiates exempt and nonexempt employees?
19. What challenges does a company face when using cloud-based payroll and personnel records?

Exercises Set A

E2-1A.
LO 2-1, 2-4

Nike Tran, a nonexempt employee at Refurbished Woods, in Marquette, Wisconsin, works a standard 7:00 a.m.–4:00 p.m. schedule with an hour for lunch each day. Nike received overtime pay for hours in excess of 40 per week. During the week, Nike worked the following schedule:
- Monday: 9.25 hours
- Tuesday: 7.5 hours
- Wednesday: 8.75 hours
- Thursday: 6.75 hours
- Friday: 8.25 hours

How many hours of overtime did Nike work this week?
1. 0 hours
2. 0.50 hours
3. 2 hours
4. 2.25 hours

E2-2A.
LO 2-1

London Weatherby is paid every other week while working for the federal government. Which of the following choices describes the pay frequency?
1. Biweekly
2. Semimonthly
3. Weekly
4. Monthly

E2-3A.
LO 2-2

Sage Rivera is a new employee for De Terra Glass. Which federal forms must be completed as part of the hiring process? (Select all that apply.)
1. W-4
2. W-2
3. SS-8
4. I-9

E2-4A.
LO 2-5, 2-6

West Matthews, a resident of Texas, resigned from employment with Grand Lake Cattle Farms on October 6, 2023. The next pay date for the company is October 13. By what date should the final pay be received?
1. October 6
2. October 13
3. October 27
4. October 31

E2-5A.
LO 2-5

Xailen Kelley is a new nonexempt sales associate for Oyondo Retail Stores. After completing the time card for the pay period, what is the next step in the payroll review process to ensure proper internal controls?
1. Submit the time card to the payroll clerk.
2. Have a friend check her math for accuracy.
3. Submit the time card to her manager for review.
4. Enter the time card data directly into the payroll system.

E2-6A.
LO 2-6

Addison Silva needs additional filing space at the end of the year in the company's off-site, secured storage. There are several boxes of payroll records marked for the current year's destruction. What methods can Addison use to dispose of the payroll records? (Select all that apply.)
1. Contact an off-site record destruction service.
2. Place the boxes containing the records in the company trash disposal.
3. Shred the records, and then dispose of the shredded paper.
4. Incinerate the payroll records marked for destruction.

E2-7A.
LO 2-1

Jaylin Blue is a payroll clerk at Quaking Aspens Antiques. Through reviews of the employee files, what information should be present for each employee? (Select all that apply.)
1. Spouse's name
2. Pay rate
3. Occupation
4. Supervisor name

E2-8A.
LO 2-2

Camryn Klein is the payroll clerk for Neolane Transportation. A colleague who is classified as an independent contractor asks to be classified as an employee. What factors should Camryn consider? (Select all that apply.)
1. Relationship of the parties
2. Behavioral control
3. Method of compensation
4. Financial control

E2-9A.
LO 2-2

What are the forms of identification that establish *employment authorization* for the I-9? (Select all that apply.)
1. Driver's license
2. Native American tribal document
3. Voter registration card
4. Social Security card

E2-10A.
LO 2-2

What are the forms of identification that establish *identity* for the I-9 for employees over the age of 25? (Select all that apply.)
1. State-issued driver's license
2. U.S. passport
3. School record
4. Certified copy of the birth certificate

E2-11A.
LO 2-3

Rylen Patil is a candidate for the position of sales manager with Retrozz Furniture. This position will be required to supervise several employees and can determine the direction in which assignments will be completed. What guidelines should be followed when classifying workers as exempt or nonexempt? (Select all that apply.)
1. OSHA
2. FLSA
3. Department of Labor
4. IRS

E2-12A.
LO 2-3

Tanner Robledo is the office manager for Wardley and Sons Auto Detailing. Because it is a small office, Tanner is required to keep track of all employee records and pay both employees and contractors. Which of the following are legal factors that will distinguish exempt from nonexempt employees? (Select all that apply.)
1. Number of hours worked
2. Type of work performed
3. Employee age and education
4. Amount of supervisor-given direction

Problems Set A

P2-1A.
LO 2-1

Sawyer Walker is a vice president of sales at Fields Brothers Autos in Davenport, Iowa, and earns an annual salary of $59,000. What is Sawyer's period pay for each of the following pay frequencies?
1. Biweekly
2. Semimonthly
3. Weekly
4. Monthly

P2-2A.
LO 2-2, 2-3

Xian Oni is a part-time worker for Senior Solvers and uses company equipment to perform job duties. Xian asks the payroll supervisor to grant independent contractor status. What should the payroll supervisor tell Xian?

P2-3A.
LO 2-5

You are the new payroll supervisor for your company. Which payroll documentation control procedures are now your responsibility?

P2-4A.
LO 2-2

Finley Figueroa is a new employee in the payroll department of Octolium Computers. After working at the company for one week, Finley asks you why it is so important to submit new-hire documentation. What guidance will you offer?

P2-5A.
LO 2-4

You are the payroll accounting clerk for your company, Conose Advertising, which has 50 employees. The controller has recently switched the firm from an in-house payroll system to an outsourced payroll provider. What are your responsibilities within the company for payroll records and employee file issues?

P2-6A.
LO 2-2

River Tallchief is a citizen of the Northern Pomo Indian Nation. In completing the I-9, River provides an official Northern Pomo Indian Nation birth certificate to establish identification and employment eligibility. Is this sufficient documentation? Why or why not?

P2-7A.
LO 2-3

Maria Rupert is the payroll supervisor at All Family Investments. Management is asking to have the investment salespeople, who are paid on an hourly basis, be classified as exempt employees because their job duties occasionally require evening and weekend work. What tests should the investment salespeople meet to achieve exempt status?

P2-8A.
LO 2-6

Twinte Cars, a California corporation, has internal corporate requirements that stipulate a three-year payroll document retention period. It enters into a contract with an international company that mandates a six-year payroll document retention requirement. How should Twinte Cars balance these requirements?

P2-9A.
LO 2-2

Teagan McCormick is a full-time life insurance agent with Centixo Insurance, a small insurance company. The company has classified Teagan as an employee. Teagan feels the classification should be independent contractor because there are no company benefits and Teagan sets the office hours. Should Teagan be reclassified as an independent contractor? Why or why not?

P2-10A.
LO 2-2

Ash Hardy is an employee of Polyent Plastics, a company with headquarters in Rock Island, Illinois. Ash lives and works in Doha, Qatar, and earns an annual salary of $97,300. The company has been withholding U.S. federal income taxes from the pay, but Ash believes the wages should be exempt as an expatriate. What course of action should Ash take?

P2-11A.
LO 2-2, 2-4

Complete the W-4 for employment at Plexivent Plastics starting 9/6/2023. The employer's address is 1 Plastics Way, Lincoln Valley, ND 58430, and EIN is 56-4658631.
Harley W. Pierce
2024 Denhoff Highway, Apartment 12
Lincoln Valley, ND 58430
SSN: 687-55-4658
Marital status: Married filing jointly with two dependents under 17
One job and spouse does not work
Does not require any additional amount to be withheld

P2-12A.
LO 2-2, 2-4

Complete the I-9 for employment at Plexivent Plastics starting 9/6/2023. The employer's address is 1 Plastics Way, Lincoln Valley, ND 58430, and the EIN is 56-4658631. Harley is starting work on 9/6/2023. Be sure to complete Section 2 of Form I-9.
Harley W. Pierce
2024 Denhoff Highway, Apartment 12
Lincoln Valley, ND 58430
SSN: 687-55-4658
Marital status: Married
Date of Birth: 8/15/1999
U.S. Citizen
Harley's North Dakota driver's license number is MKJ-462856 and expires on 8/15/2027.
Office Manager Gabriel MacMillan verified the information for the company.

Form **W-4**	**Employee's Withholding Certificate**	OMB No. 1545-0074
Department of the Treasury Internal Revenue Service	Complete Form W-4 so that your employer can withhold the correct federal income tax from your pay. Give Form W-4 to your employer. Your withholding is subject to review by the IRS.	**20**23

Step 1: Enter Personal Information

(a) First name and middle initial | Last name | (b) Social security number

Address

City or town, state, and ZIP code

Does your name match the name on your social security card? If not, to ensure you get credit for your earnings, contact SSA at 800-772-1213 or go to www.ssa.gov.

(c) ☐ **Single** or **Married filing separately**
☐ **Married filing jointly** or **Qualifying surviving spouse**
☐ **Head of household** (Check only if you're unmarried and pay more than half the costs of keeping up a home for yourself and a qualifying individual.)

Complete Steps 2–4 ONLY if they apply to you; otherwise, skip to Step 5. See page 2 for more information on each step, who can claim exemption from withholding, other details, and privacy.

Step 2: Multiple Jobs or Spouse Works

Complete this step if you (1) hold more than one job at a time, or (2) are married filing jointly and your spouse also works. The correct amount of withholding depends on income earned from all of these jobs.

Do **only one** of the following.

(a) Reserved for future use.
(b) Use the Multiple Jobs Worksheet on page 3 and enter the result in Step 4(c) below; **or**
(c) If there are only two jobs total, you may check this box. Do the same on Form W-4 for the other job. This option is generally more accurate than (b) if pay at the lower paying job is more than half of the pay at the higher paying job. Otherwise, (b) is more accurate . . . . ▶ ☐

TIP: If you have self-employment income, see page 2.

Complete Steps 3–4(b) on Form W-4 for only ONE of these jobs. Leave those steps blank for the other jobs. (Your withholding will be most accurate if you complete Steps 3–4(b) on the Form W-4 for the highest paying job.)

Step 3: Claim Dependent and Other Credits

If your total income will be $200,000 or less ($400,000 or less if married filing jointly):

Multiply the number of qualifying children under age 17 by $2,000 ▶ $ _____

Multiply the number of other dependents by $500 . . . . ▶ $ _____

Add the amounts above for qualifying children and other dependents. You may add to this the amount of any other credits. Enter the total here . . . . **3** $ _____

Step 4 (optional): Other Adjustments

(a) **Other income (not from jobs).** If you want tax withheld for other income you expect this year that won't have withholding, enter the amount of other income here. This may include interest, dividends, and retirement income . . . . **4(a)** $ _____

(b) **Deductions.** If you expect to claim deductions other than the standard deduction and want to reduce your withholding, use the Deductions Worksheet on page 3 and enter the result here . . . . **4(b)** $ _____

(c) **Extra withholding.** Enter any additional tax you want withheld each **pay period** . . **4(c)** $ _____

Step 5: Sign Here

Under penalties of perjury, I declare that this certificate, to the best of my knowledge and belief, is true, correct, and complete.

_____   _____
Employee's signature (This form is not valid unless you sign it.)   **Date**

Employers Only | Employer's name and address | First date of employment | Employer identification number (EIN)

For Privacy Act and Paperwork Reduction Act Notice, see page 3.   Cat. No. 10220Q   Form **W-4** (2023)

(Source: Internal Revenue Service)

Employment Eligibility Verification
Department of Homeland Security
U.S. Citizenship and Immigration Services

USCIS Form I-9
OMB No. 1615-0047
Expires 10/31/2022

▶ **START HERE:** Read instructions carefully before completing this form. The instructions must be available, either in paper or electronically, during completion of this form. Employers are liable for errors in the completion of this form.

ANTI-DISCRIMINATION NOTICE: It is illegal to discriminate against work-authorized individuals. Employers **CANNOT** specify which document(s) an employee may present to establish employment authorization and identity. The refusal to hire or continue to employ an individual because the documentation presented has a future expiration date may also constitute illegal discrimination.

Section 1. Employee Information and Attestation *(Employees must complete and sign Section 1 of Form I-9 no later than the first day of employment, but not before accepting a job offer.)*

Last Name (Family Name)	First Name (Given Name)	Middle Initial	Other Last Names Used (if any)

Address (Street Number and Name)	Apt. Number	City or Town	State	ZIP Code

Date of Birth (mm/dd/yyyy)	U.S. Social Security Number	Employee's E-mail Address	Employee's Telephone Number

I am aware that federal law provides for imprisonment and/or fines for false statements or use of false documents in connection with the completion of this form.

I attest, under penalty of perjury, that I am (check one of the following boxes):

☑ 1. A citizen of the United States

☐ 2. A noncitizen national of the United States *(See instructions)*

☐ 3. A lawful permanent resident   (Alien Registration Number/USCIS Number): _____

☐ 4. An alien authorized to work   until (expiration date, if applicable, mm/dd/yyyy): _____
Some aliens may write "N/A" in the expiration date field. *(See instructions)*

Aliens authorized to work must provide only one of the following document numbers to complete Form I-9:
An Alien Registration Number/USCIS Number OR Form I-94 Admission Number OR Foreign Passport Number.

1. Alien Registration Number/USCIS Number: _____
   OR
2. Form I-94 Admission Number: _____
   OR
3. Foreign Passport Number: _____
   Country of Issuance: _____

QR Code - Section 1
Do Not Write In This Space

Signature of Employee	Today's Date (mm/dd/yyyy)

Preparer and/or Translator Certification (check one):
☐ I did not use a preparer or translator.   ☐ A preparer(s) and/or translator(s) assisted the employee in completing Section 1.
(Fields below must be completed and signed when preparers and/or translators assist an employee in completing Section 1.)

I attest, under penalty of perjury, that I have assisted in the completion of Section 1 of this form and that to the best of my knowledge the information is true and correct.

Signature of Preparer or Translator	Today's Date (mm/dd/yyyy)

Last Name (Family Name)	First Name (Given Name)

Address (Street Number and Name)	City or Town	State	ZIP Code

🛑 *Employer Completes Next Page* 🛑

Form I-9 10/21/2019

Employment Eligibility Verification
Department of Homeland Security
U.S. Citizenship and Immigration Services

USCIS Form I-9
OMB No. 1615-0047
Expires 10/31/2022

Section 2. Employer or Authorized Representative Review and Verification

(Employers or their authorized representative must complete and sign Section 2 within 3 business days of the employee's first day of employment. You must physically examine one document from List A OR a combination of one document from List B and one document from List C as listed on the "Lists of Acceptable Documents.")

Employee Info from Section 1	Last Name *(Family Name)*	First Name *(Given Name)*	M.I.	Citizenship/Immigration Status

List A Identity and Employment Authorization	OR	List B Identity	AND	List C Employment Authorization

Document Title		Document Title		Document Title
Issuing Authority		Issuing Authority		Issuing Authority
Document Number		Document Number		Document Number
Expiration Date *(if any) (mm/dd/yyyy)*		Expiration Date *(if any) (mm/dd/yyyy)*		Expiration Date *(if any) (mm/dd/yyyy)*

Document Title
Issuing Authority
Document Number
Expiration Date *(if any) (mm/dd/yyyy)*

Document Title
Issuing Authority
Document Number
Expiration Date *(if any) (mm/dd/yyyy)*

Additional Information

QR Code - Sections 2 & 3
Do Not Write In This Space

Certification: I attest, under penalty of perjury, that (1) I have examined the document(s) presented by the above-named employee, (2) the above-listed document(s) appear to be genuine and to relate to the employee named, and (3) to the best of my knowledge the employee is authorized to work in the United States.

The employee's first day of employment *(mm/dd/yyyy)*: _____ *(See instructions for exemptions)*

Signature of Employer or Authorized Representative	Today's Date *(mm/dd/yyyy)*	Title of Employer or Authorized Representative
Last Name of Employer or Authorized Representative	First Name of Employer or Authorized Representative	Employer's Business or Organization Name

Employer's Business or Organization Address *(Street Number and Name)*	City or Town	State	ZIP Code

Section 3. Reverification and Rehires *(To be completed and signed by employer or authorized representative.)*

A. New Name *(if applicable)*			**B. Date of Rehire** *(if applicable)*
Last Name *(Family Name)*	First Name *(Given Name)*	Middle Initial	Date *(mm/dd/yyyy)*

C. If the employee's previous grant of employment authorization has expired, provide the information for the document or receipt that establishes continuing employment authorization in the space provided below.

Document Title	Document Number	Expiration Date *(if any) (mm/dd/yyyy)*

I attest, under penalty of perjury, that to the best of my knowledge, this employee is authorized to work in the United States, and if the employee presented document(s), the document(s) I have examined appear to be genuine and to relate to the individual.

Signature of Employer or Authorized Representative	Today's Date *(mm/dd/yyyy)*	Name of Employer or Authorized Representative

Form I-9 10/21/2019

LISTS OF ACCEPTABLE DOCUMENTS
All documents must be UNEXPIRED

Employees may present one selection from List A
or a combination of one selection from List B and one selection from List C.

LIST A Documents that Establish Both Identity and Employment Authorization	LIST B Documents that Establish Identity	LIST C Documents that Establish Employment Authorization
1. U.S. Passport or U.S. Passport Card	1. Driver's license or ID card issued by a State or outlying possession of the United States provided it contains a photograph or information such as name, date of birth, gender, height, eye color, and address	1. A Social Security Account Number card, unless the card includes one of the following restrictions: (1) NOT VALID FOR EMPLOYMENT (2) VALID FOR WORK ONLY WITH INS AUTHORIZATION (3) VALID FOR WORK ONLY WITH DHS AUTHORIZATION
2. Permanent Resident Card or Alien Registration Receipt Card (Form I-551)		
3. Foreign passport that contains a temporary I-551 stamp or temporary I-551 printed notation on a machine-readable immigrant visa	2. ID card issued by federal, state or local government agencies or entities, provided it contains a photograph or information such as name, date of birth, gender, height, eye color, and address	2. Certification of report of birth issued by the Department of State (Forms DS-1350, FS-545, FS-240)
4. Employment Authorization Document that contains a photograph (Form I-766)	3. School ID card with a photograph	3. Original or certified copy of birth certificate issued by a State, county, municipal authority, or territory of the United States bearing an official seal
5. For a nonimmigrant alien authorized to work for a specific employer because of his or her status: a. Foreign passport; and b. Form I-94 or Form I-94A that has the following: (1) The same name as the passport; and (2) An endorsement of the alien's nonimmigrant status as long as that period of endorsement has not yet expired and the proposed employment is not in conflict with any restrictions or limitations identified on the form.	4. Voter's registration card	
	5. U.S. Military card or draft record	
	6. Military dependent's ID card	4. Native American tribal document
	7. U.S. Coast Guard Merchant Mariner Card	5. U.S. Citizen ID Card (Form I-197)
	8. Native American tribal document	6. Identification Card for Use of Resident Citizen in the United States (Form I-179)
	9. Driver's license issued by a Canadian government authority	
	For persons under age 18 who are unable to present a document listed above:	7. Employment authorization document issued by the Department of Homeland Security
6. Passport from the Federated States of Micronesia (FSM) or the Republic of the Marshall Islands (RMI) with Form I-94 or Form I-94A indicating nonimmigrant admission under the Compact of Free Association Between the United States and the FSM or RMI	10. School record or report card	
	11. Clinic, doctor, or hospital record	
	12. Day-care or nursery school record	

Examples of many of these documents appear in the Handbook for Employers (M-274).

Refer to the instructions for more information about acceptable receipts.

Form I-9 10/21/2019

(Source: U.S. Citizenship and Immigration Services)

Exercises Set B

E2-1B.
LO 2-1, 2-4

Dallas Walters, a nonexempt employee of Consolidated Utilities, works a standard 10:00 a.m. to 7:00 p.m. schedule with an hour for lunch. Dallas works in Weed, California, and the state requires overtime pay for hours exceeding 8 per day and for those exceeding 40 in a week. During the week, the following schedule was worked:
- Monday: 8.75 hours
- Tuesday: 7.75 hours
- Wednesday: 8.50 hours
- Thursday: 8.00 hours
- Friday: 8.25 hours

Based on the state's requirements, how much overtime has Dallas worked during the period?
1. 2 hours
2. 1.25 hour
3. 1 hour
4. 2.75 hours

E2-2B.
LO 2-1

Micah Volkov is a salaried employee earning $49,850 annually. Micah is paid twice per month. Which of the following best describes the pay frequency?
1. Biweekly
2. Semimonthly
3. Weekly
4. Monthly

E2-3B.
LO 2-4, 2-6

On June 21, 2023, Dorian Goodman was terminated from Black Diamond Sports in New Hampshire. Black Diamond Sports pays its employees biweekly on Fridays, and the next payday is 7/7/2023. When must Dorian receive the final paycheck?
1. On the next pay date
2. Within seven days
3. Immediately upon discharge
4. Within 72 hours

E2-4B.
LO 2-4, 2-6

Kal Andrews resigned from Atlas Inks on March 21, 2023. When is the earliest that Atlas Inks may destroy Kal's payroll records?
1. March 23, 2024
2. March 23, 2025
3. March 23, 2026
4. March 23, 2027

E2-5B.
LO 2-5

Blake Brown is a new payroll accountant at Zata Imports, a company with 250 employees. After completing all time card data for the pay period, what should Blake's next step in the payroll review process be?
1. Ask employees to verify that the time Blake entered is accurate.
2. Generate paychecks and prepare them for signature.
3. Ask the supervisor to verify the accuracy of the payroll data.
4. Have another payroll clerk verify the data accuracy.

E2-6B.
LO 2-6

Jesse Oliveria needs additional filing space at the end of the year in the company's office and chooses to use off-site, secured storage. Upon arriving at the storage facility, the unit is nearly full and there are several boxes marked for destruction at the end of the calendar year. What are Jesse's options regarding the destruction of the payroll records marked for destruction? (Select all that apply.)
1. Jesse should take the oldest year's boxes to the closest recycling facility.
2. Jesse should make arrangements to pulp or burn the paper payroll records marked for destruction.
3. Jesse should arrange to have a document destruction service pick up the boxes marked for destruction.
4. Jesse should bring a shredding machine to the storage facility and prepare to shred the records marked for destruction.

E2-7B.
LO 2-1

Sam Rogers is conducting a review of the payroll files for each employee at Meejo Games. Which of the following items must be present in the file? (Select all that apply.)
1. The basis upon which compensation is paid
2. Overtime pay earned during each pay period
3. Hours worked during each pay period
4. Break times taken each day

E2-8B.
LO 2-2

Jamie McCarthy is preparing to compute employee pay and needs to determine the amount of employee federal income taxes to be withheld. Which of the following should be consulted?
1. USCIS I-9
2. IRS Publication 15-T
3. DHS Schedule F
4. SSA Schedule 8

E2-9B.
LO 2-2

Dana Baker is a new employee of Farnsdel and Babcock, LLP. Which of the following will provide proof of *employment authorization* for the completion of the I-9? (Select all that apply.)
1. U.S. passport
2. U.S. military identification card
3. U.S. citizen identification card
4. State-issued driver's license

E2-10B.
LO 2-2

Reed Pelliere is completing the I-9 as part of the new employment file with the state of New Mexico. Which of the following provides proof of *identity*? (Select all that apply.)
1. Social Security card
2. Certificate of birth abroad, issued by the U.S. Department of State
3. New Mexico driver's license
4. U.S. passport

E2-11B.
LO 2-3

Corey Watkins is a candidate for the position of marketing manager with the promotions department of Paramba Productions, earning $17.50 per hour. Corey will work occasional overtime in the new position and will not have managerial or supervisory duties as a regular part of the job description. Why should Corey be classified as a nonexempt employee? (Select all that apply.)
1. Corey's annual wages are lower than the minimum exempt salary.
2. Corey has no supervisory or managerial duties.
3. Corey has the term clerk in the job title.
4. Corey will work occasional overtime.

E2-12B.
LO 2-3

Ryan Marshall manages a ski resort with year-round and seasonal employees. Assuming that the ski resort engages in interstate commerce, what FLSA requirement(s) should Ryan consider? (Select all that apply.)
1. Hourly wages paid to employees
2. Safety of the working conditions
3. Number of hours worked per week
4. Employee age and weekly work schedule

Problems Set B

P2-1B.
LO 2-2

Stevie Webb is an independent contractor for Antimbu Exports, where you are the payroll accountant. Stevie feels entitled to employee benefits based on the number of hours dedicated to the company. What guidance could you offer Stevie?

P2-2B.
LO 2-6

Max Wexler was terminated for cause by Santel Auto Parts in North Carolina on July 20, 2023. As of the date of his termination, he had worked 22 hours of regular time. Employees at Santel Auto Parts are paid semimonthly on the 15th and last day of the month. Max would like to know when the final paycheck will be available. What will you tell him?

P2-3B.
LO 2-2

Devin Coahoma is a member of the Algonquin Indian Nation and is a new employee at Pactco Game Designs. During the process of completing the I-9, Devin claims that the only way to prove his identity is the Algonquin Indian Nation's official birth certificate. Is this document sufficient to prove identity for the purposes of the I-9? Why or why not?

P2-4B.
LO 2-2

Addison Manning is a new employee of Symity Batteries. Addison is curious about the purpose of the requirements for new-hire documentation to be forwarded to government agencies. What should you tell Addison?

P2-5B.
LO 2-3

Pax Arturo wants to start a company and hire employees. Because you are a seasoned payroll professional, Pax approaches you for guidance about the differences between exempt and nonexempt employees. What would you tell Pax?

P2-6B.
LO 2-5

Skyler Alvarez is a new payroll clerk for Remm Plumbing. Skyler is curious about the purpose of the different steps in the payroll review process and asks you, as the supervisor, for guidance. What would you tell Skyler?

P2-7B.
LO 2-4

Karsyn Aldri started as a payroll accountant at Sticktoit Adhesives, a company with 100 employees. Karsyn soon notices that the former payroll accountant had been processing payroll manually and suggested that the company immediately switch to cloud-based payroll. What types of documentation must be maintained in employee records?

P2-8B.
LO 2-5

Yael Morris, a payroll clerk, has received a promotion and is now the payroll supervisor for Fligen Enterprises. What document control items could now become part of Yael's responsibility?

P2-9B.
LO 2-2

Kennedy Watkins is in the payroll department of Neombee Plastics, a multistate company. The company has historically been filing employee information with each state. What alternative exists for multistate employers?

P2-10B.
LO 2-1

Drew Allen is the payroll supervisor for Caposis Freight. The company is preparing to merge with another distribution company that has a different pay cycle. The president of the company wants to know the difference between biweekly and semimonthly pay cycles as far as pay dates and payment amounts are concerned. What should Drew tell him?

P2-11B.
LO 2-2, 2-4

Complete the W-4 for employment starting 5/23/2023 at Martel Semiconductors, located at 2445 Manchester Road, Lakehurst, NJ 08733, EIN 26-4684136.
Tatum A. Noren
221 First Street
Lakehurst, NJ 08733
SSN: 785-56-4321
Single with no dependents
No additional tax withholding

P2-12B.
LO 2-2, 2-4

Complete the I-9 for employment starting 5/23/2023 at Martel Semiconductors, located at 2445 Manchester Road, Lakehurst, NJ 08733, EIN 26-4684136. Be sure to complete Section 2 of Form I-9.
Tatum A. Noren
221 First Street
Lakehurst, NJ 08733
SSN: 785-56-4321
Birthdate: 6/5/1998
Tatum presented a driver's license and Social Security card to Human Resources Manager Angel Andrews to review.
New Jersey driver's license #N15368497531246; expires 6/5/2027.

Form **W-4**	**Employee's Withholding Certificate**	OMB No. 1545-0074
Department of the Treasury Internal Revenue Service	Complete Form W-4 so that your employer can withhold the correct federal income tax from your pay. Give Form W-4 to your employer. Your withholding is subject to review by the IRS.	**2023**

Step 1: Enter Personal Information

(a) First name and middle initial   Last name

(b) Social security number

Address

City or town, state, and ZIP code

Does your name match the name on your social security card? If not, to ensure you get credit for your earnings, contact SSA at 800-772-1213 or go to *www.ssa.gov*.

(c) ☐ **Single** or **Married filing separately**
☐ **Married filing jointly** or **Qualifying surviving spouse**
☐ **Head of household** (Check only if you're unmarried and pay more than half the costs of keeping up a home for yourself and a qualifying individual.)

Complete Steps 2–4 ONLY if they apply to you; otherwise, skip to Step 5. See page 2 for more information on each step, who can claim exemption from withholding, other details, and privacy.

Step 2: Multiple Jobs or Spouse Works

Complete this step if you (1) hold more than one job at a time, or (2) are married filing jointly and your spouse also works. The correct amount of withholding depends on income earned from all of these jobs.

Do **only one** of the following.

(a) Reserved for future use.

(b) Use the Multiple Jobs Worksheet on page 3 and enter the result in Step 4(c) below; **or**

(c) If there are only two jobs total, you may check this box. Do the same on Form W-4 for the other job. This option is generally more accurate than (b) if pay at the lower paying job is more than half of the pay at the higher paying job. Otherwise, (b) is more accurate . . . . ☐

TIP: If you have self-employment income, see page 2.

Complete Steps 3–4(b) on Form W-4 for only ONE of these jobs. Leave those steps blank for the other jobs. (Your withholding will be most accurate if you complete Steps 3–4(b) on the Form W-4 for the highest paying job.)

Step 3: Claim Dependent and Other Credits

If your total income will be $200,000 or less ($400,000 or less if married filing jointly):

Multiply the number of qualifying children under age 17 by $2,000 $ _____

Multiply the number of other dependents by $500 . . . . . $ _____

Add the amounts above for qualifying children and other dependents. You may add to this the amount of any other credits. Enter the total here . . . . | 3 | $

Step 4 (optional): Other Adjustments

(a) **Other income (not from jobs).** If you want tax withheld for other income you expect this year that won't have withholding, enter the amount of other income here. This may include interest, dividends, and retirement income . . . . | 4(a) | $

(b) **Deductions.** If you expect to claim deductions other than the standard deduction and want to reduce your withholding, use the Deductions Worksheet on page 3 and enter the result here . . . . | 4(b) | $

(c) **Extra withholding.** Enter any additional tax you want withheld each **pay period** . . | 4(c) | $

Step 5: Sign Here

Under penalties of perjury, I declare that this certificate, to the best of my knowledge and belief, is true, correct, and complete.

_____   _____
Employee's signature (This form is not valid unless you sign it.)   **Date**

Employers Only

Employer's name and address	First date of employment	Employer identification number (EIN)

For Privacy Act and Paperwork Reduction Act Notice, see page 3.   Cat. No. 10220Q   Form **W-4** (2023)

(Source: Internal Revenue Service)

Employment Eligibility Verification
Department of Homeland Security
U.S. Citizenship and Immigration Services

USCIS Form I-9
OMB No. 1615-0047
Expires 10/31/2022

▶ **START HERE:** Read instructions carefully before completing this form. The instructions must be available, either in paper or electronically, during completion of this form. Employers are liable for errors in the completion of this form.

ANTI-DISCRIMINATION NOTICE: It is illegal to discriminate against work-authorized individuals. Employers **CANNOT** specify which document(s) an employee may present to establish employment authorization and identity. The refusal to hire or continue to employ an individual because the documentation presented has a future expiration date may also constitute illegal discrimination.

Section 1. Employee Information and Attestation *(Employees must complete and sign Section 1 of Form I-9 no later than the first day of employment, but not before accepting a job offer.)*

Last Name *(Family Name)*	First Name *(Given Name)*	Middle Initial	Other Last Names Used *(if any)*

Address *(Street Number and Name)*	Apt. Number	City or Town	State	ZIP Code

Date of Birth *(mm/dd/yyyy)*	U.S. Social Security Number	Employee's E-mail Address	Employee's Telephone Number
	___ - __ - ____		

I am aware that federal law provides for imprisonment and/or fines for false statements or use of false documents in connection with the completion of this form.

I attest, under penalty of perjury, that I am (check one of the following boxes):

☑ 1. A citizen of the United States

☐ 2. A noncitizen national of the United States *(See instructions)*

☐ 3. A lawful permanent resident   (Alien Registration Number/USCIS Number): _____

☐ 4. An alien authorized to work   until (expiration date, if applicable, mm/dd/yyyy): _____
       Some aliens may write "N/A" in the expiration date field. *(See instructions)*

Aliens authorized to work must provide only one of the following document numbers to complete Form I-9:
An Alien Registration Number/USCIS Number OR Form I-94 Admission Number OR Foreign Passport Number.

1. Alien Registration Number/USCIS Number: _____
   OR
2. Form I-94 Admission Number: _____
   OR
3. Foreign Passport Number: _____
   Country of Issuance: _____

QR Code - Section 1
Do Not Write In This Space

Signature of Employee	Today's Date *(mm/dd/yyyy)*

Preparer and/or Translator Certification (check one):

☐ I did not use a preparer or translator.   ☐ A preparer(s) and/or translator(s) assisted the employee in completing Section 1.

(Fields below must be completed and signed when preparers and/or translators assist an employee in completing Section 1.)

I attest, under penalty of perjury, that I have assisted in the completion of Section 1 of this form and that to the best of my knowledge the information is true and correct.

Signature of Preparer or Translator	Today's Date *(mm/dd/yyyy)*

Last Name *(Family Name)*	First Name *(Given Name)*

Address *(Street Number and Name)*	City or Town	State	ZIP Code

🛑 Employer Completes Next Page 🛑

Form I-9 10/21/2019

Employment Eligibility Verification
Department of Homeland Security
U.S. Citizenship and Immigration Services

USCIS
Form I-9
OMB No. 1615-0047
Expires 10/31/2022

Section 2. Employer or Authorized Representative Review and Verification
(Employers or their authorized representative must complete and sign Section 2 within 3 business days of the employee's first day of employment. You must physically examine one document from List A OR a combination of one document from List B and one document from List C as listed on the "Lists of Acceptable Documents.")

Employee Info from Section 1	Last Name *(Family Name)*	First Name *(Given Name)*	M.I.	Citizenship/Immigration Status

List A Identity and Employment Authorization	OR	List B Identity	AND	List C Employment Authorization
Document Title		Document Title		Document Title
Issuing Authority		Issuing Authority		Issuing Authority
Document Number		Document Number		Document Number
Expiration Date *(if any) (mm/dd/yyyy)*		Expiration Date *(if any) (mm/dd/yyyy)*		Expiration Date *(if any) (mm/dd/yyyy)*
Document Title				
Issuing Authority				
Document Number		Additional Information		QR Code - Sections 2 & 3 Do Not Write In This Space
Expiration Date *(if any) (mm/dd/yyyy)*				
Document Title				
Issuing Authority				
Document Number				
Expiration Date *(if any) (mm/dd/yyyy)*				

Certification: I attest, under penalty of perjury, that (1) I have examined the document(s) presented by the above-named employee, (2) the above-listed document(s) appear to be genuine and to relate to the employee named, and (3) to the best of my knowledge the employee is authorized to work in the United States.

The employee's first day of employment *(mm/dd/yyyy)*: _____ *(See instructions for exemptions)*

Signature of Employer or Authorized Representative	Today's Date *(mm/dd/yyyy)*	Title of Employer or Authorized Representative
Last Name of Employer or Authorized Representative	First Name of Employer or Authorized Representative	Employer's Business or Organization Name

Employer's Business or Organization Address *(Street Number and Name)*	City or Town	State	ZIP Code

Section 3. Reverification and Rehires *(To be completed and signed by employer or authorized representative.)*

A. New Name *(if applicable)*			B. Date of Rehire *(if applicable)*
Last Name *(Family Name)*	First Name *(Given Name)*	Middle Initial	Date *(mm/dd/yyyy)*

C. If the employee's previous grant of employment authorization has expired, provide the information for the document or receipt that establishes continuing employment authorization in the space provided below.

Document Title	Document Number	Expiration Date *(if any) (mm/dd/yyyy)*

I attest, under penalty of perjury, that to the best of my knowledge, this employee is authorized to work in the United States, and if the employee presented document(s), the document(s) I have examined appear to be genuine and to relate to the individual.

Signature of Employer or Authorized Representative	Today's Date *(mm/dd/yyyy)*	Name of Employer or Authorized Representative

Form I-9 10/21/2019

LISTS OF ACCEPTABLE DOCUMENTS
All documents must be UNEXPIRED

Employees may present one selection from List A
or a combination of one selection from List B and one selection from List C.

LIST A Documents that Establish Both Identity and Employment Authorization	LIST B Documents that Establish Identity	LIST C Documents that Establish Employment Authorization
1. U.S. Passport or U.S. Passport Card	1. Driver's license or ID card issued by a State or outlying possession of the United States provided it contains a photograph or information such as name, date of birth, gender, height, eye color, and address	1. A Social Security Account Number card, unless the card includes one of the following restrictions: (1) NOT VALID FOR EMPLOYMENT (2) VALID FOR WORK ONLY WITH INS AUTHORIZATION (3) VALID FOR WORK ONLY WITH DHS AUTHORIZATION
2. Permanent Resident Card or Alien Registration Receipt Card (Form I-551)		
3. Foreign passport that contains a temporary I-551 stamp or temporary I-551 printed notation on a machine-readable immigrant visa		
	2. ID card issued by federal, state or local government agencies or entities, provided it contains a photograph or information such as name, date of birth, gender, height, eye color, and address	2. Certification of report of birth issued by the Department of State (Forms DS-1350, FS-545, FS-240)
4. Employment Authorization Document that contains a photograph (Form I-766)		
	3. School ID card with a photograph	3. Original or certified copy of birth certificate issued by a State, county, municipal authority, or territory of the United States bearing an official seal
5. For a nonimmigrant alien authorized to work for a specific employer because of his or her status: a. Foreign passport; and b. Form I-94 or Form I-94A that has the following: (1) The same name as the passport; and (2) An endorsement of the alien's nonimmigrant status as long as that period of endorsement has not yet expired and the proposed employment is not in conflict with any restrictions or limitations identified on the form.	4. Voter's registration card	
	5. U.S. Military card or draft record	
	6. Military dependent's ID card	
	7. U.S. Coast Guard Merchant Mariner Card	4. Native American tribal document
		5. U.S. Citizen ID Card (Form I-197)
	8. Native American tribal document	6. Identification Card for Use of Resident Citizen in the United States (Form I-179)
	9. Driver's license issued by a Canadian government authority	
	For persons under age 18 who are unable to present a document listed above:	7. Employment authorization document issued by the Department of Homeland Security
6. Passport from the Federated States of Micronesia (FSM) or the Republic of the Marshall Islands (RMI) with Form I-94 or Form I-94A indicating nonimmigrant admission under the Compact of Free Association Between the United States and the FSM or RMI	10. School record or report card	
	11. Clinic, doctor, or hospital record	
	12. Day-care or nursery school record	

Examples of many of these documents appear in the Handbook for Employers (M-274).

Refer to the instructions for more information about acceptable receipts.

(Source: U.S. Citizenship and Immigration Services)

Critical Thinking

2-1. When Omnimia Graphics was looking to implement a payroll accounting system, the manufacturing firm had several options. With only 40 employees, the manual preparation of payroll through spreadsheets and handwritten time cards was a comfortable option for the firm. Another option was to convince the senior management of Omnimia Graphics to implement a software program for payroll processing. How should the company handle the maintenance of the current payroll records? What internal control issues should be addressed?

2-2. You have been hired as a consultant for Semiva Productions, a company facing an IRS audit of its accounting records. During your review, you notice anomalies in the payroll system involving overpayments of labor and payments to terminated employees. What should you do?

In the Real World: Scenario for Discussion

The Lilly Ledbetter Fair Pay Act of 2009 centered on a case in which Ms. Ledbetter discovered documents that revealed discrimination against her that resulted in unequal pay practices. The company argued that the documents were confidential and scheduled for destruction and that Ms. Ledbetter should not have had access to the information. What are the issues in this case in terms of document privacy and retention? How could the situation have been prevented in the first place?

Internet Activities

2-1. Using a search engine such as Google, Yahoo, or Bing, search the Internet for the term "new-hire packet contents." Compile a list of the different new-hire packet items that you find in at least three companies. What are some unique items that you found on the companies' lists?

2-2. Go to www.irs.gov and search for IRS e-file security. List the facts that the IRS cites about why e-filing is secure. What about these practices makes the customer's information secure? How could the IRS improve e-filing security?

2-3. Want to know more about some of the concepts discussed in this chapter? Check out

    www.uscis.gov

    www.irs.gov/businesses

    www.archives.gov/federal-register/cfr/subject-title-26.html

    www.proshred.com

    www.ironmountain.com

2-4. The Massachusetts Institute of Technology (MIT) has created a website with a living wage calculator. This tool is designed to help people compute the wages they need to earn in order to achieve their desired lifestyle. Check it out at **Living Wage Calculator**.

Continuing Payroll Project: Prevosti Farms and Sugarhouse

Prevosti Farms and Sugarhouse pays its employees according to their job classification. The following employees make up Sugarhouse's staff:

Employee Number	Name and Address	Payroll Information
A-Mille	Thomas Millen 1022 Forest School Rd Woodstock, VT 05001 802-478-5055 SSN: 031-11-3456 401(k) deduction: 3% Section 125 deduction: $155	Hire Date: 2-1-2023 DOB: 12-16-1992 Position: Production Manager PT/FT: FT, exempt M/S: Married/Joint Pay Rate: $35,000/year Dependents under 17: 3 Dependents over 17: 1 Step 4 information: none

Employee Number	Name and Address	Payroll Information
A-Towle	Avery Towle 4011 Route 100 Plymouth, VT 05102 802-967-5873 SSN: 089-74-0974 401(k) deduction: 5% Section 125 deduction: $100	Hire Date: 2-1-2023 DOB: 7-14-2001 Position: Production Worker PT/FT: FT, nonexempt M/S: Single Pay Rate: $15.00/hour Dependents under 17: 0 Dependents over 17: 0 Step 4 information: none
A-Long	Charlie Long 242 Benedict Road S. Woodstock, VT 05002 802-429-3846 SSN: 056-23-4593 401(k) deduction: 2% Section 125 deduction: $155	Hire Date: 2-1-2023 DOB: 3-16-1997 Position: Production Worker PT/FT: FT, nonexempt M/S: Married/Joint Pay Rate: $15.00/hour Dependents under 17: 2 Dependents over 17: 0 Step 4 information: none
B-Shang	Mary Shangraw 1901 Main Street #2 Bridgewater, VT 05520 802-575-5423 SSN: 075-28-8945 401(k) deduction: 3% Section 125 deduction: $100	Hire Date: 2-1-2023 DOB: 8-20-1980 Position: Administrative Assistant PT/FT: PT, nonexempt M/S: Single Pay Rate: $15.00/hour Dependents under 17: 0 Dependents over 17: 1 Step 4 information: none
B-Lewis	Kristen Lewis 840 Daily Hollow Road Bridgewater, VT 05523 802-390-5572 SSN: 076-39-5673 401(k) deduction: 4% Section 125 deduction: $155	Hire Date: 2-1-2023 DOB: 4-6-1991 Position: Office Manager PT/FT: FT, exempt M/S: Married/Joint Pay Rate: $32,000/year Dependents under 17: 2 Dependents over 17: 1 Step 4 information: none
B-Schwa	Joel Schwartz 55 Maple Farm Way Woodstock, VT 05534 802-463-9985 SSN: 021-34-9876 401(k) deduction: 5% Section 125 deduction: $100	Hire Date: 2-1-2023 DOB: 5-23-1993 Position: Sales PT/FT: FT, exempt M/S: Married/Joint Pay Rate: $32,000/year base plus 3% commission per case sold Dependents under 17: 2 Dependents over 17: 0 Step 4 information: none
B-Prevo	Toni Prevosti 820 Westminster Road Bridgewater, VT 05520 802-555-3456 SSN: 055-22-0443 401(k) deduction: 6% Section 125 deduction: $155	Hire Date: 2-1-2023 DOB: 9-19-1987 Position: Owner/President PT/FT: FT, exempt M/S: Married/Joint Pay Rate: $45,000/year Dependents under 17: 3 Dependents over 17: 2 Step 4 information: none

The company has the following departments:

Department A: Agricultural Workers

Department B: Office Workers

1. You have been hired to start on February 1, 2023, as the new accounting clerk. Your employee number is B-STUDE, where "B" denotes that you are an office worker.

Form W-4
Department of the Treasury
Internal Revenue Service

Employee's Withholding Certificate
Complete Form W-4 so that your employer can withhold the correct federal income tax from your pay.
Give Form W-4 to your employer.
Your withholding is subject to review by the IRS.

OMB No. 1545-0074

2023

Step 1:
Enter Personal Information

(a) First name and middle initial | Last name | (b) Social security number

Address

City or town, state, and ZIP code

Does your name match the name on your social security card? If not, to ensure you get credit for your earnings, contact SSA at 800-772-1213 or go to www.ssa.gov.

(c) ☐ Single or Married filing separately
☐ Married filing jointly or Qualifying surviving spouse
☐ Head of household (Check only if you're unmarried and pay more than half the costs of keeping up a home for yourself and a qualifying individual.)

Complete Steps 2–4 ONLY if they apply to you; otherwise, skip to Step 5. See page 2 for more information on each step, who can claim exemption from withholding, other details, and privacy.

Step 2:
Multiple Jobs or Spouse Works

Complete this step if you (1) hold more than one job at a time, or (2) are married filing jointly and your spouse also works. The correct amount of withholding depends on income earned from all of these jobs.

Do **only one** of the following.

(a) Reserved for future use.

(b) Use the Multiple Jobs Worksheet on page 3 and enter the result in Step 4(c) below; **or**

(c) If there are only two jobs total, you may check this box. Do the same on Form W-4 for the other job. This option is generally more accurate than (b) if pay at the lower paying job is more than half of the pay at the higher paying job. Otherwise, (b) is more accurate . . . . ☐

TIP: If you have self-employment income, see page 2.

Complete Steps 3–4(b) on Form W-4 for only ONE of these jobs. Leave those steps blank for the other jobs. (Your withholding will be most accurate if you complete Steps 3–4(b) on the Form W-4 for the highest paying job.)

Step 3:
Claim Dependent and Other Credits

If your total income will be $200,000 or less ($400,000 or less if married filing jointly):

Multiply the number of qualifying children under age 17 by $2,000 $ _____

Multiply the number of other dependents by $500 . . . . . $ _____

Add the amounts above for qualifying children and other dependents. You may add to this the amount of any other credits. Enter the total here . . . . **3** $ _____

Step 4 (optional):
Other Adjustments

(a) **Other income (not from jobs).** If you want tax withheld for other income you expect this year that won't have withholding, enter the amount of other income here. This may include interest, dividends, and retirement income . . . . **4(a)** $ _____

(b) **Deductions.** If you expect to claim deductions other than the standard deduction and want to reduce your withholding, use the Deductions Worksheet on page 3 and enter the result here . . . . **4(b)** $ _____

(c) **Extra withholding.** Enter any additional tax you want withheld each **pay period** . . **4(c)** $ _____

Step 5:
Sign Here

Under penalties of perjury, I declare that this certificate, to the best of my knowledge and belief, is true, correct, and complete.

_____ _____
Employee's signature (This form is not valid unless you sign it.)   **Date**

Employers Only | Employer's name and address | First date of employment | Employer identification number (EIN)

For Privacy Act and Paperwork Reduction Act Notice, see page 3.   Cat. No. 10220Q   Form **W-4** (2023)

(Source: Internal Revenue Service)

Employment Eligibility Verification
Department of Homeland Security
U.S. Citizenship and Immigration Services

USCIS Form I-9
OMB No. 1615-0047
Expires 10/31/2022

▶ **START HERE:** Read instructions carefully before completing this form. The instructions must be available, either in paper or electronically, during completion of this form. Employers are liable for errors in the completion of this form.

ANTI-DISCRIMINATION NOTICE: It is illegal to discriminate against work-authorized individuals. Employers **CANNOT** specify which document(s) an employee may present to establish employment authorization and identity. The refusal to hire or continue to employ an individual because the documentation presented has a future expiration date may also constitute illegal discrimination.

Section 1. Employee Information and Attestation (Employees must complete and sign Section 1 of Form I-9 no later than the **first day of employment**, but not before accepting a job offer.)

Last Name (Family Name)	First Name (Given Name)	Middle Initial	Other Last Names Used (if any)

Address (Street Number and Name)	Apt. Number	City or Town	State	ZIP Code

Date of Birth (mm/dd/yyyy)	U.S. Social Security Number	Employee's E-mail Address	Employee's Telephone Number
	___-__-____		

I am aware that federal law provides for imprisonment and/or fines for false statements or use of false documents in connection with the completion of this form.

I attest, under penalty of perjury, that I am (check one of the following boxes):

- [✓] 1. A citizen of the United States
- [ ] 2. A noncitizen national of the United States (See instructions)
- [ ] 3. A lawful permanent resident   (Alien Registration Number/USCIS Number): _____
- [ ] 4. An alien authorized to work   until (expiration date, if applicable, mm/dd/yyyy): _____
  Some aliens may write "N/A" in the expiration date field. (See instructions)

Aliens authorized to work must provide only one of the following document numbers to complete Form I-9:
An Alien Registration Number/USCIS Number OR Form I-94 Admission Number OR Foreign Passport Number.

1. Alien Registration Number/USCIS Number: _____
   OR
2. Form I-94 Admission Number: _____
   OR
3. Foreign Passport Number: _____
   Country of Issuance: _____

QR Code - Section 1 Do Not Write In This Space

Signature of Employee	Today's Date (mm/dd/yyyy)

Preparer and/or Translator Certification (check one):

- [ ] I did not use a preparer or translator.   [ ] A preparer(s) and/or translator(s) assisted the employee in completing Section 1.

(Fields below must be completed and signed when preparers and/or translators assist an employee in completing Section 1.)

I attest, under penalty of perjury, that I have assisted in the completion of Section 1 of this form and that to the best of my knowledge the information is true and correct.

Signature of Preparer or Translator	Today's Date (mm/dd/yyyy)

Last Name (Family Name)	First Name (Given Name)

Address (Street Number and Name)	City or Town	State	ZIP Code

🛑 *Employer Completes Next Page* 🛑

Form I-9 10/21/2019

Employment Eligibility Verification
Department of Homeland Security
U.S. Citizenship and Immigration Services

USCIS Form I-9
OMB No. 1615-0047
Expires 10/31/2022

Section 2. Employer or Authorized Representative Review and Verification
(Employers or their authorized representative must complete and sign Section 2 within 3 business days of the employee's first day of employment. You must physically examine one document from List A OR a combination of one document from List B and one document from List C as listed on the "Lists of Acceptable Documents.")

Employee Info from Section 1	Last Name *(Family Name)*	First Name *(Given Name)*	M.I.	Citizenship/Immigration Status

List A Identity and Employment Authorization	OR	List B Identity	AND	List C Employment Authorization
Document Title		Document Title		Document Title
Issuing Authority		Issuing Authority		Issuing Authority
Document Number		Document Number		Document Number
Expiration Date *(if any) (mm/dd/yyyy)*		Expiration Date *(if any) (mm/dd/yyyy)*		Expiration Date *(if any) (mm/dd/yyyy)*
Document Title				
Issuing Authority		Additional Information		QR Code - Sections 2 & 3 Do Not Write In This Space
Document Number				
Expiration Date *(if any) (mm/dd/yyyy)*				
Document Title				
Issuing Authority				
Document Number				
Expiration Date *(if any) (mm/dd/yyyy)*				

Certification: I attest, under penalty of perjury, that (1) I have examined the document(s) presented by the above-named employee, (2) the above-listed document(s) appear to be genuine and to relate to the employee named, and (3) to the best of my knowledge the employee is authorized to work in the United States.

The employee's first day of employment *(mm/dd/yyyy)*: _____ *(See instructions for exemptions)*

Signature of Employer or Authorized Representative	Today's Date *(mm/dd/yyyy)*	Title of Employer or Authorized Representative
Last Name of Employer or Authorized Representative	First Name of Employer or Authorized Representative	Employer's Business or Organization Name

Employer's Business or Organization Address *(Street Number and Name)*	City or Town	State	ZIP Code

Section 3. Reverification and Rehires *(To be completed and signed by employer or authorized representative.)*

A. New Name *(if applicable)*			B. Date of Rehire *(if applicable)*
Last Name *(Family Name)*	First Name *(Given Name)*	Middle Initial	Date *(mm/dd/yyyy)*

C. If the employee's previous grant of employment authorization has expired, provide the information for the document or receipt that establishes continuing employment authorization in the space provided below.

Document Title	Document Number	Expiration Date *(if any) (mm/dd/yyyy)*

I attest, under penalty of perjury, that to the best of my knowledge, this employee is authorized to work in the United States, and if the employee presented document(s), the document(s) I have examined appear to be genuine and to relate to the individual.

Signature of Employer or Authorized Representative	Today's Date *(mm/dd/yyyy)*	Name of Employer or Authorized Representative

Form I-9 10/21/2019

LISTS OF ACCEPTABLE DOCUMENTS
All documents must be UNEXPIRED

Employees may present one selection from List A
or a combination of one selection from List B and one selection from List C.

LIST A Documents that Establish Both Identity and Employment Authorization	LIST B Documents that Establish Identity	LIST C Documents that Establish Employment Authorization

1. U.S. Passport or U.S. Passport Card
2. Permanent Resident Card or Alien Registration Receipt Card (Form I-551)
3. Foreign passport that contains a temporary I-551 stamp or temporary I-551 printed notation on a machine-readable immigrant visa
4. Employment Authorization Document that contains a photograph (Form I-766)
5. For a nonimmigrant alien authorized to work for a specific employer because of his or her status:
   a. Foreign passport; and
   b. Form I-94 or Form I-94A that has the following:
    (1) The same name as the passport; and
    (2) An endorsement of the alien's nonimmigrant status as long as that period of endorsement has not yet expired and the proposed employment is not in conflict with any restrictions or limitations identified on the form.
6. Passport from the Federated States of Micronesia (FSM) or the Republic of the Marshall Islands (RMI) with Form I-94 or Form I-94A indicating nonimmigrant admission under the Compact of Free Association Between the United States and the FSM or RMI
	1. Driver's license or ID card issued by a State or outlying possession of the United States provided it contains a photograph or information such as name, date of birth, gender, height, eye color, and address
	2. ID card issued by federal, state or local government agencies or entities, provided it contains a photograph or information such as name, date of birth, gender, height, eye color, and address
	3. School ID card with a photograph
	4. Voter's registration card
	5. U.S. Military card or draft record
	6. Military dependent's ID card
	7. U.S. Coast Guard Merchant Mariner Card
	8. Native American tribal document
	9. Driver's license issued by a Canadian government authority
	For persons under age 18 who are unable to present a document listed above:
	10. School record or report card
	11. Clinic, doctor, or hospital record
	12. Day-care or nursery school record
		1. A Social Security Account Number card, unless the card includes one of the following restrictions:
		   (1) NOT VALID FOR EMPLOYMENT
		   (2) VALID FOR WORK ONLY WITH INS AUTHORIZATION
		   (3) VALID FOR WORK ONLY WITH DHS AUTHORIZATION
		2. Certification of report of birth issued by the Department of State (Forms DS-1350, FS-545, FS-240)
		3. Original or certified copy of birth certificate issued by a State, county, municipal authority, or territory of the United States bearing an official seal
		4. Native American tribal document
		5. U.S. Citizen ID Card (Form I-197)
		6. Identification Card for Use of Resident Citizen in the United States (Form I-179)
		7. Employment authorization document issued by the Department of Homeland Security

Examples of many of these documents appear in the Handbook for Employers (M-274).

Refer to the instructions for more information about acceptable receipts.

Form I-9 10/21/2019

(Source: U.S. Citizenship and Immigration Services)

Your Social Security number is 555-55-5555, you are full-time, nonexempt, and paid at a rate of $34,000 per year. You have elected to contribute 2 percent of your gross pay to your 401(k) and will have $100 per pay period for Section 125. Complete the W-4 and the I-9 to start your own employee file. You are single with only one job. You live at 1644 Smitten Road, Woodstock, VT 05001. You will not be claiming anything for section 4 of the W-4. Your phone number is (555) 555-5555. Your date of birth is 01/01/2001. You are a citizen of the United States and provide a Vermont driver's license #88110009 expiring 01/01/27 in addition to your Social Security card for verification of your identity. Mary Shangraw verified the information for the company. Prevosti Farms and Sugarhouse is located at 820 Westminster Road, Bridgewater, VT, 05520. Prevosti has an EIN of 22-6654454.

2. Complete the employee information form for each employee. Enter the pay rate earnings for each employee.

Employee Earnings Register

NAME _____ Hire Date _____ Dependent child <17 _____
ADDRESS _____ Date of Birth _____ Dependent other _____
CITY/STATE/ZIP _____ Position _____ PT / FT Step 4a W-4 Info _____
TELEPHONE _____ Filing Status _____ Step 4b W-4 Info _____
SOCIAL SECURITY NUMBER _____ Exempt/Nonexempt _____ Step 4c W-4 Info _____
 Pay Rate _____ Hr / Wk / Mo / Yr

Period Ended	Hrs Worked	Reg Pay	OT Pay	Comm	Gross Pay	Social Sec Tax	Medicare	Fed Inc Tax	State W/H Tax	Sect 125	401(k)	Total Deduc	Net Pay	YTD

EMPLOYEE EARNING RECORD

NAME _____ Hire Date _____
ADDRESS _____ Date of Birth _____
CITY/STATE/ZIP _____ Position _____
TELEPHONE _____ Filing Status _____
SOCIAL SECURITY NUMBER _____ Exempt/Nonexempt _____
POSITION _____ Pay Rate _____

Period Ended	Hrs Worked	Reg Pay	OT Pay	Holiday	Comm	Gross Pay	Ins	401(k)	Taxable Pay for Federal	Taxable Pay for FICA

Taxable Wages for Federal	Taxable Wages for FICA	Federal W/H	Social Sec. Tax	Medicare Tax	State Inc. Tax	Total Deduc	Net Pay	YTD Net Pay	YTD Gross Pay

EMPLOYEE EARNING RECORD

NAME _____ Hire Date _____

ADDRESS _____ Date of Birth _____

CITY/STATE/ZIP _____ Exempt/Nonexempt _____

TELEPHONE _____ Married/Single _____

SOCIAL SECURITY NUMBER _____ Pay Rate _____

POSITION _____

Period Ended	Hrs Worked	Reg Pay	OT Pay	Holiday	Comm	Gross Pay	Ins	401(k)	Taxable Pay for Federal	Taxable pay for FICA

Taxable Wages for Federal	Taxable Wages for FICA	Federal W/H	Social Sec. Tax	Medicare Tax	State Inc. Tax	Total Deduc	Net Pay	YTD Net Pay	YTD Gross Pay

EMPLOYEE EARNING RECORD

NAME _____ Hire Date _____

ADDRESS _____ Date of Birth _____

CITY/STATE/ZIP _____ Exempt/Nonexempt _____

TELEPHONE _____ Married/Single _____

SOCIAL SECURITY NUMBER _____ Pay Rate _____

POSITION _____

Period Ended	Hrs Worked	Reg Pay	OT Pay	Holiday	Comm	Gross Pay	Ins	401(k)	Taxable Wages for Federal	Taxable Wages for FICA

Taxable Wages for Federal	Taxable Wages for FICA	Federal W/H	Social Sec. Tax	Medicare Tax	State Inc. Tax	Total Deduc	Net Pay	YTD Net Pay	YTD Gross Pay

EMPLOYEE EARNING RECORD

NAME _____	Hire Date _____
ADDRESS _____	Date of Birth _____
CITY/STATE/ZIP _____	Exempt/Nonexempt _____
TELEPHONE _____	Married/Single _____
SOCIAL SECURITY NUMBER _____	Pay Rate _____
POSITION _____

Period Ended	Hrs Worked	Reg Pay	OT Pay	Holiday	Comm	Gross Pay	Ins	401(k)	Taxable Pay for Federal	Taxable Pay for FICA

Taxable Wages for Federal	Taxable Wages for FICA	Federal W/H	Social Sec. Tax	Medicare Tax	State Inc. Tax	Total Deduc	Net Pay	YTD Net Pay	YTD Gross Pay

EMPLOYEE EARNING RECORD

NAME _____	Hire Date _____
ADDRESS _____	Date of Birth _____
CITY/STATE/ZIP _____	Exempt/Nonexempt _____
TELEPHONE _____	Married/Single _____
SOCIAL SECURITY NUMBER _____	Pay Rate _____
POSITION _____

Period Ended	Hrs Worked	Reg Pay	OT Pay	Holiday	Comm	Gross Pay	Ins	401(k)	Taxable Pay for Federal	Taxable Pay for FICA

Taxable Wages for Federal	Taxable Wages for FICA	Federal W/H	Social Sec. Tax	Medicare Tax	State Inc. Tax	Total Deduc	Net Pay	YTD Net Pay	YTD Gross Pay

EMPLOYEE EARNING RECORD

NAME _____ Hire Date _____

ADDRESS _____ Date of Birth _____

CITY/STATE/ZIP _____ Exempt/Nonexempt _____

TELEPHONE _____ Married/Single _____

SOCIAL SECURITY NUMBER _____ Pay Rate _____

POSITION _____

Period Ended	Hrs Worked	Reg Pay	OT Pay	Holiday	Comm	Gross Pay	Ins	401(k)	Taxable Pay for Federal	Taxable Pay for FICA

Taxable Wages for Federal	Taxable Wages for FICA	Federal W/H	Social Sec. Tax	Medicare Tax	State Inc. Tax	Total Deduc	Net Pay	YTD Net Pay	YTD Gross Pay

EMPLOYEE EARNING RECORD

NAME _____ Hire Date _____

ADDRESS _____ Date of Birth _____

CITY/STATE/ZIP _____ Exempt/Nonexempt _____

TELEPHONE _____ Married/Single _____

SOCIAL SECURITY NUMBER _____ Pay Rate _____

POSITION _____

Period Ended	Hrs Worked	Reg Pay	OT Pay	Holiday	Comm	Gross Pay	Ins	401(k)	Taxable Pay for Federal	Taxable Pay for FICA

Taxable Wages for Federal	Taxable Wages for FICA	Federal W/H	Social Sec. Tax	Medicare Tax	State Inc. Tax	Total Deduc	Net Pay	YTD Net Pay	YTD Gross Pay

EMPLOYEE EARNING RECORD

NAME	_____	Hire Date	_____
ADDRESS	_____	Date of Birth	_____
CITY/STATE/ZIP	_____	Exempt/Nonexempt	_____
TELEPHONE	_____	Married/Single	_____
SOCIAL SECURITY NUMBER	_____	Pay Rate	_____
POSITION	_____		_____

Period Ended	Hrs Worked	Reg Pay	OT Pay	Holiday	Comm	Gross Pay	Ins	401(k)	Taxable Pay for Federal	Taxable Pay for FICA

Taxable Wages for Federal	Taxable Wages for FICA	Federal W/H	Social Sec. Tax	Medicare	State W/H	Total Deduc	Net Pay	YTD Net Pay	YTD Gross Pay

Answers to Stop & Check Exercises

What's in the File?

1. a, b, d, e
2. b
3. d
4. a
5. c

Who Are You?

1. Student answers will vary. One possible way to prove both identity and employment is a current U.S. passport. Alternatively, a current state-issued driver's license and a Social Security card will work for the purposes of the I-9.
2. Student answers will vary. When evaluating the earnings of more than one job, the breakdown of the includable amount by pay period is often overlooked.
3. Student answers will vary. Examples of statutory employees include the following: A driver who distributes beverages (other than milk) or meat, vegetable, fruit, or bakery products or who picks up and delivers laundry or dry cleaning if the driver is a single company's agent or is paid on commission. A full-time life insurance sales agent whose principal business activity is selling life insurance or annuity contracts, or both, primarily for one life insurance company. An individual who works at home on materials or goods that a company supplies and that must be returned to that company or a designated agent in accordance with furnished specifications for the work to be done. A full-time traveling or city salesperson who works on a single company's behalf and turns in orders from wholesalers, retailers, contractors, or operators

of hotels, restaurants, or other similar establishments. The goods sold must be merchandise for resale or supplies for use in the buyer's business operation. The work performed for that single company must be the salesperson's principal business activity.

Exempt vs. Nonexempt

1. Exempt workers are exempt from the overtime provisions of FLSA. Exempt workers tend to be employees in a company's managerial or other leadership functions, in which they may need to work more than 40 hours per week to complete their tasks. Exempt workers usually receive a fixed salary per period that is not based on the number of hours worked. Nonexempt workers tend to be compensated on an hourly basis and often do not have managerial or leadership responsibilities. It should be noted that some nonexempt workers do have managerial or leadership responsibilities and may receive a fixed salary; however, these particular employees are covered by the overtime provisions of FLSA.
2. c (40 hours)
3. The leased employee is a common-law employee of the firm, whereas the temporary employee is an employee of the temporary agency.

Worker Facts

1. Hourly workers and nonexempt workers are protected by FLSA.
2. Exempt workers receive a fixed amount of money and generally direct the actions of other employees; nonexempt workers are eligible for overtime and generally have their work directed by a manager.
3. Commission workers are typically tied to sales completed by the individual; piece-rate pay is determined by the number of pieces the employee completes during a shift or period.
4. Student answers may vary but should include: the minimum hourly rate is set by the U.S. federal government. Minimum wage rates can and do vary per state, and different parts of the same state may have different minimum wages. The minimum wage may differ from a "living wage," which is an amount needed to meet basic subsistence needs. A calculating tool was provided in the chapter for discussion on living wages in various locations.

Who Does Which Job?

Student answers will vary. The answer should reflect a clear separation of duties, cross-training, rotation of tasks, and security protocols.

Internal Controls and Audits

1. b
2. b, c
3. a, c, d

Destroy and Terminate

1. Paper payroll records should be shredded or burned. Computer records should be purged from the server and all other storage devices.
2. Apollo should receive his final pay on October 11, and no later than October 12. His employer is not required to provide him with a severance package, although he may be eligible for his accrued vacation pay.

Dollar sign made from binary numbers: Ralf Hiemisch/Getty Images

Chapter Three

Gross Pay Computation

Two important terms in payroll accounting are gross pay and net pay. **Gross pay** is the total amount of wages earned before deducting amounts for taxes or other deductions. **Net pay** is the amount of money the employee actually receives in a paycheck after all taxes and other deductions have been subtracted. In this chapter, we will focus on computing gross pay.

The calculation of an employee's gross pay is the first step for payroll processing. Employee pay may be calculated in different ways. **Hourly** employees are paid for each hour, or fraction thereof, that they work on a given day. Salaried employees are broken into two classifications based on FLSA legislation: *exempt* and *nonexempt*. Salaried exempt employees receive pay based on the job they perform, regardless of the number of hours it takes to perform the job. Salaried nonexempt employees may receive both *salary* and *overtime*. Another class of employees works on a *commission* basis, which means that some of their wages are based on sales revenue. The final classification is *piece-rate* employees. Typically found in manufacturing environments, employees are paid based upon the number of pieces completed during a work shift.

LEARNING OBJECTIVES

After studying Chapter 3, you should be able to:

LO 3-1   Analyze Minimum Wage Pay for Nonexempt Workers
LO 3-2   Compute Gross Pay for Different Pay Bases
LO 3-3   Calculate Pay Based on Hours and Fractions of Hours
LO 3-4   Calculate Overtime in Various Situations
LO 3-5   Create a Payroll Register
LO 3-6   Apply Combination Pay Methods
LO 3-7   Explain Special Pay Situations

Ink Drop/Shutterstock

Inflation, Wage Increases, and Pay Transparency Puts Pressure on Employers

A consequence of the effect of COVID on the U.S. economy has been high inflation. With unemployment at its lowest point in many years, employers have been competing more to attract workers. Many employers have discovered a need to increase employee pay to remain competitive in what has become an opportunity for workers to demand and receive the pay increases they desire. The average pay increase has been 3.9 percent among U.S. employers.

Pay transparency laws in 17 states have made it easier for job candidates to compare employers before deciding on accepting a job. Small and medium-sized employers have experienced the pressure from pay transparency laws more than large companies because of the pressure it creates to offer competitive wage packages. An interesting piece of employer pay competition is the minimum wage offered by states. Although approximately 40 percent of states have maintained the federal minimum, the other 60 percent have legislated significant increases to the minimum wage for 2023. For example, New Hampshire has maintained the federal minimum wage since its inception in 2009, while neighboring Vermont offers a minimum wage that is nearly 82 percent higher. This puts pressure on employers, especially multi-state ones, to examine their competitiveness and what actions they can take to increase their allure for job seekers.

(Sources: Comp and Benefits Today[1]; Comp and Benefits Today[2]; Department of Labor)

> **Employee pay is the focus of Chapter 3. We will examine different bases for gross pay computations, discuss how these compensation bases differ, and introduce the payroll register as a tool in pay calculation.**

LO 3-1 Analyze Minimum Wage Pay for Nonexempt Workers

Two primary classifications of employees exist: exempt and nonexempt. These classifications refer to the provisions of the Fair Labor Standards Act (FLSA). The FLSA provisions protect nonexempt employees, including clerical, factory, and other nonmanagerial employees. Nonexempt employees are operative workers whose workdays may vary in duration, whose tasks do not meet the U.S. Department of Labor guidelines for exempt employees, and who do not generally have supervisory or managerial duties. Exempt employees include employees who meet the U.S. Department of Labor guidelines for exempt classification, including job titles such as Department Supervisor or Warehouse Manager.

Sorbis/Shutterstock

For hourly workers, FLSA contains wage provisions that stipulate the *minimum wage* an employer may pay an employee. However, the law exempts some employers from the minimum wage requirements. According to the U.S. Department of Labor, the following conditions exempt an employer from paying the federal minimum wage:

- Firms that do not engage in interstate commerce as part of their business production.
- Firms with less than $500,000 of annual business volume.

Note that certain firms are always covered by the FLSA provisions, regardless of their interstate commerce or annual business volume participation. These businesses include hospitals, schools for mentally or physically disabled or gifted children, preschools, schools of any level, and governmental agencies. Under FLSA section 3(y), law enforcement and fire protection employees may have specified work periods ranging from 7 to 28 days. Employees would be paid for overtime only after a predefined number of working hours.

FLSA was modified in 1974 to include explicit provisions about domestic workers. Since 1974, minimum wage provisions cover domestic service workers, such as nannies and chauffeurs. Note that the 1974 modification specifically excluded occasional babysitters and employees who provide domestic companion services for the elderly. In 2015, the U.S. Congress further amended FLSA to include caregivers and other direct care employees who provide in-home companionship services as being subject to the federal or state minimum wage, whichever is higher. It should be noted that domestic workers who reside on the employer's premises permanently or for an extended time period are exempt from FLSA provisions.

> The pay and employment taxes of in-house employees such as nannies or elder caregivers is becoming an important issue in 2023. Issues of withholding FICA taxes are receiving scrutiny from tax authorities. The cost of caregiving activities is another issue worth considering because of its relation with minimum wage provisions under FLSA. Another issue is economic considerations because the household worker is still eligible for unemployment benefits when not terminated for cause.
>
> Other considerations include the classification of the household employee. Many households classify the worker as an independent contractor when they should be classified as an employee. Third-party payments such as Venmo or Zelle have become noticed by the IRS. Finally, the Department of Labor stipulates that household workers who are required to work on a live-in basis must receive a minimum of eight hours of sleep, five of which must be consecutive.
>
> (Source: Accounting Today, DOL)

Minimum Wage

The federal minimum wage was instituted in 1938. One purpose of the minimum wage was to protect the economy following the Great Depression that started in 1929. Another purpose was to help the lowest-paid workers who lacked the representation that wealthier employees had. It was intended to create a standard of living for the poorest Americans. The following is a chart depicting the change in the minimum wage over time, both adjusted and unadjusted for inflation.

Real and nominal value of the federal minimum wage in the United States from 1938 to 2022 (in 2022 U.S. dollars)

■ Unadjusted wage (real U.S. dollars)   ■ Inflation adjusted wage (nominal U.S. dollars)

(Source: Statista)

An important consideration of the minimum wage provision of the FLSA is the existence of separate tiers of the minimum wage. Wages for *tipped employees* are lower than those of nontipped employees. Federal wage and hour laws as of 2023 stipulate a federal minimum wage of $7.25 and a minimum hourly wage of $2.13 for tipped employees. States may enact additional minimum wage laws to address the specific economic needs of their populations. This minimizes federal legislative needs to revisit the minimum wage annually.

> In 2022, Nevada voters opted to change the two-tiered minimum wage system. The two tiers meant that employers who offered health insurance benefits to their employees could offer a lower minimum wage than employers without a health insurance benefit. Ballot question 2 made a change to the Nevada state constitution to eradicate this two-tier system and offer the same minimum wage across the state as of January 1, 2024.
>
> (Source: SHRM)

As of 2023, 29 states and the District of Columbia have minimum wage rates higher than the federal minimum wage. Note that five states have a minimum wage that is not specified. When the minimum wage is not specified, the federal minimum wage applies. These lower minimum wages may be paid by employers who are not subject to FLSA provisions because they do not conduct interstate commerce. A map depicting minimum wages for 2023 is shown in Figure 3-1, and the details of specific minimum wage rates are shown in Table 3-1. Examples involving employee pay with different minimum wages follow.

FIGURE 3-1
Minimum Wage Hourly Rates for 2023

(Source: U.S. Department of Labor, 2023)
Legend: The states highlighted in dark blue have minimum wage amounts higher than the federal minimum wage of $7.25 per hour.

TABLE 3-1
2023 Minimum Wage Hourly Rates by State

AK	$10.85	IA	$7.25	MS	None†	PA	$7.25
AL	None†	ID	7.25	MT	$9.95*	RI	13.00
AR	11.00	IL	13.00	NC	7.25	SC	None†
AZ	13.85	IN	7.25	ND	7.25	SD	10.80
CA	15.50*	KS	7.25	NE	10.50	TN	None†
CO	13.65	KY	7.25	NH	7.25	TX	7.25
CT	14.00	LA	None†	NJ	14.13	UT	7.25
D.C.	16.50	MA	15.00	NM	12.00	VA	12.00
DE	11.75	MD	13.25	NV	10.75*	VT	13.18
FL	11.00	ME	13.80	NY	14.20*	WA	15.74*
GA	7.25	MI	10.10	OH	10.10*	WI	7.25
HI	12.00	MN	10.59*	OK	7.25*	WV	8.75
		MO	12.00	OR	13.50	WY	7.25

(Source: U.S. Department of Labor, 2023)
*These states have stipulations that change the minimum wage based on different variables. Consult the state's revenue office for specific details.
†In states with no minimum wage or one lower than the federal minimum wage, the federal minimum wage prevails as long as they meet FLSA revenue and interstate commerce thresholds.

> ### EXAMPLE 1: NO STATE MINIMUM WAGE, APPLY FEDERAL MINIMUM WAGE
>
> Alix works for an employer and earns the minimum wage in South Carolina. How much would Alix earn for a 40-hour pay period?
>
> Federal minimum wage: $7.25 per hour
> 40 hours × $7.25/hour = $290
>
> Because the state does not have a minimum wage, the federal minimum wage would be applied.

> **EXAMPLE 2: STATE MINIMUM WAGE HIGHER THAN THE FEDERAL MINIMUM WAGE**
>
> West is a minimum wage worker in the State of Washington. They work for a national office supply chain and have a standard 37.5-hour workweek. How much would West earn during a 75-hour, two-week pay period?
>
> Washington minimum wage: $15.74 per hour
> 75 hours × $15.74/hour = $1,180.50
>
> Because West works for a national office supply chain, it is safe to assume that the company conducts interstate commerce and earns more than $500,000 in revenues per year. West would be compensated at the state minimum wage in any case.

Tipped Employees

Workers in professions such as waiters, waitresses, bartenders, food service workers, and some hotel service personnel may receive an hourly wage less than the minimum wage rates listed in Table 3-1. The rationale for the decreased minimum wage is that these employees can earn tips (*tipped wages*) from patrons of the establishments as a regular part of their employment. The federal minimum cash wage for tipped employees is $2.13 per hour; however, many states have different regulations about how much the employee must earn in tips to meet federal wage and hour laws.

> In 2018, voters in Washington, DC, approved Initiative 77, which will gradually increase the tipped wage through 2026 until it meets the minimum wage area. As of 2021, a final rule allowed employers to require tipped employees to pool their tips with staff for which a tip is not expected. This rule was designed to offer an incentive to traditionally nontipped restaurant employees.
>
> (Source: The Hill)

The difference between the tipped employee minimum wage and the federal minimum wage is the *tip credit*. Federal wage and hour laws mandate that the tip credit is $5.12 per hour. Note that the tip credit is the difference between the minimum wage and the tipped employee minimum wage ($7.25 − $2.13 = $5.12). Some states such as Alaska, California, and Montana do not allow tip credit; instead, all workers receive the prevailing federal or local minimum wage. Table 3-2 contains the details about tip credit for each state. Some

FIGURE 3-2
IRS Form 4070 for Tipped Employees to Report Tips

Form **4070** (Rev. August 2005) Department of the Treasury Internal Revenue Service	**Employee's Report of Tips to Employer**	OMB No. 1545-0074
Employee's name and address Landry Treeland, 224 Main Street, Berlin, NJ 08009		Social security number 087 : 13 : 8995
Employer's name and address (include establishment name, if different) Wicked Pizza 3044 Medford Highway Berlin, NJ 08009		1 Cash tips received 457.00
		2 Credit and debit card tips received 286.00
		3 Tips paid out 34.00
Month or shorter period in which tips were received from May 1, 2023, to May 31, 2023,		4 Net tips (lines **1** + **2** − **3**) 777.00
Signature *Landry Treeland*		Date 5/31/2023
For Paperwork Reduction Act Notice, see the instructions on the back of this form.	Cat. No. 41320P	Form **4070** (Rev. 8-2005)

states have requirements on employers regarding information that must be obtained before applying for a tip credit. For example, North Carolina requires a monthly or per-pay-period affidavit from employees of the total amount of tips.

Employees must report tips in excess of $20 per month to their employer using IRS form 4070. All tips, including cash, debit or credit card, or paid out must be included in this form. This form is due on the 10th of the following month (i.e., April 10 for the month ending March 31) unless the 10th is a Saturday, Sunday, or legal holiday. Figure 3-2 contains an example of a completed Form 4070.

TABLE 3-2
2023 Minimum Hourly Wages for Tipped Employees by State

Jurisdiction	Basic Combined Cash and Tip Minimum Wage Rate	Maximum Tip Credit Against Minimum Wage	Minimum Cash Wage	Definition of Tipped Employee by Minimum Tips Received (monthly unless otherwise specified)
Federal: Fair Labor Standards Act (FLSA)	$7.25	$5.12	$2.13	More than $30
State Law Does Not Allow Tip Credit				
Note: The minimum rate is the same for tipped and nontipped employees.				
Alaska			10.85	
California			15.50	
Minnesota:				
Large employer Annual receipts > $500,000 per year			10.59	
Small employer Annual receipts < $500,000 per year			8.63	
Montana:				
Business with gross annual sales exceeding $110,000			9.95	
Businesses with gross annual sales of $110,000 or less			4.00	
Nevada			10.50	With no health insurance benefits provided by the employer and received by the employee
			9.50	With health insurance benefits provided by the employer and received by the employee
Oregon			13.50	
Washington			15.74	
State Law Allows Tip Credit				
Arizona	13.85	3.00	10.85	Not specified
Arkansas	11.00	8.37	2.63	More than $20
Colorado	13.65	3.02	10.63	More than $30
Connecticut:	14.00			At least $10 weekly for full-time employees or $2.00 daily for part-time in hotels and restaurants. Not specified for other industries.
Hotel, restaurant		7.62	6.38	
Bartenders who customarily receive tips		5.77	8.23	
Delaware	11.75	9.52	2.23	More than $30
District of Columbia (D.C.)[1]	16.10	10.75	5.35	Not specified
Florida	11.00	3.02	7.98	
Hawaii	12.00	1.00	11.00	More than $20
Idaho	7.25	3.90	3.35	More than $30

Jurisdiction	Basic Combined Cash and Tip Minimum Wage Rate	Maximum Tip Credit Against Minimum Wage	Minimum Cash Wage	Definition of Tipped Employee by Minimum Tips Received (monthly unless otherwise specified)
Illinois	13.00	40% of the applicable minimum wage (5.20)	7.80	Not specified
Indiana	7.25	5.12	2.13	Not specified
Iowa	7.25	2.90	4.35	More than $30
Kansas	7.25	5.12	2.13	Not specified
Kentucky	7.25	5.12	2.13	More than $30
Maine	13.80	50% of the applicable minimum wage (6.90)	6.90	More than $30
Maryland	13.25	9.62	3.63	More than $30
Massachusetts	15.00	8.25	6.75	More than $20
Michigan	10.10	6.26	3.84	Not specified
Missouri	12.00	50% of the applicable minimum wage (6.00)	6.00	Not specified
Nebraska	10.50	8.37	2.13	Not specified
New Hampshire	7.25	55% of the applicable minimum wage (3.99)	45% of the applicable minimum wage (3.26)	More than $30
New Jersey	14.13	8.87	5.26	Not specified
New Mexico	12.00	9.00	3.00	More than $30
New York	See website[2]			Not specified
North Carolina	7.25	5.12	2.13	More than $20
North Dakota	7.25	33% of the applicable minimum wage (2.39)	4.86	More than $30
Ohio: *Applies to employees of businesses with annual gross receipts of greater than $342,000 per year*	10.10	5.05	5.05	More than $30
Oklahoma	7.25	5.12	2.13	Not specified
Pennsylvania	7.25	4.42	2.83	More than $30
Rhode Island	13.00	9.11	3.89	Not specified
South Carolina	7.25	5.12	2.13	Not specified
South Dakota	10.80	50% of the applicable minimum wage (5.40)	5.40	More than $35
Tennessee	7.25	5.12	2.13	More than $30
Texas	7.25	5.12	2.13	More than $20
Utah	7.25	5.12	2.13	More than $30
Vermont: *Employees in hotels, motels, tourist places, and restaurants who customarily and regularly receive >$120/month in tips for direct and personal customer service*	13.18	6.59	6.59	More than $120
Virginia	12.00	9.87	2.13	More than $30
West Virginia	8.75	70% of the applicable minimum wage (6.13)	2.62	Not specified
Wisconsin	7.25	4.92	2.33	Not specified
Wyoming	7.25	5.12	2.13	More than $30

(Source: U.S. Department of Labor, 2023)

> **EXAMPLE: TIPPED EMPLOYEE IN OKLAHOMA, MINIMUM WAGE MET**
>
> Argyle Hansford is a tipped employee in Stillwater, Oklahoma. During a 40-hour workweek and pay period, she earned $220 in tips.
>
> Hourly tipped minimum wage: $2.13 per hour.
> $2.13 per hour × 40 hours = $85.20 in wages
> Tips earned: $220
> Total wages and tips earned during the pay period:
> $220 + $85.20 = $305.20
>
> The federal and state minimum wage is $7.25 per hour. The minimum wage for a 40-hour workweek:
>
> $7.25 per hour × 40 hours = $290
>
> Therefore, Argyle has earned more than the federal and state minimum wage. The employer does not need to contribute to Argyle's pay during the pay period.

> **EXAMPLE: TIPPED EMPLOYEE IN RHODE ISLAND, MINIMUM WAGE *NOT* MET**
>
> Grayson Jeffries is a tipped waiter in Warwick, Rhode Island. During a 40-hour work and pay period, he earned $75 in tips.
>
> Hourly tipped minimum wage: $3.89 per hour.
> $3.89 per hour × 40 hours = $155.60 in wages
> Tips earned: $75
> Total wages and tips earned during the pay period:
> $155.60 + 75 = $230.60
>
> The state minimum wage for Rhode Island is $13.00 per hour. During a 40-hour workweek and pay period, the minimum pay for an employee is:
>
> $13.00 per hour × 40 hours = $520.00
>
> Because Grayson has not earned the minimum wage, the employer must pay the difference between the earned wages and tips and the minimum wage:
>
> $520.00 − $230.60 = $289.40 to be added to Grayson's pay by the employer to bring his pay to the minimum wage.

Pay Your Employees Correctly

Stop & Check

1. Pai works as a clerk receiving minimum wage for a pharmaceutical company in North Carolina that pays its employees biweekly. Pai is classified as nonexempt, with a standard workweek of 40 hours. During a two-week period, Pai worked 88 hours and received $638.00. Was Pai's pay correct? Explain.

2. Terry works as a publisher's representative receiving minimum wage in Maryland. This week Terry worked 39.5 hours. What should Terry's gross pay be?

3. Morgan is a temporary worker for a popular radio station, a large employer in Minnesota. Morgan receives the minimum wage and works 32 hours per week. How much should be the gross pay for two weeks of work?

4. Toby is a tipped minimum wage worker for a Montana restaurant with $615,000 in annual revenues. Toby worked 75 hours during a biweekly pay period and earned $1,000 in tips. What is Toby's gross pay (excluding tips)?

LO 3-2 Compute Gross Pay for Different Pay Bases

Salaried Workers

Employees in highly technical, qualification-driven positions within a company are generally classified as exempt from FLSA regulations. Accountants, engineers, lawyers, managers, and supervisors are included in this classification. **Section 13(a)(1)** of the FLSA defines the eligible exempt employees in the following job descriptions: Executives, administrative personnel, professionals, and outside sales representatives. **Section 13(a)(17)** of the FLSA also allows specific computer-related employees to be included in salaried workers' classification. The FLSA provides a minimum wage for salaried workers of not less than $684 per week, per the Final Rule that went into effect in January 2020. Also, the Final Rule, according to **29 CFR 778.114**, stipulates an employer may use the fluctuating workweek method if the employee works hours that vary from week to week and receives a fixed salary as straight-time compensation. The hourly rate is then computed by dividing the salary amount by the number of hours actually worked.

Pixelfit/E+/Getty Images

> Companies often use a technique called "job leveling" to determine salaries for exempt employees. This technique uses job analysis to define common types of responsibilities to generate pay grades. Although this technique intends to determine objective pay criteria, this practice has led to staffing imbalances, multiple titles for similar jobs, and employee morale issues.
>
> Since job leveling was clarified in 2015, firms have experienced mixed results regarding employee morale and engagement. Changes in work location, flexible schedules, and certain job duties have prompted additional classification to the idea of job leveling. The driving question has changed from "what the employee does" to "why is this job necessary." The focus of job leveling has become a discussion of the job's purpose within its operations' broader context.
>
> (Sources: SHRM; Lattice)

For nonexempt salaried workers, the employment contract entered into between the employee and the employer determines at what level of hourly work they would receive overtime pay. Many salaried nonexempt worker contracts, when specified, are for 45 hours per week. If the contract stipulates that 45 hours per week is the standard workweek for a salaried, nonexempt employee, then the employee is still subject to FLSA overtime rules for hours worked past 40. For this textbook, the standard workweek is five days out of a seven-day week.

> **EXAMPLE: SALARIED, NONEXEMPT EMPLOYEE**
> Dallas is a salaried, nonexempt employee, earns $1,000 per week and has a standard 45-hour workweek.
>
>   Hourly compensation: $1,000/45 hours = $22.22 per hour
>   Overtime rate = $22.22 × 1.5 = $33.33 per hour
>
> Because this employee is classified as nonexempt according to FLSA guidelines, the employee is subject to overtime compensation, and the hourly rate is needed to compute overtime pay.
>
> For the same salaried, nonexempt employee, if the contract between the employee and employer stated that all hours *exceeding* 45 were covered, the individual would need to work 45.25 hours or more in the week to qualify for overtime. These are typically non-FLSA companies.
>
> However, *if* the contract stated that only 40 hours were required before the overtime rates are applied, then the 5 hours would be paid at overtime rates.
>
> Note: A salaried *exempt* worker would be paid $1,000 per week regardless of the number of hours worked.

Employers may not prorate a salaried worker's pay when the number of hours worked is fewer than the contractual hour requirement. An exception to this would be time away from work per the employer's sick or vacation policy. The company would allow employees to take paid time off under either of these programs to supplement their missed wages. Companies may also offer salaried employees the option of leave without pay for missed days; however, contractual hours covered under leave without pay must be documented and signed by both a manager and the employee.

Salary Translation to Hourly Rates

The calculation of gross pay for salaried employees depends on the firm's choice of pay periods. An employee's gross pay is determined by dividing the annual pay by the number of pay periods in a year. For instance, if a firm paid employees every month, then the salary calculation would be $\frac{1}{12}$ of the yearly amount. It is occasionally necessary to determine the hourly rate for salaried employees. To get the hourly rate, you would use the following equation:

$$\text{Hourly rate} = \frac{\text{Annual amount}}{\text{Total hours worked per year}}$$

To arrive at the total number of hours worked per year, multiply the number of weeks in a year (52) by the number of hours worked in a standard workweek without overtime.

$$\text{Hourly rate} = \frac{\text{Annual salary}}{\text{Number of hours in a standard workweek} \times 52 \text{ weeks per year}}$$

Because the calculation of overtime, holiday, or vacation time for salaried workers could be based upon the individual's job duties, knowing how to calculate that amount will enable accurate pay.

EXAMPLE: SALARY TO HOURLY RATE COMPUTATIONS

Jesse earns a salary of $60,000 per year for ABD Industries. ABD Industries pays its employees every month.

Gross pay = $60,000 per year/12 months = $5,000 per month

If Jesse were a nonexempt employee, it would become necessary to calculate the hourly rate. When calculating the hourly rate, using the correct number of hours in a regular workweek is critical in determining the overtime pay rate. Note the following examples of computing the hourly rate using different regular workweeks.

Number of Hours in the Regular Workweek	$\dfrac{\text{Annual salary}}{\text{Number of hours} \times 52 \text{ weeks}}$	Hourly Rate
40	$\dfrac{60,000}{(40 \times 52)}$	$28.85
37.5	$\dfrac{60,000}{(37.5 \times 52)}$	$30.77
35	$\dfrac{60,000}{(35 \times 52)}$	$32.97

What happens if the salaried employee decides to take unpaid leave during a pay period? That amount must be deducted from the gross pay amount. With unpaid leave, the amount of time taken and the number of regular hours in the pay period are the major factors.

> **EXAMPLE: UNPAID LEAVE**
>
> Barre wants to take two extra days off around a holiday but has no paid time remaining for the year. ABD Industries pays Barre $60,000 annually on a biweekly basis, and there are 80 hours in a pay period. At 8 hours per day, Barre will be taking 16 hours of unpaid leave (8 hours × 2 days).
>
> Using the example of Barre's work with ABD Industries with the regular working hours as 40 hours per week, the normal salary is
> 80 hours × $28.85/hour = $2,308 per pay period
>
> To calculate the pay, including the unpaid leave, we need the proportion of the paycheck that will be unpaid. We calculate the proportion of the total paycheck Barre will be taking as unpaid leave.
>
> Unpaid portion: 16 hours
> Normal hours per pay period: 80
> Unpaid portion = 16/80 = 0.20
>
> That means Barre will receive 100 − 0.20 = 0.80 (or 80 percent) of the normal gross pay.
>
> Gross pay per period with 16 hours of unpaid time:
> $2,308 × 0.80 = $1,846.40
>
> Note: Using a rounded hourly rate (shown in this example) to compute period pay will differ from results using nonrounded hourly rates. We have also not separated the holiday pay intentionally for this example.

In many instances, nonexempt employees are paid on a salary basis to avoid paperwork such as *time cards* or pay sheets if they consistently work a fixed number of hours per week. According to **29 CFR 778.113(a)**, the employer and employee must agree on the standard number of hours to be worked each week for which the employee shall receive pay. However, if the employee is classified as nonexempt, the FLSA requires that these salaried workers be eligible for overtime. A nonexempt hourly rate is necessary to compute pay beyond the agreed-upon weekly hours per **29 CFR 778.113(a)**.

If the employee works fewer than the agreed-upon number of hours during the week, some states have provisions by which the employee's salary is adjusted to match the actual hours worked. In this case, the hourly rate is again needed to make sure the gross pay is correctly calculated.

Salaried Workers and Minimum Wage Comparisons

For a salaried nonexempt worker for whom FLSA provisions apply, the fixed weekly salary must adhere to minimum wage guidelines. The minimum wage applies to salaried nonexempt employees whose wages do not exceed $684 per week. The U.S. Department of Labor has established this salary level as one of the exemption tests from FLSA provisions.

> **EXAMPLE: SALARIED NONEXEMPT EMPLOYEE PAY**
>
> Skyler is a receptionist for KTC Incorporated, located in California, and is salaried with a schedule of 40 hours per week. Skyler is nonexempt based on the job classification as nonmanagerial.
>
> If Skyler were paid $275 per week
> Hourly wage = $275/40 hours per week = $6.88/hour
>
> *(continued)*

(concluded)

This amount is below the federal minimum wage test for exempt employees. Skyler would need to be paid a minimum of $290 per week to meet FLSA minimum wage requirements because of the weekly 40-hour work agreement with the employer. Considering that California has a much higher minimum wage than the federal minimum wage, it would be necessary to determine the appropriate minimum wage for the location, industry, and company size. The employer must contribute additional money to meet the minimum wage requirement.

Hourly Workers

Hourly workers are paid for any hours or fraction of the hours they work. These employees may be either skilled or unskilled. Hourly employees must receive overtime for hours worked more than 40 per week, according to FLSA. Overtime is the same for hourly workers as it is for salaried nonexempt workers. Hourly workers may be paid for each minute worked, and the computation of those minutes depends upon company policy. Companies may offer different work shifts and workday lengths, such as four 10-hour shifts or five 8-hour shifts, to reach the 40 hours needed. State regulations may require the company to file an election to pay no overtime for the two additional hours per day. The reason stated should not be overtime avoidance, but a deemed economic benefit for the longer schedules. For example, setup time in a manufacturing environment can eliminate anywhere from half an hour to an hour or more of productive time. By working longer schedules, manufacturing efficiency can be improved.

In Asheville, North Carolina, the city changed the working hours for employees in the public works department to 10-hour shifts. The change in working hours has led to increased employee satisfaction. Additionally, the department consumed less electricity and natural gas by closing the office one day per week. Although a four-day workweek is not appropriate for all departments and job functions, it is an option that employers may consider.

In 2020, research into the idea of longer workdays and shorter workweeks revealed that the flexibility of having shorter workweeks would be an advance for traditional U.S. companies. The possibility for increased flexibility, especially when working from home or with a hybrid work schedule, appealed to most employees.

This flexibility came to light with the COVID-19 closures and other pandemic ramifications. In January 2021, the average working week was 35 hours. There were many ups and downs, never quite reaching that point again and in January 2022 the average of 34.5 working week hours was the lowest in years.

(Sources: WLOS; SHRM; Statista)

Hourly Workers in More Than One Job Classification

An employee working for an hourly wage may work in more than one job classification. When this occurs, the employee's pay per classification may vary. For example, a manufacturing employee may work on the sales counter, where the pay differential provides an additional $1.50 per hour. When situations like this occur, the payroll accountant must be informed of hours performed for each job classification to provide accurate pay, classification, and reporting. Methods used to communicate this include notes on the time card, schedules provided to the payroll clerk, or job duty notification forms. Known in the industry as "shared employees," these individuals can solve some of a company's short-staffing issues that result from cutbacks or economic downturns.

> **EXAMPLE: HOURLY PAY WITH DIFFERENT RATES**
>
> Cabral is an hourly worker for a fast-food establishment in Louisiana and earns $7.25 per hour. Occasionally Cabral fills in as the crew chief, which results in a $2 per hour differential. During a 40-hour workweek, Cabral worked 16 hours as a crew chief and 24 hours as a regular employee. The pay would be calculated as follows:
>
> Regular pay: 24 hours × $7.25/hour = $174
>
> Crew chief pay: $7.25/hour + $2.00/hour differential = $9.25/hour
>
> 16 hours × $9.25/hour = $148
>
> Gross pay = $174 + $148 = $322

Commission Work

Commissions are compensation based on a set percentage of the sales revenue for a product or service that the company provides. Commission-based compensation is appropriate in the following types of situations:

- Retail sales personnel.
- Automotive sales personnel.
- Media databases or monitoring that pertains to media relations.
- Marketing sales agents.

> **EXAMPLE: COMMISSION WORKER PAY**
>
> An ice machine company may have sales representatives earning a 5 percent commission on all sales made. If sales representative A sells $100,000 worth of ice machines during July, the commission due is computed as follows:
>
> Sales price × Commission rate = $100,000 × 5% = $5,000
>
> Note: Commissions may be contingent upon the company's commission return/warranty policy.
>
> If sales representative A had returns of $7,500 during August, the commission for that month could be reduced:
>
> Returns × Commission rate = deduction from commissions $7,500 returns × 5% commission rate = $375 deducted from commissions during August.
>
> Note that the commission deduction policy varies among employers and is not mandated by any legislation.

An important classification of a sales representative's job is the difference between inside and outside sales. An inside sales representative conducts business via telephone, email, or other electronic means and may not travel to customer sites. An outside sales representative meets with customers either at the customer's facility or another agreed-upon location. Some inside sales representatives are covered under the FLSA and must receive at least minimum wage for their labor. Outside sales representatives are excluded from minimum wage requirements under FLSA. In a 2010 circuit court decision, the judge ruled that inside sales representatives are nonexempt from FLSA wage and hour provisions, whereas outside sales and retail sales representatives are exempt.

> **EXAMPLE: INSIDE SALES REPRESENTATIVE, LESS THAN MINIMUM WAGE**
>
> Steinel works as an inside sales representative in the company store and receives a 5 percent commission for all completed sales during the shift. During the week, there were 15 telephone sales with a total dollar value of $1,500.
>
> Commissions = Dollar value of sales × Commission rate
> Commissions = $1,500 × 5% = $75
>
> Based upon a 40-hour workweek, Steinel would have effectively earned **$1.88** per hour; thus, the employer would be responsible for meeting the minimum wage requirements under FLSA. The employer would have to adjust Steinel's compensation to meet the minimum wage requirements for the specific location and local laws.

> **EXAMPLE: OUTSIDE SALES REPRESENTATIVE, LESS THAN MINIMUM WAGE**
>
> Durant works as an outside sales representative. During the week there were $2,000 of sales with an agreed-upon commission percentage of 10 percent of total sales revenue. Commission = 2,000 × 10% = $200; $200 per week/40 hours = $5.00 per hour. As an outside sales representative, Durant is exempt from minimum wage regulations under FLSA.

Gross Pay for Commission-Based Employees

In situations where the employee is principally engaged in the sale of a product or service but in no way engaged in the item's manufacturing, a commission pay basis is appropriate. In some states, the commission-based employee may receive commissions for work, even after termination, if the sale was completed before termination. In many ways, commission-based pay is a contract between the employer and the employee to sell a product. The payment for such a contract may not be reneged upon, even after termination of employment. It should be noted that many states prohibit deductions about the cost of doing business from an employee's commission. In other words, if a customer received a product that was damaged, lost, or otherwise destroyed, the employee's commission would not be affected.

> **EXAMPLE: OUTSIDE SALESPERSON**
>
> Devin Hin works as an outside salesperson with Bayfront Watercraft in California. Devin's whole function with Bayfront is to sell the company's products to customers at the customer's facility or other agreed-upon locations. Devin receives a commission of 5 percent based on the retail price of all sales made. During May, there were sales of $20,000 in products during one week.
>
> Commission = $20,000 × 0.05 = $1,000

Syda Productions/Shutterstock

Commission pay can vary by employer, client, sales volume, and employee based on their seniority or experience with the company. Different products may also have varying commission rates, and changes in sales volume can alter commission rates. A sample of a commission tracking sheet follows.

> **EXAMPLE: COMMISSION TRACKING SHEET**
>
> | Salesperson | Client | Product or Service | Total Sales Price | Rate | Commission |
> | --- | --- | --- | --- | --- | --- |
> | **Andy Bauer** | Thompson Milbourne | RR-223 | $1,245 | 2% | $24.90 |
> | **Andy Bauer** | Kockran Heights | RS-447 | $2,016 | 5% | $100.80 |
> | **Andy Bauer** | Hoptop Ranges | RT-11 | $892 | 3.5% | $31.22 |

Commissions earned must be tracked closely for a variety of reasons:

- Employees' pay accuracy
- Sales employee performance
- Sales tracking
- Job order tracking
- Returns/reductions of commissions paid accuracy

Commission pay must still meet FLSA minimum wage standards unless the employee is classified as an exempt worker. Like salaried nonexempt employees, commission-based employees are subject to the 40-hour workweek as a basis for FLSA minimum wage computations.

EXAMPLE: EFFECTIVE PAY RATE, EXCEED MINIMUM WAGE

In the example concerning Sage Hinton at Bayfront, Sage's pay was $1,000 for 40 hours of work.

Sage's effective wage = $1,000/40 hours = $25/hour

EXAMPLE: EFFECTIVE PAY RATE, LOWER THAN THE MINIMUM WAGE

Ari Edwards, another inside sales commission-based employee at Bayfront Watercraft, made only $250 in commission for the week during the 40 hours.

Effective hourly rate = $250/40 hours = $6.25/hour

This amount is below the minimum wage in California. The employer's responsibility is to compensate the employee at the appropriate minimum wage, so Bayfront would have to adjust Ari's compensation to meet FLSA requirements.

Piece-Rate Work

Piece-rate work involves paying employees for each unit they manufacture or each action they complete. Compensation based on task completion is one of the oldest forms of performance-based pay. Dating back to the 16th century, piece-rate pay is thought to have evolved from journeyman artisans whose masters paid them per unit they completed. Before computations of hourly wages, piece rate was an accurate measure of how productive an employee was. Frederick Taylor wrote about a piece-rate system in 1896, citing that it emphasized efficiency and production. However, a criticism of Taylor's writing is that the piece-rate system overemphasizes production and may create an adversarial relationship between workers and managers.

Marianne Purdie/Getty Images

California's **AB 1513**, passed in 2016, amended California Labor Code 226.2 and mandated that piece-rate workers be paid for nonproductive time during the workday. Pay during the nonproductive time would be at a different rate than the normal piece-rate work. This nonproductive time includes the employee's time under the employer's control but not on a rest or recovery break. The argument for paid nonproductive time for piece-rate workers is that the employee remains under the employer's control despite the lack of productivity.

(Source: California Department of Industrial Relations)

FLSA requirements subjected the piece-rate system to minimum wage requirements. Piece-rate workers must be paid no less than the minimum wage for their location, forcing employers to accurately track their work. In many ways, piece-rate pay is more difficult to track and administer than other payment types. Not only must the employees be compensated for the work they complete, but they are also subject to FLSA minimum and daily break provisions, including lunch and other breaks. Piece-rate work has also fallen under some suspicion regarding the quality of work being performed. This can require adding a review to the completed work.

> **EXAMPLE: PIECE-RATE PAY, EXCEEDING THE MINIMUM WAGE**
>
> Julian is a piece-rate worker in Tennessee who receives $15 per completed piece of work. During a week, there were 30 completed pieces during 40 hours of work.
>
> Julian's pay = $15/per piece completed × 30 pieces completed = $450
> Hourly rate equivalent = $450/40 hours = $11.25/hour
>
> Since Tennessee has no minimum wage requirements, the federal minimum wage would apply. Julian's pay exceeds the FLSA minimum wage for this location, so the employer does not have to adjust Julian's compensation.

> **EXAMPLE: PIECE-RATE WORKER, BELOW MINIMUM WAGE**
>
> Kaydon McDowell works for the same employer as Julian and receives the same rate of pay. Kaydon completes 15 pieces during the week.
>
> Kaydon's pay = $15/piece × 15 = $225
> Hourly rate equivalent = $225/40 = $5.63/hour
>
> Kaydon's pay does not meet the minimum wage requirement, so the employer would have to examine Kaydon's work and pay rates to ensure that the company meets the FLSA minimum wage requirements.

A wide variety of occupations benefit from piece-rate pay systems. Some of these occupations are:

Vineyard workers	Inspectors
Carpenters	Property assessors
Machinists/fabricators	Production workers
Sheep shearers	Forest workers

The common thread is that each position has an output that is quantifiable and linked to some aspect of a manufacturing or service industry. The important part of piece-rate work is that a quantifiable base must be linked with a specified standard rate per amount of work.

Vineyard workers: Tons of grapes harvested
Inspectors: Number of items inspected
Installers: Number of items installed
Customer service agents: Number of customers assisted
Machinists/fabricators: Number of items produced
Sheep shearers: Pounds of wool gathered
Forest workers: Amount of wood chopped and/or processed

At Bayfront Watercraft, the manufacturing department has different types of fabricators, installers, and other production workers in addition to Pat (the hull maker). Let us assume that Justice works in the upholstery department, where she constructs vinyl covers for seats. Rian is in the assembly department and assembles steering mechanisms for the boats.

EXAMPLE: PIECE-RATE COMPUTATION, DIFFERENT EMPLOYEES

Worker	Number of Items	Rate per Item	Gross Pay
Pat Wu	30 hulls	$100	$3,000
Justice Yoder	100 seat covers	25	2,500
Rian Karmaran	25 steering mechanisms	40	1,000

Each worker is compensated based on the work he or she completes. In some companies, workers may work on multiple items for which different rates exist. In cases where one worker completes multiple pieces at different rates, each piece's rates must be computed.

EXAMPLE: TOTAL PAY, ONE PIECE-RATE EMPLOYEE

Worker	Item	Number of Items	Pay per Item	Total Pay
Brick Brichacek	Motor installation	10 motors	$50 per motor	$500
	Rudder installation	15 rudders	20 per rudder	300
			Total pay for John:	$800

A separate record for each employee is important in piece-rate pay, especially when the employee works with multiple production items at different rates. Overtime rates for piece-rate workers are computed differently than for hourly workers. Once the standard number of pieces per hour is determined, the amount per hour per piece can be computed. Since the hourly rate now includes the overtime hours worked, the specific overtime hours would only be multiplied by 1/2 instead of the 1-1/2 of other workers.

EXAMPLE: PIECE RATE WITH OVERTIME PAY

Bayfront determines that 50 ignition assemblies can reasonably be completed in a 40-hour workweek by one worker. Ignition assemblies are paid at a rate of $25 per assembly.

> Standard amount paid per 40-hour workweek: $1,250
> 50 assemblies × $25/assembly = $1,250
> Hourly amount = $1,250/40 hours = $31.25/hour

If the employee worked overtime, the rate would be computed as follows:

> Overtime wages = (Hourly rate + (0.5 × Hourly rate)) × Overtime hours

If an employee worked a 45-hour workweek, the pay would be computed as:

> Standard amount per week + Overtime pay
> = $1,250 + ($31.25/hour × 5 hours overtime) + ($15.625 × 5 hours overtime)
> = $1,484.375, which would be $1,484.38 (rounded)

According to FLSA provisions, piece-rate workers must have a standard number of items that can be reasonably completed each day that allows for breaks and rest periods. To increase compensation, it could be straightforward for an employee to overwork to complete more items. According to **29 CFR 525.12(h)(2)(ii)**, piece-rate employees must have a standard number of items per period, and most are subject to minimum wage provisions. However, if an employee is paid a different rate for nonproductive time, the regular rate is the regular rate and the nonproductive rate.

Computations for Different Bases

Stop & Check

1. Amari is a marketing representative who earns a 3 percent commission based on the revenue earned from the marketing campaigns completed. During the current pay period, the completed marketing campaign had $224,800 in revenue. How much commission will Amari receive from this campaign?

2. Sybil is a specialty artisan for a luxury car maker based in South Carolina. Sybil makes handcrafted dashboards and receives $550 per completed assembly. During a semimonthly pay period, Sybil completes two dashboard assemblies and works 90 hours. How much does Sybil receive for the completion of the assemblies? Does this amount comply with minimum wage requirements? Explain.

3. Karstyn is a salaried worker making $57,000 per year for a company using biweekly payroll. The standard schedule is 40 hours over five days per week. Karstyn used all available vacation time before this pay period and fell ill for three days. What effect does this have on the current pay period? Will the gross pay be the same as if Karstyn had vacation time available? (Note: Only round final calculations.)

LO 3-3 Calculate Pay Based on Hours and Fractions of Hours

Both salaried nonexempt and hourly employees are paid based on the number of hours (or fractions thereof) worked. The payroll accountant must learn how to convert a fraction of a 60-minute clock into a fraction of 100. While accounting software packages can convert minutes into payable units, the payroll accountant typically does this math. Fortunately, the math for this calculation is fairly straightforward.

Andrey_Popov/Shutterstock

> **EXAMPLE: CONVERSION OF MINUTES TO DECIMALS AND FRACTIONS**
>
> If an employee works 30 minutes, then the computation for pay purposes is:
>
> 30 minutes ÷ 60 minutes/hour = 0.5 hour or 50/100
>
> If an employee works 33 minutes, the payroll computation is
>
> 33 minutes ÷ 60 minutes/hour = 0.55 hour or 55/100
>
> Note: This calculation is necessary when the employer pays using the hundredth-hour method instead of the quarter-hour method. If this had been a quarter-hour computation, the number of minutes would have been rounded to the closest 15-minute increment, which is 0.50 hours.

Calculations of employee wages are broken down by the hour or fraction thereof. Regardless of the employee's classification, a determination of pay per pay period causes the payroll accountant to break down all wages. Salaries are determined based on a yearly salary and therefore need to be broken down per pay period (monthly, semimonthly, weekly, or biweekly). Companies may pay employees by fractions of an hour (hundredth-hour basis) or by the quarter-hour (rounded to the nearest 15-minute interval), depending upon company policy. The next section will walk you through the calculations of both the hundredth and quarterly processes.

Hourly Calculations

Depending on the company's policy, time payments can be paid either by the individual minute or rounded to the nearest designated interval. Hourly calculations are a combination of minutes and hours. Hours are broken into two categories: regular and overtime. When determining the hourly wage for a salaried individual, the number of average hours required under the salary agreement must be known. Hourly wages are commonly needed for accurate recording of paid time off and holiday pay.

> **EXAMPLE: HOURLY WAGE COMPUTATION, SALARIED EMPLOYEE**
>
> If an exempt manager is contracted to work 45 hours per week at $75,000 per year, the effective hourly wage would be:
>
> $75,000/(45 × 52 weeks) = $75,000/2,340 = $32.05 per hour (rounded)

> **EXAMPLE: WEEKLY PAY INCLUDING PAID SICK TIME**
>
> A nonexempt employee worked four days during the payroll week. The employee worked 7.5 hours on the first day, 8.75 hours on the second day, 7 hours on the third day, and 9.5 hours on the fourth day. The employee used 8 hours of paid sick leave on one day during the week. The employee is only paid overtime for any hours worked more than 40 per week.
>
> Regular hours: 7.5 + 8.75 + 7 + 9.5 = 32.75 hours
> Sick hours: 8 hours
> Gross pay = 32.75 regular hours + 8 sick = 40.75 hours
>
> Even though the employee has more than 40 hours on this payroll, the 8 hours of sick time are not considered "worked" and would therefore not be included in the calculation to determine overtime.

> **EXAMPLE: WEEKLY PAY INCLUDING PAID HOLIDAY TIME**
>
> Kit Golliff worked four days during the week with a holiday on Monday. This week's hours worked were 8.25 hours on the first day, 9 hours on the second day, 7.75 hours on the third day, and 8.5 hours on the fourth day. The company pays 8 hours for a holiday. Per policy, Kit is paid for any hours worked more than 40 hours per week.
>
> Regular hours: 8.25 + 9 + 7.75 + 8.5 = 33.5 hours
> Additionally, there will be 8 hours of regular pay for the holiday.
>
> Kit's gross pay will contain 41.5 hours of regular pay, including 8 hours of holiday pay. Kit has not worked more than 40 hours because the holiday is not included in *worked* hours, so she will not receive overtime.

Quarter-Hour System

Some employers compensate employees based on rounding working hours to the nearest 15 minutes, a system widely known as the *quarter-hour system*. The payroll accountant becomes responsible for rounding the time either up or down consistently across all individuals and pay periods. A person who worked 8 hours and 6 minutes would be paid for 8 hours. However, a person who worked for 8 hours and 8 minutes would be paid for 8 hours plus 15 minutes of overtime if the company pays for overtime on any hours worked over 8 in a day.

niroworld/123RF

> **EXAMPLE: ROUNDING MINUTES FOR THE QUARTER-HOUR SYSTEM**
>
> - 0–7 minutes past the previous 15-minute interval rounds *down* to the previous 15-minute interval.
>   Example: 10:06 a.m. would count as 10:00 a.m. in the quarter-hour system.
> - 8–15 minutes past the previous 15-minute interval rounds *up* to the next 15-minute interval.
>   Example: 10:09 a.m. would count as 10:15 a.m. in the quarter-hour system.

> **EXAMPLE: QUARTER-HOUR SYSTEM COMPUTATION, ROUNDING TO THE PREVIOUS QUARTER-HOUR**
>
> Leong worked from 8 a.m. until noon then took one hour for lunch and returned to work at 1 p.m. At the end of the day, Leong ended up leaving work at 4:20 p.m. To determine total time using the quarter-hour system:
>
> - From 8 a.m. to noon: 4 hours
> - From 1 p.m. to 4:20 p.m.: 3.25 hours, because 4:20 p.m. rounds down to 4:15 p.m. under the quarter-hour system.
> - Total time: 4 + 3.25 = 7.25 hours

> **EXAMPLE: QUARTER-HOUR SYSTEM COMPUTATION, ROUNDING TO THE NEXT QUARTER-HOUR**
>
> Peyton Fretwell worked from 8 a.m. until 12:30 p.m. before taking a half-hour lunch. Peyton returned at 1 p.m. and worked until 4:10 p.m. The employer pays on the quarter-hour system, so Peyton would be paid as follows:
>
> - From 8 a.m. to 12:30 p.m.: 4 hours, 30 minutes = 4.5 hours
> - From 1 p.m. to 4:10 p.m.: 3.25 hours, because 4:10 p.m. rounds up to 4:15 p.m. under the quarter-hour system.
> - Total time for the day: 7.75 hours

> One of the broader ethical challenges comes when an employer operates under a quarter-hour system and employees see the benefit of waiting a minute to clock out so they receive an additional 15 minutes of pay. One of the authors has seen individuals clocking in for others so the employee was not marked tardy and received unearned pay. In reciprocation, the employee would clock out the other employee later so that they both received additional pay for the period.
>
> This practice is called time theft. According to the American Payroll Association, time theft affects nearly 75 percent of businesses, and over 40 percent of employees have engaged in this practice. The use of time cards and many other time measurement systems makes time theft possible. Biometric time measurement systems have reduced this practice.
>
> (Source: Software Advice)

Hundredth-Hour System

The *hundredth-hour system* is similar to the quarter-hour system in that it calculates partial hours of work performed. Instead of rounding the employee's time to 15-minute intervals, the hundredth-hour system divides the hour into increments. The calculation of partial minutes is simple:

$$\text{Conversion of minutes to hundredth hour} = \frac{\text{Number of minutes in partial hour}}{60 \text{ minutes per hour}}$$

> **EXAMPLE: CONVERSION FROM MINUTES TO HUNDREDTH-HOUR**
> If an employee worked 4 hours and 16 minutes,
>
> 4 hours + 16 minutes/60 minutes per hour = 4.27 hours

> **EXAMPLE: HUNDREDTH-HOUR TIME COMPUTATION**
> Remy Mellor works an eight-hour shift that had 15 minutes of additional overtime. Remy's normal hourly rate is $15/hour. The pay would be computed as follows:
>
> - 8 hours × $15 per hour = $120 regular pay
> - 15 minutes overtime = 15/60 = 0.25 hour
> - Overtime = 0.25 hours × $15/hour × 1.5 = $5.63 (rounded)
> - Total pay for the day = $80 + $3.75 = $125.63

Following is an example of how the time may appear on an individual's time card. Note that an employer should choose only one method of computing partial hours—quarter-hours or hundredth-hours—and apply it to all situations and all employees.

EXAMPLE: QUARTER-HOUR COMPUTATION, WEEKLY PAY DETAILS

Employee Number 1776M

Clock In	Clock Out	Clock In	Clock Out	Hours Worked
08:00	11:00	12:00	16:54 rounds up	7 hours 54 minutes = 8.00 hours
08:00	11:30	12:30	17:05 rounds down	8 hours 5 minutes = 8.00 hours
07:00	12:09 rounds up	13:15	17:30	9 hours 24 minutes = 9.5 hours
07:30	12:20 rounds down	13:22 rounds up	17:30	8 hours 52 minutes = 8.75 hours
			Total	34.25 hours

In the next example, notice how the same employee with the same amount of time worked would have different hourly computations based on hundredth-hour computations. The difference in the hourly computations leads to a difference in compensation for the period.

EXAMPLE: HUNDREDTH-HOUR COMPUTATION, WEEKLY PAY DETAILS

Employee Number 1776M

Clock In	Clock Out	Clock In	Clock Out	Hours Worked
08:00	11:00	12:00	16:54	7 hours 54 minutes = 7.9 hours
08:00	11:30	12:30	17:05	8 hours 5 minutes = 8.08 hours
07:00	12:09	13:15	17:30	9 hours 24 minutes = 9.4 hours
07:30	12:21	13:24	17:30	8 hours 57 minutes = 8.95 hours
			Total	34.33 hours

> **BEST PRACTICE: QUARTER-HOUR OR HUNDREDTH-HOUR?**
> Debate exists around the question of which timekeeping system is better, quarter-hour or hundredth-hour. The best practices in this regard focus on consistency and accuracy. If the company feels that the hundredth-hour timekeeping system is more appropriate for its needs, it must create that policy and implement it through its payroll and timekeeping systems. The FLSA guidance is that the quarter-hour method is the federal requirement.
>
> Which is the best practice? It is up to the employer. The most accurate method of wage determination is the hundredth-hour method.

Stop & Check — Quarter-Hour vs. Hundredth-Hour

1. Blue Sky Manufacturing has historically paid its employees according to the quarter-hour system. Software changes have caused them to change to the hundredth-hour system. See the table below. What is the number of hours worked under the quarter-hour system? What is the time worked under the hundredth-hour system? (Hint: Convert to a 24-hour clock to make calculations easier.)

Employee	Time In	Time Out	Time In	Time Out	Total
A	8:06 a.m.	12:25 p.m.	1:20 p.m.	4:57 p.m.	Quarter-hour: Hundredth:
B	7:58 a.m.	12:02 p.m.	1:02 p.m.	5:05 p.m.	Quarter-hour: Hundredth:
C	8:32 a.m.	11:54 a.m.	1:05 p.m.	5:32 p.m.	Quarter-hour: Hundredth:

2. Why do discrepancies exist between the quarter-hour time and the hundredth-hour time totals?
3. Why would it be worthwhile for Blue Sky Manufacturing to switch to the hundredth-hour system?

LO 3-4 Calculate Overtime in Various Situations

fizkes/Shutterstock

Nonexempt employee overtime may occur in a variety of situations. When an employee works past the FLSA maximum hours per week, the employee must be compensated at a rate of 1.5 times the regular hourly rate. However, situations exist when employees must be compensated at more than the standard overtime premium, and others exist when exempt employees may receive overtime pay. We will explore examples of overtime compensation in a variety of situations.

Standard Overtime Pay

In general, FLSA-stipulated overtime includes hours worked more than 40 during a seven-day, 168-hour week. No limit on the number of hours an employee may work per week exists for employees over 16 years of age. No legislation stipulates that employees must be paid at overtime rates on Saturdays and Sundays as long as the total number of hours worked is less than 40 during a period of seven consecutive days. An important fact to note is that the regular pay rate may not be below the FLSA or state-based minimum wage, especially when overtime pay has been earned.

> According to the Bureau of Labor Statistics, the average number of weekly overtime hours as of November 2022 was 2.9 per employee for nonmanufacturing industries, and this continued into 2022. Although this may seem to be a relatively low number, employee overtime can become a significant amount for a large employer.
>
> For example, Kynd Hearts Home Care, LLC, was ordered to pay over $1.5 million to nearly 200 workers because it willfully did the following:
>
> - Failed to pay nonexempt employees who worked more than 40 hours during a seven-day period.
> - Reduced employees' hourly rates when they worked more hours and paid overtime at that reduced rate.
> - Did not document overtime on internal payroll records.
>
> (Sources: Bureau of Labor Statistics; Wavy.com)

The first example explains basic overtime pay computation for a nonexempt employee with a 40-hour workweek. The second part of the example reflects the bonus payment as a normal part of the employee's pay.

Overtime on retail or service salaries with a commission has two rules that must be met for the commissions to be included in the wage base for the overtime calculations: (1) the employee's regular payments must be more than 1½ times the statutory minimum wage and (2) more than one-half of the employee's compensation must be from the commissions.

> ### EXAMPLE: NONEXEMPT PAY CALCULATION
> Monroe works as a maintenance worker at a busy office building. Monroe earns $52,000 annually, is paid weekly, and is classified as nonexempt. Monroe's standard workweek is 40 hours. Since Monroe is classified as a nonexempt worker, overtime is any hours worked more than 40 per week per her employment contract.
>
> During the pay period ending April 22, Monroe worked 50 hours. As a result, Monroe would receive the weekly pay *plus* overtime calculated to include the nondiscretionary bonus. To determine the hourly wage, divide the annual pay by the total hours worked during the year. The gross earnings for the April 22 pay period would be as follows:
>
> | Name | M/S | #Dep | Hourly Rate | No. of Regular Hours | No. of Overtime Hours | Regular Earnings | Overtime Earnings | Gross Earnings |
> |---|---|---|---|---|---|---|---|---|
> | Monroe | S | 1 | 25.00 | 40 | 10 | 1,000.00 | 375.00 | 1,375.00 |
>
> Note that Monroe's regular pay and overtime pay are calculated separately and then added together to determine the gross pay.
>
> #### Hourly rate plus bonus
> If Monroe were eligible for a bonus as part of the employment agreement, the bonus would be added to the regular pay to determine an hourly rate on which the overtime is based. In this example, if Monroe received a $120 bonus for the work, the overtime computation would be as follows:
>
> | Name | M/S | #Dep | Hourly Rate | No. of Regular Hours | No. of Overtime Hours | Bonus | Regular Earnings | Overtime Earnings | Gross Earnings |
> |---|---|---|---|---|---|---|---|---|---|
> | Monroe | S | 1 | 25.00 | 40 | 10 | 120.00 | 1,000.00 | 420.00* | 1,540.00 |
>
> * Calculation: $40 * 25 = $1,000 + 120 = $1,120 / 40 = $28 * 1.5 = $42 * 10 = $420

Overtime for Employees of Hospitals and Residential Care Facilities

Overtime computation differs from the standard rate for employees who work at hospitals and residential care facilities. FLSA section **7(j)** applies a rule to these workers known as the

Eight and Eighty (8 and 80) rule. According to the 8 and 80 rule, the number of consecutive days is 14 instead of 7. Similarly, the threshold for overtime is 80 hours during the work period instead of 40. An example reflecting the 8 and 80 rule follows.

> ### EXAMPLE: 8 AND 80 OVERTIME CALCULATION
> Val is a licensed practical nurse (LPN) at Fountainside Hospital. During the period starting June 5 and ending June 18, Val worked 95 hours. Val is classified as nonexempt and earns an hourly wage of $31.50. Val's pay for the two-week period would be as follows:
>
> | Name | M/S | #W/H | Hourly Rate | No. of Regular Hours | No. of Overtime Hours | Regular Earning | Overtime Earning | Gross Earning |
> |---|---|---|---|---|---|---|---|---|
> | Val | S | 1 | 31.50 | 80 | 15 | 2,520.00 | 708.75 | 3,228.75 |
>
> Note that the first 80 hours are paid at the regular hourly rate. The 15 additional hours are paid at the overtime premium rate.

> Overtime for nurses took on a different aspect during the COVID-19 pandemic. Most nurses worked overtime as of mid-2020 to respond to the critical needs of the hospitals. Nurses in Milford, Massachusetts, involved the National Labor Relations Board in their drive to have reasonable hours and safe working conditions.
>
> In 2021, the issue of nurse pay gained an additional dimension: traveling nurses. Nurses who took on additional work during the COVID-19 pandemic received the same wages as they did before the outbreak. However, traveling nurses had more control over their time and could command higher pay. States considered increasing nurse pay but found the wage increase unsustainable for future fiscal periods.
>
> (Sources: Patch; KSLA)

Tipped Employee Overtime

Another overtime situation involves tipped employees. According to the FLSA, employers may consider tips earned by the employee when computing overtime pay. A best practice when the employer chooses to use the tips earned as part of the overtime computation is to notify employees in advance that their tips will be included in the overtime pay calculation. An example of both situations will show how wage computations differ with and without tips included.

> ### EXAMPLE: TIPPED EMPLOYEE OVERTIME
> Keegan is a nonexempt tipped employee at the Love House Bar and Grill in Arvada, Colorado. The minimum cash wage in Colorado is $10.63 per hour, and the tip credit is $3.02 per hour (i.e., the minimum wage for Colorado is $13.65 per hour). During the pay period beginning January 30, 2023, and ending February 4, 2023, Keegan worked 48 hours and earned $300 in tips.
>
> Without the consideration of tips, and based on the state minimum wage, Keegan must be paid $709.80 for the 48 hours worked, as follows:
>
> | Name | M/S | #W/H | Hourly Rate | No. of Regular Hours | No. of Overtime Hours | Tips | Regular Earning | Overtime Earning | Gross Earning |
> |---|---|---|---|---|---|---|---|---|---|
> | Keegan | S | 1 | 13.65 | 40 | 8 | | 546.00 | 163.80 | 709.80 |
>
> *Overtime pay with tips included as part of the hourly wage*
> If the employer counted the $300 in tips earned toward the minimum cash overtime wage, Keegan would not be eligible for any further compensation because the gross earnings exceeded the minimum due.

Name	M/S	#W/H	Hourly Rate	No. of Regular Hours	No. of Overtime Hours	Tips	Regular Earnings	Overtime Earnings	Gross Earnings
Keegan	S	1	10.63	40	8	300.00	725.20	217.56	942.76

Earnings calculation

Regular earnings: $300 + (10.63 × 40) = $300 + 425.20 = $725.20
Overtime earnings: $725.20/40 = $18.13/hour × 1.5 = $27.195 × 8 = $217.56

Overtime pay excluding tips as part of the hourly wage

If the employer did **not** count Keegan's tips toward the hourly wage, the pay would be computed as follows (note that overtime is omitted from minimum wage computations):

Name	M/S	#W/H	Hourly Rate	No. of Regular Hours	No. of Overtime Hours	Tips	Regular Earning	Overtime Earning	Gross Earning
Keegan	S	1	10.63	40	8	300.00	425.20	127.56	852.76

In this case, the employer would not need to pay Keegan the difference between the minimum wage and the minimum tipped wage:

$(425.20 + 127.56)/40 = $552.76/40 = $13.819/hour

Note: State laws vary as to the inclusion of tips in tipped employee overtime calculations. Additionally, the employee earned more than the state's minimum wage.

Piece-Rate Employee Overtime

Piece-rate workers are eligible for overtime on a similar basis to that of hourly nonexempt employees. However, because they are paid on a piece-rate basis, the overtime computation is based on the number of pieces completed and the total number of productive hours worked during the consecutive seven-day period.

The overtime earnings are computed based on the piece-rate earnings plus the product of the nonproductive hours times the hourly rate (which is the minimum wage in this case) to obtain the regular earnings. The overtime is computed using the sum of the piece-rate earning plus the regular earnings divided by the total number of hours worked to obtain the overtime hourly rate. The overtime hourly rate is multiplied by 0.5 and by the number of overtime hours to determine the overtime earnings. See **29 CFR 778.111**.

EXAMPLE: PIECE-RATE EMPLOYEE OVERTIME

Easton is a piece-rate employee at Snowy Day Sculptures in Terrace Lake, New Mexico. Easton earns $75 per finished sculpture. During the week of February 20, there were 48.5 hours worked and 12 sculptures completed. Easton is paid minimum wage (i.e., $12.00 per hour) for nonproductive time, of which there were four nonproductive hours. Easton's overtime would be calculated based on the productive time of 44.5 hours as follows:

Name	M/S	#W/H	Piece Rate	# of Pieces Completed	No. of Regular Hours	No. of Overtime Hours	Piece Rate Earnings	Regular Earnings	Overtime Earnings	Gross Earnings
Easton	S	1	75	12	40	4.5	900.00	48.00	47.93	995.93

Earnings calculation

Piece-rate earnings: 12 × $75 = $900
Regular earnings = 4 × $12.00 = $48.00
Overtime = $948/44.5 = $21.3034 × 0.5 = $10.6517 × 4.5 (productive hours) = $47.93

Salaried Nonexempt Overtime

When the employee is a salaried nonexempt worker, the standard number of working hours per week may depend on the hiring agreement. If the number of hours agreed upon is 40 per week, then the standard overtime examples should be followed. However, if the number of agreed-upon hours is 45 per week, the overtime is calculated using 45 hours to determine the hourly rate, and time worked more than 40 hours is subject to overtime premiums. The same principle applies to employees who work four 10-hour shifts, shifts with differential rates, or other similar arrangements.

EXAMPLE: SALARIED NONEXEMPT POSITION WITH A NORMAL 45-HOUR WORK SCHEDULE

Clay is an administrator for Strickland Farms and earns $52,000 annually, paid biweekly. Clay is a salaried nonexempt employee with a standard 45-hour workweek. During the biweekly pay period ending September 22, Clay worked 99 hours. The overtime would be computed as follows:

Name	M/S	#W/H	Salary	No. of Regular Hours	No. of Overtime Hours*	Regular Earning	Overtime Earning	Gross Earning
Clay	S	1	2,000.00	90	19	2,000.00	633.33	2,633.33

Earnings calculation

*Although Clay has a 45-hour standard workweek, per FLSA Clay must be paid overtime for all hours worked in excess of 40. The number of overtime hours is 99 − (2 weeks × 40 hours/week), or 19.
Overtime rate = $52,000/(45 × 52) = $22.22222 × 1.5 = $33.33333 × 19 = $633.33

The U.S. Department of Labor recovered over $259,000 in overtime and back wages for 330 Michigan healthcare workers from two West Michigan employers in 2021. The employers were found in violation of the 8 and 80 FLSA rules when the employers paid for overtime only after 12 hours in a day or paid straight time regardless of the number of hours worked. This brought the total recovered wages for Michigan's healthcare workers from 2019 through 2021 to $3.5 million.

(Source: DOL)

Overtime for Employees Who Work in Two or More Separate Functions

Suppose an employee works in two separate functions in the company and earns a different rate for each function. For example, the employee may work in accounts payable and as a front desk receptionist, each with different pay rates. In this case, the overtime rate is often calculated using the average of the two pay rates.

EXAMPLE: EMPLOYEE WITH TWO DIFFERENT PAY RATES FOR DIFFERENT FUNCTIONS

Kian works equally for Sidwell Industries as both an accounts payable clerk and a front desk clerk. Kian earns $18.50 in accounts payable and $15 per hour for front desk work. During the week ending October 27, Kian worked 50 hours; 26 hours were in accounts payable (6 of these hours were overtime), and the rest were at the front desk. The pay would be computed as follows:

Name	M/S	#W/H	Hourly Rate	No. of Regular Hours	No. of Overtime Hours	Regular Earning	Overtime Earning	Gross Earning
Kian—accounts payable	S	1	18.50	20	6	370.00	166.50	536.50
Kian—front desk	S	1	15.00	20	4	300.00	90.00	390.00
Total Earnings								926.50

Note that company policies on overtime pay may vary from the situations described. When in doubt, the payroll accountant should refer to the FLSA overtime calculator advisor published by the U.S. Department of Labor.

Stop & Check — How Does Overtime Affect Gross Pay?

1. A hospital worker in New Hampshire is a nonexempt salaried worker with a 40-hour workweek. Which rule governs this employee's overtime pay?

2. A salaried nonexempt employee who earns $39,000 per year, paid biweekly, with a commission is based on the sales of service contracts (represents less than half their pay). How does the commission income affect any overtime compensation?

3. A waitperson at Good Cooking Diner is a tipped employee. What are the two ways that this employer might compute overtime earnings regarding tip income?

LO 3-5 Create a Payroll Register

The *payroll register* is the payroll accountant's internal tool that helps ensure the accuracy of employee compensation. A payroll register can be completed manually, in a spreadsheet program such as Microsoft Excel, in accounting software programs such as QuickBooks, or by payroll outsourcing companies such as ADP or Paychex. Like other worksheets that accountants use, the payroll register is a company's confidential document subject to document retention and destruction rules.

Pressmaster/Shutterstock

Payroll Register Data

The payroll register is annotated at the top with the beginning and end dates of the payroll period. Each employee has a separate row in the register. The register contains columns to reflect each employee's specific payroll information, such as:

1. Employee name
2. Filing status
3. Number and type of dependents
4. Hourly rate or period salary
5. The number of regular hours worked
6. The number of overtime hours worked
7. Regular pay
8. Overtime pay
9. Gross pay

10. Federal income tax withheld
11. Social Security tax withheld
12. Medicare tax withheld
13. State income tax withheld (where applicable)
14. Other state taxes
15. Local taxes (if applicable)
16. 401(k) or other retirement plan deductions
17. Insurance deductions
18. Garnishments or levies
19. Union dues
20. Any other deductions
21. Net pay
22. Check or payment ID number

It may seem tedious to complete a register each payroll period, but the register offers more information than just employee compensation. The register also contains information about employer liabilities for taxes and the employees' voluntary deductions that the employer must remit to the appropriate places at a future date. A sample payroll register with annotations to correlate with the preceding list of items is shown in Figure 3-3.

Note that other columns may be added to meet the company's needs. Other columns that may appear on a payroll register include commission, piece rate, standby hours, and sleep time. The purpose of the payroll register is to document the employees' time and hours worked and provide totals of the compensation for each category. Employers use these categorizations as part of labor analysis and planning tasks.

A separate payroll register is maintained for each pay period. To ensure accuracy, the accountant totals, proves, and rules the register.

FIGURE 3-3
Sample Payroll Register with Annotations

*Other state and local taxes would have columns after the state withholding tax.
†Other voluntary or mandated deductions would be in this location.

> **WHAT DO *TOTAL*, *PROVE*, AND *RULE* MEAN?**
>
> *Total:* Each column and row are totaled.
>
> *Prove:* The column totals are added horizontally, and row totals are totaled vertically. The aggregate column and row totals must be equal.
>
> *Rule:* Column totals are double-underlined to show that they have been totaled.

Track Employee Compensation Using a Payroll Register

A payroll register is a tool used by payroll accountants to ensure accurate tracking of employee compensation. The following examples will demonstrate different scenarios using a payroll register.

> **EXAMPLE 1: WAGE PAYMENTS, NO OVERTIME**
>
> Bailey, a nonexempt, hourly employee of CM Bakeries, receives $12.50/hour and receives overtime for any time worked more than 40 hours/week. Bailey is single with one dependent under 17 years of age. During the week ending April 21, Bailey worked 37 hours. The payroll register would appear as follows:
>
> | Name | Filing Status | Dependents | Hourly Rate or Period Wage | No. of Regular Hours | Gross Earnings |
> |---|---|---|---|---|---|
> | Bailey | S | 1<17 | 12.50 | 37 | 462.50 |

In Example 1, the employee's hourly rate is multiplied by the number of hours worked to obtain the period's gross pay. The use of the Regular Earnings column is introduced here, although no overtime exists. Example 2 will show how overtime is included in a payroll register.

> **EXAMPLE 2: WAGE PAYMENT WITH OVERTIME**
>
> Ash is a nonexempt, hourly employee of Strong Tea Company and earns $18.50/hour. Ash is married and filing jointly with two dependents under 17 years of age. Overtime is calculated for any hours worked over 40 during a weekly period. During the period that ended September 15, Ash worked 45.75 hours. The payroll register would appear as follows:

(continued)

(concluded)

Name	Filing Status	Dependents	Hourly Rate or Period Wage	No. of Regular Hours	No. of Overtime Hours	Reg. Earnings	Overtime Earnings	Gross Earnings
Ash	MJ	2<17	18.50	40	5.75	740.00	159.56*	899.56

*Overtime earning = $18.50/hour × 5.75 hours × 1.5 (overtime premium) = $159.56.

Notice that the payroll register in Example 2 is expanded to include a breakdown of regular earnings and overtime earnings. This practice aims to facilitate computations, ensure accuracy, and allow for future analysis of overtime worked during a given period.

Example 3 contains a payroll register for a salaried, exempt employee. Notice the difference in the columns used to record the period salary.

EXAMPLE 3: SALARY PAYMENT

Rae is a manager at Tet Torr Industries. Rae is a salaried, exempt employee, married, filing jointly with three dependents under 17 and one other dependent. Rae earns a salary of $2,000 per pay period. For the period ending July 31, the payroll register would appear as follows:

Name	Filing Status	Dependents	Hourly Rate or Period Wage	Gross Earnings
Rae	MJ	3<17; 1 Other	2,000.00	2,000.00

It is common in a company to have both salaried and hourly employees, and all employees must be represented on a payroll register. Example 4 contains employees with pay variations that commonly exist in business.

EXAMPLE 4: PAYROLL REGISTER FOR MULTIPLE EMPLOYEES

PBL Freight pays its employees on a biweekly basis. The standard workweek for hourly employees is 40 hours, and employees receive overtime pay for any hours worked more than 40 during an established seven-day period. The following payroll register is for the period ending March 17:

Name	Filing Status	Dependents	Hourly Rate or Period Wage	No. of Regular Hours	No. of Overtime Hours	Reg. Earnings	Overtime Earnings	Gross Earnings
Justice	S	1<17	15.25	40		610.00		610.00
Corey	MJ	3<17	2,750.00			2,750.00		2,750.00
Sam	MJ	4<17 1 Other	21.50	40	6	860.00	193.50	1,053.50
Total						4,220.00	193.50	4,413.50

Notice how the columns are totaled in Example 4. Each earnings column is totaled vertically, and the double underline (i.e., ruling) denotes that the computations are concluded. The total in the bottom-right corner proves that the sum of the rows in the Gross Earnings column equals the Regular Earnings and Overtime Earnings columns. Once the payroll register is totaled, proved, and ruled, it is ready for the next step in the payroll process.

The Payroll Register

Stop & Check

1. What is the purpose of the payroll register?
2. What are five of the columns that usually appear in a payroll register?
3. Why are computations for regular hours and overtime hours entered in different columns?

LO 3-6 Apply Combination Pay Methods

Employers often offer *combination pay* methods. Sometimes the employee performs two different jobs for the same employer, and those two tasks have different compensation bases. Other situations involve payroll-based incentives that link to company productivity. Note how the payroll register reflects these combination pay methods in the following examples.

Base Salary Plus Commission

A common method includes a base salary plus a commission or piece rate, depending on the nature of the work performed. Another method is salary plus hourly compensation that reflects a standard set of work hours plus additional hours that are paid only when worked. The combination pay method aims to meet minimum wage requirements and encourage employees to achieve sales or production goals. The base salary offers both the employer and the employee a level of stability in pay amounts because they will know the minimum amount of compensation for each pay period. Whatever the employees earn above the base salary may vary from pay period to pay period, depending on their capabilities, production needs, and customer needs.

EXAMPLE: BASE SALARY PLUS COMMISSION

West is a salaried, exempt employee of Night Lights Security. West is single with two dependents under the age of 17. The compensation package includes a commission based on sales of security system packages to customers. During the pay period ending January 13, West earned $1,500 in salary and a 4 percent commission on $10,000 in sales.

Commission = $10,000 × 0.04 = $400

Name	Filing Status	Dependents	Hourly Rate or Period Wage	Commissions	Gross Earnings
West	S	2<17	1,500.00	400.00	1,900.00

Many types of jobs have a combination pay method because it has been found to boost employee productivity and maintain FLSA compliance. Some jobs that use combination pay methods are:

- District managers
- Recruiters
- Farmworkers
- Account executives
- Retail sales workers
- Real estate salespersons

To compute combination pay methods, it is essential to know how to compute the employee's base salary plus any variable items.

> **EXAMPLE: DIFFERENT COMBINATION METHODS, THE SAME COMPANY**
>
> Avery is an account executive for Bayfront Watercraft. Avery earns a base salary of $36,000 plus a commission of 0.5 percent on each sale made. Avery is married with six dependents: four under the age of 17 and two other dependents. Suppose that Avery sold $100,000 of boats during a biweekly pay period ending June 16.
>
> Base salary = $36,000/26 = $1,384.62.
> Commission = $100,000 × 0.5% = $500.
> Total pay for Avery: $1,884.62
>
> The payroll register for Avery's June 16 pay would appear as:
>
> | Name | Filing Status | Dependents | Hourly Rate or Period Wage | Commissions | Gross Earnings |
> |---|---|---|---|---|---|
> | Avery | MJ | 4<17; 2 Other | 1,384.62 | 500.00 | 1,884.62 |
>
> Dana installs the seating in the boats for Bayfront Watercraft. Dana is single with one dependent under the age of 17 and earns a base salary of $26,000 per year plus a piece rate of $100 for each boat completed during the pay period. During the pay period, Dana installed the seating for eight boats.
>
> Salary = $26,000/26 = $1,000
> Piece-rate pay = $100 × 8 = $800
> Total pay for Dana: $1,800
>
> The payroll register, including both employees for the June 17 pay period, would appear as follows:
>
> | Name | Filing Status | Dependents | Hourly Rate or Period Wage | Piece Rate Pay | Commissions | Gross Earnings |
> |---|---|---|---|---|---|---|
> | Avery | MJ | 4<17; 2 Other | 1,384.62 | | 500.00 | 1,884.62 |
> | Dana | S | 1<17 | 1,000.00 | 800.00 | | 1.800.00 |
> | Totals | | | 2,384.62 | 800.00 | 500.00 | 3,684.62 |

Like any other type of payment method, the important element in computing combination pay is accurate maintenance of the base salary, the variable rate, and the number of items or sales for which the variable rate must apply. The payroll register's use facilitates the computations and ensures the accuracy of the employee's gross pay.

Payroll Draw

A special situation in commission-based pay is a situation called a ***draw***. A draw generally involves an employee whose regular compensation is little more than the minimum wage, such as a retail sales position. Employees have sales goals they must meet and receive compensation on a commission basis once they meet or exceed those sales goals. If the sales goal is not met, the employee may draw a salary against future commissions. The expectation with a draw is that the employee will eventually generate enough sales to cover any draws during pay periods when sales revenues were lower than expected.

> A draw is generally associated with a commission-only job in which the employer allows new employees to receive money for expected future commissions. With a draw, it is implied that the draw may occur regularly. However, paying employees solely based on commission and draw has been challenged because it does not recognize employee rest breaks and nonproductive time. In *Bermudez Vaquero v. Stoneledge Furniture LLC,* the court upheld the FLSA rules regarding mandatory rest breaks.
>
> (Source: MorganLewis)

Salary Plus Commission and Draw

Salaried employees who receive commission may be eligible to draw against that commission at the company's discretion. This pay combination could be for external salespeople who have commissions as a relatively large portion of their regular income.

> **EXAMPLE: SALARY PLUS COMMISSION AND DRAW**
>
> Brooke is an employee in the sales department of Rozz Escape. Brooke is single with one dependent under the age of 17 and has an annual base salary of $12,000, paid monthly. Brooke is expected to earn between $1,000 and $3,000 in sales commissions each month and may draw up to $3,000 per month against future earnings.
>
> During October, Brooke earned $1,000 in commissions in addition to their salary. Brooke decided to take an additional $1,000 draw against future earnings. The payroll register would reflect this compensation as follows:
>
> | Name | Filing Status | Dependents | Hourly Rate or Period Wage | Reg. Earnings | Draw | Commissions | Gross Earnings |
> |---|---|---|---|---|---|---|---|
> | Brooke | S | 1<17 | 1,000.00 | 1,000.00 | 1,000.00 | 1,000.00 | 3,000.00 |
>
> In this case, Brooke could have withdrawn up to $3,000 against future earnings. If the employment is terminated before enough sales commission is earned to cover the draw, then the employee must repay the company the amount not earned. It is important to keep track of employee draws to ensure that the employee repays the unearned draw.

Another example where the company may allow individuals to draw on their payroll exists when the pay period is monthly. In this situation, many employers may allow their employees to draw up to 30 to 40 percent of their wages at mid-month. Some organizations may not withhold taxes from the draw, and the employee will have the full amount of taxes withdrawn upon the next payroll.

Employers must be careful when allowing employees to draw against future wages. A written and signed authorization must be obtained from the employee that specifies when the draw will be deducted from the employee's future wages to avoid legal issues with deductions, such as wage garnishments, that could be affected by the draw.

> **EXAMPLE: SALARY PLUS DRAW, EMPLOYEE INELIGIBLE FOR COMMISSION**
>
> Rowan is a new salesperson with Warm Blu, hired on September 18. Rowan has no dependents, receives a base salary of $19,500 per year, is paid biweekly, and receives a 5 percent commission once a sales quota of $20,000 during a pay period has been reached. During the pay period ending September 29, Rowan closed $10,000 in sales, and thus was ineligible for a September commission. Rowan may draw up to the minimum commission for the pay period, $20,000 × 5%, or $1,000. The payroll register would reflect his pay as follows:
>
> | Name | Filing Status | Dependents | Hourly Rate or Period Wage | Reg. Earnings | Draw | Commissions | Gross Earnings |
> |---|---|---|---|---|---|---|---|
> | Rowan | S | 0 | 750.00 | 750.00 | 1,000.00 | | 1,750.00 |
>
> Period salary = $19,500/26 pay periods = $750.00
> Commission draw = $20,000 × 0.05 = $1,000.00

Incentive Stock Options (ISOs)

Other employee compensation plans, known as *incentive stock options (ISOs)*, allow an employee to report a small base salary for tax purposes and be issued company stock that must be held for a certain period before being sold. In some instances, the stock option may be exercised after three months of employment, and in other cases, it may be after one year of employment. The purpose of ISO stock option plans is a deferral of taxes and salary liabilities for the employer and employee. This type of compensation is often found in executive pay packages.

In the class-action lawsuit *McElrath v. Uber Technologies,* the plaintiff stated that employees were offered an ISO as a significant part of the compensation package. The issue arose because Uber had accelerated the exercisability of its ISOs to make the compensation attractive. However, when employees exercised their options, the company refused to allow employees to receive the promised compensation on a tax-deferred basis consistent with an ISO. Instead, Uber changed the ISOs to nonqualified stock options (NSOs), which changed the taxation on employee compensation.

(Source: Classaction.org)

EXAMPLE: EXECUTIVE SALARY WITH ISO

Raven Wilde was hired as a regional manager with Amificat International. Amificat International's stock had a market price of $25 per share when Raven was hired. Raven was offered an annual salary of $78,000 paid biweekly and an ISO of 1,000 shares at $25 per share that could be exercised one year after the hire date.

Biweekly salary = $78,000/26 = $3,000

Note that the ISO, valued at $25,000 at the time of hire, may not be exercised for one year. The stock option's value would depend on the market price on the date that Raven exercised the stock option by selling the shares. In any case, the ISO does not appear on the payroll register but would be included in the employee's total compensation.

Stop & Check

Combination Pay Methods

1. A service administrator receives a base salary of $42,000 per year paid semimonthly, plus a $100 commission for each service contract sold to customers. During a pay period, five contracts were sold. What is the administrator's gross pay for the period?

2. A new salesperson with S&D Music receives a base salary of $36,000 paid monthly. Company policy allows the salesperson to draw 35 percent of their salary on the 15th of each month. How much will the salesperson receive at mid-month if they elect to take a draw? How much will they receive at the end of the month if they take the 35 percent draw?

3. An executive for Adarma Chemicals receives an annual salary of $75,000 plus an additional 3 percent in an ISO. What is the amount of stock received annually? What is the total annual compensation?

LO 3-7 Explain Special Pay Situations

Compensation laws have many exceptions. According to the FLSA, every aspect of labor legislation, including minimum wage and overtime provisions, has its less common applications. The introduction of new types of knowledge-based employment during the 21st century and the continuance of more traditional agricultural tasks necessitate examining these special pay situations.

Compensatory Time

The FLSA allows public employees to receive *compensatory (comp) time* in place of overtime. According to section **3(s)(1)(c)** of the FLSA, exempt public employees must receive comp time equal to 1.5 times the overtime hours worked. Therefore, if a public employee worked 5 hours of overtime, the comp time awarded must be 7.5 hours.

The private sector often misconstrues comp time. FLSA provisions for comp time are only for public-sector employees, such as government workers, law enforcement, and seasonally hired laborers. Unless specifically designated by a firm's policies, a private-sector employer is not required to offer comp time. Additionally, many private-sector employers offer comp time on a straight-line basis, meaning that they offer the same number of compensatory hours as the number of overtime hours worked. Firefighters, police, and other emergency workers may receive a maximum of 480 comp hours annually; other public-sector employees are eligible for up to 240 hours of comp time based on union-negotiated contracts. Certain union comp time contracts will only cover specific peak periods for the work being performed.

When calculating an employee's gross pay, it is prudent to know any effects that a comp time award may have on overtime pay to ensure that the employee's compensation is accurate.

> **EXAMPLE: PUBLIC EMPLOYEE COMPENSATORY TIME**
> Remy works as an exempt employee of the federal government. During the current pay period, Remy accrued 8 hours of overtime when completing additional work for an absent coworker. According to FLSA regulations, Remy must receive 12 hours of comp time since the position is not eligible for paid overtime as an exempt government employee.

On-Call Time

Some professions require employees to be available for work outside of normal working hours. This availability is known as *on-call time*, and two classes of on-call time exist: on-call at the employer's premises and on-call away from the employer's premises.

- If the employee is required to remain at the employer's premises, the employee's freedom is restricted, and they **must** be compensated for the on-call time.
- If the employee is not restricted to the employer's premises for the on-call time, compensation is **not required**.

> The town of Jay, Maine, began a pilot program in June 2020 during which firefighters received on-call pay to be available 10 hours per day. The purpose of the program was to provide fire department support during daytime hours. Each firefighter receives a stipend of $40 for being on-call in addition to regular pay. Despite the payroll cost, the response time improved, and services became more available for the surrounding towns.
>
> (Source: *Sun Journal*)

In either case, company policy must be specific regarding the conditions of the on-call time. The number of hours specified for on-call compensation must be added to the employee's gross pay. Company policy should also be specific about the pay rate for the on-call time, especially if the pay rate differs from the employee's regular pay rate.

> ### EXAMPLE: ON-CALL TIME
> Aiden works as a service representative for Hon Wolf, an equipment manufacturer. Aiden earns $19.25/hour for a standard 40-hour workweek and is married, filing separately with two dependents under the age of 17. Hon Wolf requires that each service representative rotate on-call duties in one-week increments, during which they remain available for service calls outside of working hours but may otherwise engage in personal activities. During this on-call time, company policy stipulates that on-call service representatives receive two hours of regular pay for each on-call day. Aiden was on-call during the biweekly pay period ending February 25 and would receive 14 hours of additional straight-time pay for the on-call time. The payroll register would reflect the on-call pay as follows:
>
> | Name | Filing Status | Dependents | Hourly Rate or Period Wage | No. of Regular Hours | No. of On-Call Hours | Reg. Earnings | On-Call Earnings | Gross Earnings |
> |---|---|---|---|---|---|---|---|---|
> | Aiden | MS | 2<17 | 19.25 | 80 | 14 | 1,540.00 | 269.50 | 1,809.50 |

Sleep Time, Travel Time, and Wait Time

Although a growing trend toward telecommuting exists, employees have traditionally commuted to and from work. Traveling to and from an office is not a compensable time; however, many employees do not work at a single location. Additionally, many employees travel for their employer's benefit for training or other business requirements. Similarly, employees may be required by their employer to wait, as in the case of a chauffeur or a truck driver. Other employees, such as firefighters or medical personnel, may be required to work 24-hour shifts and be given at least five consecutive hours of paid *sleep time* during that 24-hour period. An agreement between the employer and employee may exclude up to eight hours if the employer provides furnished facilities for uninterrupted sleep.

According to FLSA, the guideline that assists in determining compensable activity in these three situations is if the activity is for the employer's benefit. Travel among customer- or business-related sites are compensable as *travel time* because it directly benefits the employer. Requiring a driver to wait as part of the job description also benefits the employer and is compensated as *wait time*. Traveling from the employee's home to the office or the first customer site in the morning and returning home in the evening benefits the employee and is not compensable. In general, travel required by the employer is compensable (even overnight stays), but the travel from home at the beginning of the day and returning home at the end of the day is not compensable. Exceptions, such as emergency travel or work in another city that requires an unusual amount of travel, are compensable. See **29 CFR 790.6** and **29 CFR 785**.

> ### EXAMPLE: TRAVEL AMONG MULTIPLE JOB SITES DURING A WORKDAY
> Rani is a nonexempt employee who works from home as an equipment repair technician for AB Generators. The job demands travel among customer sites throughout the day. During the course of the day, Rani traveled as follows:
>
> Home to first customer site: 1.5 hours
>
> First customer site to second customer site: 1 hour
>
> Second customer site to third customer site: 2 hours
>
> Third customer site to home: 45 minutes

According to FLSA guidelines, Rani would be paid for the three hours of travel between worksites, but not the 2.25 hours traveling to the first customer worksite and home from the third customer worksite.

EXAMPLE: SLEEP TIME

Monroe is a first-year surgical resident at Mercy Hospital and is classified as a nonexempt employee who earns $124,000 per year, paid semimonthly. The standard workweek is 40 hours. Monroe is single with no dependents and works two 24-hour shifts per week in the regular course of employment. The employer provides a quiet sleeping area, per FLSA requirements. During a single 24-hour shift in the November 17 pay period, Monroe slept 7 hours. According to FLSA guidelines, the pay may not be reduced for the first 5 hours slept. Monroe's gross pay will reflect a 2-hour reduction for the additional sleep over the 5-hour requirement.

The hourly rate needs to be computed to determine the deduction for the excess sleep time: $124,000/(40 × 52) = $59.62 (rounded).

The payroll register would appear as follows:

Name	Filing Status	Dependents	Hourly Rate or Period Wage	Hourly Rate	Sleep Hours >5	Reg. Earnings	Less Excess Sleep Time	Gross Earnings
Monroe	S	0	5,166.67	59.62	2	5,166.67	(119.24)	5,047.43

Note the inclusion of the sleep hours over 5 and the deduction. The purpose of tracking this information is to highlight specific issues with employee performance and related costs, which leads to stronger managerial control.

Jury Duty

Employees may be summoned to serve on a jury for court cases. If an employee is required to serve jury duty, the pay given to employees for the time spent away from work in this capacity is at the employer's discretion. Some employers pay their employees their full compensation, while others pay a predetermined alternate amount. If an employee receives full compensation while on jury duty, the company may require the employee to return or reject the jury duty pay.

Image Source

Vacation and Holiday Hours

Employees commonly have paid time off in the form of holiday or vacation time. Although no legislation exists for the number of holidays observed by a company or the number of vacation hours per employee, the time for these situations should be classified using the payroll register to ensure its annotation in the employees' files. The following examples show how vacation and holiday pay should be annotated.

EXAMPLE: HOLIDAY HOURS

Tanner is an hourly employee at Naira Dram Company, earning $15.60 per hour, paid biweekly on a 40-hour-per-week basis. Tanner is single, has no dependents, and is eligible for two weeks of vacation per year. During one pay period, Tanner took three days of vacation. The payroll register would appear as follows. Notice how the regular hours and the vacation hours are recorded in different columns.

(continued)

(concluded)

	Filing Status	Dependents	Hourly rate or period salary	No. of regular hours	No. of vacation hours	Gross Earnings
Tanner	S	0	15.60	56	24	1,248.00

A similar approach is taken with holiday pay.

In November 2023, Naira Dram Company has holidays on Thursday and Friday, November 23 and 24, to celebrate Thanksgiving. A different employee, Spencer, is a nonexempt salaried employee earning $39,000 annually, paid biweekly. Spencer is married filing jointly and has two dependents under the age of 17. Spencer works five hours of overtime during this holiday period, but not during the week of the holiday. In this case, the annual salary must be converted to hourly pay to determine the amount of overtime pay, although the regular hours and holiday hours remain at the period salary.

Annual Salary = $39,000/ (52 weeks × 40 hours) = $18.75 per hour
Overtime pay = $18.75/hour × 1.5 = $28.13 (rounded) × 5 hours = $140.65

	Filing status	Dependents	Hourly rate or period salary	No. of regular hours	No. of overtime hours	No. of holiday hours	Gross Earnings
Spencer	MJ	2	1,500.00	64	5	16	1,640.63

Subminimum Wage Situations

Tipped employees are not the only workers who may legally receive compensation lower than the minimum wage. Other specific classes of employees may receive an hourly wage that is less than the FLSA minimum wage. Some states have eliminated the subminimum wage entirely or for specific classes of workers, so it is important to remain current with any state law changes.

wavebreakmedia/Shutterstock

A 1996 amendment to the FLSA, described in Section 6(g), allows workers younger than the age of 20 to be paid a minimum wage of $4.25 per hour, but only for the first 90 calendar days of employment.

Note that overtime worked by employees who are paid at subminimum wage rates may not be less than the federal minimum wage.

EXAMPLE: YOUNG EMPLOYEE

Coree is a new employee of Big Chicken, a fast-food restaurant in Glendale, Arizona, where new employees are paid minimum wage. Coree is 18 years of age and is single with no dependents. During the weekly pay period ending July 18, Coree worked 37 hours. The payroll register would appear as follows:

Name	Filing Status	Hourly Rate or Period Wage	No. of Regular Hours	Reg. Earnings	Gross Earnings
Coree	S-0	4.25	37	157.25	157.25

An employer may obtain a certificate to pay a worker with disabilities related to the work performed an amount less than the minimum wage. According to Section 14(c) of the FLSA, employers must obtain a certificate to pay less than the minimum wage.

> **EXAMPLE: DISABLED WORKER**
> Snow is employed as a call-center representative with OEC Dispatch in Provo, Utah. Snow is disabled due to a hearing impairment, and OEC Dispatch has obtained a certificate under section 14(c) of the FLSA to pay Snow $6.10/hour, which is less than Utah's minimum wage of $7.25/hour. During the weekly pay period ending March 10, Snow worked 44 hours, 4 of which were overtime. Snow is single with two dependents. The payroll register for the period would appear as follows:
>
> | Name | Filing Status | Hourly Rate or Period Wage | No. of Regular Hours | No. of Overtime Hours | Reg. Earning | Overtime Earnings | Gross Earnings |
> |---|---|---|---|---|---|---|---|
> | Snow | S-2 | 6.10 | 40 | 4 | 244.00 | 36.60 | 280.60 |

Full-time students in the employ of retail establishments, agriculture, colleges, and universities may receive a wage that is 85 percent of the federal minimum wage under FLSA Section 14(c). Like disabled employees, the employer must obtain a certificate authorizing the subminimum wage.

> **EXAMPLE: FULL-TIME STUDENT WAGE**
> Stone works in the café at Valparaiso University in Valparaiso, Indiana. Stone is a full-time student at the university and is 20 years old, single, with no dependents. According to the FLSA, Stone may receive 85 percent of the minimum wage.
>
> Indiana minimum wage: $7.25/hour
> Full-time student wage = $7.25/hour × 0.85 = $6.16/hour (rounded)
> Stone may legally be paid $6.16 per hour while continuing to be a full-time student. During the week of May 6, Stone worked 35 hours. The payroll register would appear as follows:
>
> | Name | Filing Status | Hourly Rate or Period Wage | No. of Regular Hours | Reg. Earning | Gross Earnings |
> |---|---|---|---|---|---|
> | Stone | S-0 | 6.16 | 35 | 215.60 | 215.60 |

According to **Section 14(a)** of the FLSA, student learners in vocational education programs may be paid at a rate of 75 percent of the federal minimum wage. Similar to situations involving disabled employees, the employer must obtain a certificate authorizing the subminimum wage.

> **EXAMPLE: STUDENT WORKER IN A VOCATIONAL EDUCATION PROGRAM**
> Addison is enrolled at Middlebury High School in Maine and is taking a shop class as part of the school's programs. Addison is 16, single, with no dependents. Addison works for Vining's Cabinets as an apprentice woodworker. After obtaining a certificate from the U.S. Department of Labor's Wage and Hour National Certification Team, Vining's Cabinets pays Addison an hourly wage of $10.35 ($13.80 minimum wage × 75 percent) due to the enrollment in the shop class at the high school. During the weekly pay period ending December 15, Addison worked 36 hours. The payroll register would reflect the pay as follows:
>
> *(continued)*

(concluded)

Name	Filing Status	Hourly Rate or Period Wage	No. of Regular Hours	Reg. Earnings	Gross Earnings
Addison	S-0	10.35	36	372.60	372.60

States have been working to repeal the subminimum wage. As of 2023, the following states have repealed the subminimum wage:

- Alaska
- California
- Colorado
- Delaware
- Maine
- Maryland
- New Hampshire
- Oregon
- Rhode Island
- South Carolina
- Tennessee
- Washington

Other states are currently working to remove the subminimum wage for disabled workers.

(Source: APSE)

Nonqualified Deferred Compensation

Certain employees may be subject to the nonqualified deferred compensation provisions of IRS Code **section 409(a)**. Nonqualified deferred compensation pertains to employees who earn compensation in one period but elect to receive it later. A common example of this practice involves teachers who work during the nine-month academic year but elect to receive compensation for 12 months. Under section 409(a), this type of compensation is taxed like any other employee pay.

Pension Payments

Employers occasionally offer pension plans to their employees. The percentage of employees who participate in employer-sponsored pensions has decreased due to the availability of alternate retirement plans (401(k), 403(b), etc.), and pension funding has experienced shortfalls among both private and governmental employers. When the pension enters the payout period, the retired employee receives the pension less any federal tax due. FICA taxes do not apply to pension plan payments.

Retroactive Pay

If an employee is due retroactive pay ("back pay") because of compensation increases or labor union negotiations, the wages must be issued at the earliest time, and all applicable taxes are due. To receive back pay, the FLSA has three methods available:

1. The Department of Labor's Wage and Hour Division may provide supervision for the payment.

Shutterstock / BOSANESDRA

2. The Secretary of Labor may bring a lawsuit for back pay plus an equal amount of damages.
3. The employee may initiate a lawsuit for the back pay *plus* an equal amount of damages *plus* attorney's fees and court costs.

It is important to note that the statute of limitations for back pay lawsuits is two years. However, if willful nonpayment can be proven, the statute of limitations is three years.

> In early 2019, the Gilroy Federation of Paraeducators in California agreed to grant pay raises to the educational support staff retroactive to July 1, 2017. This pay raise was spread incrementally over two fiscal years to spread the impact on the school district's budget.
>
> (Source: *Gilroy Dispatch*)

Wages for Deceased Employees

If an employee dies while being a current employee of a firm, it is important to understand the payroll implications associated with gross pay. IRS guidelines stipulate that wages earned before the employee's death must be paid as accurately as possible to reflect the amount of work performed. A special note about deceased employee pay is that the employee's pay if issued specifically in a check form may need to be reissued to the deceased employee's estate. In many states, the pay for a deceased employee goes to the surviving spouse or children (if no surviving spouse exists) as long as the pay is below state-mandated thresholds.

Trends to Watch

EMPLOYEE COMPENSATION

Employee compensation tends to be a hot topic because it affects people on a personal level. Some developments since 2019 in employee compensation include the following:

- Increased diligence in overtime tracking and compensation following a lawsuit involving large companies
- New types of incentive pay to increase employee engagement, including merchandise rewards, additional company benefits, and other nonmonetary awards
- Discussions of the legality of differential pay levels for travel time by nonexempt employees
- Discussions about gaps in wages between people with and without a college education
- An increased minimum wage for exempt employees

Future trends to watch include:

- Employee pay including flexible work location agreements
- Rising inflation driving pay increases
- Expanded salary transparency laws
- Variable pay structures increasing to recognize employee contributions
- A federal minimum wage increase to $15/hour by 2026
- Elimination of subminimum wages at the state level

Stop & Check: What Is the Correct Pay?

1. A nonexempt employee of The Silver Club (a governmental entity) works 10 hours of overtime during a pay period and asks to receive compensatory time instead of overtime pay. The Silver Club's overtime policy states that compensatory time may be offered at 1.5 times the number of hours worked more than 40. The employer grants the request and offers 10 hours of compensatory time. How much comp time should they receive? Explain.

2. A student in a vocational program at a cosmetology school accepts employment as a shampooer at Cuts & Styles Hair Salon in Alabama. The agreement between the school and the salon is that students receive the student-learner minimum wage. How much should the student be paid per hour?

Summary of Gross Pay Computation

Gross pay is the employee's compensation before taxes and other withholdings are deducted; net pay is the amount of money an employee receives after taxes and other deductions are subtracted. We discussed the different types of pay computation methods, including salary, hourly, commission, and piece-rate pay. Gross pay is complex, and various combinations exist to meet the needs of traditional, hybrid, and gig economies.

We looked at the effect of FLSA provisions and the applicability of different compensation methods and offered examples of some job classifications that could be compensated using different methods. We discussed using a payroll register in computing gross pay and explored the concepts of the total, prove, and rule to ensure accurate computation of gross pay.

We explored a variety of situations involving overtime pay and discussed the computations for different pay bases. We concluded with a discussion of special compensation situations, including on-call time, time spent unoccupied for the employer's benefit, and situations in which an employee may receive less than the FLSA minimum wage. The conclusion had an explanation of retroactive pay and other less-common pay situations.

Key Points

- Gross pay is the total amount earned by an employee before the deductions for taxes or other withholdings.
- Employees may be subject to the wage and hour provisions of the FLSA (nonexempt), or they may not (exempt), depending on the type of job and employee duties.
- Nonexempt hourly employees are compensated on the basis that recognizes an economic connection between work performed and wages paid.
- Nonexempt salaried employees work a fixed number of working hours per week and receive overtime compensation.
- Exempt employees receive a fixed salary and may work more hours than their nonexempt colleagues.
- Commission-based pay connects employee compensation with sales revenue.
- Piece-rate pay compensates employees based on the manufacturing or completion of goods or services.
- The payroll register is an integral tool to ensure the accuracy of payroll computations, especially in combination pay situations.
- Employees who work on a commission basis may have the option to draw against future earnings.

- ISOs are a means of offering compensation on a tax-deferred basis connected to the market price of the company's stock.
- Compensatory time is legally required for public-sector exempt employees and may be offered to private-sector employees at the employer's discretion.
- Overtime pay is computed according to the IRS guidelines, as appropriate to the employee's pay base.
- Employees may be compensated when they are unoccupied if they are required to be available for the employer's benefit.
- Retroactive "back pay" and pension pay are situations requiring additional care in processing to avoid lawsuits.
- In certain circumstances, employees may receive less than the FLSA minimum wage.

Vocabulary

Combination pay
Compensatory (comp) time
Draw
Eight and Eighty (8 and 80)
Gross pay
Hourly
Hundredth-hour system
Incentive stock option (ISO)

Net pay
Nonexempt
On-call time
Overtime
Prove
Quarter-hour system
Rule
Salary

Sleep time
Time card
Tip credit
Tipped employee
Tipped wage
Total
Travel time
Wait time

Review Questions

1. How is overtime pay computed for nonexempt, salaried workers?
2. For which employees do overtime rates apply?
3. How does minimum wage affect commission employees?
4. How does the tipped minimum wage differ from the FLSA minimum wage?
5. What types of occupations are typically salaried?
6. What is an ISO, and how does it affect employee pay?
7. What is the difference between a salary and a draw?
8. How is overtime computed for piece-rate employees?
9. In what situations could a salaried employee receive overtime pay?
10. What is the primary difference between commission work and piece-rate work?
11. In what situations might an employee draw money against his or her future pay?
12. What is the difference between quarter-hour and hundredth-hour pay?
13. Why are companies moving toward the hundredth-hour system?
14. What is comp time?
15. Under what circumstances may an employee receive compensation for on-call time?
16. When are wait time, travel time, and sleep time compensable?
17. Aside from tipped employees, under what circumstances may an employee receive less than the FLSA minimum wage?
18. What is one of the three methods for employees to receive retroactive pay?
19. What amount did the Final Rule stipulate as the minimum wage for salaried workers?
20. How must tipped employees report the tips they receive each month?

Exercises Set A

E3-1A.
LO 3-1

A minimum wage worker in Nevada is contemplating a move to another state. Which of the following states would be the most favorable in terms of the highest minimum wage? (Select all that apply.)
1. Idaho
2. California
3. Utah
4. Arizona

E3-2A.
LO 3-1

FLSA provisions always cover certain types of businesses. Which of the following businesses are always covered by FLSA? (Select all that apply.)
1. Fruit stands selling only locally obtained goods that conduct no interstate business
2. A school for children with learning disabilities
3. A privately run hospital
4. A Social Security Administration branch office

E3-3A.
LO 3-1

What is the minimum tipped wage for a tipped employee in Washington, DC?
1. $2.13/hour
2. $3.25/hour
3. $4.55/hour
4. $5.35/hour

E3-4A.
LO 3-1

A server at the Seven Wonders Restaurant in Honolulu, Hawaii, receives the tipped minimum wage. During a 40-hour workweek, how much must be earned in tips to meet the minimum wage requirement?
1. $30.00
2. $40.00
3. $75.20
4. $125.30

E3-5A.
LO 3-2

An employee of HyroSports is compensated based on sales of store products to customers. Which type of pay best represents this basis?
1. Piece rate
2. Hourly
3. Commission
4. Salary

E3-6A.
LO 3-3

The accounting clerk at Tenity Enterprises is paid $18.15 per hour. During a week's pay period, the employee worked 39 hours and 41 minutes. Based on a hundredth-hour pay method, what is the gross pay for the period? (Round the final answer to two decimal places.)
1. $726.00
2. $721.46
3. $716.93
4. $720.25

E3-7A.
LO 3-4

According to the FLSA, what is the basis used to determine overtime worked for standard nonexempt workers?
1. The 8 and 80 rule
2. The excess over 40 hours during any pay period
3. The excess of over 40 hours in seven consecutive days
4. The excess over 8 hours in a 24-hour period

E3-8A.
LO 3-4

A shared employee for Tetra Computers works in both the programming and the research departments and splits time equally between the roles. The employee earns $20 per hour in the programming department and $28 per hour in the research department. What is the pay rate if the employee worked overtime in the research department?
1. $30 per hour
2. $36 per hour
3. $42 per hour
4. $48 per hour

E3-9A.
LO 3-5

Of the items in the following list, which one(s) should appear in a payroll register? (Select all that apply.)
1. Name
2. Home address
3. Shifts worked
4. Hours worked

E3-10A.
LO 3-5

Mikah is a salaried, exempt employee with CaxKyat Stores. Mikah is single with one dependent under 17 and earns $35,568 per year. Complete the payroll register for the biweekly pay period ending March 10, 2023, with a pay date of March 15, 2023.

P/R End Date:										
Check Date:							Company Name:			
Name	Filing Status	Dependents	Hourly Rate or Period Wage	No. of Regular Hours	No. of Overtime Hours	Commissions	Reg. Earnings	Overtime Earnings	Gross Earnings

E3-11A.
LO 3-6

Latan is an employee of Giant Computers, where the job responsibilities include selling computers and software to customers. Latan is married and filing jointly with two dependents under 17. The annual salary is $42,000, and Latan receives a 3 percent commission on all sales. During the semimonthly pay period ending September 29, Latan sold $20,000 worth of computers and software. Complete the payroll register for the September 29 pay period with a pay date of October 4.

P/R End Date:										
Check Date:							Company Name:			
Name	Filing Status	Dependents	Hourly Rate or Period Wage	No. of Regular Hours	No. of Overtime Hours	Commissions	Reg. Earnings	Overtime Earnings	Gross Earnings

E3-12A.
LO 3-7

Jude is a full-time student working in the library at Sioux City College in Sioux City, Iowa. What is the minimum hourly wage that Jude may receive?
1. $7.25 per hour
2. $6.50 per hour
3. $6.16 per hour
4. $5.44 per hour

Problems Set A

P3-1A.
LO 3-3

Brick worked the following schedule: Monday, 9 hours; Tuesday, 7 hours 30 minutes; Wednesday, 8 hours 48 minutes; Thursday, 8 hours 25 minutes; Friday, 8 hours. The employer pays overtime for all time worked in excess of 40 hours per week. Complete the following table. Determine Brick's total time worked according to (a) the quarter-hour method and (b) the hundredth-hour method. Which is the more favorable method for Brick, quarter-hour or hundredth-hour?

	Quarter-Hour Time	Hundredth-Hour Time	More Favorable Method
Brick			

P3-2A.
LO 3-2

Bobi is a salaried exempt employee at Coric Industries. Bobi is married and filing jointly with two dependents under 17. The contract stipulates a 40-hour work week at $47,500 per year. During the week ending November 24, there was a company-paid holiday for one day. Calculate Bobi's weekly pay. Round period wages to five decimal points.

Name	Filing Status	Dependents	Hourly Rate or Period Wage	No. of Regular Hours	No. of Holiday Hours	Reg. Earnings	Holiday Earnings	Gross Earnings

P3-3A.
LO 3-2

Casey finished designing 22 custom cakes on an 18-cake contract as an employee of Yuan Fox Wedding Planners. There is a bonus earned if the individual exceeds 145 percent of their piece-rate contract. How many cakes must Casey complete in the remainder of the week to receive the bonus?

P3-4A.
LO 3-5

Lann works for Talbert Electronics. As a shared employee, Lann works in the manufacturing department and has been trained to work the sales counter when needed. During this period Lann was asked to work the sales counter for two days, five hours each day during other employees' vacations. Lann earns $17.75 per hour in the manufacturing department and a $1.50 pay differential for working the sales counter. There was a total of 38 hours and 38 minutes worked during the week. Lann is married filing jointly with no dependents. Compute Lann's pay for the week ending August 18 using the hundredth-hour system. (Use a separate line for each job classification.)

Name	Filing Status	Dependents	Hourly Rate or Period Wage	No. of Regular Hours	Reg. Earnings
Total Pay					

P3-5A.
LO 3-3

Winter submitted a pay card reflecting the following hours worked at Kicy, Inc. Winter earns $16.02 per hour. The company pays overtime only on hours worked exceeding 40 per week. The company is considering changing from quarter-hour to hundredth-hour time collection. Under the current quarter-hour system, each time the employee clocks in or out, the time is rounded to the nearest quarter-hour. Calculate Winter's time for both the quarter-hour and hundredth-hour systems. (Round your intermediate calculations and final answers to two decimal places.)

In	Out	In	Out	Total Hours with Quarter-Hour	Total Hours with Hundredth-Hour
8:00	11:22	12:17	5:22		
7:29	12:30	1:45	4:10		
9:12	11:45	12:28	3:36		
8:00	11:00	12:02	5:00		

What is Winter's total pay in a quarter-hour system? _____
What is Winter's total pay in a hundredth-hour system? _____

P3-6A.
LO 3-4

Rey is a nurse at Central City Hospital and is paid $32.50 per hour for a 40-hour standard workweek. During the biweekly pay period from January 9–20, Rey worked a total of 87 hours. What is Rey's gross pay?

P3-7A.
LO 3-5

Terry, a single employee with two dependents under the age of 17, is paid $12 per hour and receives a commission on net sales for a company in Russelville, Oklahoma. No commission is received until net sales exceed $150,000. Once the minimum net sales are reached, the 4 percent commission on sales applies. During the week of January 27, there were $87,000 of sales; however, there were $2,250 of returns from the prior week's sales. Company policy requires that commissions on sales returns are deducted from the employee's pay, regardless of current commission earnings. Compute Terry's gross pay for the 40-hour weekly pay period.

Name	Filing Status	Dependents	Hourly Rate or Period Salary	No. of Regular Hours	Reg. Earnings	Commissions	Gross Earnings

P3-8A.
LO 3-1, 3-2

Shawn, an outside sales representative for Marosh Communications in Caldwell, Idaho, receives a 20 percent commission on all new marketing packages sold within the sales territory. During the week of April 6, there were $9,700 of new subscriptions sold during 40 hours of work.
What is Shawn's gross pay?
Are the wages subject to minimum wage laws?
Why or why not?

P3-9A.
LO 3-1, 3-2

Telemarketers receive a $15 commission on all new customers that sign up for cell phone service through Movill Networks in Mississippi. Each telemarketer works 40 hours. The company ran a competition this week to see who could sign up the largest number of new customers, and the winner would get a bonus of $75. Because these employees are paid solely on commission, the employer must ensure that they earn the federal minimum wage for 40 hours each week. Compute the gross pay for each of the following outbound sales representatives.

Employee	Number of New Customers Signed	Total Commission	Difference between Commission and Minimum Pay (if the minimum is not met)	Total Gross Pay
A	25			
B	18			
C	23			
D	15			

P3-10A.
LO 3-1, 3-2

Each of the following workers is a piece-rate worker at Golden Boats in Connecticut. If the employees have a standard 40-hour workweek, what is their effective hourly wage? Based on the state's minimum wage in Connecticut, calculate each employee's minimum weekly pay. What is the difference the employer must pay between the calculated gross pay and the calculated state's minimum pay if any? (Reminder: Divide gross pay by 40 hours to determine the hourly wage.)

Worker	Number of Items	Rate per Item	Gross Pay	Gross Pay/ 40 Hours	Minimum Pay	Difference to Be Paid by the Employer
P	25 boat hulls	$25				
Q	150 seat covers	$10				
R	15 steering mechanisms	$24				

P3-11A.
LO 3-4

Corey, a nonexempt salesperson with Verent Enterprises, earns a base annual salary of $30,000 with a standard 40-hour workweek. In addition, a 3 percent commission on all sales during the pay period applies. During the weekly pay period ending August 25, Corey closed $25,000 in sales and worked four hours of overtime. What is the gross pay for the period?

P3-12A.
LO 3-1, 3-2, 3-4

Reed is a waiter at Albicious Foods in South Carolina. Reed is single with one other dependent and receives the standard tipped hourly wage. During the week ending October 20, 2023, 44 hours were worked, and Reed received $210 in tips. Calculate Reed's gross pay, assuming tips are included in the overtime rate determination.

Name	Filing Status	Dependents	Hourly Rate or Period Wage	Overtime Rate	No. of Regular Hours	No. of Overtime Hours	Reg. Earnings	Tips	Overtime Earnings	Gross Earnings

Does Albicious Foods need to contribute to Reed's wages to meet FLSA requirements? _____
If so, how much should be contributed? _____

P3-13A.
LO 3-5

Parker is a salaried, nonexempt administrator for Forise Industries and is paid biweekly. The annual salary is $63,000 with a standard workweek of 40 hours. During the pay period ending February 3, 2023, Parker worked eight hours of overtime. Parker is married filing jointly with two dependents under the age of 17. Complete the following payroll register for Parker's pay. (Round intermediate calculations to two decimal points.)
What is Parker's regular wage for the pay period? _____
What are the overtime earnings? _____
What is Parker's gross pay?

Name	Filing Status	Dependents	Period Salary	Hourly Rate	No. of Regular Hours	No. of Overtime Hours	Reg. Earnings	Overtime Earnings	Gross Earnings

P3-14A.
LO 3-7

Rico Musgrove is an 18-year-old worker in the receiving department of Trynix, Inc. in Alabama. Rico received $170.00 gross pay for 40 hours of work on the first paycheck. Did the employer pay Rico correctly? Explain.

Exercises Set B

E3-1B.
LO 3-1

A minimum wage worker in Oklahoma is contemplating moving to a state with a more favorable minimum wage. Which of the following states should be chosen? (Select all that apply.)
1. Texas
2. Arkansas
3. Louisiana
4. New Mexico

E3-2B.
LO 3-1

Which one of the following workers is covered by FLSA provisions? (Select all that apply.)
1. Factory manager for an international company
2. Part-time babysitter earning $1,000 annually
3. Professional chauffeur earning $25,000 annually
4. Assistant fire chief for a small town

E3-3B.
LO 3-1

Caelen is a tipped employee at Wild Waves in Maine. What is the minimum tipped wage for the area, assuming receipt of tips in excess of $30 per pay period?
1. $9.35/hour
2. $2.13/hour
3. $6.90/hour
4. $8.25/hour

E3-4B.
LO 3-1

Brett is a waitperson at a diner in Vermont. Brett earns the tipped minimum wage. During a 40-hour workweek in February 2023, how much must Brett earn in tips to satisfy the minimum wage requirement (without consideration of the tip credit)?
1. $85.20
2. $263.60
3. $190.00
4. $349.80

E3-5B.
LO 3-2

Amari is an interior designer for Only Qex Designs. Amari is paid based on the number and complexity of the customer designs generated. What pay basis most accurately describes this compensation?
1. Hourly
2. Commission
3. Piece rate
4. Salary

E3-6B.
LO 3-3

Dorian is a stocker at a factory outlet, paid hourly earning $12.45 per hour. During a one-week period, Dorian worked 39 hours and 19 minutes. How much would the gross pay be under the quarter-hour system? (Round your final answer to two decimal places.)
1. $485.55
2. $488.66
3. $489.49
4. $491.78

E3-7B.
LO 3-4

What are the two methods an employer may use to determine a tipped employee's overtime compensation?
1. Compute gross pay based on the minimum cash wage plus tips.
2. Compute gross pay based on an average of the minimum cash wage and the maximum tip credit.
3. Compute gross pay based on the minimum cash wage, excluding tips.
4. Compute gross pay based on the minimum cash wage multiplied by the overtime rate (i.e., 1.5).

E3-8B.
LO 3-4

Beasley is a salaried nonexempt accounting clerk contracted to work 40 hours per week. How should overtime be determined, according to FLSA?
1. Any hours worked in excess of 40 during a consecutive 7-day period
2. Any hours worked in excess of 45 during a consecutive 7-day period
3. Any hours worked in excess of 80 during a consecutive 14-day period
4. Any hours worked in excess of 45 during a consecutive 14-day period

E3-9B.
LO 3-5

Of the following items listed, which ones should appear in a payroll register? (Select all that apply.)
1. Gross pay
2. Hourly rate
3. Period ending date
4. Office number

E3-10B.
LO 3-4, 3-5

Cax is an hourly employee, single with no dependents, and earns $16.25 per hour. During a biweekly pay period ending February 17, Cax worked 88.5 hours. Complete the payroll register with the period's information, assuming a 40-hour week. (Note: Round overtime rate computation to three decimal places. All earnings should be rounded to two decimal places.)

Name	Filing Status	Dependents	Hourly Rate	Overtime Rate	No. of Regular Hours	No Overtime Hours	Regular Earnings	Overtime Earnings	Gross Earnings

E3-11B.
LO 3-6

Ret is an employee earning a base salary of $27,200 plus an 8 percent commission on all sales. Ret is married filing jointly with four dependents, three under 17 and one other. During the biweekly pay period that ended June 16, Ret made $15,000 in sales. Complete the payroll register for the pay period.

Name	Filing Status	Dependents	Period Salary	Sales	Reg. Earnings	Commission Earnings	Gross Earnings

E3-12B.
LO 3-7

Averill is 18 years of age, and a new employee in Hendersonville, Tennessee. What is the minimum hourly wage that may be received during the first 90 days of employment?
1. $9.47 per hour
2. $2.13 per hour
3. $7.25 per hour
4. $4.25 per hour

Problems Set B

P3-1B.
LO 3-3

Andy worked the following schedule: Monday, 7 hours 42 minutes; Tuesday, 8 hours 23 minutes; Wednesday, 9 hours 28 minutes; Thursday, 8 hours 12 minutes; Friday, 8 hours 6 minutes. The employer pays overtime in accordance with FLSA regulations. Determine the total time worked according to the (a) quarter-hour method and (b) the hundredth-hour method. Which is the more favorable method, quarter-hour or hundredth-hour?

	Quarter-Hour Time	Hundredth-Hour Time	More Favorable Method
Anders			

P3-2B.
LO 3-2

Kenete is a salaried exempt employee at Big State College with a contract that stipulates 35 hours per week at $57,000 per year. Kenete is married, filing jointly, with two dependents under 17. The pay period ending December 1 contained two company-paid holidays. Calculate Kenete's biweekly pay based on a standard five-day workweek. Round wages to five decimal points. (Hint: Determine Kenete's hourly wage to determine holiday pay.)

Name	Filing Status	Dependents	Period Salary	Hourly Rate	No. of Regular Hours	No. of Holiday Hours	Reg. Earnings	Holiday Earnings	Gross Earnings

P3-3B.
LO 3-2

Egon completed 1,750 pieces on a 2,000-piece contract. There is a bonus earned if the individual exceeds 115 percent of the piece contract. How many more pieces must Egon complete in the remainder of the pay period to receive the bonus?

P3-4B.
LO 3-4, 3-5

Charlie is a shared employee who works in the accounting department and has been trained to work at the front desk in times of need. During one weekly pay period, Charlie was asked to work at the front desk for four days for five hours each day. Charlie earns $17.26 per hour in the accounting department and $13.75 per hour for working at the front desk. Charlie worked a total of 45 hours during the week. Complete the payroll register using separate lines for each job classification, and place the overtime in the accounting department.

Name	Filing Status	Hourly Rate	No. of Regular Hours	No. of Overtime Hours	Reg. Earnings	Overtime Earnings	Gross Earnings

P3-5B.
LO 3-3

Devin earns $15.30 per hour at Jolly Creamery. Compute the pay under both the hundredth-hour and quarter-hour systems. The company is considering switching from a quarter-hour method to a hundredth-hour method. Devin submitted the following time card. (Hint: Convert times to a 24-hour clock for ease of computation.)

In	Out	In	Out	Total Hours with Quarter-Hour	Total Hours with Hundredth-Hour
8:10	11:54	12:47	4:52		
9:02	12:23	1:11	5:07		
7:52	11:48	12:52	4:21		
7:58	12:18	1:06	5:17		

Devin's total pay in the hundredth-hour system: _____
Devin's total pay in a quarter-hour system: _____
Which is the most beneficial for Devin? _____

P3-6B.
LO 3-4

Hayden is the concierge at Hotel Amize and is a nonexempt employee earning $18 per hour plus a $250 biweekly bonus based on customer reviews. During the pay period of November 26 through December 9, Hayden worked 85 hours and earned the entire bonus. What is Hayden's gross pay for the pay period, assuming a 40-hour standard workweek?

P3-7B.
LO 3-4, 3-5

Pat is married, filing jointly with two other dependents, is paid $17.25 per hour and receives a commission on sales. No commission is paid out until sales exceed $60,000. Once the minimum sales have been reached, a 7 percent commission on sales applies. For the week ending June 10, Pat worked 48 hours and sold $75,000 of medical supplies. Compute Pat's gross pay for the week.

Name	Filing Status	Dependents	Hourly Rate or Period Wage	No. of Regular Hours	No. of Overtime Hours	Commissions	Reg. Earnings	Overtime Earnings	Gross Earnings

P3-8B.
LO 3-1, 3-2

An outside sales representative in Albuquerque, New Mexico, receives a 4 percent commission on all new policies in the sales territory. During the pay period ending April 14, $150,000 of new policies were sold during 40 hours of work.
What is the gross pay? _____
Is this subject to minimum wage laws? _____
Why or why not? _____

P3-9B.
LO 3-1, 3-2

Outbound sales representatives at Alindu Magazines in Arizona receive a $20 commission on all new customers they sign up for new magazine subscriptions. Each Outbound sales representative works 40 hours. During a weekly competition, the Outbound sales representative who sold the most subscriptions was awarded a $125 bonus. Because these employees are paid solely on commission, the employer must ensure that they earn the federal minimum wage for 40 hours each week. Compute the gross pay for each of the following Outbound sales representatives and the difference when the commission pay is less than the gross pay at minimum wage.

Employee	New Customers Signed	Total Commission	Gross Pay at Minimum Wage	Difference between Commission and Minimum Pay (if the minimum is not met)
F	35			
G	19			
H	42			
I	29			

P3-10B.
LO 3-1, 3-2

Determine the gross pay for each of the piece-rate workers at Perigen Snowsports. If the employees have a standard 37.5-hour workweek, determine their effective hourly rate. Based on the minimum wage for New Hampshire, what is the minimum wage they must receive each week? If they are not receiving the FLSA minimum wage for the pay period, what is the difference that must be paid by the employer? (Remember: Effective hourly rate equals the gross pay divided by 37.5 hours.)

Worker	Number of Items	Rate per Item	Gross Pay	Gross Pay/ 37.5 Hours	Minimum Pay	Difference to Be Paid by the Employer
S	25 snowboards	$9.00				
A	30 helmets	$7.75				
L	80 bindings	$4.50				

P3-11B.
LO 3-4

A piece-rate employee receives $30 for each desktop computer assembled and has a standard 40-hour workweek. During the weekly pay period ending December 15, 48 computers were assembled during 44 hours, all of which are productive hours. What is the gross pay for this period?

P3-12B.
LO 3-1, 3-2

Parker is the concierge at the Trans-Canada Resort in Michigan. Parker is single with one other dependent and receives the standard tipped hourly wage for the state. During the week ending June 2, Parker worked 40 hours and received $105 in tips. Compute Parker's pay for the period.

Name	Filing Status	Dependents	Hourly Rate or Period Wage	No. of Regular Hours	Reg. Earnings	Tips	Gross Earnings

Does the Trans-Canada Resort need to contribute to Parker's wages to meet FLSA minimum wage requirements? _____
If so, how much must the employer contribute? _____

P3-13B.
LO 3-5

Preethi is a salaried, nonexempt administrative assistant and is paid semi-monthly. Preethi is married filing jointly with five dependents under 17. Annual salary is $65,000 with a standard workweek of 37.5 hours, and the employer will pay overtime for excess hours over 37.5. During the pay period, 10 hours of overtime were worked. Compute the gross pay for the period ending August 18.

Name	Filing Status	Period Salary	Hourly Rate	Overtime Rate	No. of Overtime Hours	Reg. Earnings	Overtime Earnings	Gross Earnings

P3-14B.
LO 3-7

A 19-year-old accounting clerk with Quijen Accounting Solutions (there is not a state minimum wage) received $369.75 for the first biweekly pay covering 87 regular hours. Did the employer pay the clerk correctly? Explain.

Critical Thinking

3-1. West Virginia State University has a policy of hiring students to work in its bookstores and cafeterias. Assuming that 138 students work for the university at minimum wage rates, what is the total amount of pay they will receive for a biweekly pay period, assuming each works 30 hours per week?

3-2. You are the owner of Veiled Wonders, a firm that makes window treatments. Some merchandise is custom-made to customer specifications, and some are mass-produced in standardized measurements. There are production workers who work primarily on standardized blinds and some employees who work on custom products on an as-needed basis. How should you structure the pay methods for these production workers?

In the Real World: Scenario for Discussion

Many states offer incentives to hire individuals with physical or mental disabilities. When doing so, the employer must receive a specific waiver allowing them to pay sub-minimum wage. This can be a great outreach for the employer in assisting the disabled community to obtain independence and a sense of self-worth.

Review two state agencies, determine the wages that may be paid to workers with disabilities, and what benefits two different states have. What federal incentives are there for hiring disabled workers?

Internet Activities

3-1. Using a search engine such as Google, Yahoo, or Bing, search "commission-based pay." Sites such as the Society for Human Resource Management (www.shrm.com) have many articles about commission-based pay and workplace cases. Choose a case and find out as much as you can about the company involved. Why do you think that commission-based pay is such a popular topic among human resource professionals?

3-2. Go to www.accountingtools.com/podcasts and look for payroll-related podcasts. Once you have listened to one or more podcasts, what do you feel was the most interesting information you learned?

3-3. Want to learn more about the concepts in this chapter? Check out

www.dol.gov/whd/minwage/america.htm

www.flsa.com/coverage.html

http://webapps.dol.gov/elaws/otcalculator.htm

3-4. Would you like to watch a video to learn more about FLSA's treatment of minimum wage, hours worked, and overtime? Check out the following links:

Topic 2: Minimum Wage

Topic 4: Hours Worked

Topic 5: Overtime

Continuing Payroll Project: Prevosti Farms and Sugarhouse

The first day of work for Prevosti Farms and Sugarhouse for all employees is February 1, 2023. February 10 is the end of the first pay period and includes work completed during the week of February 1–10 (weekdays only). Compute the employee gross pay using 40 hours as the standard workweek for all employees except Mary Shangraw, who works 20 hours per week and receives overtime for any time worked past that point per company policy. The other hourly employees receive overtime pay when they work more than 40 hours in one week. Joel Schwartz has made $5,000 in case sales at a 3 percent commission rate during this pay period. Remember that the employees are paid biweekly. The pay frequency for federal income tax purposes is biweekly. For nonexempt employees, over 64 hours (8 days at 8 hours per day, except Shangraw who works 4 hours per day) in the first payroll will be overtime.

February

Sunday	Monday	Tuesday	Wednesday	Thursday	Friday	Saturday
			1	2	3	4
5	6	7	8	9	10	11
12	13	14	15	16	17	18
19	20	21	22	23	24	25
26	27	28				

When determining the amount an exempt employee receives for partial weeks, take their salary divided by the number of weeks times days worked. Annual salary: $35,000/(52 × 5) = $35,000/260 = $134.61538 (rounded to five decimal points) per day. Once you have a per-day rate, multiply it by the number of days worked. Exempt employee salary information is as follows:

Name	Annual Salary	Notes
Millen	$35,000	
Lewis	$32,000	
Schwartz	$32,000	plus 3% commission on sales
Prevosti	$45,000	

The hours for the nonexempt employees are as follows:

Name	Hourly Rate	Hours Worked 2/1–2/10	Regular Time Pay	Overtime Pay	Gross Pay
Towle	$15.00	64 hours			
Long	$15.00	66 hours			
Shangraw	$15.00	32 hours			
Success (You)	$16.35	65 hours			

Complete the payroll register for the period's gross pay. Pay will be disbursed on February 14, 2023, starting with check number 6628.

February 24, 2023, is the end of the final pay period for the month and is a full biweekly payroll. Schwartz has sold $7,500 of products during this pay period at a 3 percent commission. Complete the payroll register for the period's gross pay. Pay will be disbursed on February 28, 2023, and check numbers will continue from the prior payroll.

The hours for the nonexempt employees are as follows:

Name	Hourly Rate	Hours Worked 2/11–2/24	Regular Time Pay	Overtime Pay	Gross Pay
Towle	$15.00	83 hours			
Long	$15.00	80 hours			
Shangraw	$15.00	42 hours			
Success (You)	$16.35	81 hours			

P/R End Date:

Check Date:

Company Name: _____

Name	Filing Status	Type and Number of Dependents	Hourly Rate or Period Wage	No. of Regular Hours	No. of Overtime Hours	No. of Holiday Hours	Commissions	Gross Earnings	Sec 125	401(k)	Taxable Wages for Federal and State W/H
Totals											

Name	Gross Earnings	Taxable Wages for Federal and State W/H	Taxable Wages for FICA	Federal W/H	Social Security Tax	Medicare W/H	State W/H Tax	Garnishment	United Way	Net Pay
Totals										

Answers to Stop & Check Exercises

Pay Your Employees Correctly

1. No. Pai should have received time-and-a-half for the additional 8 hours. Her pay should have been $667.00 [(80 × 7.25) + (8 × 1.5 × 7.25)].
2. $523.38 (rounded) (39.5 × 13.25)
3. $677.76 (32 × 2 × 10.59)
4. $746.25 (75 × 9.95)

Computations for Different Bases

1. $6,744.00 ($224,800 × 3%)
2. $1,100.00. Yes, because $1,100.00/90 hours = $12.22 per hour. South Carolina has no dictated minimum wage, so federal minimum wage would apply.
3. The current pay would be lower when the employee does not have paid leave available. An employee with paid leave would only have classification differences but would receive their full pay.

Standard salary per biweekly payroll: $57,000/26 = $2,192.310769
($57,000/(40 × 26 × 2)) = $27.40384 per hour × (8 × 3) for unpaid leave of $657.69216
Current pay $2,192.30769 − 657.69216 = $1,534.62 (rounded)

Quarter-Hour vs. Hundredth-Hour

1. A:
   Quarter-hour: 8.25 hours
   Hundredth-hour: 7.93 hours
   B:
   Quarter-hour: 8 hours
   Hundredth-hour: 8.12 hours
   C:
   Quarter-hour: 8 hours
   Hundredth-hour: 7.82 hours
2. The difference exists because the time worked during a quarter-hour system is rounded to the nearest quarter-hour. In a hundredth-hour system, the worker is paid for the exact number of minutes worked.
3. It would be beneficial to adopt a hundredth-hour system to reduce payroll inaccuracies that may affect both employees and company profits.

How Does Overtime Affect Gross Pay?

1. FLSA Section 7(j) covers the overtime rules for hospital and residential care facilities and would fall under the 8 and 80 rule.
2. Since the commissions do not represent more than half of her pay, they have no effect on overtime earnings.
3. This employer could include tips by adding them to gross pay based on the cash wage. This total with tips becomes the hourly rate used to determine overtime earnings. The other method would be to exclude the tip income, using the cash wage only as the basis for overtime computations.

The Payroll Register

1. To document the employees' time and hours worked as well as to provide totals of the compensation by each category.
2. Student answers should include five of the following: Name, marital status, number of withholdings, hourly rate, number of regular hours, number of overtime hours, commission, piece rate, regular earnings, overtime earnings, and gross earnings.
3. To facilitate calculations of regular and overtime, help ensure accuracy, and allow for analysis of overtime worked.

Combination Pay Methods

1. Base pay = $42,000 ÷ 24 = $1,750
   Commission = $100 × 5 = $500
   Gross pay = $2,250

2. $36,000 ÷ 12 = $3,000 per month
   $3,000 × 0.35 = $1,050 mid-month draw
   $3,000 − $1,050 draw = $1,950 received at the end of the month
3. $75,000 × 0.03 = $2,250 received in stock
   Annual compensation = $75,000 + $2,250 = $77,250

What Is the Correct Pay?

1. 15 hours because compensatory time must be awarded at 1.5 times regular hours.
2. $5.44 per hour ($7.25 × 75%)

Chapter Four

Fringe Benefits and Voluntary Deductions

Fringe benefits are noncash forms of compensation that employers use to reward an employee for company service. Examples of fringe benefits include the use of a company car, health and life insurance, dependent care, gym memberships, and many other perks offered as a privilege of working for a particular employer. Employers are not required to offer fringe benefits, and the presence of certain benefits serves as an incentive for potential employees to join the company. By offering fringe benefits, an employer can avoid the need to rely on high salary and wage amounts to attract employees and build morale. However, the cost of offering fringe benefits can impede the company's cash flow. The challenge is to provide a salary and fringe benefit package that attracts the desired employees at a manageable cost.

The IRS classifies fringe benefits as deductible from an employee's pay on either a pre-tax or a post-tax basis, depending on the type of benefit. Pre-tax deductions reduce the employee's current taxable income and may be taxed at a later time; for example, contributions to a qualifying retirement program would be a pre-tax deduction. Other fringe benefits are deducted from an employee's compensation after computing taxes, making the perk a post-tax benefit. The IRS clearly differentiates between taxable and non-taxable fringe benefits in Publication 15-B.

LEARNING OBJECTIVES

After studying Chapter 4, you should be able to:

LO 4-1	Define Fringe Benefits within the Context of Payroll
LO 4-2	Interpret Cafeteria Plan Types
LO 4-3	Describe Fringe Benefit Exclusion Rules
LO 4-4	Explain Fringe Benefit Valuation Rules
LO 4-5	Differentiate between Pre-tax and Post-tax Deductions
LO 4-6	Apply Rules for Withholding, Depositing, and Reporting Benefits

fizkes/ShutterStock

Employers Must Integrate Benefit Programs into Company Culture

With the expansion of hybrid work arrangements, it has become imperative for employers to integrate benefit offerings to match the company culture. One way to achieve this integration is to include employees in the benefits planning because of the disconnect that can occur when employers offer benefits without knowing employee needs. Employers need to include benefit topics in company meetings to remind employees of benefits they may have forgotten.

Wellness benefits are a significant topic that employees may overlook during their day-to-day work challenges. "Soft" benefits such as flexible work schedules, massages, and financial counseling are popular among employees and lead to better retention. One issue with the flexible work schedules that could be solved by integrating benefits more intentionally into company culture is the "out of sight, out of mind" phenomenon that occurs. Normalization of working from remote locations and team building events that include remote workers could alleviate the problem and keep employers aware of talented employees when internal job openings arise. One thing is certain: An increase in soft benefits leads to employee satisfaction.

(Sources: EBN, SHRM)

> **Despite the additional cost involved, fringe benefits are an important part of attracting and retaining high-quality employees. We will explore different types of fringe benefits and their treatment for payroll purposes in Chapter 4.**

LO 4-1 Define Fringe Benefits within the Context of Payroll

stoatphoto/Shutterstock

Payroll has been said to be the intersection of human resources and accounting because of the need to include employee information and record all financial transactions involving work performed. Fringe benefits are an extension of that notion because these benefits are rewards given to employees in return for their service to the company. The correlation between employee satisfaction and retention is often a result of the employer's fringe benefits.

The term *fringe* was applied to these noncash benefits because they were insignificant in total employee *compensation*. Over time, the Bureau of Labor Statistics has found that fringe benefits actually constitute an additional 25–33 percent of an employee's annual compensation. Despite the inherent monetary value, the importance of fringe benefits is best seen in terms of employee satisfaction, and long-term increases in revenue and net income. This section will examine the purpose of fringe benefits and the treatment of this form of noncash compensation as it pertains to pay and taxation.

Purpose of Fringe Benefits

Employees have often been considered one of the costs of conducting business. The employer's obligation to pay employment taxes and supply additional benefits to entice employee engagement was viewed as a necessary, albeit expensive, part of its financial structure. Research conducted during the past decade has found that the advantages gained from providing fringe benefits far outweigh the related costs in terms of employee productivity, creativity, and revenue production.

Starting in September 2021, a significant number of employees have left their jobs looking for many things, including flexibility, comprehensive benefits, and a supportive, caring culture. To employers, what this is looking like is an increase in mental health focus, steady wages, and benefits that can foster empathy while maintaining profitability.

Employers should continually introduce new or expanded benefit plans to attract, develop, and keep good employees, especially during and after COVID. Examples of companies offering such benefits include:

- PricewaterhouseCoopers and Fidelity Investments have benefits packages that include mental health and child care to support employees who work from home.
- Noodles & Company offered a program called LifeAtNoodles that included a wide range of benefits, including expanded, flexible time off, wellness initiatives, family planning, and other incentives.
- Prudential included education and support to teach coping methods during the pandemic.
- Domino's offered employees an option to receive their pay on demand at the end of daily work shifts.

In addition to a company's existing benefits, it has been noted that adding an extra benefit each year, no matter how small, goes a long way toward employee retention. Simple ideas such as the addition of a day to bring your dog to work cost the employer nothing, but the payoff in morale is huge.

(Sources: Employee Benefits News[1], Employee Benefits News[2])

Hallmarks of fringe benefits include the following indicators:

- All employees have access to the benefit because of their working relationship with the employer.
- Employees enjoy improved living conditions as a result of the benefit.

- The ability to receive the benefit is not related to employee performance.
- Fringe benefits supplement employees' cash compensation.
- These benefits may be deducted either pre- or post-tax.
- Fringe benefits promote the welfare of all employees.
- Legislative treatment of fringe benefits involves certain mandatory tax deductions from employee pay.

Fringe benefits may be included in employee pay, although they are not part of the cash compensation package. It is important to note fringe benefits are taxable unless they are specifically excluded per *Publication 15-B*. In the next section, we will explore how fringe benefits appear on an employee's pay advice.

Including Benefits in Pay

In Chapter 3, we discussed the computation of employee gross pay. Some fringe benefits may increase employee pay and could be taxable. Examples of this include but are not limited to employer-provided vehicles, mileage, leasing, and commuting. The items to be included in gross pay are valued at the level as if they were purchased through a third party, often referred to as an arms-length transaction.

> State laws regarding fringe benefits, while based on IRS regulations, may vary regarding paid sick time and paid time off. Furthermore, employees must receive an annual notice that contains details about balances accrued in sick time and paid time off categories. Employers are not required to disburse cash compensation for the accrued time at termination and can decide if the unused time may be rolled over to the next year.
>
> As a result of the COVID-19 pandemic, the landscape of fringe benefits has changed to support differences in employee needs. Health plans were redesigned to address employees' mental and financial health needs. Diversity and inclusion programs were recognized as vital elements of employee benefits programs. This new breed of benefits has been termed "lifestyle benefits" because it can be individualized to meet employee needs.
>
> (Sources: BenefitsPro; Employee Benefit News)

Fringe Benefits and Payroll Taxes

Certain fringe benefits change tax calculations, such as Federal withholding, Medicare, or Social Security taxes. Others do not affect the calculation for taxes and are considered post-tax benefits. The IRS requires that all fringe benefits that involve deductions from pay or for which the employee contributes part of regular compensation must be listed explicitly on the employee's *pay advice*. A sample pay advice is contained in Figure 4-1. The affected deductions include Federal withholding (W/H), SSI, Medicare, and State withholding (W/H), and the fringe benefits include pre-tax insurance and 401(k) voluntary deductions.

An exception to this requirement involves *de minimis* benefits. *De minimis* benefits include items with a value that is so minimal that accounting for it would be unnecessary. These items include an occasional coffee or an isolated postage stamp, both relatively small in value. However, it should be noted that when *de minimis* items become a regular benefit, such as a cup of coffee every day, instead of an occasional one, then the value aggregates to become a sum that could be treated as taxable income.

De minimis benefits, according to IRS Publication 15-B, have such minimal accounting value that the accounting for it is deemed impractical. Examples of *de minimis* benefits include (but are not limited to):

- Employee use of a company copier, as long as personal use does not exceed 15 percent of the employee's total usage of that equipment for business purposes.

FIGURE 4-1
Sample Pay Advice

Hazlitt Industries						
2210 Secours Way						
Springfield, MA 02312						199203
Stephen Torrisi			Date		11/05/20XX	
One-thousand one-hundred twenty-two and 77/100				dollars		1,122.77

Payee: Stephen Torrisi
Address: 3230 Longview Drive
City/State Zip: Agawam, MA 02249   Signed: *Mitchell North*

Payroll End Date	10/31/20XX	Payroll Pay Date	11/05/20XX	Check:	199203
Employee Name	Stephen Torrisi	Employee Number	42850	Rate	21.50

Description	Earnings	YTD Gross	Description	Deductions	YTD Deductions
Regular	1,720.00	32,680.00	Federal W/H	275.47	5,233.93
Holiday			SSI	106.64	2,026.16
Commissions			Medicare	24.94	473.86
			State W/H	88.58	1,683.02
			Pretax Insurance	50.00	950.00
Total Earnings	1,720.00	32,680.00	401(k)	51.60	980.40
			Total Deductions	597.23	11,347.37

- Noncash, low-value holiday or birthday gifts.
- Similar gifts for family illnesses or birth celebrations.
- Group-term life insurance for the death of a dependent if the life insurance face value does not exceed $2,000.
- Certain meals, occasional picnics, and parties for employees and their guests.
- Occasional tickets to sporting or theater events.
- Personal use of an employer-provided cell phone is provided primarily for non-compensatory business purposes.

Notice that *de minimis* benefits are generally classified as occasional use. If the use of a fringe benefit becomes more than occasional, such as season tickets to sporting or arts events or club memberships, the benefits are not considered *de minimis*.

(Source: IRS)

Benefits offerings often constitute the difference when a jobseeker is choosing between employers. The type and amount of benefits offerings communicate the work culture, can attract talent, and affect employee engagement and productivity.

(Source: ADP)

FIGURE 4-2
Fringe Benefits and Payroll Tax Treatment (IRS Publication 15-B)

Type of Fringe Benefit	Income Tax Exempt	FICA Taxes Exempt	FUTA Tax Exempt
Accident and health benefits*	XX	XX	XX
Achievement awards (up to $1,600 for qualified plan awards, $400 for nonqualified)	XX	XX	XX
Adoption assistance	XX		
Athletic facilities owned or leased by the employer†	XX	XX	XX
De minimis benefits	XX	XX	XX
Dependent care assistance (up to $5,000 annually)	XX	XX	XX
Education (i.e., tuition) assistance (up to $5,250 annually)	XX	XX	XX
Employee discounts (various limits apply)	XX	XX	XX
Employee stock options (depending on the type of option)	XX	XX	XX
Employer-provided cell phone (if not otherwise compensated)	XX	XX	XX
Group-term life insurance	XX	XX‡	XX
Health savings accounts (HSAs) for qualified individuals	XX	XX	XX
Lodging on the employer's premises (for the employer's convenience as a condition of employment)	XX	XX	XX
Meals (exempt if *de minimis* or for employer convenience on employer premises)	XX	XX	XX
No-additional-cost services	XX	XX	XX
Retirement planning services	XX	XX	XX
Transportation benefits (commuting and rail passes up to $300, exempt if *de minimis*)	XX	XX	XX
Tuition reduction for undergraduate education (graduate if the employee engages in teaching or research)	XX	XX	XX
Working condition benefits	XX	XX	XX

*Does not include long-term care benefits if they are included in flexible spending accounts.
†Exempt if substantially all use during the calendar year is by employees, their spouses, and their dependent children. The facility is on the employer's premises or a location owned or leased by the employer.
‡Up to cost of $50,000 of coverage. The excess over $50,000 must appear on the employee's Form W-2.
(Source: IRS)

Voluntary fringe benefits have two basic types of treatments regarding payroll taxes: They may be deducted either before or after *mandatory deductions* (i.e., taxes) have been calculated. The IRS specifies which fringe benefits may be deducted on a pre-tax basis and which must be treated as post-tax deductions in Publication 15-B, which is updated annually. Employers are responsible for promptly remitting amounts withheld for fringe benefits and reporting annual totals to employees on Form W-2. Figure 4-2 details the types of fringe benefits and their payroll tax treatment.

EXAMPLE: FRINGE BENEFIT
Rylan is an employee of Cohen Corporation, a company that offers undergraduate educational assistance as a fringe benefit. According to the IRS, the first $5,250 of Rylan's tuition assistance is not subject to payroll taxes. In 2023, Rylan received reimbursement from his employer of $7,250 in education assistance. The additional $2,000 is taxable income for Rylan.

Ground Picture/Shutterstock

Fringe Benefits 101

Stop & Check

1. What are the two main categories of fringe benefits?
2. Which of the following benefits is not considered a fringe benefit? (Use Figure 4-2 as a reference.)
   a. Educational assistance for undergraduate students
   b. Group-term life insurance over $250,000
   c. Overtime hours worked during the year
   d. Cell phones for business purposes
   e. Retirement planning services
3. Which of the following fringe benefits would also be exempt from Social Security and Medicare taxes?
   a. Working condition benefits
   b. Adoption assistance
   c. Qualified health savings accounts

LO 4-2 Interpret Cafeteria Plan Types

Rocketclips, Inc./Shutterstock

The Internal Revenue Code has a special program to assist workers with necessary healthcare expenses. Section 125 of the IRS code was initially enacted in 1978 and has been revised several times. It permits employers to offer employees a choice between two or more cash and qualified benefits. The employer must explicitly describe the plan benefit, rules governing the benefit, and ways to pay for and obtain the benefits. Employee-elected deductions for qualified cafeteria plan benefits are withheld on a pre-tax basis.

> Examples of qualified insurance benefits include:
> - Accident and health benefits.
> - Long-term care benefits.
> - Group-term life insurance (including costs not excluded from wages).
> - Health savings accounts (HSAs).

Cafeteria plans, also known as Section 125 plans, are offered by the employer and are usually deducted on a pre-tax basis to make employer-sponsored benefits more affordable for employees. In essence, a cafeteria plan allows employees to convert fringe (i.e., noncash) benefits into tax savings. Although they often pertain to health coverage, cafeteria plans may also include dependent care and other expenses. Participation in cafeteria plans potentially saves employees upward of 7.65 percent (the FICA taxes) and may save more money, depending on their income tax bracket. If an employee chooses to receive benefits under the cafeteria plan, this does not convert a fringe benefit to a taxable one.

Premium-Only Plan (POP)

A *premium-only plan (POP)* is a type of cafeteria plan that allows employees to deduct premiums for employer-sponsored group insurance on a pre-tax basis. Deducting the premium

TABLE 4-1
Types of Insurance that May Be Included in a Premium-Only Plan

Health	Dental	Vision
Prescription	Cancer	Medicare supplement
Accident	Disability	Hospital indemnity
Employee group-term life*		

*Employee group-term life insurance premiums are subject to a limit of $50,000 per employee and may be subject to a 10-employee minimum.

on a pre-tax basis allows the employee to have a lower tax liability. A list of POPs that employers may provide and that are subject to Section 125 pre-tax provisions is provided in Table 4-1. Note that not all employers offer all types of insurance coverage.

Employers benefit from offering POPs because employee premiums deducted on a pre-tax basis reduce the employer's FICA tax liability. Offering pre-tax deductions for group insurance coverage as part of their employee benefits package is also beneficial to employers because participation in health plans has been correlated with reductions in employee sick time and related healthcare costs. POPs allow employees to offset the cost of rising healthcare premiums by allowing employees to deduct the premiums on a pre-tax basis.

> **EXAMPLE: PRE-TAX DEDUCTION OF HEALTH INSURANCE PREMIUM**
>
> Stevie Hollins, an employee of Wolfe & Associates, has the option to deduct her health insurance premium on a pre-tax basis. She consulted her payroll accountant about the difference between pre-tax and post-tax premium deductions and received this analysis:
>
> | | Pre-Tax vs. Post-Tax Premium Deduction | |
> |---|---|---|
> | | Pre-Tax | Post-Tax |
> | Period gross pay | $2,500 | $2,500 |
> | Health insurance premium | 250 | 250 |
> | Taxable income | $2,250 | $2,500 |
>
> The pre-tax deduction would lower taxable income, resulting in less federal, state, and local income tax deducted from Stevie's pay.

Flexible Spending Arrangement (FSA)

Another benefit that can be included in the cafeteria plan is a *flexible spending arrangement (FSA)*. FSAs are available to assist in the payment of medical expenses, including certain co-payments and prescriptions, transportation, and certain childcare expenses. According to IRS **Publication 502**, examples of includible medical expenses are:

- Acupuncture
- Ambulance service
- Automobile expenses when traveling for medical purposes
- Braille books and magazines
- Chiropractor services
- Hearing aids
- Lead-based paint removal
- Wheelchairs

It should be noted that any employee contributions to an FSA over $3,050 annually (2023 amount) are treated as taxable income. The FSA's purpose is not to defer taxable income or to avoid paying taxes but to reduce the financial burden of healthcare costs.

Cafeteria plan-based FSAs generally have a "use it or lose it" provision, meaning that any unused funds at the end of the plan year may not be accessed afterward. However, the IRS permits employers to roll over up to $500 annually per employee at the employer's discretion. Because of the Taxpayer Certainty and Disaster Tax Relief Act of 2020, the FSA carryover increased to 20 percent of the allowable contribution for plans starting after 2020 for COVID-related expenses. The employee would need to submit documentation that the expenses were related to COVID.

> **EXAMPLE: FSA EFFECT ON ANNUAL GROSS SALARY**
>
> For plans that have a year starting after December 31, 2022, the maximum annual amount an employee may contribute to an FSA offered under Section 125 is $3,050 per person. As an example, Frankie is an employee of Kuzmeckis Doors, earns $50,000 annually, and elects to contribute $2,700 of her annual pay to an employer-sponsored FSA. Her taxable pay would be reduced as follows:
>
> $$\text{Annual pay} - \text{FSA election} = \$50{,}000 - \$2{,}700 = \$47{,}300$$
>
> Frankie has $500 remaining out of her annual FSA election at the end of the calendar year. Her employer allows her to carry over the balance to next year and requires that it be spent by March 15. She would need to spend the remaining balance on qualified medical expenses and provide documentation as required to support the expenditures. The employee would forfeit any amount remaining from the prior year after March 15.

One benefit of cafeteria plans is that employees may choose two or more benefits that consist of cash and noncash elements. For example, they may elect to have health insurance premiums *and* a flexible spending arrangement deducted on a pre-tax basis.

> **EXAMPLE: PRE-TAX VS. POST-TAX WITH A FLEXIBLE SPENDING ARRANGEMENT (FSA)**
>
> Harley can contribute to an FSA for annual out-of-pocket medical expenses and decides to use that to meet cafeteria plan requirements. Harley is paid semimonthly and decides to contribute $3,000 to a qualified FSA. The taxable income would be as follows:
>
> | | Pre-Tax vs. Post-Tax | Premium Deduction |
> | --- | --- | --- |
> | | Pre-Tax | Post-Tax |
> | Period gross pay | $2,500 | $2,500 |
> | Health insurance premium | 250 | 250 |
> | FSA ($3,000/24) | 125 | -0- |
> | **Taxable income** | **$2,125** | **$2,250** |
>
> Note the difference between the taxable incomes in both situations. The use of pre-tax deductions can significantly reduce Harley's tax liability.

> Healthcare costs have been rising, and they affect households differently, depending on their income. The following graph depicts how healthcare costs have contributed to people's stress. For people with lower levels of income, approximately 60 percent indicated an increased level of financial stress due to healthcare costs.

Percentage of U.S. adults reporting the cost of healthcare for them and their family contributed a lot or some to their stress of 2021, by income

Income	Percentage
<$24K	60%
$24K≤$48K	63%
$48K≤$90K	56%
$90K≤$120K	48%
$120K≤$180K	41%
$180K+	32%

(Source: Gallup)

Health Savings Account (HSA)

Another type of cafeteria plan is a *health savings account (HSA)* that can pay for qualified medical expenses. It is important to note that HSAs may only be used in conjunction with a cafeteria plan by employees with a *high-deductible health plan (HDHP)*. The 2023 definition of a high-deductible health plan includes the following deductible limits:

- $1,500 annual deductible (self-coverage)
- $3,000 annual deductible (family)
- $7,500 out-of-pocket expenses maximum (self-coverage)
- $15,000 out-of-pocket expenses maximum (family)

FSA vs. HSA

FSA	HSA
Must be offered by an employer.	Only permitted for employees with an HDHP (see deductible rules).
Independent contractors do not qualify.	Independent contractors do not qualify.
Employees may elect to contribute up to $3,050.	Employees may contribute to HSAs as follows: • $3,850 (single) • $7,750 (married) • $1,000 (additional catch-up amount for employees over age 55)
Employees may use any amount of the annual contribution at any time, regardless of how much they have contributed for the year.	Functions like a bank account in that the employee owns the funds contributed, although employers may also contribute funds.
The employer owns the plan, and the employer may retain unused balances in annual contributions.	All funds contributed are the property of the employee.
Employers can decide if they want to give employees a grace period (up to March 15 of the following year in most cases) to use annual elections.	Unused funds roll over each year and continue to grow with the account. Unused funds do not affect the yearly contribution limits.
Employees must provide receipts or provide evidence to support used funds.	Employees may not access more funds than they have contributed to the HSA.
FSA contributions are reported on the W-2.	Employees must report all used funds with their personal income tax returns.
Annual contributions must be elected each year.	Employees may change their annual contribution at any time.

One aspect of HSAs that differentiates them from FSAs is that the amounts employees contribute to an HSA may remain in the account for use later in life. These funds may be reserved for medical costs and long-term care and are not taxable when used for medical expenses. Money withdrawn for nonmedical expenses is subject to income taxes. Another difference is that anyone with an HDHP may establish an HSA with a trustee, even if their employer does not offer the benefit. However, not all HSAs can be considered tax-exempt. Only HSAs included as part of the company's qualifying Section 125 cafeteria plan are deemed exempt from Social Security, Medicare, and federal income taxes.

Sashkin/Shutterstock

> HDHPs are a way for employers to offer affordable insurance premiums for their employees. However, many employees have delayed care or have reported increased out-of-pocket costs while using an HDHP. Other employees with an HDHP reported that their employer offered no other healthcare option. Employees with an HSA as part of their HDHP noted an increase in their appreciation for the plan and its flexibility for future use.
>
> (Source: PR Newswire)

With HSAs, the money contributed to the account may roll over from year to year as long as the employee is part of an HDHP. Certain HSA plans allow participants to invest money in mutual funds or other investments. It should also be noted HSAs do not have the same restrictions for spending as FSAs.

Employers may make tax-exempt contributions to their employees' HSAs as long as they make comparable contributions to all company employee accounts according to the category or coverage and the employment category (e.g., full-time, part-time). Employer contributions to HSAs are exempt from federal income tax, FICA, and FUTA because sums contributed are not considered employee wages.

> An issue with cafeteria plans is the exclusion of sole proprietors, partners, and shareholders in an S corporation who have greater than a 2 percent share in the company, and members of limited liability companies (LLCs) who elect to be taxed as partnerships. According to Section 125, these individuals may not participate in a cafeteria plan. The problem is that 73 percent of business owners fall into one of these exclusions, which means that many people cannot participate in qualified cafeteria plans, missing out on the tax benefits.
>
> (Source: Financial Regulation News)

What Is Served in the Cafeteria Plan?

Stop & Check

1. Which of the following types of insurance may be included in a POP?
    a. Cancer
    b. Vision
    c. Auto
    d. Dental
2. What are two of the differences between FSAs and HSAs?
3. What constitutes an HDHP?

LO 4-3 Describe Fringe Benefit Exclusion Rules

Remember that fringe benefits are noncash compensation. We have discussed the tax treatment of benefits deducted from employee income on a pre-tax basis using a cafeteria plan. Other fringe benefits may not be included in a cafeteria plan and are generally not reported as compensation. Employers routinely offer these excluded fringe benefits, and payroll accountants need to understand specific tax rules to represent them accurately on employee W-2s.

Excluded fringe benefits exist that are not part of a cafeteria plan and, despite the cash value, do not generally constitute a taxable portion of employee pay. The value of these fringe benefits is exempt from federal income tax, FICA taxes, and FUTA tax and is not reported on the employee's W-2. Figure 4-2 contains specific details of fringe benefit exclusions and limitations of the exclusions. This section will examine fringe benefits not specifically addressed in *Publication 15-B* that are commonly offered by companies.

Prizes and Awards

Workplace prizes and awards are ways for employers to influence employee morale by offering noncash rewards for winning competitions and achieving milestones such as company tenure. In Publication 15-B, the cash-value limit on achievement awards is $1,600 annually for those given in accordance with a qualified plan; the limit for nonqualified awards is $400. A *qualified plan* is one that considers all employees equally, not favoring highly compensated employees. For the purposes of the following examples, assume that all achievement awards are on a qualified plan. According to IRS Publication 535, these types of achievement awards are for improvements to safety programs and the longevity of service to the employer. The following example contains some context for achievement awards.

Tony Tallec/Alamy Stock Photo

ACHIEVEMENT AWARDS
Logan is a sales employee at Austin Trailers and Motorsports. The company offers achievement awards regularly to reward sales employees for achieving safety goals and longevity of service. All sales staff members are eligible for these awards, including the company officers.

NONTAXABLE ACHIEVEMENT AWARD
On April 5, 2023, Logan won a noncash, quarterly achievement award valued at $500 for achieving the highest safety record during May. According to Publication 15-B, this achievement award would not be reported on Logan's W-2 as taxable income.

TAXABLE PORTION OF ACHIEVEMENT AWARD: NONCASH AWARD
As of December 29, 2023, Logan had won the quarterly award for compiling a comprehensive safety plan on four separate occasions during the calendar year. The total value of the achievement awards is $500 × 4, or $2,000. Because the achievement awards received exceeded $1,600, the additional $400 ($2,000 − $1,600) would be reflected as taxable income on Logan's W-2.

TAXABLE PORTION OF ACHIEVEMENT AWARD: CASH AWARD
In addition to winning the noncash prizes for safety achievement, Logan received cash of $1,000 for 10 years of service to the company. As the awards' values are now $3,000, the excess of the value over $1,600 (i.e., $1,400) will be reflected as taxable income. Remember that cash awards are always taxable income to the employee.

Gym Memberships

Employee discounts for gym memberships are a common fringe benefit that employers use to promote wellness initiatives. If the employer has on-site athletic facilities (either on the employer's premises or other premises owned or leased by the employer) that are restricted to

Kzenon/Shutterstock

use by employees, their spouses, and their dependents, the benefit would be nontaxable. However, if an employer provides gym memberships to off-site clubs at no additional cost to employees, the gym membership cost is taxable even on a qualified plan. Likewise, if the athletic facility is open to the public and employees and their dependents, the value of the membership would be taxable.

> **EXAMPLE: OFF-SITE GYM MEMBERSHIP**
> Carlie is an employee of Althea Productions. The employer offers memberships at a local gym as an optional benefit for employees. These memberships are at no additional cost to the employee and have a $75 per month cash value. Because the gym membership has an annual value of $900 and is not an on-site athletic facility, it must be counted as income and reported on Carlie's Form W-2.

Personal Use of Company Vehicle

Company cars are a common fringe benefit given to employees who regularly drive as part of their job. Business use of these company cars is considered a nontaxable fringe benefit because it is an asset provided to the employee for use that specifically benefits the company, much like a computer or office equipment. The taxable portion occurs when the employee uses the company-provided vehicle for personal business. Employers often request that employees document personal use of the business vehicle at the end of the calendar year to identify taxable income associated with the company car properly.

Mark Dierker/McGraw-Hill Education

> In the case of *Scott v. Scott,* an issue that arose was the value of fringe benefits used to determine the defendant's income for use in divorce proceedings. The plaintiff contended that the use of a company truck was not calculated into the value of the defendant's income that was used as the basis for calculating child support. Upon reviewing the defendant's total compensation, including all fringe benefits, the Supreme Court of Georgia found that the defendant's actual monthly income was substantially more than previously stated and increased the monthly child support obligation.
>
> (Source: Justia)

Gift Cards

If an employee received gift cards as a fringe benefit, the gift cards' cash value must be included as compensation on the employee's Form W-2. For example, if an employee entered a company-sponsored raffle at company functions during the year and won a $100 gift card to a local restaurant, the $100 must be added as compensation to the employee's Form W-2. There is no minimum amount of cash or cash equivalent gift cards that would be excluded under *de minimis* fringe benefits.

Employer-Provided Snacks and Meals

Employers often have coffeemakers and kitchen facilities available for employees. If the employer *occasionally* provides food or beverage as an employee perk, the benefit's cash value is considered *de minimis* and is not taxable. However, if the employer routinely provides food or beverages for employee consumption at no additional charge to the employees, then the cash value of those items must be reported as compensation on the employee's Form W-2.

Emilija Manevska/Moment/Getty Images

> **EXAMPLE: PIZZA FRIDAYS**
> Devin works for Excellent Embroidery and Screen Printing. On Fridays, the company provides a pizza lunch for all employees. The pizza lunch is intended to promote employee morale on Fridays and to celebrate weekly accomplishments. Although the weekly value of Friday pizza per employee of Excellent Embroidery is small, it aggregates to an additional $100 per employee over a year. Devin would see an additional $100 in compensation added to Form W-2 for this noncash fringe benefit.

Keep in mind that fringe benefits may appear in many different forms. The payroll accountant needs to be aware of the perks offered to employees and Publication 15-B guidelines. This publication fosters awareness of potential additions to employee compensation and provides accurate reports to employees and governmental authorities.

> For a fringe benefit to be excluded, the employer must be prepared to prove that providing the benefit, not simply adding it to employee gross pay, substantially improves conditions at the firm. For example, the addition of an on-site gym must provide significant benefits above what it would cost employers to add the amount associated with a gym membership to employee pay. Proving that the benefit is substantial could include tracking the number of employees who use the on-site facility versus those who request and use an external gym membership.
>
> (Source: Mondaq)

Stop & Check — Excluded Fringe Benefits

1. Glazier Foods, Inc., provides an athletic facility on the premises for employees to use. Would this benefit be taxable on employees' W-2? Why or why not?
2. Parker is an employee of the Moeller Gallery, and she has a company-issued vehicle to use to conduct business. Does this vehicle represent a fringe benefit? Why or why not?

LO 4-4 Explain Fringe Benefit Valuation Rules

Now that we have an idea about what fringe benefits are and how they fit into a payroll context, it is time to address specific rules about fringe benefits valuation. As noted in the case of *Scott v. Scott,* the value of fringe benefits potentially increases the total value of an employee's income without directly affecting the cash they receive. Note that the details for fringe-benefit valuation rules appear in Publication 15-B and are updated annually.

Proper valuation of vehicles is essential for benefits evaluation. Employers must know the value of the benefits they provide to ensure that they withhold appropriate amounts of tax for the use of company property such as vehicles.

Zoran Zeremski/Shutterstock

General Valuation Rule

The *general valuation rule (GVR)* is the most common way to determine the value of fringe benefits. The GVR uses *fair market value (FMV)* as the cornerstone of valuation. Fair market value is defined as the price a person would need to pay to obtain a good or service from a third party in an arm's-length transaction. In other words, if an employee needed to obtain a gym membership, the price paid for that individual membership would constitute the fair market value. In this section, we will explore different applications of the GVR with explanations of the method used to determine the value for payroll reporting purposes.

Personal Use of Company Vehicle: Lease-Value Rule

Access to a company car can present a challenge in evaluating the amount associated with the personal use of the asset. To compute the value of the employee's personal use of the asset, the IRS uses a complex method that involves the car's age, the fair market value of the asset, and miles driven. Three primary methods exist for determining value: the *lease-value rule*, the *commuting rule*, and the *cents-per-mile rule*. Figure 4-3 contains an example of how a company could derive the valuation using the lease-value method. Publication 15-B does provide an annual lease amount for vehicles. After the annual amount of the lease has been determined, the amount is then multiplied by the percentage of personal use of the vehicle. This amount is considered taxable income to the employee. When the employer provides the vehicle's fuel, this must also be included in the previous calculations. Employer-paid fuel is calculated at FMV or 5.5 cents per mile of personal use. If the employer does not provide fuel, then there is no addition to the calculation for fuel.

In the form provided in Figure 4-3, the employee, Leith Ofir, claims the use of a company car for personal reasons for a total of 25 percent during the calendar year. By obtaining the data requested in the form and computing the fringe benefit's value, Leith has received $2,312.50 in noncash compensation for this fringe benefit. The company has also provided fuel for the vehicle (at 5.5 cents per mile), and the number of personal miles is used to compute the personal value of fuel consumption. The total value of this benefit for Leith is $2,492.97 and must be added to Form W-2 as compensation.

FIGURE 4-3
Value of the Personal Use of a Company Car: Lease-Value Rule

Cold Naira Artisanal Brands

Worksheet to Calculate Personal Use of Company Vehicle

(Lease-Value Rule)

Employee Name: ____Leith Ofir____

Vehicle Make: ____Toyota____   Vehicle Year: __2022__

Vehicle Model: ____RAV4____

Odometer Mileage on the First Day of Use During the Year: ____5,250____

Odometer Mileage on the Last Day of Use During the Year: ____18,375____

Annual Lease Method

Fair Market Value of Vehicle: ____$34,850____

Annual Lease Value: ____$9,250____ (Use Table 3-1 in Publication 15b)

Enter Number of Days Available for Use During the Year: ____365____

Divide by the Number of Days in the Tax Year: ____365____

Prorated Annual Lease Percentage: ____100.00%____

Prorated Annual Lease Value: ____$9,250____

Percent of Personal Use During the Year (from employee statement): ____25%____

Personal Annual Lease Value: ____$2,312.50____ (Prorated Annual Lease Value x % Personal Use)

If fuel is provided by the employer, enter personal miles: 3,281.25x $0.055/mile[1] = **$180.47**

Total Personal Use Taxable Income: ____$2,312.50 + 180.47 = $2,492.97____

[1]Fuel provided by company is valued at $0.055 per mile for personal use purposes.

Note: The number of personal miles is computed by determining the total miles driven during the year (18,375 - 5,250 = 13,125 miles), then multiplying that total by the percentage of personal use (13,125 × 25% = 3,281.25 miles).

Personal Use of a Company Vehicle: Commuting Rule

Like the situation in the lease-value rule, the employee has a company vehicle for use. However, the commuting rule applies to employees strictly forbidden from using the vehicle outside of work hours and for personal purposes. The vehicle is only available for transport to and from work and during the workday. Under the commuting rule, the employee computes the number of miles driven for commuting to and from work and multiplies that by $1.50 to determine the valuation for this fringe benefit. Figure 4-4 contains an example of how this rule is applied, assuming an 18-mile round-trip commute done each day of the week.

In Figure 4-4, we see that providing a company car and charging an employee based on the number of miles in the commute can lead to a higher fringe benefit valuation than seen in the lease-value rule.

Personal Use of a Company Vehicle: Cents-per-Mile Rule

Another way to determine a company car's value as a fringe benefit is to use the IRS standard mileage rate. This rate is updated each year. For 2023, the rate is $0.655 per Publication 15-B. The cents-per-mile rule uses the number of personal miles driven and multiplies it by the standard mileage rate to determine the fringe benefit's value. The purpose of the cents-per-mile rule is to consider the costs of maintenance and insurance for the vehicle, both of which may increase for the company when the vehicle is driven for personal purposes. Figure 4-5 contains an example of applying the cents-per-mile rule.

The choice of company car valuation method rule determines the company's policy and the vehicle's actual use in terms of total miles driven for business, the value of the asset, and the primary user of the vehicle. Publication 15-B contains specific details for the payroll accountant to determine which method is the most appropriate. No matter which method is chosen, it is important to be consistent in the application of personal vehicle use valuations.

Unsafe Conditions

A special rule applies if a company vehicle is provided to an employee only because of unsafe conditions. This rule's foundation is that the employee would walk, bicycle, or use public transportation under normal conditions. An example of an unsafe condition in which this rule may apply would be in the event of a sudden snowstorm that makes the employee's normal travel mode unsafe. In this case, the IRS rule is that the employee is charged $1.50 for a one-way commute (i.e., to or from home), and this charge should be either subtracted from the employee's wages or reimbursed to the company by the employee.

Scherbinator/Shutterstock

FIGURE 4-4
Value of the Personal Use of a Company Car: Commuting Rule

Cold Naira Artisanal Brands

Worksheet to Calculate Personal Use of Company Vehicle

(Commuting Rule)

Employee Name: Leith Ofir

Vehicle Make: Toyota   Vehicle Year: 2022

Vehicle Model: RAV4

Odometer Mileage on the First Day of Use During the Year: 5,250

Odometer Mileage on the Last Day of Use During the Year: 18,375

Commuter Rule

Number of miles driven for daily commute to and from work:	18
Number of Days worked during the year:	350
Total number of commute miles driven during the year (18 x 350):	6,300
Value of company vehicle for commuting (6,300 x $1.50/mile):	$9,450

FIGURE 4-5
Value of the Personal Use of a Company Car: Cents-per-Mile Rule

Cold Naira Artisanal Brands

Worksheet to Calculate Personal Use of Company Vehicle

(Cents-per-Mile Rule)

Employee Name: _____Leith Ofir_____

Vehicle Make: _____Toyota_____   Vehicle Year: _2022_

Vehicle Model: _____RAV4_____

Odometer Mileage on the First Day of Use During the Year: _____5,250_____

Odometer Mileage on the Last Day of Use During the Year: _____18,375_____

<u>Cents-per-Mile Rule</u>

Number of miles driven during the year	<u>13,125</u>
Number of miles OR percent driven for personal use:	<u>25%</u>
Total number of commute miles driven during the year (13,125 x 0.25):	<u>3,281.25</u>
Value of company vehicle for commuting: (3,281.25x $0.655/mile):	<u>$2,149.22</u>

Other Transportation Benefits

Another transportation benefit that employers can offer is a transit pass. These provide employees access to commuter vehicles (six or more passengers required) through the pass. Employers in larger cities, where parking is at a premium, may provide parking subsidies to their employees. When there are toll roads present, employers may provide prepaid commuter passes to their employees to meet the toll roads' cost. Employers may exclude up to $300 (2023 value) from the employees' wages for these benefits. Any amount paid by the employer of more than $300 for a commuter pass would be taxable income for the employee.

> Employers in Seattle with more than 20 employees must offer pre-tax monthly deductions to employees for transit or vanpool expenses. These monies will then be used to reimburse employees for the costs of qualifying expenses.
>
> (Source: APA)

Fringe Benefit Valuations

Stop & Check

1. Ian is a field service representative whose primary job function is to visit customer sites. The primary base for computing mileage is Ian's home. In 2023, a total of 30,250 miles were driven in the company car, 15 percent of which was for personal use. Using the IRS standard mileage rate of 65.5 cents per mile, what is the value of this fringe benefit using the cents-per-mile rule?

2. Turner is a sales representative for a large pharmaceutical company. The company car is a 2022 Lexus ES, which has a fair market value of $47,000 and a lease value of $12,250. Turner has had the use of the vehicle for 180 days in 2023. Turner drove the vehicle 20 percent for personal use, and the employer does not provide fuel. Using the lease value rule, what is the value of the fringe benefit? (Round the final figure to two decimal places.)

LO 4-5 Differentiate between Pre-tax and Post-tax Deductions

Two classes of deductions exist: pre-tax and post-tax. Pre-tax deductions are those deductions withheld from an employee's *gross pay*, which is the amount of compensation before computing tax liability or applying deductions. The effect of pre-tax deductions is that they reduce the taxable income of the employee. Pre-tax deductions are *voluntary deductions* that have been legislated by the federal government as eligible for pre-tax withholding status, including certain types of insurance, retirement plans, and cafeteria plans.

Post-tax deductions are deducted from employee pay after federal, state, and local income taxes and FICA taxes have been deducted. Amounts deducted on a post-tax basis include both voluntary and court-mandated deductions. The voluntary deductions taken on a post-tax basis involve fringe benefits such as gym memberships, charitable contributions, repayment of company loans, optional insurance (e.g., auto, home), and union dues. Court-mandated deductions deducted on a post-tax basis may include child support garnishments, tax liens, credit card garnishments, and other legally directed items.

Homer W Sykes/Alamy Stock Photo

Insurance

Employers may provide subsidized health insurance coverage for their employees. The employees pay a portion of these health insurance expenses out of their paychecks, and the company makes up the difference. How much a company pays is determined by the company and could vary greatly, depending on the costs of health insurance and the employee's policy. For health insurance plans to qualify for pre-tax status, they must meet the guidelines stated in the IRS Code.

According to the IRS, the following guidelines are used to determine if a health insurance plan qualifies for pre-tax status:

- Health plans offered through the state's small or large group market.
- An employer's self-insured health plan.
- The Department of Defense's Non-Appropriated Fund Health Benefits Program.
- A governmental plan.
- COBRA health coverage.
- Retiree health coverage.

(Source: IRS)

The IRS specifies these items as pre-tax because it reflects the belief that health insurance is necessary, allowing employees to reduce their tax liability and ultimately to reduce the financial burden on families and employers by proactively supporting medical care.

EXAMPLE: PRE-TAX MEDICAL PREMIUM

Kell works for Gunderson Associates. Kell's employer offers medical insurance for which the premiums may be taken on a pre-tax basis. Kell is a salaried employee who earns $48,000 annually and is paid on a semimonthly basis. The premium for medical insurance is $125 per pay period. Consider the following difference in taxable income:

(continued)

(concluded)

	Medical Insurance Deducted on a Pre-Tax Basis	Medical Insurance NOT Deducted on a Pre-Tax Basis
Annual salary	$48,000	$48,000
Period salary	$48,000/24 = $2,000	$48,000/24 = $2,000
Medical insurance deduction	$125	$0
Taxable Income	$1,875	$2,000

In 2010, the Affordable Care Act was passed, providing small businesses a tax credit for providing health insurance coverage when their employees are at low- and moderate-income levels. The act extended coverage of children until the age of 26 to be included as an option to employees on a pre-tax basis. This is only for employees covered under a qualifying cafeteria plan.

In response to the Affordable Care Act, IRS Code 6056 changed the reporting requirements for employees' health insurance programs. Employers with more than 50 employees are required to file an information return with the IRS and must provide a detailed summary of health coverage to employees. The value of the insurance coverage contributed by the employer must be reported on the employee's W-2 year-end tax statement within box 12 using code DD. It should reflect the amounts contributed by both the employee and the employer. It is important to remember that the amounts reported on the W-2 for the employer's contribution to health insurance do not add to the employee's taxable wages.

> According to the Internal Revenue Service, the Affordable Care Act mandates that individuals have "minimum essential coverage."
>
> Examples of minimum essential coverage include:
>
> - Employer-provided health insurance.
> - Health insurance purchased through an approved health insurance exchange.
> - Coverage provided under federal auspices such as Medicare and Medicaid.
> - Privately purchased health insurance.
>
> Minimum essential coverage does not include the following limited benefit or limited-term coverage plans:
>
> - Vision and dental insurance issued on a stand-alone basis (i.e., not grouped with a medical insurance policy).
> - Workers' compensation insurance.
> - Accidental death and disability plans maintained by the employer.
>
> (Sources: Tax Cuts and Job Act; IRS)

Supplemental Health and Disability Insurance

Another option many employers are offering is a flow-through (i.e., the company does not cover any of the costs) of supplemental health and disability insurance. One of the largest insurance providers is the American Family Life Assurance Company (AFLAC). AFLAC comprises a variety of policies with separate treatment for taxation purposes (whether pre- or post-tax). The IRS Revision Ruling 2004-55 deals specifically with the tax treatment of short- and long-term disability, and IRS Code Sections 104(a)(3) and 105(a) deal with the exclusion of short- and long-term disability benefits from employees' gross wages. Long-term disability insurance is excluded from taxable income under the ruling. If an employer pays for long-term disability insurance, these amounts may be excluded from or included in gross pay, depending upon the company's election. When determining the tax treatment for supplemental health insurance, the IRS guidance provides the following: If the income derived will be estimated to be tax-free, then the cost associated will also be tax-exempt.

Note: Supplemental health and disability plan premiums are not tax-exempt for the calculation of Social Security and Medicare taxes.

> **EXAMPLE: SUPPLEMENTAL HEALTH INSURANCE DEDUCTION**
>
> Nichols is a salaried exempt employee of Mark One Restoration Services. Nichols earns $78,000 annually and is paid biweekly. The employer offers medical insurance and supplemental health insurance with premiums of $150 and $75, respectively. Nichols elects to have both premiums withheld on a pre-tax basis.
>
> | | |
> |---|---:|
> | Salary per period ($78,000/26) | $3,000.00 |
> | Less: Medical insurance premium | 150.00 |
> | Less: Supplemental medical insurance premium | 75.00 |
> | Taxable Income* | $2,775.00 |
>
> *Note: Taxable income computed here pertains to computations of federal income tax. The taxable income for Social Security and Medicare taxes would be $2,850 because supplemental medical insurance premiums are not exempt from FICA taxes.

Retirement Plans

Retirement plans were covered under the Employee Retirement Income Security Act (ERISA) of 1974 in conjunction with the Internal Revenue Code. There are two basic types of retirement plans: ***defined benefit*** and ***defined contribution***. In a defined benefit plan, the employer guarantees the employee a specific income level once retirement has been reached. For example, under a defined benefit plan, the employer may guarantee 10 percent of the average salary earned in the final five years of employment.

Zerbor/Shutterstock

In a defined contribution plan, the individual places money from his or her payroll, pre-tax, into a retirement plan, and the company may or may not match to a percentage. There are several different types of defined contribution plans, such as ***401(k)***, ***SIMPLE 401(k)***, ***403(b)***, ***457***, ***IRA***, ***SIMPLE***, ***SEP***, ***ESOP***, and profit-sharing.

Note: Although some qualified 401(k) plans may be considered cafeteria plans and may be excluded from FICA tax liability, the IRS states in Publication 15-B that most retirement plans are subject to Social Security and Medicare taxes. For this text's purposes, we will assume that the retirement plans are not included in federal or state tax calculations but are included in Social Security and Medicare tax calculations. See Table 4-2 for an explanation of the different retirement plan types.

TABLE 4-2
Retirement Plan Types

Type of Plan	Description
401(k)	A group of investments, typically invested in stock market-based or mutual fund-based plans.
403(b)	Similar to a 401(k) but offered by nonprofit employers such as governmental agencies, hospitals, and schools.
457	Similar to 401(k) and 403(b) but has no penalty for fund withdrawal before age 59-1/2. Generally offered to governmental and certain nongovernmental employees.
Savings Incentive Match Plan for Employees (SIMPLE)	The major limitation is employers may not have more than 100 employees. Funds are specifically set aside for the individual employee in a bank, mutual fund account, or stock market SIMPLE 401(k).
Individual Retirement Account (IRA)	Funds are specifically set aside for the individual employee in a bank or mutual fund account.
Employee Stock Ownership Plan (ESOP)	The company offers employees the ability to earn company stock for the duration of their employment. ESOP participation is tax-deferred while the person is employed.
Simplified Employee Pension (SEP)	A tax-favorable IRA is set up by or for the employee, and the employer contributes the funds into the account. The SEP is tax-favorable because it reduces the employee's income tax liability.

(Sources: DOL; IRS)

> **EXAMPLE: RETIREMENT PLAN EMPLOYEE CONTRIBUTION**
>
> Whit is a salaried, exempt employee of Hovey Heating and Cooling. Whit is single with one dependent under 17 years of age and receives an annual salary of $60,000, paid semi-monthly. Whit elects to contribute 6 percent per pay period to the company-sponsored 401(k) plan on a pre-tax basis. Whit's taxable income would be computed as follows:
>
> | | |
> |---|---:|
> | Salary per period ($60,000/24) | $2,500.00 |
> | Less: 6% contribution to 401(k)* | 150.00 |
> | Taxable Income | $2,350.00 |
>
> *Note: The 401(k) deduction is *not* exempt from Social Security and Medicare taxes.

> Each year, the IRS imposes a cap on pre-tax retirement plan contributions. For 2023, the limit on 401(k) contributions is $22,500. People over 50 years of age may contribute a pre-tax "catch-up" amount of up to $7,500. There are separate limits for SIMPLE 401(k) plans at $15,500 with the "catch-up" of $3,500 in 2023.
>
> (Source: IRS)

Post-Tax Deductions

After the employer withholds the pre-tax and mandatory amounts from an employee's pay, other withholdings may apply. These other withholdings, known as post-tax deductions, comprise both voluntary and *mandated deductions*. An example of a voluntary post-tax deduction is a charitable contribution elected by the employee. Mandated post-tax deductions include *garnishments* and *union dues*. Post-tax deductions are amounts that the IRS has declared cannot reduce the employee's tax liability. A general guide to garnishments is in Table 4-3.

Charitable Contributions

Many companies offer to deduct funds for approved charitable organizations directly from the employee's pay. This *charitable contribution* is typically withheld *after* taxes have been calculated. The individual will report the charitable contribution on his or her itemized tax return. There are separate requirements for meeting the deductible percentage outside the scope of this text.

TABLE 4-3
Garnishment Rules

Type of Garnishment	Maximum percentage of DISPOSABLE income
Child Support or Alimony	50% if the employee is supporting another spouse or child. 60% if the employee is not supporting another spouse or child. NOTE: If child support is >12 weeks in arrears, an additional 5% may be added to the garnishment.
U.S. Government Debts	15% of earnings over federal minimum wage weekly earnings.
Student Loans	15% of earnings over federal minimum wage weekly earnings.
Consumer Credit	25% of earnings over federal minimum wage weekly earnings.
Tax Levies	See IRS Publication 1494.
Personal Bankruptcy	Lower of 25% or 30 times the amount of weekly income over federal minimum wage.

Sources: DOL; IRS

> **EXAMPLE: NET PAY WITH A CHARITABLE CONTRIBUTION**
>
> Perri is an employee at Working Environments in Winchester, New Hampshire. Earning $29,000 annually, Perri is paid weekly and is single with one withholding allowance.

Additionally, Perri has pre-tax health insurance of $25 and a charitable contribution to the United Way of $10 per pay period. Taxable income would be as follows:

Period pay	$557.69
Less: Health insurance	25.00
Taxable income	$532.69

Note that Perri's taxable income does *not* reflect the United Way contribution. Because that contribution is computed on a post-tax basis, it does not affect taxable income.

Court-Ordered Garnishments

There are several reasons that a court may order an employer to withhold amounts from an employee's pay and redirect those funds to a regulatory agency. The most common garnishments are for child support, alimony, and student loans. Garnishments apply to *disposable income*. The amount of employee pay after legally required deductions such as income taxes have been withheld. If an employee has one garnishment order for 10 percent and receives a second for 15 percent, any further garnishment requests will be deferred until the disposable income is at a level that is available for garnishments.

> **Consumer credit:**
>
> According to **Title III** of the ***Consumer Credit Protection Act (CCPA)***, garnishments may not be more than (a) 25 percent of the employee's disposable earnings OR (b) the amount by which an employee's disposable earnings are greater than 30 times the federal minimum wage, or $217.50.
>
> **Child support:**
>
> Garnishments for child support or alimony may be up to 50 percent of disposable income, with an additional 5 percent for any child support that is more than 12 weeks in arrears.
>
> **Nontax debts owed to federal agencies:**
>
> Garnishments for nontax amounts to federal agencies may not total more than 15 percent of disposable income.

Union Dues

Luigi Morris/Shutterstock

When employees are part of a union that requires regular dues, the employer must withhold those dues from the employee as a post-tax payroll deduction. The union uses dues to fund its activities, which include representation in employee-employer negotiations and political activism. Some employers may pay the union dues for their employees as part of their noncash compensation, but there is no requirement for them to do so.

One of the changes that have come about regarding unions is in right to work states, the unions must represent all employees, regardless of their dues payment status. Since many individuals realized that they could have the protections of the union without the cost of the union, many unions saw a drop in the number of members paying dues but not a corresponding loss of the number of members covered.

> Employees of the American Civil Liberties Union (ACLU) chose to form a labor union in 2021. What distinguished the ACLU union from other labor unions is the ACLU's nonprofit status. Comprising over 300 employees in multiple cities, one purpose is to prevent staff turnover and implement robust investment strategies. Other purposes include support for employees' wages and benefits.
>
> (Source: The Washington Post)

Summary of Pre-tax and Post-tax Benefit Tax Treatments

Pre-tax	Post-tax	Either Pre- or Post-Tax*
Flexible spending arrangements (FSA)	Short-term disability insurance	Health insurance
Health savings account (HSA)	Long-term disability insurance	Dental insurance
	Voluntary additional life insurance	Vision insurance
		Voluntary retirement plans (e.g., 401(k), 403(b), 457, etc.)

*Employees may elect to have these amounts withheld pre- or post-tax.

Pre-tax vs. Post-tax Deductions

Stop & Check

1. Which act offered a small-business tax credit for employees' health insurance premiums?
2. What are examples of different retirement plans that may qualify as pre-tax withdrawals?
3. An employee has disposable pay of $1,790.00 for this biweekly pay period. The payroll department receives a court-ordered garnishment for credit card debt of $15,000. What is the maximum amount that may be withheld from the employee's pay?
4. The employee questioned the amount of the garnishment in question 3, claiming that the health insurance of $125 and union dues of $45 must also be withheld from their pay before calculating disposable pay. How much should be withheld for the garnishment? Explain.

LO 4-6 Apply Rules for Withholding, Depositing, and Reporting Benefits

Providing benefits as a condition of employment is an important part of employee compensation. In many cases, amounts of money associated with benefits are quantifiable, such as insurance premiums, employee contributions, or specific mandatory deductions. In other cases, the fringe benefit valuation rules are needed. The next piece of the puzzle is actually withholding, depositing, and reporting the organizations' benefits.

Rules for Withholding Amounts Related to Benefits

The money associated with employee voluntary withholdings for benefits should be withheld when the benefit is made available. For example, if an employee voluntarily opts for withdrawals for a gym membership benefit, the membership should be available when the employee's deduction occurs. The deduction should coincide with regularly-scheduled pay periods. Therefore, any employee contributions to cafeteria plans, FSAs, HSAs, or other benefits should be deducted from regular pay. A best practice is to document the period and annual amounts of voluntary deductions in writing for the employee to acknowledge and sign.

Sums of money related to benefits should be deducted from employee pay promptly. The IRS stipulates that the value of all noncash benefits must be determined no later than January 31 of the following year. This deadline facilitates reporting of the fringe benefits on the employees' W-2s. It also gives the employer time to deposit any necessary amounts on time.

> The IRS reported that the number of employer audits had increased because of the reporting of fringe benefits and taxes due. According to the IRS, when an audit is

> triggered because of red flags in the computer selection program, one of the first areas checked is employer valuation and fringe benefits reporting. Other items considered include the employer's internal control system and workers' classification as employees or independent contractors.
>
> (Source: Accounting Today)

An exception to the general rule is the IRS's *special accounting rule* for noncash benefits provided only in the last two months of the calendar year (i.e., November and December). Benefits given during this period may be treated as paid during the following calendar year; however, only the benefits' values may be treated as such. Although employers may opt to use the special accounting period for specific benefits, all employees who receive that benefit must also have it reported in accordance with the special accounting rule.

> **EXAMPLE: SPECIAL ACCOUNTING RULE**
> Kris is an employee of Connections, Inc., and drives a company car. According to the special accounting rule, the company deferred the taxable amount of Kris's personal use of the company car during November and December 2023 until January 2024. This practice would reduce Kris's taxable income for 2023, but Kris would still be liable for the 2024 taxes. Connections, Inc., would be required to notify Kris of its use of the special accounting rule for the personal company car use no later than January 31, 2024.

Treatment of Taxable Benefit Withholdings

No matter how the employee receives specific benefits; the employer must treat the benefit as though it was paid annually. The rationale for this treatment is to guarantee that taxable benefits are reflected appropriately on employee W-2s. The employer may change the timing of any amounts withheld for benefits as necessary for the entire company and individual employees.

One caveat to the rules for withholding involves the transfer of property associated with benefits. For example, if the benefit involved is an investment, any amount withheld from the employee must coincide with the investment transfer.

Regarding the valuation of taxable fringe benefits, employers may choose to add the periodic value of the fringe benefit to period pay and tax it at the employee's regular tax rate. Alternatively, the employer may report the total value and withhold federal income tax at the 25 percent rate. An example of this practice would involve the valuation of personal company car use if reported annually. In that case, the employer may add the full amount of the benefit valuation to a single pay period and deduct the taxes at that time.

> Employees have found that their "free" fringe benefits may be subject to taxes. Wellness programs involving gym memberships, nutritional counseling, and other services provided at no cost to employees may be added to an employee's gross income and be subject to income and FICA taxes.
>
> (Source: Forbes)

Rules for Depositing Amounts Related to Benefits

Employer deposit rules related to benefits are nearly as diverse as the benefits themselves. Like the withholdings, the deposit frequency depends on the timing of deductions from employee pay and recipient requirements (when applicable). A general rule for taxes withheld is that the deposit of these amounts must follow employer deposit rules, covered in Chapter 6. The employer should estimate the amount of the benefit transmitted on a specific date, remit taxes, and transmit any other monies as necessary.

> **EXAMPLE: DEPOSIT OF EMPLOYEE 401(K) CONTRIBUTIONS**
> Bowen, an employee of TMS Physical Therapy, contributes 4 percent of gross pay to the employer-sponsored employee stock option benefit. Bowen is paid biweekly and earns $52,000 annually. The employer makes quarterly deposits to the stockbroker. In this example, Bowen's contribution is $2,000 × 0.04, or $80, per pay period. The employer would deduct this amount from Bowen's pay and retain it in a liability account, which they would deposit with the stockbroker at the appropriate time each quarter.

Depositing taxes for noncash fringe benefits will occasionally require an estimate of the taxes due. An example of when such an estimate may occur would be employee meals. The employer would estimate the value of the meals and deposit the appropriate amount of tax because it would be a taxable fringe benefit. It is important to note that the estimate needs to be as accurate as possible. The underpayment of taxes associated with noncash fringe benefits will result in IRS penalties.

Rules for Reporting Benefits

Benefit reports occur in two different places: the employee's Form W-2 and the total compensation report. Each report serves a different purpose.

- Form W-2 serves as a report of all wages and associated taxes for a calendar year. All taxable benefits are reported as wages on the employee's Form W-2. This reporting method ensures that the employer calculates the correct amount of income taxes and that the employee's annual tax return reflects the proper amounts of income.
- The total compensation report is a report given to the employee from the company that details all benefits in monetary terms. This report allows employees to have an accurate statement of their service's cash and noncash value to the employer.

> Custom benefits software is becoming more popular among employers. Companies specializing in employee benefits provide integrated custom platforms that address employer withholding, depositing, and reporting needs.
>
> Examples of benefits management software platforms include the following companies:
>
> - BambooHR
> - Ceridian
> - Workday
>
> These platforms sometimes cost more than $100,000, making them too expensive for many small- and some medium-sized employers. Innovations in technology may ultimately make these platforms more affordable. Changes in reporting laws certainly make them necessary.
>
> (Source: Employee Benefit Adviser)

According to the IRS and the Department of Labor, some of the most common benefits errors are:

- Incorrectly defined compensation.
- Delays in the remittance of employees' contributions for benefits.
- Improper definition of employee eligibility and enrollment in benefit plans.
- Incorrect employee vesting in plans.
- Benefit forfeitures.
- Improper use of loans made to participants.
- Incorrect use of hardship distributions.
- Incorrectly recorded plan expenses.

The best way to avoid errors is to involve both the payroll and the human resources departments in benefits determinations to ensure proper implementation and internal classification of related monies. Benefit plans should be reviewed annually to ensure accuracy in legal compliance, remittance procedures, and reconciliation of employee contributions with payroll records.

Stop & Check: Employee Benefits Reporting

1. When should employers withhold amounts of money associated with benefits from employee pay?
2. Braden McLaughlin is an employee of Creighton Steel and receives several fringe benefits due to his employment. He wants to know the value of his employment, both cash and noncash. What report should he request from his employer?
3. Ali King is an employee of Nabors Drilling. When Form W-2 was distributed in January, Ali noticed that gross pay exceeded the annual salary. As the payroll accountant, you are aware of all fringe benefits available to and used by employees. What would you tell Ali to help explain the difference?

Trends to Watch

EMPLOYEE BENEFITS

Employers' attitudes toward employee benefits have changed since 2019. Benefits have become important negotiating tools for employees, which has resulted in the following:

- Large companies such as Google, Facebook, and Costco have developed a reputation for offering generous benefits.
- Employees are using sites such as Glassdoor and Salary.com to rate prospective employers' total compensation packages.
- Values associated with fringe benefits have risen in proportion to employee salaries.
- Employers are starting to offer financial wellness planning—apart from retirement planning.
- Legislation is in the works to encourage employers and employees to make student loan reduction payments.
- Many companies are adding fertility benefits for employees.

Future trends to watch include:

- Team-building experiences for in-office and remote workers.
- Employee choice of the available benefits to create customized benefits.
- Coordinated web portals for employees to view pay, personnel, and benefit information.
- Home office stipends to offset the cost of working remotely.
- Changes in the definition of "family member" through legislation for the purpose of benefits.
- Increased participation in company retirement plans because of the student loan payment matching provision of the SECURE 2.0 Act.

Summary of Fringe Benefits and Voluntary Deductions

Fringe benefits are an integral part of employee compensation and often significantly influence an employee's costs. Common forms of fringe benefits are health insurance and retirement, but they can encompass an endless variety of employee perks. Certain noncash fringe benefits are subject to employment taxes, which require an employer to be aware of the taxes associated with offering certain types of benefits.

An important category of fringe benefits involves employer-sponsored medical insurance plans. Most medical insurance plans may be deducted from an employee's pay on a pre-tax basis, which reduces the employee's tax liability. Employee medical insurance premiums are deducted on a pre-tax basis; this fringe benefit is often part of a cafeteria plan. Other pre-tax benefits, such as flexible spending arrangements (FSA), may be included.

Certain types of noncash fringe benefits are excluded from taxation. Commonly excluded fringe benefits include *de minimis* benefits, whose small value would make cost accounting for them unrealistic. Other noncash fringe benefits not subject to taxes include items employers offer for their own convenience, such as on-site meals and company cars. However, personal use of company cars is subject to tax, based on the employer's valuation method.

Many voluntary benefits are deducted from employee pay on a post-tax basis. Other post-tax deductions include court-mandated deductions and garnishments. It is important to note the legal limits of garnishing employee pay to deduct an appropriate amount. Employers are responsible for withholding, depositing, and reporting all deductions from an employee's pay, especially when those deductions are taxes. The total amount of annual compensation, including pay, taxes, and benefits, may be reported on Form W-2 and the total compensation report.

Key Points

- Fringe benefits are an important part of an employee's compensation package because they help attract and retain high-quality employees.
- Fringe benefits have been correlated with increases in employee productivity, retention, and company revenue.
- Fringe benefits may be statutory or voluntary in nature.
- Pre-tax deductions are used to reduce the taxable wage base for qualified deductions.
- Cafeteria plans allow employees to exclude medical premiums and qualified medical expenses from income tax and FICA taxes.
- Certain pre-tax deductions are subject to FICA taxes.
- Excluded fringe benefits are subject to specific IRS rules that govern amounts and taxation.
- Personal use of company vehicles is evaluated to determine the amount of income employees are taxed on Form W-2.
- Post-tax deductions include garnishments, union dues, and charitable contributions.
- Garnishments are subject to maximum percentages of disposable income, depending on the type of garnishment.
- Employer withholding of amounts associated with providing employee benefits varies depending on the benefit and is subject to taxes.
- Taxes associated with taxable noncash fringe benefits must be deposited when the benefit is transmitted to the employee.
- Employers report the valuation of noncash fringe benefits as part of the employee's Form W-2 and the total compensation report.

Vocabulary

401(k)	ESOP	Mandated deduction
403(b)	Fair market value (FMV)	Mandatory deduction
457	Flexible spending arrangement (FSA)	Pay advice
Cafeteria plan		Post-tax deduction
Cents-per-mile rule	Fringe benefit	Premium-only plan (POP)
Charitable contribution	Garnishment	Publication 15-B
Commuting rule	General valuation rule (GVR)	Qualified plan
Compensation		SEP
Consumer Credit Protection Act (CCPA)	Health savings account (HSA)	SIMPLE
		SIMPLE 401(k)
De minimis	High-deductible health plan (HDHP)	Special accounting rule
Defined benefit		Union dues
Defined contribution	IRA	Voluntary deduction
Disposable income	Lease-value rule	

Review Questions

1. Why do companies offer fringe benefits to their employees?
2. Approximately what percentage of employee compensation includes fringe benefits?
3. What are three examples of voluntary fringe benefits?
4. What are the two reports associated with fringe benefits?
5. What are two examples of voluntary deductions?
6. What are two examples of pre-tax deductions?
7. What are two types of insurance that may be deducted pre-tax under a cafeteria plan?
8. What are the four categories of cafeteria plans?
9. How does an FSA affect an employee's taxable wages?
10. What are three examples of excluded fringe benefits?
11. What are the ways that the value of a company vehicle as a fringe benefit is determined?
12. What are garnishments, and how must they be handled?
13. How do post-tax deductions differ from pre-tax deductions?
14. How does the special accounting rule affect the withholding of benefits?
15. How often must employers deposit taxes associated with taxable fringe benefits?

Exercises Set A

E4-1A.
LO 4-1, 4-4

Harper is a children's photographer for Cool Cax Digital and would like advice about using an FSA for miscellaneous prescriptions and other medical expenses. What reason(s) would you give Harper for having an FSA account? (Select all that apply.)
a. The monthly amount is deducted on a pre-tax basis.
b. The employee's income that is subject to income tax(es) is reduced.
c. The income subject to Social Security and Medicare taxes is reduced.
d. The FSA will continue from year to year if not used.

E4-2A.
LO 4-1

Dev is a metalworker at Bartleby's Metal Shop. Which of the following would likely be fringe benefits that the employer would provide because they would be needed as part of this job? (Select all that apply.)
a. Heat-resistant gloves
b. On-site cafeteria
c. Welding mask
d. Personal accounting services

E4-3A.
LO 4-2

Gem is wondering what elements are in a qualified health plan. Which of the following would be included? (Select all that apply.)
a. Mental health benefits
b. Prescription drugs
c. Pet insurance premiums
d. Preventive and wellness services

E4-4A.
LO 4-2

What is a significant difference between flexible spending arrangements (FSAs) and health savings accounts (HSAs)?
a. Only FSAs may be included as part of a cafeteria plan.
b. HSAs may accompany any type of employer-sponsored health insurance.
c. Amounts contributed to HSAs may remain in the account for use later in life.
d. No annual pre-tax contribution limit exists for FSAs.

E4-5A.
LO 4-1

Silver is an employee who receives educational assistance from their employer in the amount of $15,000 per year. How is this amount treated for tax purposes?
a. None of it is taxable
b. All of it is taxable
c. $5,250 is taxable
d. $9,750 is taxable

E4-6A.
LO 4-4

Jace is an employee of Wilson In-Home Healthcare. Jace has a company vehicle to drive to customer sites. Which of the general valuation rules would be appropriate to compute the value of the asset for any personal use? (Select all that apply.)
a. Cents-per-mile rule
b. Commuting rule
c. Unsafe conditions rule
d. Lease value rule

E4-7A.
LO 4-5

Which of the following describes the primary difference between a 401(k) and a 403(b) retirement plan?
a. The 401(k) is a defined benefit-only plan.
b. The 403(b) is a defined contribution-only plan.
c. The 401(k) is restricted to investments in stocks only.
d. The 403(b) is restricted to use by nonprofit companies.

E4-8A.
LO 4-5

Which of the following is true about fringe benefits? (Select all that apply.)
a. They represent additional cash paid directly to employees.
b. They are only available for employees and their families.
c. They represent additional compensation given for services performed.
d. The amount of the fringe benefit is never subject to income tax.

E4-9A.
LO 4-5

How is disposable income computed?
a. Gross pay less pre-tax deductions
b. Gross pay less pre-tax deductions and income taxes
c. Gross pay less mandatory deductions
d. Gross pay less Social Security and Medicare taxes

E4-10A.
LO 4-6

By what date must a company declare the value of noncash benefits used in 2023?
a. January 1, 2024
b. December 31, 2023
c. February 1, 2024
d. January 31, 2024

Problems Set A

P4-1A.
LO 4-1, 4-2

Sargent is a new employee at Tet Torr Entertainment. The company has both a POP with the opportunity for an FSA or an HDHP with an opportunity for an HSA. The POP premium is $350 per month and the annual deductible is $500. For the HDHP, the monthly premium is $200 and the annual deductible is $1,200. Explain the options of each to Sargent.

P4-2A.
LO 4-1

Emery is a computer programmer at Biosphere Communications. Emery has a garnishment for child support and would like to pay it personally and not have it automatically withdrawn from the gross pay. What advice should you offer Emery?

P4-3A.
LO 4-1, 4-2

Addison is a graphic designer at a large marketing firm and earns $56,000 annually, paid biweekly. Addison contributes 5 percent of the gross pay to a qualified 401(k) plan on a pre-tax basis and has a pre-tax medical premium of $350. What is the taxable income per pay period?

P4-4A.
LO 4-3

Kai is an employee of Dimensionworks Designs in New Mexico who received the following achievement awards from her employer during 2023:
- Best safety plan, Santa Fe County: Set of golf clubs worth: $1,200
- Top emergency plan layout, New Mexico: Television valued at: $1,600
- Ten-year employee award: iPad valued at: $750

The achievement awards are eligible under a qualified plan.
How much of Kai's achievement award income is taxable?

P4-5A.
LO 4-1, 4-3

Jona is an employee at Radiance Senior Living and received the following benefits from the employer during 2023 on the company's location for company purposes:
- Personal protective equipment: $50 per month
- Employer-provided cell phone: $50 per month
- Ten-year employee award: iPad valued at: $750

What amount of these benefits is/are taxable for 2023?

P4-6A.
LO 4-4

Dana is an account representative at Ever Pharmaceuticals. Dana has a company car for customer visits and uses it to commute from work to home on Friday nights and from home to work on Monday mornings, 50 weeks per year. The commute is 25 miles in each direction. Using the commuting rule, what is the valuation of the fringe benefit?

P4-7A.
LO 4-4

Blaine is the vice president of operations for Southern Sweets Bakery. Blaine drives a 2023 Toyota Prius as his company car, and it has a fair market value of $41,500. The vehicle's prorated annual lease value per Publication 15-B is $10,750. Blaine reported driving 34,750 miles during 2023, of which 20 percent were for personal reasons. The company pays for fuel and charges five cents per mile for fuel charges. Using the lease value rule, what is the valuation of Blaine's company car benefit?

P4-8A.
LO 4-5

Marley is a supervisor at Fantastigifts and receives an annual salary of $45,000, paid biweekly, and a garnishment for consumer credit of $375. Assuming that the disposable income is 80 percent of the gross pay per period, does the garnishment follow the CCPA? If not, what is the maximum garnishment allowed for Marley's consumer credit garnishment?

P4-9A.
LO 4-1, 4-2, 4-5

Shiloh is an employee at Jankoski Cycles and earns an annual salary of $37,765, paid semimonthly. Shiloh contributes to the following fringe benefits and other deductions:
- Medical insurance: $220 per pay period
- Dental insurance: $15 per pay period
- 401(k): 6 percent of gross pay
- Additional withholding: $125 per month

What is the total annual amount of Shiloh's fringe benefits and other deductions?

P4-10A.
LO 4-6

Jesse is the payroll accountant for Comptech Industries which decided to use the special accounting rule for 2023. Which months may be included in the special accounting rule?

P4-11A.
LO 4-1, 4-2, 4-3, 4-5

Dallas is the payroll accountant at White Box Builders and is preparing an information package about voluntary and fringe benefits. Using the following list of fringe benefits, classify each benefit as pre-tax or post-tax and as taxable or tax-exempt for federal income taxes.

Employee Benefits				
Benefit	Pre-tax	Post-tax	Taxable	Tax-Exempt
401(k)				
Medical insurance				
Off-site gym membership				
United Way contributions				
AFLAC				
Tuition assistance up to $5,250 annually				
Commuter passes up to $300 monthly				

Exercises Set B

E4-1B.
LO 4-1

Which of the following fringe benefits is exempt from federal income tax but subject to FICA tax?
a. Moving expense reimbursements
b. Tuition reduction for undergraduate education
c. Adoption assistance
d. Working condition benefits

E4-2B.
LO 4-1

Taylor is an employee of New York Boutiques, Inc., and is a traveling salesperson who routinely meets with customers at their places of business. Which of the following fringe benefits would be appropriate for the employer to provide for Taylor to conduct business? (Select all that apply.)
a. Personal stylist
b. Tuition assistance
c. Clothing allowance
d. Cell phone

E4-3B.
LO 4-2

Which of the following is a co-requisite of a health savings account (HSA)?
a. No employer-provided insurance
b. A high-deductible health plan
c. Multiple health insurance plans held by the same employee
d. A flexible spending arrangement

E4-4B.
LO 4-2

What is the annual maximum amount that an employee may contribute to a flexible savings arrangement before it becomes taxable income?
a. $2,850
b. $2,950
c. $3,050
d. $3,150

E4-5B.
LO 4-3

Marlow is an employee of All-Adventure Tours. All-Adventure Tours offers tuition reimbursement as a fringe benefit. What maximum amount may be excluded from Marlow's taxes as a fringe benefit? (Select all that apply.)
a. $4,750
b. $5,000
c. $5,250
d. $5,750

E4-6B.
LO 4-4

Grey is an employee of Convergent Technologies whose job is strictly based in the company's office. The employer has authorized the use of a company vehicle for commuting purposes as necessary. Which of the general valuation rules would be appropriate to evaluate the value of this fringe benefit? (Select all that apply.)
a. Lease value rule
b. Unsafe conditions rule
c. Commuting rule
d. Cents-per-mile rule

E4-7B.
LO 4-2

Casey is the payroll accountant for Glowing Yoga and is preparing a Section 125 cafeteria plan presentation. Which of the following items may qualify for inclusion in a cafeteria plan? (Select all that apply.)
a. Health benefits
b. Adoption assistance
c. Childcare expenses
d. Education assistance

E4-8B.
LO 4-5

Jamie is the payroll accountant of Central Communications and is researching retirement plan options for the employer. Central Communications has 135 employees and is a for-profit company. Which of the following plans should Jamie consider?
a. IRA
b. 457
c. 403(b)
d. 401(k)

E4-9B.
LO 4-1

Which of the following is/are examples of fringe benefits? (Select all that apply.)
a. Education assistance (up to $5,250 annually)
b. Dependent care assistance (up to $5,000 annually)
c. Vacation packages
d. Retirement planning services

E4-10B.
LO 4-5

Which of the following are always post-tax deductions? (Select all that apply.)
a. Garnishments
b. Qualified health insurance
c. Charitable contributions
d. Retirement plan contributions

E4-11B.
LO 4-6

To which two months does the special accounting rule pertain?
a. January and February
b. November and December
c. The last two months of the company's fiscal year
d. December and January of the following year

Problems Set B

P4-1B.
LO 4-1, 4-2

Robin is a new employee at Big Tech Computers and is debating whether to enroll in a POP with the opportunity for an FSA or an HDHP with an opportunity for an HSA. The POP premium is $550 per month and the annual deductible is $400. For the HDHP, the monthly premium is $175 and the annual deductible is $1,400. Explain the options of each to Robin.

P4-2B.
LO 4-1

Quinn is employed as a concierge at Strawberry Lodge, an upscale resort in the Adirondack Mountains. Quinn asks the payroll accountant which deductions from gross pay are considered voluntary fringe benefits. Where would you tell Quinn to look on the pay stub?

P4-3B.
LO 4-1, 4-2

Tate is a manager at Complex Ventures, Inc. Tate contributes $2,750 annually to an FSA and has medical insurance with a $500 monthly premium. Tate earns a salary of $72,200 and is paid biweekly. What is the taxable income per period?

P4-4B.
LO 4-3

Windsor is employed at Rockstar Music. Windsor is receiving education assistance of $5,750 per year from Rockstar Music to complete a bachelor's degree from an accredited college. How much of that assistance is taxable?

P4-5B.
LO 4-1, 4-3

Lane is an employee in the office of Salvaggio & Wheelers, Attorneys at Law, who received the following benefits during 2023:
- Medical insurance: $250 per month
- Commuter pass: $500 per month
- Employer-paid membership to Anytime Gym: $75 per year
- Dependent care assistance: $3,600 per year

What is the total taxable amount for Lane's 2023 benefits?

P4-6B.
LO 4-4

Shiloh is a sales representative for American Silk Mills who has a company car to visit customer sites. Shiloh drove 25,500 miles during 2023, of which 15 percent was reported as personal miles. Using the cents-per-mile rule, what is the valuation of this benefit for 2023?

P4-7B.
LO 4-4

River, president of Miller Custom Coffee Roasters, drives a 2022 Mercedes E300 with a fair market value of $57,500. The lease value is $14,750. The odometer started at 655 and was reported at 32,855 at the end of the year. The car was available all of 2023. River reported driving 32,200 miles during 2023, of which 9,800 were for personal reasons. The company pays all fuel and charges five cents per personal mile for fuel costs. What is River's 2023 valuation using the lease value rule?

P4-8B.
LO 4-5

Hayden is an employee at Finesong Jewelry and earns a salary of $38,850 per year, is paid biweekly, and has a credit card garnishment. Assuming that Hayden's disposable income is 85 percent of the gross pay, what is the maximum amount per period that may be deducted for the garnishment?

P4-9B.
LO 4-5

August is an employee at Ruby Investments, with an annual salary of $92,500, paid biweekly. August has the following fringe and voluntary benefits:
- Medical insurance: $400 per month
- 401(k): 3 percent of gross pay
- Flexible spending arrangement: $2,550 annually
- Charitable contribution: $65 per pay period

What is the total amount August contributes to fringe benefits and voluntary deductions annually?

P4-10B.
LO 4-6

Teagan is the payroll accountant for Penn & Associates Investments. The company decided on December 15, 2023, that it would invoke the special accounting rule. By what date does Teagan need to notify affected employees that the rule is being used?

P4-11B.
LO 4-1, 4-2, 4-3, 4-5

Kit is reviewing benefits with you, the payroll accountant for Silly Lemon Films. Classify the following benefits as pre-tax or post-tax deductions *and* as taxable or tax-exempt for federal income tax.

Benefits				
Benefit	Pre-Tax	Post-Tax	Taxable	Tax Exempt
Medical insurance				
FSA				
AFLAC				
Graduate school tuition at $11,000 annually				
On-site meals				

Critical Thinking

4-1. Rowan M. is a sales employee of Carefree Pools and Spas, Inc. In 2023, he was issued a company car with a fair market value of $35,000 and drove a total of 22,000 miles; used the car for 2,000 miles for personal use; and the employer paid for fuel, charging Rowan 5.5 cents per mile. Under the lease-value rule, what is the amount that must be added to Rowan's gross pay for 2023? (Use the following table for lease values.)

4-2. Rowan's employer offers the option to use the cents-per-mile rule instead of the lease-value rule for 2023. Which method will yield the lower gross income for Rowan? (Use 65.5 cents per mile in your calculations.)

(1) Automobile FMV	(2) Annual Lease
$ 0 to 999	$ 600
1,000 to 1,999	850
2,000 to 2,999	1,100
3,000 to 3,999	1,350
4,000 to 4,999	1,600
5,000 to 5,999	1,850
6,000 to 6,999	2,100
7,000 to 7,999	2,350
8,000 to 8,999	2,600
9,000 to 9,999	2,850
10,000 to 10,999	3,100
11,000 to 11,999	3,350
12,000 to 12,999	3,600
13,000 to 13,999	3,850
14,000 to 14,999	4,100
15,000 to 15,999	4,350
16,000 to 16,999	4,600
17,000 to 17,999	4,850
18,000 to 18,999	5,100
19,000 to 19,999	5,350
20,000 to 20,999	5,600
21,000 to 21,999	5,850
22,000 to 22,999	6,100
23,000 to 23,999	6,350

(1) Automobile FMV	(2) Annual Lease
24,000 to 24,999	6,600
25,000 to 25,999	6,850
26,000 to 27,999	7,250
28,000 to 29,999	7,750
30,000 to 31,999	8,250
32,000 to 33,999	8,750
34,000 to 35,999	9,250
36,000 to 37,999	9,750
38,000 to 39,999	10,250
40,000 to 41,999	10,750
42,000 to 43,999	11,250
44,000 to 45,999	11,750
46,000 to 47,999	12,250
48,000 to 49,999	12,750
50,000 to 51,999	13,250
52,000 to 53,999	13,750
54,000 to 55,999	14,250
56,000 to 57,999	14,750
58,000 to 59,999	15,250

In the Real World: Scenario for Discussion

Project labor agreements (PLAs) are used in certain states to promote pay and benefit equity for construction workers. Specifically, PLAs ensure that construction workers who choose not to join a union have access to the same pay and benefits as their union-affiliated colleagues. PLAs ensure that the presence or absence of a labor union is not a factor in the contract bidding process, therefore encouraging more contractors to bid on construction projects. Proponents of PLAs contend that they expand employment opportunities. Opponents claim that the PLA cannot exist in at-will employment states.

Which side is more correct? How can at-will employment laws exist where PLAs are allowed?

Internet Activities

4-1. Health insurance is a rapidly changing and evolving field. Employers have many options and concerns to consider. Check out www.npr.org/sections/health-care/ to listen to podcasts about health insurance and employer issues. What issues do employers currently face?

4-2. Using a site such as Google, Yahoo, or Safari, search for the term "fringe benefits." Sites such as Zywave and Employee Benefit Adviser contain insights into fringe benefits and guidance about the tax treatment for benefits. Why do you think that fringe benefits are important enough to influence an employee's choice of an employer?

4-3. Go to Talking Benefits and search for benefits-related podcasts. Once you have listened to one or more podcasts, describe the insights you gained from the information presented.

4-4. Want to know more about the topics discussed in this chapter? Go to the following links:

www.healthcare.gov/law/index.html

www.aflac.com

www.investopedia.com

www.irs.gov/pub/irs-pdf/p15b.pdf

www.dol.gov/general/topic/wages/garnishments

4-5. Can employers charge employees for their uniforms? Check out the U.S. Department of Labor video at

https://www.youtube.com/watch?v=PoZCux0rTN8&feature=youtu.be

Continuing Payroll Project: Prevosti Farms and Sugarhouse

Although the company has already established medical and retirement plan benefits, Toni Prevosti wants to consider other benefits to attract employees. As the company's accountant, you have been tasked with annotating employee earnings records with benefit elections for each employee. The following sheet contains details of employee choices. These costs are employer-paid and will take effect on the first pay period of March.

Multiply the employee's annual salary by 1 percent to calculate the life insurance benefit. For example, if an employee earned $50,000 per year, the life insurance would be $50,000 × 0.01 = $500.

Employee	Flex-Time	Childcare Assistance (under $5,000 annually)	FSA (annual)	Educational Assistance ($4,000 annually)	Life Insurance (at 1% of annual salary value)	Long-Term Care Insurance ($15 per period)	Gym Membership ($15 per month)
Millen	Yes	Yes	$500.00	No	Yes	No	Yes
Towle	No	No	1,200.00	Yes	No	No	Yes
Long	Yes	Yes	700.00	Yes	Yes	No	Yes
Shangraw	Yes	No	200.00	No	Yes	No	No
Lewis	No	No	1,600.00	No	Yes	Yes	No
Schwartz	No	No	450.00	Yes	Yes	No	Yes
Prevosti	Yes	No	900.00	No	Yes	No	Yes
Student	No	No	300.00	Yes	No	No	Yes

Annotate the Employee Earning Records with payroll-related benefit elections. The amount per period should be included in the record. As an example, if an employee elected to contribute $1,300 to his or her FSA, the period payroll deduction would be $1,300/26, or $50. The estimated yearly earnings used for insurance purposes for the hourly employees are computed as follows: (hourly wages times number of hours worked per week × 52) then divide by 26 pay periods to get an amount per pay period. For example, if Shangraw worked 20 hours per week, the computation is 20 hours × $15/hour × 52 weeks = $15,600 per year. Insurance is computed as $15,600 × 1% = $156/26 = $6.00 per pay period.

EMPLOYEE EARNING RECORD

NAME	Thomas Millen	Hire Date	2/1/2023
ADDRESS	1022 Forest School Road	Date of Birth	12/16/1992
CITY/STATE/ZIP	Woodstock, VT 05001	Position	Production Manager
TELEPHONE	802-478-5055	Filing Status	Married/Joint
SOCIAL SECURITY NUMBER	031-11-3456	Exempt/Nonexempt	Exempt
		Pay Rate	$35,000.00

Dependent child < 17	3	
Dependent other	1	
PT/(FT) Step 4a W-4 Info	none	
Step 4b W-4 Info	none	
Step 4c W-4 Info	none	
Hr / Wk / Mo /(Yr)		

Flex-Time	Child Care	FSA Amount	Educational Assistance	Life Ins.	Long-Term Care	Gym Membership	Total Benefit

212 Chapter 4 *Fringe Benefits and Voluntary Deductions*

EMPLOYEE EARNING RECORD

NAME	Avery Towle	Hire Date	2/1/2023
ADDRESS	4011 Route 100	Date of Birth	7/14/2001
CITY/STATE/ZIP	Plymouth, VT 05102	Position	Production Worker PT/(FT)
TELEPHONE	802-967-5873	Filing Status	Single
SOCIAL SECURITY NUMBER	089-74-0974	Exempt/Nonexempt	Non-exempt
		Pay Rate	$15.00 (Hr)/ Wk / Mo / Yr

Dependent child < 17	0
Dependent other	0
Step 4a W-4 Info	none
Step 4b W-4 Info	none
Step 4c W-4 Info	none

Flex-Time	Child Care	FSA Amount	Educational Assistance	Life Ins.	Long-Term Care	Gym Membership	Total Benefit

---

EMPLOYEE EARNING RECORD

NAME	Charlie Long	Hire Date	2/1/2023
ADDRESS	242 Benedict Road S.	Date of Birth	3/16/1997
CITY/STATE/ZIP	Woodstock, VT 05002	Position	Production Worker PT/(FT)
TELEPHONE	802-429-3846	Filing Status	Married/Joint
SOCIAL SECURITY NUMBER	056-23-4593	Exempt/Nonexempt	Non-exempt
		Pay Rate	$15.00 (Hr)/ Wk / Mo / Yr

Dependent child < 17	2
Dependent other	0
Step 4a W-4 Info	none
Step 4b W-4 Info	none
Step 4c W-4 Info	none

Flex-Time	Child Care	FSA Amount	Educational Assistance	Life Ins.	Long-Term Care	Gym Membership	Total Benefit

---

EMPLOYEE EARNING RECORD

NAME	Mary Shangraw	Hire Date	2/1/2023
ADDRESS	1901 Main Street #2	Date of Birth	8/20/1980
CITY/STATE/ZIP	Bridgewater, VT 05520	Position	Administrative Assistant (PT)/FT
TELEPHONE	802-575-5423	Filing Status	Single
SOCIAL SECURITY NUMBER	075-28-8945	Exempt/Nonexempt	Non-exempt
		Pay Rate	$15.00 (Hr)/ Wk / Mo / Yr

Dependent child < 17	0
Dependent other	1
Step 4a W-4 Info	none
Step 4b W-4 Info	none
Step 4c W-4 Info	none

Flex-Time	Child Care	FSA Amount	Educational Assistance	Life Ins.	Long-Term Care	Gym Membership	Total Benefit

EMPLOYEE EARNING RECORD

NAME	Kristen Lewis	Hire Date	2/1/2023	Dependent child < 17	2
ADDRESS	840 Daily Hollow Road	Date of Birth	4/6/1991	Dependent other	1
CITY/STATE/ZIP	Bridgewater, VT 05523	Position	Office Manager	PT/(FT) Step 4a W-4 Info	none
TELEPHONE	802-390-5572	Filing Status	Married/Joint	Step 4b W-4 Info	none
SOCIAL SECURITY NUMBER	076-39-5673	Exempt/Nonexempt	Exempt	Step 4c W-4 Info	none
		Pay Rate	$32,000.00	Hr / Wk / Mo /(Yr)	

Flex-Time	Child Care	FSA Amount	Educational Assistance	Life Ins.	Long-Term Care	Gym Membership	Total Benefit

EMPLOYEE EARNING RECORD

NAME	Joel Schwartz	Hire Date	2/1/2023	Dependent child < 17	2
ADDRESS	55 Maple Farm Way	Date of Birth	5/23/1993	Dependent other	0
CITY/STATE/ZIP	Woodstock, VT 05534	Position	Sales	PT/(FT) Step 4a W-4 Info	none
TELEPHONE	802-463-9985	Filing Status	Married/Joint	Step 4b W-4 Info	none
SOCIAL SECURITY NUMBER	021-34-9876	Exempt/Nonexempt	Exempt	Step 4c W-4 Info	none
		Pay Rate	$32,000 + Commiss	Hr / Wk / Mo /(Yr)	

Flex-Time	Child Care	FSA Amount	Educational Assistance	Life Ins.	Long-Term Care	Gym Membership	Total Benefit

EMPLOYEE EARNING RECORD

NAME	Toni Prevosti	Hire Date	2/1/2023	Dependent child < 17	3
ADDRESS	820 Westminster Road	Date of Birth	9/19/1987	Dependent other	2
CITY/STATE/ZIP	Bridgewater, VT 05521	Position	Owner/President	PT/(FT) Step 4a W-4 Info	none
TELEPHONE	802-555-3456	Filing Status	Married/Joint	Step 4b W-4 Info	none
SOCIAL SECURITY NUMBER	055-22-0443	Exempt/Nonexempt	Exempt	Step 4c W-4 Info	none
		Pay Rate	$45,000.00	Hr / Wk / Mo /(Yr)	

Flex-Time	Child Care	FSA Amount	Educational Assistance	Life Ins.	Long-Term Care	Gym Membership	Total Benefit

EMPLOYEE EARNING RECORD

NAME	Student Success	Hire Date	2/1/2023	Dependent child < 17	0
ADDRESS	1644 Smitten Road	Date of Birth	1/1/2001	Dependent other	0
CITY/STATE/ZIP	Woodstock, VT 05001	Position	Accounting Clerk PT/(FT)	Step 4a W-4 Info	none
TELEPHONE	555-555-5555	Filing Status	Single	Step 4b W-4 Info	none
SOCIAL SECURITY NUMBER	555-55-5555	Exempt/Nonexempt	Non-exempt	Step 4c W-4 Info	none
		Pay Rate	$34,000.00	Hr / Wk / Mo/(Yr)	

Flex-Time	Child Care	FSA Amount	Educational Assistance	Life Ins.	Long-Term Care	Gym Membership	Total Benefit

Answers to Stop & Check Exercises

Fringe Benefits 101

1. Fringe benefits will fall under the pre-tax or post-tax categories.
2. b and c.
3. a, c, and d.

What Is Served in the Cafeteria Plan?

1. a, b, and d.
2. A flexible spending arrangement (FSA) can be taxable when the employee's contributions are over $3,050 annually. The purpose is to defer, not avoid, paying taxes, and there is typically a "use it or lose it" policy where the funds expire at a point in time when not used. Health savings accounts (HSAs) may only be used in conjunction with a cafeteria plan where there is a high deductible, and the funds may be available longer for related medical care.
3. An HDHP has the following limits: $1,500 annual deductible (single), $3,000 annual deductible (family), $7,500 out-of-pocket expenses maximum (single), and $15,000 out-of-pocket expenses maximum (family).

Excluded Fringe Benefits

1. No, because it is provided on the employer's premises and is operated by the company and is restricted to use by its employees, their spouses, and dependents.
2. A portion of the cost of the car that would represent the personal use portion of mileage will be included in Parker's gross income. However, any amount that is directly related to the job would be excluded under the Working Conditions Benefits.

Fringe Benefit Valuations

1. $2,972.06 (30,250 miles × 15% × 0.655).
2. The value of the fringe benefit is $1,208.22, computed as follows (round the final figure to two decimals):

Fair market value of the vehicle:	$ 47,000
Annual lease value:	12,250
Prorated annual lease value:	49.315%
Percent of personal use during the year:	20%
Personal annual lease value:	$1,208.22

Pre-tax vs. Post-tax Deductions

1. Affordable Care Act.
2. 401(k); 403(b); Savings Incentive Match Plan for Employees (SIMPLE); Individual Retirement Account (IRA); Employee Stock Ownership Plan (ESOP); Simplified Employee Pension (SEP).
3. $447.50 calculated as: $1,790 disposable income × 25%.
4. Union dues and health insurance are not legally required and thus would not affect the amount of disposable income available for garnishments.

Employee Benefits Reporting

1. Monies should be withheld from the employee when the benefit is made available; normal practice is to deduct these as the employees receive their pay (daily, weekly, biweekly, semimonthly, monthly, annually).
2. The total compensation report can be given to Braden to explain the total cost of benefits and compensation received.
3. There are several fringe benefits that must be included in taxable income of the employees. These include personal use of a company-provided vehicle, commuting paid by the employer, and lease of a vehicle.

Chapter Five

Employee Net Pay and Pay Methods

Death and taxes are two certainties in life. Taxes are withheld from employees' earnings and remitted to the governing body. Companies operate as the collectors and depositors of income taxes, garnishments, and other deductions on behalf of the employee. The tax code permits certain qualifying deductions to be taken out of an employee's pay before calculating income taxes. These deductions are called pre-tax deductions. Other deductions are removed from the employee's pay after income taxes have been calculated; these are called post-tax deductions. Circular E, also known as **Publication 15** (and all supplemental materials), from the Internal Revenue Service provides a comprehensive list of employee taxes, employer responsibilities, and guidance for special situations. **Publication 15-T** was introduced in 2020 and contains the wage-bracket tables and percentage method computation amounts.

Taxes and both voluntary and mandated deductions all reduce the gross pay that we computed in Chapter 3. This chapter will explore the effects of these deductions and any other fringe benefits on employee take-home pay, also called *net pay*.

LEARNING OBJECTIVES

After studying Chapter 5, you should be able to:

- **LO 5-1** Compute Employee Net Pay
- **LO 5-2** Determine Federal Income Tax Withholding Amounts
- **LO 5-3** Compute Social Security and Medicare Tax Withholding
- **LO 5-4** Calculate State and Local Income Taxes
- **LO 5-5** Apply Post-Tax Deductions
- **LO 5-6** Discuss Employee Pay Methods

Naruedol Reelaong/Shutterstock

Flexible Pay Draws Employees to Employers

For decades, waiting until payday to receive the cash for your work has been the norm. The concept of living paycheck to paycheck affects over 60 percent of workers and has become an aspect of the definition of financial health. Other dire statistics such as the notion of how most households could not afford a $400 emergency have also emerged.

Employers started offering flexible pay options, which is the ability to access your pay before the set pay date. Ninety percent of employees reported an improvement in their financial situation because of the ability to access the money they had earned instead of incurring credit card debt or using short-term lenders to meet financial needs. Flexible pay is most common among shift workers and other lower-pay occupations because it empowers people to control their finances, and 78 percent of workers said they would be reluctant to accept a job offer from a company that did not offer such flexible pay options.

At the Dee Set Group, the employer offered this policy of flexible pay to its employees along with access to financial education options. The option for flexible pay and education options has resulted in the company attracting more talent to add to its workforce. Flexible pay is one aspect of the trend of flexibility as a desired benefit and has already shown positive results.

(Sources: CNBC; Comp and Benefits Today; Employee Benefits)

> **Net pay computations and payment methods affect employee take-home pay and access to earned income. Chapter 5 will explore the computations of employee net pay and the methods used to transmit that pay to the employees.**

LO 5-1 Compute Employee Net Pay

Now that we have discussed the computation of gross income, it is time to focus on the various taxes and miscellaneous voluntary or court-ordered deductions withheld and to determine the employee's *net pay,* which is the amount of cash an employee receives in a physical check, cash, direct deposit, or a paycard. The process of computing gross pay involves several steps, each of which must be completed accurately. We will explore the details of pre-tax deductions, tax computations, and post-tax deductions in the following sections of this chapter.

In 2020, the Tax Cuts and Jobs Act of 2017 led to a new Form W-4 and different tax tables. For those who filed the 2020 (or later) Form W-4, an employee's federal income tax is computed based on the employee's tax filing status, pay frequency, taxable earnings, and spouse's employment status—a vast difference from prior years. We will be using the current year's Form W-4 exclusively.

Once the employer has computed the employee's gross pay, the next step is to deduct mandatory (i.e., legislated), voluntary, and mandated (i.e., court-ordered or union-regulated) amounts. These deductions include federal income tax, Medicare, and Social Security taxes, which are the primary mandatory deductions. Other mandatory deductions that the employee may be subject to include *state income taxes*, city or county income taxes, and regional taxes. For example, Denver has a "head tax" for those employees working within the city and county; Mountain View, California, instituted a similar tax because of Google's presence in the city. Federal unemployment tax is the sole employer-only tax. Some states require employees to contribute to the state unemployment tax, whereas other states consider it an employer-only tax.

Pay Computation Steps

The following steps show the process for computing each employee's pay:

1. Start with the employee's gross pay.
2. Subtract the pre-tax deductions to get the total taxable earnings.
3. Compute the taxes to be withheld from the total taxable earnings.
4. Deduct the taxes.
5. Deduct any other voluntary or mandated deductions.
6. The result is the employee's net pay.

The easiest way to keep track of all deductions and ensure pay accuracy is to use a payroll register. In the following examples, we will show the computations and a sample of the payroll register representation.

EXAMPLE: NET PAY COMPUTATION

Myle receives a salary of $2,000 paid biweekly has earned $46,000 year-to-date, is married, filing jointly with one dependent under 17. The checkbox in Step 2 is not checked, and the W-4 is from 2020 or later. Myle works for KOR, Inc., in Charleston, West Virginia, where the state income tax is 6.5 percent. The pre-tax deductions include medical insurance of $50, a cafeteria plan of $75, and a 401(k) of 3 percent of gross salary per pay period. There is a charitable contribution of $10, union dues of $62, and a court-ordered garnishment of $120. Taxable income computation is the same for both federal and state income tax purposes. Let us compute Myle's net pay step by step:

Gross pay	$2,000.00
Less: Pre-tax medical insurance deduction	−50.00
Less: Cafeteria plan	−75.00
Less: 401(k) contribution	−60.00
Total taxable earnings	$1,815.00
Less: Federal income tax*	0.00
Less: Social Security tax†	−116.25
Less: Medicare tax‡	−27.19
Less: West Virginia state income tax§	−117.98
Less: Charitable contribution	−10.00
Less: Union dues	−62.00
Less: Garnishment	−120.00
Net pay	$1,361.58

*$1,815 has a tax bracket of $74.00 and the $2,000 credit for a dependent under 17 is divided by 26 for a per pay period credit amount of $76.92, leaving no federal income tax.
†$2,000 − 50 − 75 = 1,875 \times 0.062 = 116.25$
‡$2,000 − 50 − 75 = 1,875 \times 0.0145 = 27.19$
§$1,815 \times 0.065 = 117.98$

The payroll register for Myle's pay would appear as follows:

Name	Filing Status	Dependents	Hourly Rate or Period Wage	No. of Regular Hours	No. of Overtime Hours	No. of Holiday Hours	Gross Earnings	401(k)	Insurance	Cafeteria Plan	Taxable Wages for Federal W/H	Taxable Wages for FICA
Myle	MJ	1 < 17	2,000.00				2,000.00	60.00	50.00	75.00	1,815.00	1,875.00

Name	Gross Earning	Taxable Wages for Federal W/H	Taxable Wages for FICA	Federal W/H	Social Security Tax	Medicare Tax	State W/H Tax	Charitable Contribution	Union Dues	Garnishment	Net Pay
Myle	2,000.00	1,815.00	1,875.00	0.00	116.25	27.19	117.98	10.00	62.00	120.00	1,361.58

Grossed-Up Pay

An employer will occasionally want to pay an employee a specific net amount, perhaps as a bonus. However, all federal, state, and local taxes must be applied. The employee's pay must be "grossed up" to satisfy tax liabilities and achieve the net pay desired.

Andrey_Popov/Shutterstock

> **EXAMPLE: "GROSSING UP" AN EMPLOYEE'S PAY**
>
> Sawyer is an employee of Pacifica Enterprises, located in the state of Washington. The firm's president wants to award Sawyer a $150 bonus at the end of the year. Use the following steps to compute the gross-up amount:
>
> 1. Compute the tax rate for federal income tax and FICA. The tax rate on bonuses is 22 percent, per Publication 15 (Section 7). Social Security (6.2 percent) and Medicare taxes (1.45 percent) must be added to this rate. For bonuses, the total tax rate equals 22% + 6.2% + 1.45%, or 29.65%. (For nonbonus gross-up, compute the tax rate using amounts from Appendix C.) Add any state or local income tax rates to this computation as necessary.
>
> 2. To calculate the net tax rate, subtract the tax rate percentage from 100 percent (i.e., 100% − tax rate) to get the net tax rate. This bonus is 100% − 29.65%, or 70.35%, because no state or local income tax rates apply.
>
> 3. The gross-up amount equals the net pay divided by the net tax rate.
>
> **For example, for Sawyer to receive a $150 bonus, the equation to calculate the gross pay is $150/70.35% = $213.22.**
>
> Note: Typically, voluntary pre-tax or post-tax deductions are not withheld from bonus checks.

> In Ada County, Idaho, the highway district examined its commissioner's compensation package. When he was hired in 2020, he was given a three-year contract. If the commissioner were released from the contract early or resigned, he would receive a grossed-up lump sum for his health coverage in addition to the annual $169,750 salary and other payments.
>
> (Source: *Idaho Statesman*)

Differentiating between Gross and Net Pay

Stop & Check

1. What is the difference between gross pay and net pay?
2. What are three items that may be deducted from gross pay?
3. What does it mean to "gross up" an amount paid to an employee?

LO 5-2 Determine Federal Income Tax Withholding Amounts

Now let us shift our focus to *mandatory deductions* that must be withheld from employee pay. The first class of mandatory deductions is the federal income tax. This is an employee-only tax, meaning that the employer does not contribute a matching amount for the federal income tax withheld from an employee's pay.

Federal Income Taxes

The first tax we will cover is the *federal income tax*. The federal income tax represents amounts to be withheld from employed persons, calculated using the information reported by the employee on Form W-4. The withheld tax is the employee's deposit

Andrii Yalanskyi/Shutterstock

against income taxes. The employer acts as a collector and depositor for these funds. When an individual files the income tax return, the amount withheld from his or her pay during the year reduces the amount he or she may have to pay with the return. Federal taxable income is reduced by the pre-tax deductions discussed previously.

There are two commonly used methods to calculate the employee's federal income tax in manual systems: wage bracket and percentage. Starting in 2020, the IRS issued Publication 15-T for the sole purpose of income tax calculations, given that two types of Forms W-4 were in use at that time. We will explain the federal income tax computation methods using the 2023 Form W-4. It is important to note that employees hired prior to the change in income tax laws may retain their 2019 or earlier W-4 and new employees need to use the W-4 for the year of hire. Regardless of the method used for calculating federal income taxes, the reduction for pre-tax items will remain the same. Publication 15-T contains tax tables to match the new criteria. The following examples reflect how tax deductions affect employee pay.

Federal Income Pre-Tax Computation Examples

EXAMPLE: GROSS PAY LESS 401(K) AND INSURANCE

Bellamy's gross wages are $950. Bellamy is subscribed to the company's cafeteria plan and has agreed to a 10 percent contribution to a qualified 401(k) plan. Bellamy's portion of the health insurance is $56.90 per pay period. To calculate the taxable pay, we must first determine the 401(k) deduction: $950 × 10% = $95. Therefore, taxable pay is:

$950.00	gross pay
−95.00	401(k) deduction
−56.90	health insurance
$798.10	taxable income

EXAMPLE: EFFECT OF FIXED AMOUNT VS. PERCENTAGE DEDUCTION FOR 401(K) CONTRIBUTION ON TAXABLE WAGES

Channing has gross wages of $1,125, participates in the company's 401(k) program at $100 per pay period, and has health insurance and AFLAC (all pre-tax) totaling $113.80. The calculation of Channing's taxable income is:

$1,125.00	gross pay
−100.00	401(k) deduction
−113.80	health insurance and AFLAC
$ 911.20	taxable income

If Channing participated in the company's 401(k) at a percentage instead of a fixed dollar amount, the percentage would be calculated before other deductions. For instance, if the investment was 3 percent of gross pay, taxable income would be:

$1,125.00	
× 0.03	
33.75	401(k) contribution
$1,125.00	gross pay
−33.75	401(k) contribution
−113.80	health insurance and AFLAC
$ 977.45	taxable income

Note: Gross pay − Qualified medical = Taxable wages for FICA. $1,125 − 113.80 = $1,011.20 would be the taxable amount for Social Security and Medicare because retirement contributions are not exempt from FICA taxes.

Starting in 2020, Form W-4 was very different in appearance than in years prior. The criteria for amounts withheld from employee payroll focused more on annual taxes than the employee's marital status and the number of dependents. The employee federal income tax criteria used starting in 2020 included the following:

- Filing status (Single, Married Filing Jointly, Married Filing Separately, and Head of Household)
- Multiple jobs or spouse's employment
- Dependents under the age of 17
- Other dependents

In prior years, the marital status and number of dependents served as the determinants for how much tax should be withheld. This method resulted in too little tax being withheld each pay period. The current Form W-4 focuses on marital status, annual income, and dependents. The filing status was expanded to match the categories used on the annual tax return. The reality of an employee supporting other nonchild dependents was included as part of the form.

> If the employee (and spouse, when applicable) has more than one job, they should check the box at Step 2(c) on Form W-4 and
>
> - Complete page 3 of Form W-4 **OR**
> - Use the IRS tax estimator at www.irs.gov/w4app

The following examples show how to compute the federal withholding tax using the manual method in Publication 15-T and Form W-4. In the example, the employee is married to a spouse who also has a job. No pre-tax deductions are contained in the first example.

Note: If an employee has more than one job or is married to a spouse who is also employed, they should complete Step 4 of Form W-4 to have the appropriate amount of federal income tax withheld. Step 4(c) specifically addresses the amount of withholding when the employee has a multiple jobs situation.

EXAMPLE: MANUAL PAYROLL TAX COMPUTATION USING FORM W-4, NO PRE-TAX DEDUCTIONS

Rene works for Tru-Deal Homebuilders and earns $48,550, paid semimonthly. There are no other deductions. Rene is married, filing jointly with two dependents under 17 years of age. Rene's spouse earns $42,675 annually, paid biweekly, so the box in Step 2(c) has been checked.

Steps 3 through 4 of her W-4 would appear as follows:

Step 3: Claim Dependent and Other Credits	If your total income will be $200,000 or less ($400,000 or less if married filing jointly):		
	Multiply the number of qualifying children under age 17 by $2,000 $ ____4000____		
	Multiply the number of other dependents by $500 . . . . . $ _____		
	Add the amounts above for qualifying children and other dependents. You may add to this the amount of any other credits. Enter the total here	3 $	4000
Step 4 (optional): Other Adjustments	(a) Other income (not from jobs). If you want tax withheld for other income you expect this year that won't have withholding, enter the amount of other income here. This may include interest, dividends, and retirement income	4(a) $	
	(b) Deductions. If you expect to claim deductions other than the standard deduction and want to reduce your withholding, use the Deductions Worksheet on page 3 and enter the result here	4(b) $	
	(c) Extra withholding. Enter any additional tax you want withheld each **pay period** . .	4(c) $	155

Form W-4 (2023) Page **3**

Step 2(b)—Multiple Jobs Worksheet *(Keep for your records.)*

If you choose the option in Step 2(b) on Form W-4, complete this worksheet (which calculates the total extra tax for all jobs) on **only ONE** Form W-4. Withholding will be most accurate if you complete the worksheet and enter the result on the Form W-4 for the highest paying job. To be accurate, submit a new Form W-4 for all other jobs if you have not updated your withholding since 2019.

Note: If more than one job has annual wages of more than $120,000 or there are more than three jobs, see Pub. 505 for additional tables.

1. **Two jobs.** If you have two jobs or you're married filing jointly and you and your spouse each have one job, find the amount from the appropriate table on page 4. Using the "Higher Paying Job" row and the "Lower Paying Job" column, find the value at the intersection of the two household salaries and enter that value on line 1. Then, **skip** to line 3 . . . . 1 $ _____3720_____

2. **Three jobs.** If you and/or your spouse have three jobs at the same time, complete lines 2a, 2b, and 2c below. Otherwise, skip to line 3.

    a Find the amount from the appropriate table on page 4 using the annual wages from the highest paying job in the "Higher Paying Job" row and the annual wages for your next highest paying job in the "Lower Paying Job" column. Find the value at the intersection of the two household salaries and enter that value on line 2a . . . . 2a $ _____

    b Add the annual wages of the two highest paying jobs from line 2a together and use the total as the wages in the "Higher Paying Job" row and use the annual wages for your third job in the "Lower Paying Job" column to find the amount from the appropriate table on page 4 and enter this amount on line 2b . . . . 2b $ _____

    c Add the amounts from lines 2a and 2b and enter the result on line 2c . . . . 2c $ _____

3. Enter the number of pay periods per year for the highest paying job. For example, if that job pays weekly, enter 52; if it pays every other week, enter 26; if it pays monthly, enter 12, etc. . . . . 3 _____24_____

4. **Divide** the annual amount on line 1 or line 2c by the number of pay periods on line 3. Enter this amount here and in **Step 4(c)** of Form W-4 for the highest paying job (along with any other additional amount you want withheld) . . . . 4 $ _____155_____

Page 4 of Form W-4 gives us the amount to deduct for Rene and the spouse's jobs. Following is an excerpt from page 4 as it pertains to Rene.

Form W-4 (2023) Page **4**

Married Filing Jointly or Qualifying Surviving Spouse

Higher Paying Job Annual Taxable Wage & Salary	Lower Paying Job Annual Taxable Wage & Salary											
	$0 - 9,999	$10,000 - 19,999	$20,000 - 29,999	$30,000 - 39,999	$40,000 - 49,999	$50,000 - 59,999	$60,000 - 69,999	$70,000 - 79,999	$80,000 - 89,999	$90,000 - 99,999	$100,000 - 109,999	$110,000 - 120,000
$0 - 9,999	$0	$0	$850	$850	$1,000	$1,020	$1,020	$1,020	$1,020	$1,020	$1,020	$1,870
$10,000 - 19,999	0	930	1,850	2,000	2,200	2,220	2,220	2,220	2,220	2,220	3,200	4,070
$20,000 - 29,999	850	1,850	2,920	3,120	3,320	3,340	3,340	3,340	3,340	4,320	5,320	6,190
$30,000 - 39,999	850	2,000	3,120	3,320	3,520	3,540	3,540	3,540	4,520	5,520	6,520	7,390
$40,000 - 49,999	1,020	2,220	3,320	3,520	3,720	3,740	3,740	4,720	5,720	6,720	7,720	8,590
$50,000 - 59,999	1,020	2,220	3,340	3,540	3,740	3,760	4,750	5,750	6,750	7,750	8,750	9,610
$60,000 - 69,999	1,020	2,220	3,340	3,540	3,740	4,750	5,750	6,750	7,750	8,750	9,750	10,610
$70,000 - 79,999	1,020	2,220	3,340	3,540	4,720	5,750	6,750	7,750	8,750	9,750	10,750	11,610
$80,000 - 99,999	1,020	2,220	4,170	5,370	6,570	7,600	8,600	9,600	10,600	11,600	12,600	13,460
$100,000 - 149,999	1,870	4,070	6,190	7,390	8,590	9,610	10,610	11,660	12,860	14,060	15,260	16,330
$150,000 - 239,999	2,040	4,440	6,760	8,160	9,560	10,780	11,980	13,180	14,380	15,580	16,780	17,850
$240,000 - 259,999	2,040	4,440	6,760	8,160	9,560	10,780	11,980	13,180	14,380	15,580	16,780	17,850
$260,000 - 279,999	2,040	4,440	6,760	8,160	9,560	10,780	11,980	13,180	14,380	15,580	16,780	18,140
$280,000 - 299,999	2,040	4,440	6,760	8,160	9,560	10,780	11,980	13,180	14,380	15,870	17,870	19,740
$300,000 - 319,999	2,040	4,440	6,760	8,160	9,560	10,780	11,980	13,470	15,470	17,470	19,470	21,340
$320,000 - 364,999	2,040	4,440	6,760	8,550	10,750	12,770	14,770	16,770	18,770	20,770	22,770	24,640
$365,000 - 524,999	2,970	6,470	9,890	12,390	14,890	17,220	19,520	21,820	24,120	26,420	28,720	30,880
$525,000 and over	3,140	6,840	10,460	13,160	15,860	18,390	20,890	23,390	25,890	28,390	30,890	33,250

Notice that the circled result, $3,720, appears on Step 2, line 1 of the Multiple Jobs Worksheet.

Note that the extra withholding from line 4(c) is rounded to the nearest dollar. Using the wage bracket in Publication 15-T, the federal withholding amount would be $163 per pay period. Since Rene has the two dependents under 17, this is reduced by $166.67 ($4,000/24) and would give Rene no federal income taxes. However, the extra withholding of $155.00 must be added to the amount shown in the wage-bracket tables or the result of the percentage method. The federal income tax withheld from Rene's pay would be **$155.00** per pay period.

This next example shows the manual federal tax computation for a married employee with dependents and pre-tax deductions. Form W-4 should be completed first to obtain the IRS Withholding Tax Assistant's data to work properly.

EXAMPLE: MANUAL PAYROLL TAX COMPUTATION USING FORM W-4 AND THE IRS INCOME TAX WITHHOLDING ASSISTANT WITH PRE-TAX DEDUCTIONS

Bai is an employee at Benson Architects who earns $75,500 annually, is paid biweekly, and is married. Bai's spouse is employed, earning $54,000 annually, and paid semi-monthly, so box 2(c) is checked. They have three dependents under the age of 17 and one other dependent. Bai has elected to contribute 5 percent of gross pay to a 401(k) plan and has pre-tax medical insurance of $250 per pay period.

Steps 2 through 4 of Bai's W-4 would appear as follows:

Step 2: Multiple Jobs or Spouse Works

Complete this step if you (1) hold more than one job at a time, or (2) are married filing jointly and your spouse also works. The correct amount of withholding depends on income earned from all of these jobs.

Do **only one** of the following.

(a) Reserved for future use.

(b) Use the Multiple Jobs Worksheet on page 3 and enter the result in Step 4(c) below; **or**

(c) If there are only two jobs total, you may check this box. Do the same on Form W-4 for the other job. This option is generally more accurate than (b) if pay at the lower paying job is more than half of the pay at the higher paying job. Otherwise, (b) is more accurate . . . . ☐

TIP: If you have self-employment income, see page 2.

Complete Steps 3–4(b) on Form W-4 for only ONE of these jobs. Leave those steps blank for the other jobs. (Your withholding will be most accurate if you complete Steps 3–4(b) on the Form W-4 for the highest paying job.)

Step 3: Claim Dependent and Other Credits

If your total income will be $200,000 or less ($400,000 or less if married filing jointly):

Multiply the number of qualifying children under age 17 by $2,000 $ 6000

Multiply the number of other dependents by $500 . . . . . $ 500

Add the amounts above for qualifying children and other dependents. You may add to this amount of any other credits. Enter the total here . . . . **3** $ 6500

Step 4 (optional): Other Adjustments

(a) **Other income (not from jobs).** If you want tax withheld for other income you expect this year that won't have withholding, enter the amount of other income here. This may include interest, dividends, and retirement income . . . . **4(a)** $

(b) **Deductions.** If you expect to claim deductions other than the standard deduction and want to reduce your withholding, use the Deductions Worksheet on page 3 and enter the result here . . . . **4(b)** $

(c) **Extra withholding.** Enter any additional tax you want withheld each **pay period** . . **4(c)** $ 221.15

To determine the amount for Step 4(c), Bai would need to complete the Multiple Jobs Worksheet on page 3 of Form W-4 as follows:

Form W-4 (2023) Page **3**

Step 2(b)—Multiple Jobs Worksheet *(Keep for your records.)*

If you choose the option in Step 2(b) on Form W-4, complete this worksheet (which calculates the total extra tax for all jobs) on **only ONE** Form W-4. Withholding will be most accurate if you complete the worksheet and enter the result on the Form W-4 for the highest paying job. To be accurate, submit a new Form W-4 for all other jobs if you have not updated your withholding since 2019.

Note: If more than one job has annual wages of more than $120,000 or there are more than three jobs, see Pub. 505 for additional tables.

1. **Two jobs.** If you have two jobs or you're married filing jointly and you and your spouse each have one job, find the amount from the appropriate table on page 4. Using the "Higher Paying Job" row and the "Lower Paying Job" column, find the value at the intersection of the two household salaries and enter that value on line 1. Then, **skip** to line 3 . . . . **1** $ 5750

2. **Three jobs.** If you and/or your spouse have three jobs at the same time, complete lines 2a, 2b, and 2c below. Otherwise, skip to line 3.

   a. Find the amount from the appropriate table on page 4 using the annual wages from the highest paying job in the "Higher Paying Job" row and the annual wages for your next highest paying job in the "Lower Paying Job" column. Find the value at the intersection of the two household salaries and enter that value on line 2a . . . . **2a** $

   b. Add the annual wages of the two highest paying jobs from line 2a together and use the total as the wages in the "Higher Paying Job" row and use the annual wages for your third job in the "Lower Paying Job" column to find the amount from the appropriate table on page 4 and enter this amount on line 2b . . . . **2b** $

   c. Add the amounts from lines 2a and 2b and enter the result on line 2c . . . . **2c** $

3. Enter the number of pay periods per year for the highest paying job. For example, if that job pays weekly, enter 52; if it pays every other week, enter 26; if it pays monthly, enter 12, etc. **3** 26

4. **Divide** the annual amount on line 1 or line 2c by the number of pay periods on line 3. Enter this amount here and in **Step 4(c)** of Form W-4 for the highest paying job (along with any other additional amount you want withheld) . . . . **4** $ 221.15

To determine the amount on line 1 of the Multiple Jobs Worksheet, Bai would use page 4 of Form W-4 as follows:

Form W-4 (2023) — Page 4

Married Filing Jointly or Qualifying Surviving Spouse

Higher Paying Job Annual Taxable Wage & Salary	Lower Paying Job Annual Taxable Wage & Salary										
	$0 - 9,999	$10,000 - 19,999	$20,000 - 29,999	$30,000 - 39,999	$40,000 - 49,999	$50,000 - 59,999	$60,000 - 69,999	$70,000 - 79,999	$80,000 - 89,999	$90,000 - 99,999	$100,000 - 109,999	$110,000 - 120,000
$0 - 9,999	$0	$0	$850	$850	$1,000	$1,020	$1,020	$1,020	$1,020	$1,020	$1,020	$1,870
$10,000 - 19,999	0	930	1,850	2,000	2,200	2,220	2,220	2,220	2,220	2,220	3,200	4,070
$20,000 - 29,999	850	1,850	2,920	3,120	3,320	3,340	3,340	3,340	3,340	4,320	5,320	6,190
$30,000 - 39,999	850	2,000	3,120	3,320	3,520	3,540	3,540	3,540	4,520	5,520	6,520	7,390
$40,000 - 49,999	1,000	2,200	3,320	3,520	3,720	3,740	3,740	4,720	5,720	6,720	7,720	8,590
$50,000 - 59,999	1,020	2,220	3,340	3,540	3,740	3,760	4,750	5,750	6,750	7,750	8,750	9,610
$60,000 - 69,999	1,020	2,220	3,340	3,540	3,740	4,750	5,750	6,750	7,750	8,750	9,750	10,610
$70,000 - 79,999	1,020	2,220	3,340	3,540	4,720	5,750	6,750	7,750	8,750	9,750	10,750	11,610
$80,000 - 99,999	1,020	2,220	4,170	5,370	6,570	7,600	8,600	9,600	10,600	11,600	12,600	13,460
$100,000 - 149,999	1,870	4,070	6,190	7,390	8,590	9,610	10,610	11,660	12,860	14,060	15,260	16,330
$150,000 - 239,999	2,040	4,440	6,760	8,160	9,560	10,780	11,980	13,180	14,380	15,580	16,780	17,850
$240,000 - 259,999	2,040	4,440	6,760	8,160	9,560	10,780	11,980	13,180	14,380	15,580	16,780	17,850
$260,000 - 279,999	2,040	4,440	6,760	8,160	9,560	10,780	11,980	13,180	14,380	15,580	16,780	18,140
$280,000 - 299,999	2,040	4,440	6,760	8,160	9,560	10,780	11,980	13,180	14,380	15,870	17,870	19,740
$300,000 - 319,999	2,040	4,440	6,760	8,160	9,560	10,780	11,980	13,470	15,470	17,470	19,470	21,340
$320,000 - 364,999	2,040	4,440	6,760	8,550	10,750	12,770	14,770	16,770	18,770	20,770	22,770	24,640
$365,000 - 524,999	2,970	6,470	9,890	12,390	14,890	17,220	19,520	21,820	24,120	26,420	28,720	30,880
$525,000 and over	3,140	6,840	10,460	13,160	15,860	18,390	20,890	23,390	25,890	28,390	30,890	33,250

Notice that the circled result, $5,750, appears on Step 2, line 1 of the Multiple Jobs Worksheet.

Before we compute the federal withholding tax per period, we need to apply the pre-tax deductions:

Period salary: $75,500/26	$2,903.85
Less: 401(k) at 5% of salary	−145.19
Less: Pre-tax medical insurance	250.00
Taxable income	$2,508.66*
Federal tax per Publication 15-T	$ 3.00**
Additional withholding (Box 4(c) is checked)	221.15
Total federal income tax	$ 224.15

*Note: Gross pay − Qualified medical = Taxable wages for FICA. $2,903.85 − 250.00 = $2,653.85 would be the taxable amount for Social Security and Medicare because retirement contributions are not exempt from FICA taxes.
** Since the employee has three dependents under 17 and one other (for a total of three dependents), the resulting federal withholding of $253 is reduced by a $250 dependent deduction for a total of $3.

Wage-Bracket Method

Using the *wage-bracket method*, the payroll clerk identifies the individual's marital status, number of exemptions, and taxable income level and then follows the chart in Publication 15-T for the amount to be withheld. If manually calculating the wage-bracket method, it is important to apply the appropriate number of withholding variables before calculating the tax amounts. The wage-bracket method is useful for manual payroll preparation because the process of federal tax withholding is an estimate for the year-end amount of taxes due. To determine taxes to withhold using Appendix C, the payroll clerk may use Publication 15-T. If the payroll clerk uses an automated system, periodic checking and ensuring that year-end updates do not run before the last payroll are important to ensuring the system's validity.

EXAMPLE: WAGE-BRACKET COMPUTATION OF FEDERAL INCOME TAX, SINGLE, BIWEEKLY

Gerry is an employee at Vosgienne Farms. The employee is single with no dependents and earns $48,000 annually, paid biweekly. Using the wage bracket tables in Appendix C, we will determine Gerry's federal income tax in different situations.

(continued)

(concluded)

1. NO PRE-TAX DEDUCTIONS

Period pay ($48,000/26)	$1,846.15
Taxable income	1,846.15
Federal income tax	150.00

2. PRE-TAX HEALTH INSURANCE, $75, PRE-TAX SUPPLEMENTAL HEALTH INSURANCE, $55

Period pay ($48,000/26)	$1,846.15
Less: health insurance	75.00
Less: supplemental health insurance	55.00
Taxable income*	$1,716.15
Federal income tax	$ 133.00

3. PRE-TAX HEALTH INSURANCE, $75, PRE-TAX SUPPLEMENTAL HEALTH INSURANCE, $55, 401(K) CONTRIBUTION, $100

Period pay ($48,000/26)	$1,846.15
Less: health insurance	75.00
Less: supplemental health insurance	55.00
Less: 401(k) contribution	100.00
Taxable income*	$1,616.15
Federal income tax	$ 121.00

*Note: The taxable income for Social Security and Medicare tax is $1,846.15 − 75 − 55 = $1,716.15.

When using the wage-bracket tables, it should be noted that many wage amounts are the same number as the beginning and the end of a range. If the number is the exact number of the range in these events, the next bracket should be used. For example, refer to the below image. It is important to notice the language at the top of the column: "And the wages are— At least. . . But less than." If the wages were $3,324.99, then the top row would be used. If the wages were precisely $3,325, then the second row would be used.

EXAMPLE: WAGE-BRACKET COMPUTATION OF FEDERAL INCOME TAX, MARRIED FILING JOINT, SEMIMONTHLY PAY PERIOD

Robin is an employee of Centerspot Photo Designs. Robin earns $36,000 per year, is paid semimonthly, and is single with no dependents. Box 2 is not checked. Using the wage-bracket tables in Appendix C, we will determine Robin's federal income tax in different situations.

1. NO VOLUNTARY PRE-TAX DEDUCTIONS

Period pay ($36,000/24)	$1,500.00
Taxable income	1,500.00
Federal income tax	$ 101.00

2. PRE-TAX HEALTH INSURANCE DEDUCTION, $150

Period pay ($36,000/24)	$1,500.00
Less: health insurance	150.00
Taxable income*	$1,350.00
Federal income tax	$ 84.00

3. PRE-TAX HEALTH INSURANCE DEDUCTION, $150, AND 401(K) CONTRIBUTION, 4%

Period pay ($36,000/24)	$1,500.00
Less: health insurance	150.00
Less: 401(k) contribution	80.00
Taxable income*	$1,270.00
Federal income tax	$ 75.00

*Note: The taxable income for Social Security and Medicare tax is $2,000 − 150 = $1,850.

Percentage Method

There are many tables in IRS Publication 15-T to assist employers with the correct amount of withholding. The *percentage method* for calculating employee withholding is tiered, with each layer building upon the previous layer. In 2020, the changes to tax credits drastically altered the computation method, focusing on consistency between the annual tax filing and the federal income tax per pay period. We will go through an example in which we complete the percentage method using a manual system.

Note that the wage-bracket and percentage methods will yield similar results as to income tax withholding. The percentage method shown in Figure 5-1 allows more flexibility for calculations involving high-wage earners or uncommon pay periods, but the wage-bracket method is simpler for manual payroll computations.

FIGURE 5-1
2023 Percentage Method Tables for Income Tax

2023 Percentage Method Tables for Manual Payroll Systems With Forms W-4 from 2020 or Later

WEEKLY Payroll Period

STANDARD Withholding Rate Schedules (Use these if the box in Step 2 of Form W-4 is NOT checked)					Form W-4, Step 2, Checkbox, Withholding Rate Schedules (Use these if the box in Step 2 of Form W-4 IS checked)				
If the Adjusted Wage Amount (line 1h) is:		The tentative amount to withhold is:	Plus this percentage—	of the amount that the Adjusted Wage exceeds—	If the Adjusted Wage Amount (line 1h) is:		The tentative amount to withhold is:	Plus this percentage—	of the amount that the Adjusted Wage exceeds—
At least—	But less than—				At least—	But less than—			
A	B	C	D	E	A	B	C	D	E
Married Filing Jointly					**Married Filing Jointly**				
$0	$533	$0.00	0%	$0	$0	$266	$0.00	0%	$0
$533	$956	$0.00	10%	$533	$266	$478	$0.00	10%	$266
$956	$2,253	$42.30	12%	$956	$478	$1,126	$21.20	12%	$478
$2,253	$4,201	$197.94	22%	$2,253	$1,126	$2,100	$98.96	22%	$1,126
$4,201	$7,537	$626.50	24%	$4,201	$2,100	$3,768	$313.24	24%	$2,100
$7,537	$9,427	$1,427.14	32%	$7,537	$3,768	$4,713	$713.56	32%	$3,768
$9,427	$13,874	$2,031.94	35%	$9,427	$4,713	$6,937	$1,015.96	35%	$4,713
$13,874		$3,588.39	37%	$13,874	$6,937		$1,794.36	37%	$6,937
Single or Married Filing Separately					**Single or Married Filing Separately**				
$0	$266	$0.00	0%	$0	$0	$133	$0.00	0%	$0
$266	$478	$0.00	10%	$266	$133	$239	$0.00	10%	$133
$478	$1,126	$21.20	12%	$478	$239	$563	$10.60	12%	$239
$1,126	$2,100	$98.96	22%	$1,126	$563	$1,050	$49.48	22%	$563
$2,100	$3,768	$313.24	24%	$2,100	$1,050	$1,884	$156.62	24%	$1,050
$3,768	$4,713	$713.56	32%	$3,768	$1,884	$2,357	$356.78	32%	$1,884
$4,713	$11,384	$1,015.96	35%	$4,713	$2,357	$5,692	$508.14	35%	$2,357
$11,384		$3,350.81	37%	$11,384	$5,692		$1,675.39	37%	$5,692
Head of Household					**Head of Household**				
$0	$400	$0.00	0%	$0	$0	$200	$0.00	0%	$0
$400	$702	$0.00	10%	$400	$200	$351	$0.00	10%	$200
$702	$1,551	$30.20	12%	$702	$351	$775	$15.10	12%	$351
$1,551	$2,234	$132.08	22%	$1,551	$775	$1,117	$65.98	22%	$775
$2,234	$3,902	$282.34	24%	$2,234	$1,117	$1,951	$141.22	24%	$1,117
$3,902	$4,847	$682.66	32%	$3,902	$1,951	$2,424	$341.38	32%	$1,951
$4,847	$11,517	$985.06	35%	$4,847	$2,424	$5,759	$492.74	35%	$2,424
$11,517		$3,319.56	37%	$11,517	$5,759		$1,659.99	37%	$5,759

(continued)

2023 Percentage Method Tables for Manual Payroll Systems With Forms W-4 from 2020 or Later
BIWEEKLY Payroll Period

STANDARD Withholding Rate Schedules (Use these if the box in Step 2 of Form W-4 is NOT checked)					Form W-4, Step 2, Checkbox, Withholding Rate Schedules (Use these if the box in Step 2 of Form W-4 IS checked)				
If the Adjusted Wage Amount (line 1h) is:		The tentative amount to withhold is:	Plus this percentage—	of the amount that the Adjusted Wage exceeds—	If the Adjusted Wage Amount (line 1h) is:		The tentative amount to withhold is:	Plus this percentage—	of the amount that the Adjusted Wage exceeds—
At least—	But less than—				At least—	But less than—			
A	B	C	D	E	A	B	C	D	E
Married Filing Jointly					**Married Filing Jointly**				
$0	$1,065	$0.00	0%	$0	$0	$533	$0.00	0%	$0
$1,065	$1,912	$0.00	10%	$1,065	$533	$956	$0.00	10%	$533
$1,912	$4,506	$84.70	12%	$1,912	$956	$2,253	$42.30	12%	$956
$4,506	$8,402	$395.98	22%	$4,506	$2,253	$4,201	$197.94	22%	$2,253
$8,402	$15,073	$1,253.10	24%	$8,402	$4,201	$7,537	$626.50	24%	$4,201
$15,073	$18,854	$2,854.14	32%	$15,073	$7,537	$9,427	$1,427.14	32%	$7,537
$18,854	$27,748	$4,064.06	35%	$18,854	$9,427	$13,874	$2,031.94	35%	$9,427
$27,748		$7,176.96	37%	$27,748	$13,874		$3,588.39	37%	$13,874
Single or Married Filing Separately					**Single or Married Filing Separately**				
$0	$533	$0.00	0%	$0	$0	$266	$0.00	0%	$0
$533	$956	$0.00	10%	$533	$266	$478	$0.00	10%	$266
$956	$2,253	$42.30	12%	$956	$478	$1,126	$21.20	12%	$478
$2,253	$4,201	$197.94	22%	$2,253	$1,126	$2,100	$98.96	22%	$1,126
$4,201	$7,537	$626.50	24%	$4,201	$2,100	$3,768	$313.24	24%	$2,100
$7,537	$9,427	$1,427.14	32%	$7,537	$3,768	$4,713	$713.56	32%	$3,768
$9,427	$22,768	$2,031.94	35%	$9,427	$4,713	$11,384	$1,015.96	35%	$4,713
$22,768		$6,701.29	37%	$22,768	$11,384		$3,350.81	37%	$11,384
Head of Household					**Head of Household**				
$0	$800	$0.00	0%	$0	$0	$400	$0.00	0%	$0
$800	$1,404	$0.00	10%	$800	$400	$702	$0.00	10%	$400
$1,404	$3,102	$60.40	12%	$1,404	$702	$1,551	$30.20	12%	$702
$3,102	$4,467	$264.16	22%	$3,102	$1,551	$2,234	$132.08	22%	$1,551
$4,467	$7,804	$564.46	24%	$4,467	$2,234	$3,902	$282.34	24%	$2,234
$7,804	$9,694	$1,365.34	32%	$7,804	$3,902	$4,847	$682.66	32%	$3,902
$9,694	$23,035	$1,970.14	35%	$9,694	$4,847	$11,517	$985.06	35%	$4,847
$23,035		$6,639.49	37%	$23,035	$11,517		$3,319.56	37%	$11,517

2023 Percentage Method Tables for Manual Payroll Systems With Forms W-4 from 2020 or Later
SEMIMONTHLY Payroll Period

STANDARD Withholding Rate Schedules (Use these if the box in Step 2 of Form W-4 is NOT checked)					Form W-4, Step 2, Checkbox, Withholding Rate Schedules (Use these if the box in Step 2 of Form W-4 IS checked)				
If the Adjusted Wage Amount (line 1h) is:		The tentative amount to withhold is:	Plus this percentage—	of the amount that the Adjusted Wage exceeds—	If the Adjusted Wage Amount (line 1h) is:		The tentative amount to withhold is:	Plus this percentage—	of the amount that the Adjusted Wage exceeds—
At least—	But less than—				At least—	But less than—			
A	B	C	D	E	A	B	C	D	E
Married Filing Jointly					**Married Filing Jointly**				
$0	$1,154	$0.00	0%	$0	$0	$577	$0.00	0%	$0
$1,154	$2,071	$0.00	10%	$1,154	$577	$1,035	$0.00	10%	$577
$2,071	$4,881	$91.70	12%	$2,071	$1,035	$2,441	$45.80	12%	$1,035
$4,881	$9,102	$428.90	22%	$4,881	$2,441	$4,551	$214.52	22%	$2,441
$9,102	$16,329	$1,357.52	24%	$9,102	$4,551	$8,165	$678.72	24%	$4,551
$16,329	$20,425	$3,092.00	32%	$16,329	$8,165	$10,213	$1,546.08	32%	$8,165
$20,425	$30,060	$4,402.72	35%	$20,425	$10,213	$15,030	$2,201.44	35%	$10,213
$30,060		$7,774.97	37%	$30,060	$15,030		$3,887.39	37%	$15,030
Single or Married Filing Separately					**Single or Married Filing Separately**				
$0	$577	$0.00	0%	$0	$0	$289	$0.00	0%	$0
$577	$1,035	$0.00	10%	$577	$289	$518	$0.00	10%	$289
$1,035	$2,441	$45.80	12%	$1,035	$518	$1,220	$22.90	12%	$518
$2,441	$4,551	$214.52	22%	$2,441	$1,220	$2,276	$107.14	22%	$1,220
$4,551	$8,165	$678.72	24%	$4,551	$2,276	$4,082	$339.46	24%	$2,276
$8,165	$10,213	$1,546.08	32%	$8,165	$4,082	$5,106	$772.90	32%	$4,082
$10,213	$24,666	$2,201.44	35%	$10,213	$5,106	$12,333	$1,100.58	35%	$5,106
$24,666		$7,259.99	37%	$24,666	$12,333		$3,630.03	37%	$12,333

	Head of Household					Head of Household			
$0	$867	$0.00	0%	$0	$0	$433	$0.00	0%	$0
$867	$1,521	$0.00	10%	$867	$433	$760	$0.00	10%	$433
$1,521	$3,360	$65.40	12%	$1,521	$760	$1,680	$32.70	12%	$760
$3,360	$4,840	$286.08	22%	$3,360	$1,680	$2,420	$143.10	22%	$1,680
$4,840	$8,454	$611.68	24%	$4,840	$2,420	$4,227	$305.90	24%	$2,420
$8,454	$10,502	$1,479.04	32%	$8,454	$4,227	$5,251	$739.58	32%	$4,227
$10,502	$24,954	$2,134.40	35%	$10,502	$5,251	$12,477	$1,067.26	35%	$5,251
$24,954		$7,192.60	37%	$24,954	$12,477		$3,596.36	37%	$12,477

2023 Percentage Method Tables for Manual Payroll Systems With Forms W-4 from 2020 or Later
MONTHLY Payroll Period

STANDARD Withholding Rate Schedules (Use these if the box in Step 2 of Form W-4 is **NOT** checked)					Form W-4, Step 2, Checkbox, Withholding Rate Schedules (Use these if the box in Step 2 of Form W-4 **IS** checked)				
If the Adjusted Wage Amount (line 1h) is:		The tentative amount to withhold is:	Plus this percentage—	of the amount that the Adjusted Wage exceeds—	If the Adjusted Wage Amount (line 1h) is:		The tentative amount to withhold is:	Plus this percentage—	of the amount that the Adjusted Wage exceeds—
At least—	But less than—				At least—	But less than—			
A	B	C	D	E	A	B	C	D	E
	Married Filing Jointly					Married Filing Jointly			
$0	$2,308	$0.00	0%	$0	$0	$1,154	$0.00	0%	$0
$2,308	$4,142	$0.00	10%	$2,308	$1,154	$2,071	$0.00	10%	$1,154
$4,142	$9,763	$183.40	12%	$4,142	$2,071	$4,881	$91.70	12%	$2,071
$9,763	$18,204	$857.92	22%	$9,763	$4,881	$9,102	$428.90	22%	$4,881
$18,204	$32,658	$2,714.94	24%	$18,204	$9,102	$16,329	$1,357.52	24%	$9,102
$32,658	$40,850	$6,183.90	32%	$32,658	$16,329	$20,425	$3,092.00	32%	$16,329
$40,850	$60,121	$8,805.34	35%	$40,850	$20,425	$30,060	$4,402.72	35%	$20,425
$60,121		$15,550.19	37%	$60,121	$30,060		$7,774.97	37%	$30,060
	Single or Married Filing Separately					Single or Married Filing Separately			
$0	$1,154	$0.00	0%	$0	$0	$577	$0.00	0%	$0
$1,154	$2,071	$0.00	10%	$1,154	$577	$1,035	$0.00	10%	$577
$2,071	$4,881	$91.70	12%	$2,071	$1,035	$2,441	$45.80	12%	$1,035
$4,881	$9,102	$428.90	22%	$4,881	$2,441	$4,551	$214.52	22%	$2,441
$9,102	$16,329	$1,357.52	24%	$9,102	$4,551	$8,165	$678.72	24%	$4,551
$16,329	$20,425	$3,092.00	32%	$16,329	$8,165	$10,213	$1,546.08	32%	$8,165
$20,425	$49,331	$4,402.72	35%	$20,425	$10,213	$24,666	$2,201.44	35%	$10,213
$49,331		$14,519.82	37%	$49,331	$24,666		$7,259.99	37%	$24,666
	Head of Household					Head of Household			
$0	$1,733	$0.00	0%	$0	$0	$867	$0.00	0%	$0
$1,733	$3,042	$0.00	10%	$1,733	$867	$1,521	$0.00	10%	$867
$3,042	$6,721	$130.90	12%	$3,042	$1,521	$3,360	$65.40	12%	$1,521
$6,721	$9,679	$572.38	22%	$6,721	$3,360	$4,840	$286.08	22%	$3,360
$9,679	$16,908	$1,223.14	24%	$9,679	$4,840	$8,454	$611.68	24%	$4,840
$16,908	$21,004	$2,958.10	32%	$16,908	$8,454	$10,502	$1,479.04	32%	$8,454
$21,004	$49,908	$4,268.82	35%	$21,004	$10,502	$24,954	$2,134.40	35%	$10,502
$49,908		$14,385.22	37%	$49,908	$24,954		$7,192.60	37%	$24,954

2023 Percentage Method Tables for Manual Payroll Systems With Forms W-4 from 2020 or Later
DAILY Payroll Period

STANDARD Withholding Rate Schedules (Use these if the box in Step 2 of Form W-4 is **NOT** checked)					Form W-4, Step 2, Checkbox, Withholding Rate Schedules (Use these if the box in Step 2 of Form W-4 **IS** checked)				
If the Adjusted Wage Amount (line 1h) is:		The tentative amount to withhold is:	Plus this percentage—	of the amount that the Adjusted Wage exceeds—	If the Adjusted Wage Amount (line 1h) is:		The tentative amount to withhold is:	Plus this percentage—	of the amount that the Adjusted Wage exceeds—
At least—	But less than—				At least—	But less than—			
A	B	C	D	E	A	B	C	D	E
	Married Filing Jointly					Married Filing Jointly			
$0.00	$106.50	$0.00	0%	$0.00	$0.00	$53.30	$0.00	0%	$0.00
$106.50	$191.20	$0.00	10%	$106.50	$53.30	$95.60	$0.00	10%	$53.30
$191.20	$450.60	$8.47	12%	$191.20	$95.60	$225.30	$4.23	12%	$95.60
$450.60	$840.20	$39.60	22%	$450.60	$225.30	$420.10	$19.79	22%	$225.30
$840.20	$1,507.30	$125.31	24%	$840.20	$420.10	$753.70	$62.65	24%	$420.10
$1,507.30	$1,885.40	$285.41	32%	$1,507.30	$753.70	$942.70	$142.71	32%	$753.70
$1,885.40	$2,774.80	$406.41	35%	$1,885.40	$942.70	$1,387.40	$203.19	35%	$942.70
$2,774.80		$717.70	37%	$2,774.80	$1,387.40		$358.84	37%	$1,387.40

(continued)

	Single or Married Filing Separately					Single or Married Filing Separately			
$0.00	$53.30	$0.00	0%	$0.00	$0.00	$26.60	$0.00	0%	$0.00
$53.30	$95.60	$0.00	10%	$53.30	$26.60	$47.80	$0.00	10%	$26.60
$95.60	$225.30	$4.23	12%	$95.60	$47.80	$112.60	$2.12	12%	$47.80
$225.30	$420.10	$19.79	22%	$225.30	$112.60	$210.00	$9.90	22%	$112.60
$420.10	$753.70	$62.65	24%	$420.10	$210.00	$376.80	$31.32	24%	$210.00
$753.70	$942.70	$142.71	32%	$753.70	$376.80	$471.30	$71.36	32%	$376.80
$942.70	$2,276.80	$203.19	35%	$942.70	$471.30	$1,138.40	$101.60	35%	$471.30
$2,276.80		$670.13	37%	$2,276.80	$1,138.40		$335.08	37%	$1,138.40
	Head of Household					Head of Household			
$0.00	$80.00	$0.00	0%	$0.00	$0.00	$40.00	$0.00	0%	$0.00
$80.00	$140.40	$0.00	10%	$80.00	$40.00	$70.20	$0.00	10%	$40.00
$140.40	$310.20	$6.04	12%	$140.40	$70.20	$155.10	$3.02	12%	$70.20
$310.20	$446.70	$26.42	22%	$310.20	$155.10	$223.40	$13.21	22%	$155.10
$446.70	$780.40	$56.45	24%	$446.70	$223.40	$390.20	$28.23	24%	$223.40
$780.40	$969.40	$136.53	32%	$780.40	$390.20	$484.70	$68.27	32%	$390.20
$969.40	$2,303.50	$197.01	35%	$969.40	$484.70	$1,151.70	$98.51	35%	$484.70
$2,303.50		$663.95	37%	$2,303.50	$1,151.70		$331.96	37%	$1,151.70

(Source: Internal Revenue Service)

The IRS has published guidance for using the percentage method tables manually. The process published in 2023 differs significantly from the process that existed prior to 2020 because of the changes to Form W-4 and income tax laws.

FIGURE 5-2
2023 Percentage Method Tables Directions

4. Percentage Method Tables for Manual Payroll Systems With Forms W-4 From 2020 or Later

If you compute payroll manually, your employee has submitted a Form W-4 for 2020 or later, and you prefer to use the Percentage Method or you can't use the Wage Bracket Method tables because the employee's annual wages exceed $100,000, use the worksheet below and the Percentage Method tables that follow to figure federal income tax withholding. This method works for any amount of wages.

Worksheet 4. Employer's Withholding Worksheet for Percentage Method Tables for Manual Payroll Systems With Forms W-4 From 2020 or Later

Keep for Your Records

Table 5	Monthly	Semimonthly	Biweekly	Weekly	Daily
	12	24	26	52	260

Step 1. Adjust the employee's wage amount
- 1a Enter the employee's total taxable wages this payroll period .... 1a $ _____
- 1b Enter the number of pay periods you have per year (see Table 5) .... 1b _____
- 1c Enter the amount from Step 4(a) of the employee's Form W-4 .... 1c $ _____
- 1d Divide line 1c by the number on line 1b .... 1d $ _____
- 1e Add lines 1a and 1d .... 1e $ _____
- 1f Enter the amount from Step 4(b) of the employee's Form W-4 .... 1f $ _____
- 1g Divide line 1f by the number on line 1b .... 1g $ _____
- 1h Subtract line 1g from line 1e. If zero or less, enter -0-. This is the **Adjusted Wage Amount** ...... 1h $ _____

Step 2. Figure the Tentative Withholding Amount
based on your pay frequency, the employee's Adjusted Wage Amount, filing status (Step 1(c) of Form W-4), and whether the box in Step 2 of Form W-4 is checked.

- 2a Find the row in the *STANDARD Withholding Rate Schedules* (if the box in Step 2 of Form W-4 is NOT checked) or the *Form W-4, Step 2, Checkbox, Withholding Rate Schedules* (if it HAS been checked) of the Percentage Method tables in this section in which the amount on line 1h is at least the amount in column A but less than the amount in column B, then enter here the amount from column A of that row .... 2a $ _____

2b	Enter the amount from column C of that row	2b $ _____
2c	Enter the percentage from column D of that row	2c _____ %
2d	Subtract line 2a from line 1h	2d $ _____
2e	Multiply the amount on line 2d by the percentage on line 2c	2e $ _____
2f	Add lines 2b and 2e. This is the **Tentative Withholding Amount**	2f $ _____
Step 3.	**Account for tax credits**	
3a	Enter the amount from Step 3 of the employee's Form W-4	3a $ _____
3b	Divide the amount on line 3a by the number of pay periods on line 1b	3b $ _____
3c	Subtract line 3b from line 2f. If zero or less, enter -0-	3c $ _____
Step 4.	**Figure the final amount to withhold**	
4a	Enter the additional amount to withhold from Step 4(c) of the employee's Form W-4	4a $ _____
4b	Add lines 3c and 4a. **This is the amount to withhold from the employee's wages this pay period**	4b $ _____

(Source: Internal Revenue Service)

Using the percentage method can be confusing, so let's look at a step-by-step example. This first example uses data from the employee's Form W-4 and prior year income tax filing information.

> **EXAMPLE: SINGLE EMPLOYEE, PERCENTAGE METHOD**
>
> CS is single and has two dependents under the age of 17 reported on Form W-4 from 2023. CS is paid semimonthly and earns $51,000 per year, does not receive any other income, and does not itemize deductions. Form W-4, Step 2 box has not been checked. CS has no pre-tax deductions.
>
> The following image is an excerpt from the Percentage Method Tables with an outline around the row to be used for Step 2.
>
> **2023 Percentage Method Tables for Manual Payroll Systems With Forms W-4 from 2020 or Later**
> **SEMIMONTHLY Payroll Period**
>
> | STANDARD Withholding Rate Schedules (Use these if the box in Step 2 of Form W-4 is NOT checked) | | | | | Form W-4, Step 2, Checkbox, Withholding Rate Schedules (Use these if the box in Step 2 of Form W-4 IS checked) | | | | |
> |---|---|---|---|---|---|---|---|---|---|
> | If the Adjusted Wage Amount (line 1h) is: | | The tentative amount to withhold is: | Plus this percentage— | of the amount that the Adjusted Wage exceeds— | If the Adjusted Wage Amount (line 1h) is: | | The tentative amount to withhold is: | Plus this percentage— | of the amount that the Adjusted Wage exceeds— |
> | At least— | But less than— | | | | At least— | But less than— | | | |
> | A | B | C | D | E | A | B | C | D | E |
> | **Married Filing Jointly** | | | | | **Married Filing Jointly** | | | | |
> | $0 | $1,154 | $0.00 | 0% | $0 | $0 | $577 | $0.00 | 0% | $0 |
> | $1,154 | $2,071 | $0.00 | 10% | $1,154 | $577 | $1,035 | $0.00 | 10% | $577 |
> | $2,071 | $4,881 | $91.70 | 12% | $2,071 | $1,035 | $2,441 | $45.80 | 12% | $1,035 |
> | $4,881 | $9,102 | $428.90 | 22% | $4,881 | $2,441 | $4,551 | $214.52 | 22% | $2,441 |
> | $9,102 | $16,329 | $1,357.52 | 24% | $9,102 | $4,551 | $8,165 | $678.72 | 24% | $4,551 |
> | $16,329 | $20,425 | $3,092.00 | 32% | $16,329 | $8,165 | $10,213 | $1,546.08 | 32% | $8,165 |
> | $20,425 | $30,060 | $4,402.72 | 35% | $20,425 | $10,213 | $15,030 | $2,201.44 | 35% | $10,213 |
> | $30,060 | | $7,774.97 | 37% | $30,060 | $15,030 | | $3,887.39 | 37% | $15,030 |
> | **Single or Married Filing Separately** | | | | | **Single or Married Filing Separately** | | | | |
> | $0 | $577 | $0.00 | 0% | $0 | $0 | $289 | $0.00 | 0% | $0 |
> | $577 | $1,035 | $0.00 | 10% | $577 | $289 | $518 | $0.00 | 10% | $289 |
> | **$1,035** | **$2,441** | **$45.80** | **12%** | **$1,035** | $518 | $1,220 | $22.90 | 12% | $518 |
> | $2,441 | $4,551 | $214.52 | 22% | $2,441 | $1,220 | $2,276 | $107.14 | 22% | $1,220 |
> | $4,551 | $8,165 | $678.72 | 24% | $4,551 | $2,276 | $4,082 | $339.46 | 24% | $2,276 |
> | $8,165 | $10,213 | $1,546.08 | 32% | $8,165 | $4,082 | $5,106 | $772.90 | 32% | $4,082 |
> | $10,213 | $24,666 | $2,201.44 | 35% | $10,213 | $5,106 | $12,333 | $1,100.58 | 35% | $5,106 |
> | $24,666 | | $7,259.99 | 37% | $24,666 | $12,333 | | $3,630.03 | 37% | $12,333 |
>
> | **Step 1: Adjust the employee's wage amount** | 1a | Total taxable wages for the period (Note: This is the amount after pre-tax deductions for insurance, etc.) | $51,000/24 = $2,125 |
> |---|---|---|---|
> | | 1b | Number of pay periods per year | 24 |
> | | 1c | Amount from Step 4(a) of CS's W-4 (other income not from jobs) | $0 |
>
> *(continued)*

232 Chapter 5 *Employee Net Pay and Pay Methods*

(concluded)

	1d	Divide the amount on 1c by the number on 1b.	0
	1e	Add lines 1a and 1d.	$2,125
	1f	Enter the amount from Step 4(b) of the employee's Form W-4.	$0
	1g	Divide line 1f by the number on line 1b.	0
	1h	Subtract 1g from 1e. This is the adjusted wage amount.	$2,125
Step 2: Figure the tentative withholding amount	**2a**	Since Box 2 on CS's Form W-4 was not checked, use the left-hand tables on the Percentage Method Tables for the semimonthly pay period. For CS, this is row 3 in the section labeled "Single or Married Filing Separately." Enter the amount from Column A of that row.	Column A: $1,035
	2b	Enter the amount of Column C of that row.	$45.80
	2c	Enter the percentage from Column D of that row.	12%
	2d	Subtract line 2a from 1h.	$2,125 − 1,035 = $1,090
	2e	Multiply the amount on 2d by the percentage on 2c.	$1,090 × 12% = $130.80
	2f	Add lines 2b and 2e. This is the tentative withholding amount.	$45.80 + $130.80 = $176.60
Step 3: Account for tax credits	**3a**	Enter the amount from Step 3 of CS's Form W-4. Since CS has two dependents under the age of 17, the amount would be:	$2,000 × 2 = $4,000
	3b	Divide the amount on line 3a by the number of pay periods on line 1b.	$4,000/24 = $166.67
	3c	Subtract line 3b from line 2f. If zero or less, enter –0–.	$176.60 − $166.67 = $9.93
Step 4: Figure the final amount to withhold	**4a**	Enter the additional amount to withhold from Step 4(c) of CS's Form W-4. CS has entered no additional amounts.	0
	4b	Add lines 3c and 4a. This is the amount to withhold from the employee's wages this pay period.	$9.93

(Source: Internal Revenue Service)

The amount of federal income tax withholding may differ slightly between the wage bracket and percentage methods. However, the computation method is similar. Let's revisit the tax computation for CS's tax using the wage-bracket method and compare the two amounts side by side. Only the totals from each step are included because the other information remains the same in both methods.

> **EXAMPLE: SINGLE EMPLOYEE, PERCENTAGE METHOD VS. WAGE-BRACKET TABLE**
>
> CS is single and has two dependents under the age of 17 reported on Form W-4 from 2023. CS is paid semimonthly and earns $51,000 per year, does not receive any other income, and does not itemize deductions. Form W-4, Step 2 box has not been checked.
>
> The following image is an excerpt from the wage-bracket method tables with an outline around the amount to be used for Step 2.

2023 Wage Bracket Method Tables for Manual Payroll Systems with Forms W-4 From 2020 or Later
SEMIMONTHLY Payroll Period

If the Adjusted Wage Amount (line 1h) is		Married Filing Jointly		Head of Household		Single or Married Filing Separately	
		Standard withholding	Form W-4, Step 2, Checkbox withholding	Standard withholding	Form W-4, Step 2, Checkbox withholding	Standard withholding	Form W-4, Step 2, Checkbox withholding
At least	But less than			The Tentative Withholding Amount is:			
$1,885	$1,905	$74	$149	$110	$190	$149	$256
$1,905	$1,925	$76	$151	$113	$195	$151	$260
$1,925	$1,945	$78	$154	$115	$199	$154	$264
$1,945	$1,965	$80	$156	$118	$204	$156	$269
$1,965	$1,985	$82	$159	$120	$208	$159	$273
$1,985	$2,005	$84	$161	$122	$212	$161	$278
$2,005	$2,025	$86	$163	$125	$217	$163	$282
$2,025	$2,045	$88	$166	$127	$221	$166	$286
$2,045	$2,065	$90	$168	$130	$226	$168	$291
$2,065	$2,085	$92	$171	$132	$230	$171	$295
$2,085	$2,105	$95	$173	$134	$234	$173	$300
$2,105	$2,125	$97	$175	$137	$239	$175	$304
$2,125	$2,145	$99	$178	$139	$243	$178	$308
$2,145	$2,165	$102	$180	$142	$248	$180	$313
$2,165	$2,185	$104	$183	$144	$252	$183	$317

Comparison of Percentage and Wage-Bracket Methods

	Percentage method	Wage-bracket method
Step 1: Adjusted wage amount	$2,125.00	$2,125.00
Step 2: Tentative withholding amount	$176.60	$178.00
Step 3: Account for tax credits	$166.67	$166.67
Step 4: Figure the final amount to withhold	$176.60 − 166.67 = $9.93	$178.00 − 166.67 = $11.33

(Source: Internal Revenue Service)

Note that the amount to withhold differs slightly between the percentage method and the wage-bracket method. The cause for this discrepancy is rounding inherent to the wage-bracket method.

If using a manual payroll tax system, the wage-bracket method will be simpler to compute federal income tax amounts. However, note that the percentage method will yield more accurate results. If the company uses a software package to complete its payroll, the percentage method will be used by default.

Stop & Check — How Much Tax to Withhold?

1. Asa earns $75,000 annually, is married filing jointly with two dependents not under 17, a spouse that does not work (box 2 is not checked), and is paid semimonthly; the W-4 is from 2023. Calculate the amount to be withheld using (a) the wage-bracket method and (b) the percentage method.

2. If Asa elected to deduct $100 per pay period for a 401(k), how much would that change the tax withheld from the paycheck? (Use the wage-bracket method.)

3. How much would Asa's federal income tax be if $75 health insurance and $55 AFLAC premiums were deducted each pay period pre-tax? (Use the wage-bracket method, independent of question 2.)

LO 5-3 Compute Social Security and Medicare Tax Withholding

The Social Security Act of 1935 mandated the withholding of certain taxes in addition to federal income tax. Employers collect only federal income taxes on employees without making a corresponding contribution. Social

Security and Medicare, collectively known as *FICA (Federal Insurance Contribution Act) taxes*, contain both the employer's and the employee's portion. When the employer deposits the federal withholding tax, it deposits the Social Security and Medicare amounts simultaneously. The deposits are usually done online but may be made by standard mail in certain circumstances. The report provided to the IRS does not provide a breakdown of tax amounts for individual employees. Specific questions about Social Security or Medicare tax situations should be directed to the Social Security Administration at www.ssa.gov or via telephone at 800-772-1213.

Social Security Tax

Social Security tax, formerly known as OASDI, was designed to cover people for illness, retirement, disability, and old age. As a social insurance method by which communities will help provide for people who are unable to work, Social Security has evolved into a tax that is levied upon all employees until their annual income reaches a specified level. The maximum income, known as the *wage base*, for the Social Security tax changes annually. In 2023, the wage base is $160,200. This means only the first $160,200 of wages earned are subject to the 6.2 percent tax. Every dollar earned above $160,200 will not be subject to Social Security tax. The tax rate on employee pay is 6.2 percent of eligible wages. Remember that eligible wages can be different from gross pay because of pre-tax deductions and the wage base maximum.

An important part of determining Social Security tax when an employee is close to the wage base is to compute the amount of year-to-date (YTD) pay. In programs such as QuickBooks, this computation occurs automatically. The following is a guide to computing Social Security taxable pay.

You will need the following information to complete this computation:

- Period pay.
- Pay frequency.
- The number of prior pay periods in the calendar year.

The computation aims to ensure that the employee does not overpay tax as they approach the annual wage base.

	Period Pay	Pay Frequency	Number of Prior Pay Periods	YTD Pay (Period Pay × # of Prior Pay Periods)	Social Security Taxable Pay for Next Pay Period
Employee 1	$3,500	Weekly	47	$3,500 × 47 = $164,500	–0–
Employee 2	$6,850	Biweekly	23	$6,850 × 23 = $157,550	$160,200 – 157,550 = $2,650
Employee 3	$7,800	Semimonthly	20	$7,800 × 20 = $156,000	$160,200 – 156,000 = $4,200

Note that these computations are used primarily in two instances:

- Highly paid employees
- Pay periods near the end of the calendar year

Examples of Social Security Tax Computations

Employee	Period Wages	YTD Salary at the End of Previous Pay Period	Social Security Tax Computation	Social Security Tax Amount to Be Withheld
1	$1,700	$ 55,600	$1,700 × 6.2%	$105.40
2	2,850	90,000	2,850 × 6.2%	176.70
3	7,200	158,400	1,800 × 6.2%*	111.60
4	8,200	155,800	4,400 × 6.2%†	272.80
5	10,500	195,000	0‡	0

*The employee's wage base reaches the maximum during this pay period; thus, only the amount under the $160,200 cap is taxed for Social Security: $160,200 − $158,400 = $1,800, so only the $1,800 is taxed.
†The employee's wage base reaches the maximum during this pay period; thus, only the amount under the $160,200 cap is taxed for Social Security: $160,200 − $155,800 = $4,400, so only the $4,400 is taxed.
‡The employee's wage base maximum was met before the current pay period, so no Social Security taxes are withheld.

The employee earnings record is vital in computing and tracking the Social Security taxes due for each employee. Current records allow payroll accountants to keep track of annual salaries for each employee to avoid exceeding the maximum wage base, preventing excess deductions from employees' pay.

The employer and employee pay the same amount for the Social Security tax. Remember, the Social Security tax has a maximum annual wage amount, known as the wage base, for which taxes may be withheld. After reaching that maximum annual wage, neither the employee nor the employer pays any more Social Security tax for the remainder of the year.

> With the increase in the retirement age to 67 to qualify for full Social Security benefits (anyone born after 1960 or turning 62 in 2023), employers may find more people in the workforce longer. This represents the latest increase in the retirement age since the 1950s. Semi-retired employees (under qualified retirement age) also need to keep an eye on how much they are earning as their Social Security benefits also begin to phase out at $19,560, by $1 of benefits for every $2 over the cap. In the year the employee reaches the qualified retirement age, he or she may earn up to $51,960, and the phase-out is $1 of benefits for every $3 over the cap. Employees over the full retirement age do not have a benefits phase-out on their earnings.
>
> Any higher-waged individual who caps out of Social Security ($160,200 for 2023) will find the wages over the cap are also not used in calculating future Social Security benefits. Employees working in retirement may also increase their future benefits.
>
> (Sources: Fox Business; U.S. News Money)

Medicare Tax

Medicare taxes differ from Social Security taxes in a couple of significant ways. *Medicare taxes* were levied on employers and employees to help provide basic health coverage for all individuals qualified to enroll in Medicare benefits. The Medicare tax amount for employee wages is 1.45 percent on all wages earned; there is **no maximum wage base** for Medicare taxes.

The Affordable Care Act of 2010 levied an *additional Medicare tax* of 0.9 percent on certain workers, known as highly compensated employees. Only the employee pays this additional tax, and no employer match is required. The wage base for this additional Medicare tax depends on the marital and tax filing statuses reported on the employee's Form W-4 as follows:

- $200,000 for employees who report that they are single, head of household, qualifying widow(er) with a dependent child.
- $250,000 for employees who report that they are married and file taxes jointly.
- $125,000 for employees who report that they are married and file taxes separately.

This made the simple computations and tracking for Medicare taxes a little more challenging for payroll accountants and increased the employee earnings report's need for accuracy. Note the additional Medicare tax is levied *only* on the employees, so there is no employer match. Unless otherwise noted, this text will use $200,000 as the cap.

Examples of Medicare Tax Computations

Employee	Period Wages	YTD Salary at the End of Previous Pay Period	Medicare Tax Computation	Total Medicare Tax Liability (Employee and Employer)
1	$ 1,700	$ 55,600	$1,700 × 1.45%	$24.65 × 2 = $ 49.30
2	2,850	90,000	2,850 × 1.45%	41.33 × 2 = 82.66
3	7,200	112,600	7,200 × 1.45%	104.40 × 2 = 208.80
4	6,200	118,000	6,200 × 1.45%	89.90 × 2 = 179.80
5	10,500	195,000	Employee: ($10,500 × 0.0145*) + ($5,500† × 0.009) = $201.75	Employee: $201.75 + Employer: $152.25‡ Total = $354.00

*10,500 * 0.0145 = 152.25
†195,000 + 10,500 = 205,500. 205,500 − 200,000 = 5,500
‡The employer does not pay the additional Medicare tax.

Remember the applicable wages may have pre-tax deductions. Social Security and Medicare taxes apply to the employee's gross pay if an employee elects to have a 401(k) deduction. However, qualified Section 125 (cafeteria) plans are exempt from FICA taxes. When computing employee taxes, understanding the pre-tax deductions' tax effect is important in computing accurate FICA deductions.

EXAMPLE: COMPUTATION OF SOCIAL SECURITY AND MEDICARE TAXES WITH PRE-TAX DEDUCTIONS

Brooklyn is an employee who earns an annual salary of $58,000, paid biweekly, and is single with no dependents. Brooklyn has pre-tax deductions, including $155 for health insurance and a contribution of 5 percent of gross pay to a 401(k) plan. Let's compute Brooklyn's net pay using Publication 15-T to determine federal income tax under the wage-bracket method, using the information for Form W-4 after 2020 in Appendix C.

Gross pay per period (58,000/26)	$2,230.77
Less: health insurance	155.00
Less: 401(k) (2,230.77 × 0.05)	111.54
Taxable income*	$1,964.23
Federal income tax	164.00
Social Security tax†	128.70
Medicare tax†	30.10
Net pay	$1,641.43

*This taxable income is for federal income tax only.
†Social Security and Medicare taxes are computed on taxable income of $2,230.77 − $155.00 = $2,075.77, then $2,075.77 × 0.062 (Social Security) and $2,075.77 × 0.0145 (Medicare).

EXAMPLE: COMPUTATION OF NET PAY, HIGHLY COMPENSATED EMPLOYEE

Malone is the CEO and president of Martians Flooring. Malone's annual salary is $320,000, paid biweekly, married with no dependents, files taxes jointly, and has pre-tax deductions for health insurance of $250 and 401(k) of $1,000; the box in Step 2 is not checked.

In June, Malone will exceed the Social Security wage base and incur the additional Medicare tax in September. Let's look at the net pay computations on January 14, July 15, and October 21.

FEDERAL INCOME TAX COMPUTATION

Federal income tax is computed as follows, using the percentage tables in Publication 15-T or Appendix C:

Gross pay per period	$12,307.69
Less: health insurance	250.00
Less: 401(k)	1,000.00
Taxable income	$11,057.69
Total federal income tax	$ 1,890.47*

*Using the percentage method in 2023 Publication 15-T for Form W-4 after 2020: $11,057.69 − 8,402 = $2,655.69 × 24% = $637.37 (rounded) + 1,253.10 = $1,890.47.

JANUARY 14 PAY PERIOD

Gross pay per period	$12,307.69
Less: health insurance	250.00
Less: 401(k)	1,000.00
Taxable income*	$11,057.69
Federal income tax	1,890.47
Social Security tax†	747.58
Medicare tax†	174.84
Net pay	$ 8,244.82

*This taxable income is for federal income tax only.
†Social Security and Medicare taxes are computed using a base of $12,307.69 − 250 = $12,057.69.

JULY 15 PAY PERIOD

As of July 1, Malone has earned year-to-date FICA taxable pay of $156,749.97 ($12,057.69 × 13 pay periods). The next payroll will exceed the Social Security wage base. Malone's salary is only taxable for Social Security wages up to the wage base of $160,200 (2023 amount), so the amount that may be taxed is $160,200 −$156,749.97 − $250 = $3,200.03. After the July 15 pay period, there will be no more Social Security tax deducted. This net pay for July 15 will be as follows:

Gross pay per period	$12,307.69
Less: health Insurance	250.00
Less: 401(k)	1,000.00
Taxable income*	$11,057.69
Federal income tax	1,890.47
Social Security tax†	198.40
Medicare tax‡	174.84
Net pay	$ 8,793.98

*This taxable income is for federal income tax only.
†Social Security tax is computed as $3,200.03 × 0.062 = $198.40.
‡Medicare tax is computed using a base of $12,057.69 * 0.0145 = $174.84.

OCTOBER 21 PAY PERIOD

As of October 7, Malone has earned year-to-date pay of $241,153.80 (12,057.69 × 20 pay periods). The next paycheck will be subject to the additional Medicare tax of 0.9 percent, levied only on employees (i.e., no employer match). Since the employee is

(continued)

(concluded)

married, the additional Medicare tax applies once their pay reaches $250,000. The net pay for October 21 will be computed as follows:

Gross pay per period	$12,307.69
Less: health insurance	250.00
Less: 401(k)	1,000.00
Taxable income*	$11,057.69
Federal income tax	1,890.47
Social Security tax	–0–
Medicare tax†	203.74
Net pay	$ 8,896.48

*This taxable income is for federal income tax only.
†Medicare taxes are computed as: $12,307.69 − $250.00 = $12,057.69 *.0145 = $174.84 and ($12,057.69 * 20 payrolls = $253,211.54 − $250,000 = $3,211.54 * .009 = $28.90) for a total Medicare tax of $203.74.

Maintaining accurate records of taxes withheld through payroll registers and employee earnings records is a critical part of calculating proper FICA tax deductions. Whether a company uses a manual system, an automated system, or outsources the payroll duties, it remains responsible for the accuracy of the deductions and maintenance of associated records.

Stop & Check — FICA Taxes

1. Peyton is an employee who earned $68,640 before the current pay period. The current gross pay for the period is $5,280. What amount must be withheld for Social Security tax? For Medicare tax?

2. For Peyton's FICA taxes, what is the total tax liability, including employee and employer share?

3. Shae is the CEO of a company and earns $250,000 per year. The year-to-date salary for the 19th pay period of the year was $197,916.67. Shae is single, contributes 5 percent of gross pay to 401(k), and has a qualified Section 125 deduction of $75 per semimonthly pay period.

    a. For the 20th pay period, what is the Social Security tax liability? Medicare tax liability?

    b. For the 21st pay period, what is the Medicare tax liability?

LO 5-4 Calculate State and Local Income Taxes

Many states and localities apply taxes in addition to the federal income tax, Social Security, and Medicare. According to the IRS, all but nine states withhold income taxes. As budgets become tighter and the unfunded pension liabilities come due, these states may look to income tax as a means for covering budget or pension shortfalls. The nine states are:

Alaska	New Hampshire*	Tennessee
Florida	South Dakota	Washington
Nevada	Texas	Wyoming

*New Hampshire does not charge a payroll tax but obtains revenue from individual taxpayers through taxes on dividends and investments.

(Source: Tax Admin)

> Due to the effect of inflation and other economic influences, 38 states have notable changes to personal income tax rates. Eleven states reduced their tax rates on personal income, and three states changed from a progressive tax structure to a flat tax. Only Massachusetts increased its personal income tax rates.
>
> (Source: Tax Foundation)

State-Specific Taxes

All states except for the nine just mentioned withhold income tax from their employees, and many apply other taxes as well. For instance, employees in California pay State Disability Insurance (SDI) of 0.9 percent of gross pay (up to a maximum wage of $153,164 in 2023) in addition to the personal income tax (PIT) that the state levies. Like federal income tax, California's PIT amounts vary by income level, pay frequency, and marital status. Like many other states, California offers both the wage bracket and the percentage method of determining the PIT amount due. In contrast, Pennsylvania charges a flat rate of 3.07 percent on all employees for its state withholding tax. (See Appendix D for state income tax information.)

If a firm operates only in one state, deciphering state income tax requirements is reasonably simple but becomes increasingly complex as it does business in more locations. Due to employee mobility in the wake of the COVID pandemic, some firms have employees working in states different from their previous locations, and it is important to file the appropriate state and local taxes for the employee's work locations.

State income tax information is readily available through each state's revenue department and most computerized payroll software programs. (See Appendix E for a state revenue department list.)

> California ranks as the highest state in *per capita* state tax. The marginal tax rate in 2022 ranged from 1.0 percent to 13.3 percent, depending on income. While California has the lowest marginal tax bracket in the country (1 percent), the highest tax bracket is 12.3 percent plus an additional 1 percent mental health tax for people whose annual income exceeds $1 million.
>
> Thomas Barwick/Getty Images
>
> (Source: World Population Review)

Some states require the collection and remittance of income taxes based on all wages earned within their state. This could result in the company having several state employer identification numbers, even if it does not have a physical presence in the state. For example, if a Floridian paper mill worker is stationed at its St. Marys, Georgia, location, the employer could be required to remit the employee's income taxes in Georgia. Other types of payroll taxes can include Oregon's public transportation payroll tax for any services performed within the state, regardless of residency status.

> **EXAMPLE: NET PAY WITH STATE INCOME TAX**
>
> Angel receives wages of $850 per week in Joliet, Illinois. Angel is married, filing jointly (box 2 is not checked) with one dependent under 17, and is paid weekly. We will use the wage bracket table for Forms W-4 after 2020 in Appendix C to determine federal
>
> *(continued)*

(concluded)

income tax. There are pre-tax deductions of $50 for qualified insurance and $50 for 401(k). Using the Illinois state tax rate of 4.95 percent,

Taxable income ($850 − 50 − 50)	$750.00
State income tax ($750 × 0.0495)	$ 37.13

The net pay would be computed as follows:

Name	Marital Status	Dependents	Hourly Rate or Period Wage	No. of Regular Hours	No. of Overtime Hours	No. of Holiday Hours	Gross Earnings	401(k)	Insurance	Cafeteria Plan	Taxable Wages for Federal W/H	Taxable Wages for FICA
Angel	MJ	1 < 17	850.00				850.00	50.00	50.00		750.00	800.00

Name	Gross Earnings	Taxable Wages for Federal W/H	Taxable Wages for FICA	Federal W/H	Social Security Tax	Medicare W/H Tax	State W/H Tax	Charitable Contribution	Union Dues	Garnishment	Net Pay
Angel	850.00	750.00	800.00	0.00*	49.60†	11.60††	37.13				651.67

*Federal income tax represents no liability due to dependents.
†Social Security tax: $800 × 0.062.
††Medicare tax = $800 × 0.0145.

Local Income Taxes

Another mandatory tax is the *local income tax* levied by certain municipalities and counties. Payroll accountants need to be aware of any local taxes that apply to their business. Information about applicable local taxes may be found through city and county governments, often through their Internet sites.

> Denver, Colorado, has a local tax called the Occupational Privilege Tax (OPT), also known as the "head tax." The OPT is $5.75 per month for employees and $4 for employers of any business with any activity in Denver, even if the employee or business does not exist or reside in Denver itself, on wages exceeding $500. The local income tax is applied after any pre-tax deductions.
>
> (Source: City and County of Denver)

EXAMPLE: NET PAY WITH LOCAL INCOME TAX

Shale is an employee at Keiser and Sons in Denver, Colorado, earns $39,000 annually, and is paid biweekly. Shale is married, filing jointly with no dependents, and box 2(c) is not checked. Shale has pre-tax deductions, including $100 for health insurance and a contribution of 6 percent of gross pay to a 401(k) plan. We will use the Wage-Bracket table in Appendix C to compute Shale's federal income tax. Colorado's state income tax is 4.40 percent. The net pay would be as follows:

Name	Filing Status	Dependents	Hourly Rate or Period Wage	No. of Regular Hours	No. of Overtime Hours	No. of Holiday Hours	Gross Earnings	401(k)	Insurance	Cafeteria Plan	Taxable Wages for Federal W/H	Taxable Wages for FICA
Shale	MJ	0	1,500.00				1,500.00	90.00	100.00		1,310.00	1,400.00

Name	Gross Earnings	Taxable Wages for Federal W/H	Taxable Wages for FICA	Federal W/H Tax	Social Security W/H Tax	Medicare W/H Tax	State W/H Tax	Denver OPT	Union Dues	Garnishment	Net Pay
Shale	1,500.00	1,310.00	1,400.00	24.00	86.80*	20.30†	57.64‡	2.65**			1,118.61

*$1,400 × 0.062 = $86.80
†$1,400 × 0.0145 = $20.30
‡$1,310 × 0.044 = $57.64
**Occupational privilege − ($5.75/month × 12 months)/26 = $2.65 rounded

State and Local Income Taxes

Stop & Check

1. Ever works as a research scientist in Amasa, Michigan; earns $62,500 annually; is married filing jointly with no dependents (box 2 is not checked); and is paid biweekly. Ever has a pre-tax deduction of $150 for a 401(k) and $80 for qualified health insurance. Using the state tax listed in Appendix D, what is the state income tax?

2. Jodie works as an accountant in Denver, Colorado. Colorado has a state income tax of a flat 4.4 percent. Colorado's OPT is $5.75 per month per employee. If Jodie is paid monthly and earns $2,850 after pre-tax deductions, what are the state and local taxes?

LO 5-5 Apply Post-Tax Deductions

Once the payroll clerk determines each employee's gross pay, pre-tax deductions, and taxes withheld, the post-tax deductions are applied to the remaining amount. All deductions, both voluntary and mandatory, should be listed on an attachment to the paycheck, in both pay period and year-to-date amounts.

Post-tax deductions may include court-mandated or governmental debts as well as employee repayments of advances or overpayments. This section will explore examples of post-tax deductions and how they are included in net pay computations.

Rob Byron/Shutterstock

Charitable Contributions

Employees may choose to contribute part of their pay to charitable organizations as an automatic deduction. This deduction is taken on a post-tax basis because the employee may deduct it from gross income on the annual tax return.

EXAMPLE: CHARITABLE CONTRIBUTION

Jan is an employee at Working Environments in Winchester, New Hampshire; earns $29,000 annually; and is paid weekly. Jan is single with no dependents, has a pre-tax health insurance premium of $25, and a charitable contribution of $10 per pay period. The net pay would be as follows using the wage-bracket method for Forms W-4 after 2020:

Name	Filing Status	Dependents	Hourly Rate or Period Wage	No. of Regular Hours	No. of Overtime Hours	No. of Holiday Hours	Gross Earnings	401(k)	Insurance	Cafeteria Plan	Taxable Wages for Federal W/H	Taxable Wages for FICA
Jan	S	0	557.69				557.69		25.00		532.69	532.69

(continued)

(concluded)

Name	Gross Earnings	Taxable Wages for Federal W/H	Taxable Wages for FICA	Federal W/H	Social Security Tax	Medicare W/H	State W/H Tax	Charitable Contribution	Union Dues	Garnishment	Net Pay
Jan	557.69	532.69	532.69	27.00	33.03	7.72		10.00			454.94

Garnishments

Remember garnishments are for court-mandated deductions such as child support obligations, liens, and consumer credit repayment. Title III of the CCPA limits the amount or percentage of pay deductions for garnishments. These deductions are taken on a post-tax basis because they are viewed as an obligation of the employee that must be paid out of post-tax income.

Table 5-1 reflects the maximum that may be garnished based on disposable income and pay frequency under Title III.

TABLE 5-1
Garnishment Maximum Based on Pay Frequency at the Federal Minimum Wage*

Weekly	Biweekly	Semimonthly	Monthly
Less than $217.50: $0	Less than $435.00: $0	Less than $471.25: $0	Less than $942.50: $0
$217.50 > $290.00: Only the amount over $217.50 may be garnished	$435.00 > $580.00: Only the amount over $435.00 may be garnished	$471.25 > $628.33: Only the amount over $471.25 may be garnished	$942.50 > $1,256.66: Only the amount over $942.50 may be garnished
Over $290.00: 25%	Over $580.00: 25%	Over $628.33: 25%	Over $1,256.66: 25%

(Source: U.S. DOL)
*In the case of bankruptcy, government tax liens, and child support, these maximums do not apply.

Garnishments are subject to a maximum of 25 percent of disposable income for many situations. However, child support garnishment may be up to 60 percent, depending on how many people are supported financially. Table 5-2 contains an explanation of the type of garnishment and maximum allowed.

TABLE 5-2
Garnishments Maximum Percentage by Type

Garnishment Type	Maximum Percentage
Child Support or Alimony	50% if the employee is supporting a spouse or child 60% if the employee is not supporting a spouse or child 5% additional if child support is in arrears
Federal Student Loan	15%
Credit Card Debt	Up to 25%
Medical Debt	Up to 25%
Other Court-Related Judgments	Up to 25%

(Source: Nolo)

> Federal student loan garnishment was suspended because of the COVID-19 pandemic until June 20, 2023, pending litigation with the Department of Education. Before the garnishment suspension, student loan debt could constitute up to 15 percent of an employee's discretionary income. Although the suspension applied to federal student loan garnishments, private student loans were not covered by the suspension mandate.
>
> (Source: Student Aid)

EXAMPLE: CHILD SUPPORT

Ash is an employee of Kennesaw Mills, earns $49,500 annually, and is paid semi-monthly. Ash is single with one dependent under 17, has a pre-tax health insurance deduction of $100, and contributes 3 percent of gross pay to his 401(k) per pay period. The state income tax rate is 6 percent. Ash has a court-ordered garnishment of $300 per pay period for child support. Specific computations used in the payroll register follow immediately below the register. Use the percentage method for federal income taxes from Publication 15-T or Appendix C.

Name	Filing Status	Dependent	Hourly Rate or Period Wage	No. of Regular Hours	No. of Overtime Hours	No. of Holiday Hours	Gross Earnings	401(k)	Insurance	Cafeteria Plan	Taxable Wages for Federal W/H	Taxable Wages for FICA
Ash	S	1 < 17	2,062.50				2,062.50	61.88	100.00		1,900.62	1,962.50

Name	Gross Earnings	Taxable Wages for Federal W/H	Taxable Wages for FICA	Federal W/H Tax	Social Security Tax	Medicare W/H	State W/H Tax	Charitable Contribution	Union Dues	Garnishment	Net Pay
Ash	2,062.50	1,900.62	1,962.50	66.34	121.68	28.46	114.04			300.00	1,270.10

Payroll Register Computations

Payroll Register Column	Computation
Period wage	$49,500/24 = $2,062.50
Health insurance	$100.00
401(k)	$2,062.50 × 0.03 = $61.88
Taxable wages for federal and state	$2,062.50 − 61.88 − 100 = $1,900.62
Taxable wages for FICA	$2,062.50 − 100 = $1,962.50
Federal income tax	$1,900.62 − column A $1,035 = $865.62 $865.62 × 12% = $103.87 + column C $45.80 = $149.67 less credit of $2,000 / 24 = $83.33 for federal taxes = $66.34
Social Security tax	$1,962.50 × 0.062 = $121.68
Medicare tax	$1,962.50 × 0.0145 = $28.46
State income tax	$1,900.62 × 0.06 = $114.04
Garnishment	$300.00
Net pay	$2,062.50 − 61.88 − 100 − 66.34 − 121.68 − 28.46 − 114.04 − 300 = $1,270.10

DISPOSABLE INCOME: CHILD SUPPORT

It is important to consider Ash's disposable income to ensure the garnishment does not exceed legal maximums. The disposable income is computed as follows:

Gross pay	$2,062.50
Less: federal income tax	66.34
Less: state income tax	114.04
Less: Social Security tax	121.68
Less: Medicare tax	28.46
Total disposable income	$1,731.98
Percent of garnishment to disposable income	17.3%*

*$300 / $1,731.98 = 0.1732 = 17.3% (rounded)

Consumer Credit

Like other post-tax deductions such as student loans, consumer credit is considered an obligation to be paid out of a person's after-tax earnings. The next example shows the effect of a consumer credit garnishment on an employee's wages. In this case, the 25 percent maximum garnishment rule applies.

Jelica Videnovic/Shutterstock

EXAMPLE: CONSUMER CREDIT

Marion is an employee of Level Two Gallery in Ogden, Utah; earns $38,500 annually; and is paid biweekly. Marion is single with no dependents. The state income tax rate is 4.85 percent, and there are pre-tax deductions of $50 for health insurance and $30 for the 401(k) plan. Post-tax deductions include contributing $15 to charity. There is a court-ordered consumer credit garnishment of $100 per pay period. Using the percentage method from Publication 15-T or Appendix C, calculating the net pay would appear as follows:

Name	Filing Status	Dependents	Hourly Rate or Period Wage	No. of Regular Hours	No. of Overtime Hours	Gross Earnings	401(k)	Section 125	Taxable Wages for Federal W/H	Taxable Wages for FICA
Marion	S	0	1,480.77			1,480.77	30.00	50.00	1,400.77	1,430.77

Name	Gross Earnings	Taxable Wages for Federal/State W/H	Taxable Wages for FICA	Federal W/H	Social Security Tax	Medicare W/H Tax	State W/H Tax	Charitable Contribution	Garnishment	Net Pay
Marion	1,480.77	1,400.77	1,430.77	95.67	88.71	20.75	67.94	15.00	100.00	1,012.70

Payroll Register Computations

Payroll Register Column	Computation
Period wage	$38,500 / 26 = $1,480.77
401(k)	$30.00
Health insurance	$50.00
Taxable wages for federal and state	$1,480.77 − 30 − 50 = $1,400.77
Taxable wages for FICA	$1,480.77 − 50 = $1,430.77
Federal income tax	$1,400.77 − column A $956 = $444.77 × 12% = $53.37 + column C $42.30 = $95.67
Social Security tax	$1,430.77 × .062 = $88.71
Medicare tax	$1,430.77 × .0145 = $20.75
State income tax	$1,400.77 × .0485 = $67.94
Charitable contribution	$15
Garnishment	$100
Net pay	$1,480.77 − 30 − 50 − 95.67 − 88.71 − 20.75 − 67.94 − 15 − 100 = $1,012.70

DISPOSABLE INCOME: CONSUMER CREDIT

Let's ensure Marion's consumer credit garnishment is within legal guidelines:

Gross pay	$1,480.77
Less: federal income tax	95.67
Less: state income tax	67.94
Less: Social Security tax	88.71
Less: Medicare tax	20.75
Total disposable income	$1,207.70
Percent of garnishment to disposable income	8.3%*

*$100 / $1,207.70 = 0.0832 = 8.3% (rounded)

> A discussion topic between the American Payroll Association and the Wage and Hour Division of the Department of Labor has been the treatment of lump-sum distributions when a garnishment is imposed on an employee. The general guideline for considering a distribution as subject to garnishment is the concept of "personal service." If the distribution was for services rendered by the employee, then the amount may be garnished. Specific examples of lump-sum distributions that are subject to garnishment include the following:
>
> - Sign-on bonuses
> - Any performance or productivity bonus
> - Commissions
> - Holiday pay
> - Retroactive pay
> - Termination pay
> - Any other bonuses or incentive payments
>
> (Source: U.S. Department of Labor)

Union Dues

Employees who belong to a collective bargaining unit usually pay dues to the unit for their representation. The CCPA disposable income limits do not pertain to union dues because those dues are not court-mandated. The following example shows how union dues affect employee pay. It should be noted that the employee's deduction for union dues is voluntary.

> **EXAMPLE: UNION DUES**
> Foster is an employee of Pacific High School in Washington State. Foster takes part in a collective bargaining unit (i.e., a labor union) that negotiates salary, benefits, and working conditions and has dues of $50 per pay period. Foster earns $67,500 annually and is paid biweekly, is married filing jointly with 2 dependents under 17 (box 2 is not checked), and has a 2023 W-4. There are pre-tax deductions of $150 for a 401(k) plan and $100 for a qualified Section 125 cafeteria plan. Using the wage-bracket tables from Publication 15-T or Appendix C (remember to adjust for the two dependents under 17), the net pay would appear as follows:

Name	Filing Status	Dependents	Hourly Rate or Period Wage	No. of Regular Hours	No. of Overtime Hours	Gross Earnings	401(k)	Section 125	Taxable Wages for Federal W/H	Taxable Wages for FICA
Foster	MJ	2 < 17	2,596.15			2,596.15	150.00	100.00	2,346.15	2,496.15

Name	Gross Earnings	Taxable Wages for Federal W/H	Taxable Wages for FICA	Federal W/H	Social Security Tax	Medicare W/H Tax	State W/H Tax	Charitable Contribution	Union Dues	Net Pay
Foster	2,596.15	2,346.15	2,496.15	0	154.76	36.19			50.00	2,105.20

Employee Advances and Overpayments

Employees may have an opportunity for an advance of money in anticipation of their pay. The timing of the repayment of advances depends on the agreement between the employee and employer. When the advance becomes due for repayment, it is treated as a post-tax deduction. The same concept applies to situations in which the employee is overpaid due to an error in computation or reporting.

At Maricopa County Community College, a payroll system upgrade caused employees to be under- or overpaid, sometimes by thousands of dollars. The new payroll system's rollout caused issues with understanding the differences between the new and old systems. Accountants worked with managers and employees to ensure that all discrepancies were addressed promptly.

Another underpayment issue that arose during the COVID-19 pandemic was the omission of hazard pay to essential workers. Although they remained at work, they often did not receive additional pay for working in hazardous conditions.

(Sources: AZCentral; Brookings)

Stop & Check

Post-tax Deductions

1. Which of the following is a debt that may be collected via wage garnishment?
   a. Student loans
   b. Child support
   c. Debt to family members
   d. Tax liens
   e. Union dues
   f. Charitable contributions
2. An electrician who is a member of the IBEW union asks you, the payroll accountant, if they may pay the union dues with a personal check instead of a post-tax deduction. The IBEW requires that the employer remit collected dues. What advice would you offer the employee?

LO 5-6 Discuss Employee Pay Methods

Once the net pay is computed, the next step is to give the employees access to their money. Four common types of payment methods are available: cash, check, direct deposit, and paycard. Each method has its advantages and disadvantages. We will explore each method separately.

Cash

Cash is one of the oldest forms of paying employees but is not widely used as a contemporary payroll practice. The most common use of cash as a payment method involves paying for day laborers, temporary helpers, and odd jobs. Cash is one of the most difficult payroll forms to manage because it is difficult to track and control. Payments for wages in cash should involve a written receipt signed by the employee. Companies paying by cash must physically have the cash on hand for payroll, which increases the risk of theft from both internal and external sources. Payroll taxes must be withheld, which requires prior preparation so that the appropriate amount of cash is available to pay precisely what is due for each employee. For employees, cash is a very convenient payment method because of its inherent liquidity.

Romariolen/Shutterstock

Cash wage payment challenges the security of the funds for both the employer and the employee. For the employer, ensuring the employee receives and acknowledges the appropriate payment amount is the key. When using cash as a payment method for employees, a receipt that contains information about gross pay, deductions, and net pay is important. The critical piece is to have the employee sign and date a copy acknowledging the receipt of the correct amount of cash on the specific date. Obtaining the employee's signature and the date received can prevent future problems with perceived problems involving timely employee compensation payments.

Check

Paper checks are a common method of remitting employee compensation. For the employer, a paper check offers accounting record traceability and simplicity. The use of checks instead of cash means the employer does not have to maintain large amounts of cash, reducing the vulnerability of keeping currency on hand. QuickBooks and Sage100 Cloud allow employers to print paychecks directly from the program on specifically designed, preprinted forms. Checks offer a security level that cash does not because they are issued to a specific employee, and they are the only person who can legally convert the check into cash.

The disadvantage of using paper checks for payroll purposes involves bank account reconciliation. Once issued, the employee may choose not to deposit it into their bank account, which can complicate the firm's reconciliation process. Paper checks could be lost or destroyed, requiring voiding the old check and issuance of a new one. Additionally, employees might not have a bank account, which makes cashing paychecks challenging and potentially costly. Paper checks may soon be phased out of current practice as other employee pay methods grow in popularity because of the convenience for both the employer and the employee.

Forecasted number of digital banking users in the United States from 2021 to 2025 (in millions)

Year	Number of digital banking users in million
2021	196.8
2022	203
2023	208
2024	212.8
2025	216.8

According to Insider Intelligence, over 208 million people used digital banking in the United States as of 2021. This number is expected to increase to nearly 217 million by 2025. The practice of payroll disbursement using paper checks is declining as people shift from traditional banking methods to a culture of electronic money management. It is important to remember that payment in cryptocurrencies for normal compensation is not covered by the Fair Labor Standards Board as an acceptable method.

(Source: Insider Intelligence)

For employers who use paper checks as a compensation method, two significant best practices exist: (1) The use of a payroll-only checking account and (2) a procedure for the handling of the payroll checks themselves. A separate payroll-dedicated checking account prevents problems that could occur if the company has difficulties (such as insufficient funds) in the business's main account. It also prevents embezzlement by falsified company checks if multiple people are involved in the check creation and approval process.

For the checks themselves, the payroll accountant needs to maintain a record that notes the use of each and every check, especially for checks that are voided, lost, or never cashed. If a company issues checks, it needs to maintain an unclaimed property account for payroll checks that the employee has never cashed. The process of leaving a check uncashed, especially if it is a payroll check, results in the *escheatment* of the payroll check because the payee of the check has never claimed the property (i.e., the payroll money) and is subject to state laws about the handling and distribution of such unclaimed money. Compliance with state escheatment laws is mandatory but not largely enforced—but that does not relieve the employer of the obligation to pay its employees. The use of a record in which the payroll accountant annotates each check's use (i.e., cashed, voided, or lost) is imperative.

> According to the State Controller of New York's office, the policy for escheatment is that uncashed payroll checks are escheated as of predetermined dates. As of 2023, about $17.5 billion in escheated funds remained in the custody of the state.
>
> (Source: Office of New York State Comptroller)

When a company pays employees by check, the check's numerical amount must also be represented in specific words for the bank to accept the check for payment to the payee. It is important to note banks pay the check based on the amount written in words on the check. The highlighted area in the image in Figure 5-3 shows how the information should appear on the check's face, specifically the written-out amount of the check. Figure 5-3 contains a sample of a paycheck.

FIGURE 5-3
Sample Paycheck

| Wings of the North |
| 121 Nicholas Street |
| North Pole, AK 99705 | Check No. 23445 |

| Petra Smith | Date | 1/3/20XX |
| One Thousand One Hundred Twenty-four and 13/100 | dollars | 1,124.13 |

Payee: Petra Smith
Address: 426 Candy Cane Lane
City/State Zip: North Pole, AK 99705   Signed: *Rudolph Donner*

A relevant concept in using checks for payroll is the potential for fraud by manipulating the checks' information. The check issuer (i.e., the employer) may be liable for the funds until the fraudulent activity is proven. Some red flags that may indicate check fraud include the following:

- Changes in font type between the company's address and the employee's name.
- Low check numbers (e.g., 1,001–1,500) because payroll fraud often involves new accounts.
- Evidence of typewriter use on the check (most payroll checks are generated via computerized programs).

- Stains or discolorations on the check.
- Notations in the memo line that contain the word "payroll" or "load."
- Handwritten additions to the check, such as the recipient's phone number.
- Absence of the bank's or the recipient's address.
- The check number is either absent or is the same on all checks.

(Source: Federal Trade Commission)

Paper checks are more vulnerable to fraud than electronic transfers because of the ease of obtaining preprinted checks. Many employers are transitioning to either direct deposits or paycards to protect company assets.

> There has been growing interest in receiving pay on demand. Companies such as Zelle, Venmo, and Paycor have been working with companies to facilitate prompt payment from the company to employees. Individuals may request up to a predetermined amount of their earned pay from the participating employer ahead of the normally scheduled payroll date. This does come with a fee, which can be either paid by the employer as part of fringe benefits or passed on to the employee for convenience. This can also create tax calculation and remittance issues that the payroll accountant should be aware of, such as tax reporting, a lack of visibility into errors in pay disbursement, and the need to issue pay advices to employees who use these services.

Direct Deposit

Direct deposit of employee compensation into the individual's bank account offers employers some of the same advantages as checks. Like checks, employee compensation is traceable through both the employer's bank and the optional paper pay advice issued to the employee. Employees often prefer direct deposit because their pay is immediately available in their bank account, eliminating the need to travel to the bank to deposit the paper check. However, for employees to receive their pay through direct deposit, they must have a bank account.

> As of late 2022, a survey by the American Payroll Association found that approximately 93 percent of employees used direct deposit to receive payroll amounts. The remaining percentage comprised paper checks, cash, and paycards. The use of direct deposit means that the employee's paycheck is in their account on payday. Depending on the bank, employees may be able to access payroll funds earlier than the pay date.
>
> (Source: NACHA)

An advantage of direct deposit is that it prevents paper waste, promoting "green" business practices. According to the Association for Financial Professionals, the savings per employee per pay period is approximately $5.91 per employee. Although this may seem like a small amount, when multiplied by the number of employees and pay periods annually, it creates a potentially large saving for employers. These savings come from lower waste collection, paper usage, and recycling costs. Not only does direct deposit save a company money, but it also reduces the time needed for payroll processing, which frees payroll accountants to complete other tasks.

When using a direct deposit as an employee compensation method, a suggested best practice is to grant the employees access to a website or online portal by which they can securely view their *pay advice* and pay history, as this may substitute for paper payroll advice. Because direct deposit involves electronic data transmittal, the posting of the pay advice on a secure site could be linked with the human resources data, allowing

Comstock/PunchStock

the employee an element of self-maintenance in payroll records. The potential pitfall in using a website for these susceptible records is the vulnerability of the information to computer hacking. Employers who choose to use a website in this manner must take steps to prevent hacking through data encryption, identity verification, and site security.

> The Federal Communications Commission (FCC) published guidelines for employer data security procedures, especially as it pertains to employee information on websites and the use of paycards. The FCC guidelines include advice about selecting data to be included on employee-accessible websites, password strength guidelines, update intervals, and data archiving.
>
> (Source: FCC)

Paycards

Paycards have been growing in popularity since the beginning of the 21st century. These cards are debit cards onto which an employer electronically transmits the employee's pay. The use of payroll cards started in the 1990s as a convenient way to compensate over-the-road truck drivers who could not be in a predictable place on each payday. Comerica started issuing paycards that could be used anywhere a conventional MasterCard was accepted, which is nearly everywhere. Unlike the use of paper checks or direct deposits, the paycard does not require an employee to maintain a bank account to access their pay. The convenience and ease of use for employees make the paycard an option that millions of workers in the United States have chosen to use.

TARIK KIZILKAYA/Getty Images

> Paycards have grown in popularity because of their inherent flexibility for sending and receiving money. The paycard may be used as a debit card by people without bank accounts, which also grants them the ability to participate in online purchases even if they cannot qualify for a credit card. For the approximately 10 million unbanked households in the United States, paycards grant the financial freedom and accessibility they may otherwise not have and allow unbanked employees to avoid check-cashing fees.
>
> (Source: American Payroll Association)

What is the disadvantage of paycard use? Unlike the limits to access that a bank has for its account holders, a paycard can be lost or stolen. Some employees may encounter challenges such as withdrawal limits or cash back at point-of-sale (POS) purchases. Like paper checks, paycards may be subject to state escheatment laws that govern unclaimed funds.

An issue that haunted the early use of paycards was **Regulation E** of the Federal Deposit Insurance Corporation (FDIC), which protects consumers from loss of the availability of their funds on deposit in the event of bank losses. Until 2006, Regulation E applied to funds on deposit in an FDIC-insured institution. Regulation E was extended to cover payroll funds transferred to paycards, according to **12 CFR Part 205**. As a payment method growing in popularity among employers and employees, paycards offer more compensation options for employers.

Paycards require different security types than the other types of employee compensation, but most elements remain the same. In addition to tracking hours and accurately compensating employees based on their marital status and withholdings, the employer must keep the employee's paycard number in a secure file. Software such as QuickBooks offers password encryption abilities for the files of employees who have paycards.

nito/Shutterstock

Like any other debit card, the funds are electronically coded to the account number. The card issuer (not the employer) must remain compliant with Regulation E as far as card loss or theft is concerned. Still, the employer is responsible for ensuring this extra step of payroll security.

> Visa, Inc., introduced an improvement to its Visa Advanced Authorization technology, making compensation via paycards more secure and reliable. This new technology improved real-time fraud detection and was projected to prevent nearly $200 million in fraud within a five-year period. Since its inception, technology has evolved to include predictive analytics that detect unusual card usage.
>
> (Source: Visa)

Cryptocurrency

An emerging wage payment method involves *cryptocurrency*, such as Bitcoin or Ethereum, and *blockchain* technology. Cryptocurrency uses Internet technology to transmit money securely from one "wallet," or account, to a recipient. The cryptocurrency itself is not a physical currency, as it exists only in electronic form. Transmission of wages is thought to be secure because blockchain technology makes it very difficult for wages to be diverted from the intended recipient. After all, the blockchain involves the transmission of packets of data through many computers, making a single transaction difficult to isolate.

Zapp2Photo/Shutterstock

The advantage of using cryptocurrency is that it is not subject to international exchange rates, and it is transferred almost instantaneously. The disadvantage of using cryptocurrency is that no centralized authority oversees the value of the currency, making it extremely volatile in value, which could lead to employees' underpayment if the currency loses value. In addition, the Fair Labor Standards Board does not recommend the use of cryptocurrencies since they are not an instrument that is considered "cash or a negotiable instrument at par." There are additional recordkeeping requirements for any employer using cryptocurrencies to ensure the value paid out in the cryptocurrency is equivalent to the amount that would be paid out in cash or cash equivalents.

In March 2022, President Joe Biden signed Executive Order 14067 to responsibly look into the application of cryptocurrencies as a mode of payment by establishing the development of a U.S. Central Bank Digital Currency. This marked a governmental awareness and potential acceptance of digital assets as a form of payment by connecting digital payments to the National Security Agency, the Federal Trade Commission, The Consumer Finance Protection Bureau, and other federal bodies. Some state and local governments have started implementing the use of cryptocurrencies for accounts payable vendors. From a payroll perspective, it is essential that proper record-keeping be followed to avoid issues. If a company uses cryptocurrencies as a form of payment, the date, time, transaction amount, and exchange rate must all be recorded and retained. Since cryptocurrencies are not (as of the writing of this book) backed by the banking industries, this executive order would research and design a centralized bank for digital currencies.

> The company BitPay, which started in 2013, offered payroll via cryptocurrency in 2020. The service allowed employers to disburse payments without a Bitcoin account. Using BitPay, employers transmit payroll directly to the employees' cryptocurrency wallets and charge each party a 1 percent fee for the service.

(continued)

(concluded)

Bitpay announced in 2021 that the use of cryptocurrency worked well as a payment for international and gig economy workers. It offers immediate access to funds and fosters ease in global payments.

(Sources: CoinDesk; SHRM)

Stop & Check — Pay Methods

1. What are the different employee pay methods?
2. What regulation governs paycard loss or theft?
3. For which pay method(s) must an employee have a bank account?
4. What type of payments may be made to employees through cryptocurrencies?

Trends to Watch

TAXES AND PAYMENT METHODS

Employee net pay changes each year because of legal developments regarding deductions and payment methods. Developments in employee withholdings since 2019 include the following:

- Changes to employee net pay because of the Affordable Care Act health insurance requirements for employers.
- Changes to sick-leave compensation at the state and local levels.
- Changes in the amounts that employees may contribute on a tax-deferred basis to pension plans.
- Increased public awareness of the effect of pay raises, especially for the cost of living, on net pay.
- Expanded regulatory guidance regarding data privacy and security, similar to the General Data Protection Regulation (GDPR) mandated in the European Union, to protect electronic employee payroll transmission.

Future trends to watch include:

- Same-day payroll processing and possible shorter payroll cycles due to the use of existing technology.
- Increased governmental guidance about the use of earned wage access regarding tax and other withholding amounts.
- On-demand pay through which employees can access earned payroll amounts at their discretion.
- Increasing regulation on digital payroll in response to online security and accessibility needs.
- Increased splitting of earned wage and salary payments using both direct deposit and paycards that grants flexibility in the way employees receive their pay.
- Movement toward payment with digital assets.

Summary of Employee Net Pay and Pay Methods

Employee pay is subject to various deductions that can be mandatory, mandated by a court or other authority, or voluntary. In 2020, the introduction of the new Form W-4 changed the factors by which federal income tax withholding was determined. Deductions such as federal income tax and Medicare tax are virtually inescapable. Other taxes such as Social Security, state taxes, and local taxes are not applicable in every employee's situation and depend on various factors such as year-to-date pay and state of residence. Of the other deductions, some can be withheld from an employee's pay before taxes are deducted, which benefits employees by reducing their payroll tax liability. Other deductions must be taken after taxes are withheld. Understanding the difference between gross pay and net pay is vital for payroll accountants because the net pay, not the gross, is the pay that the employee actually receives.

The question of employee pay methods is complex. Which payment method is the best? It is not an easy answer. An employer should consider the employees' needs and the business to decide if one method will suit everyone. Sometimes a combination of payment methods is the best solution, although it adds complexity for the payroll accountant. The most appropriate method for the organization will depend on many different factors. Attention to these factors, including payroll frequency, employee types, and the nature of the business itself, helps inform employer decisions about employee pay methods.

Key Points

- Net pay is gross pay less all deductions.
- Federal income tax applies to all workers, and the changes in federal income tax deductions changed because of the implementation of provisions of the Tax Cuts and Jobs Act.
- After January 1, 2020, employees are subject to different factors as part of federal income tax computation and need to use the new W-4 forms. Employees hired in 2019 and prior years may continue to use their existing W-4.
- Social Security tax has a maximum wage base that can change each year.
- Medicare tax has no maximum wage base, and an additional Medicare tax is levied on highly compensated employees.
- Employees subject to mandated deductions such as garnishments for child support and consumer credit liens have certain protections as to the percent of disposable income that may be withheld.
- Employees' pay may be disbursed in cash, by check, by paycard, or via direct deposit.
- Uncashed employee paychecks are turned over to state authorities as escheatments and become unclaimed property.
- Electronic means of transmitting pay, such as paycards, continue to grow in popularity because of employee access and transmittal ease.
- Cryptocurrency is increasingly used as a way for employers to transmit funds to employees and state agencies, although the standardization of cryptocurrency rules does not yet exist. Funds transmitted cannot be wages or overtime, but can include bonuses or commissions.

Vocabulary

Additional Medicare tax
Blockchain
Cryptocurrency
Direct deposit
Escheatment
Federal income tax
Local income tax
Percentage method
Regulation E
Social Security tax
State income taxes
Wage base
Wage-bracket method

Review Questions

1. What factors affect how much federal income tax is withheld from an employee's pay using Form W-4?
2. How should employees complete their Form W-4 if they have multiple jobs or have a spouse who works?
3. How is Social Security tax computed? What is the maximum wage base?
4. How is Medicare tax computed? What is the maximum wage base?
5. Name four states that do not have an employee income tax.
6. How is an employee's net income computed?
7. Why is the difference between gross pay and taxable income important?
8. What are two of the five different payment methods?
9. What are an advantage and a disadvantage of paycards?
10. What are an advantage and a disadvantage of direct deposit?
11. How does the percentage method work using Form W-4 information?
12. When should the percentage method be used instead of the wage-bracket method?
13. What are two examples of garnishments?
14. Why are garnishments deducted on a post-tax basis?
15. Why are union dues not considered a garnishment?
16. How does cryptocurrency function as a payroll payment method?

Exercises Set A

E5-1A.
LO 5-1

The payroll accountant needs to compute net pay for the employees for Hay Industries. Place the following steps in the proper order.
a. Compute income taxes.
b. Subtract pre-tax deductions from gross pay.
c. Compute Social Security and Medicare taxes.
d. Subtract taxes and all other deductions from gross pay.
e. Determine gross pay.
Order: _____

E5-2A.
LO 5-1

The owner of Padua Products wants to reward the employees for their work during the year and has asked you to gross-up their bonuses so that they receive the full amount as net pay. What amount(s) should you consider when computing the grossed-up pay? (Select all that apply.)
a. Desired bonus amount
b. Garnishments
c. Court or government-mandated deductions
d. Income tax(es)

E5-3A.
LO 5-2

A new employee at Financial Technologies, Ltd. is married with children, and the spouse works. What items need to be considered for appropriate Form W-4 completion? (Select all that apply.)
a. Children's ages
b. Tax filing status
c. Spouse's income
d. Spouse's birthdate

E5-4A.
LO 5-3

Under which circumstances could the percentage method be used to determine federal income tax withholding amounts? (Select all that apply.)
a. When the employee's taxable income exceeds the maximum amount on the appropriate wage-bracket table
b. When using a computerized accounting system to compute payroll deductions
c. When using a manual accounting system for a small number of low-pay employees
d. When computational accuracy is critical

E5-5A.
LO 5-3

Which of the following is true about Social Security and Medicare taxes as they pertain to earnings limits?
a. Social Security tax applies only to earnings greater than the wage base.
b. Highly compensated employees are subject to additional Medicare tax withholding.
c. Employers must match all Medicare contributions for highly compensated employees.
d. Employees contribute the same percentage of gross pay to Medicare regardless of their YTD gross pay.

E5-6A.
LO 5-3

What is the Social Security wage base for 2023?
a. $128,400
b. $142,800
c. $147,000
d. $160,200

E5-7A.
LO 5-4

Which of the following statements are true about state and local income taxes? (Select all that apply.)
a. All states tax employee earnings.
b. State tax rates on employee earnings vary among states.
c. Certain states have no personal income tax deduction.
d. Some localities levy income tax on employees.

E5-8A.
LO 5-6

The owner of All Grains Bakery is considering offering additional payroll disbursal methods for the employees. Which of the following would be the safest for employees without a bank account?
a. Check
b. Paycard
c. Cash
d. Direct deposit

E5-9A.
LO 5-2

What are the two methods payroll accountants use to determine federal income tax withholding amounts? (Select all that apply.)
a. Percentage method
b. Salary-bracket method
c. Wage-salary method
d. Wage-bracket method

E5-10A.
LO 5-3

At what income level do many employees contribute an additional percentage to their Medicare tax deduction?
a. $150,000
b. $160,200
c. $175,000
d. $200,000

Problems Set A

P5-1A.
LO 5-1, 5-2, 5-3

Compute the net pay for Briar Khan and Hollis Hart. Assume that they are paid a $2,500 salary biweekly, subject to federal income tax (use the wage-bracket method) in Appendix C and FICA taxes and have no other deductions from their pay. They have a state tax rate of 3 percent. If they choose to participate in the cafeteria plan, the deduction for the pay period is $100; otherwise, there is no deduction for the cafeteria plan. The cafeteria plan qualifies under Section 125. You do not need to complete the number of hours. Additional information for Briar: Box 2 is not checked, and the dependents are under 17.

Name	Filing Status	Dependents	Hourly Rate or Period Wage	No. of Regular Hours	No. of Overtime Hours	No. of Holiday Hours	Commissions	Gross Earnings	Cafeteria Plan	Taxable Wages for Federal/State W/H	Taxable Wages for FICA
Briar Khan—no cafeteria plan	MJ	2 < 17	2,500.00								
Briar Khan—cafeteria plan	MJ	2 < 17	2,500.00								
Hollis Hart—no cafeteria plan	S	0	2,500.00								
Hollis Hart—cafeteria plan	S	0	2,500.00								

Name	Gross Earnings	Taxable Wages for Federal/State W/H	Taxable Wages for FICA	Federal W/H	Social Security Tax	Medicare W/H Tax	State W/H Tax	Net Pay
Briar Khan—no cafeteria plan								
Briar Khan—cafeteria plan								
Hollis Hart—no cafeteria plan								
Hollis Hart—cafeteria plan								

P5-2A.
LO 5-1, 5-2, 5-3, 5-5

Enlightened Eats in Anchorage, Alaska, has six employees who are paid semimonthly. Calculate the net pay from the information provided here for the November 15 pay date. Assume that all wages are subject to Social Security and Medicare taxes. All 401(k) and Section 125 amounts are pre-tax deductions. Use the percentage method for manual payroll systems with Forms W-4 from 2020 or later in Appendix C to compute federal income taxes. You do not need to complete the number of hours.

a. W. Packer
   Married/Joint, two dependents <17, box 2 checked
   Annual pay: $35,500
   401(k) deduction: $125 per pay period
b. K. Ela
   Married/Separate, two dependents <17, box 2 checked
   Annual pay: $53,400
   401(k) deduction: $250 per pay period
c. G. Laureano
   Single, no dependents, box 2 not checked
   Annual pay: $50,400
   Section 125 deduction: $75 per pay period
   401(k) deduction: $50 per pay period

d. T. Spraggins
   Married/joint, one dependent <17, box 2 not checked
   Annual pay: $45,000
   Charitable contribution: $50 per pay period
   Garnishment: $50 per pay period
e. M. Christman
   Single, two dependents <17, one other dependent, box 2 checked
   Annual pay: $58,800
   Section 125 deduction: $50 per pay period
   401(k) deduction: 6 percent of gross pay per pay period
f. J. Cherry
   Married/joint, one other dependent, box 2 checked
   Annual pay: $48,400
   401(k) deduction: $75 per pay period

Name	Filing Status	Dependents	Hourly Rate or Period Wage	No. of Regular Hours	No. of Overtime Hours	No. of Holiday Hours	Commissions	Gross Earnings	401(k)	Section 125	Taxable Wages for Federal / State W/H	Taxable Wages for FICA

Name	Gross Earnings	Taxable Wages for Federal/State W/H	Taxable Wages for FICA	Federal W/H	Social Security Tax	Medicare W/H Tax	State W/H Tax	Garnishments	United Way	Net Pay

P5-3A.
LO 5-1, 5-2, 5-3, 5-4, 5-5

The following salaried employees of Mountain Stone Brewery in Fort Collins, Colorado, are paid semimonthly. Some employees have union dues or garnishments deducted from their pay. Calculate their net pay using the percentage method for manual payroll systems with Forms W-4 from 2020 or later in Appendix C to determine federal income tax. Assume box 2 is *not* checked for any employee. Include Colorado income tax of 4.40 percent of taxable pay. No employee has exceeded the maximum FICA limit. You do not need to complete the number of hours.

Employee	Filing Status, Dependents	Pay	Union Dues per Period	Garnishment per Period
S. Bergstrom	MJ-0	$1,700		$ 50
C. Pare	MJ-2 (<17)	3,500	$120	
L. Van der Hooven	S-1 (Other)	3,225	240	75
S. Lightfoot	MJ-0	2,850		100

Name	Filing Status	Dependents	Hourly Rate or Period Wage	No. of Regular Hours	No. of Overtime Hours	No. of Holiday Hours	Commissions	Gross Earnings	401(k)	Section 125	Taxable Wages for Federal/State W/H	Taxable Wages for FICA

Name	Gross Earnings	Taxable Wages for Federal/State W/H	Taxable Wages for FICA	Federal W/H	Social Security Tax	Medicare W/H Tax	State W/H Tax	Union Dues	Garnishment	Net Pay

P5-4A.
LO 5-1, 5-2, 5-3, 5-4, 5-5

Lexington is the payroll accountant at All's Fair Gifts. The employees of All's Fair Gifts are paid semimonthly. Asa comes to Lexington on April 7 and requests a pay advance of $1,000, which Asa will pay back in equal parts on the April 14 and May 15 paychecks. Asa is single, with one dependent under 17, is paid $50,000 per year, contributes 3 percent of gross pay to a 401(k), and has $125 per paycheck deducted for a Section 125 plan. Compute the net pay on Asa's April 14 paycheck. The applicable state income tax rate is 5.25 percent. Use the wage-bracket method for manual payroll systems with Forms W-4 from 2020 or later in Appendix C to determine the federal income tax. Assume box 2 is *not* checked.

Name	Filing Status	Dependents	Hourly Rate or Period Wage	No. of Regular Hours	No. of Overtime Hours	No. of Holiday Hours	Commissions	Gross Earnings	401(k)	Section 125	Taxable Wages for Federal/State W/H	Taxable Wages for FICA
Asa												

Name	Gross Earnings	Taxable Wages for Federal/State W/H	Taxable Wages for FICA	Federal W/H	Social Security Tax	Medicare W/H Tax	State W/H Tax	Advance	Net Pay
Asa									

P5-5A.
LO 5-1, 5-2

Milligan's Millworks pays its employees weekly. Use the wage-bracket tables from Appendix C to compute the federal income tax withholdings for the following employees of Milligan's Millworks. Assume that no pre-tax deductions exist for any employee, box 2 is not checked for all employees, and a manual payroll system is used.

Employee	Filing Status	Dependents	Weekly Pay	Federal Tax
D. Balestreri	Single	2 <17	$ 845	
Y. Milligan	Single	One Other	1,233	
H. Curran	Married/Joint	2 < 17, One Other	682	
D. Liberti	Head of Household	1 < 17	755	

P5-6A.
LO 5-2

Moravanti Italian Imports has four employees and pays biweekly. On Form W-4, complete Step 2, the Multiple Jobs Worksheet (when applicable) to obtain the amount for Step 4(c). Calculate the federal income tax withholding using the wage-bracket tables in Appendix C. Assume that box 2 is not checked for L. Torabi and R. Beninati and is checked for G. Fisher and J. Tillman.

Employee	Filing Status	Dependents	Annual Salary	Spouse Annual Salary/Pay Frequency	Federal Income Tax per Period
L. Torabi	S	None	$39,500	n/a	
R. Beninati	S	One Other	48,500	n/a	
G. Fisher	MJ	3 < 17	45,300	$75,600/biweekly	
J. Tillman	MJ	2 < 17	42,000	$27,500/weekly	

Form W-4
Department of the Treasury
Internal Revenue Service

Employee's Withholding Certificate
Complete Form W-4 so that your employer can withhold the correct federal income tax from your pay.
Give Form W-4 to your employer.
Your withholding is subject to review by the IRS.

OMB No. 1545-0074

2023

Step 1: Enter Personal Information

(a) First name and middle initial | Last name | (b) Social security number

Address

Does your name match the name on your social security card? If not, to ensure you get credit for your earnings, contact SSA at 800-772-1213 or go to www.ssa.gov.

City or town, state, and ZIP code

(c) ☐ Single or Married filing separately
☐ Married filing jointly or Qualifying surviving spouse
☐ Head of household (Check only if you're unmarried and pay more than half the costs of keeping up a home for yourself and a qualifying individual.)

Complete Steps 2–4 ONLY if they apply to you; otherwise, skip to Step 5. See page 2 for more information on each step, who can claim exemption from withholding, other details, and privacy.

Step 2: Multiple Jobs or Spouse Works

Complete this step if you (1) hold more than one job at a time, or (2) are married filing jointly and your spouse also works. The correct amount of withholding depends on income earned from all of these jobs.

Do **only one** of the following.

(a) Reserved for future use.

(b) Use the Multiple Jobs Worksheet on page 3 and enter the result in Step 4(c) below; **or**

(c) If there are only two jobs total, you may check this box. Do the same on Form W-4 for the other job. This option is generally more accurate than (b) if pay at the lower paying job is more than half of the pay at the higher paying job. Otherwise, (b) is more accurate . . . . ☐

TIP: If you have self-employment income, see page 2.

Complete Steps 3–4(b) on Form W-4 for only ONE of these jobs. Leave those steps blank for the other jobs. (Your withholding will be most accurate if you complete Steps 3–4(b) on the Form W-4 for the highest paying job.)

Step 3: Claim Dependent and Other Credits

If your total income will be $200,000 or less ($400,000 or less if married filing jointly):

Multiply the number of qualifying children under age 17 by $2,000 $ _____

Multiply the number of other dependents by $500 . . . . . $ _____

Add the amounts above for qualifying children and other dependents. You may add to this the amount of any other credits. Enter the total here . . . . **3** $ _____

Step 4 (optional): Other Adjustments	(a) **Other income (not from jobs).** If you want tax withheld for other income you expect this year that won't have withholding, enter the amount of other income here. This may include interest, dividends, and retirement income	4(a)	$
	(b) **Deductions.** If you expect to claim deductions other than the standard deduction and want to reduce your withholding, use the Deductions Worksheet on page 3 and enter the result here	4(b)	$
	(c) **Extra withholding.** Enter any additional tax you want withheld each **pay period** . .	4(c)	$

Step 5: Sign Here	Under penalties of perjury, I declare that this certificate, to the best of my knowledge and belief, is true, correct, and complete.	
	Employee's signature (This form is not valid unless you sign it.)	**Date**

Employers Only	Employer's name and address	First date of employment	Employer identification number (EIN)

For Privacy Act and Paperwork Reduction Act Notice, see page 3. Cat. No. 10220Q Form **W-4** (2023)

Form W-4 (2023) Page **3**

Step 2(b)—Multiple Jobs Worksheet *(Keep for your records.)*

If you choose the option in Step 2(b) on Form W-4, complete this worksheet (which calculates the total extra tax for all jobs) on **only ONE** Form W-4. Withholding will be most accurate if you complete the worksheet and enter the result on the Form W-4 for the highest paying job. To be accurate, submit a new Form W-4 for all other jobs if you have not updated your withholding since 2019.

Note: If more than one job has annual wages of more than $120,000 or there are more than three jobs, see Pub. 505 for additional tables.

1 **Two jobs.** If you have two jobs or you're married filing jointly and you and your spouse each have one job, find the amount from the appropriate table on page 4. Using the "Higher Paying Job" row and the "Lower Paying Job" column, find the value at the intersection of the two household salaries and enter that value on line 1. Then, **skip** to line 3 . . . . **1** $ _____

2 **Three jobs.** If you and/or your spouse have three jobs at the same time, complete lines 2a, 2b, and 2c below. Otherwise, skip to line 3.

  a Find the amount from the appropriate table on page 4 using the annual wages from the highest paying job in the "Higher Paying Job" row and the annual wages for your next highest paying job in the "Lower Paying Job" column. Find the value at the intersection of the two household salaries and enter that value on line 2a . . . . **2a** $ _____

  b Add the annual wages of the two highest paying jobs from line 2a together and use the total as the wages in the "Higher Paying Job" row and use the annual wages for your third job in the "Lower Paying Job" column to find the amount from the appropriate table on page 4 and enter this amount on line 2b . . . . **2b** $ _____

  c Add the amounts from lines 2a and 2b and enter the result on line 2c . . . . **2c** $ _____

3 Enter the number of pay periods per year for the highest paying job. For example, if that job pays weekly, enter 52; if it pays every other week, enter 26; if it pays monthly, enter 12, etc. . . . . . **3** _____

4 **Divide** the annual amount on line 1 or line 2c by the number of pay periods on line 3. Enter this amount here and in **Step 4(c)** of Form W-4 for the highest paying job (along with any other additional amount you want withheld) . . . . **4** $ _____

Step 4(b)—Deductions Worksheet *(Keep for your records.)*

1 Enter an estimate of your 2023 itemized deductions (from Schedule A (Form 1040)). Such deductions may include qualifying home mortgage interest, charitable contributions, state and local taxes (up to $10,000), and medical expenses in excess of 7.5% of your income . . . . **1** $ _____

2 Enter: • $27,700 if you're married filing jointly or a qualifying surviving spouse
         • $20,800 if you're head of household
         • $13,850 if you're single or married filing separately . . . . **2** $ _____

3 If line 1 is greater than line 2, subtract line 2 from line 1 and enter the result here. If line 2 is greater than line 1, enter "-0-" . . . . **3** $ _____

4 Enter an estimate of your student loan interest, deductible IRA contributions, and certain other adjustments (from Part II of Schedule 1 (Form 1040)). See Pub. 505 for more information . . . . **4** $ _____

5 **Add** lines 3 and 4. Enter the result here and in **Step 4(b)** of Form W-4 . . . . **5** $ _____

Privacy Act and Paperwork Reduction Act Notice. We ask for the information on this form to carry out the Internal Revenue laws of the United States. Internal Revenue Code sections 3402(f)(2) and 6109 and their regulations require you to provide this information; your employer uses it to determine your federal income tax withholding. Failure to provide a properly completed form will result in your being treated as a single person with no other entries on the form; providing fraudulent information may subject you to penalties. Routine uses of this information include giving it to the Department of Justice for civil and criminal litigation; to cities, states, the District of Columbia, and U.S. commonwealths and territories for use in administering their tax laws; and to the Department of Health and Human Services for use in the National Directory of New Hires. We may also disclose this information to other countries under a tax treaty, to federal and state agencies to enforce federal nontax criminal laws, or to federal law enforcement and intelligence agencies to combat terrorism.

You are not required to provide the information requested on a form that is subject to the Paperwork Reduction Act unless the form displays a valid OMB control number. Books or records relating to a form or its instructions must be retained as long as their contents may become material in the administration of any Internal Revenue law. Generally, tax returns and return information are confidential, as required by Code section 6103.

The average time and expenses required to complete and file this form will vary depending on individual circumstances. For estimated averages, see the instructions for your income tax return.

If you have suggestions for making this form simpler, we would be happy to hear from you. See the instructions for your income tax return.

Form W-4 (2023)   Page **4**

Married Filing Jointly or Qualifying Surviving Spouse

Higher Paying Job Annual Taxable Wage & Salary	$0 - 9,999	$10,000 - 19,999	$20,000 - 29,999	$30,000 - 39,999	$40,000 - 49,999	$50,000 - 59,999	$60,000 - 69,999	$70,000 - 79,999	$80,000 - 89,999	$90,000 - 99,999	$100,000 - 109,999	$110,000 - 120,000
$0 - 9,999	$0	$0	$850	$850	$1,000	$1,020	$1,020	$1,020	$1,020	$1,020	$1,020	$1,870
$10,000 - 19,999	0	930	1,850	2,000	2,200	2,220	2,220	2,220	2,220	2,220	3,200	4,070
$20,000 - 29,999	850	1,850	2,920	3,120	3,320	3,340	3,340	3,340	3,340	4,320	5,320	6,190
$30,000 - 39,999	850	2,000	3,120	3,320	3,520	3,540	3,540	3,540	4,520	5,520	6,520	7,390
$40,000 - 49,999	1,000	2,200	3,320	3,520	3,720	3,740	3,740	4,720	5,720	6,720	7,720	8,590
$50,000 - 59,999	1,020	2,220	3,340	3,540	3,740	3,760	4,750	5,750	6,750	7,750	8,750	9,610
$60,000 - 69,999	1,020	2,220	3,340	3,540	3,740	4,750	5,750	6,750	7,750	8,750	9,750	10,610
$70,000 - 79,999	1,020	2,220	3,340	3,540	4,720	5,750	6,750	7,750	8,750	9,750	10,750	11,610
$80,000 - 99,999	1,020	2,220	4,170	5,370	6,570	7,600	8,600	9,600	10,600	11,600	12,600	13,460
$100,000 - 149,999	1,870	4,070	6,190	7,390	8,590	9,610	10,610	11,660	12,860	14,060	15,260	16,330
$150,000 - 239,999	2,040	4,440	6,760	8,160	9,560	10,780	11,980	13,180	14,380	15,580	16,780	17,850
$240,000 - 259,999	2,040	4,440	6,760	8,160	9,560	10,780	11,980	13,180	14,380	15,580	16,780	17,850
$260,000 - 279,999	2,040	4,440	6,760	8,160	9,560	10,780	11,980	13,180	14,380	15,580	16,780	18,140
$280,000 - 299,999	2,040	4,440	6,760	8,160	9,560	10,780	11,980	13,180	14,380	15,870	17,870	19,740
$300,000 - 319,999	2,040	4,440	6,760	8,160	9,560	10,780	11,980	13,470	15,470	17,470	19,470	21,340
$320,000 - 364,999	2,040	4,440	6,760	8,550	10,750	12,770	14,770	16,770	18,770	20,770	22,770	24,640
$365,000 - 524,999	2,970	6,470	9,890	12,390	14,890	17,220	19,520	21,820	24,120	26,420	28,720	30,880
$525,000 and over	3,140	6,840	10,460	13,160	15,860	18,390	20,890	23,390	25,890	28,390	30,890	33,250

Single or Married Filing Separately

Higher Paying Job Annual Taxable Wage & Salary	$0 - 9,999	$10,000 - 19,999	$20,000 - 29,999	$30,000 - 39,999	$40,000 - 49,999	$50,000 - 59,999	$60,000 - 69,999	$70,000 - 79,999	$80,000 - 89,999	$90,000 - 99,999	$100,000 - 109,999	$110,000 - 120,000
$0 - 9,999	$310	$890	$1,020	$1,020	$1,020	$1,860	$1,870	$1,870	$1,870	$1,870	$2,030	$2,040
$10,000 - 19,999	890	1,630	1,750	1,750	2,600	3,600	3,600	3,600	3,600	3,760	3,960	3,970
$20,000 - 29,999	1,020	1,750	1,880	2,720	3,720	4,720	4,730	4,730	4,890	5,090	5,290	5,300
$30,000 - 39,999	1,020	1,750	2,720	3,720	4,720	5,720	5,730	5,890	6,090	6,290	6,490	6,500
$40,000 - 59,999	1,710	3,450	4,570	5,570	6,570	7,700	7,910	8,110	8,310	8,510	8,710	8,720
$60,000 - 79,999	1,870	3,600	4,730	5,860	7,060	8,260	8,460	8,660	8,860	9,060	9,260	9,280
$80,000 - 99,999	1,870	3,730	5,060	6,260	7,460	8,660	8,860	9,060	9,260	9,460	10,430	11,240
$100,000 - 124,999	2,040	3,970	5,300	6,500	7,700	8,900	9,110	9,610	10,610	11,610	12,610	13,430
$125,000 - 149,999	2,040	3,970	5,300	6,500	7,700	9,610	10,610	11,610	12,610	13,610	14,900	16,020
$150,000 - 174,999	2,040	3,970	5,610	7,610	9,610	11,610	12,610	13,750	15,050	16,350	17,650	18,770
$175,000 - 199,999	2,720	5,450	7,580	9,580	11,580	13,870	15,180	16,480	17,780	19,080	20,380	21,490
$200,000 - 249,999	2,900	5,930	8,360	10,660	12,960	15,260	16,570	17,870	19,170	20,470	21,770	22,880
$250,000 - 399,999	2,970	6,010	8,440	10,740	13,040	15,340	16,640	17,940	19,240	20,540	21,840	22,960
$400,000 - 449,999	2,970	6,010	8,440	10,740	13,040	15,340	16,640	17,940	19,240	20,540	21,840	22,960
$450,000 and over	3,140	6,380	9,010	11,510	14,010	16,510	18,010	19,510	21,010	22,510	24,010	25,330

Head of Household

Higher Paying Job Annual Taxable Wage & Salary	$0 - 9,999	$10,000 - 19,999	$20,000 - 29,999	$30,000 - 39,999	$40,000 - 49,999	$50,000 - 59,999	$60,000 - 69,999	$70,000 - 79,999	$80,000 - 89,999	$90,000 - 99,999	$100,000 - 109,999	$110,000 - 120,000
$0 - 9,999	$0	$620	$860	$1,020	$1,020	$1,020	$1,020	$1,650	$1,870	$1,870	$1,890	$2,040
$10,000 - 19,999	620	1,630	2,060	2,220	2,220	2,220	2,850	3,850	4,070	4,090	4,290	4,440
$20,000 - 29,999	860	2,060	2,490	2,650	2,650	3,280	4,280	5,280	5,520	5,720	5,920	6,070
$30,000 - 39,999	1,020	2,220	2,650	2,810	3,440	4,440	5,440	6,460	6,880	7,080	7,280	7,430
$40,000 - 59,999	1,020	2,220	3,130	4,290	5,290	6,290	7,480	8,680	9,100	9,300	9,500	9,650
$60,000 - 79,999	1,500	3,700	5,130	6,290	7,480	8,680	9,880	11,080	11,500	11,700	11,900	12,050
$80,000 - 99,999	1,870	4,070	5,690	7,050	8,250	9,450	10,650	11,850	12,260	12,460	12,870	13,820
$100,000 - 124,999	2,040	4,440	6,070	7,430	8,630	9,830	11,030	12,230	13,190	14,190	15,190	16,150
$125,000 - 149,999	2,040	4,440	6,070	7,430	8,630	9,980	11,980	13,980	15,190	16,190	17,270	18,530
$150,000 - 174,999	2,040	4,440	6,070	7,980	9,980	11,980	13,980	15,980	17,420	18,720	20,020	21,280
$175,000 - 199,999	2,190	5,390	7,820	9,980	11,980	14,060	16,360	18,660	20,170	21,470	22,770	24,030
$200,000 - 249,999	2,720	6,190	8,920	11,380	13,680	15,980	18,280	20,580	22,090	23,390	24,690	25,950
$250,000 - 449,999	2,970	6,470	9,200	11,660	13,960	16,260	18,560	20,860	22,380	23,680	24,980	26,230
$450,000 and over	3,140	6,840	9,770	12,430	14,930	17,430	19,930	22,430	24,150	25,650	27,150	28,600

P5-7A.
LO 5-3

The employees of Ethereal Bank are paid on a semimonthly basis. Compute the FICA taxes for the employees for the November 30 payroll. All employees have been employed for the entire calendar year. All employees are single. There are no pre-tax deductions.

Employee	Semimonthly Pay	YTD Pay for Nov. 15 Pay Date	Social Security Tax for Nov. 30 Pay Date	Medicare Tax for Nov. 30 Pay Date
R. Bellagio	$9,500			
B. Khumalo	6,700			
S. Schriver	6,800			
K. Saetang	7,250			
T. Ahmad	9,750			
M. Petrova	8,100			

P5-8A.
LO 5-4

Fannon's Chocolate Factory operates in North Carolina. Calculate the state income tax for each employee using the state income tax rate of 4.75 percent. Assume that no pre-tax deductions exist for any employee.

Employee	Amount per Pay Period	North Carolina Income Tax
K. Jamieson	$550	
D. Macranie	4,895	
G. Lockhart	3,225	
K. McIntyre	1,795	

P5-9A.
LO 5-2

Using the percentage method for manual payroll with W-4s from 2020 or later in Appendix C, calculate the federal withholding amounts for the following employees. No information was included in Step 4 of the W-4, and no box was checked in Step 2.

Employee	Filing Status	Dependents	Pay Frequency	Amount per Pay Period	Federal Income Tax
S. Calder	MJ	3 < 17	Monthly	$10,000	
P. Singh	HH	1 < 17	Biweekly	3,300	
B. Nelson	MJ	None	Daily	500	

P5-10A.
LO 5-6

You are the new accountant for a start-up company, Peaceful Skunk Builders. The company has cross-country drivers, warehouse personnel, and office staff at the main location. The company is looking at options that allow its employees flexibility in receiving their pay. You have been asked to present the advantages and disadvantages of the various payment methods for senior management. Which would be the best option for each class of workers?

Exercises Set B

E5-1B.
LO 5-1

The payroll accountant needs to compute net pay for the employees of Happy Crab Marketing. Place the following steps in the proper order after the determination of gross pay has been completed.
a. Compute Social Security and Medicare tax withholding
b. Compute income tax withholding(s)
c. Compute pre-tax deductions
d. Compute post-tax deductions
Order: _____

E5-2B.
LO 5-1

The payroll accountant has received a court order for garnishment for an employee's student loan payments. What must be considered in computing the garnishment? (Select all that apply.)
a. Year-to-date pay
b. Hourly wage
c. Disposable income
d. Pay frequency

E5-3B.
LO 5-2

Lux of Trade Secrets Importing is preparing payroll taxes manually. As Lux prepares to use the wage-bracket tables to determine federal income tax withholdings for each employee, which information should be available? (Select all that apply.)
a. Filing status
b. Job title
c. Year-to-date earnings
d. Age, type, and number of dependents

E5-4B.
LO 5-2

Which of the following are steps in computing federal income tax withholding using the percentage method? (Select all that apply.)
a. Compute and record dependents.
b. Apply the tax rate to the taxable portion of the earnings.
c. Determine if the employee is exempt or nonexempt.
d. Add the marginal tax.

E5-5B.
LO 5-3

Which of the following is true about Social Security and Medicare tax deductions?
a. They are applied to the gross pay.
b. Contributions to a 401(k) plan are exempt from these taxes.
c. Medicare taxes apply to all earnings at the same rate.
d. Certain pre-tax deductions are exempt from Social Security and Medicare tax computations.

E5-6B.
LO 5-3

Scout is the vice president for marketing at Sun Field Industries, earns $175,000 annually, and is paid on a semimonthly basis. As of November 15, Scout has year-to-date earnings of $153,125. The Social Security wage base is $160,200. What is the maximum amount of taxable earnings that may be subject to Social Security tax for the November 30 pay period?
a. $5,833.27
b. $6,235.33
c. $7,291.67
d. $7,074.93

E5-7B.
LO 5-4

Which of the following is(are) true about state and local income tax? (Select all that apply.)
a. Pre-tax deduction rules for federal income tax are generally the same for state and local income taxes.
b. Nine states do not have a personal income tax on earnings.
c. All localities levy income taxes on employees.
d. State income tax computations vary among states.

E5-8B.
LO 5-6

Which of the following is(are) true about employee pay methods? (Select all that apply.)
a. Employees must be able to access the full amount of their net pay on the pay date.
b. Employers must keep a record of all pay disbursements.
c. Employees do not need to own a bank account to receive their pay via direct deposit.
d. Employees must request the transfer of payroll earnings to their paycard each period.

E5-9B.
LO 5-4

Which of the following is(are) true about child support garnishments? (Select all that apply.)
a. They are based on gross pay.
b. The garnishment may be as high as 65 percent.
c. Only the minimum wage amount of an employee's pay is subject to garnishment.
d. Title III of the CCPA protects employees.

E5-10B.
LO 5-6

You are preparing a training session for your colleagues about payroll check fraud. Which of the following may be indicators of check fraud? (Select all that apply.)
a. Changes in font type between company address and employee name.
b. Company logo on the face of the check.
c. The check number is missing from the check.
d. Only one signature is required from the company.

Problems Set B

P5-1B.
LO 5-1, 5-2, 5-3

Compute the net pay for Merritt Gamal and Cove Green. Assume that they are paid biweekly, subject to federal income tax (use the wage-bracket method in Appendix C) and FICA taxes, and have no other deductions from their pay. Merritt's deduction with participation in the cafeteria plan is $75; Cove's is $250. There is no deduction if they do not participate in the cafeteria plan. The cafeteria plan qualifies for Section 125. There are no state income taxes, and you do not need to complete the number of hours. All W-4s were received in 2023, and there is no information for Step 4. Cove did check the box in Step 2.

Name	Filing Status	Dependents	Hourly Rate or Period Wage	No. of Regular Hours	No. of Overtime Hours	No. of Holiday Hours	Commissions	Gross Earnings	Cafeteria Plan	Taxable Wages for Federal / State W/H	Taxable Wages for FICA
Merritt Gamal—no cafeteria plan	S	None	1,600.00								
Merritt Gamal—cafeteria plan	S	None	1,600.00								
Cove Green—no cafeteria plan	MJ	2 < 17 One Other	1,875.00								
Cove Green—cafeteria plan	MJ	2 < 17 One Other	1,875.00								

Name	Gross Earnings	Taxable Wages for Federal / State W/H	Taxable Wages for FICA	Federal W/H	Social Security Tax	Medicare W/H	Net Pay
Merritt Gamal—no cafeteria plan							
Merritt Gamal—cafeteria plan							
Cove Green—no cafeteria plan							
Cove Green—cafeteria plan							

P5-2B.
LO 5-1, 5-2, 5-3, 5-5, 5-6

Teton Tours in Evanston, Wyoming, has six employees who are paid on a biweekly basis. Calculate the net pay from the information provided for the July 14 pay date. Assume that all wages are subject to Social Security and Medicare taxes. Use the wage-bracket tables in Appendix C to determine the federal income tax withholding. You do not need to complete the number of hours. No one has checked the box in Step 2, and there is no additional information in Step 4.

a. A. Bowman
Married/joint, two dependents <17
Annual pay $36,320
401(k) deduction: 2 percent of gross pay per pay period

b. J. Raz
Single, no dependents
Annual pay: $46,350
401(k) deduction: $220 per pay period

c. G. Koskoris
Single, one dependent <17, one other dependent
Annual pay: $55,120
Section 125 deduction: $25 per pay period
401(k) deduction: $150 per pay period

d. S. Hays-Smith
Married/joint, three dependents <17
Annual pay: $40,820
United Way deduction: $25 per pay period
Garnishment: $75 per period

e. H. Inhofe
Married/joint, no dependents
Annual pay: $55,000
Section 125 deduction: $100 per period
401(k) deduction: 4 percent of gross pay

f. D. Wong
Single, one other dependent
Annual pay: $38,600
401(k) deduction: $120 per period

Name	Filing Status	Dependents	Hourly Rate or Period Wage	No. of Regular Hours	No. of Overtime Hours	No. of Holiday Hours	Gross Earnings	401(k)	Section 125	Taxable Wages for Federal / State W/H	Taxable Wages for FICA

266 Chapter 5 Employee Net Pay and Pay Methods

Name	Gross Earnings	Taxable Wages for Federal/State W/H	Taxable Wages for FICA	Federal W/H Tax	Social Security Tax	Medicare Tax	State Tax	United Way	Garnishment	Net Pay

P5-3B.
LO 5-1, 5-2, 5-3, 5-4, 5-5

The following employees of Concordian Construction of Walla Walla, Washington, are paid biweekly. Some employees have union dues or garnishments deducted from their pay. Calculate their net pay. Use the percentage method for manual payrolls with Form W-4 from 2020 or later in Appendix C to determine federal income tax. No employee has exceeded the maximum FICA limits. You do not need to complete the number of hours. No one checked the box in Step 2, and there is no additional information in Step 4.

Employee	Filing Status	Dependents	Annual Pay	Union Dues per Period	Garnishment per Period
J. Johnson	Married/joint	1 < 17	$45,000	$102	
V. Roberson	Single	None	33,800		$70
T. Major	Married/joint	None	65,650	110	90
M. Reice	Head of household	1 < 17	76,600		45

Name	Filing Status	Dependents	Hourly Rate or Period Wage	No. of Regular Hours	No. of Overtime Hours	No. of Holiday Hours	Commissions	Gross Earnings	401(k)	Section 125	Taxable Wages for Federal/State W/H	Taxable Wages for FICA

Name	Gross Earnings	Taxable Wages for Federal/State W/H	Taxable Wages for FICA	Federal W/H	Social Security Tax	Medicare W/H Tax	State W/H	Union Dues	Garnishment	Net Pay

P5-4B.
LO 5-1, 5-2, 5-3, 5-4, 5-5

You are the payroll accountant for Multi Winds Energy of Cornelius, North Carolina, whose employees are paid biweekly. An employee, Larson, comes to you on September 14 and requests a pay advance of $1,000, which will be paid back in equal parts on the September 22 and October 20 paychecks. Larson is single, has no dependents, is paid $52,500 per year, contributes 5 percent of gross pay to a 401(k) plan, and has $250 per paycheck deducted for a court-ordered garnishment. Compute the net pay for Larson's September 24 paycheck. The state income tax rate is 4.75 percent. Use the wage-bracket tables in Appendix C to determine the federal income tax withholding amount. You do not need to complete the number of hours. Assume that no pre-tax deductions exist for the employee and box 2 is not checked.

Name	Filing Status	Dependents	Hourly Rate or Period Wage	No. of Regular Hours	No. of Overtime Hours	No. of Holiday Hours	Commissions	Gross Earnings	401(k)	Section 125	Taxable Wages for Federal/ State W/H	Taxable Wages for FICA
Larson												

Name	Gross Earnings	Taxable Wages for Federal / State W/H	Taxable Wages for FICA	Federal W/H	Social Security Tax	Medicare Tax	State Tax	Garnishment	Advance	Net Pay
Larson										

P5-5B.
LO 5-2

Wolfe Industries pays its employees on a semimonthly basis. Using the wage-bracket tables in Appendix C, compute the federal income tax deductions for the following employees of Wolfe Industries. No information was included in Step 4 of any W-4; McCollum checked the box in Step 2c. Assume that no pre-tax deductions exist for any employee and box 2 is not checked for all other employees. Do not round intermediate calculations. Round your final answers to the nearest cent.

Employee	Marital Status	Dependents	Semimonthly Pay	Federal Income Tax
T. Canter	Single	None	$1,450	
M. McCollum	Married/joint	2 < 17	1,690	
C. Hai	Head of household	1 < 17	1,795	
T. Elliott	Single	1 other	2,165	

P5-6B.
LO 5-2

Country Pet Industries has employees with pay schedules that vary based on job classification. Compute each employee's federal income tax liability using the percentage method for manual payroll systems in Appendix C. All Form W-4s were received in 2022. No one checked the box in Step 2, and there was no additional information in Step 4.

Employee	Filing Status	Dependents	Pay Frequency	Pay Amount	Federal Income Tax
X. Gander	Married/joint	1 < 17	Biweekly	$1,825	
M. Stanley	Married/separately	None	Weekly	750	
N. Heim	Single	1 < 17	Weekly	875	
D. Young	Head of household	1 Other	Semimonthly	2,025	

P5-7B.
LO 5-3

The employees of Lillian's Interiors are paid on a semimonthly basis. Compute the FICA taxes for the employees for the December 29, 2023, pay period. All employees are single and have been employed for the entire calendar year.

Employee	Semimonthly Pay	YTD Pay for Dec. 15 Pay Date	Social Security Tax Dec. 29 Pay Date	Medicare Tax for Dec. 29 Pay Date
W. Babish	$8,325			
G. Hanoush	6,275			
R. Fezzeti	9,250			
T. Gomez	4,550			
N. Bertraud	5,705			
R. LaPonte	4,950			

P5-8B.
LO 5-4

Christensen Ranch operates in Pennsylvania. Calculate the state income tax for each employee using the state income tax rate of 3.07 percent. Assume that no pre-tax deductions exist for any employee.

Employee	Amount per Pay Period	Pennsylvania Income Tax
G. Zonis	$1,325	
V. Sizemore	1,710	
R. Dawson	925	
C. Couture	2,550	

P5-9B.
LO 5-2

Using the wage-bracket method for manual payroll systems with Form W-4 from 2020 or later in Appendix C, calculate the federal withholding amounts for the following employees. No box was checked in Step 2, and no additional information was included in Step 4.

Employee	Filing Status	Dependents	Pay Frequency	Amount per Pay Period	Federal Income Tax
L. Abbey	Head of household	2 < 17	Semimonthly	$2,500	
G. Narleski	Married/joint	None	Weekly	1,000	
T. Leider	Single	1 other	Monthly	4,000	

P5-10B.
LO 5-6

You have been retained as a consultant for Marionet Industries. The company has had difficulty with its cross-country drivers receiving their pay in a timely manner because they are often away from their home banks. The company is looking at options that offer its employees flexibility in receiving their pay. Prepare a presentation for senior management depicting the advantages and disadvantages of the various payment methods.

Critical Thinking

For the Critical Thinking problems, use the following steps to compute the gross-up amount:

1. Compute tax rate: The tax rate on bonuses is 22 percent. Social Security (6.2 percent) and Medicare taxes (1.45 percent) must be added to this rate. For bonuses, the total tax rate equals 22% + 6.2% + 1.45%, or 29.65%.
2. Subtract 100 percent − tax rate percentage to get the net tax rate. For bonuses, it is 100% − 29.65%, or 70.35%.
3. Gross-up amount = net pay / net tax rate. For example, if you want the employee to receive a $150 bonus, the equation is $150/70.35% = $213.22.
    (Note: Typically voluntary pre-tax and post-tax deductions are not withheld from bonus checks.)

5-1. Arden, an employee of Sweet Shoppe Industries, receives a bonus of $5,000 for stellar work this period. Arden's boss wants the net check to be $5,000. Arden contributes 3 percent to a pre-tax 401(k) deduction. Calculate the gross pay amount that would result in $5,000 paid to Arden.

5-2. Your boss approaches you in mid-December and requests that you pay certain employees their gross pay amount as if there were no deductions as their year-end bonuses. None of the employees have reached the Social Security wage base for the year, and the company pays semimonthly. What is the gross-up amount for each of the following employees? (Use the tax rate for bonuses and no state taxes.)

Employee	Regular Gross Pay per Period	Grossed-Up Amount
Onyx St. John	$2,500	
Indigo Johnson	3,380	
Zion Hale	3,178	

In the Real World: Scenario for Discussion

The state of Kansas passed legislation that allowed employers to select their employee pay method. The legislation was known as the "paperless payroll law," and many employers opted to give their employees paycards instead of cash, check, or direct deposit. This practice spread to many other states, including New York. In 2017, the law was revoked because it made employers into *de facto* financial institutions.

What are the issues with this practice? What are the benefits?

Internet Activities

5-1. Did you know that you can use an online calculator to see how your voluntary deductions will affect your paycheck? Many different payroll calculators exist. Go to one or more of the following sites and use the payroll calculator:

www.paycheckcity.com/

www.surepayroll.com/resources/calculator

www.adp.com/tools-and-resources/calculators-and-tools/payroll-calculators.aspx

5-2. Want to know more about the concepts in this chapter? Check out these sites:

https://www.irs.gov/pub/irs-pdf/p15t.pdf

www.americanpayroll.org/Visa-Paycard-Portal/

5-3. Would you like to preview employee apps used to enter time and calculate payroll disbursements? Check out these links:

DOL Timesheet: https://itunes.apple.com/us/app/dol-timesheet/id433638193?mt=8

Intuit payroll: https://payroll.intuit.com/additional-services/mobile-payroll-apps/

Sure payroll: https://www.surepayroll.com/payroll/mobile

Continuing Payroll Project: Prevosti Farms and Sugarhouse

For the February 10, 2023, pay period, use the gross pay totals from the end of Chapter 3 to compute each employee's net pay. Once you have computed the net pay (use the wage-bracket tables in Appendix C), the state withholding tax for Vermont is computed at 3.35 percent of taxable wages (i.e., gross pay less pre-tax deductions). Note that the first pay period comprises only eight days of work during the February 10 pay period. The federal income tax should be determined using the biweekly tables in Appendix C.

Initial pre-tax deductions for each employee are as follows:

Name	Deduction
Millen	Insurance: $155/paycheck/401(k): 3% of gross pay
Towle	Insurance: $100/paycheck/401(k): 5% of gross pay
Long	Insurance: $155/paycheck/401(k): 2% of gross pay
Shangraw	Insurance: $100/paycheck/401(k): 3% of gross pay
Lewis	Insurance: $155/paycheck/401(k): 4% of gross pay
Schwartz	Insurance: $100/paycheck/401(k): 5% of gross pay
Prevosti	Insurance: $155/paycheck/401(k): 6% of gross pay
You	Insurance: $100/paycheck/401(k): 2% of gross pay

February 10 is the end of the first pay period and includes work completed during February 1–10. Compute the net pay for the February 10 pay period using the payroll register. All insurance and 401(k) deductions are pre-tax for federal and state. Update the Employee Earnings Records as of February 10, 2023. Joel Schwartz has made $5,000 in case sales at a 3 percent commission rate during this pay period. Recall that this is not a complete two-week pay period.

February

Sunday	Monday	Tuesday	Wednesday	Thursday	Friday	Saturday
			1	2	3	4
5	6	7	8	9	10	11
12	13	14	15	16	17	18
19	20	21	22	23	24	25
26	27	28				

Name	Filing Status	Dependents	Hourly Rate or Period Wage	No. of Regular Hours	No. of Overtime Hours	No. of Holiday Hours	Commission	Gross Earnings	401(k)	Sec 125	Taxable Wages for Federal/State W/H	Taxable Wages for FICA
T. Millen				64								
A. Towle				64								
C. Long				64	2							
M. Shangraw				32								
K. Lewis				64								
J. Schwartz				64			150.00					
T. Prevosti				64								
S. Success				64	1							

Name	Gross Earnings	Taxable Wages for Federal/State W/H	Taxable Wages for FICA	Federal W/H Tax	Social Security Tax	Medicare W/H Tax	State W/H Tax	Total Deduct	Net Pay	Check No.

February 24, 2023, is the end of the final pay period for the month. Schwartz has sold $7,500 of products during this pay period at a 3 percent commission. Complete the payroll register for the period's gross pay. Pay will be disbursed on February 28, 2023, and check numbers will continue from the prior payroll.

Name	Filing Status	Dependents	Hourly Rate or Period Wage	No. of Regular Hours	No. of Overtime Hours	No. of Holiday Hours	Commission	Gross Earnings	401(k)	Sec 125	Taxable Wages for Federal W/H	Taxable Wages for FICA
T. Millen				80								
A. Towle				80	3							
C. Long				80								
M. Shangraw				40	2							
K. Lewis				80								
J. Schwartz				80			225.00					
T. Prevosti				80								
S. Success				80	1							

Name	Gross Earnings	Taxable Wages for Federal/State W/H	Taxable Wages for FICA	Federal W/H Tax	Social Security Tax	Medicare W/H Tax	State W/H Tax	Total Deduct	Net Pay	Check No.
T. Millen										
A. Towle										
C. Long										
M. Shangraw										
K. Lewis										
J. Schwartz										
T. Prevosti										
S. Success										

EMPLOYEE EARNING RECORD

Name	Thomas Millen	Hire Date	2/1/2023
Address	1022 Forest School Rd	Date of Birth	12/16/1992
City/State/Zip	Woodstock, VT 05001	Exempt/Nonexempt	Exempt
Telephone	802-478-5055	Filing Status	Married/joint
Social Security Number	031-11-3456	No. of Dependents	3 < 17; 1 other
Position	Production Manager	Pay Rate	$35,000/year

Flex-Time	Child Care	FSA Amount	Educ. Assist.	Life Ins.	Long-Term Care	Gym

Period Ended	Hrs Worked	Reg Pay	OT Pay	Holiday	Comm	Gross Pay	401(k)	Sec 125	Taxable Wages for Federal W/H	Taxable Wages for FICA

272   Chapter 5   *Employee Net Pay and Pay Methods*

Taxable Wages for Federal	Taxable Wages for FICA	Federal W/H	Social Security Tax	Medicare Tax	State W/H	Total Deduct	Net Pay	YTD Net Pay	YTD Gross Pay	Benefits Election

EMPLOYEE EARNING RECORD

Name	Avery Towle	Hire Date	2/1/2023
Address	4011 Route 100	Date of Birth	7/14/2001
City/State/Zip	Plymouth, VT 05102	Exempt/Nonexempt	Nonexempt
Telephone	802-967-5873	Filing Status	Single
Social Security Number	089-74-0974	No. of Dependents	None
Position	Production Worker	Pay Rate	$15.00/hour

Flex-Time	Child Care	FSA Amount	Educ. Assist.	Life Ins.	Long-Term Care	Gym	Total Benefit

Period Ended	Hrs Worked	Reg Pay	OT Pay	Holiday	Comm	Gross Pay	401(k)	Sec 125	Taxable Wages for Federal W/H	Taxable Wages for FICA

Taxable Wages for Federal	Taxable Wages for FICA	Federal W/H	Social Security Tax	Medicare Tax	State W/H	Total Deduct	Net Pay	YTD Net Pay	YTD Gross Pay	Benefits Election

EMPLOYEE EARNING RECORD

Name	Charlie Long	Hire Date	2/1/2023
Address	242 Benedict Rd	Date of Birth	3/16/1997
City/State/Zip	S. Woodstock, VT 05002	Exempt/Nonexempt	Nonexempt
Telephone	802-429-3846	Filing Status	Married/joint
Social Security Number	056-23-4593	No. of Dependents	2 < 17
Position	Production Worker	Pay Rate	$15.00/hour

Flex-Time	Child Care	FSA Amount	Educational Assistance	Life Ins.	Long-Term Care	Gym	Total Benefit

Period Ended	Hrs Worked	Reg Pay	OT Pay	Holiday	Comm	Gross Pay	401(k)	Sec 125	Taxable Wages for Federal W/H	Taxable Wages for FICA

Taxable Wages for Federal	Taxable Wages for FICA	Federal W/H	Social Security Tax	Medicare Tax	State W/H	Total Deduc	Net Pay	YTD Net Pay	YTD Gross Pay	Benefits Election

EMPLOYEE EARNING RECORD

Name	Mary Shangraw	Hire Date	2/1/2023
Address	1901 Main St #2	Date of Birth	8/20/1980
City/State/Zip	Bridgewater, VT 05520	Exempt/Nonexempt	Exempt
Telephone	802-575-5423	Filing Status	Single
Social Security Number	075-28-8945	No. of Dependents	1 other
Position	Administrative Assistant	Pay Rate	$15.00/hour

Flex-Time	Child Care	FSA Amount	Educational Assistance	Life Ins.	Long-Term Care	Gym	Total Benefit

Period Ended	Hrs Worked	Reg Pay	OT Pay	Holiday	Comm	Gross Pay	401(k)	Sec 125	Taxable Wages for Federal W/H	Taxable Wages for FICA

Taxable Wages for Federal	Taxable Wages for FICA	Federal W/H	Social Security Tax	Medicare Tax	State W/H	Total Deduct	Net Pay	YTD Net Pay	YTD Gross Pay	Benefits Election

EMPLOYEE EARNING RECORD

Name	Kristen Lewis	Hire Date	2/1/2023
Address	840 Daily Hollow Rd	Date of Birth	4/6/1991
City/State/Zip	Bridgewater, VT 05523	Exempt/Nonexempt	Exempt
Telephone	802-390-5572	Filing Status	Married/joint
Social Security Number	076-39-5673	No. of Dependents	2 < 17; 1 other
Position	Office Manager	Pay Rate	$32,000/year

Flex-Time	Child Care	FSA Amount	Educational Assistance	Life Ins.	Long-Term Care	Gym	Total Benefit

Period Ended	Hrs Worked	Reg Pay	OT Pay	Holiday	Comm	Gross Pay	401(k)	Sec 125	Taxable Wages for Federal W/H	Taxable Wages for FICA

Taxable Wages for Federal	Taxable Wages for FICA	Federal W/H	Social Security Tax	Medicare Tax	State W/H	Total Deduct	Net Pay	YTD Net Pay	YTD Gross Pay	Benefits Election

EMPLOYEE EARNING RECORD

Name	Joel Schwartz	Hire Date	2/1/2023
Address	55 Maple Farm Way	Date of Birth	5/23/1993
City/State/Zip	Woodstock, VT 05534	Exempt/Nonexempt	Exempt
Telephone	802-463-9985	Filing Status	Married/joint
Social Security Number	021-34-9876	No. of Dependents	2 < 17
Position	Sales	Pay Rate	$32,000/year + commission

Flex-Time	Child Care	FSA Amount	Educational Assistance	Life Ins.	Long-Term Care	Gym	Total Benefit

Period Ended	Hrs Worked	Reg Pay	OT Pay	Holiday	Comm	Gross Pay	401(k)	Sec 125	Taxable Wages for Federal W/H	Taxable Wages for FICA

Taxable Wages for Federal	Taxable Wages for FICA	Federal W/H	Social Security Tax	Medicare Tax	State W/H	Total Deduct	Net Pay	YTD Net Pay	YTD Gross Pay	Benefits Election

EMPLOYEE EARNING RECORD

Name	Toni Prevosti	Hire Date	2/1/2023
Address	820 Westminster Rd	Date of Birth	9/19/1987
City/State/Zip	Bridgewater, VT 05521	Exempt/Nonexempt	Exempt
Telephone	802-673-2636	Filing Status	Married/joint
Social Security Number	055-22-0443	No. of Dependents	3 < 17; 2 other
Position	Owner/President	Pay Rate	$45,000/year

Flex-Time	Child Care	FSA Amount	Educational Assistance	Life Ins.	Long-Term Care	Gym	Total Benefit

Period Ended	Hrs Worked	Reg Pay	OT Pay	Holiday	Comm	Gross Pay	401(k)	Sec 125	Taxable Wages for Federal W/H	Taxable Wages for FICA

Taxable Wages for Federal	Taxable Wages for FICA	Federal W/H	Social Security Tax	Medicare Tax	State W/H	Total Deduct	Net Pay	YTD Net Pay	YTD Gross Pay	Benefits Election

EMPLOYEE EARNING RECORD

Name	Student Success	Hire Date	2/1/2023
Address	1644 Smitten Rd	Date of Birth	1/1/2001
City/State/Zip	Woodstock, VT 05001	Exempt/Nonexempt	Nonexempt
Telephone	(555) 555-5555	Filing Status	Single
Social Security Number	555-55-5555	No. of Dependents	None
Position	Accounting Clerk	Pay Rate	$34,000/year

Flex-Time	Child Care	FSA Amount	Educational Assistance	Life Ins.	Long-Term Care	Gym	Total Benefit

Period Ended	Hrs Worked	Reg Pay	OT Pay	Holiday	Comm	Gross Pay	401(k)	Sec 125	Taxable Wages for Federal W/H	Taxable Wages for FICA

Taxable Wages for Federal	Taxable Wages for FICA	Federal W/H	Social Security Tax	Medicare Tax	State W/H	Total Deduct	Net Pay	YTD Net Pay	YTD Gross Pay	Benefits Election

Answers to Stop & Check Exercises

Differentiating between Gross and Net Pay

1. Gross pay consists of wages or commissions earned by the employee before deductions. Net pay is the amount of cash the employee receives after all deductions.
2. Student answers may vary but could include qualifying medical or dental plans, Internal Revenue Code Section 125 plans, 401(k) retirement plans, federal income tax, Medicare tax, Social Security tax, state income tax, garnishments, charitable contributions, and union dues.
3. To "gross-up" a payroll amount is to calculate the amount of gross pay necessary to receive a net pay result. This is most often done for bonuses.

How Much Tax to Withhold?

1. $75,000 paid semimonthly would give per period of $3,125, $75,000/24 = $3,125. The dependent deduction of (2 × $500)/24 pay periods is $41.67.
   (a) $220 tentative tax − $41.67 dependents = $178.33; (b) $218.18 tentative tax − $41.67 dependents = $176.51.

2. $3,125 gross pay − $100 for 401(k) deduction per pay period = $3,025 taxable pay. This is the amount used in conjunction with the wage-bracket table to calculate the federal income tax withheld of $208 less dependents of $41.67 gives $166.33. The difference in taxes with the 401(k) deduction is $12 = $178.33 − $166.33.
3. $3,125 gross pay − $75 health insurance − $55 AFLAC = $2,995 taxable pay. This is the new amount used in conjunction with the wage bracket table to calculate the federal income tax withheld of $203 less dependents of $41.67 gives $161.33. The difference in taxes with the health insurance and AFLAC deductions is $17 = $178.33–$161.33.

FICA Taxes

1. Social Security = $327.36 = $5,280 × 0.062; Medicare = $76.56 = $5,280 × 0.0145.
2. Total liability = $807.84 = ($327.36 + $76.56) × 2.
3. $250,000/24 = $10,416.67 per pay period − $75 for Section 125 deduction = $10,341.67 subject to FICA taxes each period.
   (a) $0 Social Security liability because the maximum amount of wages taxable for Social Security is $160,200 and the employee has exceeded that. Year-to-date gross wages of $197,916.67 less qualified deduction of $1,425 ($75 × 19) gives $196,491.67 of YTD Medicare taxable earnings. Medicare base for this payroll is $200,000 − 196,491.67 = $3,508.33 to reach the $200,000 cap and $6,833.34 ($10,416.67 − 3,508.33 − 75.00) that will be charged the surcharge, so ($3,508.33 × 1.45%) + ($6,833.37 × 2.35%) = $50.87 + 160.58 = $211.45 Medicare tax.
   (b) Medicare liability will be: ($10,416.67 − 75.00) × (0.0145 + 0.009) = $243.03.

State and Local Income Taxes

1. Ever's state income tax: $92.39 ($62,500 annual salary/26 biweekly = $2,403.85 gross pay − $150 for 401(k) pre-tax deduction − $80 health insurance pre-tax deduction = $2,173.85 taxable pay × 4.25% = $92.39 from Appendix D.
2. Jodie's state income tax: $125.40 ($2,850 × 4.4%) state, $5.75 local.

Post-tax Deductions

1. a, b, d
2. Because the unions typically require that employees' union dues be remitted by the employer, the amount due must be deducted on a post-tax basis from each period pay.

Pay Methods

1. Cash, check, direct deposit, paycard, and cryptocurrencies
2. Regulation E
3. Direct deposit
4. Bonuses and commissions (currently)

Chapter Six

Employer Payroll Taxes and Labor Planning

All facets of payroll accounting are important because they affect the company's success and its employees. An essential piece of the payroll puzzle is the employer's payroll tax responsibility. The reporting and remittance of payroll taxes is a significant aspect that requires scrupulous attention to detail. Many different tax forms exist that must be filed at regular intervals and with varying governmental bodies. Tax filing requires organizational skills, time management, and continued accuracy. Tax reporting is a huge responsibility for the business and its payroll accountant because of governmental oversight. Additionally, employment tax revenue remittances represent 70 percent of all federal revenue. Therefore, employment tax remittances are a vital part of the U.S. economy.

Employers must also consider payroll responsibilities as part of labor planning. Besides taxes, other aspects of an employer's payroll responsibilities include maintaining workers' compensation insurance, forwarding amounts withheld through employees' voluntary and mandated deductions, and determining labor expenses and employee benefits. The Internal Revenue Service and state employment departments have websites that contain important information about filing requirements, due dates, guidelines, and penalties (see Appendix E for state employment department contact information). Insurance responsibilities are a vital consideration when determining labor expenses and employee benefits because they are a significant element in the cost of doing business.

LEARNING OBJECTIVES

After studying Chapter 6, you should be able to:

LO 6-1   List Employer-Paid and Employee-Paid Obligations

LO 6-2   Discuss Reporting Periods and Requirements for Employer Tax Deposits

LO 6-3 Prepare Mid-Year and Year-End Employer Tax Reporting and Deposits

LO 6-4 Describe Payroll within the Context of Business Expenses

LO 6-5 Relate Labor Expenses to Company Profitability

LO 6-6 Complete Benefit Analysis as a Function of Payroll

Alex-VN / Alamy Stock Photo

Labor Costs Cause Layoffs at Disney

Labor costs are often an employer's most significant expense. The Walt Disney Corporation is famous for its in-character and friendly employees, but the sharp increase in inflation during 2022 sparked questions about cost reductions within the company. In early 2023, the Disney Corporation announced an impending layoff of 7,000 employees that would save the company over $5 billion in labor costs alone.

The Department of Labor announced in early 2023 that labor costs were growing more slowly than predicted. The drop in labor costs led to slower economic growth and curbed inflation. Disney's layoffs reflect a part of that trend: By reducing labor costs, Disney could redirect that money to other parts of the company that were feeling the effect of rapid economic inflation. A reduction in labor costs allowed the company to refrain from increasing ticket prices, which might have reduced the number of visitors to theme parks, and potentially prevented a similar contraction in Disney's streaming media service. The reduction in labor costs, either through layoffs or reduced wage and salary increases, all led to relatively lower employer costs across the United States.

(Sources: Variety; Reuters; Bloomberg)

> Labor costs potentially constitute a significant portion of a company's expenses. Employee benefits such as company contributions to retirement plans, temporary disability insurance, and educational reimbursements represent additional business expenses. Chapter 6 will examine employer payroll tax responsibilities and how payroll is a tool in labor planning.

LO 6-1 List Employer-Paid and Employee-Paid Obligations

Employers must pay some of the same taxes that the employees do. However, a firm has additional liabilities that employees do not, such as certain unemployment taxes and workers' compensation insurance. A comparison of employee-paid and employer-paid taxes is given in Table 6-1.

The taxes an employer must pay are often known as ***statutory deductions***, meaning that governmental statutes have made the tax a mandatory, legally obligated deduction. An important element of employer tax responsibility is that it continues after disbursing the employees' pay, often extending well after leaving the firm. Employers must file mandatory reconciliation reports detailing the amounts they have withheld from employee pay, track the employees throughout the company's accounting system, and maintain the personnel files for current and terminated employees per the firm's payroll practices and governmental regulations.

Diego Cervo/Shutterstock

Social Security and Medicare Taxes

The ***FICA*** taxes, which include both the Social Security and Medicare taxes, are among the statutory withholdings employees and employers pay. Employees and employers must each contribute 6.2 percent (for a total of 12.4 percent) of the employee's pay up to the maximum withholding amount for Social Security of $160,200 for 2023. Employers must match the employees' payroll deductions for the Medicare tax in the amount of 1.45 percent (for a total

TABLE 6-1
Employee-Paid and Employer-Paid Taxes

Tax	Employee Pays	Employer Pays
Social Security	XX	XX
Medicare	XX	XX
Federal Income Tax	XX	
Federal Unemployment Tax (FUTA)		XX
State Income Tax (where applicable)	XX	
State Unemployment Tax (SUTA)	Sometimes both are responsible at different percentages; see your local taxation authority for specific details.	XX
Local Income Taxes	XX	
Local Occupational Taxes (where applicable)	XX	XX
Workers' Compensation Premiums		XX
401(k)/Pension (if a matching policy exists)	XX	XX
Other Voluntary Deductions	XX	

of 2.9 percent) of the employees' gross pay less any applicable deductions. Remember that the Affordable Care Act mandated an additional tax for highly compensated employees. The employer does not match this additional Medicare tax.

> The CARES Act in 2020 offered employers relief from payroll-related income taxes. Employers had the option of tax deferrals and tax credit programs to help their businesses remain solvent during the COVID-19 pandemic. Certain CARES programs allowed employers to defer full remittance of payroll taxes until December 2022.
>
> (Source: RSM)

Let's look at an example of how the employee's and the employer's share of the FICA tax works.

> **EXAMPLE: EMPLOYEE AND EMPLOYER SHARE, SOCIAL SECURITY TAX**
>
> Russe works as an hourly worker who earns an annual salary of $36,000 and is paid biweekly. The gross pay is $1,384.62 per pay period ($36,000 per year/26 pay periods).
>
> | | |
> |---|---:|
> | Russe's share of the Social Security tax: | $1,384.62 × 6.2% = $ 85.85 |
> | The employer's share of the Social Security tax: | $1,384.62 × 6.2% = $ 85.85 |
> | Total Social Security tax liability for Russe's pay this period: | $ 171.70 |

As shown in the example, the employer and employee contribute the same amounts for the Social Security tax. Remember, the Social Security tax has a maximum withholding per year based on the employee's salary, which is $160,200 for 2023. After reaching that maximum, neither the employee nor the employer contributes any more Social Security tax.

> **EXAMPLE: EMPLOYEE AND EMPLOYER SHARE SOCIAL SECURITY TAXES, HIGHLY COMPENSATED EMPLOYEE**
>
> Alix Perry is the vice president of Sunny Glassworks. The annual salary is $243,000, which is paid semimonthly. Alix's gross pay per period is $10,125.00 ($243,000/24 pay periods), and there are no pre-tax deductions. For the 16th pay period of the year, the Social Security tax withholding is as follows:
>
> | | |
> |---|---:|
> | Alix's share of the Social Security tax: | $10,125 × 6.2% = $ 627.75 |
> | Sunny Glassworks' share of Alix's Social Security tax: | $10,125 × 6.2% = 627.75 |
> | Total Social Security tax liability for Alix's pay this period: | $1,255.50 |
>
> After the 15th pay period, Alix's year-to-date pay is $10,125 × 15 = $151,875. After the 16th pay period, Alix's year-to-date pay will be $10,125 × 16 = $162,000. The amount subject to Social Security tax for the 17th pay period equals the wage base minus the 15th pay period YTD pay:
>
> $160,200 − $162,000 = $200 of Alix's pay during the 17th pay period is subject to Social Security tax. Neither Alix nor his employer will be taxed on the remaining amount.
>
> | | |
> |---|---:|
> | Alix's share of the Social Security tax: | $200 × 6.2% = $12.40 |
> | Sunny Glassworks' share of Alix's Social Security tax: | $200 × 6.2% = $12.40 |
> | Total Social Security tax liability for Alix's pay this period that must be remitted by Sunny Glassworks: | $24.80 |

Medicare tax, the other piece of the FICA taxes, has no maximum but does have an additional tax for high-wage employees. Let's look at Russe's pay again to see how the Medicare tax works and the total FICA tax for the pay period.

> ### EXAMPLE: EMPLOYEE AND EMPLOYER SHARE, MEDICARE TAXES
>
> | | |
> |---|---:|
> | Russe's share of the Medicare tax: | $1,384.62 × 1.45% = $ 20.08 |
> | The employer's share of the Medicare tax: | $1,384.62 × 1.45% =   20.08 |
> | Total Medicare tax liability for Russe's pay this period that must be remitted by Sunny Glassworks: | $ 40.16 |
> | Total FICA responsibility from Russe's pay this period ($171.70 + $40.16): | $211.86 |

Now let's look at Medicare and total FICA taxes for Alix. Note the additional Medicare tax and how the employer does not match it.

> ### EXAMPLE: EMPLOYEE AND EMPLOYER SHARE MEDICARE TAXES, HIGHLY COMPENSATED EMPLOYEE
>
> As of the 20th pay period of the year, Alix's YTD pay is $202,500. Amount subject to the additional Medicare tax: $2,500.
>
> | | |
> |---|---:|
> | Medicare tax amounts: | |
> | Alix's standard Medicare tax liability: | $10,125 × 1.45% = $ 146.81 |
> | Sunny Glassworks' Medicare tax liability: | $10,125 × 1.45% =   146.81 |
> | Alix's additional Medicare tax liability: | $2,500 × 0.9% =   22.50 |
> | Total Medicare tax liability: | $ 316.12 |
> | Total FICA responsibility for Alix's pay this period: | $ 316.12 |
>
> Remember, no Social Security tax applies because Alix has already exceeded the wage base.

Social Security and Medicare amounts may be listed separately when the company makes its tax deposit. The employer's tax deposit will also include the amount deducted from the employee for federal income tax.

Maintaining accurate records of taxes withheld through payroll registers and employee earnings records is critical in calculating proper FICA tax deductions. Whether a company uses a manual system, has an automated system, or outsources payroll duties, it remains responsible for the accuracy of the deductions and maintenance of associated records.

Federal and State Unemployment Taxes

Another set of employer-paid payroll taxes includes those mandated by the *Federal Unemployment Tax Act (FUTA)* and *State Unemployment Tax Act (SUTA)*. FUTA and SUTA are unemployment compensation funds established to provide for workers who have lost their jobs. Generally, the FUTA tax rate is lower than that for the SUTA tax because (1) the states govern the disbursement of unemployment funds, and (2) unemployment rates vary by region. FUTA taxes pay for the administrative expenses of the unemployment insurance fund. SUTA tax rates provide a localized and individual focus for employer taxes. The unemployment insurance fund pays for half of the extended unemployment benefits and provides a fund of additional benefits against which states may borrow as necessary to cover unemployment claims. An interesting note is that FUTA and SUTA are employer-only taxes in all but three states: Alaska, New Jersey, and Pennsylvania.

Vitalii Vodolazskyi/Shutterstock

FUTA pertains only to U.S. citizens and workers employed by American companies. According to the IRS, to be classified as an American company, an employer must meet the following criteria:

- An individual who is a resident of the United States,
- A partnership, if two-thirds or more of the partners are residents of the United States,
- A trust, if all of the trustees are residents of the United States, or
- A corporation organized under the U.S. laws of any state or the District of Columbia.

> American citizens who work for companies outside of the United States who are not classified as American employers are not subject to FUTA provisions. Certain resident aliens and professions are exempt from FUTA provisions, as stipulated by Income Tax Regulation §31.3301-1. The professions from which employee compensation is exempt from FUTA provisions are:
>
> - Agricultural workers
> - Household employees unless the compensation exceeds $1,000 during any calendar quarter of the current year or prior year
> - Employees of religious, charitable, educational, or certain other tax-exempt organizations
> - Employees of the U.S. government or any of its agencies
> - Employees of the government of any U.S. state or any of its political subdivisions
> - Employees of the government of the District of Columbia or any of its political subdivisions

The FUTA tax's full 2023 tax is 6.0 percent of the first $7,000 of an employee's wages paid during a calendar year. The employer pays FUTA. Employees who move to a different company will have the new employer paying additional FUTA taxes. Therefore, if an employer has a high turnover rate among its employees (i.e., a large number of employees remain employed for only a short period before terminating employment), the firm will pay FUTA tax for all employees for the first $7,000 of earnings, including the ones who remained in their employ for only a short time.

> Due to the COVID-19 outbreak, employers were granted a refundable tax credit of 50 percent of wages paid between April 2, 2020, and December 31, 2020, by certain employers who met the following criteria:
>
> - Operations were suspended, partially or in full, because of the outbreak.
> - Gross sales declined 50 percent or more because of the outbreak.*
> - Tax-exempt businesses were also eligible for this break.
>
> Also, a payroll tax credit was extended for businesses that continued to pay wages (up to $10,000 of compensation per employee, including fringe health benefits paid), as follows:
>
> - For businesses with more than 100 employees, compensation for services not provided due to COVID-19 reasons.
> - For businesses with fewer than 100 employees, all employee wages qualified for the credit.
>
> *The gross sales tax credit eligibility ceased once the business's sales receipts reached 80 percent of the same amount earned during the same quarter of the prior calendar year.
>
> (Source: U.S. Congress)

With the credit, the employer's FUTA rate will be 0.6 percent on the first $7,000 of every employee's wage. The minimum FUTA tax rate is 0.6 percent, which means that a minimum of $42 ($7,000 × 0.006) may be paid per employee. Note that the FUTA tax liability is always reported for the prior year, which means that the FUTA tax liability in 2023 will increase with the first payroll and reflect both 2022 and 2023 liability if the 940 has not been filed yet. If the employer makes quarterly deposits, then the full 2022 liability would not be part of the FUTA Tax Payable account in 2023.

> ### EXAMPLE: FUTA TAX COMPUTATION, ALL EMPLOYEES EARNING MORE THAN $7,000
> Snowborn, Inc., is a company based in Great Falls, Montana. In 2023, the company had 178 employees, all of whom earned more than $7,000 in wages and salaries. Only 145 employees remained with the company at the end of the year. The 2023 FUTA tax liability for Snowborn, Inc., would be computed as follows:
>
> | Number of Employees During 2023 | Multiplied by the First $7,000 of Wages | Multiplied by 0.6% Tax Rate | FUTA Tax Liability for 2023 |
> |---|---|---|---|
> | 178 | $7,000 | 0.006 | $7,476 |
>
> Note that Snowborn, Inc., is liable for the FUTA tax on all employees who worked for the company, even if they left employment with the company. The FUTA tax filing is due on January 31, 2024.

What happens when the employees earn less than $7,000 during the calendar year? The employer is still responsible for the FUTA tax on the employees' earnings and the amount earned during the calendar year.

> ### EXAMPLE: FUTA TAX, EMPLOYEES WITH EARNINGS LESS THAN $7,000 DURING THE YEAR
> Baja Brothers Wines, based in Tucson, Arizona, has 62 employees and the following is employee data for FUTA taxes:
>
> | Number of Employees Who Earned More Than $7,000 During 2023 | Multiplied by the First $7,000 of Wages | Multiplied by 0.6% Tax Rate | FUTA Tax Liability for 2023 |
> |---|---|---|---|
> | 59 | $7,000.00 | 0.006 | $ 2,478.00 |
> | **Employees Who Earned Less Than $7,000 During 2023** | **Multiplied by the Amount of Wages Earned in 2023** | **Multiplied by 0.6% Tax Rate** | |
> | Employee A | $5,894.00 | 0.006 | $ 35.36 |
> | Employee B | 3,198.00 | 0.006 | 19.19 |
> | Employee C | 975.00 | 0.006 | 5.85 |
> | | | **Total FUTA tax** | **$2,538.40** |

The establishment of the SUTA in each state provided states with the local authority to offer unemployment or jobless benefits. Designed as an unemployment insurance program after the Great Depression of the 1930s, SUTA payments' remittance follows many of the same procedures as other payroll taxes. As a state-run fund, each state can establish its own qualification requirements for individual claims and business payments, the wage base for employers in the state, and the tax rate. The SUTA wage base and rate fluctuate among states and can be an incentive for businesses to change operations from one state to another. Note that all states' wage bases exceed the minimum required by the law, but the tax rate is variable.

FUTA Credit Reduction

As we noted, the nominal FUTA tax is 6.0 percent, of which the employer remits 0.6 percent to the federal government. A caveat to this 0.6 percent employer rate involves Title XII advances issued from the federal government to assist with payments of unemployment liabilities. This can occur when a high period of unemployment happens due to layoffs or economic downturns. FUTA is subject to a 5.4 percent reduction, for which employers may qualify on two conditions.

1. Employers make SUTA deposits on time and in full.
2. The state is not a credit reduction state.

If a state defaults on its repayment of these federal loans, the credit taken against the 6.0 percent FUTA rate may be reduced. Each year, states have until November 10 to repay the prior year's loan. If the loan remains unpaid for more than one year, the FUTA credit will continue to be reduced in the third and fifth years after the loan is due. An example of the FUTA credit reduction follows.

> ### EXAMPLE: FUTA CREDIT REDUCTION
> State Z had a loan taken in 2022 to supplement amounts paid for unemployment insurance liabilities. The balance of that loan would be due on November 10, 2023. If the balance is not paid by that date, the credit against the FUTA rate for the next calendar year would be as follows:
>
> | FUTA Rate | Standard FUTA Rate after Credit | Additional FUTA Tax | FUTA Rate after Credit Reduction |
> |---|---|---|---|
> | 6.0% | 0.6% | 1.8% | 2.4% |
>
> The credit would be reduced further in future years if the loan remains unpaid. Employers report the credit reduction on Form 940. In 2023, there are four states and one territory with a FUTA credit reduction: California, Connecticut, Illinois, and New York have a 0.3 percent reduction, and the U.S. Virgin Islands has a 3.6 percent reduction.
>
> (Source: Federal Register)

State Unemployment Taxes

The SUTA is limited to wages collected, and the 5.4 percent rate is a guideline. State rates vary based on employee retention and other factors. States examine employee turnover during an established period and determine if employers qualify for a credit against the nominal SUTA rate. Depending upon the company's state, this limit may be equal to, higher, or lower than the SUTA rate. For example, Alaska's SUTA wage base is $47,100 in 2023. A chart containing the SUTA wage base and rates is shown in Table 6-2.

TABLE 6-2
SUTA Wage Base and Rates 2023

State	Wage Base	Min/Max Rate
Alabama	$ 8,000	0.65%–6.8%
Alaska	$47,100	1.0%–5.4%
Arizona	$ 8,000	0.03%–7.79%
Arkansas	$ 7,000	0.9%–12.8%
California	$ 7,000	1.5%–6.2%
Colorado	$20,400	0.78%–10.2%

(continued)

TABLE 6-2
SUTA Wage Base and Rates 2023 *(concluded)*

State	Wage Base	Min/Max Rate
Connecticut	$15,000	1.9%–6.8%
Delaware	$10,500	0.3%–8.2%
District of Columbia	$9,000	1.6%–7.0%
Florida	$7,000	0.59%–5.4%
Georgia	$9,500	0.04%–8.1%
Hawaii	$56,700	0.2%–5.8%
Idaho	$49,900	0.453%–7.5%
Illinois	$13,271	0.55%–8.15%
Indiana	$9,500	0.51%–7.548%+surcharge
Iowa	$36,100	0.0%–7.5%
Kansas	$14,000	0.09%–9.4%
Kentucky	$11,100	1.0%–10.0%
Louisiana	$7,700	0.10%–6.2%
Maine	$12,000	0.89%–8.27%
Maryland	$8,500	0.3%–7.5%
Massachusetts	$15,000	0.79%–11.19%
Michigan	$9,500	0.26%–10.3%
Minnesota	$40,000	0.1%–9.1%
Mississippi	$14,000	0.2%–5.4%
Missouri	$10,500	0.0%–9.7%
Montana	$40,500	0.8%–6.3%
Nebraska	$9,000/$24,000*	0.0%–5.4%
Nevada	$40,100	0.25%–5.4%
New Hampshire	$14,000	1.0%–8.5%
New Jersey	$41,100	1.2%–7.0%
New Mexico	$30,100	0.1%–5.4%
New York	$12,300	1.5%–9.9%
North Carolina	$29,600	0.072%–6.912%
North Dakota	$40,800	0.16%–9.76%
Ohio	$9,000	0.3%–10.6%
Oklahoma	$25,700	0.2%–7.3%
Oregon	$50,900	2.2%–5.4%
Pennsylvania	$10,000	2.8%–15.1%
Rhode Island	$28,200/$29,700*	1.9%–10.0%
South Carolina	$14,000	0.089%–7.805%
South Dakota	$15,000	0.0%–10.03%
Tennessee	$7,000	0.15%–19.0%
Texas	$9,000	0.54%–7.35%
Utah	$44,800	1.1%–9.5%
Vermont	$13,500	1.3%–8.4%
Virginia	$8,000	0.52%–6.62%
Washington	$67,600	0.02%–7.85%
West Virginia	$9,000	1.5%–8.5%
Wisconsin	$14,000	0.27%–9.8%
Wyoming	$29,100	0.63%–10.0%

*Applies only to employers assigned the maximum rate.

(Source: American Payroll Association)

An employer's SUTA rate is determined by a mix of state unemployment rates and company experience ratings. The SUTA rate for company A may be different from the rate for company B. For example, a construction company may experience higher unemployment claims because of the seasonal nature and higher risk associated with the industry; therefore, its rate could be 4.54 percent, whereas a similar-sized company in a professional services industry may have an unemployment rate of 3.28 percent. States issue letters annually to companies with the individually determined SUTA rate for the following year.

The first example is a company with a SUTA rate of 5.4 percent, and all employees have earned more than $7,000 for the year.

EXAMPLE: FUTA AND SUTA LIABILITY; SUTA = 5.4 PERCENT

JayMac Communications, a Tennessee company, has 15 employees, all of whom have met the FUTA tax's $7,000 threshold. The state portion for which JayMac is liable is 5.4 percent. The unemployment tax obligations are

FUTA:	15 employees × $7,000 × 0.006 =	$ 630
SUTA:	15 employees × $7,000 × 0.054 =	5,670
Total unemployment tax liability:		$6,300

The next example is a company in Georgia with a SUTA rate of 2.3 percent and some employees who have earned less than $7,000 during the year.

EXAMPLE: FUTA AND SUTA LIABILITY; SUTA = 2.3 PERCENT

Charmer Industries of Georgia has 20 employees: 18 employees have met the FUTA and SUTA thresholds, and 2 employees have not, earning $5,400 and $2,500, respectively. The state obligation for Charmer is 2.3 percent due to a favorable employer rating. Charmer's unemployment taxes would be computed as follows:

FUTA:	18 employees × $7,000 × 0.006 =	$ 756.00
	($5,400 + $2,500) × 0.006 =	47.40
	Total FUTA liability:	$ 803.40
SUTA:	18 employees × $9,500 × 0.023 =	$3,933.00
	($5,400 + $2,500) × 0.023 =	181.70
	Total SUTA liability:	$4,114.70
Total unemployment tax liability:		$4,918.10

Tips to Minimize SUTA Taxes

Experience-Rating System
• Know how your company compares to other similar companies in the same industry in terms of hiring and retention of employees.
Experience Rate Charges
• The employer's account is charged each time a former employee files for unemployment. Be careful to avoid improper use of the account by dumping employees into other states to avoid SUTA taxation.
Review the SUTA Account Regularly
• Ensure that charges to the employer's account are accurate, and promptly alert the state unemployment office if inaccuracies occur.
Carefully Select New Employees
• All employees should be assessed before hiring to ensure that they are an appropriate fit for the company culture and have the needed skills for their job requirements.

Time Temporary or Seasonal Layoffs to Avoid Partial Weeks	
• Partial weeks of unemployment can lead to large amounts being charged to the employer's SUTA account.	
Employee Separation Review and Documentation	
• Maintain documentation about employees' departure from the company to ensure that they do not improperly claim SUTA benefits.	
Former Employees and Retirement	
• The offer of retirement with the possibility of rehiring can reduce unemployment claims because a retired employee cannot claim unemployment insurance.	
Use State-Issued Forms if Contesting an Unemployment Claim	
• This will make the processing quicker and ensure the accuracy and remediation of any disputes.	
Pay SUTA Taxes on Time	
• A record of timely SUTA payments adds to the company's experience rating and allows the employer to avoid penalties or other fees.	
Use Historical SUTA Reports to Estimate Future Unemployment Charges	
• Knowing what to expect ahead of time will help with budgeting, hiring, and estimating future labor costs.	

Other State and Local Employer-Only Payroll Taxes

Some states have employer-only taxes unique to the area. Delaware, Colorado, Hawaii, and several other states have additional taxes remitted under different names. Some examples of these types of taxes include:

- Maine has an employer-paid Competitive Skills Scholarship Program tax of 0.07 percent and a 0.15 percent unemployment program administrative fund assessment.
- In California, employers pay an Employment Training Tax (ETT) of 0.1 percent on all wages up to the first $7,000 of wages.

As a payroll accountant, you must be familiar with the tax withholding and employer responsibilities for each state where the company has employees residing, even if there is not a business office located there. It is also important to be aware of any required forms within the state where the company has employees.

Individual counties and cities can also impose occupational taxes on businesses within their jurisdiction. The reporting periods for the local and city taxes are separate from federal or state tax filing requirements. The payroll accountant must review all tiers of taxes to ensure compliance in collection, submission, and reporting.

Workers' Compensation Insurance

Workers' compensation insurance is another type of employer payroll responsibility. Although it is not considered a tax, states enforce workers' compensation statutes; the Federal Employment Compensation Act protects federal employees. Workers' compensation statutes are designed to protect workers who are injured (temporarily or permanently) or killed during the performance of their job-related duties.

Because workers' compensation is an insurance policy maintained by employers, premiums vary based on employees' job classifications and the risk of injury they typically encounter in the normal course of work. Premium amounts are expressed as amounts per $100 of payroll for each job classification. Premium amounts are estimated based on expected payroll amounts for the coming year and then adjusted at the end of the year once the actual payroll amounts are finalized.

Fertnig/Getty Images

EXAMPLE: WORKERS' COMPENSATION PREMIUM COMPUTATION

Callaway is the owner of Eastern Freight Lines. The company has three categories of employees: drivers, loaders, and administrative staff. The workers' compensation premium rates are as follows:

- Drivers: $1.45/$100 of payroll
- Loaders: $2.50/$100 of payroll
- Administrative staff: $0.40/$100 of payroll

For 20XX, the Eastern Freight Lines payroll is expected to be the following:

Job Classification	Premium per $100 of Payroll	Estimated Payroll	Premium Due Jan. 1
Driver	$1.45	$387,500	$ 5,618.75*
Loader	2.50	435,200	10,880.00†
Administrative Staff	0.40	320,000	1,280.00‡
Total premium due Jan. 1			$17,778.75

*($387,500/$100) × $1.45 = $5,618.75
†($435,200/$100) × $2.50 = $10,880
‡($320,000/$100) × $0.40 = $1,280

The 20XX premium is adjusted based on the actual payroll. The difference between the paid estimated premium and the premium based on actual payroll results must either be remitted to the insurance company or refunded to the employer. An analysis of the actual payroll as of December 31, 20XX, revealed the following results:

Job Classification	Premium per $100 of Payroll	Actual Payroll	Premium Due Dec. 31
Driver	$1.45	$410,563	$ 5,953.16*
Loader	2.50	478,290	11,957.25†
Administrative staff	0.40	338,945	1,355.78‡
Total actual premium due December 31			$19,266.19
Less: Premium paid on Jan. 1			17,778.75
Difference to be remitted to the insurance company			$ 1,487.44

*($410,563/$100) × $1.45 = $5,953.16
†($478,290/$100) × $2.50 = $11,957.25
‡($338,945/$100) × $0.40 = $1,355.78

Eastern Freight Lines must remit $1,487.44 to the insurance company due to the difference between the estimated and the actual payroll for 20XX.

Workers' compensation premium rates may also vary based on the employer's safety record. For example, a company with multiple job-related injuries would have a higher premium than another company with few or no injuries. Employer compliance with OSHA guidelines is important to controlling the cost of workers' compensation insurance.

The majority of workers' compensation insurance claims occur in five main categories of injuries:

1. Sprains and strains.
2. Punctures or cuts.
3. Bruises or other contusions.
4. Inflammation.
5. Fractured bones.

Most work-related injuries can be avoided through employee safety training, attention to the facility's walking and working conditions, and employer diligence.

(Source: *Insurance Journal*)

FUTA, SUTA, and Workers' Compensation

Stop & Check

1. AMS Enterprises in New Mexico has 30 employees. Of these, 25 have exceeded the FUTA and SUTA wage bases. This is the first quarter of the year, and AMS Enterprises has not yet paid FUTA or SUTA taxes for the year. The other five employees' YTD wages are as follows: Employee A, $15,800; Employee B, $7,800; Employee C, $11,115; Employee D, $22,800; Employee E, $2,575. AMS Enterprises receives the full FUTA tax credit and pays a SUTA rate of 4.2 percent (see Table 6-2 for SUTA taxable wage maximum). How much are AMS Enterprises' FUTA and SUTA liabilities?

2. Noodle Noggins of Maine has 12 employees and is eligible for the full FUTA tax credit; the SUTA rate is 3.26 percent. Ten of the 12 employees have exceeded the FUTA wage base. Eight employees have exceeded the SUTA wage base (see Table 6-2 for the SUTA taxable wage maximum). The remaining employees have the following YTD wages: $5,500, $6,800, $11,100, and $9,850. Noodle's YTD total wages are $279,580. What are the FUTA and SUTA tax liabilities for Noodle Noggins?

3. High Flyers Jump School has two classifications of employees: clerical employees and jump instructors. The workers' compensation premium rates are $0.45/$100 for clerical employees and $3.75/$100 for jump instructors. During 20XX, the estimated payroll amounts were $104,550 for clerical employees and $215,690 for jump instructors. How much would the estimated workers' compensation insurance policy cost High Flyers Jump School during 20XX?

LO 6-2 Discuss Reporting Periods and Requirements for Employer Tax Deposits

The frequency of depositing federal income tax and FICA taxes depends on the size of the company's payroll. The depositing schedules have nothing to do with a company's pay frequency, although some of the names are similar. The IRS stipulates five different schedules for an employer's deposit of payroll taxes:

1. Annually
2. Quarterly
3. Monthly
4. Semiweekly
5. Next business day

Of these, the most common deposit schedules are monthly and semiweekly. Electronic tax deposits are usually processed through the *Electronic Federal Tax Payment System (EFTPS)* website. However, the IRS allows employers to transmit payments through certain financial institutions via *Automated Clearing House (ACH)* or wire transfer. When using the EFTPS, the employer must register with the IRS to access the site. The EFTPS is used for Form 941 (federal income tax, Social Security tax, and Medicare tax) and annual Form 940 FUTA tax deposit.

Lookback Period

The frequency of each company's deposits is determined through a *lookback period*, which is the amount of payroll taxes an employer has reported in the 12-month period before June 30 of the previous year. For example, the lookback period that the IRS would use for 2023 tax deposit frequency would be the period from July 1, 2021, through June 30, 2022.

Employers receive notification about their deposit requirements in writing from the IRS in October of each year. Table 6-3 shows the lookback period.

TABLE 6-3
Lookback Period

Lookback Period for 2023 Taxes			
July 1, 2021, through	October 1, 2021, through	January 1, 2022, through	April 1, 2022, through
September 30, 2021	December 31, 2021	March 31, 2022	June 30, 2022

(Source: Internal Revenue Service)

> Section 2302(a)(1) and (a)(2) of the CARES Act allowed employers to defer eligible amounts of Social Security tax remittances in response to cash needs during the COVID-19 pandemic as follows:
>
> - 50 percent of the eligible deferred amount must be paid by December 31, 2021.
> - If 50 percent of the eligible deferred amount was paid by December 31, 2021, the employer could defer the remainder of the eligible amount until December 31, 2022.
>
> (Source: Internal Revenue Service)

Deposit Frequencies

The IRS informs businesses in writing if they need to deposit their payroll taxes annually, monthly, or semiweekly based on the deposits during the lookback period. All new companies are monthly schedule depositors unless they have a total payroll liability over $100,000 during any pay period. It is important to note that the tax deposit due date is based on the payroll disbursement date, not the pay period ending date. For example, if a company's pay period ended on June 28, but the payroll was not disbursed until July 1, the payroll tax deposit date would be based on the July 1 disbursement. Table 6-4 outlines the criteria for differences among deposit frequencies.

TABLE 6-4
Criteria for Deposit Frequencies

Frequency	Criteria	Due Date
Annually	$1,000 or less in employment taxes to be remitted annually with Form 944.	January 31 of the following year.
Quarterly	For any amounts not deposited during the quarter that may be due to rounding errors or other undeposited amounts.	The 15th of the month following the end of the quarter.
Monthly	$50,000 or less in payroll tax liability during the lookback period. The amount of total tax liability is also found on Form 941, line 10. All new businesses are monthly schedule depositors unless they accrue more than $100,000 in payroll taxes for any pay period. (See the Next Business Day rule frequency.)	The 15th of the month following the month during which the company accrued payroll tax deposits. For example, taxes on the March payroll would be due on **April 15** or the next business day if April 15 falls on a weekend or a holiday.
Semiweekly	More than $50,000 in payroll tax liability during the lookback period. The amount of total tax liability is also found on Form 941, line 10. The exception to the semiweekly deposit schedule is the Next Business Day rule.	For payroll paid on a Wednesday, Thursday, or Friday, the payroll tax deposit is due by the following **Wednesday.** For payroll paid on a Saturday, Sunday, Monday, or Tuesday, the payroll tax is due by the following **Friday.**
Next business day	$100,000 or more in payroll tax liability for any payroll period.	The payroll tax deposit is due on the **next business day.**

> **EXAMPLE: MONTHLY SCHEDULE DEPOSITOR**
>
> Generational Coffee is a company based in Wenatchee, Washington. During the lookback period ending June 30, 2022, the company had **$36,549** in total payroll tax liability. Generational Coffee would be a *monthly* schedule depositor. Payroll tax deposits would be due on the 15th of the following month (e.g., June 15 for May payroll taxes).

Notice the amount of total payroll tax for Generational Coffee. Because the total amount was less than $50,000, it is classified as a monthly schedule payroll tax depositor, and the due dates are the 15th of the following month.

> **EXAMPLE: SEMIWEEKLY SCHEDULE DEPOSITOR**
>
> Pollak Woolens is a company based in Sault Ste. Marie, Michigan. During the lookback period ending June 30, 2022, it had **$75,984** in total payroll tax liability. Pollak Woolens would be a semiweekly schedule depositor. Depending on the payroll date, tax deposits are due on either the Wednesday or the Friday following the payroll date.
>
> Notice the total tax liability during the lookback period. For Pollak Woolens, the amount exceeded $50,000 but is less than $100,000; this makes it a semiweekly schedule depositor.

Because payroll tax deposits for semiweekly depositors are driven by the day of the week upon which payroll was paid, deposits may be due either on Wednesday or on Friday. For companies with a biweekly payroll frequency, the tax deposit date may remain the same, with a few exceptions due to holidays. For companies with semimonthly payroll frequencies, the day of the tax deposit will likely vary.

> **EXAMPLE: NEXT-BUSINESS-DAY DEPOSITOR**
>
> Cornell Companies, based in Ohio, is a semiweekly schedule payroll tax depositor because of the total payroll tax liability of $693,259 during the lookback period ending June 30, 2022. The company had a total payroll tax liability of **$110,290** during the August 18, 2023, payroll period. August 18 is a Friday, so the payroll deposit would be due on Monday, August 21, because it exceeds $100,000.

In this example, Cornell Companies is already a semiweekly schedule depositor because of its payroll tax liability during the lookback period. Because the company's tax liability exceeds $100,000 for the payroll period, Cornell Companies must deposit those payroll taxes by the next business day.

> **EXAMPLE: ANNUAL SCHEDULE DEPOSITOR**
>
> Wallflower Guitars is based in Ocean Springs, Mississippi. During the lookback period ending June 30, 2022, the company had a total payroll tax liability of $954. The payroll tax deposit schedule for Wallflower Guitars would be annual because of the small total tax liability. As long as the total payroll tax liability remains less than $1,000 during 2023, the company may deposit its payroll taxes with its annual payroll tax return using Form 944.

In this example, Wallflower Guitars has a minimal payroll tax liability. It should be noted that *annual schedule depositors* are assumed to have a minimal tax liability. If the company's payroll tax liability grows during the calendar year, the schedule depositors should be mindful of the monthly schedule deposit rules. However, the company will not become a monthly schedule depositor until notified in writing by the IRS.

Stop & Check — Reporting Periods

1. Perry Plastics had $46,986 in payroll taxes during the lookback period. How often must the company deposit its payroll taxes?
2. For Perry Plastics, when is the deposit for June payroll taxes due?
3. Charlie's Kitchens has a payroll tax liability of $126,463 on its Friday payroll. When is the payroll tax deposit due?

LO 6-3 Prepare Mid-Year and Year-End Employer Tax Reporting and Deposits

Companies and payroll accountants are responsible for the timely filing of the various tax documents required by governmental authorities. Note that the dates for depositing and reporting taxes are not always the same. For example, an employer may be required to file payroll tax deposits through the EFTPS daily, semiweekly, or monthly, depending upon their payroll tax liability during the lookback period. However, that same employer would not be required to file tax forms until after the quarter. Like personal tax reporting, business reporting of statutory tax obligations has specific forms that employers must use. The most common forms used to deposit federal income tax and FICA taxes are Forms 941 (quarterly) and 944 (annual). An additional form used by agricultural businesses is Form 943, which serves the same purpose as Form 941.

pattarawat/Shutterstock

> Employer tax remittance forms changed significantly during the calendar year 2021 because of the CARES Act provisions. Since employers had the option to defer certain payroll taxes, the accounting for those tax amounts needed to be documented for financial tracking purposes.

Form 941

Monthly, semiweekly, and next-business-day payroll tax depositors file *Form 941* (see Figure 6-1), the employer's quarterly report of taxes deposited and taxes due. The form is used to reconcile the firm's deposits with the tax liability derived through mathematical computations. It is common to encounter minor adjustments due to rounding differences incurred during monthly tax deposits while completing the form. Form 941 has specific instructions for its completion, as shown in Table 6-5. Note that the IRS changed Form 941 in July 2021 due to revisions in COVID-19 tax credits and changes that went into effect for COBRA premiums with the *American Rescue Plan Act (ARPA)*. This new form was mandatory for employer tax reporting for the second quarter of 2021 but not for previous reporting periods.

The IRS again changed Form 941 twice during 2022, and another revision was issued in February 2023. The changes to Form 941 are in part related to the COVID-19 tax credits and to new changes designed to increase the form's usability over many years, as has been done to other forms.

Schedule B

Semiweekly depositors must file Schedule B (Figure 6-2) in addition to Form 941. This form allows firms to enter the details of payroll tax liabilities that occur multiple times during a month. On *Schedule B*, the payroll tax liability is entered on the days of the month on which the payroll occurred. The total tax liability for each month is entered in the right column. The total tax liability for the quarter must equal line 10 of Form 941.

TABLE 6-5
Instructions for Completing Form 941

Part 1: Data for Chalmette Company

Finley Wagner is the president of Chalmette Company, EIN 67-3983240, located at 572 Rue Bon Temps, New Orleans, Louisiana, 70116. The company's phone number is 504-555-2039. The following Form 941 is for the first quarter of the year. Chalmette Company had 12 employees during the first quarter.

Name	Gross Earning	Taxable Wages for Federal W/H	Taxable Wages for FICA	Taxable Wages for FUTA	Total Federal W/H	Total Social Security Tax	Total Medicare W/H	FUTA Tax	SUTA Tax	Net Pay
YTD Totals	128,356.74	128,356.74	94,569.00	84,000.00	18,432.50	11,726.56	2,742.50	504.00	5,106.73	
Line # on Form 941		2	5a & 5c		3	5a	5c			

Line 1: The number of employees during the quarter reported, as indicated in the box in the upper-right-hand corner.
Line 2: Total wages subject to federal income tax (less pre-tax deductions) for the quarter.
Line 3: Federal income tax withheld from wages paid during the quarter.
Line 4: Check the box only if no wages paid during the quarter were subject to taxes. (This is uncommon.)
Lines 5a–d: Column 1 is for the wages and tips subject to Social Security and Medicare taxes; column 2 is the number of wages multiplied by the tax percent specified on the form.
Line 5e: Total of column 2, lines 5a–5d.
Line 5f: Tax on unreported tips.
Line 6: Total taxes due before adjustments.
Lines 7–9: Quarterly tax adjustments.
Line 10: Total tax after adjustments: line 6 minus lines 7, 8, and 9.
Line 11a: Qualified business tax credit for research activities.
Line 11b: CARES Act nonrefundable adjustments.
Line 11c: Reserved for future use.
Line 11d: CARES Act nonrefundable portion of credit for qualified sick and family leave.
Lines 11e–f: Reserved for future use.
Line 11g: Total nonrefundable credits.
Line 12: Total taxes due, after adjustments and credits.
Line 13a: Total taxes deposited during the quarter.
Line 13b: Reserved for future use.
Line 13c: CARES Act refundable adjustments.
Line 13d: Reserved for future use.
Line 13e: Total deposits and refundable credits.
Line 13f: Total advances received from Form(s) 7200 per quarter.
Line 13g: Total deposits and refundable credits less advances.
Lines 13h–i: Reserved for future use.
Line 14: Balance due.
Line 15: Overpayment.

Part 2:

Check the first box if the tax liability for the quarter is less than $2,500.
OR
Check the second box if the tax liability is greater than $2,500 and enter the taxes deposited each month during the quarter.
The total deposits must equal the total liability in Part 1.
If the business is a semiweekly depositor, then Schedule B must be completed.

> ### EXAMPLE: PAYROLL TAX LIABILITY
> Jem Katzenberg is the owner of a company that pays its employees on the 15th and the last day of the month. All employees are salaried, exempt workers. Pay dates that fall on the weekend are paid on the preceding Friday. According to the lookback period, the company is required to deposit payroll taxes on a semiweekly basis. Because Katzenberg is a semiweekly schedule depositor, the company must file Schedule B in addition to Form 941. For the first quarter of 2023, Katzenberg's company had the following pay dates and payroll tax liabilities:
>
> | Pay Date | Payroll Tax Liability |
> |---|---|
> | January 13 | $ 41,486.47 |
> | January 31 | 41,486.47 |
> | February 15 | 41,486.47 |
> | February 28 | 41,486.47 |
> | March 15 | 41,486.47 |
> | March 31 | 41,486.47 |
> | **Total Tax Liability for the Quarter** | $248,918.82 |
>
> Note: The payroll tax liability is (a) listed on the payroll date and (b) includes the FICA taxes (employee and employer share) and the federal income tax withheld.

State Tax Remittance

Each state that charges income tax has its own form for employee income *tax remittance* purposes. State tax forms are similar to federal forms as far as the information included is concerned and generally have similar due dates. An important note is that each state has its own unique taxes. For example, California has an employee-only State Disability Insurance (SDI) tax of 0.9 percent on earnings up to $153,164 per employee (2023 figure). California also has an employer-only Employment Training Tax (ETT) of 0.1 percent and an unemployment insurance tax, both on the first $7,000 of each employee's earnings. These additional taxes are included on the state's payroll tax return. Figure 6-3 contains an example of a completed California quarterly tax return. As of 2023, many states require online submission of quarterly wage reports. See Appendix E for state revenue office contact information.

Additionally, employers are responsible for reporting any other local or regional taxes. Employers must abide by the filing requirements for each of the taxes or face fines or penalties, depending upon the state and local tax codes. The purpose of these taxes can include the provision of social services and the funding of infrastructure costs. The Denver Head Tax was designed to fulfill both of these purposes in response to the increase in infrastructure and municipal programs' availability for residents. An example of the Denver Occupational Privilege Tax Return quarterly form is located in Figure 6-4.

Form 944

Firms with a total annual tax liability of less than $1,000 use *Form 944* (see Figure 6-5). Like Form 941, the firm enters the details of wages paid and computes the taxes due. The firm reports the monthly deposits and liabilities in Part 2. However, instead of entering a quarterly liability, the firm enters the annual liability, which is the sum of all the monthly liabilities. The IRS must notify a company in writing of the requirement to file Form 944 before its use.

> ### EXAMPLE: FORM 944
> Gavi Jennings owns Forest Dog Walkers. Forest Dog Walkers is a sole proprietorship with one part-time employee who works only five months of the year. The IRS has notified Gavi that Forest Dog Walkers must report federal payroll tax liabilities using Form 944. The total wages paid to the employee during 2022 were $2,380.78. The federal income tax liability was $274, and the total payroll tax liability for the year was $638.26. Because the total annual payroll tax liability is less than $1,000, Forest Dog Walkers must file an annual return. The due date for Form 944 is January 31 of the following year.

FIGURE 6-1
Form 941

Form 941 for 2023: Employer's QUARTERLY Federal Tax Return
(Rev. March 2023) Department of the Treasury — Internal Revenue Service

950122
OMB No. 1545-0029

Employer identification number (EIN): 67-3983240

Name (not your trade name): Finley Wagner

Trade name (if any): Chalmette Company

Address: 572 Rue Bon Temps
New Orleans, LA 70116

Report for this Quarter of 2023 (Check one.)
- [X] 1: January, February, March
- [ ] 2: April, May, June
- [ ] 3: July, August, September
- [ ] 4: October, November, December

Go to www.irs.gov/Form941 for instructions and the latest information.

Read the separate instructions before you complete Form 941. Type or print within the boxes.

Part 1: Answer these questions for this quarter.

Line	Description	Value
1	Number of employees who received wages, tips, or other compensation for the pay period including: Mar. 12 (Quarter 1), June 12 (Quarter 2), Sept. 12 (Quarter 3), or Dec. 12 (Quarter 4)	12
2	Wages, tips, and other compensation	128,356.74
3	Federal income tax withheld from wages, tips, and other compensation	18,432.50
4	If no wages, tips, and other compensation are subject to social security or Medicare tax ☐ Check and go to line 6.	

5a	Taxable social security wages*	94,569.00	× 0.124 =	11,726.56
5a(i)	Qualified sick leave wages*	.	× 0.062 =	.
5a(ii)	Qualified family leave wages*	.	× 0.062 =	.
5b	Taxable social security tips	.	× 0.124 =	.
5c	Taxable Medicare wages & tips	94,569.00	× 0.029 =	2,742.50
5d	Taxable wages & tips subject to Additional Medicare Tax withholding	.	× 0.009 =	.

*Include taxable qualified sick and family leave wages paid in this quarter of 2023 for leave taken after March 31, 2021, and before October 1, 2021, on line 5a. Use lines 5a(i) and 5a(ii) **only** for taxable qualified sick and family leave wages paid in this quarter of 2023 for leave taken after March 31, 2020, and before April 1, 2021.

Line	Description	Value
5e	Total social security and Medicare taxes. Add Column 2 from lines 5a, 5a(i), 5a(ii), 5b, 5c, and 5d	14,469.06
5f	Section 3121(q) Notice and Demand—Tax due on unreported tips (see instructions)	.
6	Total taxes before adjustments. Add lines 3, 5e, and 5f	32,901.56
7	Current quarter's adjustment for fractions of cents	.01
8	Current quarter's adjustment for sick pay	.
9	Current quarter's adjustments for tips and group-term life insurance	.
10	Total taxes after adjustments. Combine lines 6 through 9	32,901.57
11a	Qualified small business payroll tax credit for increasing research activities. Attach Form 8974	.
11b	Nonrefundable portion of credit for qualified sick and family leave wages for leave taken before April 1, 2021	.
11c	Reserved for future use	.

You MUST complete all three pages of Form 941 and SIGN it.

For Privacy Act and Paperwork Reduction Act Notice, see the back of the Payment Voucher. Cat. No. 17001Z Form **941** (Rev. 3-2023)

				951222
Name *(not your trade name)*			**Employer identification number (EIN)**	
Finley Wanger			67 – 3983240	

Part 1: Answer these questions for this quarter. *(continued)*

11d	Nonrefundable portion of credit for qualified sick and family leave wages for leave taken after March 31, 2021, and before October 1, 2021	11d	.
11e	Reserved for future use	11e	.
11f	Reserved for future use		
11g	Total nonrefundable credits. Add lines 11a, 11b, and 11d	11g	.
12	Total taxes after adjustments and nonrefundable credits. Subtract line 11g from line 10 .	12	32,901 . 57
13a	Total deposits for this quarter, including overpayment applied from a prior quarter and overpayments applied from Form 941-X, 941-X (PR), 944-X, or 944-X (SP) filed in the current quarter	13a	.
13b	Reserved for future use	13b	.
13c	Refundable portion of credit for qualified sick and family leave wages for leave taken before April 1, 2021	13c	.
13d	Reserved for future use	13d	.
13e	Refundable portion of credit for qualified sick and family leave wages for leave taken after March 31, 2021, and before October 1, 2021	13e	.
13f	Reserved for future use	13f	.
13g	Total deposits and refundable credits. Add lines 13a, 13c, and 13e	13g	32,901 . 57
13h	Reserved for future use	13h	.
13i	Reserved for future use	13i	.
14	**Balance due.** If line 12 is more than line 13g, enter the difference and see instructions . . .	14	. 00
15	**Overpayment.** If line 13g is more than line 12, enter the difference [.] Check one: ☐ Apply to next return. ☐ Send a refund.		

Part 2: Tell us about your deposit schedule and tax liability for this quarter.

If you're unsure about whether you're a monthly schedule depositor or a semiweekly schedule depositor, see section 11 of Pub. 15.

16 Check one: ☐ Line 12 on this return is less than $2,500 or line 12 on the return for the prior quarter was less than $2,500, and you didn't incur a $100,000 next-day deposit obligation during the current quarter. If line 12 for the prior quarter was less than $2,500 but line 12 on this return is $100,000 or more, you must provide a record of your federal tax liability. If you're a monthly schedule depositor, complete the deposit schedule below; if you're a semiweekly schedule depositor, attach Schedule B (Form 941). Go to Part 3.

☒ **You were a monthly schedule depositor for the entire quarter.** Enter your tax liability for each month and total liability for the quarter, then go to Part 3.

Tax liability:	Month 1	10,967 . 19
	Month 2	10,967 . 19
	Month 3	10,967 . 19
	Total liability for quarter	32,901 . 57 Total must equal line 12.

☐ **You were a semiweekly schedule depositor for any part of this quarter.** Complete Schedule B (Form 941), Report of Tax Liability for Semiweekly Schedule Depositors, and attach it to Form 941. Go to Part 3.

You MUST complete all three pages of Form 941 and SIGN it.

Name *(not your trade name)*
Finley Wagner

Employer identification number (EIN)
67 – 3983240

Part 3: Tell us about your business. If a question does NOT apply to your business, leave it blank.

17 If your business has closed or you stopped paying wages . . . . ☐ Check here, and

 enter the final date you paid wages ___/___/___ ; also attach a statement to your return. See instructions.

18 If you're a seasonal employer and you don't have to file a return for every quarter of the year . . . ☐ Check here.

19 Qualified health plan expenses allocable to qualified sick leave wages for leave taken before April 1, 2021 19 _____ .

20 Qualified health plan expenses allocable to qualified family leave wages for leave taken before April 1, 2021 20 _____ .

21 Reserved for future use . . . . 21 _____ .

22 Reserved for future use . . . . 22 _____ .

23 Qualified sick leave wages for leave taken after March 31, 2021, and before October 1, 2021 23 _____ .

24 Qualified health plan expenses allocable to qualified sick leave wages reported on line 23 24 _____ .

25 Amounts under certain collectively bargained agreements allocable to qualified sick leave wages reported on line 23 . . . . 25 _____ .

26 Qualified family leave wages for leave taken after March 31, 2021, and before October 1, 2021 26 _____ .

27 Qualified health plan expenses allocable to qualified family leave wages reported on line 26 27 _____ .

28 Amounts under certain collectively bargained agreements allocable to qualified family leave wages reported on line 26 . . . . 28 _____ .

Part 4: May we speak with your third-party designee?

Do you want to allow an employee, a paid tax preparer, or another person to discuss this return with the IRS? See the instructions for details.

☐ Yes. Designee's name and phone number _____ _____

 Select a 5-digit personal identification number (PIN) to use when talking to the IRS. ☐ ☐ ☐ ☐ ☐

☒ No.

Part 5: Sign here. You MUST complete all three pages of Form 941 and SIGN it.

Under penalties of perjury, I declare that I have examined this return, including accompanying schedules and statements, and to the best of my knowledge and belief, it is true, correct, and complete. Declaration of preparer (other than taxpayer) is based on all information of which preparer has any knowledge.

Sign your name here *Finley Wagner*

Print your name here: Finley Wagner
Print your title here: President

Date 4/12/2023

Best daytime phone 504-555-2039

Paid Preparer Use Only   Check if you're self-employed . . . ☐

Preparer's name	
Preparer's signature	
Firm's name (or yours if self-employed)	
Address	
City	State

PTIN	
Date	/ /
EIN	
Phone	
ZIP code	

Page 3   Form **941** (Rev. 3-2023)

(Source: Internal Revenue Service)

FIGURE 6-2
Schedule B for Form 941

Schedule B (Form 941):
Report of Tax Liability for Semiweekly Schedule Depositors

960311

(Rev. January 2017) — Department of the Treasury — Internal Revenue Service

OMB No. 1545-0029

Employer identification number (EIN): 98-7654322

Name (not your trade name): Jem Katzenberg

Calendar year: 2022 (Also check quarter)

Report for this Quarter... (Check one.)
- [X] 1: January, February, March
- [ ] 2: April, May, June
- [ ] 3: July, August, September
- [ ] 4: October, November, December

Use this schedule to show your TAX LIABILITY for the quarter; don't use it to show your deposits. When you file this form with Form 941 or Form 941-SS, don't change your tax liability by adjustments reported on any Forms 941-X or 944-X. You must fill out this form and attach it to Form 941 or Form 941-SS if you're a semiweekly schedule depositor or became one because your accumulated tax liability on any day was $100,000 or more. Write your daily tax liability on the numbered space that corresponds to the date wages were paid. See Section 11 in Pub. 15 for details.

Month 1

Day	Amount	Day	Amount	Day	Amount	Day	Amount
1		9		17		25	
2		10		18		26	
3		11		19		27	
4		12		20		28	
5		13		21		29	
6		14	41486.47	22		30	
7		15		23		31	41486.47
8		16		24			

Tax liability for Month 1: 82972.94

Month 2

Day	Amount	Day	Amount	Day	Amount	Day	Amount
1		9		17		25	
2		10		18		26	
3		11		19		27	
4		12		20		28	41486.47
5		13		21		29	
6		14		22		30	
7		15	41486.47	23		31	
8		16		24			

Tax liability for Month 2: 82972.94

Month 3

Day	Amount	Day	Amount	Day	Amount	Day	Amount
1		9		17		25	
2		10		18		26	
3		11		19		27	
4		12		20		28	
5		13		21		29	
6		14		22		30	
7		15	41486.47	23		31	41486.47
8		16		24			

Tax liability for Month 3: 82972.94

Fill in your total liability for the quarter (Month 1 + Month 2 + Month 3) ▶
Total must equal line 12 on Form 941 or Form 941-SS.

Total liability for the quarter: 248918.82

For Paperwork Reduction Act Notice, see separate instructions. IRS.gov/form941 Cat. No. 11967Q Schedule B (Form 941) (Rev. 1-2017)

(Source: Internal Revenue Service)

FIGURE 6-3
Example of Completed California Quarterly Contribution Return and Report of Wages

EDD — Employment Development Department, State of California

QUARTERLY CONTRIBUTION RETURN AND REPORT OF WAGES

REMINDER: File your DE 9 and DE 9C together.
PLEASE TYPE THIS FORM—DO NOT ALTER PREPRINTED INFORMATION

00090112

YR 23   QTR 3

QUARTER ENDED 09/30/2023   DUE 10/15/2023   DELINQUENT IF NOT POSTMARKED OR RECEIVED BY 10/15/2023

EMPLOYER ACCOUNT NO. 392-1002-3

Four Mountains Inn
19283 Aracita Boulevard
Jackson, California 94453

DO NOT ALTER THIS AREA — DEPT. USE ONLY
Pt, P2, C, P, U, S, A
T
EFFECTIVE DATE   Mo. Day Yr.

FEIN 58-3020493

A. NO WAGES PAID THIS QUARTER ☐
B. OUT OF BUSINESS/NO EMPLOYEES ☐
B1. OUT OF BUSINESS DATE M M D D Y Y Y Y

ADDITIONAL FEINS

C. TOTAL SUBJECT WAGES PAID THIS QUARTER 48394.78

D. UNEMPLOYMENT INSURANCE (UI) (Total Employee Wages up to $_____ per employee per calendar year)

(D1) UI Rate % 3.8   TIMES   (D2) UI TAXABLE WAGES FOR THE QUARTER 28422.00   =   (D3) UI CONTRIBUTIONS 1080.04

E. EMPLOYMENT TRAINING TAX (ETT)

(E1) ETT Rate % 0.1   TIMES   UI Taxable Wages for the Quarter (D2) ...... =   (E2) ETT CONTRIBUTIONS 28.42

F. STATE DISABILITY INSURANCE (SDI) (Total Employee Wages up to $_____ per employee per calendar year)

(F1) SDI Rate % 1.1   TIMES   (F2) SDI TAXABLE WAGES FOR THE QUARTER 48394.78   =   (F3) SDI EMPLOYEE CONTRIBUTIONS WITHHELD 532.34

G. CALIFORNIA PERSONAL INCOME TAX (PIT) WITHHELD 3275.29

H. SUBTOTAL (Add Items D3, E2, F3, and G) 4874.09

I. LESS: CONTRIBUTIONS AND WITHHOLDINGS PAID FOR THE QUARTER 4874.09
(DO NOT INCLUDE PENALTY AND INTEREST PAYMENTS)

J. TOTAL TAXES DUE OR OVERPAID (Item H minus Item I) 0

If amount due, prepare a *Payroll Tax Deposit* (DE 88), include the correct payment quarter, and mail to: Employment Development Department, P.O. Box 826276, Sacramento, CA 94230-6276. **NOTE:** Do not mail payments along with the DE 9 and *Quarterly Contribution Return and Report of Wages (Continuation)* (DE 9C), as this may delay processing and result in erroneous penalty and interest charges. **Mandatory Electronic Funds Transfer (EFT)** filers must remit all SDI/PIT deposits by EFT to avoid a noncompliance penalty.

K. I declare that the above, to the best of my knowledge and belief, is true and correct. If a refund was claimed, a reasonable effort was made to refund any erroneous deductions to the affected employee(s).

Signature *Angel Sistare*   Title President (Owner, Accountant, Preparer, etc.)   Phone (909) 555-6478   Date 10/10/2023

SIGN AND MAIL TO: State of California / Employment Development Department / P.O. Box 989071 / West Sacramento CA 95798-9071

DE 9 Rev. 1 (1-12) (INTERNET)   Page 1 of 2

Fast, Easy, and Convenient! Visit EDD's Web site at www.edd.ca.gov

(Source: State of California)

FIGURE 6-4
Example of a Denver Occupational Privilege Tax Return

Denver Occupational Privilege Tax Return
Quarterly

City and County of Denver
Department of Finance, Treasury Division
P.O. Box 660859
Dallas, TX 75266-0859
www.DenverGov.org/eBizTax

Business Name: Mile High Gifts
Account Number: 209-1495010
Phone Number: 303-555-8883

Primary Business Location: 6667 16th Avenue, Denver, CO 80123
Period End Date: 3/31/2023

▶ YOU **MUST** FILE A RETURN EVEN IF YOU HAVE DETERMINED NO TAX IS DUE
▶ IMPORTANT INFORMATION IS ON THE BACK

If the number of employees for which the business is liable (Line 2) is different from the number of employees from whom the tax was withheld (Line 3) or if no tax is due, you must attach an explanation.

I. BUSINESS OCCUPATIONAL PRIVILEGE TAX

Line 1. Enter the number of self-employed individuals, owners, partners or managers. Multiply this number by $4.00 and enter the total.

NOTE: This line is for self-employed proprietors, partners, or managers of the business. There is no minimum level of monthly earnings required for self-employed proprietors, partners, or managers to be liable.

NOTE: All businesses located in Denver or performing work in Denver, regardless of the length or duration, are required to pay the minimum $4.00 Business Occupational Privilege Tax (OPT) for each month even when there are no taxable employees.

Line 2. Enter the number of employees for which the business is liable. Multiply this number by $4.00 and enter the total.

Liable employees are those who worked all or part of their time in Denver and received gross compensation of at least $500 for the month for services performed in Denver. Include all qualifying employees, even if some have another employer that is withholding this tax. The business is still liable for the business portion if the compensation was $500 or more. In the case of corporations for purposes of this tax, everyone, including all corporate officers, are considered employees.

II. EMPLOYEE OCCUPATIONAL PRIVILEGE TAX

Line 3. Enter the number of employees liable for this tax. Multiply this number by $5.75 and enter the total.

This line is for all employees who received gross compensation of at least $500 for the month for services performed in Denver. Corporations under the Business OPT ordinance are considered to only have employees, not owners. Therefore all corporate officers meeting the earnings requirement in Denver, should be included here. If any employee has another employer who is withholding this tax, Form TD-269 must be furnished to the secondary employer verifying the primary employer is withholding the tax.

Line 4a. If the return is filed or paid after the due date, enter 15% of Line 4, or $25.00, whichever is greater.
Line 4b. If the return is filed or paid after the due date enter 1% of Line 4 for each month or part of a month past due.
Line 5. Add Line 3, Line 4a, Line 4b. Enter the total. This is the total amount owed. Include a check or money order made payable to **Manager of Finance.**

RETURN LOWER PORTION - DETACH HERE

DENVER OCCUPATIONAL PRIVILEGE TAX RETURN

☐ CHECK HERE IF THIS IS AN AMENDED RETURN
ACCOUNT NUMBER: 209-1495010
TaxType: Occupational Privilege Tax
Period End: 3/31
Due Date: 3/31
Media #: 000000000005

NAME
PRIMARY BUSINESS LOCATION: 6667 16th Street, Denver, CO 80123

I hereby certify, under penalty of perjury, that the statements made herein are to the best of my knowledge true and correct.
Signature (Required): Kira Gardner
Title: President
Date: 3/31/2023

BUSINESS OCCUPATIONAL PRIVILEGE TAX

1 Enter the number of liable self-employed individuals, owners, partners or managers for each month, add across and enter the total.

Month 1	Month 2	Month 3	Total			
1	1	1	3	Multiply Total by $4.00	12	00

2 Enter the number of employees the business is liable for each month, add across and enter total.

Month 1	Month 2	Month 3	Total			
5	5	5	15	Multiply Total by $4.00	60	00

EMPLOYEE OCCUPATIONAL PRIVILEGE TAX

3 Enter the number of liable employees for each month, add across and enter total.

Month 1	Month 2	Month 3	Total			
5	5	5	15	Multiply Total by $5.75	86	25

4 Total Tax: Add Lines 1, 2 and 3 — 158 | 25

5 Late Filing - if return is filed after the due date - Add:
  a Penalty: the greater of 15% of Line 4 or $25.00
  b Interest: 1% of Line 4 for each month that the return is late

6 TOTAL DUE AND PAYABLE: Add Line 4, 5a, 5b. This is the total due. Include a check or money order payable to **MANAGER OF FINANCE** — 158 | 25

000000000000 5 000000000 5

(Source: City of Denver)

302 Chapter 6 *Employer Payroll Taxes and Labor Planning*

FIGURE 6-5
Form 944: Note that a company that files Form 944 has the opportunity to remit payroll taxes using Form 944-V, a payment voucher.

Form **944 for 2022:** Employer's ANNUAL Federal Tax Return
Department of the Treasury — Internal Revenue Service

OMB No. 1545-2007

Employer identification number (EIN): 32-9876566

Name (not your trade name): Gavi Jennings

Trade name (if any): Forest Dog Walkers

Address: 403 Lake Road
Number / Street / Suite or room number

Rouse Point / NY / 12809
City / State / ZIP code

Foreign country name / Foreign province/county / Foreign postal code

Who Must File Form 944
You must file annual Form 944 instead of filing quarterly Forms 941 **only if the IRS notified you in writing.**
Go to *www.irs.gov/Form944* for instructions and the latest information.

Read the separate instructions before you complete Form 944. Type or print within the boxes.

Part 1: Answer these questions for this year. Employers in American Samoa, Guam, the Commonwealth of the Northern Mariana Islands, the U.S. Virgin Islands, and Puerto Rico can skip lines 1 and 2, unless you have employees who are subject to U.S. income tax withholding.

1. Wages, tips, and other compensation **1** 2380.78

2. Federal income tax withheld from wages, tips, and other compensation **2** 274.00

3. If no wages, tips, and other compensation are subject to social security or Medicare tax **3** ☐ Check and go to line 5.

4. Taxable social security and Medicare wages and tips:

	Column 1		Column 2
4a Taxable social security wages*	2380.78	× 0.124 =	295.22
4a (i) Qualified sick leave wages*	.	× 0.062 =	.
4a (ii) Qualified family leave wages*	.	× 0.062 =	.
4b Taxable social security tips	2380.78	× 0.124 =	69.04
4c Taxable Medicare wages & tips	.	× 0.029 =	.
4d Taxable wages & tips subject to Additional Medicare Tax withholding	.	× 0.009 =	.

*Include taxable qualified sick and family leave wages paid in 2022 for leave taken after March 31, 2021, and before October 1, 2021, on line 4a. Use lines 4a(i) and 4a(ii) **only** for taxable qualified sick and family leave wages paid in 2022 for leave taken after March 31, 2020, and before April 1, 2021.

4e Total social security and Medicare taxes. Add Column 2 from lines 4a, 4a(i), 4a(ii), 4b, 4c, and 4d **4e** 364.26

5. Total taxes before adjustments. Add lines 2 and 4e **5** 638.26

6. Current year's adjustments (see instructions) . . . . **6** .

7. Total taxes after adjustments. Combine lines 5 and 6 . . . . **7** 638.26

8a. Qualified small business payroll tax credit for increasing research activities. Attach Form 8974 **8a** .

8b. Nonrefundable portion of credit for qualified sick and family leave wages for leave taken before April 1, 2021 . . . . **8b** .

8c. Reserved for future use . . . . **8c** .

8d. Nonrefundable portion of credit for qualified sick and family leave wages for leave taken after March 31, 2021, and before October 1, 2021 . . . . **8d** .

You MUST complete all three pages of Form 944 and SIGN it.

For Privacy Act and Paperwork Reduction Act Notice, see the back of the Payment Voucher. Cat. No. 39316N Form **944** (2022)

Name (not your trade name)
Gavi Jennings

Employer identification number (EIN)
32 — 9876566

Part 1: Answer these questions for this year. *(continued)*

8e	Nonrefundable portion of COBRA premium assistance credit 8e	
8f	Number of individuals provided COBRA premium assistance [ ]	
8g	Total nonrefundable credits. Add lines 8a, 8b, 8d, and 8e 8g	
9	Total taxes after adjustments and nonrefundable credits. Subtract line 8g from line 7 . . 9	638 . 26
10a	Total deposits for this year, including overpayment applied from a prior year and overpayments applied from Form 944-X, 944-X (SP), 941-X, or 941-X (PR) 10a	638 . 26
10b	Reserved for future use 10b	
10c	Reserved for future use 10c	
10d	Refundable portion of credit for qualified sick and family leave wages for leave taken before April 1, 2021 . . . . 10d	
10e	Reserved for future use 10e	
10f	Refundable portion of credit for qualified sick and family leave wages for leave taken after March 31, 2021, and before October 1, 2021 . . . . 10f	
10g	Refundable portion of COBRA premium assistance credit 10g	
10h	Total deposits and refundable credits. Add lines 10a, 10d, 10f, and 10g 10h	638 . 26
10i	Reserved for future use 10i	
10j	Reserved for future use 10j	
11	**Balance due.** If line 9 is more than line 10h, enter the difference and see instructions . . . 11	. 00
12	**Overpayment.** If line 10h is more than line 9, enter the difference [ ] . Check one: [ ] Apply to next return. [ ] Send a refund.	

Part 2: Tell us about your deposit schedule and tax liability for this year.

13 Check one: [X] Line 9 is less than $2,500. Go to Part 3.

[ ] Line 9 is $2,500 or more. Enter your tax liability for each month. If you're a semiweekly schedule depositor or you became one because you accumulated $100,000 or more of liability on any day during a deposit period, you must complete Form 945-A instead of the boxes below.

	Jan.		Apr.		July		Oct.
13a		13d		13g		13j	
	Feb.		May		Aug.		Nov.
13b		13e		13h		13k	
	Mar.		June		Sept.		Dec.
13c		13f		13i		13l	

Total liability for year. Add lines 13a through 13l. Total must equal line 9.   13m [ ]

You MUST complete all three pages of Form 944 and SIGN it.

Name *(not your trade name)*	Employer identification number (EIN)
Gavi Jennings	32 – 9876566

Part 3: Tell us about your business. If any question does NOT apply to your business, leave it blank.

14. If your business has closed or you stopped paying wages . . . . ☐ Check here, and

    enter the final date you paid wages [__ / __ / __]; also attach a statement to your return. See instructions.

15. Qualified health plan expenses allocable to qualified sick leave wages for leave taken before April 1, 2021 **15** [.   ]

16. Qualified health plan expenses allocable to qualified family leave wages for leave taken before April 1, 2021 **16** [.   ]

17. Reserved for future use **17**

18. Reserved for future use **18**

19. Qualified sick leave wages for leave taken after March 31, 2021, and before October 1, 2021 **19** [.   ]

20. Qualified health plan expenses allocable to qualified sick leave wages reported on line 19 **20** [.   ]

21. Amounts under certain collectively bargained agreements allocable to qualified sick leave wages reported on line 19 . . . . **21** [.   ]

22. Qualified family leave wages for leave taken after March 31, 2021, and before October 1, 2021 **22** [.   ]

23. Qualified health plan expenses allocable to qualified family leave wages reported on line 22 **23** [.   ]

24. Amounts under certain collectively bargained agreements allocable to qualified family leave wages reported on line 22 . . . . **24** [.   ]

25. Reserved for future use **25**

26. Reserved for future use **26**

Part 4: May we speak with your third-party designee?

Do you want to allow an employee, a paid tax preparer, or another person to discuss this return with the IRS? See the instructions for details.

☐ Yes. Designee's name and phone number [   ] [   ]

Select a 5-digit personal identification number (PIN) to use when talking to the IRS. [ ][ ][ ][ ][ ]

☒ No.

Part 5: Sign here. You MUST complete all three pages of Form 944 and SIGN it.

Under penalties of perjury, I declare that I have examined this return, including accompanying schedules and statements, and to the best of my knowledge and belief, it is true, correct, and complete. Declaration of preparer (other than taxpayer) is based on all information of which preparer has any knowledge.

Sign your name here	*Gavi Jennings*	Print your name here	Gavi Jennings
		Print your title here	Owner
Date	1/15/2023	Best daytime phone	518-555-4395

Paid Preparer Use Only   Check if you're self-employed ☐

Preparer's name		PTIN	
Preparer's signature		Date	
Firm's name (or yours if self-employed)		EIN	
Address		Phone	
City		State		ZIP code	

Form **944** (2022)

(Source: Internal Revenue Service)

Unemployment Tax Reporting

Form 940 is the employer's annual report of federal unemployment taxes due, based on employee wages paid during the year. This report is for a calendar year and is due by January 31 of the following year.

According to **26 IRC Section 3306**, certain fringe benefits are not subject to federal unemployment taxes because they represent non-cash compensation that is not intended to be used as disposable income. Specific examples of these fringe benefits are employer contributions to employee retirement plans, such as 401(k) and 403(b), and payments for benefits excluded under qualified Section 125 cafeteria plans.

EXAMPLE: EMPLOYER CONTRIBUTIONS TO RETIREMENT PLANS

Winterguard Products offers its employees a matching 401(k) contribution of 0.5 percent for each 1 percent of the employee's salary. In 2023, Kendall Stark, an employee of Winterguard Products, contributed 4 percent of the $36,500 annual salary to a 401(k) plan.

Kendall's contribution	$36,500 × 0.04 =	$1,460.00
Winterguard's contribution match	Half of the employee's contribution =	730.00
Amount exempt from FUTA tax		$ 730.00

The $730 would be listed on line 4 of Form 940 as exempt from FUTA taxes.

Fringe benefits that may be exempt from FUTA taxes are those excluded from cafeteria plans, such as the ones in the following example:

EXAMPLE: EXCLUDED FRINGE BENEFITS NOT SUBJECT TO FUTA TAXES

Hutcheson Medical Products offers its employees the following fringe benefits:

Benefit	Annual Value	Amount Paid during the Calendar Year
Adoption assistance	$5,000 per employee	$ 15,000.00
Achievement awards	$250 per employee	10,000.00
Meals	$300 per employee	15,000.00
Total the annual value of excluded fringe benefits		$40,000.00

Hutcheson Medical Products would list $40,000 on Form 940 line 4, "Payments exempt from FUTA tax."

Other fringe benefits specifically exempt from FUTA tax and reported on line 4 include:

- Dependent care (up to $2,500 per employee or $5,000 per married couple).
- Employer contributions to group-term life insurance.
- Certain other noncash payments, as outlined in the instructions for **Form 940**.

For tax reporting purposes, amounts contributed by employees to these exempt items must be treated in one of two ways on Form 940:

1. Deducted from Line 3 "Total payments to all employees."
2. Reported on Line 4 "Payments exempt from FUTA taxes."

EXAMPLE: ANNUAL FUTA TAX LIABILITY LESS THAN $500

Kimbro Painting has an annual FUTA liability of $392 during 2022. During the first three quarters of 2022, it would leave Part 5 blank because the tax liability is less than $500, and the liability would roll over to the next quarter. They would complete Part 5 to report the year-end FUTA deposit.

According to IRS Tax Topic 759, they should deposit since it is year-end: "If your total FUTA tax liability for the year is $500 or less, you can either deposit the amount or pay the tax with your Form 940 by January 31." Because they have a total liability of $392 for the year, they should have an amount in Section 5 and make the payment with the year-end filing.

EXAMPLE: FORM 940

London DuVault owns Mustang Motorsports, EIN 79-5312249. London filed the Annual FUTA Tax Return (Form 940) to report unemployment tax contributions during 2022. Mustang Motorsports has 12 employees, all of whom earned over the FUTA wage base. Lines 9 through 11 are adjustments to the FUTA deposited, rare, and do not apply in this scenario. (See pages 8–10 of Publication 15 for more details.)

Name	Gross Earnings (including fringe benefits and retirement)	Fringe Benefits	Retirement/ Pension	Payments Exempt from FUTA	Payments over $7,000 per Employee	Taxable Wages for FUTA	FUTA Tax
YTD Totals	$364,039.32	$24,868.00	$38,496.00	$63,364.00	$216,675.32	$84,000.00	$504.00
Line on Form 940	3			4	5	7	8

Line 1a: If the company pays the unemployment tax in only one state, then the state abbreviation is entered here; otherwise, the company must check the box on line 1b and complete Schedule A. Mustang Motorsports has only one location, which is in California.

Line 3: All wages paid during the calendar year are entered here ($364,039.32).

Line 4: Payments exempt from the FUTA tax. Mustang Motorsports has fringe benefits ($24,868.00) and retirement plan contributions ($38,496.00) that are exempt from the FUTA tax.

Line 5: Wages for the year that are more than $7,000 per employee are entered here. The FUTA wage base is $7,000 per employee. In this example, all employees worked for the entire calendar year, so Mustang Motorsports is responsible for the FUTA tax of $7,000 per employee. To compute line 5:

Total wages	$364,039.32
Less: payments exempt from FUTA	(63,364.00)
Less: FUTA wage base ($7,000 × 12 employees)	(84,000.00)
Wages over $7,000	$216,675.32

Line 6: This is the sum of lines 4 and 5.
Line 7: FUTA taxable wages, which are $84,000 for Mustang Motorsports.
Line 8: FUTA tax ($84,000 × 0.006) or $504.
Line 12: Total FUTA tax of $504.
Line 13: Total FUTA tax deposited during the year. This total must match line 16 (side 2). Because all of Mustang Motorsports' employees exceeded their wage base by the end of the second quarter of 2022, all FUTA tax for the year has been deposited before the completion of the tax return.

> **Lines 16a and 16b:** Tax liability during each quarter. These boxes report the employer's FUTA tax liability based on wages paid or accrued during the quarter. In this case, Mustang Motorsports had a FUTA liability of $350 for the first quarter of 2022 and $104 for the second quarter of 2022. The sum of these liabilities (and any other quarterly liability, which does not exist in this example) is recorded on line 17. The total on line 17 must match the total on line 13 (side 1).
>
> An example of Form 940 for Mustang Motorsports is found in Figure 6-6.

Matching Final Annual Pay to Form W-2

One of the more common questions payroll accountants receive following the release of W-2s from the employees at the end of the year is, "Why doesn't this match my final paycheck?" In short, it should—if you know how to calculate the income that belongs in each block of the W-2. The W-2 reflects all gross wages received by the employee, less any pre-tax deductions: health insurance, qualified retirement contributions, and other deductions adding any taxable fringe benefits. The total federal income taxes that the employer withheld from the employee and remitted as part of the 941 tax deposits also appear on the W-2 and act as supporting documentation for the total wages reported on Forms 941 and 940.

As a result of the Affordable Care Act, employers must report their contributions to employee health coverage on Form W-2. Amounts contributed by the employer should appear in box 12 using code DD to designate the employer's share of the healthcare premium.

REPORTING OF EMPLOYER-SPONSORED HEALTHCARE COVERAGE

Type of Coverage	Form W-2, Box 12, Code DD		
	Must Report	Optional	Do Not Report
Major medical insurance	X		
Dental insurance, either as part of major medical or a separate, voluntary election		X	
Health FSA funded only by salary reduction (reported in box 14)			X
Health FSA value over employee salary deduction for qualified benefits	X		
Health saving arrangement contribution (employer or employee funded)			X
Hospital indemnity or specified illness funded by employee pre-tax deduction or by employer	X		
Multi-employer plans		X	
Domestic partner coverage is included in gross income	X		
The governmental plan provided for members of the military and their families			X
Federally recognized Indian tribal government plans			X
Accident or disability income			X
Long-term care			X
Workers' compensation			X
Excess reimbursement to highly compensated individuals			X
Payment or reimbursement of premium to 2 percent shareholder-employee, included in gross income			X
Employers are required to file fewer than 250 W-2 forms in the preceding calendar year		X	
Form W-2 furnished to the terminated employee before the end of the calendar year		X	
Form W-2 provided by the third-party sick-pay provider to employees of other employers		X	

(Source: Internal Revenue Service)

FIGURE 6-6
Form 940

Form **940 for 2022:** Employer's Annual Federal Unemployment (FUTA) Tax Return
Department of the Treasury — Internal Revenue Service

850113
OMB No. 1545-0028

Employer identification number (EIN): 79-5312249

Name (not your trade name): London DuVault

Trade name (if any): Mustang Motorsports

Address: 12298 El Toro Boulevard

City: Martinez **State:** CA **ZIP code:** 93378

Type of Return (Check all that apply.)
- [ ] a. Amended
- [ ] b. Successor employer
- [ ] c. No payments to employees in 2022
- [ ] d. Final: Business closed or stopped paying wages

Go to www.irs.gov/Form940 for instructions and the latest information.

Read the separate instructions before you complete this form. Please type or print within the boxes.

Part 1: Tell us about your return. If any line does NOT apply, leave it blank. See instructions before completing Part 1.

1a If you had to pay state unemployment tax in one state only, enter the state abbreviation . . . **1a** CA

1b If you had to pay state unemployment tax in more than one state, you are a multi-state employer . . . **1b** ☐ Check here. Complete Schedule A (Form 940).

2 If you paid wages in a state that is subject to CREDIT REDUCTION . . . **2** ☐ Check here. Complete Schedule A (Form 940).

Part 2: Determine your FUTA tax before adjustments. If any line does NOT apply, leave it blank.

3 Total payments to all employees . . . **3** 364,039.32

4 Payments exempt from FUTA tax . . . **4** 63,364.00

Check all that apply: **4a** [X] Fringe benefits **4c** [X] Retirement/Pension **4e** ☐ Other
4b ☐ Group-term life insurance **4d** ☐ Dependent care

5 Total of payments made to each employee in excess of $7,000 . . . **5** 216,675.32

6 **Subtotal** (line 4 + line 5 = line 6) . . . **6** 280,039.32

7 **Total taxable FUTA wages** (line 3 – line 6 = line 7). See instructions . . . **7** 84,000.00

8 **FUTA tax before adjustments** (line 7 × 0.006 = line 8) . . . **8** 504.00

Part 3: Determine your adjustments. If any line does NOT apply, leave it blank.

9 If ALL of the taxable FUTA wages you paid were excluded from state unemployment tax, multiply line 7 by 0.054 (line 7 × 0.054 = line 9). Go to line 12 . . . **9** .

10 If SOME of the taxable FUTA wages you paid were excluded from state unemployment tax, OR you paid ANY state unemployment tax late (after the due date for filing Form 940), complete the worksheet in the instructions. Enter the amount from line 7 of the worksheet . . **10** .

11 If credit reduction applies, enter the total from Schedule A (Form 940) . . . **11** .

Part 4: Determine your FUTA tax and balance due or overpayment. If any line does NOT apply, leave it blank.

12 **Total FUTA tax after adjustments** (lines 8 + 9 + 10 + 11 = line 12) . . . **12** 504.00

13 FUTA tax deposited for the year, including any overpayment applied from a prior year . **13** 504.00

14 **Balance due.** If line 12 is more than line 13, enter the excess on line 14.
- If line 14 is more than $500, you must deposit your tax.
- If line 14 is $500 or less, you may pay with this return. See instructions . . . **14** 0.00

15 **Overpayment.** If line 13 is more than line 12, enter the excess on line 15 and check a box below **15** .

You MUST complete both pages of this form and SIGN it. Check one: ☐ Apply to next return. ☐ Send a refund.

For Privacy Act and Paperwork Reduction Act Notice, see the back of the Payment Voucher. Cat. No. 11234O Form **940** (2022)

Name (not your trade name)	Employer identification number (EIN)
London DuVault	79 – 5312249

850212

Part 5: Report your FUTA tax liability by quarter only if line 12 is more than $500. If not, go to Part 6.

16 Report the amount of your FUTA tax liability for each quarter; do NOT enter the amount you deposited. If you had no liability for a quarter, leave the line blank.

16a	1st quarter (January 1 – March 31)	16a	252 . 00
16b	2nd quarter (April 1 – June 30)	16b	252 . 00
16c	3rd quarter (July 1 – September 30)	16c	0 . 00
16d	4th quarter (October 1 – December 31)	16d	0 . 00
17	Total tax liability for the year (lines 16a + 16b + 16c + 16d = line 17)	17	504 . 00 Total must equal line 12.

Part 6: May we speak with your third-party designee?

Do you want to allow an employee, a paid tax preparer, or another person to discuss this return with the IRS? See the instructions for details.

☐ Yes. Designee's name and phone number

Select a 5-digit personal identification number (PIN) to use when talking to the IRS.

☒ No.

Part 7: Sign here. You MUST complete both pages of this form and SIGN it.

Under penalties of perjury, I declare that I have examined this return, including accompanying schedules and statements, and to the best of my knowledge and belief, it is true, correct, and complete, and that no part of any payment made to a state unemployment fund claimed as a credit was, or is to be, deducted from the payments made to employees. Declaration of preparer (other than taxpayer) is based on all information of which preparer has any knowledge.

Sign your name here	*London DuVault*	Print your name here	London DuVault
		Print your title here	Owner
Date	1 / 15 / 2023	Best daytime phone	714-555-2309

Paid Preparer Use Only   Check if you are self-employed ☐

Preparer's name		PTIN	
Preparer's signature		Date	/ /
Firm's name (or yours if self-employed)		EIN	
Address		Phone	
City		State	ZIP code

Form **940** (2022)

(Source: Internal Revenue Service)

Similarly, Form W-2 contains the employee's Social Security and Medicare wages. These wages are not reduced by contributions by the employee to qualified pension accounts (401(k), 403(b), etc.), and therefore may be higher than box 1. The only difference between boxes 3 and 5 will come when employees earn more than the maximum Social Security wage in the given year, that is, $160,200 for 2023. When this occurs, the Medicare wages reported in box 5 will be greater than the Social Security wages displayed in box 3. Boxes 4 and 6 contain the Social Security and Medicare taxes withheld from the employee and remitted through 941 deposits.

Tipped employees will have amounts represented in boxes 7 and 8 for their reported tips via Form 4070. Box 10 is used to report Dependent Care Benefits. Contributions to nonqualifying retirement plans will be represented in box 11. Employee contributions to qualifying plans are represented in box 12. An alphabetical code is assigned to the specific type of qualified retirement plan to which the contributions are made (A through EE). Box 13 denotes specific contributions to deferred compensation plans. Box 14 is used to report other information to employees, such as union dues, health insurance premiums (not pre-tax), educational assistance payments, and other similar items. State and local taxes and wages are represented in boxes 15 through 20.

The following is an explanation of each box and its contents for Form W-2.

Instructions for Completing Form W-2	
Box	Explanation
a	Employee's Social Security number, based on their Social Security card and/or Form W-4.
b	Employer Identification Number (EIN)
c	Employer address: This should match the address reported on other tax reports, such as Form 941 and Form 940.
d	Optional. This could be used for the company's employee number.
e–f	Employee's name and address as shown on the Social Security card and Form W-4.
1	Wages paid during the calendar year, including any additional amounts from • Bonuses • Cash value of prizes • Awards • Noncash value of fringe benefits • Educational assistance programs (over $5,250) • Group-term life insurance • Roth contributions made to certain retirement plans • Payments to statutory employees • HSA contributions • Nonqualified moving expenses and expense reimbursements • Any other compensation
2	Federal income tax withheld during the year.
3	Social Security wages: Wages paid subject to employees' Social Security tax but not including Social Security and allocated tips. • Educational assistance programs (over $5,250)
4	Social Security tax withheld (employee share only)
5	Medicare wages and tips: This should be the same as the Social Security wages in box 3 unless employees reach the Social Security wage cap. • Educational assistance programs (over $5,250)
6	Medicare tax withheld (employee share only)
7	Social Security tips: Any tips reported to you by the employee go in this box.
8	Allocated tips: Use this box if the company allocates tips among employees.
9	Verification code: Used if the employer participates in the W-2 Verification Code pilot.
10	Dependent care benefits: Report all dependent care benefits paid during the calendar year under a dependent care benefit program.
11	Nonqualified plans: Used by the Social Security Administration.
12	Codes (see Figure 6-7)
13	Check the boxes for the following circumstances: • Statutory employee: Earnings are subject to Social Security and Medicare taxes but not federal income tax. • Retirement plan: If the employee was an active participant in a defined benefit or defined contribution plan. • Third-party sick pay: Used when reporting sick pay benefits.
14	Other: Used to report the annual lease value of an employee's company car if the employer paid 100 percent.
15–20	Used for reporting state and local tax information. Deductions and inclusions would follow state laws.

(Source: Internal Revenue Service)

FIGURE 6-7
Box 12 Codes for Form W-2 and Retirement Plan Checkbox Decisions Chart

Form W-2 Reference Guide for Box 12 Codes

A	Uncollected social security or RRTA tax on tips	L	Substantiated employee business expense reimbursements	Y	Deferrals under a section 409A nonqualified deferred compensation plan
B	Uncollected Medicare tax on tips (but not Additional Medicare Tax)	M	Uncollected social security or RRTA tax on taxable cost of group-term life insurance over $50,000 (former employees only)	Z	Income under a nonqualified deferred compensation plan that fails to satisfy section 409A
C	Taxable cost of group-term life insurance over $50,000	N	Uncollected Medicare tax on taxable cost of group-term life insurance over $50,000 (but not Additional Medicare Tax) (former employees only)	AA	Designated Roth contributions under a section 401(k) plan
D	Elective deferrals under a section 401(k) cash or deferred arrangement plan (including a SIMPLE 401(k) arrangement)	P	Excludable moving expense reimbursements paid directly to members of the Armed Forces	BB	Designated Roth contributions under a section 403(b) plan
E	Elective deferrals under a section 403(b) salary reduction agreement	Q	Nontaxable combat pay	DD	Cost of employer-sponsored health coverage
F	Elective deferrals under a section 408(k)(6) salary reduction SEP	R	Employer contributions to an Archer MSA	EE	Designated Roth contributions under a governmental section 457(b) plan
G	Elective deferrals and employer contributions (including nonelective deferrals) to a section 457(b) deferred compensation plan	S	Employee salary reduction contributions under a section 408(p) SIMPLE plan	FF	Permitted benefits under a qualified small employer health reimbursement arrangement
H	Elective deferrals to a section 501(c)(18)(D) tax-exempt organization plan	T	Adoption benefits	GG	Income from qualified equity grants under section 83(i)
J	Nontaxable sick pay	V	Income from exercise of nonstatutory stock option(s)	HH	Aggregate deferrals under section 83(i) elections as of the close of the calendar year
K	20% excise tax on excess golden parachute payments	W	Employer contributions (including employee contributions through a cafeteria plan) to an employee's health savings account (HSA)		

Form W-2 Box 13 Retirement Plan Checkbox Decision Chart

Type of Plan	Conditions	Check Retirement Plan Box?
Defined benefit plan (for example, a traditional pension plan)	Employee qualifies for employer funding into the plan, due to age/years of service—even though the employee may not be vested or ever collect benefits	Yes
Defined contribution plan (for example, a 401(k) or 403(b) plan, a Roth 401(k) or 403(b) account, but not a 457 plan)	Employee is eligible to contribute but does not elect to contribute any money in this tax year	No
Defined contribution plan (for example, a 401(k) or 403(b) plan, a Roth 401(k) or 403(b) account, but not a 457 plan)	Employee is eligible to contribute and elects to contribute money in this tax year	Yes
Defined contribution plan (for example, a 401(k) or 403(b) plan, a Roth 401(k) or 403(b) account, but not a 457 plan)	Employee is eligible to contribute but does not elect to contribute any money in this tax year, but the employer does contribute funds	Yes
Defined contribution plan (for example, a 401(k) or 403(b) plan, a Roth 401(k) or 403(b) account, but not a 457 plan)	Employee contributed in past years but not during the current tax year under report	No (even if the account value grows due to gains in the investments)
Profit-sharing plan	Plan includes a grace period after the close of the plan year when profit sharing can be added to the participant's account	Yes, unless the employer contribution is purely discretionary and no contribution is made by end of plan year

(Source: Internal Revenue Service)

When completing *Form W-2*, you will have several copies of the same form. A sample Form W-2 is found in Figure 6-8. According to the order in which they print, the copies of Form W-2 are as follows:

Which Copy?	What Is It For?
Copy A	Social Security Administration
Copy 1	State, City, or Local Tax Department
Copy B	Filing with the Employee's Federal Tax Return
Copy C	Employee's Records
Copy 2	State, City, or Local Tax Department
Copy D	Employer

> **EXAMPLE: FORM W-2**
>
> Baylor Christopherson, Social Security number 238-90-7653, worked for Sunnystyles Senior Community Center in 2023. Baylor's address is 5978 Route 202, Pawtucket, Rhode Island, 02862. Sunnystyles Senior Community Center is located at 228 Maple Street, Pawtucket, Rhode Island, 02862, and has an EIN of 23-8907653 and a state ID number of 382948374. The following is on Baylor's W-2 for 2023:
>
> **Box 1** contains the wages, tips, and other compensation. Baylor earned $36,523.34 in 2023.
>
> **Box 2** contains the federal income tax withheld: Baylor had $3,671.04 withheld based on the W-4 information.
>
> **Boxes 3 and 5** contain the Social Security and Medicare wages. Note that these two boxes contain a higher amount than box 1. Baylor contributed $2,000 during 2023 into a retirement plan.
>
> **Boxes 4 and 6** contain the Social Security tax withheld ($2,388.45) and the Medicare tax withheld ($558.59).
>
> **Box 12** contains amounts for nontaxable items. Codes for box 12 are contained in Figure 6-7.
>
> **Boxes 15–17** contain the state tax information. Baylor had $1,369.63 withheld for state taxes based on the state withholding certificate filed in January 2024.

Figure 6-8 is an example of a Form W-2 for Baylor Christopherson.

FIGURE 6-8
Form W-2

Box	Field	Value
a	Employee's social security number	238-90-7653
	OMB No.	1545-0008
b	Employer identification number (EIN)	23-8907653
c	Employer's name, address, and ZIP code	Sunnystyles Senior Community Center, 228 Maple Street, Pawtucket, Rhode Island, 02862
e	Employee's first name and initial / Last name	Baylor Christopherson
f	Employee's address and ZIP code	5978 Route 202, Pawtucket, Rhode Island, 02862
1	Wages, tips, other compensation	36,523.34
2	Federal income tax withheld	3,671.04
3	Social security wages	38,523.34
4	Social security tax withheld	2,388.45
5	Medicare wages and tips	38,523.34
6	Medicare tax withheld	558.59
13	Retirement plan	X
12a	Code D	2,000.00
15	State / Employer's state ID number	RI / 382948374
16	State wages, tips, etc.	36,523.34
17	State income tax	1,369.63

Form **W-2** Wage and Tax Statement — 2023
Copy 1—For State, City, or Local Tax Department
Department of the Treasury—Internal Revenue Service

(Source: Internal Revenue Service)

Form W-3 is the transmittal form that accompanies the submission of Copy A to the Social Security Administration. It contains the aggregate data for all W-2s issued by an employer. Form W-3 and all accompanying W-2s must be mailed or electronically transmitted by January 31 of the following year (i.e., W-2s and W-3s for 2023 must be transmitted on or before January 31, 2024). The total annual wages reported on the W-3 must match the annual wages reported on Forms 941 and 940. The following is an explanation of the boxes on Form W-3.

Instructions for Completing Form W-3	
Box	Explanation
a	Control number (optional)
b	Kind of payer: The employer indicates if one or more of the following applies: • Form 941 *and* no other category applies • Military • Form 943 (agricultural employers) • Form 944 *and* no other category applies • CT-1 (railroad employers) • Hshld. Emp. (household employers) • Medicare govt. emp. (if Form W-2 is for employees subject only to Medicare tax) Kind of employer: Employers check the box that applies to them: • None, if none of the situations apply • 501c non-govt. (for tax-exempt non-governmental employers, such as private foundations, charities, social and recreational clubs, and veterans organizations) • State/local non-501c (for state/local governments or other entities with governmental authority) • State/local 501c (for state/local governments that have a tax-exempt designation) • Federal govt. (for federal government entities) Third-party sick pay: Employers who have indicated on Form W-2 that they issue third-party sick pay must check this box.
c	Total number of Form W-2s submitted with the W-3
d	Establishment number: Used to identify separate establishments within the same business.
e	Employer Identification Number (EIN)
f–g	Employer name and address
h	Any other EIN used during the year
	Employer contact information
1–8	Same as boxes 1–8 on Form W-2. The numbers in these boxes should reflect the total of each box for all forms submitted with Form W-3.
9	Leave blank.
10	Dependent care benefits: Report all dependent care benefits paid during the calendar year under a dependent care benefit program as a total of all Form W-2s.
11	The total reported in box 11 of Form W-2s
12a	Deferred compensation: Enter the total of all amounts reported with codes D-H, S, Y, AA, BB, and EE in box 12 of Form W-2s. No code should be entered in box 12a.
13	For third-party sick pay use only. Leave the box blank.
15	State/Employer's state ID number: Place the two-letter state abbreviation and the ID number. If Form W-2s are from more than one state, enter X in this box and omit the ID number.
16–19	Enter the state/local total wages and income tax withheld in the corresponding boxes.

The following example from Longston Aesthetics depicts the completion of Form W-3 for a company (see Figure 6-9).

> ### EXAMPLE: FORM W-3
> Tracy Longston is the owner of Longston Aesthetics, 2849 Water Street, Falls Church, Virginia, 22043, EIN 84-9943043, phone number 703-555-0904, fax number 703-555-0906. The email address is tlongston@longstonaesthetics.com.
> **Box b:** Longston Aesthetics will file Form 941 to report quarterly tax liability, so box 941 is checked.
>
> *(continued)*

(concluded)

> **Box c:** Longston Aesthetics had 25 employees who received W-2s.
> **Box 1:** Wages and tips for 2023 were $654,087.35.
> **Box 2:** The amount of federal income tax withheld from 2023 wages was $117,735.
> **Box 3:** Social Security wages were $546,333.35.
> **Box 4:** Social Security tax withheld was $33,872.67.
> **Box 5:** Medicare wages and tips were $546,333.35.
> **Box 6:** Medicare tax withheld was $7,921.83.
> **Box 7:** Social Security tips were $24,505.
> **Box 12a:** Deferred compensation was $83,249.
> **Box 15:** VA; Employer's state ID number: 66-2245538849A-238.
> **Box 16:** State wages, tips, etc. were $654,087.35.
> **Box 17:** State income tax withheld was $41,403.73.
>
> Note: Taxable tips reported in box 7 should be reported on IRS Form 4070.
>
> (Source: Internal Revenue Service)

FIGURE 6-9
Form W-3

Field	Value
a Control number	33333
For Official Use Only: OMB No. 1545-0008	
b Kind of Payer	941 (X)
Kind of Employer	None apply (X)
c Total number of Forms W-2	25
e Employer identification number (EIN)	84-9943043
f Employer's name	Longston Aesthetics
g Employer's address and ZIP code	2849 Water Street, Falls Church, VA 22043
1 Wages, tips, other compensation	654,087.35
2 Federal income tax withheld	117,735.00
3 Social security wages	546,333.35
4 Social security tax withheld	33,872.67
5 Medicare wages and tips	546,333.35
6 Medicare tax withheld	7,921.83
7 Social security tips	24,505.00
12a Deferred compensation	83,249.00
15 State	VA
Employer's state ID number	66-2245538849A-238
16 State wages, tips, etc.	654,087.35
17 State income tax	41,403.73
Employer's contact person	Tracy Longston
Employer's telephone number	703-555-0904
Employer's fax number	703-555-0906
Employer's email address	tlongston@longstonaesthetics.com
Signature	Tracy Longston
Title	Owner
Date	1/28/2024

Form **W-3** Transmittal of Wage and Tax Statements **2023**

Department of the Treasury
Internal Revenue Service

(Source: Internal Revenue Service)

Employers may occasionally need to correct filed tax forms. In this case, the employer should use the X version of the form (i.e., Form 941-X, Form 940-X, etc.). Note that any additional tax amounts owed that are discovered during the correction process should be remitted as soon as the employer completes the correction form. During the correction process, if an employer has withheld too much federal income tax or FICA from one or more employees, the employee has the option to recover these overages using **IRS Form 843**.

Jacob Lund/Shutterstock

Payroll professionals should consider creating a checklist of the activities they need to complete at year's end. The following activities are an example of specific activities to consider:

Before Year End	After Year End
Check employee data (e.g. pay information, Social Security number, etc.) for accuracy	Check for information discrepancies, terminated employee records to be purged, etc.
Check tax deposits, wages paid and accrued, and benefit contribution deposit details	Check the new year's tax wage, and benefits data (e.g., check for new tax rates, discrepancies between company and government versions of Forms W-2 and W-3, etc.)
Check any special procedures (e.g. bonuses, Special Accounting Rule deferments, issued manual paychecks, etc.)	Check on payroll-related dates for the year, such as pay dates, holidays, and reporting dates.

(Source: ADP)

Stop & Check

Tax Forms

1. Jacobucci Enterprises is a monthly schedule depositor. According to the information it reported on Form 941, its quarterly tax liability is $8,462.96. During the quarter, it made deposits of $2,980.24 and $3,068.24. How much must it remit with its tax return?

2. Cary's Corrals paid annual wages totaling $278,452.76 to 15 employees. Assuming that all employees were employed for the entire year, what is the amount of FUTA wages?

3. For Cary's Corrals in the previous question, what is the FUTA tax liability?

4. Skyrockets, Inc., had the following wage information reported in box 1 of its W-2s:

   Employee A: $25,650
   Employee B: $30,025
   Employee C: $28,550
   Employee D: $31,970

   What amount must it report as total wages on its Form W-3?

LO 6-4 Describe Payroll within the Context of Business Expenses

Andrey_Popov/Shutterstock

Taxes and Other Deductions Remittance

Understanding employer payroll expenses are important because of the wide range of mandatory activities and lesser-known expenses associated with maintaining employees. Compensation expenses and employer payroll-related liabilities must be accurately maintained in an accounting system. The scope of payroll-related employer responsibilities contributes to the need for knowledgeable payroll accountants.

According to the Bureau of Labor Statistics in 2022, employers' average hourly cost for employees was $41.86, of which wages were $28.88 and benefits totaled $12.98. Wages comprised 69 percent and benefits were the other 31 percent. Additionally, worker costs increased by 1.0 percent between September 2022 and December 31, 2022. Benefits costs rose by 0.8 percent during the same period.

(Source: BLS$_1$, BLS$_2$)

The amounts withheld from employee pay and employer liabilities must be deposited promptly with the appropriate authorities. The omission of any of the required filings, activities, or inaccuracies in the accounting system could lead to problems that could include governmental sanctions and penalties. No statute of limitations exists for unpaid taxes. If a company outsources its payroll processing, it is still liable for any late or unremitted payroll taxes.

> **The IRS will waive penalties under two conditions:**
> 1. The shortfall amount does not exceed the greater of $100 or 2 percent of the required tax deposit.
> 2. The amount of the shortfall is deposited either (a) by the due date of the period return (monthly and semi-weekly depositors) or (b) on the first Wednesday or Friday that falls after the 15th of the month (semiweekly depositors only).

jjvallee/123RF

Tax Penalties

Penalties fall into two classifications: (1) failure to deposit and (2) failure to file. The following penalties apply:

Failure to Deposit

- 2% Deposits made 1 to 5 days late.
- 5% Deposits were made 6 to 15 days late.
- 10% Deposits were made 16 or more days late. It also applies to amounts paid within 10 days of the date of the first notice the IRS sent asking for the tax due.
- 10% Amounts (that should have been deposited) are paid directly to the IRS or paid with your tax return. See payment with the return, earlier in this section, for an exception.
- 15% Amounts still unpaid more than 10 days after the date of the first notice the IRS sent asking for the tax due or the day on which you received notice and demand for immediate payment, whichever is earlier.

(Source: Internal Revenue Service)

> ### EXAMPLE: FAILURE TO DEPOSIT PENALTY
> Mane Street Hairstylists is a monthly schedule payroll tax depositor. The company owed $4,552 in payroll tax liabilities during July. The owner, Darian James, failed to deposit the July payroll taxes until August 28.
>
> The failure to deposit penalty would be calculated as follows:
>
> | Tax Due | Number of Days Late | % Penalty | Total Penalty |
> |---|---|---|---|
> | $4,552.00 | 13 | 5% | $227.60 |

Failure to File

The failure to file penalty applies to amounts on Form 941 and is 5 percent of the unpaid tax due with the return. This penalty accrues for each month or partial month that the tax remains unpaid.

> ### EXAMPLE: FAILURE TO FILE AND FAILURE TO DEPOSIT PENALTIES
> Devin Warren, president of Great Meadows Farms, outsourced the payroll for the company during October 2023. On February 15, 2024, the company received a notice that Form 941 for the fourth quarter of 2023 was not filed. After contacting the payroll service, Devin determined that $32,860 in payroll taxes due with Form 941 was never deposited. The penalties for this oversight would be as follows:

	Failure to File Penalty		
Tax Due	Number of Months Late	% Penalty per Month	Penalty
$ 32,860	2*	5%	$3,286

	Failure to Deposit Penalty		
Tax Due	Number of Days Late	% Penalty	Penalty
$ 32,860	30	10%	$3,286
		Total penalties due	**$6,572**

*The number of months is two because the failure to file penalty is based on both months and partial months. Because the notice was issued in February, the penalty would be for two months.

Notice how quickly the penalties can accrue for unfiled and undeposited taxes. The maximum penalty rate for failure to file is 25 percent, and the maximum for failure to deposit is 15 percent. Also, keep in mind that the penalties may be subject to interest charges.

A quick summary of general employer payroll expenses and responsibilities follows:

Employee Compensation	Tax Withholding	Tax Matching (FICA taxes only)
Tax remittance	Voluntary deductions from employee pay	Remittance of voluntary deductions
Tax reporting	Tax deposits	Accountability

It is important to understand employers' responsibility for remitting the federal income tax and FICA tax amounts withheld from employees. According to **IRS §6672**, any responsible person within the company who *willfully* does not remit the withheld employee taxes—meaning they did not remit the taxes due to something as innocuous as a lack of funds—is subject to a 100 percent penalty for those unremitted funds. It is important to note this penalty only applies to employee federal income tax and FICA taxes, not the employer's share of the FICA taxes or the FUTA tax. The following diagram explains who is considered a responsible party for payroll tax deposits.

Who Has the Responsibility to Remit Payroll Tax withheld from Employees?

- Any signer on the firm's checking account
- Anyone designated in the firm's by-laws
- Anyone with the authority to hire/fire employees
- Any corporate officer
- Anyone who has authority to sign tax returns

(Source: Green & Sklarz, LLC)

Employees and Company Framework

Beyond the payroll accounting system's expenses and responsibilities is understanding how the employees fit within the company's larger framework. Payroll is one part of the cost of employing people. Before the employee ever becomes productive for a company, employers will incur recruiting, hiring, and training costs that vary based on the company's location and minimum job requirements. Other costs include any tools, uniforms, and specific equipment that employees need to perform their jobs. Expenses associated with hiring and retaining well-qualified employees may comprise a significant amount of a company's overhead.

Singkham/Shutterstock

> According to a study conducted by Hundred5, the cost to hire and train new employees averages 15 to 25 percent of the employee's salary. For a manager earning $36,000 per year, the cost to hire and train employees could total approximately $9,000.
>
> While the employee is being hired and trained, the loss of productive time could range from 1 to 2.5 percent of company revenue. Although this may seem to be a minimal amount, companies with high turnover could realize a significant revenue loss because of training costs.
>
> (Source: Hundred5)

Tracking employee payroll expenses is an important duty of payroll accountants. Payroll reports foster cost analysis that informs accounting and human resource professionals of specific details needed for budget purposes. Companies need the information generated by payroll records to ensure profitability and competitiveness.

> Project-based companies face more challenges than other types of companies. Employees could work on multiple projects, and their salaries must be allocated appropriately to measure the actual costs of labor used for different projects. Furthermore, if bonuses are given for certain projects, those employee payments must be allocated correctly for cost analysis purposes.
>
> (Source: ADP)

Payroll-Related Business Expenses

Stop & Check

1. What are the two types of penalties associated with payroll taxes?
2. How do payroll expenses relate to other business functions?

LO 6-5 Relate Labor Expenses to Company Profitability

Compensating employees is far more complex than simply paying the hourly wage. The employer's expenses related to taxes, insurance, and benefits are an addition to the employee's annual salary (see Figure 6-10). Having employees affects a company's profitability but is vital for doing business. Managers need to associate the proper amount of payroll costs with their department so they can make informed decisions about employee productivity and future budgets.

Jirapong Manustrong/Shutterstock

FIGURE 6-10
Percent of Employee Compensation Component to Total Payroll Expense

Compensation Component	Civilian Workers	Private Industry	State and Local Government
Wages and salaries	69.0%	70.5%	61.9%
Benefits	31.0	29.5	38.1
Paid leave	7.4	7.4	7.4
Supplemental pay	3.1	3.6	1.0
Insurance	8.3	7.6	11.4
Health benefits	7.8	7.1	11.1
Retirement and savings	5.1	3.4	12.9
Legally required	7.2	7.5	5.4

(Source: Bureau of Labor Statistics)

The Labor Distribution Report

The number of employees in a department is known as its *labor distribution*. Payroll accounting is a powerful tool for understanding the labor distribution of a company. Accounting records facilitate departmental identification of the number and type of employees, time worked, overtime used, and benefits paid. Integrating the department information into the employee earnings records facilitates labor distribution analysis.

For example, ABD Industries has three departments: administration, sales, and manufacturing. The employees are distributed as follows:

| Administration: 15 | Sales: 10 | Manufacturing: 60 |

Without *departmental classification*, the payroll costs associated with the 85 employees at ABD would be allocated evenly among the departments. This allocation would result in the administration and sales departments absorbing an amount of the payroll costs that are disproportionate to the number of employees. The departmental classification yields an accurate picture of how labor is distributed across a company.

> **EXAMPLE: LABOR DISTRIBUTION, NO DEPARTMENTAL CLASSIFICATION**
> Total payroll amount for ABD Industries = $500,000
> Number of departments = 3
> Payroll cost assigned to each department:
> $500,000/3 = $166,666.67

Assigning payroll costs without departmental classification works when each department is composed of an equal number of employees with reasonably similar skills and job titles.

> **EXAMPLE: LABOR DISTRIBUTION WITH DEPARTMENTAL CLASSIFICATION**
> Total payroll for ABD: $500,000 or
> Payroll cost per employee: $500,000/85 employees = $5,882.35 per employee (if allocated evenly per employee).
> **Departmental allocation:**
> Administration payroll costs = $5,882.35 × 15 = $88,235.25
> Sales payroll costs = $5,882.35 × 10 = $58,823.50
> Manufacturing payroll costs = $5,882.35 × 60 = $352,941

Allocating costs according to the number of employees in each department yields a more accurate amount than the equal distribution of the labor costs across the three departments at ABD. However, allocating by the number of departmental employees assumes that each employee has equal compensation, which is improbable. A payroll accounting system allows accurate allocation based on the precise amounts paid to each employee per payroll period.

Labor distribution reports are among the tools that managers use to determine the productivity and costs specifically associated with their department.

> Labor distribution reports may be used to reveal whatever information is important to a business. Funding sources, payroll accuracy, and budget projections are three common uses of labor distribution reports. Vanderbilt University uses a labor distribution report to ensure that payroll costs are linked to appropriate departments and to specific grant funding.
>
> (Source: *Small Business Chronicle*)

Stop & Check

Labor Distribution Report

1. Pine Banks Tree Farms has 10 employees on staff: three office staff, five agricultural workers, and two drivers. The annual payroll expense is $300,000.
    a. What would be the labor distribution if Pine Banks Tree Farms uses departmental classification?
    b. What would be the labor distribution if Pine Banks Tree Farms does not use departmental classification?
2. Which method—departmental classification or non-departmental classification—is most appropriate? Why?

LO 6-6 Complete Benefit Analysis as a Function of Payroll

The need for companies to offer employee benefits to retain employees after the initial hire and to remain competitive within their industry is a movement that is gaining momentum at a time when employees can choose where they want to work. The problem with offering benefits is that the cost of the benefits directly affects a company's profitability. The challenge is to find ways to promote employee engagement, reduce employee turnover, and maintain company profitability. Payroll data plays an important role in completing an analysis of the benefits offered and their strategic advantage.

kentoh/Shutterstock

Wages and salaries are often a company's largest employee expense. The second-largest expense to employers is employee benefits. According to Paychex, employee benefits potentially add 25–33 percent to an employee's base pay. Benefits may include paid time off, holiday pay, bonuses, and low-cost insurance. Many companies pay a percentage of the employee's insurance benefits, ranging from 70 percent to 100 percent in some cases. With the rising costs and mandatory nature of health insurance for certain employers, employee costs have become a major budget concern for many managers.

> With the growing number of available jobs in the United States, employees are feeling empowered to demand the benefits they want. Health and well-being top the list of requested benefits, especially in the wake of the COVID-19 pandemic. Diversity, equity, and inclusion are not benefits in the original meaning of the word. However, employees are seeking more diverse and inclusive workplaces. Access to the benefits they want is a large influence among contemporary jobseekers.
>
> (Source: Paychex)

Payroll-related employee costs need to be compared to the advantages of maintaining the employee, namely, the department's profitability and the company. To achieve the analysis required, a *benefit analysis* report needs to be compiled. Compiling a benefit analysis report is an important tool in maintaining a balance between employee retention and profitability. The company's payroll records facilitate the compilation of the benefit analysis report.

> **IMPORTANCE OF THE BENEFIT ANALYSIS REPORT**
>
> The analysis of employee benefits considers all of the variables that comprise their compensation. Many managers are unaware of the full cost of having an employee added to or removed from their department, so the benefit analysis report serves the following purposes:
>
> - Benefit analysis helps employers benchmark their employees' compensation to other companies with similar profiles or in certain geographic locations.
> - The report helps employers with labor distribution and budgeting tasks by providing data for decision-making.
> - The benefit analysis facilitates managerial understanding of departmental impacts before hiring or dismissing employees.
>
> Sebastiaan Blockmans/Alamy Stock Photo

Accurate reporting of the benefits costs to employers provides the management with guidance for budget analysis and employee compensation. A sample benefit analysis report is contained in Figure 6-11.

Note the differences between total employee benefit costs and total employer benefit costs. Mandatory and voluntary employee payroll deductions represent a significant monetary investment. When added to the employee's wages and the costs involved with recruitment and hiring, the amount of money dedicated to labor costs becomes a significant portion of a company's expenses.

Taking the information prepared above, the payroll accountant can determine each employee's cost to the company. This information can also determine the total cost of offering a particular benefit to the employees. The latter is used when the company is looking at annual renewals of health insurance benefits for comparison.

Annual Total Compensation Report

Some companies provide their employees with an *annual total compensation report*. The annual total compensation report is similar to the benefit analysis report because it contains a detailed analysis of employee costs. The difference between the two reports is the intended audience. The benefit analysis report is an internal report for the company's management, and the annual total compensation report is meant to be distributed to the employee. The work going into the total compensation report can come from either the human resources department or the accounting department, depending on its structure. Either way, the payroll accountant contributes vital information to the report.

> Total compensation reports are a tool for employers to show employees the complete picture of their cash pay plus benefits. Sedgwick started using total compensation reports as an employee retention tool in 2014 to demonstrate the full value of their compensation packages. These reports illustrate, using facts and visuals, the value the employer brings to its employees. Furthermore, transparency about employee pay and benefits builds trust between employers and employees and allows employees to make informed decisions about their careers.
>
> (Source: EBN)

FIGURE 6-11
Sample Benefit Analysis Report
Statement for: Hayden M. Charette
Annual Gross Salary: $44,137.60
Total Hours Worked Annually: 2,080 Hours

Health & Welfare Benefits	Annual Employee Cost	Annual Employer Cost
Medical/Dental:	$ 600.00	$ 6,000.00
Life insurance:	0	1,200.00
AD&D coverage:	0	980.00
Dependent life insurance:	300.00	600.00
Disability insurance:	600.00	3,000.00
Total health & welfare:	$1,500.00	$ 11,780
Retirement Plan Benefits:	**Employee Cost**	**Employer Cost**
401(k) employee contribution:	$1,324.13	$ 662.07
Profit sharing:	0	3,000.00
Total retirement plan:	$1,324.13	$ 3,662.07
PTO & Holiday Pay:	**Employee Cost**	**Employer Cost**
Paid time off:	$ 0	$ 1,697.60
Holiday pay:	0	1,867.36
Total PTO and holiday pay:	$ 0	$ 3,564.96
Additional Compensation:	**Employee Cost**	**Employer Cost**
Annual bonus:	$ 0	$ 2,500.00
Bereavement pay:	0	509.28
Production bonus:	0	500.00
Tuition reimbursement:	0	5,250.00
Total additional comp:	$ 0	$ 8,759.28
Government-Mandated:	**Employee Cost**	**Employer Cost**
Social Security:	$2,736.53	$ 2,736.53
Medicare:	640.00	640.00
Federal unemployment:	0	253.28
State unemployment:	0	2,279.53
Workers' compensation:	0	353.10
Total government mandated:	$3,376.53	$ 6,262.44
Total cost of benefit provided by WLA Industries	$6,200.66	$34,028.75
Total cost of employing H. M. Charette*		$78,166.35*

*44,137.60 + 34,028.75 = $78,166.35.

To prepare the information for the benefit analysis and total compensation reports, the payroll accountant will gather information from many sources: payroll registers, accounts payable invoices, *payroll tax reports*, and contributions to retirement programs (when employer matching is involved). The payroll accountant will start by printing the annual earnings report for the employee in question. A computerized earnings register can be configured to include taxes and other deductions from the employee's pay. When the total compensation report covers periods greater than one year, it may be necessary for the payroll accountant to obtain Social Security and Medicare tax rates for the years in question. Employer portions of unemployment insurance, workers' compensation, and taxes are added to the employees' benefits in determining the total cost.

The payroll accountant will request copies of invoices for health insurance, life insurance, and any other benefits the employer provides, such as on-site meals and gym facilities/memberships, from the accounts payable accountant. Other items that may be added to the cost per

LJSphotography / Alamy Stock Photo

employee for benefit analysis could be company-provided awards, meals, clothing, or special facilities (break room, locker room, etc.). Once complete, the annual compensation report is distributed to employees to inform them of their annual compensation's total value. A sample total compensation report is in Figure 6-12.

FIGURE 6-12
Total Compensation Report

CASH COMPENSATION AND BENEFITS SUMMARY

The amount of your total compensation from ABC Company is much more than what is indicated in your yearly earnings statement. In addition to direct pay, it includes the value of your healthcare insurance, disability and life insurance, retirement benefits, and government-mandated benefits. Below, we break out your total compensation.

CASH COMPENSATION				Amount
Base Salary				$52,000.00
Total:				**$52,000.00**

BENEFITS	Plan	Coverage	Your Contribution	Company Contribution
Medical Insurance	ABC One		$600.00	$5,400.00
Vision Insurance	ABC Vision		$0.00	$600.00
Dental Insurance	NL Dental		$120.00	$1,080.00
Total:			**$720.00**	**$7,080.00**

Your Contribution 9.23%

Company Contribution 90.77%

TOTAL COMPENSATION VALUE

The true value of your ABC Company total compensation includes your direct pay, the company's contribution to your benefits, and the consequent tax savings to you.

Cash Compensation $52,000

Benefits $7,080

Tax Savings $0

Benefit Analysis Report

Stop & Check

1. What are the purposes of compiling a benefit analysis report?
2. What is the difference between a benefit analysis report and an annual total compensation report?

Trends to Watch

EMPLOYER TAXES AND BENEFIT ANALYSIS

Employers' tax rates and remittance methods tend to change annually based on federal, state, and local directives. Some developments in employer taxes that have changed since 2018 include the following:

- Continuing focus on employee wellness that includes health incentives as part of employees' total compensation package.
- Flexible scheduling will become the norm instead of the exception for many employees.
- Increased access to Employee Assistance Programs (EAPs) will acknowledge employee mental health needs.
- Employee development programs allowing employees to gain skills on demand will become an important part of the benefits package.

Future trends to watch include:

- Increased employer focus on diversity and inclusion programs to attract prospective employees
- Employee-driven benefit packages resulting from low unemployment
- Demand for physical and mental health benefits to improve employee retention
- On-demand pay as part of employee benefits packages
- Benefits packages that include retirement fund perks for paying student loans in a timely manner

Summary of Employer Payroll Taxes and Labor Planning

Taxes are a part of conducting business. Whether taxes are income or employee-related, a business must abide by timely submission and tax reporting regulations. Employers have responsibilities for collecting federal income tax, Social Security, and Medicare taxes from their employees. The company is also responsible for setting aside federal unemployment taxes per employee based on taxable wages. Apart from the federal taxes, employers may be liable for collecting, reporting, and submitting state and local income and unemployment taxes. Privilege taxes, such as the Denver Head Tax, may also be collected in specific districts. Employers who fail to meet the reporting, deposit, or submission requirements may be subject to fines and penalties.

Understanding the connection between Form W-2 and the final paycheck of the year can save payroll accountants hours of work searching to find the answers to each employee's query. When the payroll accountant can explain the elements of the W-2 with confidence, fewer employees will come to ask about the difference, especially if the payroll accountant provides a written explanation with the final annual paycheck or W-2.

Although the human resources department could prepare the benefit analysis report, this duty can fall to the payroll accountant in smaller companies. Even in larger organizations, the human resources department will need specific information from the payroll accountant to feed into the benefit analysis report. Managers can examine the benefit analysis to understand how much their employees cost their department. Upon receiving a total annual compensation report, the employee has a complete understanding of the compensation package, thereby evoking wage discussions and building a data-driven understanding of cost changes.

Key Points

- Employers share some of the same tax obligations as their employees. Some examples are Social Security, Medicare, and (in some states) SUTA taxes.
- FUTA taxes are paid only on the first $7,000 of each employee's annual taxable wage; SUTA tax wage base limits vary by state.
- Workers' compensation is a state-mandated insurance that employers carry to protect employees injured or killed while performing normal work duties.
- Workers' compensation insurance premium costs vary according to labor classifications.
- Payroll tax deposit frequency is determined by the amount of payroll taxes paid during a "lookback" period.
- All new employers are monthly schedule depositors until the next lookback period.
- Most employers file quarterly payroll tax returns on Form 941.
- Employers who deposit payroll taxes on a semiweekly basis must also file a Schedule B with their Form 941.
- Employers with less than $2,500 of annual tax liability file a Form 944 at the end of the calendar year.
- Employers report FUTA tax liability on an annual basis by using Form 940.
- Employers file an annual Form W-2 for each employee with the Social Security Administration.
- Form W-3 is the transmittal form used to transmit a company's aggregate annual wages and withholdings as reported on Form W-2.
- Labor distribution affects company profitability, and benefit costs are significant in managerial decisions.
- A total annual compensation report is used to communicate to employees the complete compensation package that they receive.
- Benefits packages are a strategic part of attracting high-quality candidates.

Vocabulary

Annual schedule depositor
Annual total compensation report
Automated Clearing House (ACH)
Benefit analysis
Departmental classification
Electronic Federal Tax Payment System (EFTPS)
Form 940
Form 941
Form 944
Form W-2
Form W-3
Labor distribution
Lookback period
Monthly depositor
Next business day depositors
Payroll tax report
Quarterly depositor
Schedule B
Semiweekly depositor
Statutory deductions
Tax remittance

Review Questions

1. What taxes are paid only by the employer in most states?
2. What taxes are the shared responsibility of the employer and employee?
3. What taxes are paid by the employee only?
4. What determines the deposit requirements for employer taxes?
5. How often must a company report Form 941 earnings/withholdings?
6. How often must a company report Form 940 earnings/withholdings?
7. Which of the mandatory taxes have a maximum wage base?
8. How did the Affordable Care Act change Medicare tax withholding percentages?
9. What is the purpose of Form 941?
10. Which employers must use Schedule B?
11. How do employers know that they must use Form 944?
12. What is the purpose of Form 940?
13. What are three ways employers could reduce their SUTA tax liability?
14. What is the difference between Form W-2 and Form W-3?
15. What are the employer's payroll responsibilities as far as taxes and other withholdings are concerned?
16. How does payroll relate to a company's costs of doing business?
17. What is meant by the term *labor distribution*?
18. How do payroll records inform managers about labor distribution?
19. What is a benefit analysis report?
20. How can a manager use the benefit analysis report in the decision-making process?
21. How do the payroll reports inform managers about department and company profitability?
22. How do total compensation reports assist employers with hiring and retention?

Exercises Set A

E6-1A.
LO 6-1

Which of the following are *always* employer-only payroll obligations? (Select all that apply.)
a. Social Security tax
b. SUTA
c. Employee income tax
d. FUTA

E6-2A.
LO 6-1

As of 2023, which of the following accurately represents the full FUTA rate and wage base?
a. 0.6 percent, $160,200
b. Varies by state
c. 6.0 percent, $7,000
d. 0.6 percent, $7,000

E6-3A.
LO 6-1

Dylan Reyes is the accountant for Heads Up Hat Corporation. In preparing the payroll for the semimonthly pay period ending December 15, Dylan notices that some of the year-to-date executives' salaries have exceeded $200,000. What payroll tax responsibilities does Heads Up Hat Corporation have, especially regarding FICA taxes? (Select all that apply.)
a. Social Security tax must be deducted from the executives' pay for those under the cap and matched by the corporation.
b. An additional 0.9 percent Medicare tax must be deducted from the employees' pay for those over the base and matched by the corporation.
c. An additional 0.9 percent Medicare tax must be deducted from the employee pay for those over the base, but no corporate match is required.
d. Medicare taxes should be deducted from all employees' pay and matched by the corporation.

E6-4A.
LO 6-2

Phoenix Booker is a payroll clerk at Elemental Exports. The company receives written notice from the IRS that the company is a monthly schedule depositor. How is the deposit schedule determined?
a. The age of the company
b. The owner's choice or remittance frequency
c. The payroll tax liability during the lookback period
d. The total SUTA tax for the previous year

E6-5A.
LO 6-2

Match the amount of payroll tax liabilities from the lookback period with the appropriate tax deposit schedule.

a. $205,684 payroll tax for one pay period   1. Monthly
b. $1,000 annual payroll taxes   2. Annually
c. $165,450 annual payroll taxes   3. Semiweekly
d. $48,350 annual payroll taxes   4. Next business day

E6-6A.
LO 6-3

Which form(s) should be prepared and filed by companies with employees and payroll tax liabilities exceeding $50,000 as of December 31, 20XX? (Select all that apply.)
a. Form 940
b. Form W-4
c. Form 941
d. Form W-2

E6-7A.
LO 6-4

Gold Star Printing made its required tax deposits. However, it filed its third-quarter Form 941 on December 10, after receiving a written notice from the IRS regarding the missing form. What is the failure to file penalty for Gold Star Printing?
a. 2 percent
b. 5 percent
c. 10 percent
d. 15 percent

E6-8A.
LO 6-4, 6-5

Which of the following is true about the cost of employees within a business context? (Select all that apply.)
a. Employees constitute a high cost of conducting business.
b. Hiring employees involves a significant overhead cost.
c. Costs associated with employees include only salary and limited hiring expenses.
d. The cost of providing employee benefits is minimal and of little importance.

E6-9A.
LO 6-6

Which of the following represents the purpose(s) of the benefit analysis report? (Select all that apply.)
a. Benchmarking with other companies
b. Understanding of employer and employee benefits costs
c. Billing employees for benefits costs
d. Identification of opportunities for increasing profitability

E6-10A.
LO 6-6

Why is it important to prepare the benefit analysis report or the total compensation report? (Select all that apply.)
a. The reports promote employee education about the total value of their salary and benefits.
b. The reports inform labor planning and employer cost strategies.
c. The reports may be used as employee contracts.
d. The reports may be used to accompany benefits billing.

E6-11A.
LO 6-1, 6-4

Which of the following is a characteristic of workers' compensation? (Select all that apply.)
a. Workers' compensation is an insurance policy.
b. Private employers are federally mandated to provide workers' compensation.
c. The cost of workers' compensation represents a labor expense to the business.
d. Workers' compensation is provided to cover employees who are injured or killed while performing work duties.

Problems Set A

P6-1A.
LO 6-1

River Signorini works for New & Old Apparel, which pays employees on a semimonthly basis. River's annual salary is $184,000. Calculate the following:

Pay Date	Prior YTD Earnings	Social Security Taxable Wages	Medicare Taxable Wages	Employer Share Social Security Tax	Employer Share Medicare Tax
October 13					
December 29					

P6-2A.
LO 6-1, 6-3

White Lemon Cameras has the following employees:

Employee Name	Annual Taxable Wages
M. Haskell	$26,000
V. Papadopoulos	35,000
P. Anderson	32,000
C. Billingmeier	29,000
C. Johnson	46,000

White Lemon Cameras's SUTA tax rate is 5.4 percent and applies to the first $8,000 of employee wages. What is the annual amount due for each employee?

Employee	FUTA Due	SUTA Due
M. Haskell		
V. Papadopoulos		
P. Anderson		
C. Billingmeier		
C. Johnson		

P6-3A.
LO 6-1, 6-2, 6-3

El Arroyo North has 22 employees within Denver City and County. All the employees worked a predominant number of hours within the city. The employees earned $17.50 per hour and worked 160 hours each during the month. The employer must remit $4.00 per month per employee who earns more than $500 per month. Additionally, employees who earn more than $500 per month must have $5.75 withheld from their pay. What are the employee and company Occupational Privilege Tax for the employees of El Arroyo North?

Employee: _____
Employer: _____

P6-4A.
LO 6-1, 6-3

Greer Utsey earned $47,500 in 2023 for a company in Kentucky. Greer is single with one dependent under 17 and is paid weekly. Compute the following employee share of the taxes using the percentage method in Appendix C and the state information in Appendix D. The box in Step 2 was not checked.

Federal income tax withholding: _____
Social Security tax: _____
Medicare tax: _____
State income tax withholding: _____

P6-5A.
LO 6-3

Using the information from P6-4A, compute the employer's share of the taxes. The FUTA rate in Kentucky for 2023 is 0.6 percent on the first $7,000 of employee wages, and the SUTA rate is 5.4 percent with a wage base of $11,100.

Federal income tax withholding: _____
Social Security tax: _____
Medicare tax: _____
FUTA tax: _____
SUTA tax: _____
State income tax withholding: _____

P6-6A.
LO 6-2

Veryclear Glassware is a new business owned by Skyler Peoples, the company president. Skyler's first year of operation commenced on January 1, 2023. What schedule depositor would Veryclear Glassware be for the first year of operations?

P6-7A.
LO 6-3

Using the information from P6-6A, complete the following Form 941 for the first quarter of 2023. The report was signed on April 14, 2023.

EIN: 78-7654398
Address: 23051 Old Redwood Highway, Sebastopol, California, 95482, phone 707-555-5555
Number of employees: 7
Wages, tips, and other compensation paid during the first quarter of 2023: $244,798
Income tax withheld from employees: $48,000
Social Security tax withheld from employees: $15,177.48
Medicare tax withheld from employees: $3,549.57
Monthly tax liability:

January	$28,484.70
February	28,484.70
March	28,484.70

Form 941 for 2023: Employer's QUARTERLY Federal Tax Return

(Rev. March 2023)
Department of the Treasury — Internal Revenue Service

950122
OMB No. 1545-0029

Employer identification number (EIN) [ ][ ] – [ ][ ][ ][ ][ ][ ][ ]

Name (not your trade name)

Trade name (if any)

Address
Number Street
Suite or room number
City State ZIP code
Foreign country name Foreign province/county Foreign postal code

Report for this Quarter of 2023
(Check one.)

- [ ] **1:** January, February, March
- [ ] **2:** April, May, June
- [ ] **3:** July, August, September
- [ ] **4:** October, November, December

Go to www.irs.gov/Form941 for instructions and the latest information.

Read the separate instructions before you complete Form 941. Type or print within the boxes.

Part 1: Answer these questions for this quarter.

1. Number of employees who received wages, tips, or other compensation for the pay period including: *Mar. 12* (Quarter 1), *June 12* (Quarter 2), *Sept. 12* (Quarter 3), or *Dec. 12* (Quarter 4) .... **1** [   ]

2. Wages, tips, and other compensation .... **2** [   ]

3. Federal income tax withheld from wages, tips, and other compensation .... **3** [   ]

4. If no wages, tips, and other compensation are subject to social security or Medicare tax .... [ ] Check and go to line 6.

		Column 1		Column 2
5a	Taxable social security wages*	[ ]	× 0.124 =	[ ]
5a	(i) Qualified sick leave wages*	[ ]	× 0.062 =	[ ]
5a	(ii) Qualified family leave wages*	[ ]	× 0.062 =	[ ]
5b	Taxable social security tips	[ ]	× 0.124 =	[ ]
5c	Taxable Medicare wages & tips	[ ]	× 0.029 =	[ ]
5d	Taxable wages & tips subject to Additional Medicare Tax withholding	[ ]	× 0.009 =	[ ]

*Include taxable qualified sick and family leave wages paid in this quarter of 2023 for leave taken after March 31, 2021, and before October 1, 2021, on line 5a. Use lines 5a(i) and 5a(ii) **only** for taxable qualified sick and family leave wages paid in this quarter of 2023 for leave taken after March 31, 2020, and before April 1, 2021.

5e. Total social security and Medicare taxes. Add Column 2 from lines 5a, 5a(i), 5a(ii), 5b, 5c, and 5d .... **5e** [   ]

5f. Section 3121(q) Notice and Demand—Tax due on unreported tips (see instructions) .... **5f** [   ]

6. Total taxes before adjustments. Add lines 3, 5e, and 5f .... **6** [   ]

7. Current quarter's adjustment for fractions of cents .... **7** [   ]

8. Current quarter's adjustment for sick pay .... **8** [   ]

9. Current quarter's adjustments for tips and group-term life insurance .... **9** [   ]

10. Total taxes after adjustments. Combine lines 6 through 9 .... **10** [   ]

11a. Qualified small business payroll tax credit for increasing research activities. Attach Form 8974 .... **11a** [   ]

11b. Nonrefundable portion of credit for qualified sick and family leave wages for leave taken before April 1, 2021 .... **11b** [   ]

11c. Reserved for future use .... **11c** [   ]

You MUST complete all three pages of Form 941 and SIGN it.

For Privacy Act and Paperwork Reduction Act Notice, see the back of the Payment Voucher. Cat. No. 17001Z Form **941** (Rev. 3-2023)

Name *(not your trade name)* | **Employer identification number (EIN)**

951222

Part 1: Answer these questions for this quarter. *(continued)*

11d Nonrefundable portion of credit for qualified sick and family leave wages for leave taken after March 31, 2021, and before October 1, 2021 . . . . **11d** ☐

11e Reserved for future use . . . . **11e** ▓

11f Reserved for future use . . . . ▓

11g Total nonrefundable credits. Add lines 11a, 11b, and 11d . . . . **11g** ☐

12 Total taxes after adjustments and nonrefundable credits. Subtract line 11g from line 10 . **12** ☐

13a Total deposits for this quarter, including overpayment applied from a prior quarter and overpayments applied from Form 941-X, 941-X (PR), 944-X, or 944-X (SP) filed in the current quarter **13a** ☐

13b Reserved for future use . . . . **13b** ▓

13c Refundable portion of credit for qualified sick and family leave wages for leave taken before April 1, 2021 . . . . **13c** ☐

13d Reserved for future use . . . . **13d** ▓

13e Refundable portion of credit for qualified sick and family leave wages for leave taken after March 31, 2021, and before October 1, 2021 . . . . **13e** ☐

13f Reserved for future use . . . . **13f** ▓

13g Total deposits and refundable credits. Add lines 13a, 13c, and 13e . . . . **13g** ☐

13h Reserved for future use . . . . **13h** ▓

13i Reserved for future use . . . . **13i** ▓

14 **Balance due.** If line 12 is more than line 13g, enter the difference and see instructions . . . **14** ☐

15 **Overpayment.** If line 13g is more than line 12, enter the difference ☐ Check one: ☐ Apply to next return. ☐ Send a refund.

Part 2: Tell us about your deposit schedule and tax liability for this quarter.

If you're unsure about whether you're a monthly schedule depositor or a semiweekly schedule depositor, see section 11 of Pub. 15.

16 Check one: ☐ Line 12 on this return is less than $2,500 or line 12 on the return for the prior quarter was less than $2,500, and you didn't incur a $100,000 next-day deposit obligation during the current quarter. If line 12 for the prior quarter was less than $2,500 but line 12 on this return is $100,000 or more, you must provide a record of your federal tax liability. If you're a monthly schedule depositor, complete the deposit schedule below; if you're a semiweekly schedule depositor, attach Schedule B (Form 941). Go to Part 3.

☐ **You were a monthly schedule depositor for the entire quarter.** Enter your tax liability for each month and total liability for the quarter, then go to Part 3.

Tax liability: Month 1 ☐

Month 2 ☐

Month 3 ☐

Total liability for quarter ☐ Total must equal line 12.

☐ **You were a semiweekly schedule depositor for any part of this quarter.** Complete Schedule B (Form 941), Report of Tax Liability for Semiweekly Schedule Depositors, and attach it to Form 941. Go to Part 3.

You MUST complete all three pages of Form 941 and SIGN it.

Form **941** (Rev. 3-2023)

Name *(not your trade name)* | **Employer identification number (EIN)**

950922

Part 3: Tell us about your business. If a question does NOT apply to your business, leave it blank.

17 If your business has closed or you stopped paying wages . . . . ☐ Check here, and

   enter the final date you paid wages ___/___/___ ; also attach a statement to your return. See instructions.

18 If you're a seasonal employer and you don't have to file a return for every quarter of the year . . . ☐ Check here.

19 Qualified health plan expenses allocable to qualified sick leave wages for leave taken before April 1, 2021   19 _____ .

20 Qualified health plan expenses allocable to qualified family leave wages for leave taken before April 1, 2021   20 _____ .

21 Reserved for future use . . . .   21 _____ .

22 Reserved for future use . . . .   22 _____ .

23 Qualified sick leave wages for leave taken after March 31, 2021, and before October 1, 2021   23 _____ .

24 Qualified health plan expenses allocable to qualified sick leave wages reported on line 23   24 _____ .

25 Amounts under certain collectively bargained agreements allocable to qualified sick leave wages reported on line 23 . . . .   25 _____ .

26 Qualified family leave wages for leave taken after March 31, 2021, and before October 1, 2021   26 _____ .

27 Qualified health plan expenses allocable to qualified family leave wages reported on line 26   27 _____ .

28 Amounts under certain collectively bargained agreements allocable to qualified family leave wages reported on line 26 . . . .   28 _____ .

Part 4: May we speak with your third-party designee?

Do you want to allow an employee, a paid tax preparer, or another person to discuss this return with the IRS? See the instructions for details.

☐ Yes. Designee's name and phone number _____ _____

   Select a 5-digit personal identification number (PIN) to use when talking to the IRS. ☐ ☐ ☐ ☐ ☐

☐ No.

Part 5: Sign here. You MUST complete all three pages of Form 941 and SIGN it.

Under penalties of perjury, I declare that I have examined this return, including accompanying schedules and statements, and to the best of my knowledge and belief, it is true, correct, and complete. Declaration of preparer (other than taxpayer) is based on all information of which preparer has any knowledge.

Sign your name here _____

Print your name here _____

Print your title here _____

Date ___/___/___   Best daytime phone _____

Paid Preparer Use Only   Check if you're self-employed . . . ☐

Preparer's name _____   PTIN _____

Preparer's signature _____   Date ___/___/___

Firm's name (or yours if self-employed) _____   EIN _____

Address _____   Phone _____

City _____   State ____   ZIP code _____

Page **3**   Form **941** (Rev. 3-2023)

(Source: Internal Revenue Service)

P6-8A.
LO 6-3

Using the information from P6-6A and P6-7A for Veryclear Glassware (California Employer Account Number 999-9999-9), complete the following State of California Form DE-9, Quarterly Contribution, and Report of Wages. Use 5.4 percent as the UI rate with a cap of $7,000 per employee, 0.1 percent as the ETT rate with a cap of $7,000 per employee, and 0.9 percent as the SDI rate with a cap of $153,164 per employee. All employees have worked the full quarter with the company, and all wages are subject to UI, ETT, and SDI. The California PIT taxes withheld for the quarter are $4,068. The company has deposited $6,656.18 for the quarter. Skyler Peoples submitted the form on 4/15/2023.

(Source: Employment Development Department)

P6-9A. LO 6-3

The Content Rabbit Graphics Company paid its 25 employees a total of $863,428.49 in 2022. Of these wages, $9,850 is exempt from retirement benefits (employer contributions to 401(k) plans). All employees have worked there for the full calendar year and reached the FUTA wage base during the first quarter; taxes were deposited then. The Content Rabbit Graphics Company is located at 3874 Palm Avenue, Sebring, Florida, 20394. The owner is Eden Parks, EIN is 99-2039485, and the phone number is 461-555-9485. Complete Form 940, submitting it on January 13, 2023.

Form 940 for 2022: Employer's Annual Federal Unemployment (FUTA) Tax Return
Department of the Treasury — Internal Revenue Service

850113
OMB No. 1545-0028

Employer identification number (EIN): 99-2039485

Name (not your trade name): Eden Parks

Trade name (if any): The Content Rabbit Graphics Company

Address: 3874 Palm Avenue
City: Sebring   **State:** FL   **ZIP code:** 20394

Type of Return (Check all that apply.)
- [ ] a. Amended
- [ ] b. Successor employer
- [ ] c. No payments to employees in 2022
- [ ] d. Final: Business closed or stopped paying wages

Part 1: Tell us about your return.

Line	Description	Amount
1a	If you had to pay state unemployment tax in one state only, enter the state abbreviation	FL
1b	If you had to pay state unemployment tax in more than one state, you are a multi-state employer	☐
2	If you paid wages in a state that is subject to CREDIT REDUCTION	☐

Part 2: Determine your FUTA tax before adjustments.

Line	Description	Amount
3	Total payments to all employees	863,428.49
4	Payments exempt from FUTA tax	9,850.00
	4a ☐ Fringe benefits 4c ☒ Retirement/Pension 4e ☐ Other	
	4b ☐ Group-term life insurance 4d ☐ Dependent care	
5	Total of payments made to each employee in excess of $7,000	678,578.49
6	Subtotal (line 4 + line 5 = line 6)	688,428.49
7	Total taxable FUTA wages (line 3 – line 6 = line 7)	175,000.00
8	FUTA tax before adjustments (line 7 × 0.006 = line 8)	1,050.00

Part 3: Determine your adjustments.

Line	Description	Amount
9	If ALL of the taxable FUTA wages you paid were excluded from state unemployment tax, multiply line 7 by 0.054	
10	If SOME of the taxable FUTA wages you paid were excluded from state unemployment tax, OR you paid ANY state unemployment tax late	
11	If credit reduction applies, enter the total from Schedule A (Form 940)	

Part 4: Determine your FUTA tax and balance due or overpayment.

Line	Description	Amount
12	Total FUTA tax after adjustments (lines 8 + 9 + 10 + 11 = line 12)	1,050.00
13	FUTA tax deposited for the year, including any overpayment applied from a prior year	1,050.00
14	Balance due.	0.00
15	Overpayment.	

You MUST complete both pages of this form and SIGN it.   Check one: ☐ Apply to next return.   ☐ Send a refund.

For Privacy Act and Paperwork Reduction Act Notice, see the back of the Payment Voucher.   Cat. No. 11234O   Form **940** (2022)

Name (not your trade name)	**Employer identification number (EIN)**

850212

Part 5: Report your FUTA tax liability by quarter only if line 12 is more than $500. If not, go to Part 6.

16 Report the amount of your FUTA tax liability for each quarter; do NOT enter the amount you deposited. If you had no liability for a quarter, leave the line blank.

- 16a 1st quarter (January 1 – March 31) . . . . 16a [.   ]
- 16b 2nd quarter (April 1 – June 30) . . . . 16b [.   ]
- 16c 3rd quarter (July 1 – September 30) . . . . 16c [.   ]
- 16d 4th quarter (October 1 – December 31) . . . . . . 16d [.   ]

17 Total tax liability for the year (lines 16a + 16b + 16c + 16d = line 17) 17 [.   ] Total must equal line 12.

Part 6: May we speak with your third-party designee?

Do you want to allow an employee, a paid tax preparer, or another person to discuss this return with the IRS? See the instructions for details.

☐ Yes. Designee's name and phone number [   ] [   ]

Select a 5-digit personal identification number (PIN) to use when talking to the IRS. [ ][ ][ ][ ][ ]

☐ No.

Part 7: Sign here. You MUST complete both pages of this form and SIGN it.

Under penalties of perjury, I declare that I have examined this return, including accompanying schedules and statements, and to the best of my knowledge and belief, it is true, correct, and complete, and that no part of any payment made to a state unemployment fund claimed as a credit was, or is to be, deducted from the payments made to employees. Declaration of preparer (other than taxpayer) is based on all information of which preparer has any knowledge.

Sign your name here [   ] Print your name here [   ]

Print your title here [   ]

Date [/ /] Best daytime phone [   ]

Paid Preparer Use Only Check if you are self-employed ☐

Preparer's name	[ ]	PTIN	[ ]
Preparer's signature	[ ]	Date	[/ /]
Firm's name (or yours if self-employed)	[ ]	EIN	[ ]
Address	[ ]	Phone	[ ]
City	[ ] State [ ]	ZIP code	[ ]

Page **2** Form **940** (2022)

(Source: Internal Revenue Service)

P6-10A.
LO 6-3

Leda, Inc., is located at 433 Augusta Road, Caribou, Maine, 04736, phone number 207-555-1212. The Federal EIN is 54-3910394, and it has a Maine Revenue Services number of 3884019. Owner Kieran Leda has asked you to prepare Form W-2 for each of the following employees of Leda, Inc., as of December 31, 2023. The same deductions are allowed for state tax as they are for federal tax.

Form W-2 Wage and Tax Statement 2023

Copy 1—For State, City, or Local Tax Department

(Source: Internal Revenue Service)

Nova C. Niehaus
122 Main Street, #3
Caribou, ME 04736
SSN: 477-30-2234
Dependent Care Benefit: $1,800.00

Total 2023 wages: $34,768.53
401(k) contribution: $1,043.06
Section 125 contribution: $1,500.00
Federal income tax withheld: $2,028.00
Social Security tax withheld: $2,062.65
Medicare tax withheld: $482.39
State income tax withheld $1,869.08

Kennedy S. Law
1503 22nd Street
New Sweden, ME 04762
SSN: 493-55-2049

Total 2023 wages: $36,729.37
401(k) contribution: $1,469.18
Section 125 contribution: $1,675.00
Federal income tax withheld: none
Social Security tax withheld: $2,173.37
Medicare tax withheld: $508.29
State income tax withheld $1,947.94

Sterling E. Manning
1394 West Highway 59
Woodland, ME 04694
SSN: 390-39-1002
Tuition in excess of $5,250: $1,575.00
(Include in boxes 1, 3, 5, 16)

Total 2023 wages: $30,034.87
401(k) contribution: $712.75
Section 125 contribution: $1,000.00
Federal income tax withheld: none
Social Security tax withheld: $1,897.81
Medicare tax withheld: $443.84
State income tax withheld $1,734.03

Briar A. Hendrix
1387 Rimbaud Avenue
Caribou, ME 04736
SSN: 288-30-5940

Total 2023 wages: $22,578.89
401(k) contribution: $1,354.73
Section 125 contribution: $2,250.00
Federal income tax withheld: $648.00
Social Security tax withheld: $1,260.39
Medicare tax withheld: $294.77
State income tax withheld $1,100.50

Ashton K. Sutter
3664 Fairfield Street
Washburn, ME 04786
SSN: 490-55-0293

Total 2023 wages: $45,908.34
401(k) contribution: $2,754.50
Section 125 contribution: $1,750.00
Federal income tax withheld: $3,288.00
Social Security tax withheld: $2,737.82
Medicare tax withheld: $640.30
State income tax withheld $2,401.42

P6-11A.
LO 6-3

Using the information from P6-10A for Leda, Inc., completed Form W-3 must accompany the company's W-2 forms. Leda, Inc., is a 941 payer and is a private, for-profit company. Kieran Leda is the owner; the phone number is 207-555-1212; no email address to disclose; the fax number is 207-555-9898. No third-party sick pay was applied for 2023. The form was signed on January 19, 2024.

33333	a Control number		For Official Use Only: OMB No. 1545-0008		
b **Kind of Payer** (Check one)	941 ☐ Military ☐ 943 ☐ 944 ☐ CT-1 ☐ Hshld. emp. ☐ Medicare govt. emp. ☐		**Kind of Employer** (Check one)	None apply ☐ 501c non-govt. ☐ State/local non-501c ☐ State/local 501c ☐ Federal govt. ☐	Third-party sick pay (Check if applicable) ☐
c Total number of Forms W-2		d Establishment number	1 Wages, tips, other compensation	2 Federal income tax withheld	
e Employer identification number (EIN)			3 Social security wages	4 Social security tax withheld	
f Employer's name			5 Medicare wages and tips	6 Medicare tax withheld	
			7 Social security tips	8 Allocated tips	
			9	10 Dependent care benefits	
			11 Nonqualified plans	12a Deferred compensation	
g Employer's address and ZIP code					
h Other EIN used this year			13 For third-party sick pay use only	12b	
15 State Employer's state ID number			14 Income tax withheld by payer of third-party sick pay		
16 State wages, tips, etc.		17 State income tax	18 Local wages, tips, etc.	19 Local income tax	
Employer's contact person			Employer's telephone number	For Official Use Only	
Employer's fax number			Employer's email address		

Under penalties of perjury, I declare that I have examined this return and accompanying documents, and, to the best of my knowledge and belief, they are true, correct, and complete.

Signature: Title: Date:

Form **W-3** Transmittal of Wage and Tax Statements   **2023**   Department of the Treasury Internal Revenue Service

(Source: Internal Revenue Service)

P6-12A.
LO 6-4, 6-6

Park Mischner owns Old Times Buttons, which employs 20 people. Park wants to perform a benefits analysis report for one of the employees, Avery Bower, for the year. Avery's benefits package is as follows:
  Annual salary: $35,650
  401(k) contribution: 6 percent of annual salary. The company match is 75 percent of the employee's contribution up to 4 percent.
  Medical insurance deduction: $230 per month
  Dental insurance: $15 per month
  Complete the following Benefits Analysis Report for Avery Bower for the year. Do not include the FUTA and SUTA taxes. (Round your final answers to two decimal places.)

Yearly Benefit Costs	Company Cost	Avery's Cost
Medical insurance	$7,200	$
Dental insurance	1,000	$
Life insurance	200	–0–
AD&D	50	–0–
Short-term disability	500	–0–
Long-term disability	250	–0–
401(k)	$	$
Social Security	$	$
Medicare	$	$
Tuition reimbursement	5,200	–0–
Total yearly benefit costs	$	$
Avery's annual salary	$	
Total yearly benefit costs	$	
The total value of Avery's compensation	$	

P6-13A.
LO 6-4, 6-5

Snow Mountain Equipment has 24 employees distributed among the following departments:

Sales: 5   Factory: 12   Administration: 7

The total annual payroll for Snow Mountain Equipment is $846,000. Compute the labor distribution based on an equal distribution among the departments.

Sales: _____
Factory: _____
Administration: _____

P6-14A.
LO 6-4, 6-5

For Snow Mountain Equipment in P6-13A, compute the labor distribution based on the number of employees per department:

Sales: _____
Factory: _____
Administration: _____

P6-15A.
LO 6-1, 6-4

Small Orange Fine Foods is a specialty grocery store. The employees are classified according to job titles for workers' compensation insurance premium computation purposes.

a. Based on the payroll estimates as of January 1, what is the total estimated workers' compensation premium for 20XX?

Employee Classification	Rate per $100 of Payroll	Estimated Payroll for 20XX	Workers' Compensation Premium
Grocery Clerk	$0.75	$192,500	
Shelf Stocker	1.90	212,160	
Stock Handler	2.40	237,120	
		Total Premium =	

b. The actual payroll for 20XX follows. What is the workers' compensation premium based on the actual payroll?

Employee Classification	Rate per $100 of Payroll	Actual Payroll for 20XX	Workers' Compensation Premium
Grocery Clerk	$0.75	$196,588	
Shelf Stocker	1.90	215,220	
Stock Handler	2.40	242,574	
		Total Premium =	

c. What is the difference between the actual and the estimated premiums?
_____

Exercises Set B

E6-1B.
LO 6-1
Of the following taxes, which one(s) is/are examples of mandatory and voluntary employee deductions? (Select all that apply.)
a. Social Security tax
b. Employee federal income tax
c. FUTA
d. 401(k) contributions

E6-2B.
LO 6-1
Which of the following is/are true about FUTA obligations? (Select all that apply.)
a. FUTA is an employer-only tax.
b. FUTA is subject to a 5.4 percent reduction based on employer and state factors.
c. FUTA is subject to a $20,000 wage base per employee.
d. FUTA applies to all companies.

E6-3B.
LO 6-1
Of the IRS-stipulated lookback periods, which one(s) is/are the most commonly used? (Select all that apply.)
a. Monthly
b. Semiweekly
c. Next business day
d. Annually

E6-4B.
LO 6-2
The Putney Youth Theater has annual payroll taxes of $3,564 during the most recent lookback period. Which payroll deposit frequency will the company have, based on that lookback period?
a. Quarterly
b. Monthly
c. Semiweekly
d. Annually

E6-5B.
LO 6-3
Shay Kinderton is a new payroll accountant with Sal's Diamond Mart, Inc., in New York, NY. The company had a payroll tax liability of $49,580 during the most recent lookback period. For the quarter ending September 30, 2023, which federal form should be filed to remit payroll taxes? (Select all that apply.)
a. Form 940
b. Form W-2
c. Form SS-8
d. Form 941

E6-6B.
LO 6-3
Which of the following is a form that must accompany all Forms W-2 submitted to the Social Security Administration?
a. Form 941
b. Form 940
c. Form W-3
d. Form W-4

E6-7B.
LO 6-4
What are the penalties associated with the lack of reporting and remitting payroll taxes? (Select all that apply.)
a. Failure to report
b. Failure to file
c. Failure to deposit
d. Failure to remit

E6-8B.
LO 6-4
Rory Briggs is the accounting supervisor for Cheeky Cat Furnishings, which has chosen to maintain its payroll on an in-house basis. For this purpose, they have hired new accounting clerks. Which of the following are the payroll responsibilities of Cheeky Cat Furnishings? (Select all that apply.)
a. Timely remittance of payroll taxes
b. Remittance of voluntary deductions
c. Accountability to employees and governmental agencies
d. Publication of salary data in company-wide publications

E6-9B.
LO 6-5

Which of the following represents the difference between the benefit analysis report and the annual total compensation report? (Select all that apply.)
a. The benefit analysis report is designed for review by company managers.
b. The annual total compensation report's intended audience is employees.
c. The benefit analysis report reflects actual benefit costs, and the annual total compensation report includes salary data.
d. The reports are maintained as public records.

E6-10B.
LO 6-5

Which of the following represents the purpose(s) of the labor distribution report? (Select all that apply.)
a. Accurate payroll cost allocation among departments
b. Explanation of individual employee costs
c. Evaluation of labor planning efforts
d. Determination of departmental performance

E6-11B.
LO 6-1, 6-4

Sunny Day Flooring has employees in its manufacturing, sales, and administrative departments. Which department will have the highest rate for its workers' compensation insurance?
a. Manufacturing
b. Sales
c. Administrative
d. All departments will have the same rate.

Problems Set B

P6-1B.
LO 6-1

Campbell Whitman works for Schaum, Whitney, & Matte, LLP, in Washington, DC, which pays employees on a biweekly basis. Campbell's annual salary is $170,000. The company began operations in 2023. Calculate the following:

Pay Period End	Prior YTD Earnings	Social Security Taxable Wages	Medicare Taxable Wages	Employer Share Social Security Tax	Employer Share Medicare Tax
September 22					
December 29					

P6-2B.
LO 6-1, 6-3

Mi Casa Restaurants of Las Cruces, New Mexico, has the following employees as of December 31. The SUTA rate for Mi Casa is 4.3 percent and the cap is $30,100 per employee. Compute the FUTA and SUTA taxes for each employee.

Employee Name	Annual Taxable Wages
A. Shelby	$48,120
M. Gomez	35,975
C. Wardly	22,350
E. Burgess	40,950
S. Black	32,295

Employee	FUTA Due	SUTA Due
A. Shelby		
M. Gomez		
C. Wardly		
E. Burgess		
S. Black		

P6-3B.
LO 6-1, 6-2, 6-3

Deep Mouse Designs has 22 employees within Denver City and County. The employees earned $13.65 per hour and worked 160 hours each during the month. The employer must remit $4.00 per month per employee who earns more than $500 per month. Additionally, employees who earn more than $500 per month must have $5.75 withheld from their pay. What are the employee and company Occupational Privilege Taxes for these employees?

Employee: _____

Employer: _____

P6-4B.
LO 6-1, 6-2, 6-3

Journey Clark earned $55,875 in 2023 for Weather Gurus in Concord, New Hampshire. Weather Gurus' SUTA rate is 2.3 percent and has a wage base of $14,000 during 2023. The FUTA rate is 0.6 percent. Compute Weather Gurus' share of Journey's annual salary.

Social Security tax: _____

Medicare tax: _____

FUTA tax: _____

SUTA tax: _____

P6-5B.
LO 6-2, 6-3

Storm Murphy is the owner of Stormy Banana Films in West Hollywood, California. Stormy Banana Films had 15 employees with total annual wages of $214,750 in 2023 (no one exceeded the Medicare tax surcharge or Social Security cap). The FUTA rate for California in 2023 is 0.6 percent. Stormy Banana Films has a SUTA rate of 3.2 percent for 2023 with a wage base of $7,000. Compute the following employer taxes:

Social Security tax: _____

Medicare tax: _____

FUTA tax: _____

SUTA tax: _____

P6-6B.
LO 6-1

Peaceful Cat Pet Foods is a new business owned by Wren Hammond. The first year of operations commenced on January 1, 2023. What schedule depositor would the company be for the first year of operations? Why?

P6-7B.
LO 6-3

Using the information from P6-6B, complete the following form 941 for the first quarter of 2023. The form was signed by the owner on April 11, 2023.

EIN: 98-0050036

Address: 1021 Old Plainfield Road, Salina, California, 95670

Phone: 707-555-0303

Number of employees: 8

Wages, tips, and other compensation paid during the first quarter of 2023: $302,374

Social Security taxable wages: $280,000

Medicare taxable wages: $280,000

Income tax withheld: $51,000

Monthly tax liability:
    January $31,280.00
    February   31,280.00
    March   31,280.00

Form 941 for 2023: Employer's QUARTERLY Federal Tax Return

(Rev. March 2023)
Department of the Treasury — Internal Revenue Service

950122
OMB No. 1545-0029

Employer identification number (EIN) ☐☐ – ☐☐☐☐☐☐☐

Name (not your trade name)

Trade name (if any)

Address
Number Street Suite or room number
City State ZIP code
Foreign country name Foreign province/county Foreign postal code

Report for this Quarter of 2023
(Check one.)

☐ 1: January, February, March
☐ 2: April, May, June
☐ 3: July, August, September
☐ 4: October, November, December

Go to www.irs.gov/Form941 for instructions and the latest information.

Read the separate instructions before you complete Form 941. Type or print within the boxes.

Part 1: Answer these questions for this quarter.

1. Number of employees who received wages, tips, or other compensation for the pay period including: *Mar. 12* (Quarter 1), *June 12* (Quarter 2), *Sept. 12* (Quarter 3), or *Dec. 12* (Quarter 4) ..... 1 ☐

2. Wages, tips, and other compensation ..... 2 ☐

3. Federal income tax withheld from wages, tips, and other compensation ..... 3 ☐

4. If no wages, tips, and other compensation are subject to social security or Medicare tax ..... ☐ Check and go to line 6.

	Column 1		Column 2
5a Taxable social security wages*	☐	× 0.124 =	☐
5a (i) Qualified sick leave wages*	☐	× 0.062 =	☐
5a (ii) Qualified family leave wages*	☐	× 0.062 =	☐
5b Taxable social security tips	☐	× 0.124 =	☐
5c Taxable Medicare wages & tips	☐	× 0.029 =	☐
5d Taxable wages & tips subject to Additional Medicare Tax withholding	☐	× 0.009 =	☐

*Include taxable qualified sick and family leave wages paid in this quarter of 2023 for leave taken after March 31, 2021, and before October 1, 2021, on line 5a. Use lines 5a(i) and 5a(ii) **only** for taxable qualified sick and family leave wages paid in this quarter of 2023 for leave taken after March 31, 2020, and before April 1, 2021.

5e. Total social security and Medicare taxes. Add Column 2 from lines 5a, 5a(i), 5a(ii), 5b, 5c, and 5d ..... 5e ☐

5f. Section 3121(q) Notice and Demand—Tax due on unreported tips (see instructions) ..... 5f ☐

6. Total taxes before adjustments. Add lines 3, 5e, and 5f ..... 6 ☐

7. Current quarter's adjustment for fractions of cents ..... 7 ☐

8. Current quarter's adjustment for sick pay ..... 8 ☐

9. Current quarter's adjustments for tips and group-term life insurance ..... 9 ☐

10. Total taxes after adjustments. Combine lines 6 through 9 ..... 10 ☐

11a. Qualified small business payroll tax credit for increasing research activities. Attach Form 8974 ..... 11a ☐

11b. Nonrefundable portion of credit for qualified sick and family leave wages for leave taken before April 1, 2021 ..... 11b ☐

11c. Reserved for future use ..... 11c ☐

You MUST complete all three pages of Form 941 and SIGN it.

For Privacy Act and Paperwork Reduction Act Notice, see the back of the Payment Voucher. Cat. No. 17001Z Form **941** (Rev. 3-2023)

951222

Name (not your trade name) _____ Employer identification number (EIN) ___-_____

Part 1: Answer these questions for this quarter. *(continued)*

11d Nonrefundable portion of credit for qualified sick and family leave wages for leave taken after March 31, 2021, and before October 1, 2021 . . . . 11d _____ .

11e Reserved for future use . . . . 11e _____ .

11f Reserved for future use . . . . [ ]

11g Total nonrefundable credits. Add lines 11a, 11b, and 11d . . . . 11g _____ .

12   Total taxes after adjustments and nonrefundable credits. Subtract line 11g from line 10 . 12 _____ .

13a Total deposits for this quarter, including overpayment applied from a prior quarter and overpayments applied from Form 941-X, 941-X (PR), 944-X, or 944-X (SP) filed in the current quarter 13a _____ .

13b Reserved for future use . . . . 13b _____ .

13c Refundable portion of credit for qualified sick and family leave wages for leave taken before April 1, 2021 . . . . 13c _____ .

13d Reserved for future use . . . . 13d _____ .

13e Refundable portion of credit for qualified sick and family leave wages for leave taken after March 31, 2021, and before October 1, 2021 . . . . 13e _____ .

13f Reserved for future use . . . . 13f _____ .

13g Total deposits and refundable credits. Add lines 13a, 13c, and 13e . . . . 13g _____ .

13h Reserved for future use . . . . 13h _____ .

13i Reserved for future use . . . . 13i _____ .

14   Balance due. If line 12 is more than line 13g, enter the difference and see instructions . . . 14 _____ .

15   Overpayment. If line 13g is more than line 12, enter the difference _____ .   Check one: ☐ Apply to next return. ☐ Send a refund.

Part 2: Tell us about your deposit schedule and tax liability for this quarter.

If you're unsure about whether you're a monthly schedule depositor or a semiweekly schedule depositor, see section 11 of Pub. 15.

16 Check one: ☐ Line 12 on this return is less than $2,500 or line 12 on the return for the prior quarter was less than $2,500, and you didn't incur a $100,000 next-day deposit obligation during the current quarter. If line 12 for the prior quarter was less than $2,500 but line 12 on this return is $100,000 or more, you must provide a record of your federal tax liability. If you're a monthly schedule depositor, complete the deposit schedule below; if you're a semiweekly schedule depositor, attach Schedule B (Form 941). Go to Part 3.

☐ **You were a monthly schedule depositor for the entire quarter.** Enter your tax liability for each month and total liability for the quarter, then go to Part 3.

Tax liability: Month 1 _____ .

Month 2 _____ .

Month 3 _____ .

Total liability for quarter _____ .   Total must equal line 12.

☐ **You were a semiweekly schedule depositor for any part of this quarter.** Complete Schedule B (Form 941), Report of Tax Liability for Semiweekly Schedule Depositors, and attach it to Form 941. Go to Part 3.

You MUST complete all three pages of Form 941 and SIGN it.

Form **941** (Rev. 3-2023)

		950922
Name *(not your trade name)*		**Employer identification number (EIN)**

Part 3: Tell us about your business. If a question does NOT apply to your business, leave it blank.

17 If your business has closed or you stopped paying wages . . . . ☐ Check here, and

   enter the final date you paid wages [/ /] ; also attach a statement to your return. See instructions.

18 If you're a seasonal employer and you don't have to file a return for every quarter of the year . . . ☐ Check here.

19 Qualified health plan expenses allocable to qualified sick leave wages for leave taken before April 1, 2021 . . . 19 [.]

20 Qualified health plan expenses allocable to qualified family leave wages for leave taken before April 1, 2021 . . . 20 [.]

21 Reserved for future use . . . . 21 [.]

22 Reserved for future use . . . . 22 [.]

23 Qualified sick leave wages for leave taken after March 31, 2021, and before October 1, 2021 . . . 23 [.]

24 Qualified health plan expenses allocable to qualified sick leave wages reported on line 23 . . . 24 [.]

25 Amounts under certain collectively bargained agreements allocable to qualified sick leave wages reported on line 23 . . . . 25 [.]

26 Qualified family leave wages for leave taken after March 31, 2021, and before October 1, 2021 . . . 26 [.]

27 Qualified health plan expenses allocable to qualified family leave wages reported on line 26 . . . 27 [.]

28 Amounts under certain collectively bargained agreements allocable to qualified family leave wages reported on line 26 . . . . 28 [.]

Part 4: May we speak with your third-party designee?

Do you want to allow an employee, a paid tax preparer, or another person to discuss this return with the IRS? See the instructions for details.

☐ Yes. Designee's name and phone number [   ] [   ]

  Select a 5-digit personal identification number (PIN) to use when talking to the IRS. [ ][ ][ ][ ][ ]

☐ No.

Part 5: Sign here. You MUST complete all three pages of Form 941 and SIGN it.

Under penalties of perjury, I declare that I have examined this return, including accompanying schedules and statements, and to the best of my knowledge and belief, it is true, correct, and complete. Declaration of preparer (other than taxpayer) is based on all information of which preparer has any knowledge.

Sign your name here [   ] Print your name here [   ]

  Print your title here [   ]

  Date [/ /] Best daytime phone [   ]

Paid Preparer Use Only Check if you're self-employed . . . ☐

Preparer's name		PTIN	
Preparer's signature		Date	/ /
Firm's name (or yours if self-employed)		EIN	
Address		Phone	
City		State [ ] ZIP code	

Page **3** Form **941** (Rev. 3-2023)

(Source: Internal Revenue Service)

P6-8B.
LO 6-3

Using the information from P6-6B and P6-7B for Peaceful Cat Pet Foods, complete the following State of California Form DE-9, Quarterly Contribution Return and Report of Wages. The California employer account number is 989-8877-1. Use 5.4 percent as the UI rate, 0.1 percent as the ETT rate, and 0.9 percent as the SDI rate. California UI and ETT wage caps are $7,000, while the SDI cap is $153,164 per employee. No employee has reached the SDI limit. All employees have worked with the company since January 1. The California PIT taxes withheld for the quarter are $40,000. The company has deposited no taxes for the quarter. Form DE-9 was completed and signed on April 11, 2023, with a due date of April 15, 2023.

P6-9B.
LO 6-3

Jealous Frog Toys paid its nine employees a total of $432,586.40 in 2022. All employees have worked there for the full calendar year and reached the FUTA wage base during the first quarter. Taxes were deposited on time. The employer contributed $12,470 to retirement plans during the year (exempt from the FUTA). Jealous Frog Toys is located at 783 Morehead Street, Fargo, ND, 68383, phone number 701-555-3432. The owner is Kyle Jackson, and the EIN is 73-4029848. Complete Form 940. The form was signed and submitted on January 6, 2023.

P6-10B.
LO 6-3

Reese Castor, the owner of Castor Corporation, is located at 1310 Garrick Way, Sun Valley, Arizona, 86029, phone number is 928-555-8842. The federal EIN is 20-1948348, and the state employer identification number is 9040-2038-1. Prepare the Form W-2 for each of the following employees of Castor Corporation as of December 31, 2023. The same deductions are allowed for state income tax as for federal. The form was submitted on January 12, 2024.

Montana M. Parsons 5834 Moon Drive Sun Valley, AZ 86029 SSN: 578-33-3049	Total 2023 wages: $47,203.78 401(k) contribution: $2,832.23 Section 125 contribution: $1,400.00 Federal income tax withheld: $1,794.00 Social Security tax withheld: $2,839.83 Medicare tax withheld: $664.15 State income tax withheld: $1,435.25
Taylen Y. Maddox 32 Second Street Holbrook, AZ 86025 SSN: 734-00-1938 Tuition in excess of $5,250: $750 (Include in boxes 1, 3, 5, 16)	Total 2023 wages: $37,499.02 401(k) contribution: $1,124.97 Section 125 contribution: $500.00 Federal income tax withheld: $1,612.00 Social Security tax withheld: $2,340.44 Medicare tax withheld: $547.36 State income tax withheld: $1,223.24
Sky J. Featherstone 7784 Painted Desert Road Sun Valley, AZ 86029 SSN: 290-03-4992	Total 2023 wages: $41,904.29 401(k) contribution: $1,885.69 Federal income tax withheld: $3,146.00 Social Security tax withheld: $2,598.07 Medicare tax withheld: $607.61 State income tax withheld: $1,336.62
Dakota L. Clearwater 7384 Ridge Road Woodruff, AZ 85942 SSN: 994-20-4837	Total 2023 wages: $29,874.37 401(k) contribution: $597.49 Section 125 contribution: $250.00 Federal income tax withheld: $390.00 Social Security tax withheld: $1,836.71 Medicare tax withheld: $429.55 State income tax withheld: $969.50
Woods L. Millen 229 Second Street #4A Holbrook, AZ 86025 SSN: 477-30-2234	Total 2023 wages: $15,889.04 Federal income tax withheld: $494.00 Social Security tax withheld: $985.12 Medicare tax withheld: $230.39 State income tax withheld: $411.53

P6-11B.
LO 6-3

Using the information from P6-10B for Castor Corporation, complete Form W-3, which must accompany the company's Form W-2s. Castor Corporation is a 941 payer and is a private, for-profit company. No third-party sick pay was applied for 2023. The W-3 was signed and submitted on January 12, 2024.

QUARTERLY CONTRIBUTION RETURN AND REPORT OF WAGES

EDD — Employment Development Department, State of California

REMINDER: File your DE 9 and DE 9C together.
PLEASE TYPE THIS FORM—DO NOT ALTER PREPRINTED INFORMATION

00090112

YR | QTR

QUARTER ENDED | DUE | DELINQUENT IF NOT POSTMARKED OR RECEIVED BY

EMPLOYER ACCOUNT NO.

DO NOT ALTER THIS AREA (DEPT. USE ONLY)
P1 | P2 | C | P | U | S | A
T
EFFECTIVE DATE — Mo. Day Yr.

FEIN _____

A. NO WAGES PAID THIS QUARTER ☐
B. OUT OF BUSINESS/NO EMPLOYEES ☐
B1. OUT OF BUSINESS DATE — M M D D Y Y Y Y

ADDITIONAL FEINS _____ _____

C. TOTAL SUBJECT WAGES PAID THIS QUARTER ....

D. UNEMPLOYMENT INSURANCE (UI) (Total Employee Wages up to $_____ per employee per calendar year)

(D1) UI Rate % _____ TIMES (D2) UI TAXABLE WAGES FOR THE QUARTER _____ = (D3) UI CONTRIBUTIONS 0.00

E. EMPLOYMENT TRAINING TAX (ETT)

(E1) ETT Rate % _____ TIMES UI Taxable Wages for the Quarter (D2) ...... = (E2) ETT CONTRIBUTIONS 0.00

F. STATE DISABILITY INSURANCE (SDI) (Total Employee Wages up to $_____ per employee per calendar year)

(F1) SDI Rate % _____ TIMES (F2) SDI TAXABLE WAGES FOR THE QUARTER _____ = (F3) SDI EMPLOYEE CONTRIBUTIONS WITHHELD 0.00

G. CALIFORNIA PERSONAL INCOME TAX (PIT) WITHHELD ....

H. SUBTOTAL (Add Items D3, E2, F3, and G) 0.00

I. LESS: CONTRIBUTIONS AND WITHHOLDINGS PAID FOR THE QUARTER .... (**DO NOT** INCLUDE PENALTY AND INTEREST PAYMENTS)

J. TOTAL TAXES DUE OR OVERPAID (Item H minus Item I) 0.00

If amount due, prepare a *Payroll Tax Deposit* (DE 88), include the correct payment quarter, and mail to: Employment Development Department, P.O. Box 826276, Sacramento, CA 94230-6276. **NOTE:** Do not mail payments along with the DE 9 and *Quarterly Contribution Return and Report of Wages (Continuation)* (DE 9C), as this may delay processing and result in erroneous penalty and interest charges. **Mandatory Electronic Funds Transfer (EFT)** filers must remit all SDI/PIT deposits by EFT to avoid a noncompliance penalty.

K. I declare that the above, to the best of my knowledge and belief, is true and correct. If a refund was claimed, a reasonable effort was made to refund any erroneous deductions to the affected employee(s).

Signature *Required* _____ Title _____ (Owner, Accountant, Preparer, etc.) Phone (___) _____ Date _____

SIGN AND MAIL TO: State of California / Employment Development Department / P.O. Box 989071 / West Sacramento CA 95798-9071

DE 9 Rev. 1 (1-12) (INTERNET) — Page 1 of 2

Fast, Easy, and Convenient! Visit EDD's Web site at www.edd.ca.gov

(Source: State of California)

Form **940 for 2022:** Employer's Annual Federal Unemployment (FUTA) Tax Return

Department of the Treasury — Internal Revenue Service

850113

OMB No. 1545-0028

Employer identification number (EIN) ☐☐ – ☐☐☐☐☐☐☐

Name *(not your trade name)*

Trade name *(if any)*

Address
- Number / Street / Suite or room number
- City / State / ZIP code
- Foreign country name / Foreign province/county / Foreign postal code

Type of Return (Check all that apply.)
- ☐ a. Amended
- ☐ b. Successor employer
- ☐ c. No payments to employees in 2022
- ☐ d. Final: Business closed or stopped paying wages

Go to *www.irs.gov/Form940* for instructions and the latest information.

Read the separate instructions before you complete this form. Please type or print within the boxes.

Part 1: Tell us about your return. If any line does NOT apply, leave it blank. See instructions before completing Part 1.

1a If you had to pay state unemployment tax in one state only, enter the state abbreviation . . 1a ☐☐

1b If you had to pay state unemployment tax in more than one state, you are a multi-state employer . . . 1b ☐ Check here. Complete Schedule A (Form 940).

2 If you paid wages in a state that is subject to CREDIT REDUCTION . . . . 2 ☐ Check here. Complete Schedule A (Form 940).

Part 2: Determine your FUTA tax before adjustments. If any line does NOT apply, leave it blank.

3 Total payments to all employees . . . . 3 ☐

4 Payments exempt from FUTA tax . . . . 4 ☐

   Check all that apply: 4a ☐ Fringe benefits   4c ☐ Retirement/Pension   4e ☐ Other
                            4b ☐ Group-term life insurance   4d ☐ Dependent care

5 Total of payments made to each employee in excess of $7,000 . . . . 5 ☐

6 **Subtotal** (line 4 + line 5 = line 6) . . . . 6 ☐

7 **Total taxable FUTA wages** (line 3 – line 6 = line 7). See instructions . . . . 7 ☐

8 **FUTA tax before adjustments** (line 7 × 0.006 = line 8) . . . . 8 ☐

Part 3: Determine your adjustments. If any line does NOT apply, leave it blank.

9 If ALL of the taxable FUTA wages you paid were excluded from state unemployment tax, multiply line 7 by 0.054 (line 7 × 0.054 = line 9). Go to line 12 . . . . 9 ☐

10 If SOME of the taxable FUTA wages you paid were excluded from state unemployment tax, OR you paid ANY state unemployment tax late (after the due date for filing Form 940), complete the worksheet in the instructions. Enter the amount from line 7 of the worksheet . . 10 ☐

11 If credit reduction applies, enter the total from Schedule A (Form 940) . . . . 11 ☐

Part 4: Determine your FUTA tax and balance due or overpayment. If any line does NOT apply, leave it blank.

12 **Total FUTA tax after adjustments** (lines 8 + 9 + 10 + 11 = line 12) . . . . 12 ☐

13 FUTA tax deposited for the year, including any overpayment applied from a prior year . 13 ☐

14 **Balance due.** If line 12 is more than line 13, enter the excess on line 14.
- If line 14 is more than $500, you must deposit your tax.
- If line 14 is $500 or less, you may pay with this return. See instructions . . . . 14 ☐

15 **Overpayment.** If line 13 is more than line 12, enter the excess on line 15 and check a box below 15 ☐

   You **MUST** complete both pages of this form and **SIGN** it.   Check one: ☐ Apply to next return.   ☐ Send a refund.

For Privacy Act and Paperwork Reduction Act Notice, see the back of the Payment Voucher.   Cat. No. 11234O   Form **940** (2022)

Name *(not your trade name)*	Employer identification number (EIN)
	—

850212

Part 5: Report your FUTA tax liability by quarter only if line 12 is more than $500. If not, go to Part 6.

16 Report the amount of your FUTA tax liability for each quarter; do NOT enter the amount you deposited. If you had no liability for a quarter, leave the line blank.

16a **1st quarter** (January 1 – March 31) . . . . 16a [.   ]

16b **2nd quarter** (April 1 – June 30) . . . . 16b [.   ]

16c **3rd quarter** (July 1 – September 30) . . . . 16c [.   ]

16d **4th quarter** (October 1 – December 31) . . . . . . 16d [.   ]

17 **Total tax liability for the year** (lines 16a + 16b + 16c + 16d = line 17) 17 [.   ] Total must equal line 12.

Part 6: May we speak with your third-party designee?

Do you want to allow an employee, a paid tax preparer, or another person to discuss this return with the IRS? See the instructions for details.

☐ **Yes.** Designee's name and phone number [   ]   [   ]

Select a 5-digit personal identification number (PIN) to use when talking to the IRS. [ ][ ][ ][ ][ ]

☐ **No.**

Part 7: Sign here. You MUST complete both pages of this form and SIGN it.

Under penalties of perjury, I declare that I have examined this return, including accompanying schedules and statements, and to the best of my knowledge and belief, it is true, correct, and complete, and that no part of any payment made to a state unemployment fund claimed as a credit was, or is to be, deducted from the payments made to employees. Declaration of preparer (other than taxpayer) is based on all information of which preparer has any knowledge.

Sign your name here [   ]

Print your name here [   ]

Print your title here [   ]

Date [/ /]

Best daytime phone [   ]

Paid Preparer Use Only   Check if you are self-employed ☐

Preparer's name		PTIN	
Preparer's signature		Date	/ /
Firm's name (or yours if self-employed)		EIN	
Address		Phone	
City		State		ZIP code	

Page **2**   Form **940** (2022)

(Source: Internal Revenue Service)

Form W-2 Wage and Tax Statement (2023)

22222	**a** Employee's social security number		
	OMB No. 1545-0008		
b Employer identification number (EIN)		**1** Wages, tips, other compensation	**2** Federal income tax withheld
c Employer's name, address, and ZIP code		**3** Social security wages	**4** Social security tax withheld
		5 Medicare wages and tips	**6** Medicare tax withheld
		7 Social security tips	**8** Allocated tips
d Control number		**9**	**10** Dependent care benefits
e Employee's first name and initial — Last name — Suff.		**11** Nonqualified plans	**12a** Code
		13 Statutory employee / Retirement plan / Third-party sick pay	**12b** Code
		14 Other	**12c** Code
			12d Code
f Employee's address and ZIP code			
15 State — Employer's state ID number	**16** State wages, tips, etc. — **17** State income tax	**18** Local wages, tips, etc. — **19** Local income tax	**20** Locality name

Form **W-2** Wage and Tax Statement — **2023** — Department of the Treasury—Internal Revenue Service

Copy 1—For State, City, or Local Tax Department

(Source: Internal Revenue Service)

Form W-3 Transmittal of Wage and Tax Statements (2023)

33333	**a** Control number	For Official Use Only: OMB No. 1545-0008
b Kind of Payer (Check one): 941 / Military / 943 / 944 / CT-1 / Hshld. emp. / Medicare govt. emp.	**Kind of Employer** (Check one): None apply / 501c non-govt. / State/local non-501c / State/local 501c / Federal govt.	Third-party sick pay (Check if applicable)
c Total number of Forms W-2 — **d** Establishment number	**1** Wages, tips, other compensation	**2** Federal income tax withheld
e Employer identification number (EIN)	**3** Social security wages	**4** Social security tax withheld
f Employer's name	**5** Medicare wages and tips	**6** Medicare tax withheld
	7 Social security tips	**8** Allocated tips
	9	**10** Dependent care benefits
	11 Nonqualified plans	**12a** Deferred compensation
g Employer's address and ZIP code		
h Other EIN used this year	**13** For third-party sick pay use only	**12b**
15 State — Employer's state ID number	**14** Income tax withheld by payer of third-party sick pay	
16 State wages, tips, etc. — **17** State income tax	**18** Local wages, tips, etc.	**19** Local income tax
Employer's contact person	Employer's telephone number	For Official Use Only
Employer's fax number	Employer's email address	

Under penalties of perjury, I declare that I have examined this return and accompanying documents, and, to the best of my knowledge and belief, they are true, correct, and complete.

Signature: _____ Title: _____ Date: _____

Form **W-3** Transmittal of Wage and Tax Statements — **2023** — Department of the Treasury Internal Revenue Service

(Source: Internal Revenue Service)

P6-12B.
LO 6-5, 6-6

Oak Cove Resorts has eight employees. The owner wants to perform a benefit analysis report for the year for one of its employees, Tristan Cassidy. Tristan's benefits package is as follows:

Annual salary: $42,950

401(k) contribution: 8 percent of annual salary; the company match is half of the employee's contribution, up to 5 percent of the employee's annual salary.

Medical insurance deduction: $340 per month

Dental insurance: $21 per month

Complete the following Benefits Analysis Report for Tristan Cassidy for 2023.

Yearly Benefit Costs	Company Cost	Tristan's Cost
Medical insurance	$9,600	$
Dental insurance	800	$
Life insurance	1,200	-0-
AD&D	125	-0-
Short-term disability	500	-0-
Long-term disability	250	-0-
401(k)	$	$
Social Security	$	$
Medicare	$	$
Tuition reimbursement	$2,500	-0-
Total yearly benefit costs	$	
Tristan's annual salary	$	
Total value of Tristan's compensation	$	

P6-13B.
LO 6-4, 6-5

Superfan Sportsgear has 30 employees distributed among the following departments:

   Sales: 7   Factory: 13   Administration: 10

The total annual payroll for Superfan Sportsgear is $975,580.

Compute the labor distribution based on the equal distribution among the departments.

Sales: _____
Factory: _____
Administration: _____

P6-14B.
LO 6-4, 6-5

For Superfan Sportsgear in P6-13B, compute the labor distribution based on the number of employees per department:

Sales: _____
Factory: _____
Administration: _____

P6-15B.
LO 6-1, 6-4

At Fox Furniture, employees are classified according to the job title for workers' compensation insurance premium computation purposes.

a. Based on the following payroll estimates as of January 1, what is the estimated workers' compensation insurance premium for the year 2023?

Employee Classification	Rate per $100 of Payroll	Estimated Payroll for 2023	Workers' Compensation Premium
Sales Associate	$0.55	$213,680	
Loader	2.15	155,240	
Furniture Builder	2.95	102,590	
		Total Premium =	

b. The actual payroll for 2023 is listed below. What is the workers' compensation premium based on the actual payroll?

Employee Classification	Rate per $100 of Payroll	Actual Payroll for 2023	Workers' Compensation Premium
Sales Associate	$0.55	$228,944	
Loader	2.15	163,743	
Furniture Builder	2.95	105,389	
		Total Premium =	

c. What is the difference between the actual and the estimated premiums?

_____

Critical Thinking

6-1. Burton Book Memorabilia is a semiweekly depositor. Following a special project's success, Keller Burton, the owner, pays each of the 250 employees a $2,000 bonus on August 11, 2023. Assume a 22 percent income tax rate. When will Keller need to deposit the payroll taxes?

6-2. Kai is the president of Zebra Antiques. An employee, Reese Francis, is due a raise. Reese's current benefit analysis is as follows:

Yearly Benefit Costs	Company Cost (Current)	Employee Cost (Current)
Medical insurance	$ 8,000.00	$ 1,200
Dental insurance	120.00	120
Life insurance	300.00	-0-
AD&D	150.00	-0-
Short-term disability	60.00	-0-
Long-term disability	30.00	-0-
401(k)	750.00	1,500
Social Security	3,018.16	3,018.16
Medicare	705.86	705.86
Tuition reimbursement	2,000.00	-0-
Total yearly benefit costs (employer)	15,134.02	
Employee's annual salary	50,000.00	
The total value of employee's compensation	$65,134.02	

Compute the benefit analysis assuming:
- 3 percent increase in pay.
- Reese will increase the 401(k) contribution to 8 percent with a company match of 50 percent up to a 3 percent contribution by the employer.
- 15 percent increase in medical and dental insurance premiums.

Yearly Benefit Costs	Company Cost (New)	Employee Cost (New)
Medical insurance	$	$
Dental insurance	$	$
Life insurance	$300	-0-
AD&D	$150	-0-
Short-term disability	$60	-0-
Long-term disability	$30	-0-
401(k)	$	$
Social Security	$	$
Medicare	$	$
Tuition reimbursement	$2,000	-0-
Total yearly benefit costs (employer)	$	
Dwight's annual salary	$	
The total value of the employee's compensation	$	

In the Real World: Scenario for Discussion

In Shavertown, Pennsylvania, the Wilkes-Barre Bookkeeping LLC owner was indicted for embezzling over $376,225 of his clients' payroll tax remittances between 2010 and 2016 and for lying to clients about his actions. Additionally, he embezzled nearly $70,000 from a nonprofit for which he was the treasurer. He was sentenced to 38 months in prison and ordered to pay restitution totaling nearly $500,000. Do you think this was a fair sentence? Why or why not?

Internet Activities

6-1. Would you like to know more about the Employment Cost Index? Check out the videos from the Bureau of Labor Statistics: www.bls.gov/eci/videos.htm

6-2. Go to https://www.firstnonprofit.com/suta-state-unemployment-tax-2023-cost-changes and check out the unemployment tax rates for your state.

6-3. Want to know more about the concepts in this chapter? Go to one or more of the following sites. What are two or three things you notice about the information on the site?

www.smallbusiness.chron.com/example-employee-compensation-plan-10068.xhtml

http://yourbusiness.azcentral.com/labor-cost-distribution-report-26061.xhtml www.irs.gov/publications/p80/ar02.xhtml

6-4. Check out the employer payroll tax estimation tool at https://gusto.com/tools/employer-tax-calculator

6-5. Would you like to explore specific topics about being an employer in more depth? Check out https://www.employer.gov/

Continuing Payroll Project: Prevosti Farms and Sugarhouse

The first-quarter tax return needs to be filed for Prevosti Farms and Sugarhouse by April 30, 2023. For the taxes, assume the second February payroll amounts were duplicated for the March 10 and March 24 payroll periods, and the new benefit elections went into effect as planned (see Chapter 4). The form was completed and signed on April 11, 2023.

Benefit Information	Exempt Federal	FICA
Health insurance	Yes	Yes
Life insurance	Yes	Yes
Long-term care	Yes	Yes
FSA	Yes	Yes
401(k)	Yes	No
Gym	No	No

Owner's name: Toni Prevosti Address: 820 Westminster Road, Bridgewater, VT 05520 Phone: 802-555-3456

Number of employees	8
Gross quarterly wages (exclusive of fringe benefits)	$38,720.96
Federal income tax withheld	469.00
401(k) contributions	1,514.27
Section 125 withheld	4,080.00
Gym membership (add to all taxable wages, not included above)	90.00
Month 1 Deposit	–0–
Month 2 Deposit	2,691.49
Month 3 Deposit	3,077.58

Complete Form 941 for Prevosti Farms and Sugarhouse. Prevosti Farms and Sugarhouse was assigned EIN 22-6654454.

Form **941 for 2023:** Employer's QUARTERLY Federal Tax Return
(Rev. March 2023)   Department of the Treasury — Internal Revenue Service

950122

OMB No. 1545-0029

Employer identification number (EIN) ☐☐ – ☐☐☐☐☐☐☐

Name *(not your trade name)*

Trade name *(if any)*

Address
Number   Street   Suite or room number
City   State   ZIP code
Foreign country name   Foreign province/county   Foreign postal code

Report for this Quarter of 2023
(Check one.)

☐ **1:** January, February, March
☐ **2:** April, May, June
☐ **3:** July, August, September
☐ **4:** October, November, December

Go to *www.irs.gov/Form941* for instructions and the latest information.

Read the separate instructions before you complete Form 941. Type or print within the boxes.

Part 1:   Answer these questions for this quarter.

1. Number of employees who received wages, tips, or other compensation for the pay period including: *Mar. 12* (Quarter 1), *June 12* (Quarter 2), *Sept. 12* (Quarter 3), or *Dec. 12* (Quarter 4)   **1** ☐

2. Wages, tips, and other compensation . . . . **2** ☐

3. Federal income tax withheld from wages, tips, and other compensation . . . . . **3** ☐

4. If no wages, tips, and other compensation are subject to social security or Medicare tax   ☐ Check and go to line 6.

     Column 1   **Column 2**

5a   Taxable social security wages* . .   ☐   × 0.124 =   ☐

5a (i)   Qualified sick leave wages* . .   ☐   × 0.062 =   ☐

5a (ii)   Qualified family leave wages* . .   ☐   × 0.062 =   ☐

5b   Taxable social security tips . . .   ☐   × 0.124 =   ☐

5c   Taxable Medicare wages & tips . .   ☐   × 0.029 =   ☐

5d   Taxable wages & tips subject to Additional Medicare Tax withholding   ☐   × 0.009 =   ☐

*Include taxable qualified sick and family leave wages paid in this quarter of 2023 for leave taken after March 31, 2021, and before October 1, 2021, on line 5a. Use lines 5a(i) and 5a(ii) **only** for taxable qualified sick and family leave wages paid in this quarter of 2023 for leave taken after March 31, 2020, and before April 1, 2021.

5e   Total social security and Medicare taxes. Add Column 2 from lines 5a, 5a(i), 5a(ii), 5b, 5c, and 5d   **5e** ☐

5f   Section 3121(q) Notice and Demand—Tax due on unreported tips (see instructions) . .   **5f** ☐

6. Total taxes before adjustments. Add lines 3, 5e, and 5f . . . .   **6** ☐

7. Current quarter's adjustment for fractions of cents . . . .   **7** ☐

8. Current quarter's adjustment for sick pay . . . .   **8** ☐

9. Current quarter's adjustments for tips and group-term life insurance . . . . .   **9** ☐

10. Total taxes after adjustments. Combine lines 6 through 9 . . . .   **10** ☐

11a. Qualified small business payroll tax credit for increasing research activities. Attach Form 8974   **11a** ☐

11b. Nonrefundable portion of credit for qualified sick and family leave wages for leave taken before April 1, 2021 . . . .   **11b** ☐

11c. Reserved for future use . . . .   **11c** ▓

You MUST complete all three pages of Form 941 and SIGN it.

For Privacy Act and Paperwork Reduction Act Notice, see the back of the Payment Voucher.   Cat. No. 17001Z   Form **941** (Rev. 3-2023)

Name (not your trade name)	Employer identification number (EIN)
	951222
	—

Part 1: Answer these questions for this quarter. *(continued)*

11d Nonrefundable portion of credit for qualified sick and family leave wages for leave taken after March 31, 2021, and before October 1, 2021 . . . . 11d ▢ .

11e Reserved for future use . . . . 11e ▨ .

11f Reserved for future use . . . . ▨

11g **Total nonrefundable credits.** Add lines 11a, 11b, and 11d . . . . 11g ▢ .

12 **Total taxes after adjustments and nonrefundable credits.** Subtract line 11g from line 10 . 12 ▢ .

13a Total deposits for this quarter, including overpayment applied from a prior quarter and overpayments applied from Form 941-X, 941-X (PR), 944-X, or 944-X (SP) filed in the current quarter 13a ▢ .

13b Reserved for future use . . . . 13b ▨ .

13c Refundable portion of credit for qualified sick and family leave wages for leave taken before April 1, 2021 . . . . 13c ▢ .

13d Reserved for future use . . . . 13d ▨ .

13e Refundable portion of credit for qualified sick and family leave wages for leave taken after March 31, 2021, and before October 1, 2021 . . . . 13e ▢ .

13f Reserved for future use . . . . 13f ▨ .

13g **Total deposits and refundable credits.** Add lines 13a, 13c, and 13e . . . . . . 13g ▢ .

13h Reserved for future use . . . . 13h ▨ .

13i Reserved for future use . . . . 13i ▨ .

14 **Balance due.** If line 12 is more than line 13g, enter the difference and see instructions . . . 14 ▢ .

15 **Overpayment.** If line 13g is more than line 12, enter the difference ▢ . Check one: ☐ Apply to next return. ☐ Send a refund.

Part 2: Tell us about your deposit schedule and tax liability for this quarter.

If you're unsure about whether you're a monthly schedule depositor or a semiweekly schedule depositor, see section 11 of Pub. 15.

16 Check one: ☐ Line 12 on this return is less than $2,500 or line 12 on the return for the prior quarter was less than $2,500, and you didn't incur a $100,000 next-day deposit obligation during the current quarter. If line 12 for the prior quarter was less than $2,500 but line 12 on this return is $100,000 or more, you must provide a record of your federal tax liability. If you're a monthly schedule depositor, complete the deposit schedule below; if you're a semiweekly schedule depositor, attach Schedule B (Form 941). Go to Part 3.

☐ **You were a monthly schedule depositor for the entire quarter.** Enter your tax liability for each month and total liability for the quarter, then go to Part 3.

Tax liability: Month 1 ▢ .

Month 2 ▢ .

Month 3 ▢ .

Total liability for quarter ▢ . Total must equal line 12.

☐ **You were a semiweekly schedule depositor for any part of this quarter.** Complete Schedule B (Form 941), Report of Tax Liability for Semiweekly Schedule Depositors, and attach it to Form 941. Go to Part 3.

You MUST complete all three pages of Form 941 and SIGN it.

Page **2** Form **941** (Rev. 3-2023)

Name *(not your trade name)*	Employer identification number (EIN)
	—

950922

Part 3: Tell us about your business. If a question does NOT apply to your business, leave it blank.

17 If your business has closed or you stopped paying wages . . . . ☐ Check here, and

enter the final date you paid wages ___/___/___ ; also attach a statement to your return. See instructions.

18 If you're a seasonal employer and you don't have to file a return for every quarter of the year . . . ☐ Check here.

19 Qualified health plan expenses allocable to qualified sick leave wages for leave taken before April 1, 2021   19 _____

20 Qualified health plan expenses allocable to qualified family leave wages for leave taken before April 1, 2021   20 _____

21 Reserved for future use . . . . 21 _____

22 Reserved for future use . . . . 22 _____

23 Qualified sick leave wages for leave taken after March 31, 2021, and before October 1, 2021   23 _____

24 Qualified health plan expenses allocable to qualified sick leave wages reported on line 23   24 _____

25 Amounts under certain collectively bargained agreements allocable to qualified sick leave wages reported on line 23 . . . . 25 _____

26 Qualified family leave wages for leave taken after March 31, 2021, and before October 1, 2021   26 _____

27 Qualified health plan expenses allocable to qualified family leave wages reported on line 26   27 _____

28 Amounts under certain collectively bargained agreements allocable to qualified family leave wages reported on line 26 . . . . 28 _____

Part 4: May we speak with your third-party designee?

Do you want to allow an employee, a paid tax preparer, or another person to discuss this return with the IRS? See the instructions for details.

☐ Yes. Designee's name and phone number _____   _____

Select a 5-digit personal identification number (PIN) to use when talking to the IRS. ☐ ☐ ☐ ☐ ☐

☐ No.

Part 5: Sign here. You MUST complete all three pages of Form 941 and SIGN it.

Under penalties of perjury, I declare that I have examined this return, including accompanying schedules and statements, and to the best of my knowledge and belief, it is true, correct, and complete. Declaration of preparer (other than taxpayer) is based on all information of which preparer has any knowledge.

Sign your name here

Print your name here _____

Print your title here _____

Date ___/___/___   Best daytime phone _____

Paid Preparer Use Only   Check if you're self-employed . . . ☐

Preparer's name		PTIN	
Preparer's signature		Date	___/___/___
Firm's name (or yours if self-employed)		EIN	
Address		Phone	
City		State ____ ZIP code	

Page **3**   Form **941** (Rev. 3-2023)

Form 941-V, Payment Voucher

Purpose of Form

Complete Form 941-V if you're making a payment with Form 941. We will use the completed voucher to credit your payment more promptly and accurately, and to improve our service to you.

Making Payments With Form 941

To avoid a penalty, make your payment with Form 941 **only if**:

- Your total taxes after adjustments and nonrefundable credits (Form 941, line 12) for either the current quarter or the preceding quarter are less than $2,500, you didn't incur a $100,000 next-day deposit obligation during the current quarter, and you're paying in full with a timely filed return; or

- You're a monthly schedule depositor making a payment in accordance with the Accuracy of Deposits Rule. See section 11 of Pub. 15 for details. In this case, the amount of your payment may be $2,500 or more.

Otherwise, you must make deposits by electronic funds transfer. See section 11 of Pub. 15 for deposit instructions. Don't use Form 941-V to make federal tax deposits.

⚠ **CAUTION** Use Form 941-V when making any payment with Form 941. However, if you pay an amount with Form 941 that should've been deposited, you may be subject to a penalty. See Deposit Penalties in section 11 of Pub. 15.

Specific Instructions

Box 1—Employer identification number (EIN). If you don't have an EIN, you may apply for one online by visiting the IRS website at *www.irs.gov/EIN*. You may also apply for an EIN by faxing or mailing Form SS-4 to the IRS. If you haven't received your EIN by the due date of Form 941, write "Applied For" and the date you applied in this entry space.

Box 2—Amount paid. Enter the amount paid with Form 941.

Box 3—Tax period. Darken the circle identifying the quarter for which the payment is made. Darken only one circle.

Box 4—Name and address. Enter your name and address as shown on Form 941.

- Enclose your check or money order made payable to "United States Treasury." Be sure to enter your EIN, "Form 941," and the tax period ("1st Quarter 2023," "2nd Quarter 2023," "3rd Quarter 2023," or "4th Quarter 2023") on your check or money order. Don't send cash. Don't staple Form 941-V or your payment to Form 941 (or to each other).

- Detach Form 941-V and send it with your payment and Form 941 to the address in the Instructions for Form 941.

Note: You must also complete the entity information above Part 1 on Form 941.

Detach Here and Mail With Your Payment and Form 941.

Form 941-V
Department of the Treasury
Internal Revenue Service

Payment Voucher

Don't staple this voucher or your payment to Form 941.

OMB No. 1545-0029

2023

1 Enter your employer identification number (EIN).

2 Enter the amount of your payment.
Make your check or money order payable to "**United States Treasury**."

Dollars | Cents

3 Tax Period
- ○ 1st Quarter
- ○ 2nd Quarter
- ○ 3rd Quarter
- ○ 4th Quarter

4 Enter your business name (individual name if sole proprietor).

Enter your address.

Enter your city, state, and ZIP code; or your city, foreign country name, foreign province/county, and foreign postal code.

(Source: Internal Revenue Service)

Answers to Stop & Check Exercises

FUTA, SUTA, and Workers' Compensation

1.
FUTA: $7,000 × 29 × 0.006 =		$ 1,218.00
$2,575 × 0.006		15.45
FUTA liability		$ 1,233.45
SUTA: $30,100 × 25 × 0.042 =		$31,605.00
$60,090 × 0.042 =		2,523.78
(under the cap: 15,800 + 7,800 + 11,115 + 22,800 + 2,575)		
SUTA liability		$34,128.78
Total combined FUTA/SUTA liability = $1,218.00 + 34,128.78 =		$35,362.23

2.
FUTA: $7,000 × 10 × 0.006 =		420.00
($5,500 + 6,800) × 0.006 =		73.80
Total FUTA liability	$	493.80
SUTA: $12,000 × 8 × 0.0326 =		$ 3,129.60
$33,250 × 0.0326 =		1,083.95
(under the cap: 5,500 + 6,800 + 11,100 + 9,850)		
Total SUTA liability		$ 4,213.55
Total FUTA and SUTA =		$ 4,707.35

3.
Job Classification	Premium per $100 of Payroll	Estimated Payroll	Premium Due
Clerical Workers	$0.45	$104,550	$470.48
Jump Instructors	3.75	215,690	8,088.38
			$8,558.86

Reporting Periods

1. Monthly.
2. July 15.
3. Monday, the next business day.

Tax Forms

1. $2,414.48 = $8,462.96 − 2,980.24 − 3,068.24.
2. $105,000 (15 employees × $7,000).
3. $630.00 ($105,000 (from problem 2) × 0.006 FUTA rate).
4. $116,195 = $25,650 + 30,025 + 28,550 + 31,970.

Payroll-Related Business Expenses

1. Failure to file and failure to deposit penalties.
2. Payroll expenses relate to the company's profitability, worker productivity analyses, employee retention, and business competitiveness.

Labor Distribution Report

1. a. $300,000/10 employees = $30,000 per employee; office, $90,000; agricultural, $150,000; drivers, $60,000.
   b. Each department would be allocated $100,000 of the payroll.
2. Student answers may vary but should include: Department classification is the most appropriate because it matches the costs more closely to each department.

Benefit Analysis Report
1. Student answers may vary but should include: One of the purposes of compiling a benefit analysis report is to represent graphically all of the variables that make up an employee's compensation package. The benefit analysis report provides managers and supervisors with a budgetary tool to understand the full cost of hiring or dismissing employees. Additionally, the benefit analysis allows companies to compare benefits and employee costs to geographic or industry standards.
2. The benefit analysis report is an internal report for the company's management, and the annual total compensation report is meant to be distributed to the employee.

Chapter Seven

The Payroll Register, Employees' Earnings Records, and Accounting System Entries

This chapter will integrate the payroll register with the employees' earnings records and financial statements. In previous chapters, we have examined the effects of payroll on employees, employers, and governmental agencies. This chapter links *Generally Accepted Accounting Principles (GAAP)* with payroll elements we have explored in Chapters 1–6. We will discuss the debits and credits associated with payroll accrual and payment. For this chapter, we will use the accrual basis of accounting, which means that transactions are recognized when they take place.

Accounting entries are the transactions that place the payroll amounts into the correct ledger accounts. In automated systems, the software is designed to code each payroll item automatically to the correct General Ledger account. However, manual entries are necessary for the payroll accountant to record accurate expenses and period-end accruals in the correct month. This is the final step of the payroll cycle for each pay period and is the most important piece of the process from an accounting perspective. The final piece of this chapter will include examining how payroll costs affect a company's financial reports.

LEARNING OBJECTIVES

After studying Chapter 7, you should be able to:

LO 7-1	Connect the Payroll Register to the Employees' Earnings Records
LO 7-2	Describe Financial Accounting Concepts
LO 7-3	Complete Payroll-Related General Journal Entries
LO 7-4	Generate Payroll-Related General Ledger Entries

LO 7-5 Describe Payroll Effects on the Accounting System

LO 7-6 Explain Payroll Entries in Accounting Reports

GaudiLab/Shutterstock

The Accountant Shortage Caused by a Perfect Storm of Events

There is a shortage of accountants in the United States. The COVID-19 pandemic exacerbated the problem with remote working, the Great Resignation, and losses due to the disease. The shift of the profession to the use of technology and artificial intelligence (AI) affected accountants by causing stress as accountants learned how to use technology in ways not previously experienced. The stress caused by all these factors led to burnout among accountants, many of whom have left the profession.

Organizations such as the Institute of Management Accountants (IMA), the American Institute of Certified Professional Accountants (AICPA), and the American Accounting Association (AAA) are keenly aware of this trifecta of issues and is working to attract students to the profession. Although the profession may not be perceived as "cool" by outsiders and starting salaries are a little lower than those of other white-collar professions, organizations within the industry are working to address the issues and make the profession more attractive.

The simple fact is this: Accountants are needed by businesses, movie franchises, and people seeking assistance with their income tax filings. The profession is still growing, and professional organizations and postsecondary institutions are working to increase the number of students preparing to be accountants.

(Sources: AICPA; Going Concern; The CPA Journal)

> **Accurate reporting of payroll costs in the financial statements is a key part of GAAP compliance and decision-making. In Chapter 7, we will examine the accounting system entries for payroll costs, the effect on the company's financial reports, and how those reports influence managerial decisions.**

LO 7-1 Connect the Payroll Register to the Employees' Earnings Records

In previous chapters, we completed the payroll register, which is the primary tool used to compute payroll amounts. The payroll register has a related set of documents called employee earnings records. Information from the payroll register is used to complete payroll accounting entries in the General Journal.

Employee earnings records form the link between the accounting and the human resource departments and connect closely with the payroll register. The information contained within each row of the payroll register is transferred to the employee's earnings record, as shown in Figure 7-1.

The employee earnings record is the master document accountants use to track employees' filing status, deductions (mandatory, voluntary, and court-mandated), and year-to-date earnings. Remember, Social Security, FUTA, and SUTA taxes have annual earnings limits for each employee. Accountants update the employees' earnings records during each pay period to track all pay and tax deductions. Any employee changes, including pay rate and filing status, should be annotated in the earnings records as soon as possible to ensure the accuracy of the payroll.

Andrey_Popov/Shutterstock

FIGURE 7-1
Employee Earnings Record

EMPLOYEE EARNING RECORD

NAME		Hire Date		Dependent child <17	
ADDRESS		Date of Birth		Dependent other	
CITY/STATE/ZIP		Position		Step 4a W-4 Info	
TELEPHONE		Filing Status		Step 4b W-4 Info	
SOCIAL SECURITY				Step 4c W-4 Info	
NUMBER		Pay Rate		Hr/Wk/Mo/Yr	

Period Ended	Hrs Worked	Reg Pay	OT Pay	Holiday	Comm	Gross Pay	Sect 125	401(k)	Taxable Pay for Federal W/H	Taxable Pay for FICA

Pay for Federal W/H	Taxable Pay for FICA	Fed Inc. Tax	Social Sec. Tax	Medicare	Total Deduc	Net Pay	YTD Net Pay	YTD Gross Pay	Current Taxable for FUTA	Current Taxable for SUTA

> ### EXAMPLE: EMPLOYEE EARNINGS RECORD, INDIVIDUAL EMPLOYEE
> Using Emerson Quinn's example at Granite Hill Products, we will enter the data into the employee earnings record. Emerson is paid semimonthly.
>
> **EMPLOYEE EARNING RECORD**
>
> | | | | | | |
> |---|---|---|---|---|---|
> | Name | Emerson Quinn | Hire Date | 3/1/20XX | Dependent child <17 | 2 |
> | Address | 3450 Pine Street | Date of Birth | 12/15/19XX | Dependent other | 1 |
> | City/State/Zip | Laurel, DE 19956 | Position | Manager | Step 4a W-4 Info | none |
> | Telephone | 302-555-3948 | Filing Status | Married/Joint | Step 4b W-4 Info | none |
> | Social Security Number | 392-20-1030 | Pay Rate | $2,500 semimonthly | Step 4c W-4 Info | none |
>
> | Period Ended | Reg Hours Worked | OT Hours Worked | Regular Pay | OT Pay | Gross Pay | 401(k) | Section 125 | Taxable Pay for Federal | Taxable Pay for FICA |
> |---|---|---|---|---|---|---|---|---|---|
> | 8/31/20xx | | | 2,500.00 | | 2,500.00 | 150.00 | 225.00 | 2,125.00 | 2,275.00 |
> | | | | | | | | | | |
>
> | Taxable Pay for Federal | Taxable Pay for FICA | Fed Inc. Tax | Social Sec. Tax | Medicare | State Inc. Tax | Net Pay | YTD Net Pay | YTD Gross Pay | YTD FUTA |
> |---|---|---|---|---|---|---|---|---|---|
> | 2,125.00 | 2,275.00 | - | 141.05 | 32.99 | 82.88 | 1,868.09 | 16,085.00 | 30,000.00 | 7,000.00 |
>
> Note how the following employee information is reflected in the employee earnings record:
>
> - Address
> - Telephone number
> - Social Security number
> - Amount paid per month
> - Filing status
> - Pay basis
> - Hire date
> - Birthdate
> - Position
> - Pay rate
> - Pay period date
> - Year-to-date net pay
> - Year-to-date gross pay
>
> These items are common to most employee earnings records because of the connection between payroll and human resources. The information contained in the employee earnings record is used as the basis for the employee's Form W-2 and other company tax and benefits reporting.

The Employees' Earnings Records and Periodic Tax Reports

Period totals are also included in the earnings record. These totals facilitate the preparation of the quarterly and annual reports. Like any payroll record, the earnings records should be retained and destroyed simultaneously with other accounting records. Earnings records are typically included as supporting documents for internal copies of quarterly filings of Form 941 and state and local tax returns (where applicable). During a payroll audit, the documentation attached to the tax returns verifies the reports' information. A secondary use is that, in the event of a computer data failure, documents attached to payroll records can be used to re-create files.

In the village of Bellows Falls, Vermont, employees of the Windham Northeast Supervisory Union, the school district for the area, experienced payroll problems for several months. These problems involved overpayment or underpayment of earnings, missing or delayed deposits of retirement deductions, and other anomalies. The Supervisory Union attributed the problem to new payroll software with which employees were undertrained before use. An audit later found that the finance director committed material financial misstatement.

(Sources: Brattleboro Reformer; VTDigger)

Stop & Check

Employees' Earnings Register

1. How do the employees' earnings records relate to the payroll register?
2. Which of the following fields exist in both the payroll register and the employees' earnings records?
   a. Name
   b. Pay rate
   c. Job title
   d. Net pay
   e. Address
3. What reports and forms use information from the employees' earnings records?

LO 7-2 Describe Financial Accounting Concepts

kenchiro168/Shutterstock

Now that we have explored computing and reporting payroll data principles, it is time to connect the information to financial accounting concepts. In financial accounting, the fundamental accounting equation is **Assets = Liabilities + Owners' Equity.**

EXAMPLE: FINANCIAL ACCOUNTING CATEGORIES

Assets: Cash or other items used in the business's operation and amounts *owed* to the business by customers.

Liabilities: Amounts *owed* by the business to other people or companies.

Owners' equity: The net investment that the owner has in the business, including earnings kept in the business.

Financial business transactions, such as the movement of cash used in paying employees and remitting amounts to third parties, are tracked using the accounting system. A fundamental concept in accounting involves the accounting equation, which must remain in balance at all times. As such, transactions will either increase an account (or multiple accounts), decrease an account (or multiple accounts), or a combination thereof. To understand the concept of equation balance, T-accounts are the first step in understanding the classification process that is part of transaction analysis.

EXAMPLE: TRANSACTION ANALYSIS USING T-ACCOUNTS

Cassian Rossman, the owner of Rossman Designs, paid an independent contractor $4,000 for work done during the course of business on August 1, 2023. Accountants classify the transaction into two accounts: Assets and owners' equity. The cash account (asset) would decrease because the money was paid from the business. Cassian's expenses would increase because the company paid a contractor, which appears as an expense of the company and decreases the amount of owner's equity Cassian has in the business. Using the T-account approach, the transaction would look like this:

Contractor Expense	
Dr.	Cr.
4,000.00	

Cash	
Dr.	Cr.
	4,000.00

Debits and Credits

If accountants were to maintain T-accounts for all of a business's transactions, their work would be tedious and vulnerable to many errors. To simplify the addition and subtraction involved, accountants use the terms *debit* (abbreviated Dr.) and *credit* (abbreviated Cr.) to explain the transaction. In accounting parlance, *debit* means "the left side of the T-account," and *credit* means "the right side of the T-account." No connotation exists about good or bad with the use of these terms in accounting.

EXAMPLE: DEBIT AND CREDIT RULES

Debits Increase:	Credits Increase:
Expenses	Liabilities
Assets	Equity (Capital)
Dividends	Revenue

The General Journal

To simplify using T-accounts, accountants use a journal (called the *General Journal*) to record daily financial transactions. The transactions in the General Journal are recorded in chronological order. The General Journal is essentially one big T-account, has columns to record the debits and credits involved in each transaction, and contains a chronologically ordered list of transactions. Complementing the General Journal is the *General Ledger*, in which all journal transactions are recorded chronologically in their specific accounts.

In the transaction above, the transaction would appear in the General Journal as follows:

EXAMPLE: TRANSACTION IN THE GENERAL JOURNAL

Trans.	Date	Account Name & Description	Post Ref	Debit	Credit
1	8/1/2023	Contractor Expense	501	4,000.00	
		Cash	101		4,000.00
		Paid contractor			

Note certain accounting conventions present in the journal entry:

- The date of the transaction is noted.
- The debit part of the transaction is on the first line and is flush left in the column.
- The credit part of the transaction is on the second line and is indented slightly.
- A brief description of the transaction is on the third line.
- Account numbers are annotated in the Post Reference (Post Ref) column.
- The post reference in the General Journal is the General Ledger account number.

The General Ledger

Once the transaction has been recorded in the General Journal, the accountant posts the entry to corresponding General Ledger accounts. The following table notes that (1) the transaction itself is listed, and (2) the balance of each account is adjusted accordingly.

EXAMPLE: GENERAL LEDGER POSTING

Account: 101 – Cash

Date	Description	Post Ref.	Debit	Credit	Balance
8/1/2023	Paid contractor	J1		4,000.00	4,000.00

Account: 501 – Contractor Expense

Date	Description	Post Ref.	Debit	Credit	Balance
8/1/2023	Paid contractor	J1	4,000.00		4,000.00

The General Ledger account balances are used to generate the payroll reports discussed so far. The elements of the General Ledger and specific posting practices will appear later in this chapter.

> Despite the increase in accounting software use, the need for payroll accountants is growing in importance. Accountants are needed to monitor accuracy in recorded transactions and adapt to industry changes, especially the integration of technology and the growing use of artificial intelligence. Payroll accountants are particularly in demand because of the specific skills involved and the increasing need for complex payroll accounting demands.
>
> (Sources: Bloomberg BNA; In the Black)

Financial Accounting Concepts

Stop & Check

1. What is the fundamental accounting equation?
2. What increases the Wages and Salaries Payable account: a debit or a credit?
3. What increases the Wages and Salaries Expense account: a debit or a credit?

LO 7-3 Complete Payroll-Related General Journal Entries

Recording the specific General Journal entries that correspond to payroll activities is the next step in the process. General Journal entries are the original entry point for events to be recorded within the accounting system. A sample period payroll for L&L Grain follows.

> **EXAMPLE: L&L GRAIN PAYROLL DATA**
>
> L&L Grain pays its employees biweekly and operates on a calendar fiscal year (i.e., the year-end is December 31). The payroll accountant for L&L Grain has completed the payroll register for the January 27, 2023, payroll. Paychecks will be issued on January 31. Payroll totals are as follows:
>
> Gross pay: $18,050.00
> Federal income tax withheld: $1,500.00
> Social Security tax withheld: $1,084.38
> Medicare tax withheld: $253.61
> State income tax withheld: $577.60
> 401(k) contributions withheld: $750.00
> Health insurance premiums withheld: $560.00
> United Way contributions withheld: $180.00
> Net pay: $13,144.41
>
> The totals row of the payroll register would appear as follows:
>
> | Name | Gross Earnings | 401(k) Contributions | Insurance | Federal W/H | Social Security Tax | Medicare Tax | State W/H | United Way | Net Pay | Check No. |
> |---|---|---|---|---|---|---|---|---|---|---|
> | Totals | $18,050.00 | $750.00 | $560.00 | $1,500.00 | $1,084.38 | $253.61 | $577.60 | $180.00 | $13,144.41 | |

The payroll register is the tool used by payroll accountants to create pay-related journal entries. Notice the General Journal account in the following table and its connection to the payroll register. Here's how it works:

> **EXAMPLE: PAYROLL REGISTER TO GENERAL JOURNAL ENTRIES**
>
> | Payroll Register Column | General Journal Account | L&L Grain Amount |
> |---|---|---|
> | Gross Earnings | Salaries and Wages Expense | $18,050.00 |
> | 401(k) Contributions | 401(k) Contributions Payable | 750.00 |
> | Insurance | Health Insurance Premiums Payable | 560.00 |
> | Federal W/H | FIT Payable | 1,500.00 |
> | Social Security Tax | Social Security Tax Payable | 1,084.38 |
> | Medicare Tax | Medicare Tax Payable | 253.61 |
> | State W/H | State Income Tax Payable | 577.60 |
> | United Way | United Way Contributions Payable | 180.00 |
> | Net Pay | Salaries and Wages Payable | 13,144.41 |

As the payroll data is transferred from the payroll register to the General Journal, notice the following accounting categories:

- Account names ending with the word "expense" are classified as Expense accounts (remember Debit increases an expense).

- Account names ending with the word "payable" are classified as Liability accounts (remember Credit increases a liability).

Employee Pay-Related Journal Entries

The General Journal entry to record the employees' portion of the payroll and the issuance of the checks to employees is in two parts: the pay period end date and the pay disbursement date. In the following example, notice how the Salaries and Wages Payable account on the pay period date (January 27) relates to the pay disbursement date (January 31).

EXAMPLE: L&L GRAIN GENERAL JOURNAL PAYROLL ENTRIES—EMPLOYEE PAYROLL TRANSACTION

Date	Description	Account	Debit	Credit
Jan. 27	Salaries and Wages Expense	511	$18,050.00	
	FIT Payable	221		$ 1,500.00
	Social Security Tax Payable	222		1,084.38
	Medicare Tax Payable	223		253.61
	State Income Tax Payable	224		577.60
	401(k) Contributions Payable	225		750.00
	Health Insurance Premiums Payable	226		560.00
	United Way Contributions Payable	227		180.00
	Salaries and Wages Payable	231		13,144.41
Jan. 31	Salaries and Wages Payable	231	13,144.41	
	Cash	101		13,144.41

Employer Payroll-Related Journal Entries

The employer's share of the payroll is similarly recorded. L&L Grain's share of the payroll expenses follows:

EXAMPLE: L&L GRAIN EMPLOYER PAYROLL TAX OBLIGATIONS DATA

Social Security tax: $1,084.38
Medicare tax: $253.61
FUTA tax: $104.94
SUTA tax: $944.46

The General Journal entry for the employer's share of the payroll taxes follows. Notice that there is only one entry and that it is on the pay period date. Disbursements to tax authorities are often made at a later date.

EXAMPLE: L&L GRAIN GENERAL JOURNAL PAYROLL ENTRIES—EMPLOYER PAYROLL TAX TRANSACTION

Date	Description	Account	Debit	Credit
Jan. 27	Payroll Taxes Expense	512	$2,387.39	
	Social Security Tax Payable	222		$1,084.38
	Medicare Tax Payable	223		253.61
	FUTA Tax Payable	228		104.94
	SUTA Tax Payable	229		944.46

> Governmental audits in Louisiana found that although the number of employees decreased in 2020, payroll costs rose 5 percent. Auditors found the overall decrease in employees was due to employee resignation or retirement. The increase in payroll costs resulted from civil service wage and salary increases (averaging 16 percent from 2013 to 2020), additional overtime resulting from natural disasters during the same time period, and the increased use of independent contractors.
>
> (Source: Greater Baton Rouge Business Report)

Other Payroll-Related Journal Entries

What about the other deductions that L&L Grain withheld from its employees' pay? These other deductions, including federal and state income tax, 401(k) contributions, health insurance premiums, and United Way contributions, are liabilities of the company. These amounts will remain in the liability accounts until L&L Grain *remits* them, which means sending the collected money to the appropriate entity. Upon remittance, the General Journal entries will appear as a debit (decrease) to the Liability account and a credit (decrease) to Cash. An example of the January 27 payroll's voluntary deductions, paid to the appropriate companies on January 31, follows:

EXAMPLE: L&L GRAIN GENERAL JOURNAL PAYROLL ENTRIES—VOLUNTARY DEDUCTIONS REMITTANCE

Date	Description	Account	Debit	Credit
Jan. 31	401(k) Contributions Payable	225	$750.00	
	Health Insurance Payable	226	560.00	
	United Way Contribution Payable	227	180.00	
	Cash	101		$1,490.00

Remember, the remittance for governmental taxes has a specific schedule. The General Journal entry for the tax remittances would follow the same pattern as the voluntary deductions: Debit the liability account(s) and credit Cash.

Payroll Accruals and Reversals

A common occurrence is that a payroll period may be split between two months, as will be the case for L&L Grain. For example, most of the pay for the end of March will be paid on the March 24, 2023, pay date, but the payroll for March 27–31 will be paid on April 4. For accounting purposes, the accountant needs to record the payroll's accrual for March to represent the *expenses* and liabilities incurred during the period accurately, according to the matching principle of accounting. Some companies choose to record the period's expenses by *adjusting entries* and then reverse the entries after starting the next period to prevent confusion in the payroll accounting process.

Employee payroll data for L&L Grain is given below, followed by the related adjusting entry for the end of March:

EXAMPLE: L&L GRAIN ADJUSTING ENTRY—EMPLOYEE PAYROLL DATA

Gross pay: $16,245.00
Federal income tax withheld: $1,350.00
Social Security tax withheld: $1,007.19
Medicare tax withheld: $235.55
State income tax withheld: $519.84
Net pay: $13,132.42

The adjusting entry for March 31, 2023, would be as follows:

EXAMPLE: L&L GRAIN GENERAL JOURNAL—EMPLOYEE DATA ADJUSTING ENTRIES

Date	Description	Account	Debit	Credit
Mar. 31	Salaries and Wages Expense	511	$16,245.00	
	FIT Payable	221		$1,350.00
	Social Security Tax Payable	222		1,007.19
	Medicare Tax Payable	223		235.55
	State Income Tax Payable	224		519.84
	Salaries and Wages Payable	231		13,132.42

The amount for the employer's share would be as follows:

EXAMPLE: L&L GRAIN GENERAL JOURNAL—EMPLOYER PAYROLL TAX DATA ADJUSTING ENTRIES

Date	Description	Account	Debit	Credit
Mar. 31	Payroll Taxes Expense	512	$2,217.44	
	Social Security Tax Payable	222		$1,007.19
	Medicare Tax Payable	223		235.55
	FUTA Tax Payable (16,245 × 0.006)	228		97.47
	SUTA Tax Payable (16,245 × 0.054)	229		877.23

On April 3, 2023, the accountant could record a reversing entry as follows:

EXAMPLE: L&L GRAIN GENERAL JOURNAL—EMPLOYEE DATA REVERSING ENTRIES

Date	Description	Account	Debit	Credit
Apr. 3	FIT Payable	221	$ 1,350.00	
	Social Security Tax Payable	222	1,007.19	
	Medicare Tax Payable	223	235.55	
	State Income Tax Payable	224	519.84	
	Salaries and Wages Payable	231	13,132.42	
	Salaries and Wages Expense	511		$16,245.00

The *reversal* of the General Journal entries, used in accrual-based accounting to represent accrued employer payroll expenditures and liabilities at the end of the prior month, would be as follows:

EXAMPLE: L&L GRAIN GENERAL JOURNAL—EMPLOYER PAYROLL TAX DATA REVERSING ENTRIES

Date	Description	Account	Debit	Credit
Apr. 3	Social Security Tax Payable	222	$1,007.19	
	Medicare Tax Payable	223	235.55	
	FUTA Tax Payable	224	97.47	
	SUTA Tax Payable	229	877.23	
	Payroll Taxes Expense	512		$2,217.44

Note that not all companies and accountants use reversing entries. An advantage of using the reversing entry is that it simplifies the payroll process by avoiding calculating partial payroll periods due to the period's end. A disadvantage is a reversing entry becomes an additional entry that the accountant has to journalize and post. The use of reversing entries is at the company's discretion.

Stop & Check — Payroll and the General Journal

1. In the following General Journal entry, which account represents the employees' gross pay?

Description	Debit	Credit
Wages and Salaries Expense	$124,785.00	
Federal Income Tax Payable		$15,280.00
Social Security Tax Payable		7,736.67
Medicare Tax Payable		1,809.38
State Income Tax Payable		4,741.83
Wages and Salaries Payable		95,217.12

2. Based on the preceding General Journal entry, what would be the entry for the employer's share of the payroll taxes? Omit FUTA/SUTA taxes.

3. Lilac's Craft Warehouse has created a journal entry to accrue the payroll to be paid out in the following period. The accrual amounts are as follows:

	Debit	Credit
Wages and Salaries Expense	$42,795.00	
Federal Income Tax Payable		$6,234.00
Social Security Tax Payable		2,653.29
Medicare Tax Payable		620.53
State Income Tax Payable		1,626.21
Wages and Salaries Payable		31,660.97

What would be the reversing entry?

LO 7-4 Generate Payroll-Related General Ledger Entries

As mentioned before, the process of updating the General Ledger accounts with the transactions that the accountant records in the General Journal is called *posting*. Each account used in the General Journal has a corresponding General Ledger account used to track individual balances.

For the January 27 payroll and January 31 disbursements and remittances for L&L Grain that we discussed in the previous section, the General Ledger's postings would appear as depicted in Figure 7-2. Note that the entries shown reflect only the payroll entries for the end of January and February. April 3, 2023, is used as the reversing entry date because it is the first business day in the month.

> Human input and payroll software have been a growing area of concern for computer security. Phishing attacks, where a computer hacker tries to breach a company's software security, have been increasing in number and type, including situations in which a company's accounting data is compromised. These attacks have led to an increase in training costs for accounting personnel to educate them about the impacts of accounting breaches to ensure payroll accuracy.
>
> (Source: ADP)

FIGURE 7-2
L&L Grain's General Ledger

Account: 101—Cash

Date		Description	Post Ref	Debit	Credit	Balance Debit	Balance Credit
Jan	31	Beginning Balance				122,367.43	
Jan	31		J1		13,144.41	109,223.02*	
Jan	31		J4		1,490.00	107,733.02	

*Cash has a normal debit balance. It will decrease when the account is credited. 122,367.43 − 13,144.91 = 109,223.02.

Account: 221—FIT Payable

Date		Description	Post Ref	Debit	Credit	Balance Debit	Balance Credit
Jan	27		J1		1,500.00		1,500.00
Mar	31	Accrue Payroll	J5		1,350.00		2,850.00*
Apr	3	Reverse Payroll	J7	1,350.00			1,500.00

*Payable is a liability account. It will increase with a credit. 1,500 + 1,350 = 2,850.

Account: 222—Social Security Tax Payable

Date		Description	Post Ref	Debit	Credit	Balance Debit	Balance Credit
Jan	27		J1		1,084.38		1,084.38
Jan	27		J1		1,084.38		2,168.76
Mar	31	Accrue Payroll	J5		1,007.19		3,175.95
Mar	31	Accrue Payroll—Employer	J6		1,007.19		4,183.14
Apr	3	Reverse Payroll	J7	1,007.19			3,175.95
Apr	3	Reverse Payroll—Employer	J7	1,007.19			2,168.76

Account: 223—Medicare Tax Payable

Date		Description	Post Ref	Debit	Credit	Balance Debit	Balance Credit
Jan	27		J1		253.61		253.61
Jan	27		J1		253.61		507.22
Mar	31	Accrue Payroll	J5		235.55		742.77
Mar	31	Accrue Payroll—Employer	J6		235.55		978.32
Apr	3	Reverse Payroll	J7	235.55			742.77
Apr	3	Reverse Payroll—Employer	J8	235.55			507.22

Account: 224—State Income Tax Payable

Date		Description	Post Ref	Debit	Credit	Balance Debit	Balance Credit
Jan	27		J1		577.60		577.60
Mar	31	Accrue Payroll	J5		519.84		1,097.44
Apr	3	Reverse Payroll	J7	519.84			577.60

Account: 225—401(k) Contributions Payable

Date		Description	Post Ref	Debit	Credit	Balance Debit	Balance Credit
Jan	27		J1		750.00		750.00
Jan	31		J4	750.00			—

Account: 226—Health Insurance Payable

Date		Description	Post Ref	Debit	Credit	Balance Debit	Balance Credit
Jan	27		J1		560.00		560.00
Jan	31		J4	560.00			—

Account: 227—United Way Contributions Payable

Date		Description	Post Ref	Debit	Credit	Balance Debit	Balance Credit
Jan	27		J1		180.00		180.00
Jan	31		J4	180.00			—

Account: 228—FUTA Tax Payable

Date		Description	Post Ref	Debit	Credit	Balance Debit	Balance Credit
Jan	27		J1		104.94		104.94
Mar	31	Accrue Payroll—Employer	J6		97.47		202.41
Apr	3	Reverse Payroll—Employer	J8	97.47			104.94

Account: 229—SUTA Tax Payable

Date		Description	Post Ref	Debit	Credit	Balance Debit	Balance Credit
Jan	27		J1		944.46		944.46
Mar	31	Accrue Payroll—Employer	J6		877.23		1,821.69
Apr	3	Reverse Payroll—Employer	J8	877.23			944.46

Account: 231—Salaries and Wages Payable

Date		Description	Post Ref	Debit	Credit	Balance Debit	Balance Credit
Jan	27		J1		13,144.41		13,144.41
Jan	31		J1	13,144.41			—
Mar	31	Accrue Payroll	J5		13,132.42		13,132.42
Apr	3	Reverse Payroll	J7	13,132.42			—

Account: 512—Payroll Taxes Expense

Date		Description	Post Ref	Debit	Credit	Balance Debit	Balance Credit
Jan	27		J1	2,387.39		2,387.39	
Mar	31	Accrue Payroll	J6	2,217.44		4,604.83	
Apr	3	Reverse Payroll	J7		2,217.44	2,387.39	

Account: 511—Salaries and Wages Expense

Date		Description	Post Ref	Debit	Credit	Balance Debit	Balance Credit
Jan	27		J1	18,050.00		18,050.00	
Mar	31	Accrue Payroll	J6	16,245.00		34,295.00	
Apr	3	Reverse Payroll	J7		16,245.00	18,050.00	

General Ledger Posting Practices

Note that the columns in the General Ledger are similar to those in the General Journal. Some specific practices in the General Ledger are worth noting:

- Each line has a date. (In the General Journal, only the first line of each transaction is dated, except for month and year changes.)
- The description is usually left blank, except for adjusting, closing, and reversing entries.

The post reference number is a combination of letters and numbers. The letters denote the journal with which the entry correlates. In this case, "J" means that the original entry may be found in the General Journal. The number in the Post Ref column reflects the journal's page on which the entry is recorded.

The first pair of Debit and Credit columns is used to record the General Journal entry. If the account had a debit in the General Journal transaction, then the amount would appear in the Debit column in the first pair of columns in the General Ledger. The same practice is used for credits.

wk1003mike/Shutterstock

Account: Salaries and Wages Payable   Account No:

	Date	Description	Post Ref.	Debit	Credit	Balance Debit	Balance Credit	
1								1
2								2
3								3
4								4

Account: Payroll Taxes Expense   Account No:

	Date	Description	Post Ref.	Debit	Credit	Balance Debit	Balance Credit	
1								1
2								2
3								3
4								4

Jeanette Landin

The second pair of Debit and Credit columns is used to maintain a running balance of the account's total. These account balances are the foundation for the accountant's financial reports and are reviewed by managers, officers, customers, vendors, and governmental agencies.

Payroll Account Reconciliation

It is necessary for accountants to reconcile the payroll to ensure accuracy. If the payroll register has been completed correctly, then the reconciliation process should be smooth. However, errors could occur, and changes may need to be made after the payroll period ends. Since payroll accuracy is vital, the reconciliation process is strongly recommended. The following steps will help you reconcile your payroll:

Step	Actions
1. **Review hours worked and pay rate**	Check the accuracy of the employees' information, especially the hours worked and pay rate. If the firm has more than 20 employees, it may be best to check for new employees only.
2. **Review deductions**	Ensure that all deductions are accurate. It would be worthwhile to review the W-4s, especially for new employees, to make sure their tax deductions are correct. Check the computation of the deductions to ascertain the net pay figures.

Step	Actions
3. **Verify the General Journal and General Ledger**	Make sure your payroll entries are correct in both the General Journal and the General Ledger. Remember that the pay disbursed is a debit and that all deductions from employee pay are credits.
4. **Check your pay period and deposit schedule tax amounts**	Run or create a report in which you check your payroll taxes for monthly, semiweekly, or next-business-day tax deposits. This involves reviewing the General Ledger entries and checking them against the employees' payroll deductions. This will help prevent tax reporting errors.
5. **At the end of the quarter, check your tax deposits again**	Double-check your deposited tax amounts in your General Ledger and verify that you are depositing the correct amount with the quarterly return (if applicable).
6. **Verify the accuracy of each employee's W-2**	You should check the W-2 against the previous year's form to check for any discrepancies. Run a payroll register for the entire year to make sure that all deductions match the W-2s. You can also verify this information against the quarterly tax deposits, when applicable. Once you have verified the accuracy of the W-2s, ensure that Form W-3 accurately reports all amounts by verifying totals against the year's payroll register.

(Source: Nowsta)

Stop & Check

General Ledger Entries

1. The Medicare Tax Payable account for Gulf Coast Shrimp had a credit balance on June 23 of $2,540. As of the June 30 payroll, credits totaling $220 were posted to the Medicare Tax Payable account. What is the balance in the account as of June 30?

2. The post reference for the June 30 journal entry is J34. What does this post reference mean?

LO 7-5 Describe Payroll Effects on the Accounting System

create jobs 51/Shutterstock

Entries in the payroll system are posted in the General Ledger. When a company has an automated payroll system, the previously updated journal entries are automatically updated in the General Ledger. A payroll accountant needs to understand how the accounts should look after a payroll period is completed to ensure the automated system has performed correctly. Glitches within computer programs, although uncommon, may cause the payroll entry to be one-sided, in which only the debit or credit entry will flow through to the General Ledger. When this occurs, the payroll accountant must discover what has not been posted to ensure the entire transaction posts correctly.

Payroll-Related Business Expenses

Payroll represents an expense to the business. As such, it reduces the company's profitability proportional to the wages earned and taxes paid. When the payroll accountant accrues the payroll expenses, the company's expenses will also increase. Companies that operate using a cash basis (i.e., recording activities only when cash is received or spent) will see the effect of payroll expenses because those expenses reduce the income when wages and salaries are paid to the employees, when taxes are remitted to governmental agencies, and when other contributions are remitted.

> The pandemic created many opportunities for companies to utilize technology that expedited the move toward artificial intelligence (AI). A 2020 Deloitte survey showed that over 70 percent of organizations were either using or moving toward cloud-based payroll processing. AI can make many data entry and verification processes quicker and more accurate. AI can also assist employees by increasing the ability to offer early wage access. Compliance can also be improved through the increased use of automation for calculations and scheduling of deposits or auditing. With the increased number of remote workers, AI can also be useful for monitoring time reporting and labor expenses for any anomalies.
>
> AI was designed to solve many problems with data entry, such as human error and the time needed to ensure accuracy. Automating these transactions enables payroll accountants to strengthen their skill set and become better suited for higher critical thinking components of the payroll planning process. Creating a value-added component to the payroll accounting staff enables growth and positive employee morale and motivation.
>
> (Source: Oracle)

Besides administering specific payroll tasks, the payroll accountant's responsibility is to allocate employee expenses to specific accounts, departments, or business activities. Regardless of the employee's job description, some time can be allocated to jobs or customers. For example, a fabric manufacturing company will have sewing, accounting, and managerial staff. The bulk of the sewing staff's time will be allocated to specific jobs; however, some time will be considered overhead, such as cleaning or meetings, for example. The bulk of the accounting department's time will be considered overhead. However, if the accountant is working on analyzing a specific client's project, that time may be billed to the client. Managerial positions may also have specific times allocated to jobs depending on the client's needs and the position.

Payroll-Related Liabilities

Unpaid payroll obligations represent a liability to the company. These liabilities include amounts due to employees and money to be remitted for voluntary, mandatory, and mandated deductions. Until the money is remitted, the company holds it in its accounts. Specific examples of payroll liabilities include, but are certainly not limited to, the following:

Natee Meepian/Shutterstock

- Federal income tax
- FICA taxes
- Health insurance premiums
- Retirement plan contributions
- Child support garnishments
- Union dues

Employers have a *fiduciary* responsibility to remit all amounts withheld from employee pay. Remember that the Current Tax Payment Act requires employers to remit taxes promptly, according to governmental guidelines. For the other deductions, according to **29 CFR 2510**, employers are subject to ERISA provisions to protect all amounts due to employees and other recipients.

> The Employee Benefits Security Administration, a division of the Department of Labor, oversees employee contributions and estimated that there were approximately 73,000 employer-sponsored 401(k) plans in which employees had invested nearly $445 billion during 2020. The number of participants has historically increased at a rate of about 3 percent per year since 1975.
>
> (Source: DOL)

Chapter 7 The Payroll Register, Employees' Earnings Records, and Accounting System Entries 377

The Business Effects of Payroll

Stop & Check

1. Does the payment of employee wages increase or decrease the profitability of a business?
2. Why is it important to allocate payroll-related expenses properly?

LO 7-6 Explain Payroll Entries in Accounting Reports

When examining the *income statement, balance sheet*, and post-closing *trial balance* (Figures 7-3, 7-4, 7-5), payroll accountants must know what effect their work has on each statement. The financial statements are the key to integrating payroll accounting data and human resources information.

Natee Meepian/Shutterstock

Let's start with the income statement, which reports all revenue and expenses for a specific time period. These periods are usually monthly, quarterly, and annually. The income statement's function is to correlate all money received during the course of business operations with the money spent to earn that income. Within the expense section of the income statement, you will see several accounts that relate to payroll. The Salaries and Wages Expense represents the gross pay from the period. Each of the taxes we have discussed is listed. Note the expenses related to the taxes are paid by the employer and forwarded to the taxing authority; thus, there is no accrued federal income tax expense. Expenses related to the employer portion of retirement fund matching, health benefits, or other benefits are also located within the income statement.

FIGURE 7-3
Income Statement Presentation (Partial)

L&L Grain Income Statement For the Quarter Ended March 31, 2023		
Revenue:		
Sales Revenue		$78,303.40
Expenses:		
Salaries and Wages Expense	$34,295.00	
Payroll Taxes Expense	4,604.83	
Utilities Expense	1,725.00	
Telephone Expense	884.00	
Rent Expense	5,175.00	
Total Expenses		46,683.83
Net Income for Quarter		$31,619.57

The balance sheet is prepared for a single date, unlike the income statement. In the balance sheet, any unpaid liabilities to be paid during the next 12 months will be reported in the current liability section. In accrual accounting, there may also be end-of-period entries to accrue for payroll earned by the employees. Additional liability accounts for accrued salaries, accrued hourly wages, accrued holiday pay, and accrued paid time off could also appear, depending on the end of the period and the types of employees and benefits which the company operates. If employees have taken payroll advances, which are amounts to be repaid by the employee, these are reported in the current assets section as receivables.

The trial balance contains all accounts the company uses, spanning all of the financial statements. Like the balance sheet, the trial balance is a report on a single date. The accounts listed on the trial balance appear in the order of the chart of accounts. In the United States, these are typically listed assets first: short-term and then long-term. Following that are the liabilities:

FIGURE 7-4
Balance Sheet Presentation (Partial)

L&L Grain Balance Sheet March 31, 2023		
Assets:		
Cash		$110,058.03
Accounts Receivable		39,723.67
Equipment		15,289.00
Inventory		225,960.00
Total Assets		$391,030.70
Liabilities:		
Accounts Payable		4,085.27
FIT Payable		2,850.00
Social Security Tax Payable		4,183.14
Medicare Tax Payable		978.32
State Income Tax Payable		1,097.44
Health Insurance Payable		560.00
FUTA Tax Payable		202.41
SUTA Tax Payable		1,821.69
Salaries and Wages Payable		13,132.42
Total Liabilities		28,910.69
Owners' Equity		
L. Wilson, Capital		330,500.74
Retained Earnings		31,619.27
Total Owners' Equity		362,120.01
Total Liabilities and Owners' Equity		$391,030.70

FIGURE 7-5
Post-Closing Trial Balance Presentation

L&L Grain Post-Closing Trial Balance March 31, 2023		
Account	Debit	Credit
Cash	$110,058.03	
Accounts Receivable	39,723.67	
Inventory	225,960.00	
Equipment	15,289.00	
Accounts Payable		$ 4,085.27
FIT Payable		2,850.00
Social Security Tax Payable		4,183.14
Medicare Tax Payable		978.32
State Income Tax Payable		1,097.44
Health Insurance Payable		560.00
FUTA Tax Payable		202.41
SUTA Tax Payable		1,821.69
Salaries and Wages Payable		13,132.42
L. Wilson, Capital		330,500.74
Retained Earnings		31,619.27
	$391,030.70	$391,030.70

short-term and then long-term. Equity accounts are listed next, followed by revenues and expenses. When examining the trial balance, the important thing to remember is that it must balance: Debits must equal credits. Should one side not balance with the other, the accountant must determine why and correct the error. A post-closing trial balance will have already closed the revenue, expense, and dividends accounts into the retained earnings account.

The purpose of all financial statements is to provide information to the stakeholders of a company. Stakeholders of a company include (but are certainly not limited to) company managers, governmental agencies, creditors, and employees who use the information to decide the business. Financial statements are prepared per GAAP guidelines to facilitate the presentation of the statements among various businesses. Managers of a company, in particular, use financial reports to make decisions about labor and benefits planning.

> Companies are increasingly using application programming interfaces (APIs) to integrate financial data among their departments. The use of APIs fosters the sharing of information to improve company performance, employee access to their payroll and employment records, and transparency of financial data within the business. This software also allows payroll accountants to engage more fully in decision-making and other functions that involve critical thought and planning.
>
> (Source: What's Next Media)

Labor Reports

The payroll accountant may provide specific *labor reports* to management or department heads. These reports may have a variety of names and content depending on the needs of the business.

- The *labor usage* report designates where the labor is used within the company. When a company has several employees who work in different departments, the labor usage report can help determine overhead *allocations* by the department and the need for increased or decreased staff within a specific department.
- The *billable vs. nonbillable* report tracks the time employees have spent specifically on projects for which customers are paying. This report allows managers to determine if the time allocated to the job-costing process is accurate, if the company is operating efficiently, or if the employee is taking too long on a specific job.
- *Overtime* reports allow managers to determine how much overtime has been paid to employees during a specified time period. This report allows managers to monitor labor distribution and scheduling to ensure adherence to budget guidelines.
- Employers can also make use of *trend reports* for payroll staffing needs. Trend reports of income over the period of a year or two can reveal seasonal increases or decreases in business. An informed business manager will know if the company needs to have seasonal or temporary workers for short-term increases. If the trend reflects a steady increase in business, the manager may determine that hiring a new employee would be beneficial. Analyzing the company's staffing needs compared to income projections may also lead managers to know if they need to lay off personnel, reduce the hours of existing employees, or restructure company operations.

> As of 2022, over 164 million Americans were employed and worked at least 15 hours per week. According to the Bureau of Labor Statistics, the level of employment in the United States has grown since 2010 and is projected to continue doing so through 2029. Because the number and type of employees are increasing, payroll accounting will become more complex. Understanding payroll accounting is a vital skill needed by all industries, government employers, and private-sector companies. It is safe to state that payroll accounting is a profession that will continue to be needed for the foreseeable future.
>
> (Source: BLS)

Labor Reports

Stop & Check

1. Which of the following reports are affected by the payroll of an organization?
   a. Trial balance
   b. Statement of owners' equity
   c. Interest statement
   d. Income statement
   e. Balance sheet
2. What is a specific type of report that the payroll accountant provides to managerial staff?
3. What are trend reports?

FIGURE 7-6
Payroll Process Flowchart

Company with employees?
- Is it payday?
- How much should each employee be paid?
- Is managerial approval needed?

Computed deductions?
- Pre-tax deductions?
- Mandatory deductions?
- Voluntary deductions?
- Mandated deductions?

Payroll register completion?
- Total, prove, and rule?
- Approval for pay disbursement?
- Correct pay method selected?
- Pay disbursed at the right time?

Payroll tax remittance?
- Payroll tax deposits and remittance forms completed?
- Forms and remittances checked for accuracy?
- Payroll taxes deposited on time?

Voluntary deductions remittances?
- Are all outgoing remittances verified?
- Are all outgoing remittances submitted on time?

Accounting entries?
- Journalize and post employee payroll?
- Journalize and post the employer's share of the payroll?
- Employee earnings records updated?
- Are all financial statements completed?

Trends to Watch

ECONOMIC EFFECTS OF PAYROLL

Although payroll accounting principles remain relatively stable, the role that payroll plays in the broader context of a business are subject to change. Some developments in payroll accounting in the business context that have changed since 2018 include the following:

- Accountants seeking roles as consultants (as opposed to technicians) because of increases in automation and technology that foster lower-level work completion.
- Increases in labor costs for employers resulting from changes to the minimum wage.
- Expansion of the gig economy has led to judicial review of employment practices.
- Expanded integration of financial technology to improve the automation of accounting transactions.
- Changes to federal reporting requirements to streamline and standardize company submissions.

Future trends to watch include:

- Payroll accounting will become more centralized to work with a remote workforce.
- Increased automation will lead to added transparency and communication among company personnel.
- Company resource allocation will adjust because of increased automation of tasks.
- Company growth will change because of remote work abilities.

Summary of the Payroll Register, Employees' Earnings Records, and Accounting System Entries

The payroll register and employees' earnings records are two tools that payroll accountants need to accurately maintain their work. Both records track employee compensation and contain information about company liabilities to governmental agencies and other organizations. These records also provide information for company decision-makers by yielding data about labor distribution and cost allocation. Payroll records provide information about benefits given to employees and how those benefits affect a business's profitability. Information contained in these sources and tools used by payroll accountants provides integral insights for managerial functions.

The final piece of the payroll cycle is the creation of accounting system entries. Like other business transactions, recording, paying the payroll, and remitting money to governmental agencies and other firms require General Journal and General Ledger entries. Business owners and departmental managers use this accounting information to measure business plans' effectiveness and plan both short- and long-term strategies. As an integral part of business operations, payroll-related expenses and liabilities represent an employer's financial duty, affect the financial reports, and influence its viability.

With this chapter's explanation of accounting system entries, we have now completed our journey through the payroll process. We have investigated the history of payroll, its many aspects and functions, and the importance of employee compensation within a business context.

We hope that after finishing this book, you will understand that payroll accounting is complex, involves many different decisions along the way, and deserves your close attention.

Key Points

- The payroll register connects directly to the employees' earnings records.
- The employees' earnings records link accounting and human resources and contain information from the payroll register.
- Accounting principles assist in the classification of payroll costs and organizational performance.

- Payroll transactions are recorded in the General Journal and posted to General Ledger accounts.
- The balances in the General Ledger accounts form the foundation of financial reports.
- Payroll costs represent an expense of the business.
- Employees are assigned to departments to foster accurate measurements of business segment profitability.
- Accounting reports provide managers with insights into company profitability and stability.
- Payroll-related transactions contain both the expenses and liabilities of a company.
- Employers have a fiduciary duty to ensure that all amounts deducted from employee pay are remitted to the appropriate entity.
- The increase in the automation of accounting information points to a need for educated, competent payroll professionals.
- Trend reports offer business leaders insight into changes in labor costs over a period.
- Financial reports contain the data that connects the payroll and human resources functions within a company.

Vocabulary

Accrual	Fiduciary	Liability
Adjusting entries	General Journal	Owners' equity
Allocation	General Ledger	Posting
Asset	Generally Accepted	Remit
Balance sheet	Accounting Principles	Reversal
Credit	(GAAP)	Trial balance
Debit	Income statement	Trend Report
Expense	Labor usage	

Review Questions

1. What types of accounts does a debit increase?
2. What types of accounts does a credit increase?
3. Where are the first accounting entries recorded?
4. Once recorded, where are the entries posted?
5. What is the purpose of the payroll register?
6. What information is contained in employees' earnings records?
7. How are the payroll register and the employees' earnings records related?
8. What type of account is debited for the gross pay?
9. What are three of the accounts that may be credited for the employee payroll?
10. What two accounts are affected upon issuance of paychecks?
11. What accounts are debited and credited for the employer's share of the payroll expenses?
12. How do payroll expenses affect the income statement and balance sheet?
13. How can companies use payroll information that is reported in the financial statements to determine labor distribution?
14. How can a company's payroll information contained in financial reports assist in corporate planning?
15. How do the payroll register and employees' earnings records help employers meet their responsibilities to different groups, such as the employees and governmental agencies?
16. What is the term for the responsibility that employers have for payroll deductions under ERISA?

Exercises Set A

E7-1A.
LO 7-1

Which column exists in the employees' earnings records but not in the payroll register?
a. Gross pay
b. Net pay
c. YTD net pay
d. 401(k) contributions

E7-2A.
LO 7-1

What is the connection between the employees' earnings records and payroll tax reporting? (Select all that apply.)
a. Employees' earnings records do not connect with payroll tax reporting.
b. Employees' earnings records may be used to ensure the accuracy of payroll tax reporting.
c. Employees' earnings records contain details of payroll tax reporting and may be considered as source documents.
d. Employees' earnings records contain year-to-date gross pay, which reflects when employees reach tax bases.

E7-3A.
LO 7-2

A credit increases which of the following types of accounts? (Select all that apply.)
a. Liabilities
b. Expenses
c. Revenues
d. Assets

E7-4A.
LO 7-3

Which amounts on the payroll register reduce federal withholding tax but are *not* deducted for FICA tax computations? (Select all that apply.)
a. Charitable contributions
b. Nonqualified pre-tax insurance
c. Retirement plan (e.g., 401(k)) contributions
d. Garnishments

E7-5A.
LO 7-4

What is always true about the General Ledger? (Select all that apply.)
a. The process of transferring amounts from the General Journal to the General Ledger is called posting.
b. The General Ledger is a way to represent monthly groupings of entire General Journal entries.
c. The General Ledger contains information about the individual accounts used in General Journal transactions.
d. A debit to an account in a General Journal transaction is a debit to that account in the General Ledger.

E7-6A.
LO 7-4, 7-5, 7-6

How does a payroll accountant use the information in the General Ledger? (Select all that apply.)
a. The account balances form the basis for accounting reports.
b. The payroll accountant uses General Ledger balances to determine the effectiveness of individual employees.
c. General Ledger account balances aggregate data to determine payroll costs.
d. Payroll expenses contained in the General Ledger are not used to make personnel decisions.

E7-7A.
LO 7-6

Which of the following accounts would appear on the balance sheet? (Select all that apply.)
a. Payroll taxes expense
b. 401(k) contributions payable
c. 401(k) employer contributions expense
d. Social Security tax payable

E7-8A.
LO 7-6

What is always true about the income statement? (Select all that apply.)
a. Only accounts with balances at the end of the period are included.
b. All income and expense accounts are included in the report.
c. All liabilities are included in the report.
d. The report is prepared for a single date.

E7-9A.
LO 7-6

The purpose of a labor report is to do what? (Select all that apply.)
a. Report an individual employee's regular time and overtime.
b. Reflect all expenses of a firm.
c. Promote analysis of payroll expenses.
d. Update managers about payroll on a daily basis.

E7-10A.
LO 7-5, 7-6

Which law governs the fiduciary responsibility that employers have with regard to employees' payroll deductions?
a. FICA
b. FLSA
c. ERISA
d. ACA

Problems Set A

P7-1A.
LO 7-1

Harper Morgan owns White Mountain Assessments in Laconia, New Hampshire. The standard workweek is 40 hours. For the weekly payroll ending September 8, 2023, disbursements dated September 13, 2023, complete the payroll register. Use the wage-bracket method in the federal tax table from Appendix C. No employee has exceeded the Social Security tax wage base. All employees submitted a 2023 Form W-4, and no box was checked in Step 2. Total, prove, and rule the entries.

P/R End Date: 9/8/2023 Company Name: White Mountain Assessments
P/R Date: 9/13/2023 Disbursement Date:

Name	Filing Status	Dependents	Hourly Rate or Period Wage	No. of Regular Hours	No. of Overtime Hours	No. of Holiday Hours	Commissions	Gross Earnings	401(k)	Sect. 125	Taxable Wages for Federal W/H	Taxable Wages for FICA
Rosenberg, A.	Single	2 < 17	$16.25	40					$50.00			
Cintron, G.	Married/Joint	2 < 17; 1 Other	$18.20	39.25					$75.00			
Freeman, S.	Married/Joint	1 Other	$17.55	36								
Crosby, L.	Single	None	$19.25	40	4							
Kepes, T.	Single	2 Other	$16.75	37.5					$60.00	$20.00		
Hankard, J.	Married/Joint	2 < 17	$18.45	40					$75.00			
Nguyen, L.	Single	1 < 17	$15.75	40	7					$15.00		
Totals												

Name	Gross Earnings	Taxable Wages for Federal W/H	Taxable Wages for FICA	Federal W/H	Social Security Tax	Medicare Tax	State W/H	Garnishment	United Way	Net Pay	Check No.
Rosenberg, A.											
Cintron, G.									$10.00		
Freeman, S.								$100.00			
Crosby, L.									$25.00		
Kepes, T.											
Hankard, J.									$10.00		
Nguyen, L.											
Totals											

P7-2A.
LO 7-1

The employee earnings record for Lyric Crosby of White Mountain Assessments is listed below. Record the earnings from the September 8 weekly pay in P7-1A.

EMPLOYEE EARNING RECORD

NAME	Lyric Crosby	Hire Date	April 1, 2018	Dependent child <17	0
ADDRESS	1856 Henniker Road	Date of Birth	February 1, 1985	Dependent other	0
CITY/STATE/ZIP	Weare, NH 03558	Position	Assessor	Step 4a W-4 Info	none
TELEPHONE	603-555-7895	Filing Status	Single	Step 4b W-4 Info	none
SOCIAL SECURITY NUMBER	634-98-1463	Pay Rate	$19.25/hour	Step 4c W-4 Info	none

Period Ended	Regular Hours Worked	Overtime Hours Worked	Regular Pay	Overtime Pay	Gross Pay	401(k)	Section 125	Taxable Wages for Federal W/H	Taxable Wages for FICA
9/1/2023	40		$770.00		$770.00	—	—	$770.00	$770.00
9/8/2023									

Taxable Wages for Federal W/H	Taxable Wages for FICA W/H	Fed W/H	Social Sec. Tax	Medicare Tax	State W/H	United Way	Net Pay	YTD Net Pay	YTD Gross Pay
$770.00	$770.00	$56.00	$47.74	$11.17	—	$25.00	$627.09	$22,748.15	$27,750.00

P7-3A.
LO 7-2, 7-3

Using the payroll register from P7-1A for White Mountain Assessments, complete the General Journal entry for the employees' pay for the September 8 pay date. Paychecks will be issued on September 13.

	Date	Description	Post Ref.	Debit	Credit	
1						1
2						2
3						3
4						4
5						5
6						6
7						7
8						8
9						9
10						10
11						11
12						12

P7-4A.
LO 7-2, 7-3

Using the payroll register from P7-1A for White Mountain Assessments, complete the General Journal entry for the employer's share of the payroll taxes for the September 8 payroll end date. Assume 5.4 percent SUTA and 0.6 percent FUTA tax rates and that only $3,542.50 is subject to FUTA and SUTA taxes.

	Date	Description	Post Ref.	Debit	Credit	
1						1
2						2
3						3
4						4
5						5
6						6
7						7
8						8
9						9

P7-5A. Using the employee payroll entry from P7-3A, post the September 8 employee pay for White Mountain Assessments to the selected General Ledger accounts shown next. This will have a Posting Reference of J4.

LO 7-2, 7-3

Account: Salaries and Wages Payable

	Date	Description	Post Ref.	Debit	Credit	Balance Debit	Balance Credit	
1								1
2								2
3								3
4								4
5								5
6								6

Account: Employee Federal Income Tax Payable

	Date	Description	Post Ref.	Debit	Credit	Balance Debit	Balance Credit	
1								1
2								2
3								3
4								4
5								5
6								6

Account: Social Security Tax Payable

	Date	Description	Post Ref.	Debit	Credit	Balance Debit	Balance Credit	
1								1
2								2
3								3
4								4
5								5
6								6

Account: Medicare Tax Payable

	Date	Description	Post Ref.	Debit	Credit	Balance Debit	Balance Credit	
1								1
2								2
3								3
4								4
5								5
6								6

Account: Salaries and Wages Expense

	Date	Description	Post Ref.	Debit	Credit	Balance Debit	Balance Credit	
1								1
2								2
3								3
4								4
5								5
6								6
7								7

P7-6A. Using the employee payroll entry from P7-3A, complete the General Journal entry for the issuance of the pay for the September 8 payroll end date. The date of the checks is September 13, 2023.

LO 7-2, 7-3

	Date	Description	Post Ref.	Debit	Credit	
1						1
2						2
3						3
4						4
5						5

P7-7A. Using the employer payroll entry from P7-4A, post the employees' share of the Social Security and Medicare taxes along with the employer's share of payroll taxes for September 8 pay at White Mountain Assessments to the appropriate General Ledger accounts.

LO 7-2, 7-3, 7-4

Account: Social Security Tax Payable

	Date	Description	Post Ref.	Debit	Credit	Balance Debit	Balance Credit	
1								1
2								2
3								3
4								4
5								5
6								6
7								7

Account: Medicare Tax Payable

	Date	Description	Post Ref.	Debit	Credit	Balance Debit	Balance Credit	
1								1
2								2
3								3
4								4
5								5
6								6
7								7

Account: Federal Unemployment Tax Payable

	Date	Description	Post Ref.	Debit	Credit	Balance Debit	Balance Credit	
1								1
2								2
3								3
4								4
5								5
6								6
7								7

Account: State Unemployment Tax Payable

	Date	Description	Post Ref.	Debit	Credit	Balance Debit	Balance Credit	
1								1
2								2
3								3
4								4
5								5
6								6
7								7

Account: Payroll Taxes Expense

	Date	Description	Post Ref.	Debit	Credit	Balance Debit	Balance Credit	
1								1
2								2
3								3
4								4
5								5
6								6
7								7

P7-8A.
LO 7-2, 7-3

KMH Industries is a monthly schedule depositor of payroll taxes. For the month of August 2023, the payroll taxes (employee and employer share combined) were as follows:

Social Security tax: $3,252.28
Medicare tax: $760.61
Employee federal income tax: $2,520.00

Create the General Journal entry for the remittance of the taxes. The entry should be dated September 13, 2023. Use check 2052 in the description.

	Date	Description	Post Ref.	Debit	Credit	
1						1
2						2
3						3
4						4
5						5
6						6
7						7
8						8

P7-9A.
LO 7-2, 7-3

Oakley Breeders has the following voluntary withholdings to remit:
AFLAC payable: $560.00
401(k) payable: $1,280.00
Garnishments payable: $375.00
United Way contributions payable: $200.00

Create the General Journal entry on June 9, 2023, for the remittance of these withheld amounts.

	Date	Description	Post Ref.	Debit	Credit	
1						1
2						2
3						3
4						4
5						5
6						6
7						7

P7-10A.
LO 7-5, 7-6

Brighton Rowe is the payroll accountant for Great Lake Lamps. The company's management has requested an analysis of the payroll effects on the expenses of the company. Explain which accounting report(s) Brighton would use to construct the analysis. How would Brighton explain the purpose of labor expenses as they affect company productivity?

P7-11A.
LO 7-6

The new vice president of marketing for your company has asked to meet with you regarding the purpose and location of payroll entries in accounting reports. What is your response to the vice president?

Exercises Set B

E7-1B.
LO 7-1

Which of the following exists in both the employees' earnings records and the payroll register? (Select all that apply.)
a. Employee birthdate
b. Social Security number
c. Hourly rate or period wage
d. Employee name

E7-2B.
LO 7-1

How do the payroll register and employees' earnings records connect with payroll tax determination and remittance? (Select all that apply.)
a. Payroll register column totals contain information about pay period tax withholdings.
b. Employees' earnings records have pertinent information to determine individual taxable wage base attainment.
c. Payroll registers records reflect which employees have reached the Medicare additional tax.
d. Payroll registers contain specific information about each employee's raise history.

E7-3B.
LO 7-2

Which of the following are categories contained in the fundamental accounting equation? (Select all that apply.)
a. Liabilities
b. Revenues
c. Expenses
d. Owners' equity

E7-4B. LO 7-2

Which of the following principles are always true about financial accounting? (Select all that apply.)
a. Transactions are posted first to the General Ledger.
b. Debits = Credits.
c. Each transaction involves at least two accounts.
d. The balance sheet contains all accounts.

E7-5B. LO 7-3

What is true about expenses and liabilities? (Select all that apply.)
a. Expenses usually have the word "expense" in the account title.
b. Expenses represent additional sums earned by the company.
c. Liabilities represent sums of money owed by third parties to the company.
d. Liabilities usually have the word "payable" in the account title.

E7-6B. LO 7-3, 7-4, 7-5

How do payroll-related expenses affect financial statements? (Select all that apply.)
a. Payroll expenses may be allocable to work performed for a firm's vendors.
b. Payroll expense accounts are reported on the income statement.
c. The period's gross earnings are reported on the balance sheet.
d. Payroll expenses reduce the net income of a company.

E7-7B. LO 7-6

Which of the following payroll-related accounts appear on the balance sheet? (Select all that apply.)
a. Wages and salaries payable
b. Medicare tax expense
c. Employee federal income tax payable
d. FUTA tax expense

E7-8B. LO 7-2, 7-5

What is the purpose of payroll-related accrual and reversal entries on financial statements? (Select all that apply.)
a. Accrual entries represent payroll amounts incurred but not yet paid.
b. Reversing entries represent the disbursement of accrued payroll prior to the end of the payroll period.
c. Accrual entries are used to improve the accuracy of the net income for a period.
d. Reversing entries are omitted from financial statements.

E7-9B. LO 7-6

Managers use labor reports to do which of the following? (Select all that apply.)
a. Analyze labor trends
b. Determine staffing needs
c. Ensure FLSA wage and hour compliance
d. Formulate strategic plans for the company

E7-10B. LO 7-5, 7-6

To which parties does an employer have a fiduciary duty when it incurs payroll liabilities? (Select all that apply.)
a. Customers
b. Employees
c. Government
d. Vendors

Problems Set B

P7-1B. LO 7-1

Nat Crossman owns Appalachian Limited Home Design in Versailles, Kentucky. Complete the payroll register for the weekly payroll dated March 10, 2023. Checks will be issued on March 15, 2023. Use the wage-bracket method in the federal tax table in Appendix C. Assume 5 percent state income tax, and the same deductions for federal tax apply to the state. No employee has exceeded the Social Security wage base. Assume all employees submitted a 2023 Form W-4. For employees with M/S (Married, filing single), use the single rate. Total, prove, and rule the entries.

P/R End Date: 3/10/2023
Check Date: 3/15/2023
Company Name: Appalachian Limited Home Design
Check Date:

Name	Filing Status	Dependents	Hourly Rate or Period Wage	No. of Regular Hours	No. of Overtime Hours	No. of Holiday Hours	Commissions	Gross Earnings	401(k)	Sect. 125	Taxable Wages for Federal W/H	Taxable Wages for FICA
Brooks, S.	Single	2 < 17	$15.25	40					$50.00			
Choi, L.	Married/Joint	3 < 17, 1 Other	$19.70	40	4					$20.00		
Hammersmith, R.	Married/Single	1 < 17, 2 Other	$17.25	38						$35.00	$10.00		
Agarwal, K.	Single	1 < 17	$18.20	36					$20.00			
Potter, D.	Married/Joint	1 Other	$15.50	40	7							
Ito, C.	Single	None	$16.85	40								
Crocker, T.	Married/Joint	2 < 17	$15.00	38.5					$45.00	$10.00		
Kollie, A.	Married/Joint	None	$18.10	40					$25.00			
Totals												

Name	Gross Earnings	Taxable Wages for Federal W/H	Taxable Wages for FICA	Federal W/H	Social Security Tax	Medicare W/H	State W/H Tax	Garnishment	United Way	Net Pay	Check No.
Brooks, S.									$10.00		
Choi, L.											
Hammersmith, R.											
Agarwal, K.									$60.00		
Potter, D.									$50.00		
Ito, C.											
Crocker, T.											
Kollie, A.											
Totals											

P7-2B.
LO 7-1

The employee earnings record for Carson Ito of Appalachian Limited Home Design follows. Record the earnings during the March 10, 2023, pay period from P7-1B.

EMPLOYEE EARNINGS RECORD

NAME: Carson Ito Hire Date: 7/1/2018 Dependents <17: 0
ADDRESS: 150 Palomino Drive Date of Birth: 8/28/1994 Dependents other: 0
CITY/STATE/ZIP: Versailles/KY/42235 Position: Graphic Designer Step 4a W-4 Info: none
TELEPHONE: 502-555-4395 Filing Status: Single Step 4b W-4 Info: none
SOCIAL SECURITY NUMBER: 789-25-6431 Pay Rate: $16.85/hour Step 4c W-4 Info: none

Period Ended	Hrs Worked	Reg Pay	OT Pay	Holiday	Comm	Gross Pay	401(k)	Sect. 125	Taxable Pay for Federal W/H	Taxable Pay for FICA
3/3/2023	40	$674.00				$674.00			$674.00	$674.00

Taxable Pay for Federal W/H	Taxable Pay for FICA	Fed Inc.	Social Sec. Tax	Medicare	State Inc. Tax	Garnishment	United Way	Net Pay	YTD Net Pay	YTD Gross Pay
$674.00	$674.00	$44.00	$41.79	$9.77	$33.70			$544.74	$5,447.40	$6,740.00

P7-3B.
LO 7-1, 7-2, 7-3

Using the payroll register from P7-1B for Appalachian Limited Home Design, complete the General Journal entry for the employees' pay for the March 10, 2023, payroll end date. Employees' paychecks will be issued on March 15.

	Date	Description	Post Ref.	Debit	Credit
1					
2					
3					
4					
5					
6					
7					
8					
9					

P7-4B.
LO 7-1, 7-2, 7-3

Using the payroll register from P7-1B for Appalachian Limited Home Design, complete the General Journal entry for the employer's share of the payroll taxes for the March 10, 2023, pay date. Assume a 5.4 percent SUTA rate and 0.6 percent FUTA rate, and assume that only $2,721.85 of the gross pay is subject to SUTA and FUTA taxes.

	Date	Description	Post Ref.	Debit	Credit
1					
2					
3					
4					
5					
6					
7					
8					
9					

P7-5B.
LO 7-3, 7-4

Using the employee payroll entry from P7-3B, post the March 10 employee payroll end date for Appalachian Limited Home Design to the selected General Ledger accounts. The Posting Reference will be J1.

Account: Salaries and Wages Payable

	Date	Description	Post Ref.	Debit	Credit	Balance Debit	Balance Credit
1							
2							
3							
4							
5							
6							

Account: Employee Federal Income Tax Payable

	Date	Description	Post Ref.	Debit	Credit	Balance Debit	Balance Credit
1							
2							
3							
4							
5							
6							

Account: Social Security Tax Payable

	Date	Description	Post Ref.	Debit	Credit	Balance Debit	Balance Credit
1							
2							
3							
4							
5							
6							

Account: Medicare Tax Payable

	Date	Description	Post Ref.	Debit	Credit	Balance Debit	Balance Credit
1							
2							
3							
4							
5							
6							

Account: Employee State Income Tax Payable

	Date	Description	Post Ref.	Debit	Credit	Balance Debit	Balance Credit
1							
2							
3							
4							
5							
6							

Account: Salaries and Wages Expense

	Date	Description	Post Ref.	Debit	Credit	Balance Debit	Balance Credit
1							
2							
3							
4							
5							
6							
7							

P7-6B.
LO 7-3, 7-4

Using the employee payroll entry from P7-3B, complete the General Journal entry for the issuance of Appalachian Limited Home Design pay on March 15, 2023.

	Date	Description	Post Ref.	Debit	Credit	
1						1
2						2
3						3
4						4
5						5

P7-7B.
LO 7-3, 7-4

Using the employer payroll entry from P7-4B, post the employer's share of payroll taxes for the March 10 pay period at Appalachian Limited Home Design to the appropriate General Ledger accounts. Employees are paid weekly. Assume a 5.4 percent SUTA rate and 0.6 percent FUTA rate, and assume that only $954.05 of the gross pay is subject to SUTA and FUTA taxes. Note: FUTA and SUTA taxes are only employer share.

Account: Payroll Taxes Expense

	Date	Description	Post Ref.	Debit	Credit	Balance Debit	Balance Credit	
1								1
2								2
3								3
4								4
5								5
6								6
7								7

Account: Social Security Tax Payable

	Date	Description	Post Ref.	Debit	Credit	Balance Debit	Balance Credit	
1								1
2								2
3								3
4								4
5								5
6								6
7								7

Account: Medicare Tax Payable

	Date	Description	Post Ref.	Debit	Credit	Balance Debit	Balance Credit	
1								1
2								2
3								3
4								4
5								5
6								6
7								7

Account: Federal Unemployment Tax Payable

	Date	Description	Post Ref.	Debit	Credit	Balance Debit	Balance Credit	
1								1
2								2
3								3
4								4
5								5
6								6
7								7

Account: State Unemployment Tax Payable

	Date	Description	Post Ref.	Debit	Credit	Balance Debit	Balance Credit	
1								1
2								2
3								3
4								4
5								5
6								6
7								7

P7-8B.
LO 7-2, 7-3

Legends Leadworks is a monthly schedule depositor of payroll taxes. For the month of April 2023, the payroll taxes (employee and employer share) were as follows:

Social Security tax: $5,386.56
Medicare tax: $1,259.76
Employee federal income tax: $4,978.00

Create the General Journal entry for the remittance of the taxes on May 13, 2023. Use check 1320 in the description.

	Date	Description	Post Ref.	Debit	Credit	
1						1
2						2
3						3
4						4
5						5
6						6
7						7
8						8

P7-9B.
LO 7-2, 7-3

Candy Café has the following voluntary withholdings to remit as of September 30, 2023:

AFLAC payable: $687.00
Workers' compensation insurance payable: $1,042.00
401(k) contributions payable: $2,104.00
Garnishments payable: $450.00
U.S. savings bonds payable: $200.00

Create the General Journal entry for the remittance of these withheld amounts on October 13, 2023.

	Date	Description	Post Ref.	Debit	Credit	
1						1
2						2
3						3
4						4
5						5
6						6
7						7
8						8

P7-10B.
LO 7-5, 7-6

Pax Martinson is the controller for HHT Industries. Pax has been asked to explain the payroll accounts on the financial statements for the preceding month. What information is available about payroll on the financial statements?

P7-11B.
LO 7-5, 7-6

You are interviewing for a position with Limelight Photography. The president of the company asks you to explain how payroll is both an expense and a liability of the company. How will you answer?

Critical Thinking

7-1. Your boss asks you for a five-year labor cost trend chart. The labor costs per year are as follows:

2019	$175,248
2020	165,225
2021	151,250
2022	170,312
2023	161,344

Construct a line chart to depict the data. What conclusions can you derive from the data about labor costs and trends over the past five years? Why?

7-2. Giblin's Goodies pays employees weekly on Fridays. However, the company notices that May 31 is a Wednesday, and the pay period will end on June 2. The payroll data for May 30–31 is as follows:

Gross pay: $4,500.00
Federal income tax: $520.00
Social Security tax: $279.00
Medicare tax: $65.25
State income tax: $90.00
Federal unemployment tax: $27.00
State unemployment tax: $243.00

Give the adjusting entry in the General Journal to recognize the employee and employer share of the payroll for May 30–31. The date of the entry is May 31. Then record the journal entry to reverse the adjustment on June 1, 2023.

	Date	Description	Post Ref.	Debit	Credit	
1						1
2						2
3						3
4						4
5						5
6						6
7						7

	Date	Description	Post Ref.	Debit	Credit	
8						8
9						9
10						10
11						11
12						12
13						13
14						14
15						15
16						16
17						17
18						18
19						19
20						20
21						21
22						22
23						23
24						24
25						25
26						26
27						27
28						28
29						29
30						30

In the Real World: Scenario for Discussion

An ongoing discussion among business managers is the return on employee investment (ROEI). Employers want to maximize business profitability, and employees are a significant part of organizational success. Investments in employee training and professional development constitute a significant part of many companies' budgets. Measures including providing tablet computers for employees to pursue flexible learning opportunities and self-paced classes allow employers to reduce training and development costs. What are the pros and cons of this practice?

Internet Activities

7-1. Would you like to know about personal experiences as a payroll accountant? How about videos that detail the completion of payroll-related forms? Go to www.youtube.com and search the term *payroll accounting* to read personal perspectives about payroll practice, outsourcing, and tax form completion. What were three insights new to you?

7-2. Would you like to build your own favorites list of payroll accounting tools? Go to one or more of the following sites. What are three important items you noticed?

    www.accountingtools.com

    www.accountantsworld.com

    www.americanpayroll.org

7-3. Join a conversation about payroll accounting with industry professionals. Go to www.linkedin.com and establish a profile (if you do not have one). Search groups for payroll accounting and follow the conversations. Which topics did you choose? Why?

7-4. Want to know more about the concepts in this chapter? Check out:

    www.moneyinstructor.com/lesson/accountingconcepts.asp

    https://www.accountingcoach.com/accounting-basics/outline

Continuing Payroll Project: Prevosti Farms and Sugarhouse

Complete the Payroll Register for the February and March biweekly pay periods, assuming benefits went into effect as anticipated.

Use the Wage-Bracket Method Tables for Income Tax Withholding in Appendix C (or the IRS federal income tax withholding assistant). Complete the General Journal entries as follows:

February 10	Journalize the employee pay.
February 10	Journalize the employer payroll tax for the February 10 pay period. Use 5.4 percent SUTA and 0.6 percent FUTA. No employees will exceed the FUTA or SUTA wage base.
February 14	Issue the employee pay.
February 24	Journalize the employee pay.
February 24	Journalize the employer payroll tax for the February 24 pay period. Use 5.4 percent SUTA and 0.6 percent FUTA. No employee will exceed the FUTA or SUTA wage base.
February 28	Issue the employee pay.
February 28	Issue payment for the payroll liabilities.
March 10	Journalize the employee pay.
March 10	Journalize the employer payroll tax for the March 10 pay period. Use 5.4 percent SUTA and 0.6 percent FUTA. No employees will exceed the FUTA or SUTA wage base.
March 14	Issue the employee pay.
March 24	Journalize the employee pay.
March 24	Journalize the employer payroll tax for the March 24 pay period. Use 5.4 percent SUTA and 0.6 percent FUTA. No employees will exceed the FUTA or SUTA wage base.
March 28	Issue the employee pay.
March 28	Issue payment for the payroll liabilities.

	Date	Description	Post Ref.	Debit	Credit	
1						1
2						2
3						3
4						4
5						5
6						6
7						7
8						8
9						9
10						10
11						11
12						12
13						13
14						14
15						15
16						16
17						17
18						18
19						19
20						20
21						21
22						22
23						23

	Date	Description	Post Ref.	Debit	Credit	
24						24
25						25
26						26
27						27
28						28
29						29
30						30
31						31
32						32
33						33
34						34
35						35

Post all journal entries to the appropriate General Ledger accounts.

Account: Cash   **101**

	Date	Description	Post Ref.	Debit	Credit	Balance Debit	Balance Credit	
1		Beg. Bal.				47 0 0 0 00		1
2								2
3								3
4								4
5								5
6								6

Account: Employee Federal Income Tax Payable   **203**

	Date	Description	Post Ref.	Debit	Credit	Balance Debit	Balance Credit	
1								1
2								2
3								3
4								4
5								5
6								6

Account: Social Security Tax Payable   **204**

	Date	Description	Post Ref.	Debit	Credit	Balance Debit	Balance Credit	
1								1
2								2
3								3
4								4
5								5
6								6

Account: Medicare Tax Payable   205

	Date	Description	Post Ref.	Debit	Credit	Balance Debit	Balance Credit	
1								1
2								2
3								3
4								4
5								5
6								6

Account: Employee State Income Tax Payable   206

	Date	Description	Post Ref.	Debit	Credit	Balance Debit	Balance Credit	
1								1
2								2
3								3
4								4
5								5
6								6

Account: 401(k) Contributions Payable   208

	Date	Description	Post Ref.	Debit	Credit	Balance Debit	Balance Credit	
1								1
2								2
3								3
4								4
5								5
6								6

Account: Health Insurance Payable   209

	Date	Description	Post Ref.	Debit	Credit	Balance Debit	Balance Credit	
1								1
2								2
3								3
4								4
5								5
6								6

Account: Salaries and Wages Payable   210

	Date	Description	Post Ref.	Debit	Credit	Balance Debit	Balance Credit	
1								1
2								2
3								3
4								4
5								5
6								6

Account: FUTA Tax Payable   211

	Date	Description	Post Ref.	Debit	Credit	Balance Debit	Balance Credit	
1								1
2								2
3								3
4								4
5								5
6								6

Account: SUTA Tax Payable   212

	Date	Description	Post Ref.	Debit	Credit	Balance Debit	Balance Credit	
1								1
2								2
3								3
4								4
5								5
6								6

Account: Payroll Taxes Expense   514

	Date	Description	Post Ref.	Debit	Credit	Balance Debit	Balance Credit	
1								1
2								2
3								3
4								4
5								5
6								6

Account: Salaries and Wages Expense   515

	Date	Description	Post Ref.	Debit	Credit	Balance Debit	Balance Credit	
1								1
2								2
3								3
4								4
5								5
6								6

Answers to Stop & Check Exercises

Employees' Earnings Records
1. The payroll register contains the period payroll information for all employees. The employees' earnings record lists all payroll data for a single employee.
2. a. Name
   b. Pay rate
   d. Net pay
3. Quarterly and annual tax reports use the totals from the employees' earnings records.

Financial Accounting Concepts

1. Assets = Liabilities + Owners' Equity
2. Credit
3. Debit

Payroll and the General Journal

1. Wages and Salaries Expense

2.
Account	Debit	Credit
Payroll Taxes Expense	$9,546.05	
Social Security Tax Payable		$7,736.67
Medicare Tax Payable		$1,809.38

3.
Account	Debit	Credit
Federal Income Tax Payable	$ 6,234.00	
Social Security Tax Payable	2,653.29	
Medicare Tax Payable	620.53	
State Income Tax Payable	1,626.21	
Wages and Salaries Payable	31,660.97	
Wages and Salaries Expense		$42,795.00

General Ledger Entries

1. $2,760 Cr.
2. The transaction may be found in the General Journal earlier in this section.

The Business Effects of Payroll

1. The payment of employee wages decreases profitability because it increases the expenses of a business.
2. Allocation of payroll expenses to specific jobs, clients, and so on allows the company to understand the costs associated with the activity.

Labor Reports

1. a. Trial balance
   b. Statement of owners' equity
   d. Income statement
   e. Balance sheet
2. Labor reports
3. Trend reports are used by managers to identify business patterns, needs, and opportunities.

Appendix A

Comprehensive Payroll Project: Wayland Custom Woodworking

Wayland Custom Woodworking is a firm that manufactures custom cabinets and woodwork for business and residential customers. Students will have the opportunity to establish payroll records and complete a month of payroll information for Wayland.

Wayland Custom Woodworking is located at 12850 Old Highway 50, Glenbrook, Nevada, 89413, phone number 775-555-9877. The owner is Mark Wayland. Wayland's EIN is 91-7444533, and the Nevada Employer Account Number is E6462582020-6. Wayland has determined it will pay its employees on a semimonthly basis. Federal income tax should be computed using the *percentage* method for manual payrolls with Forms W-4 from 2020 or later.

Students will complete the payroll for the final quarter of 2023 and will file the fourth quarter and annual tax reports on the appropriate dates. At the instructor's discretion, students may complete a short version, which contains the payroll transactions beginning December 1. Directions for completion of the short version follow the November 30 transactions.

Rounding can create a challenge. For these exercises, the rate for the individuals is not rounded. Take the employee's salary and divide it by 2,080 (52 weeks at 40 hours per week) for full-time, nonexempt employees. Note: Leave the hourly rate rounded to five decimal places, as shown in the next example. *After* the gross pay has been calculated, then round the result to two decimal points before calculating taxes or other withholdings.

EXAMPLE: ANNUAL SALARY TO AN HOURLY RATE, NONEXEMPT EMPLOYEE

Employee Cooper's annual salary is $62,000 and he is a nonexempt employee.

Hourly rate = $62,000/(52 × 40) = $62,000/2,080

Hourly rate = $29.80769 per hour

> **EXAMPLE: PERIOD GROSS PAY, SALARIED EMPLOYEE**
>
> Employee Chinson earns an annual salary of $48,000 and is paid semimonthly.
>
> Period gross pay = $48,000/24 = $2,000 gross pay
>
> For pay periods with holiday hours: determine the amount paid per day, and multiply by the number of days applicable to each pay period.
>
> Annual salary: $48,000/(52 × 5) = $48,000/260 = $184.61538 (rounded to five decimal points) per day. Once you have the holiday pay, subtract it from their salary for the period for regular time.

Employees are paid for the following holidays occurring during the final quarter:

- Thanksgiving day and the day after, Thursday and Friday, November 23–24.
- Christmas is on Monday. Employees receive holiday pay for Monday, December 25.

For the completion of this project, students will use the percentage method for federal income tax located in Appendix C. Employees' 401(k) and insurance are pre-tax for federal income tax. The SUTA (UI) rate for Wayland Custom Woodworking is 2.95 percent on the first $40,100 of employee wages. There is an additional 0.05 percent for Career Enhancement Program (CEP). FUTA, SUTA, and CEP allow for a deduction for Section 125 contributions, not for 401(k) contributions. Employer contribution of Section 125 is 1.5 times the employee portion and should be added to the wages for the completion of FUTA and SUTA forms.

No employee has additional information in Step 4 of their W-4s, all W-4s were received in 2023, and Box 2c has not been checked.

Semimonthly Federal Percentage Method for Manual Payrolls with Forms W-4 from 2020 or Later Tax Table	Appendix C
Federal Unemployment Rate (employer only) (less Section 125)	0.6% on the first $7,000 of wages
State Unemployment Rate (employer only) (less Section 125)	2.95% on the first $40,100 of wages
Career Enhancement Program (employer only) (less Section 125)	0.05% on the first $40,100 of wages

October 1

Wayland Custom Woodworking (WCW) pays its employees according to their job classification. Wayland's staff comprises the following employees:

Employee Number	Name and Address	Payroll Information
00-Chins	Anthony Chinson 530 Chimney Rock Road Stateline, NV 89449 775-555-1212 Job title: Account Executive	Married/Joint; 2 < 17 Exempt $48,000/year + commission Start Date: 10/1/2023 SSN: 511-22-3333
00-Wayla	Mark Wayland 1650 Power House Drive Glenbrook, NV 89413 775-555-1110 Job title: President/Owner	Married/Joint; 3 < 17, 1 Other Exempt $85,000/year Start Date: 10/1/2023 SSN: 505-33-1775

Employee Number	Name and Address	Payroll Information
01-Peppi	Sylvia Peppinico 1575 Flowers Avenue Glenbrook, NV 89413 775-555-2244 Job title: Craftsman	Married/Joint; 1 < 17, 1 Other Exempt $58,500/year Start Date: 10/1/2023 SSN: 047-55-9951
01-Coope	Stevon Cooper 2215 Lands End Drive Glenbrook, NV 89413 775-555-9981 Job title: Craftsman	Single; None Nonexempt $62,000/year Start Date: 10/1/2023 SSN: 022-66-1131
02-Hisso	Leonard Hissop 333 Engine House Circle Glenbrook, NV 89413 775-555-5858 Job title: Purchasing/Shipping	Single; 1 Other Nonexempt $51,500/year Start Date: 10/1/2023 SSN: 311-22-6698

Voluntary deductions for each employee are as follows:

Name	Deduction
Chinson	Insurance: $50/paycheck 401(k): 3% of gross pay
Wayland	Insurance: $75/paycheck 401(k): 6% of gross pay
Peppinico	Insurance: $75/paycheck 401(k): $50 per paycheck
Cooper	Insurance: $50/paycheck 401(k): 4% of gross pay
Hissop	Insurance: $75/paycheck 401(k): 3% of gross pay
Success	Insurance: $50/paycheck 401(k): 3% of gross pay

Pre-tax Deductions—Federal Income, FICA, State Income

Stop & Check

1. Should the insurance be excluded when calculating federal and state taxable wages? FICA taxable wages?
2. Should the 401(k) be excluded when calculating federal and state income taxable wages? FICA taxable wages?

Complete the headers of the Employee Earnings Record for all company employees. Enter the YTD earnings for each employee. The departments are as follows:

Department 00: Sales and Administration

Department 01: Factory Workers

Department 02: Delivery and Customer Service

1. You have been hired as of October 2 as the new accounting clerk. Your employee number is 00-SUCCE. Your name is STUDENT SUCCESS. Your address is 16 Kelly Circle

#2, Glenbrook, NV 89413. Your phone number is 775-556-1211, you were born on July 16, 2001, your Nevada driver's license number is 168575381944 expiring on your birthday in 2027, and your Social Security number is 555-55-5555. You are nonexempt and paid at a rate of $42,000 per year as an accounting clerk. Complete Form W-4 and, using the given information, complete the I-9 form to start your employee file. The forms were reviewed by Mark Wayland. Complete it as if you are single with no dependents or other income, you contribute 3 percent to a 401(k), and health insurance is $50 per pay period.

The balance sheet for WCW as of September 30, 2023, is as follows:

Wayland Custom Woodworking
Balance Sheet
September 30, 2023

Assets		Liabilities & Equity	
Cash	$1,125,000.00	Accounts Payable	$ 112,490.00
Supplies	27,240.00	Salaries and Wages Payable	
Office Equipment	87,250.00	Federal Unemployment Tax Payable	
Inventory	123,000.00	Social Security Tax Payable	
Vehicle	25,000.00	Medicare Tax Payable	
Accumulated Depreciation, Vehicle		State Unemployment Tax Payable	
Building	164,000.00	Career Enhancement Program Payable	
Accumulated Depreciation, Building		Employee Federal Income Tax Payable	
Land	35,750.00	Employee State Income Tax Payable	
Total Assets	1,587,240.00	401(k) Contributions Payable	
		Employee Medical Premiums Payable	
		Notes Payable	224,750.00
		Total Liabilities	337,240.00
		Owners' Equity	1,250,000.00
		Retained Earnings	—
		Total Equity	1,250,000.00
		Total Liabilities and Equity	1,587,240.00

October 15

October 15 is the end of the first pay period for the month of October. Employee pay will be disbursed on October 18, 2023. Any time worked in excess of 80 hours during this pay period is considered overtime for nonexempt employees. Remember that the employees are paid on a semimonthly basis. The hours for the employees are as follows:

Name	Hourly Rate or Period Wage (round to 5 decimals)	Pay Period Hours 10/1–10/15	Regular (round to 2 decimals)	Overtime (round to 2 decimals)	Commission
Chinson		80 hours (exempt)			$1,500.00
Wayland		80 hours (exempt)			
Peppinico		80 hours (exempt)			
Cooper		80 hours			
Hissop		85.25 hours			
Success		82 hours			

October 2023

Sunday	Monday	Tuesday	Wednesday	Thursday	Friday	Saturday
1	2	3	4	5	6	7
8	9	10	11	12	13	14
15	16	17	18	19	20	21
22	23	24	25	26	27	28
29	30	31				

Complete the Payroll Register for October 15. Round wages to five decimal points and all other final answers to two decimal points. Update the Employee Earnings Records for the period's pay and update the YTD amounts. Insurance qualifies for Section 125 treatment. Use the percentage method for manual payroll systems with Forms W-4 from 2020 or later in Appendix C for the federal income tax. The starting check number is 4215.

Voluntary deductions for each employee are as follows:

Name	Deduction
Chinson	Insurance: $50/paycheck
	401(k): 3% of gross pay
Wayland	Insurance: $75/paycheck
	401(k): 6% of gross pay
Peppinico	Insurance: $75/paycheck
	401(k): $50 per paycheck
Cooper	Insurance: $50/paycheck
	401(k): 4% of gross pay
Hissop	Insurance: $75/paycheck
	401(k): 3% of gross pay
Success	Insurance: $50/paycheck
	401(k): 3% of gross pay

> **EXAMPLE: CALCULATING AN EMPLOYEE'S NET INCOME WITH DEDUCTIONS:**
>
> 1. Determine employee gross wages by taking their annual salary and dividing it by the number of pay periods ($48,000/24 pay periods = $2,000 per pay period). Or when the employee is nonexempt, take this one step further to determine the hourly rate ($48,000/(52 weeks × 40 hours per week)) = $23.07692 per hour.
> 2. Multiply the hourly rate by the number of regular hours worked by hourly employees. 80 hours × $23.07692 = $1,846.15 in regular wages.
> 3. Multiply any overtime worked by the overtime rate. 3 hours × $23.07692 × 1.5 = $103.85 in overtime wages.
> 4. Total wages earned: $1,846.15 + 103.85 = $1,950.00.
> 5. Determine federal and state taxable wages: $1,950 − 50 (insurance) − 58.50 (3% of gross for 401(k) plan deduction) = $1,841.50.
> 6. Determine FICA taxable wages: $1,950 − 50 (insurance) = $1,900.00.
> 7. Find the federal taxes in the appropriate tax table in Appendix C.
> 8. Multiply the FICA taxable wages by the Social Security rate (6.2%).
> 9. Multiply the FICA taxable wages by the Medicare rate (1.45%).
> 10. Multiply the federal taxable wages by the state tax rate.
> 11. Subtract all deductions from gross wages to obtain net income.

Appendix A Comprehensive Payroll Project: Wayland Custom Woodworking   409

Complete the Payroll Register for October 15

P/R End Date _____   Company Name Wayland Custom Woodworking
Check Date _____

Name	Filing Status	Dependents	Hourly Rate or Period Wage	No. of Regular Hours	No. of Overtime Hours	No. of Holiday Hours	Commissions	Gross Earnings	Sec 125	401(k)	Taxable Wages for Federal W/H	Taxable Wages for FICA
Anthony Chinson												
Mark Wayland												
Sylvia Peppinico												
Stevon Cooper												
Leonard Hissop												
Student Success												
Totals												

Name	Gross Earnings	Taxable Wages for Federal W/H	Taxable Wages for FICA	Federal W/H	Social Security Tax	Medicare W/H	Total Deduc.	Net Pay	Check No.
Anthony Chinson									4215
Mark Wayland									4216
Sylvia Peppinico									4217
Stevon Cooper									4218
Leonard Hissop									4219
Student Success									4220
Totals									

EMPLOYEE EARNING RECORD

NAME _____   Hire Date _____   Dependent child <17 _____
ADDRESS _____   Date of Birth _____   Dependent other _____
CITY/STATE/ZIP _____   Position _____   Step 4a W-4 Info _____
TELEPHONE _____   Filing Status _____   Step 4b W-4 Info _____
SOCIAL SECURITY NUMBER _____   Pay Rate _____   Step 4c W-4 Info _____
   Hr/Wk/Mo/Yr

Period Ended	Hrs Worked	Reg Pay	OT Pay	Holiday	Comm	Gross Pay	Ins	401(k)	Taxable Pay for Federal	Taxable Pay for FICA

Taxable Pay for Federal	Taxable Pay for FICA	Fed Inc. Tax	Social Sec. Tax	Medicare	Total Deduc	Net Pay	YTD Net Pay	YTD Gross Pay	Current Taxable for FUTA	Current Taxable for SUTA

EMPLOYEE EARNING RECORD

NAME		Hire Date		Dependent child <17	
ADDRESS		Date of Birth		Dependent other	
CITY/STATE/ZIP		Position		Step 4a W-4 Info	
TELEPHONE		Filing Status		Step 4b W-4 Info	
SOCIAL SECURITY NUMBER		Pay Rate		Step 4c W-4 Info Hr/Wk/Mo/Yr	

Period Ended	Hrs Worked	Reg Pay	OT Pay	Holiday	Comm	Gross Pay	Ins	401(k)	Taxable Pay for Federal	Taxable Pay for FICA

Taxable Pay for Federal	Taxable Pay for FICA	Fed Inc. Tax	Social Sec. Tax	Medicare	Total Deduc	Net Pay	YTD Net Pay	YTD Gross Pay	Current Taxable for FUTA	Current Taxable for SUTA

EMPLOYEE EARNING RECORD

NAME		Hire Date		Dependent child <17	
ADDRESS		Date of Birth		Dependent other	
CITY/STATE/ZIP		Position		Step 4a W-4 Info	
TELEPHONE		Filing Status		Step 4b W-4 Info	
SOCIAL SECURITY NUMBER		Pay Rate		Step 4c W-4 Info Hr/Wk/Mo/Yr	

Period Ended	Hrs Worked	Reg Pay	OT Pay	Holiday	Comm	Gross Pay	Ins	401(k)	Taxable Pay for Federal	Taxable Pay for FICA

Taxable Pay for Federal	Taxable Pay for FICA	Fed Inc. Tax	Social Sec. Tax	Medicare	Total Deduc	Net Pay	YTD Net Pay	YTD Gross Pay	Current Taxable for FUTA	Current Taxable for SUTA

EMPLOYEE EARNING RECORD

NAME _____ Hire Date _____ Dependent child <17 _____
ADDRESS _____ Date of Birth _____ Dependent other _____
CITY/STATE/ZIP _____ Position _____ Step 4a W-4 Info _____
TELEPHONE _____ Filing Status _____ Step 4b W-4 Info _____
SOCIAL SECURITY _____ Step 4c W-4 Info _____
NUMBER _____ Pay Rate _____ Hr/Wk/Mo/Yr

Period Ended	Hrs Worked	Reg Pay	OT Pay	Holiday	Comm	Gross Pay	Ins	401(k)	Taxable Pay for Federal	Taxable Pay for FICA

Taxable Pay for Federal	Taxable Pay for FICA	Fed Inc. Tax	Social Sec. Tax	Medicare	Total Deduc	Net Pay	YTD Net Pay	YTD Gross Pay	Current Taxable for FUTA	Current Taxable for SUTA

EMPLOYEE EARNING RECORD

NAME _____ Hire Date _____ Dependent child <17 _____
ADDRESS _____ Date of Birth _____ Dependent other _____
CITY/STATE/ZIP _____ Position _____ Step 4a W-4 Info _____
TELEPHONE _____ Filing Status _____ Step 4b W-4 Info _____
SOCIAL SECURITY _____ Step 4c W-4 Info _____
NUMBER _____ Pay Rate _____ Hr/Wk/Mo/Yr

Period Ended	Hrs Worked	Reg Pay	OT Pay	Holiday	Comm	Gross Pay	Ins	401(k)	Taxable Pay for Federal	Taxable Pay for FICA

Taxable Pay for Federal	Taxable Pay for FICA	Fed Inc. Tax	Social Sec. Tax	Medicare	Total Deduc	Net Pay	YTD Net Pay	YTD Gross Pay	Current Taxable for FUTA	Current Taxable for SUTA

EMPLOYEE EARNING RECORD

NAME _____ Hire Date _____ Dependent child <17 _____
ADDRESS _____ Date of Birth _____ Dependent other _____
CITY/STATE/ZIP _____ Position _____ Step 4a W-4 Info _____
TELEPHONE _____ Filing Status _____ Step 4b W-4 Info _____
SOCIAL SECURITY _____ Step 4c W-4 Info _____
NUMBER _____ Pay Rate _____ Hr/Wk/Mo/Yr

Period Ended	Hrs Worked	Reg Pay	OT Pay	Holiday	Comm	Gross Pay	Ins	401(k)	Taxable Pay for Federal	Taxable Pay for FICA

Taxable Pay for Federal	Taxable Pay for FICA	Fed Inc. Tax	Social Sec. Tax	Medicare	Total Deduc	Net Pay	YTD Net Pay	YTD Gross Pay	Current Taxable for FUTA	Current Taxable for SUTA

Employee Earnings Records

Stop & Check

1. What is the purpose of the Current Taxable for FUTA column?
2. What is the purpose of the Dependent information?

General Journal Entries

Complete the General Journal entries as follows:

15-Oct	Journalize employee pay.
15-Oct	Journalize employer payroll tax for the October 15 pay date.
18-Oct	Journalize the payment of payroll.

Post all journal entries to the appropriate General Ledger accounts.

Date	Description	Post Ref.	Debit	Credit

October 31

October 31 is the end of the final pay period for the month. Employee pay will be disbursed on November 3, 2023. Due to customer demand, all employees worked some hours on 10/21 in addition to normal weekdays. Any hours exceeding 96 during this pay period are considered overtime for nonexempt employees. Compute the employee pay. Update the Employee Earnings Records for the period's pay and update the YTD amount.

Complete the Payroll Register for October 31. Round wages to five decimal points and all other final answers to two decimal points.

The hours for the employees are as follows:

Name	Hourly Rate or Period Wage (round to 5 decimals)	Hours Worked 10/16–10/31	Regular (round to 2 decimals)	Overtime (round to 2 decimals)	Commission
Chinson		96 hours (exempt)			$ 1,750.00
Wayland		96 hours (exempt)			
Peppinico		96 hours (exempt)			
Cooper		98 hours			
Hissop		97 hours			
Success		99 hours			

October 2023

Sunday	Monday	Tuesday	Wednesday	Thursday	Friday	Saturday
1	2	3	4	5	6	7
8	9	10	11	12	13	14
15	16	17	18	19	20	21
22	23	24	25	26	27	28
29	30	31				

Complete the Payroll Register for October 31.

P/R End Date: _____   Company Name: Wayland Custom Woodworking

Check Date: _____

Name	Filing Status	Dependents	Hourly Rate or Period Wage	No. of Regular Hours	No. of Overtime Hours	No. of Holiday Hours	Commissions	Gross Earnings	Sec 125	401(k)	Taxable Wages for Federal W/H	Taxable Wages for FICA
Anthony Chinson												
Mark Wayland												
Sylvia Peppinico												
Stevon Cooper												
Leonard Hissop												
Student Success												
Totals												

Name	Gross Earnings	Taxable Wages for Federal W/H	Taxable Wages for FICA	Federal W/H	Social Security Tax	Medicare W/H	Total Deduc.	Net Pay	Check No.
Anthony Chinson									4221
Mark Wayland									4222
Sylvia Peppinico									4223
Stevon Cooper									4224
Leonard Hissop									4225
Student Success									4226
Totals									

General Journal Entries

Complete the General Journal entries as follows:

31-Oct	Journalize employee pay.
31-Oct	Journalize employer payroll tax for the October 31 pay date.
03-Nov	Journalize the payment of payroll to employees. (Use one entry for all disbursements.)
03-Nov	Journalize remittance of 401(k) and Section 125 health insurance premiums deducted.
03-Nov	Journalize remittance of monthly payroll taxes.

Post all journal entries to the appropriate General Ledger accounts.

Date	Description	Post Ref.	Debit	Credit

Employer's Role

Stop & Check

Explain the employer's role in the collection and remittance of payroll withholdings for taxes, insurance, and 401(k) plans.

November 15

Compute the pay for each employee. Update the Employee Earnings Record for the period's pay and the new YTD amount. Employee pay will be disbursed on November 20, 2023. Any hours exceeding 88 during this pay period are considered overtime for nonexempt employees. Remember that the employees are paid semimonthly.

Complete the Payroll Register for November 15. Round wages to five decimal points and all other final answers to two decimal points.

Appendix A Comprehensive Payroll Project: Wayland Custom Woodworking

The hours for the employees are as follows:

Name	Hourly Rate or Period Wage (round to 5 decimals)	Pay Period Hours 11/01–11/15	Regular (round to 2 decimals)	Overtime (round to 2 decimals)	Commission
Chinson		88 hours (exempt)			$1,050.00
Wayland		88 hours (exempt)			
Peppinico		88 hours (exempt)			
Cooper		90 hours			
Hissop		91 hours			
Success		92 hours			

November 2023

Sunday	Monday	Tuesday	Wednesday	Thursday	Friday	Saturday
			1	2	3	4
5	6	7	8	9	10	11
12	13	14	15	16	17	18
19	20	21	22	23	24	25
26	27	28	29	30		

Complete the Payroll Register for November 15

P/R End Date _____   Company Name Wayland Custom Woodworking
Check Date _____

Name	Filing Status	Dependents	Hourly Rate or Period Wage	No. of Regular Hours	No. of Overtime Hours	No. of Holiday Hours	Commissions	Gross Earnings	Sec 125	401(k)	Taxable Wages for Federal W/H	Taxable Wages for FICA
Anthony Chinson												
Mark Wayland												
Sylvia Peppinico												
Stevon Cooper												
Leonard Hissop												
Student Success												
Totals												

Name	Gross Earnings	Taxable Wages for Federal W/H	Taxable Wages for FICA	Federal W/H	Social Security Tax	Medicare Tax	Total Deduc.	Net Pay	Check No.
Anthony Chinson									4227
Mark Wayland									4228
Sylvia Peppinico									4229
Stevon Cooper									4230
Leonard Hissop									4231
Student Success									4232
Totals									

General Journal Entries

Complete the General Journal entries as follows:

15-Nov	Journalize employee pay.
15-Nov	Journalize employer payroll tax for the November 15 pay date.
18-Nov	Journalize payment of payroll to employees.

Post all journal entries to the appropriate General Ledger accounts.

Date	Description	Post Ref.	Debit	Credit

November 30

Compute the Net Pay for each employee. Employee pay will be disbursed on December 5, 2023. Update the Employee Earnings Records with the November 30 pay and the new YTD amount.

The company is closed and pays for the Friday following Thanksgiving. The employees will receive holiday pay for Thanksgiving and the Friday following. All the hours over 88 are eligible for overtime for nonexempt employees because they were worked during the non-holiday week.

The hours for the employees are as follows:

Name	Hourly Rate or Period Wage (round to 5 decimals)	Pay Period Hours 11/16—11/30	Regular (round to 2 decimals)	Overtime (round to 2 decimals)	Holiday (round to 2 decimals)	Commission
Chinson		88 hours (exempt—16 hours holiday)				$2,325.00
Wayland		88 hours (exempt—16 hours holiday)				
Peppinico		88 hours (exempt—16 hours holiday)				
Cooper		90 hours (16 hours holiday)				
Hissop		91 hours (16 hours holiday)				
Success		89 hours (16 hours holiday)				

> **EXAMPLE**
> Holiday pay can result in less overtime for nonexempt employees. Since hours must be worked to be considered for overtime, it is important to know when the employees entered overtime during the pay period.
>
> - Employee A worked overtime for this pay period during the week preceding the holiday; therefore, the hours worked would be eligible for overtime pay. Employee A worked 42 hours in the week preceding the holiday; during a standard 40-hour week, the two additional hours would be at the overtime premium.
> - Employee B worked the extra hours for this pay period during the week with the holiday; as a result, the number of hours worked would not be eligible for overtime. Employee B worked 33 hours in the week that had an 8-hour holiday included; therefore, the employee would not be eligible for overtime.

November 2023

Sunday	Monday	Tuesday	Wednesday	Thursday	Friday	Saturday
			1	2	3	4
5	6	7	8	9	10	11
12	13	14	15	16	17	18
19	20	21	22	23	24	25
26	27	28	29	30		

Appendix A Comprehensive Payroll Project: Wayland Custom Woodworking   419

Complete the Payroll Register for November 30. Round wages to five decimal points and all other final answers to two decimal points.

Complete the Payroll Register for November 30

P/R End Date _____   Company Name Wayland Custom Woodworking
Check Date   _____

Name	Filing Status	Dependents	Hourly Rate or Period Wage	No. of Regular Hours	No. of Overtime Hours	No. of Holiday Hours	Commissions	Gross Earnings	Sec 125	401(k)	Taxable Wages for Federal W/H	Taxable Wages for FICA
Anthony Chinson												
Mark Wayland												
Sylvia Peppinico												
Stevon Cooper												
Leonard Hissop												
Student Success												
Totals												

Name	Gross Earnings	Taxable Wages for Federal W/H	Taxable Wages for FICA	Federal W/H	Social Security Tax	Medicare Tax	Total Deduc.	Net Pay	Check No.
Anthony Chinson									4233
Mark Wayland									4234
Sylvia Peppinico									4235
Stevon Cooper									4236
Leonard Hissop									4237
Student Success									4238
Totals									

General Journal Entries

Complete the General Journal entries as follows:

30-Nov	Journalize employee pay.
30-Nov	Journalize employer payroll tax for the November 30 pay date.
05-Dec	Journalize payment of payroll to employees.
05-Dec	Journalize remittance of 401(k) and health insurance premiums deducted.
05-Dec	Journalize remittance of monthly payroll taxes.

Post all journal entries to the appropriate General Ledger accounts.

Date	Description	Post Ref.	Debit	Credit

Short Version, One-Month Option:

Wayland Custom Woodworking
Balance Sheet
November 30, 2023

Assets		Liabilities & Equity	
Cash	$1,075,351.27	Accounts Payable	$ 112,747.25
Supplies	42,240.11	Salaries and Wages Payable	14,120.74
Office Equipment	87,250.00	Federal Unemployment Tax Payable	60.37
Inventory	167,068.96	Social Security Tax Payable	4,004.50
Vehicle	25,000.00	Medicare Tax Payable	936.58
Accumulated Depreciation, Vehicle		State Unemployment Tax Payable	952.68
Building	164,000.00	Career Enhancement Program Payable	16.15
Accumulated Depreciation, Building		Employee Federal Income Tax Payable	1,290.47
Land	35,750.00	401(k) Contributions Payable	1,211.83
Total Assets	$1,596,660.34	Employee Medical Premiums Payable	750.00
		Notes Payable	210,569.77
		Total Liabilities	346,660.34
		Owner's Equity	1,250,000.00
		Retained Earnings	—
		Total Equity	1,250,000.00
		Total Liabilities and Equity	$1,596,660.34

Students will complete the payroll for the final month of 2023 and will file the fourth quarter and annual tax reports on the appropriate dates. Wayland Custom Woodworking is located at 12850 Old Highway 50, Glenbrook, Nevada, 89413, phone number 775-555-9877. The owner is Mark Wayland. Wayland's EIN is 91-7444533. Wayland has determined it will pay its employees on a semimonthly basis. Federal income tax should be computed using the ***percentage*** method for manual payrolls with Forms W-4 from 2020 or later.

Rounding can create a challenge. For these exercises, the rate for the individuals is not rounded. For full-time, exempt employees, take their salary and divide it by 24 pay periods to get a period wage. For full-time, nonexempt employees, take their salary and divide by 2,080 (52 weeks at 40 hours per week). Note: Leave the hourly rate rounded to five decimal places, as shown in the example at the start of Appendix A. *After* the gross pay has been calculated, then round the result to two decimal points prior to calculating taxes or other withholdings.

December 15

Compute the net pay and update the Employee Earnings Records with the December 15 pay and the new YTD information. Employee pay will be disbursed on December 20, 2023. Any hours worked in excess of 88 hours during this pay period are considered overtime for non-exempt employees.

The hours for the employees are as follows:

Name	Hourly Rate or Period Wage (round to 5 decimals)	Pay Period Hours 12/01–12/15	Regular (round to 2 decimals)	Overtime (round to 2 decimals)	Holiday (round to 2 decimals)	Commission
Chinson		88 hours (exempt)				$1,680.00
Wayland		88 hours (exempt)				
Peppinico		88 hours (exempt)				
Cooper		92 hours				
Hissop		88 hours				
Success		91 hours				

December 2023

Sunday	Monday	Tuesday	Wednesday	Thursday	Friday	Saturday
					1	2
3	4	5	6	7	8	9
10	11	12	13	14	15	16
17	18	19	20	21	22	23
24	25	26	27	28	29	30
31						

Determining Overtime

Stop & Check

When employers pay under a semimonthly cycle, there can be more than 10 days in the pay period. For the first December pay period, how many hours are available under regular hours? How would you keep track of the number of hours in a pay period under the semimonthly cycle?

Complete the Payroll Register for December 15. Round wages to five decimal points and all other final answers to two decimal points.

Complete the Payroll Register for December 15.

P/R End Date: _____   Company Name: Wayland Custom Woodworking

Check Date: _____

Name	Filing Status	Dependents	Hourly Rate or Period Wage	No. of Regular Hours	No. of Overtime Hours	No. of Holiday Hours	Commissions	Gross Earnings	Sec 125	401(k)	Taxable Wages for Federal W/H	Taxable Wages for FICA
Anthony Chinson												
Mark Wayland												
Sylvia Peppinico												
Stevon Cooper												
Leonard Hissop												
Student Success												
Totals												

Name	Gross Earnings	Taxable Wages for Federal W/H	Taxable Wages for FICA	Federal W/H	Social Security Tax	Medicare W/H	Total Deduc.	Net Pay	Check No.
Anthony Chinson									4239
Mark Wayland									4240
Sylvia Peppinico									4241
Stevon Cooper									4242
Leonard Hissop									4243
Student Success									4244
Totals									

General Journal Entries

Complete the General Journal entries as follows:

15-Dec	Journalize employee pay.
15-Dec	Journalize employer payroll tax for the December 15 pay date.
20-Dec	Journalize payment of payroll to employees.

Post all journal entries to the appropriate General Ledger accounts.

Date	Description	Post Ref.	Debit	Credit

December 31

The final pay period of the year will not be paid to employees until January 4, 2024. The company will accrue the wages for the final pay period only. Since the pay period is complete, there will not be a reversing entry for the accrual.

The company pays holiday pay for December 25, 2023. Due to demand, the employees worked extra hours on Wednesday, December 27. Reminder: Holidays and vacations are not included as hours *worked* for the calculation of overtime.

Employee pay will be disbursed and reflected on the Employee Earnings Record when paid. The remainder of the employer liability will be paid with the final filing for the year. Complete all state and federal tax forms for the year-end. Generate Forms W-2 and W-3 for employees, and recall that these forms only reflect wages actually paid during the calendar year. Employer amounts for health coverage should be reported as 1.5 times the employee's premium in Box 12, using Code DD. The forms will be signed on January 12, 2024.

The hours for the employees are as follows:

Name	Hourly Rate or Period Wage (round to 5 decimals)	Pay Period Hours 12/16–12/31	Regular (round to 2 decimals)	Overtime (round to 2 decimals)	Holiday (round to 2 decimals)	Commission
Chinson		80 hours (exempt—8 hours holiday)				$1,015.00
Wayland		80 hours (exempt—8 hours holiday)				
Peppinico		80 hours (exempt—8 hours holiday)				
Cooper		82 hours (8 hours holiday)*				
Hissop		81 hours (8 hours holiday)*				
Success		83 hours (8 hours holiday)*				

*Employees worked extra hours on Wednesday, 12/28. Reminder, holidays and vacations are not included as hours *worked* for calculation of overtime.

December 2023						
Sunday	Monday	Tuesday	Wednesday	Thursday	Friday	Saturday
					1	2
3	4	5	6	7	8	9
10	11	12	13	14	15	16
17	18	19	20	21	22	23
24	25	26	27	28	29	30
31						

Complete the Payroll Register for December 31.

Run Date _____   Company Name Wayland Custom Woodworking

P/R Date _____

Name	Filing Status	Dependents	Hourly Rate or Period Wage	No. of Regular Hours	No. of Overtime Hours	No. of Holiday Hours	Commissions	Gross Earnings	Sec 125	401(k)	Taxable Wages for Federal W/H	Taxable Wages for FICA
Anthony Chinson												
Mark Wayland												
Sylvia Peppinico												
Stevon Cooper												
Leonard Hissop												
Student Success												
Totals												

Name	Gross Earnings	Taxable Wages for Federal W/H	Taxable Wages for FICA	Federal W/H	Social Security Tax	Medicare W/H	Total Deduc.	Net Pay	Check No.
Anthony Chinson									4245
Mark Wayland									4246
Sylvia Peppinico									4247
Stevon Cooper									4248
Leonard Hissop									4249
Student Success									4250
Totals									

General Journal Entries

Complete the General Journal entries as follows:

31-Dec	Accrue employee pay.
31-Dec	Accrue employer payroll tax for the December 31 pay date.

Post all journal entries to the appropriate General Ledger accounts.

Date	Description	Post Ref.	Debit	Credit

Handling Accruals

Stop & Check — There are two typical ways of handling accruals in the following period: reversing the accrual in total or adjusting the accrual for the actual amount. What are the benefits of each method?

Employment Eligibility Verification
Department of Homeland Security
U.S. Citizenship and Immigration Services

USCIS Form I-9
OMB No. 1615-0047
Expires 10/31/2022

▶ **START HERE:** Read instructions carefully before completing this form. The instructions must be available, either in paper or electronically, during completion of this form. Employers are liable for errors in the completion of this form.

ANTI-DISCRIMINATION NOTICE: It is illegal to discriminate against work-authorized individuals. Employers **CANNOT** specify which document(s) an employee may present to establish employment authorization and identity. The refusal to hire or continue to employ an individual because the documentation presented has a future expiration date may also constitute illegal discrimination.

Section 1. Employee Information and Attestation *(Employees must complete and sign Section 1 of Form I-9 no later than the first day of employment, but not before accepting a job offer.)*

Last Name (Family Name)	First Name (Given Name)	Middle Initial	Other Last Names Used (if any)

Address (Street Number and Name)	Apt. Number	City or Town	State	ZIP Code

Date of Birth (mm/dd/yyyy)	U.S. Social Security Number	Employee's E-mail Address	Employee's Telephone Number
	___-__-____		

I am aware that federal law provides for imprisonment and/or fines for false statements or use of false documents in connection with the completion of this form.

I attest, under penalty of perjury, that I am (check one of the following boxes):

☐ 1. A citizen of the United States
☐ 2. A noncitizen national of the United States *(See instructions)*
☐ 3. A lawful permanent resident   (Alien Registration Number/USCIS Number): _____
☐ 4. An alien authorized to work   until (expiration date, if applicable, mm/dd/yyyy): _____
    Some aliens may write "N/A" in the expiration date field. *(See instructions)*

Aliens authorized to work must provide only one of the following document numbers to complete Form I-9:
An Alien Registration Number/USCIS Number OR Form I-94 Admission Number OR Foreign Passport Number.

1. Alien Registration Number/USCIS Number: _____
   OR
2. Form I-94 Admission Number: _____
   OR
3. Foreign Passport Number: _____
   Country of Issuance: _____

QR Code - Section 1
Do Not Write In This Space

Signature of Employee	Today's Date (mm/dd/yyyy)

Preparer and/or Translator Certification (check one):
☐ I did not use a preparer or translator.   ☐ A preparer(s) and/or translator(s) assisted the employee in completing Section 1.
(Fields below must be completed and signed when preparers and/or translators assist an employee in completing Section 1.)

I attest, under penalty of perjury, that I have assisted in the completion of Section 1 of this form and that to the best of my knowledge the information is true and correct.

Signature of Preparer or Translator	Today's Date (mm/dd/yyyy)

Last Name (Family Name)	First Name (Given Name)

Address (Street Number and Name)	City or Town	State	ZIP Code

🛑 *Employer Completes Next Page* 🛑

Form I-9 10/21/2019

(Source: USCIS)

Employment Eligibility Verification
Department of Homeland Security
U.S. Citizenship and Immigration Services

USCIS
Form I-9
OMB No. 1615-0047
Expires 10/31/2022

Section 2. Employer or Authorized Representative Review and Verification

(Employers or their authorized representative must complete and sign Section 2 within 3 business days of the employee's first day of employment. You must physically examine one document from List A OR a combination of one document from List B and one document from List C as listed on the "Lists of Acceptable Documents.")

Employee Info from Section 1	Last Name *(Family Name)*	First Name *(Given Name)*	M.I.	Citizenship/Immigration Status

List A Identity and Employment Authorization	OR	List B Identity	AND	List C Employment Authorization
Document Title		Document Title		Document Title
Issuing Authority		Issuing Authority		Issuing Authority
Document Number		Document Number		Document Number
Expiration Date *(if any) (mm/dd/yyyy)*		Expiration Date *(if any) (mm/dd/yyyy)*		Expiration Date *(if any) (mm/dd/yyyy)*
Document Title				
Issuing Authority		Additional Information		QR Code - Sections 2 & 3 Do Not Write In This Space
Document Number				
Expiration Date *(if any) (mm/dd/yyyy)*				
Document Title				
Issuing Authority				
Document Number				
Expiration Date *(if any) (mm/dd/yyyy)*				

Certification: I attest, under penalty of perjury, that (1) I have examined the document(s) presented by the above-named employee, (2) the above-listed document(s) appear to be genuine and to relate to the employee named, and (3) to the best of my knowledge the employee is authorized to work in the United States.

The employee's first day of employment *(mm/dd/yyyy)*: _____ *(See instructions for exemptions)*

Signature of Employer or Authorized Representative	Today's Date *(mm/dd/yyyy)*	Title of Employer or Authorized Representative
Last Name of Employer or Authorized Representative	First Name of Employer or Authorized Representative	Employer's Business or Organization Name
Employer's Business or Organization Address *(Street Number and Name)*	City or Town	State	ZIP Code

Section 3. Reverification and Rehires *(To be completed and signed by employer or authorized representative.)*

A. New Name *(if applicable)*			B. Date of Rehire *(if applicable)*
Last Name *(Family Name)*	First Name *(Given Name)*	Middle Initial	Date *(mm/dd/yyyy)*

C. If the employee's previous grant of employment authorization has expired, provide the information for the document or receipt that establishes continuing employment authorization in the space provided below.

Document Title	Document Number	Expiration Date *(if any) (mm/dd/yyyy)*

I attest, under penalty of perjury, that to the best of my knowledge, this employee is authorized to work in the United States, and if the employee presented document(s), the document(s) I have examined appear to be genuine and to relate to the individual.

Signature of Employer or Authorized Representative	Today's Date *(mm/dd/yyyy)*	Name of Employer or Authorized Representative

Form I-9 10/21/2019

(Source: USCIS)

LISTS OF ACCEPTABLE DOCUMENTS
All documents must be UNEXPIRED

Employees may present one selection from List A
or a combination of one selection from List B and one selection from List C.

LIST A Documents that Establish Both Identity and Employment Authorization	LIST B Documents that Establish Identity	LIST C Documents that Establish Employment Authorization
1. U.S. Passport or U.S. Passport Card	1. Driver's license or ID card issued by a State or outlying possession of the United States provided it contains a photograph or information such as name, date of birth, gender, height, eye color, and address	1. A Social Security Account Number card, unless the card includes one of the following restrictions: (1) NOT VALID FOR EMPLOYMENT (2) VALID FOR WORK ONLY WITH INS AUTHORIZATION (3) VALID FOR WORK ONLY WITH DHS AUTHORIZATION
2. Permanent Resident Card or Alien Registration Receipt Card (Form I-551)		
3. Foreign passport that contains a temporary I-551 stamp or temporary I-551 printed notation on a machine-readable immigrant visa		
	2. ID card issued by federal, state or local government agencies or entities, provided it contains a photograph or information such as name, date of birth, gender, height, eye color, and address	2. Certification of report of birth issued by the Department of State (Forms DS-1350, FS-545, FS-240)
4. Employment Authorization Document that contains a photograph (Form I-766)		
	3. School ID card with a photograph	3. Original or certified copy of birth certificate issued by a State, county, municipal authority, or territory of the United States bearing an official seal
5. For a nonimmigrant alien authorized to work for a specific employer because of his or her status: a. Foreign passport; and b. Form I-94 or Form I-94A that has the following: (1) The same name as the passport; and (2) An endorsement of the alien's nonimmigrant status as long as that period of endorsement has not yet expired and the proposed employment is not in conflict with any restrictions or limitations identified on the form.	4. Voter's registration card	
	5. U.S. Military card or draft record	
	6. Military dependent's ID card	
	7. U.S. Coast Guard Merchant Mariner Card	4. Native American tribal document
		5. U.S. Citizen ID Card (Form I-197)
	8. Native American tribal document	6. Identification Card for Use of Resident Citizen in the United States (Form I-179)
	9. Driver's license issued by a Canadian government authority	
	For persons under age 18 who are unable to present a document listed above:	7. Employment authorization document issued by the Department of Homeland Security
6. Passport from the Federated States of Micronesia (FSM) or the Republic of the Marshall Islands (RMI) with Form I-94 or Form I-94A indicating nonimmigrant admission under the Compact of Free Association Between the United States and the FSM or RMI	10. School record or report card	
	11. Clinic, doctor, or hospital record	
	12. Day-care or nursery school record	

Examples of many of these documents appear in the Handbook for Employers (M-274).

Refer to the instructions for more information about acceptable receipts.

Form I-9 10/21/2019

(Source: USCIS)

Form **W-4**	**Employee's Withholding Certificate**	OMB No. 1545-0074
Department of the Treasury Internal Revenue Service	Complete Form W-4 so that your employer can withhold the correct federal income tax from your pay. Give Form W-4 to your employer. Your withholding is subject to review by the IRS.	2023

Step 1:

Enter Personal Information

(a) First name and middle initial   Last name

(b) Social security number

Address

City or town, state, and ZIP code

Does your name match the name on your social security card? If not, to ensure you get credit for your earnings, contact SSA at 800-772-1213 or go to *www.ssa.gov*.

(c) ☐ Single or Married filing separately
☐ Married filing jointly or Qualifying surviving spouse
☐ Head of household (Check only if you're unmarried and pay more than half the costs of keeping up a home for yourself and a qualifying individual.)

Complete Steps 2–4 ONLY if they apply to you; otherwise, skip to Step 5. See page 2 for more information on each step, who can claim exemption from withholding, other details, and privacy.

Step 2:

Multiple Jobs or Spouse Works

Complete this step if you (1) hold more than one job at a time, or (2) are married filing jointly and your spouse also works. The correct amount of withholding depends on income earned from all of these jobs.

Do **only one** of the following.

(a) Reserved for future use.

(b) Use the Multiple Jobs Worksheet on page 3 and enter the result in Step 4(c) below; **or**

(c) If there are only two jobs total, you may check this box. Do the same on Form W-4 for the other job. This option is generally more accurate than (b) if pay at the lower paying job is more than half of the pay at the higher paying job. Otherwise, (b) is more accurate . . . . ▶ ☐

TIP: If you have self-employment income, see page 2.

Complete Steps 3–4(b) on Form W-4 for only ONE of these jobs. Leave those steps blank for the other jobs. (Your withholding will be most accurate if you complete Steps 3–4(b) on the Form W-4 for the highest paying job.)

Step 3:

Claim Dependent and Other Credits

If your total income will be $200,000 or less ($400,000 or less if married filing jointly):

Multiply the number of qualifying children under age 17 by $2,000 $ _____

Multiply the number of other dependents by $500 . . . . . $ _____

Add the amounts above for qualifying children and other dependents. You may add to this the amount of any other credits. Enter the total here . . . . **3** $ _____

Step 4 (optional):

Other Adjustments

(a) **Other income (not from jobs).** If you want tax withheld for other income you expect this year that won't have withholding, enter the amount of other income here. This may include interest, dividends, and retirement income . . . . **4(a)** $ _____

(b) **Deductions.** If you expect to claim deductions other than the standard deduction and want to reduce your withholding, use the Deductions Worksheet on page 3 and enter the result here . . . . **4(b)** $ _____

(c) **Extra withholding.** Enter any additional tax you want withheld each **pay period** . . **4(c)** $ _____

Step 5:

Sign Here

Under penalties of perjury, I declare that this certificate, to the best of my knowledge and belief, is true, correct, and complete.

_____   _____
Employee's signature (This form is not valid unless you sign it.)   **Date**

Employers Only	Employer's name and address	First date of employment	Employer identification number (EIN)

For Privacy Act and Paperwork Reduction Act Notice, see page 3.   Cat. No. 10220Q   Form **W-4** (2023)

(Source: IRS)

Form W-4 (2023) Page **3**

Step 2(b)—Multiple Jobs Worksheet *(Keep for your records.)*

If you choose the option in Step 2(b) on Form W-4, complete this worksheet (which calculates the total extra tax for all jobs) on **only ONE** Form W-4. Withholding will be most accurate if you complete the worksheet and enter the result on the Form W-4 for the highest paying job. To be accurate, submit a new Form W-4 for all other jobs if you have not updated your withholding since 2019.

Note: If more than one job has annual wages of more than $120,000 or there are more than three jobs, see Pub. 505 for additional tables.

1. **Two jobs.** If you have two jobs or you're married filing jointly and you and your spouse each have one job, find the amount from the appropriate table on page 4. Using the "Higher Paying Job" row and the "Lower Paying Job" column, find the value at the intersection of the two household salaries and enter that value on line 1. Then, **skip** to line 3 . . . . 1 $ _____

2. **Three jobs.** If you and/or your spouse have three jobs at the same time, complete lines 2a, 2b, and 2c below. Otherwise, skip to line 3.

    a Find the amount from the appropriate table on page 4 using the annual wages from the highest paying job in the "Higher Paying Job" row and the annual wages for your next highest paying job in the "Lower Paying Job" column. Find the value at the intersection of the two household salaries and enter that value on line 2a . . . . 2a $ _____

    b Add the annual wages of the two highest paying jobs from line 2a together and use the total as the wages in the "Higher Paying Job" row and use the annual wages for your third job in the "Lower Paying Job" column to find the amount from the appropriate table on page 4 and enter this amount on line 2b . . . . 2b $ _____

    c Add the amounts from lines 2a and 2b and enter the result on line 2c . . . . 2c $ _____

3. Enter the number of pay periods per year for the highest paying job. For example, if that job pays weekly, enter 52; if it pays every other week, enter 26; if it pays monthly, enter 12, etc. . . . . . 3 _____

4. **Divide** the annual amount on line 1 or line 2c by the number of pay periods on line 3. Enter this amount here and in **Step 4(c)** of Form W-4 for the highest paying job (along with any other additional amount you want withheld) . . . . 4 $ _____

Step 4(b)—Deductions Worksheet *(Keep for your records.)*

1. Enter an estimate of your 2023 itemized deductions (from Schedule A (Form 1040)). Such deductions may include qualifying home mortgage interest, charitable contributions, state and local taxes (up to $10,000), and medical expenses in excess of 7.5% of your income . . . . 1 $ _____

2. Enter:
   - $27,700 if you're married filing jointly or a qualifying surviving spouse
   - $20,800 if you're head of household
   - $13,850 if you're single or married filing separately
   . . . . . 2 $ _____

3. If line 1 is greater than line 2, subtract line 2 from line 1 and enter the result here. If line 2 is greater than line 1, enter "-0-" . . . . 3 $ _____

4. Enter an estimate of your student loan interest, deductible IRA contributions, and certain other adjustments (from Part II of Schedule 1 (Form 1040)). See Pub. 505 for more information . . . . 4 $ _____

5. **Add** lines 3 and 4. Enter the result here and in **Step 4(b)** of Form W-4 . . . . 5 $ _____

Privacy Act and Paperwork Reduction Act Notice. We ask for the information on this form to carry out the Internal Revenue laws of the United States. Internal Revenue Code sections 3402(f)(2) and 6109 and their regulations require you to provide this information; your employer uses it to determine your federal income tax withholding. Failure to provide a properly completed form will result in your being treated as a single person with no other entries on the form; providing fraudulent information may subject you to penalties. Routine uses of this information include giving it to the Department of Justice for civil and criminal litigation; to cities, states, the District of Columbia, and U.S. commonwealths and territories for use in administering their tax laws; and to the Department of Health and Human Services for use in the National Directory of New Hires. We may also disclose this information to other countries under a tax treaty, to federal and state agencies to enforce federal nontax criminal laws, or to federal law enforcement and intelligence agencies to combat terrorism.

You are not required to provide the information requested on a form that is subject to the Paperwork Reduction Act unless the form displays a valid OMB control number. Books or records relating to a form or its instructions must be retained as long as their contents may become material in the administration of any Internal Revenue law. Generally, tax returns and return information are confidential, as required by Code section 6103.

The average time and expenses required to complete and file this form will vary depending on individual circumstances. For estimated averages, see the instructions for your income tax return.

If you have suggestions for making this form simpler, we would be happy to hear from you. See the instructions for your income tax return.

(Source: IRS)

Form W-4 (2023) Page 4

Married Filing Jointly or Qualifying Surviving Spouse

Higher Paying Job Annual Taxable Wage & Salary	Lower Paying Job Annual Taxable Wage & Salary											
	$0 - 9,999	$10,000 - 19,999	$20,000 - 29,999	$30,000 - 39,999	$40,000 - 49,999	$50,000 - 59,999	$60,000 - 69,999	$70,000 - 79,999	$80,000 - 89,999	$90,000 - 99,999	$100,000 - 109,999	$110,000 - 120,000
$0 - 9,999	$0	$0	$850	$850	$1,000	$1,020	$1,020	$1,020	$1,020	$1,020	$1,020	$1,870
$10,000 - 19,999	0	930	1,850	2,000	2,200	2,220	2,220	2,220	2,220	2,220	3,200	4,070
$20,000 - 29,999	850	1,850	2,920	3,120	3,320	3,340	3,340	3,340	3,340	4,320	5,320	6,190
$30,000 - 39,999	850	2,000	3,120	3,320	3,520	3,540	3,540	3,540	4,520	5,520	6,520	7,390
$40,000 - 49,999	1,000	2,200	3,320	3,520	3,720	3,740	3,740	4,720	5,720	6,720	7,720	8,590
$50,000 - 59,999	1,020	2,220	3,340	3,540	3,740	3,760	4,750	5,750	6,750	7,750	8,750	9,610
$60,000 - 69,999	1,020	2,220	3,340	3,540	3,740	4,750	5,750	6,750	7,750	8,750	9,750	10,610
$70,000 - 79,999	1,020	2,220	3,340	3,540	4,720	5,750	6,750	7,750	8,750	9,750	10,750	11,610
$80,000 - 99,999	1,020	2,220	4,170	5,370	6,570	7,600	8,600	9,600	10,600	11,600	12,600	13,460
$100,000 - 149,999	1,870	4,070	6,190	7,390	8,590	9,610	10,610	11,660	12,860	14,060	15,260	16,330
$150,000 - 239,999	2,040	4,440	6,760	8,160	9,560	10,780	11,980	13,180	14,380	15,580	16,780	17,850
$240,000 - 259,999	2,040	4,440	6,760	8,160	9,560	10,780	11,980	13,180	14,380	15,580	16,780	17,850
$260,000 - 279,999	2,040	4,440	6,760	8,160	9,560	10,780	11,980	13,180	14,380	15,580	16,780	18,140
$280,000 - 299,999	2,040	4,440	6,760	8,160	9,560	10,780	11,980	13,180	14,380	15,870	17,870	19,740
$300,000 - 319,999	2,040	4,440	6,760	8,160	9,560	10,780	11,980	13,470	15,470	17,470	19,470	21,340
$320,000 - 364,999	2,040	4,440	6,760	8,550	10,750	12,770	14,770	16,770	18,770	20,770	22,770	24,640
$365,000 - 524,999	2,970	6,470	9,890	12,390	14,890	17,220	19,520	21,820	24,120	26,420	28,720	30,880
$525,000 and over	3,140	6,840	10,460	13,160	15,860	18,390	20,890	23,390	25,890	28,390	30,890	33,250

Single or Married Filing Separately

Higher Paying Job Annual Taxable Wage & Salary	Lower Paying Job Annual Taxable Wage & Salary											
	$0 - 9,999	$10,000 - 19,999	$20,000 - 29,999	$30,000 - 39,999	$40,000 - 49,999	$50,000 - 59,999	$60,000 - 69,999	$70,000 - 79,999	$80,000 - 89,999	$90,000 - 99,999	$100,000 - 109,999	$110,000 - 120,000
$0 - 9,999	$310	$890	$1,020	$1,020	$1,020	$1,860	$1,870	$1,870	$1,870	$1,870	$2,030	$2,040
$10,000 - 19,999	890	1,630	1,750	1,750	2,600	3,600	3,600	3,600	3,600	3,760	3,960	3,970
$20,000 - 29,999	1,020	1,750	1,880	2,720	3,720	4,720	4,730	4,730	4,890	5,090	5,290	5,300
$30,000 - 39,999	1,020	1,750	2,720	3,720	4,720	5,720	5,730	5,890	6,090	6,290	6,490	6,500
$40,000 - 59,999	1,710	3,450	4,570	5,570	6,570	7,700	7,910	8,110	8,310	8,510	8,710	8,720
$60,000 - 79,999	1,870	3,600	4,730	5,860	7,060	8,260	8,460	8,660	8,860	9,060	9,260	9,280
$80,000 - 99,999	1,870	3,730	5,060	6,260	7,460	8,660	8,860	9,060	9,260	9,460	10,430	11,240
$100,000 - 124,999	2,040	3,970	5,300	6,500	7,700	8,900	9,110	9,610	10,610	11,610	12,610	13,430
$125,000 - 149,999	2,040	3,970	5,300	6,500	7,700	9,610	10,610	11,610	12,610	13,610	14,900	16,020
$150,000 - 174,999	2,040	3,970	5,610	7,610	9,610	11,610	12,610	13,750	15,050	16,350	17,650	18,770
$175,000 - 199,999	2,720	5,450	7,580	9,580	11,580	13,870	15,180	16,480	17,780	19,080	20,380	21,490
$200,000 - 249,999	2,900	5,930	8,360	10,660	12,960	15,260	16,570	17,870	19,170	20,470	21,770	22,880
$250,000 - 399,999	2,970	6,010	8,440	10,740	13,040	15,340	16,640	17,940	19,240	20,540	21,840	22,960
$400,000 - 449,999	2,970	6,010	8,440	10,740	13,040	15,340	16,640	17,940	19,240	20,540	21,840	22,960
$450,000 and over	3,140	6,380	9,010	11,510	14,010	16,510	18,010	19,510	21,010	22,510	24,010	25,330

Head of Household

Higher Paying Job Annual Taxable Wage & Salary	Lower Paying Job Annual Taxable Wage & Salary											
	$0 - 9,999	$10,000 - 19,999	$20,000 - 29,999	$30,000 - 39,999	$40,000 - 49,999	$50,000 - 59,999	$60,000 - 69,999	$70,000 - 79,999	$80,000 - 89,999	$90,000 - 99,999	$100,000 - 109,999	$110,000 - 120,000
$0 - 9,999	$0	$620	$860	$1,020	$1,020	$1,020	$1,020	$1,650	$1,870	$1,870	$1,890	$2,040
$10,000 - 19,999	620	1,630	2,060	2,220	2,220	2,220	2,850	3,850	4,070	4,090	4,290	4,440
$20,000 - 29,999	860	2,060	2,490	2,650	2,650	3,280	4,280	5,280	5,520	5,720	5,920	6,070
$30,000 - 39,999	1,020	2,220	2,650	2,810	3,440	4,440	5,440	6,460	6,880	7,080	7,280	7,430
$40,000 - 59,999	1,020	2,220	3,130	4,290	5,290	6,290	7,480	8,680	9,100	9,300	9,500	9,650
$60,000 - 79,999	1,500	3,700	5,130	6,290	7,480	8,680	9,880	11,080	11,500	11,700	11,900	12,050
$80,000 - 99,999	1,870	4,070	5,690	7,050	8,250	9,450	10,650	11,850	12,260	12,460	12,870	13,820
$100,000 - 124,999	2,040	4,440	6,070	7,430	8,630	9,830	11,030	12,230	13,190	14,190	15,190	16,150
$125,000 - 149,999	2,040	4,440	6,070	7,430	8,630	9,980	11,980	13,980	15,190	16,190	17,270	18,530
$150,000 - 174,999	2,040	4,440	6,070	7,980	9,980	11,980	13,980	15,980	17,420	18,720	20,020	21,280
$175,000 - 199,999	2,190	5,390	7,820	9,980	11,980	14,060	16,360	18,660	20,170	21,470	22,770	24,030
$200,000 - 249,999	2,720	6,190	8,920	11,380	13,680	15,980	18,280	20,580	22,090	23,390	24,690	25,950
$250,000 - 449,999	2,970	6,470	9,200	11,660	13,960	16,260	18,560	20,860	22,380	23,680	24,980	26,230
$450,000 and over	3,140	6,840	9,770	12,430	14,930	17,430	19,930	22,430	24,150	25,650	27,150	28,600

(Source: IRS)

State of Nevada New Hire Report

All employers are required to report certain information on newly hired or rehired employees (those separated from your employment at least 60 consecutive days). Use of this form is not mandatory. It is provided for your convenience.

Federal Tax I.D. # _____
Company Name: _____
Company Address: _____
City, State, Zip: _____
Contact Person: _____
Phone Number: _____

Social Security Number Required	First Name Middle Initial Last Name Required	Address, Street City, State, Zip Required	Date of Birth	Start Date Required	State of Hire

Please return this form by fax to (775) 684-6379 or mail to:
Department of Employment, Training and Rehabilitation
Employment Security Division – New Hire Unit
500 East Third Street, Carson City, Nevada 89713-0033

Revised 02/12

(Source: State of Nevada)

Account: Cash 101

	Date		Description	Post Ref.	Debit	Credit	Balance Debit	Balance Credit	
Beg Bal									
1									1
2									2
3									3
4									4
5									5
6									6
7									7
8									8
9									9
10									10
11									11
12									12
13									13
14									14
15									15

Account: Employee Federal Income Tax Payable 203

	Date		Description	Post Ref.	Debit	Credit	Balance Debit	Balance Credit	
1									1
2									2
3									3
4									4
5									5
6									6
7									7
8									8
9									9

Account: Social Security Tax Payable 204

	Date		Description	Post Ref.	Debit	Credit	Balance Debit	Balance Credit	
1									1
2									2
3									3
4									4
5									5
6									6
7									7
8									8
9									9
10									10
11									11
12									12
13									13
14									14
15									15

Account: Medicare Tax Payable 205

	Date	Description	Post Ref.	Debit	Credit	Balance Debit	Balance Credit	
1								1
2								2
3								3
4								4
5								5
6								6
7								7
8								8
9								9
10								10
11								11
12								12
13								13
14								14
15								15

Account: 401(k) Contributions Payable 208

	Date	Description	Post Ref.	Debit	Credit	Balance Debit	Balance Credit	
1								1
2								2
3								3
4								4
5								5
6								6
7								7
8								8
9								9
10								10

Account: Employee Medical Premiums Payable 209

	Date	Description	Post Ref.	Debit	Credit	Balance Debit	Balance Credit	
1								1
2								2
3								3
4								4
5								5
6								6
7								7
8								8
9								9
10								10

Account: Salaries and Wages Payable 210

	Date		Description	Post Ref.	Debit	Credit	Balance		
							Debit	Credit	
1									1
2									2
3									3
4									4
5									5
6									6
7									7
8									8
9									9
10									10
11									11
12									12

Account: Federal Unemployment Tax Payable 211

	Date		Description	Post Ref.	Debit	Credit	Balance		
							Debit	Credit	
1									1
2									2
3									3
4									4
5									5
6									6
7									7
8									8
9									9
10									10

Account: State Unemployment Tax Payable 212

	Date		Description	Post Ref.	Debit	Credit	Balance		
							Debit	Credit	
1									1
2									2
3									3
4									4
5									5
6									6
7									7
8									8
9									9
10									10

Account: Career Enhancement Program Payable 213

	Date	Description	Post Ref.	Debit	Credit	Balance Debit	Balance Credit	
1								1
2								2
3								3
4								4
5								5
6								6
7								7
8								8
9								9
10								10

Account: Payroll Taxes Expense 514

	Date	Description	Post Ref.	Debit	Credit	Balance Debit	Balance Credit	
1								1
2								2
3								3
4								4
5								5
6								6
7								7
8								8
9								9
10								10

Account: Salaries and Wages Expense 515

	Date	Description	Post Ref.	Debit	Credit	Balance Debit	Balance Credit	
1								1
2								2
3								3
4								4
5								5
6								6
7								7
8								8
9								9
10								10

Form 941 for 2023: Employer's QUARTERLY Federal Tax Return

(Rev. March 2023)   Department of the Treasury — Internal Revenue Service

950122
OMB No. 1545-0029

Employer identification number (EIN) [ ][ ] – [ ][ ][ ][ ][ ][ ][ ]

Name (not your trade name)

Trade name (if any)

Address
- Number   Street   Suite or room number
- City   State   ZIP code
- Foreign country name   Foreign province/county   Foreign postal code

Report for this Quarter of 2023 (Check one.)

- [ ] 1: January, February, March
- [ ] 2: April, May, June
- [ ] 3: July, August, September
- [ ] 4: October, November, December

Go to *www.irs.gov/Form941* for instructions and the latest information.

Read the separate instructions before you complete Form 941. Type or print within the boxes.

Part 1: Answer these questions for this quarter.

1. Number of employees who received wages, tips, or other compensation for the pay period including: *Mar. 12* (Quarter 1), *June 12* (Quarter 2), *Sept. 12* (Quarter 3), or *Dec. 12* (Quarter 4)   **1** [ ]

2. Wages, tips, and other compensation   **2** [ ]

3. Federal income tax withheld from wages, tips, and other compensation   **3** [ ]

4. If no wages, tips, and other compensation are subject to social security or Medicare tax   [ ] Check and go to line 6.

		Column 1		Column 2
5a	Taxable social security wages*	[ ]	× 0.124 =	[ ]
5a (i)	Qualified sick leave wages*	[ ]	× 0.062 =	[ ]
5a (ii)	Qualified family leave wages*	[ ]	× 0.062 =	[ ]
5b	Taxable social security tips	[ ]	× 0.124 =	[ ]
5c	Taxable Medicare wages & tips	[ ]	× 0.029 =	[ ]
5d	Taxable wages & tips subject to Additional Medicare Tax withholding	[ ]	× 0.009 =	[ ]

*Include taxable qualified sick and family leave wages paid in this quarter of 2023 for leave taken after March 31, 2021, and before October 1, 2021, on line 5a. Use lines 5a(i) and 5a(ii) **only** for taxable qualified sick and family leave wages paid in this quarter of 2023 for leave taken after March 31, 2020, and before April 1, 2021.

5e. Total social security and Medicare taxes. Add Column 2 from lines 5a, 5a(i), 5a(ii), 5b, 5c, and 5d   **5e** [ ]

5f. Section 3121(q) Notice and Demand—Tax due on unreported tips (see instructions)   **5f** [ ]

6. Total taxes before adjustments. Add lines 3, 5e, and 5f   **6** [ ]

7. Current quarter's adjustment for fractions of cents   **7** [ ]

8. Current quarter's adjustment for sick pay   **8** [ ]

9. Current quarter's adjustments for tips and group-term life insurance   **9** [ ]

10. Total taxes after adjustments. Combine lines 6 through 9   **10** [ ]

11a. Qualified small business payroll tax credit for increasing research activities. Attach Form 8974   **11a** [ ]

11b. Nonrefundable portion of credit for qualified sick and family leave wages for leave taken before April 1, 2021   **11b** [ ]

11c. Reserved for future use   **11c** [ ]

    You MUST complete all three pages of Form 941 and SIGN it.

For Privacy Act and Paperwork Reduction Act Notice, see the back of the Payment Voucher.   Cat. No. 17001Z   Form **941** (Rev. 3-2023)

(Source: Internal Revenue Service)

Appendix A *Comprehensive Payroll Project: Wayland Custom Woodworking* 439

951222

Name *(not your trade name)*	Employer identification number (EIN)
	—

Part 1: Answer these questions for this quarter. *(continued)*

11d Nonrefundable portion of credit for qualified sick and family leave wages for leave taken after March 31, 2021, and before October 1, 2021 . . . . 11d [_____.__]

11e Reserved for future use . . . . 11e [_____.__]

11f Reserved for future use . . . . [_____]

11g Total nonrefundable credits. Add lines 11a, 11b, and 11d . . . . 11g [_____.__]

12 Total taxes after adjustments and nonrefundable credits. Subtract line 11g from line 10 . 12 [_____.__]

13a Total deposits for this quarter, including overpayment applied from a prior quarter and overpayments applied from Form 941-X, 941-X (PR), 944-X, or 944-X (SP) filed in the current quarter 13a [_____.__]

13b Reserved for future use . . . . 13b [_____.__]

13c Refundable portion of credit for qualified sick and family leave wages for leave taken before April 1, 2021 . . . . 13c [_____.__]

13d Reserved for future use . . . . 13d [_____.__]

13e Refundable portion of credit for qualified sick and family leave wages for leave taken after March 31, 2021, and before October 1, 2021 . . . . 13e [_____.__]

13f Reserved for future use . . . . 13f [_____.__]

13g Total deposits and refundable credits. Add lines 13a, 13c, and 13e . . . . 13g [_____.__]

13h Reserved for future use . . . . 13h [_____.__]

13i Reserved for future use . . . . 13i [_____.__]

14 Balance due. If line 12 is more than line 13g, enter the difference and see instructions . . . 14 [_____.__]

15 Overpayment. If line 13g is more than line 12, enter the difference [_____.__] Check one: ☐ Apply to next return. ☐ Send a refund.

Part 2: Tell us about your deposit schedule and tax liability for this quarter.

If you're unsure about whether you're a monthly schedule depositor or a semiweekly schedule depositor, see section 11 of Pub. 15.

16 Check one: ☐ **Line 12 on this return is less than $2,500 or line 12 on the return for the prior quarter was less than $2,500, and you didn't incur a $100,000 next-day deposit obligation during the current quarter.** If line 12 for the prior quarter was less than $2,500 but line 12 on this return is $100,000 or more, you must provide a record of your federal tax liability. If you're a monthly schedule depositor, complete the deposit schedule below; if you're a semiweekly schedule depositor, attach Schedule B (Form 941). Go to Part 3.

☐ **You were a monthly schedule depositor for the entire quarter.** Enter your tax liability for each month and total liability for the quarter, then go to Part 3.

Tax liability: Month 1 [_____.__]

Month 2 [_____.__]

Month 3 [_____.__]

Total liability for quarter [_____.__] Total must equal line 12.

☐ **You were a semiweekly schedule depositor for any part of this quarter.** Complete Schedule B (Form 941), Report of Tax Liability for Semiweekly Schedule Depositors, and attach it to Form 941. Go to Part 3.

You MUST complete all three pages of Form 941 and SIGN it.

(Source: Internal Revenue Service)

Name (not your trade name)	Employer identification number (EIN)
	950922

Part 3: Tell us about your business. If a question does NOT apply to your business, leave it blank.

17 If your business has closed or you stopped paying wages . . . . ☐ Check here, and

   enter the final date you paid wages ___/___/___ ; also attach a statement to your return. See instructions.

18 If you're a seasonal employer and you don't have to file a return for every quarter of the year . . . ☐ Check here.

19 Qualified health plan expenses allocable to qualified sick leave wages for leave taken before April 1, 2021   19 ☐ .

20 Qualified health plan expenses allocable to qualified family leave wages for leave taken before April 1, 2021   20 ☐ .

21 Reserved for future use . . . .   21 ▓ .

22 Reserved for future use . . . .   22 ▓ .

23 Qualified sick leave wages for leave taken after March 31, 2021, and before October 1, 2021   23 ☐ .

24 Qualified health plan expenses allocable to qualified sick leave wages reported on line 23   24 ☐ .

25 Amounts under certain collectively bargained agreements allocable to qualified sick leave wages reported on line 23 . . . .   25 ☐ .

26 Qualified family leave wages for leave taken after March 31, 2021, and before October 1, 2021   26 ☐ .

27 Qualified health plan expenses allocable to qualified family leave wages reported on line 26   27 ☐ .

28 Amounts under certain collectively bargained agreements allocable to qualified family leave wages reported on line 26 . . . .   28 ☐ .

Part 4: May we speak with your third-party designee?

Do you want to allow an employee, a paid tax preparer, or another person to discuss this return with the IRS? See the instructions for details.

☐ Yes. Designee's name and phone number _____   _____

Select a 5-digit personal identification number (PIN) to use when talking to the IRS.   ☐ ☐ ☐ ☐ ☐

☐ No.

Part 5: Sign here. You MUST complete all three pages of Form 941 and SIGN it.

Under penalties of perjury, I declare that I have examined this return, including accompanying schedules and statements, and to the best of my knowledge and belief, it is true, correct, and complete. Declaration of preparer (other than taxpayer) is based on all information of which preparer has any knowledge.

Sign your name here _____

Print your name here _____

Print your title here _____

Date ___/___/___

Best daytime phone _____

Paid Preparer Use Only

Check if you're self-employed . . . ☐

Preparer's name	_____	PTIN	_____
Preparer's signature	_____	Date	___/___/___
Firm's name (or yours if self-employed)	_____	EIN	_____
Address	_____	Phone	_____
City	_____ State ____	ZIP code	_____

Page 3

Form **941** (Rev. 3-2023)

(Source: Internal Revenue Service)

Appendix A *Comprehensive Payroll Project: Wayland Custom Woodworking* 441

Form 941-V, Payment Voucher

Purpose of Form

Complete Form 941-V if you're making a payment with Form 941. We will use the completed voucher to credit your payment more promptly and accurately, and to improve our service to you.

Making Payments With Form 941

To avoid a penalty, make your payment with Form 941 **only if**:

- Your total taxes after adjustments and nonrefundable credits (Form 941, line 12) for either the current quarter or the preceding quarter are less than $2,500, you didn't incur a $100,000 next-day deposit obligation during the current quarter, and you're paying in full with a timely filed return; or

- You're a monthly schedule depositor making a payment in accordance with the Accuracy of Deposits Rule. See section 11 of Pub. 15 for details. In this case, the amount of your payment may be $2,500 or more.

Otherwise, you must make deposits by electronic funds transfer. See section 11 of Pub. 15 for deposit instructions. Don't use Form 941-V to make federal tax deposits.

⚠ *Use Form 941-V when making any payment with Form 941. However, if you pay an amount with Form 941 that should've been deposited, you may be subject to a penalty. See* Deposit Penalties *in section 11 of Pub. 15.*

Specific Instructions

Box 1—Employer identification number (EIN). If you don't have an EIN, you may apply for one online by visiting the IRS website at *www.irs.gov/EIN*. You may also apply for an EIN by faxing or mailing Form SS-4 to the IRS. If you haven't received your EIN by the due date of Form 941, write "Applied For" and the date you applied in this entry space.

Box 2—Amount paid. Enter the amount paid with Form 941.

Box 3—Tax period. Darken the circle identifying the quarter for which the payment is made. Darken only one circle.

Box 4—Name and address. Enter your name and address as shown on Form 941.

- Enclose your check or money order made payable to "United States Treasury." Be sure to enter your EIN, "Form 941," and the tax period ("1st Quarter 2023," "2nd Quarter 2023," "3rd Quarter 2023," or "4th Quarter 2023") on your check or money order. Don't send cash. Don't staple Form 941-V or your payment to Form 941 (or to each other).

- Detach Form 941-V and send it with your payment and Form 941 to the address in the Instructions for Form 941.

Note: You must also complete the entity information above Part 1 on Form 941.

Detach Here and Mail With Your Payment and Form 941.

Form 941-V
Department of the Treasury
Internal Revenue Service

Payment Voucher

Don't staple this voucher or your payment to Form 941.

OMB No. 1545-0029

2023

1 Enter your employer identification number (EIN).

2 **Enter the amount of your payment.**
Make your check or money order payable to "**United States Treasury**."

Dollars | Cents

3 Tax Period
- ○ 1st Quarter
- ○ 2nd Quarter
- ○ 3rd Quarter
- ○ 4th Quarter

4 Enter your business name (individual name if sole proprietor).

Enter your address.

Enter your city, state, and ZIP code; or your city, foreign country name, foreign province/county, and foreign postal code.

(Source: Internal Revenue Service)

Form 940 for 2022: Employer's Annual Federal Unemployment (FUTA) Tax Return

Department of the Treasury — Internal Revenue Service

850113

OMB No. 1545-0028

Employer identification number (EIN)

Name (not your trade name)

Trade name (if any)

Address
- Number, Street, Suite or room number
- City, State, ZIP code
- Foreign country name, Foreign province/county, Foreign postal code

Type of Return (Check all that apply.)
- a. Amended
- b. Successor employer
- c. No payments to employees in 2022
- d. Final: Business closed or stopped paying wages

Go to www.irs.gov/Form940 for instructions and the latest information.

Read the separate instructions before you complete this form. Please type or print within the boxes.

Part 1: Tell us about your return. If any line does NOT apply, leave it blank. See instructions before completing Part 1.

1a If you had to pay state unemployment tax in one state only, enter the state abbreviation . . . **1a**

1b If you had to pay state unemployment tax in more than one state, you are a multi-state employer . . . **1b** ☐ Check here. Complete Schedule A (Form 940).

2 If you paid wages in a state that is subject to CREDIT REDUCTION . . . **2** ☐ Check here. Complete Schedule A (Form 940).

Part 2: Determine your FUTA tax before adjustments. If any line does NOT apply, leave it blank.

3 Total payments to all employees . . . **3**

4 Payments exempt from FUTA tax . . . **4**

Check all that apply:
- 4a ☐ Fringe benefits
- 4b ☐ Group-term life insurance
- 4c ☐ Retirement/Pension
- 4d ☐ Dependent care
- 4e ☐ Other

5 Total of payments made to each employee in excess of $7,000 . . . **5**

6 Subtotal (line 4 + line 5 = line 6) . . . **6**

7 Total taxable FUTA wages (line 3 – line 6 = line 7). See instructions . . . **7**

8 FUTA tax before adjustments (line 7 × 0.006 = line 8) . . . **8**

Part 3: Determine your adjustments. If any line does NOT apply, leave it blank.

9 If ALL of the taxable FUTA wages you paid were excluded from state unemployment tax, multiply line 7 by 0.054 (line 7 × 0.054 = line 9). Go to line 12 . . . **9**

10 If SOME of the taxable FUTA wages you paid were excluded from state unemployment tax, OR you paid ANY state unemployment tax late (after the due date for filing Form 940), complete the worksheet in the instructions. Enter the amount from line 7 of the worksheet . . . **10**

11 If credit reduction applies, enter the total from Schedule A (Form 940) . . . **11**

Part 4: Determine your FUTA tax and balance due or overpayment. If any line does NOT apply, leave it blank.

12 Total FUTA tax after adjustments (lines 8 + 9 + 10 + 11 = line 12) . . . **12**

13 FUTA tax deposited for the year, including any overpayment applied from a prior year . . . **13**

14 Balance due. If line 12 is more than line 13, enter the excess on line 14.
- If line 14 is more than $500, you must deposit your tax.
- If line 14 is $500 or less, you may pay with this return. See instructions . . . **14**

15 Overpayment. If line 13 is more than line 12, enter the excess on line 15 and check a box below **15**

You MUST complete both pages of this form and SIGN it. Check one: ☐ Apply to next return. ☐ Send a refund.

For Privacy Act and Paperwork Reduction Act Notice, see the back of the Payment Voucher. Cat. No. 11234O Form **940** (2022)

(Source: Internal Revenue Service)

Name *(not your trade name)* | **Employer identification number (EIN)**

850212

Part 5: Report your FUTA tax liability by quarter only if line 12 is more than $500. If not, go to Part 6.

16 Report the amount of your FUTA tax liability for each quarter; do NOT enter the amount you deposited. If you had no liability for a quarter, leave the line blank.

   16a   1st quarter (January 1 – March 31) 16a

   16b   2nd quarter (April 1 – June 30) 16b

   16c   3rd quarter (July 1 – September 30) 16c

   16d   4th quarter (October 1 – December 31) 16d

17 Total tax liability for the year (lines 16a + 16b + 16c + 16d = line 17) 17 — Total must equal line 12.

Part 6: May we speak with your third-party designee?

Do you want to allow an employee, a paid tax preparer, or another person to discuss this return with the IRS? See the instructions for details.

☐ Yes. Designee's name and phone number

Select a 5-digit personal identification number (PIN) to use when talking to the IRS.

☐ No.

Part 7: Sign here. You MUST complete both pages of this form and SIGN it.

Under penalties of perjury, I declare that I have examined this return, including accompanying schedules and statements, and to the best of my knowledge and belief, it is true, correct, and complete, and that no part of any payment made to a state unemployment fund claimed as a credit was, or is to be, deducted from the payments made to employees. Declaration of preparer (other than taxpayer) is based on all information of which preparer has any knowledge.

Sign your name here

Print your name here

Print your title here

Best daytime phone

Date   /   /

Paid Preparer Use Only   Check if you are self-employed ☐

Preparer's name | PTIN

Preparer's signature | Date   /   /

Firm's name (or yours if self-employed) | EIN

Address | Phone

City | State | ZIP code

Page **2**   Form **940** (2022)

(Source: Internal Revenue Service)

Form 940-V, Payment Voucher

Purpose of Form

Complete Form 940-V if you're making a payment with Form 940. We will use the completed voucher to credit your payment more promptly and accurately, and to improve our service to you.

Making Payments With Form 940

To avoid a penalty, make your payment with your 2022 Form 940 **only if** your FUTA tax for the fourth quarter (plus any undeposited amounts from earlier quarters) is $500 or less. If your total FUTA tax after adjustments (Form 940, line 12) is more than $500, you must make deposits by electronic funds transfer. See *When Must You Deposit Your FUTA Tax?* in the Instructions for Form 940. Also see sections 11 and 14 of Pub. 15 for more information about deposits.

Use Form 940-V when making any payment with Form 940. However, if you pay an amount with Form 940 that should've been deposited, you may be subject to a penalty. See Deposit Penalties *in section 11 of Pub. 15.*

Specific Instructions

Box 1—Employer identification number (EIN). If you don't have an EIN, you may apply for one online by visiting the IRS website at *www.irs.gov/EIN*. You may also apply for an EIN by faxing or mailing Form SS-4 to the IRS. If you haven't received your EIN by the due date of Form 940, write "Applied For" and the date you applied in this entry space.

Box 2—Amount paid. Enter the amount paid with Form 940.

Box 3—Name and address. Enter your name and address as shown on Form 940.

- Enclose your check or money order made payable to "United States Treasury." Be sure to enter your EIN, "Form 940," and "2022" on your check or money order. Don't send cash. Don't staple Form 940-V or your payment to Form 940 (or to each other).

- Detach Form 940-V and send it with your payment and Form 940 to the address provided in the Instructions for Form 940.

Note: You must also complete the entity information above Part 1 on Form 940.

Detach Here and Mail With Your Payment and Form 940.

Form **940-V**
Department of the Treasury
Internal Revenue Service

Payment Voucher

Don't staple or attach this voucher to your payment.

OMB No. 1545-0028

2022

1 Enter your employer identification number (EIN).

2 Enter the amount of your payment.
Make your check or money order payable to "**United States Treasury**"

Dollars | Cents

3 Enter your business name (individual name if sole proprietor).

Enter your address.

Enter your city, state, and ZIP code; or your city, foreign country name, foreign province/county, and foreign postal code.

(Source: Internal Revenue Service)

Appendix A *Comprehensive Payroll Project: Wayland Custom Woodworking*

Page 1

DO NOT STAPLE THIS FORM

State of Nevada
Department of Employment, Training & Rehabilitation
EMPLOYMENT SECURITY DIVISION
500 E. Third St., Carson City, NV 89713-0030
Telephone (775) 687-4540

EMPLOYER'S QUARTERLY CONTRIBUTION AND WAGE REPORT

PLEASE CORRECT ANY NAME OR ADDRESS INFORMATION BELOW. 1a. EMPLOYER ACCOUNT NUMBER	1b. FOR QUARTER ENDING	1e. FEDERAL I.D. NO.
	1c. DELINQUENT AFTER	**IMPORTANT** FOR YOUR PROTECTION, VERIFY YOUR FEDERAL I.D. NO. ABOVE. IF IT IS IN ERROR, PLEASE ENTER THE CORRECT NUMBER HERE
	1d. YOUR RATES	

A REPORT MUST BE FILED
INSTRUCTIONS ENCLOSED

	Dollars	Cents	
3. TOTAL GROSS WAGES (INCLUDING TIPS) PAID THIS QUARTER (If you paid no wages, write "NONE," sign report and return.) (See Instructions)			**2. REPORT OF CHANGES** If any of the following changes have occurred, please check the appropriate box and provide details on page 2. ☐ Business Discontinued ☐ Ownership Change ☐ Entire Business Sold ☐ Part of Business Sold ☐ Legal Ownership Change ☐ Business Added
4. LESS WAGES IN EXCESS OF _____ PER INDIVIDUAL (Cannot exceed amount in Item 3.) (See Instructions)			
5. TAXABLE WAGES PAID THIS QUARTER (Item 3 less Item 4.)			
6. UI AMOUNT DUE THIS QUARTER (Item 5 x your UI Rate shown in Item 1d.)			
7. CEP AMOUNT DUE THIS QUARTER (Item 5 x the CEP Rate in Item 1d.) (Add) (Do not include the CEP amount on federal unemployment tax return Form 940.)			
8. PRIOR CREDIT (Attach "Statement of Employer Account") (Subtract)			
9. CHARGE FOR LATE FILING OF THIS REPORT (Add) (One or more days late add $5.00 forfeit.)			(FOR DIVISION USE ONLY)
10. ADDITIONAL CHARGE FOR LATE FILING, AFTER 10 DAYS (Add) (Item 5 x 1/10% (.001) for each month or part of month delinquent.)			
11. INTEREST ON PAST DUE UI CONTRIBUTIONS (Add) (Item 6 x 1% (.01) for each month or part of month delinquent.) (See Instructions)			
12. TOTAL PAYMENT DUE (Total Items 6 through 11.) MAKE PAYABLE TO NEVADA EMPLOYMENT SECURITY DIVISION. Please enter Employer Account Number on check.			

13. SOCIAL SECURITY NUMBER	14. EMPLOYEE NAME Do not make adjustments to prior quarters.	15. TOTAL TIPS REPORTED Dollars / Cents	16. TOTAL GROSS WAGES INCLUDING TIPS Dollars / Cents	
				17. NUMBER OF WORKERS LISTED ON THIS REPORT
				18. FOR EACH MONTH, REPORT THE NUMBER OF WORKERS WHO WORKED DURING OR RECEIVED PAY FOR THE PAYROLL PERIOD WHICH INCLUDES THE 12TH OF THE MONTH. 1 MO / 2 MO / 3 MO
19. TOTAL PAGES THIS REPORT	20. TOTAL TIPS AND TOTAL WAGES THIS PAGE →	$	$	

21. I certify that the information contained on this report and the attachments is true and correct.

_____ Signed/Title

_____ Name of Preparer if Other Than Employer

( ) _____ _____ ( ) _____ _____ ( ) _____ _____ _____
Area Code Fax Number   Area Code Telephone Number   Area Code Telephone Number   Date

NUCS-4072 (Rev.9-02)

(Source: State of Nevada)

22222	VOID ☐	a Employee's social security number	For Official Use Only OMB No. 1545-0008		
b Employer identification number (EIN)			1 Wages, tips, other compensation	2 Federal income tax withheld	
c Employer's name, address, and ZIP code			3 Social security wages	4 Social security tax withheld	
			5 Medicare wages and tips	6 Medicare tax withheld	
			7 Social security tips	8 Allocated tips	
d Control number			9	10 Dependent care benefits	
e Employee's first name and initial	Last name	Suff.	11 Nonqualified plans	12a See instructions for box 12	
			13 Statutory employee ☐ Retirement plan ☐ Third-party sick pay ☐	12b	
			14 Other	12c	
				12d	
f Employee's address and ZIP code					
15 State Employer's state ID number	16 State wages, tips, etc.	17 State income tax	18 Local wages, tips, etc.	19 Local income tax	20 Locality name

Form **W-2** Wage and Tax Statement   **2023**

Department of the Treasury—Internal Revenue Service

Copy A—For Social Security Administration. Send this entire page with Form W-3 to the Social Security Administration; photocopies are **not** acceptable.

For Privacy Act and Paperwork Reduction Act Notice, see the separate instructions.

Cat. No. 10134D

Do Not Cut, Fold, or Staple Forms on This Page

(Source: Internal Revenue Service)

33333	a Control number	For Official Use Only: OMB No. 1545-0008			
b Kind of Payer (Check one)	941 ☐ Military ☐ 943 ☐ 944 ☐ CT-1 ☐ Hshld. emp. ☐ Medicare govt. emp. ☐	**Kind of Employer** (Check one)	None apply ☐ 501c non-govt. ☐ State/local non-501c ☐ State/local 501c ☐ Federal govt. ☐		Third-party sick pay (Check if applicable) ☐
c Total number of Forms W-2	**d** Establishment number	**1** Wages, tips, other compensation		**2** Federal income tax withheld	
e Employer identification number (EIN)		**3** Social security wages		**4** Social security tax withheld	
f Employer's name		**5** Medicare wages and tips		**6** Medicare tax withheld	
		7 Social security tips		**8** Allocated tips	
		9		**10** Dependent care benefits	
		11 Nonqualified plans		**12a** Deferred compensation	
g Employer's address and ZIP code					
h Other EIN used this year		**13** For third-party sick pay use only		**12b**	
15 State Employer's state ID number		**14** Income tax withheld by payer of third-party sick pay			
16 State wages, tips, etc.	**17** State income tax	**18** Local wages, tips, etc.		**19** Local income tax	
Employer's contact person		Employer's telephone number		For Official Use Only	
Employer's fax number		Employer's email address			

Under penalties of perjury, I declare that I have examined this return and accompanying documents, and, to the best of my knowledge and belief, they are true, correct, and complete.

Signature: _____ Title: _____ Date: _____

Form **W-3** Transmittal of Wage and Tax Statements   **2023**   Department of the Treasury Internal Revenue Service

(Source: Internal Revenue Service)

Appendix B

Special Classes of Federal Tax Withholding

Special Classes of Employment and Special Types of Payments	Treatment under Employment Taxes		
	Income Tax Withholding	Social Security and Medicare (Including Additional Medicare Tax When Wages Are Paid in Excess of $200,000)	FUTA
Aliens, Nonresident	See Publication 515, "Withholding of Tax on Nonresident Aliens and Foreign Entities," and Publication 519, "U.S. Tax Guide for Aliens."		
Aliens, Resident			
1. Service performed in the United States	Same as U.S. citizens.	Same as U.S. citizens. (Exempt if any part of service as a crew member of foreign vessel or aircraft is performed outside the United States.)	Same as U.S. citizens.
2. Service performed outside the United States	Withhold	Taxable if (1) working for an American employer or (2) an American employer by agreement covers U.S. citizens and residents employed by its foreign affiliates.	Exempt unless on or in connection with an American vessel or aircraft and performed under a contract made in the United States, or alien is employed on such vessel or aircraft when it touches U.S. port.
Cafeteria Plan Benefits under Section 125	If an employee chooses cash, subject to all employment taxes. If an employee chooses another benefit, the treatment is the same as if the benefit was provided outside the plan. See Publication 15-B for more information.		
Deceased Worker			
1. Wages paid to beneficiary or estate in the same calendar year as worker's death. See the "Instructions for Forms W-2 and W-3" for details.	Exempt	Taxable	Taxable
2. Wages paid to beneficiary or estate after calendar year of worker's death	Exempt	Exempt	Exempt

Special Classes of Employment and Special Types of Payments	Treatment under Employment Taxes		
	Income Tax Withholding	Social Security and Medicare (Including Additional Medicare Tax When Wages Are Paid in Excess of $200,000)	FUTA
Dependent Care Assistance Programs	Exempt to the extent it is reasonable to believe amounts are excludable from gross income under Section 129.		
Disabled Worker's Wages paid after the year in which worker became entitled to disability insurance benefits under the Social Security Act.	Withhold	Exempt, if the worker did not perform service for the employer during the period for which payment is made.	Taxable
Employee Business Expense Reimbursement			
1. Accountable plan			
a. Amounts not exceeding specified government rate for per diem or standard mileage	Exempt	Exempt	Exempt
b. Amounts in excess of specified government rate for per diem or standard mileage.	Withhold	Taxable	Taxable
2. Nonaccountable plan. See Section 5 of IRS Publication 15 for details.	Withhold	Taxable	Taxable
Family Employees			
1. A child employed by the parent (or partnership in which each partner is a parent of the child)	Withhold	Exempt until age 18; age 21 for domestic service.	Exempt until age 21.
2. Parent employed by a child	Withhold	Taxable if in course of the son's or daughter's business. For domestic services, see Section 3 of IRS Publication 15.	Exempt
3. Spouse employed by a spouse. See Section 3 of IRS Publication 15 for more information.	Withhold	Taxable if in course of a spouse's business.	Exempt
Fishing and Related Activities	See Publication 334, "Tax Guide for Small Business."		
Foreign Governments and International Organizations	Exempt	Exempt	Exempt
Foreign Service by U.S. Citizens			
1. As U.S. government employees	Withhold	Same as within the United States.	Exempt
2. For foreign affiliates of American employers and other private employers	Exempt if at the time of payment (1) it is reasonable to believe the employee is entitled to an exclusion from income under Section 911 or (2) the employer is required by the law of the foreign country to withhold income tax on such payment.	Exempt unless (1) an American employer by agreement covers U.S. citizens employed by its foreign affiliates or (2) U.S. citizen works for an American employer.	Exempt unless (1) on American vessel or aircraft and work is performed under contract made in United States or worker is employed on vessel when it touches U.S. port or (2) U.S. citizen works for American employer (except in a contiguous country with which the United States has an agreement for unemployment compensation) or in the U.S. Virgin Islands.

	Treatment under Employment Taxes		
Special Classes of Employment and Special Types of Payments	**Income Tax Withholding**	**Social Security and Medicare (Including Additional Medicare Tax When Wages Are Paid in Excess of $200,000)**	**FUTA**
Fringe Benefits	Taxable on the excess of the fair market value of the benefit over the sum of an amount paid for it by the employee and any amount excludable by law. However, special valuation rules may apply. Benefits provided under cafeteria plans may qualify for exclusion from wages for Social Security, Medicare, and FUTA taxes. See Publication 15-B for details.		
Government Employment State/local governments and political subdivisions, employees of			
1. Salaries and wages (includes payments to most elected and appointed officials)	Withhold	Generally taxable for (1) services performed by employees who are either (a) covered under a Section 218 agreement or (b) not covered under a Section 218 agreement and not a member of a public retirement system (mandatory Social Security and Medicare coverage), and (2) (Medicare tax only) services performed by employees hired or rehired after 3/31/86 who are not covered under a Section 218 agreement or the mandatory Social Security provisions, unless specifically excluded by law. See Publication 963.	Exempt
2. Election workers. Election workers are individuals who are employed to perform services for state or local governments at election booths in connection with national, state, or local elections.	Exempt	Taxable if paid $2,000 or more in 2023 (lesser amount if specified by a Section 218 Social Security agreement). See Revenue Ruling 2000-6.	Exempt
Note: File Form W-2 for payments of $600 or more even if no Social Security or Medicare taxes were withheld.			
3. Emergency workers. Emergency workers who were hired on a temporary basis in response to a specific unforeseen emergency and are not intended to become permanent employees.	Withhold	Exempt if serving on a temporary basis in case of fire, storm, snow, earthquake, flood, or similar emergency.	Exempt
U.S. federal government employees	Withhold	Taxable for Medicare. Taxable for Social Security unless hired before 1984. See Section 3121(b)(5).	Exempt
Homeworkers (Industrial, Cottage Industry)			
1. Common-law employees	Withhold	Taxable	Taxable
2. Statutory employees. See Section 2 of IRS Publication 15 for details.	Exempt	Taxable if paid $100 or more in cash in a year.	Exempt

Special Classes of Employment and Special Types of Payments	Treatment under Employment Taxes		
	Income Tax Withholding	Social Security and Medicare (Including Additional Medicare Tax When Wages Are Paid in Excess of $200,000)	FUTA
Hospital Employees			
1. Interns	Withhold	Taxable	Exempt
2. Patients	Withhold	Taxable (exempt for state or local government hospitals).	Exempt
Household Employees			
1. Domestic service in private homes. Farmers, see Publication 51 (Circular A).	Exempt (withhold if both employer and employee agree)	Taxable if paid $2,600 or more in cash in 2023. Exempt if performed by an individual younger than age 18 during any portion of the calendar year and is not the principal occupation of the employee.	Taxable if the employer paid total cash wages of $1,000 or more in any quarter in the current or preceding calendar year.
2. Domestic service in college clubs, fraternities, and sororities	Exempt (withhold if both employer and employee agree)	Exempt if paid to regular students; also exempt if an employee is paid less than $100 in a year by an income-tax-exempt employer.	Taxable if the employer paid total cash wages of $1,000 or more in any quarter in the current or preceding calendar year.
Insurance for Employees			
1. Accident and health insurance premiums under a plan or system for employees and their dependents generally or for a class or classes of employees and their dependents	Exempt (except 2% shareholder-employees of S corporations)	Exempt	Exempt
2. Group-term life insurance costs. See Publication 15-B for details.	Exempt	Exempt, except for the cost of group-term life insurance includible in the employee's gross income. Special rules apply to former employees.	Exempt
Insurance Agents or Solicitors			
1. Full-time life insurance salesperson	Withhold only if an employee under common law. See Section 2 of IRS Publication 15.	Taxable	Taxable if (1) employee under common law and (2) not paid solely by commissions.
2. Other salespeople of life, casualty, and so on, insurance	Withhold only if an employee under common law.	Taxable only if an employee under common law.	Taxable if (1) employee under common law and (2) not paid solely by commissions.
Interest on Loans with Below-Market Interest Rates (forgone interest and deemed original issue discount)	See Publication 15-A, "Employer's Supplemental Tax Guide."		
Leave-Sharing Plans Amounts paid to an employee under a leave-sharing plan	Withhold	Taxable	Taxable

Special Classes of Employment and Special Types of Payments	Treatment under Employment Taxes		
	Income Tax Withholding	Social Security and Medicare (Including Additional Medicare Tax When Wages Are Paid in Excess of $200,000)	FUTA
Newspaper Carriers and Vendors Newspaper carriers younger than age 18; newspaper and magazine vendors buying at fixed prices and retaining receipts from sales to customers. See Publication 15-A for information on statutory nonemployee status.	Exempt (withhold if both employer and employee voluntarily agree)	Exempt	Exempt
Noncash Payments 1. For household work, agricultural labor, and service not in the course of the employer's trade or business 2. To certain retail commission salespersons ordinarily paid solely on a cash commission basis	Exempt (withhold if both employer and employee voluntarily agree) Optional with the employer, except to the extent employee's supplemental wages during the year exceed $1 million.	Exempt Taxable	Exempt Taxable
Nonprofit Organizations	See Publication 15-A.		
Officers or Shareholders of an S-Corporation Distributions and other payments by an S-corporation to a corporate officer or shareholder must be treated as wages to the extent the amounts are reasonable compensation for services to the corporation by an employee. See the instructions for Form 1120-S.	Withhold	Taxable	Taxable
Partners: Payments to general or limited partners of a partnership. See Publication 541, "Partnerships," for partner reporting rules.	Exempt	Exempt	Exempt
Railroads: Payments subject to the Railroad Retirement Act. See Publication 915, Social Security and Equivalent Railroad Retirement Benefits, and the instructions for Form CT-1 for more details.	Withhold	Exempt	Exempt
Religious Exemptions	See Publication 15-A and Publication 517, "Social Security and Other Information for Members of the Clergy and Religious Workers."		

	Treatment under Employment Taxes		
Special Classes of Employment and Special Types of Payments	Income Tax Withholding	Social Security and Medicare (Including Additional Medicare Tax When Wages Are Paid in Excess of $200,000)	FUTA
Retirement and Pension Plans			
1. Employer contributions to a qualified plan	Exempt	Exempt	Exempt
2. Elective employee contributions and deferrals to a plan containing a qualified cash or deferred compensation arrangement (for example, 401(k))	Generally exempt, but see Section 402(g) for limitation.	Taxable	Taxable
3. Employer contributions to individual retirement accounts under a simplified employee pension plan (SEP)	Generally exempt, but see Section 402(g) for salary reduction SEP limitation.	Exempt, except for amounts contributed under a salary reduction SEP agreement.	Exempt, except for amounts contributed under a salary reduction SEP agreement.
4. Employer contributions to Section 403(b) annuities	Generally exempt, but see Section 402(g) for limitation.	Taxable if paid through a salary reduction agreement (written or otherwise).	Taxable if paid through a salary reduction agreement (written or otherwise).
5. Employee salary reduction contributions to a SIMPLE retirement account	Exempt	Taxable	Taxable
6. Distributions from qualified retirement and pension plans and Section 403(b) annuities. See Publication 15-A for information on pensions, annuities, and employer contributions to nonqualified deferred compensation arrangements.	Withhold, but the recipient may elect exemption on Form W-4P in certain cases; mandatory 20% withholding applies to an eligible rollover distribution that is not a direct rollover; exempt for a direct rollover. See Publication 15-A.	Exempt	Exempt
7. Employer contributions to a Section 457(b) plan	Generally exempt, but see Section 402(g) limitation.	Taxable	Taxable
8. Employee salary reduction contributions to a Section 457(b) plan	Generally exempt, but see Section 402(g) salary reduction limitation.	Taxable	Taxable
Salespersons			
1. Common-law employees	Withhold	Taxable	Taxable
2. Statutory employees	Exempt	Taxable	Taxable, except for full-time life insurance sales agents.
3. Statutory nonemployees (qualified real estate agents, direct sellers, and certain companion sitters). See Publication 15-A for details.	Exempt	Exempt	Exempt
Scholarships and Fellowship Grants (Includible in Income under Section 117(c))	Withhold	Taxability depends on the nature of employment and the status of the organization. See Students, Scholars, Trainees, Teachers, etc., below.	
Severance or Dismissal Pay	Withhold	Taxable	Taxable

Special Classes of Employment and Special Types of Payments	Treatment under Employment Taxes		
	Income Tax Withholding	Social Security and Medicare (Including Additional Medicare Tax When Wages Are Paid in Excess of $200,000)	FUTA
Service Not in the Course of the Employer's Trade or Business (Other Than on a Farm Operated for Profit or for Household Employment in Private Homes)	Withhold only if an employee earns $50 or more in cash in a quarter and works on 24 or more different days in that quarter or in the preceding quarter.	Taxable if an employee receives $100 or more in cash in a calendar year.	Taxable only if an employee earns $50 or more in cash in a quarter and works on 24 or more different days in that quarter or in the preceding quarter.
Sick Pay See Publication 15-A for more information.	Withhold	Exempt after the end of 6 calendar months after the calendar month employee last worked for the employer.	
Students, Scholars, Trainees, Teachers, etc. 1. A student enrolled and regularly attending classes, performing services for			
a. Private school, college, or university	Withhold	Exempt	Exempt
b. The auxiliary nonprofit organization operated for and controlled by the school, college, or university	Withhold	Exempt unless services are covered by a Section 218 (Social Security Act) agreement.	Exempt
c. Public school, college, or university	Withhold	Exempt unless services are covered by a Section 218 (Social Security Act) agreement.	Exempt
2. Full-time student performing service for academic credit, combining instruction with work experience as an integral part of the program	Withhold	Taxable	Exempt unless the program was established for or on behalf of an employer or group of employers.
3. Student nurses performing part-time services for nominal earnings at a hospital as an incidental part of the training	Withhold	Exempt	Exempt
4. A student employed by organized camps	Withhold	Taxable	Exempt
5. Student, scholar, trainee, teacher, and so on, as nonimmigrant alien under Section 101(a)(15)(F), (J), (M), or (Q) of Immigration and Nationality Act (that is, aliens holding F-1, J-1, M-1, or Q-1 visas).	Withhold unless excepted by regulations.	Exempt if service is performed for the purpose specified in Section 101(a)(15)(F), (J), (M), or (Q) of Immigration and Nationality Act. However, these taxes may apply if the employee becomes a resident alien. See the special residency tests for exempt individuals in Chapter 1 of Pub. 519, Tax Guide for Aliens.	
Supplemental Unemployment Compensation Plan Benefits	Withhold	Exempt under certain conditions. See Publication 15-A.	
Tips 1. If $20 or more in a month	Withhold	Taxable	Taxable for all tips reported in writing to the employer.
2. If less than $20 in a month. See Section 6 of IRS Publication 15 for more information.	Exempt	Exempt	Exempt
Workers' Compensation	Exempt	Exempt	Exempt

(Source: Internal Revenue Service)

Appendix C

Federal Income Tax Tables*

The following is information about federal income tax withholding for 2023 using Publication 15-T. Specific questions about federal income taxes and business situations may be directed to the Internal Revenue Service via the IRS website at https://www.irs.gov/businesses.

*Note: Appendix C is derived from IRS Publication 15-T. A comment to refer to pages 44 and 47 exists at the section end for wage-bracket tables when the taxable wages exceed the table. These page references are for Publication 15-T itself and not to pages within this text.

4. Percentage Method Tables for Manual Payroll Systems With Forms W-4 From 2020 or Later

If you compute payroll manually, your employee has submitted a Form W-4 for 2020 or later, and you prefer to use the Percentage Method or you can't use the Wage Bracket Method tables because the employee's annual wages exceed the amount from the last bracket of the table (based on marital status and pay period), use the worksheet below and the Percentage Method tables that follow to figure federal income tax withholding. This method works for any amount of wages.

Worksheet 4. Employer's Withholding Worksheet for Percentage Method Tables for Manual Payroll Systems With Forms W-4 From 2020 or Later

Keep for Your Records

Table 6	Monthly	Semimonthly	Biweekly	Weekly	Daily
	12	24	26	52	260

Step 1. Adjust the employee's wage amount
- 1a Enter the employee's total taxable wages this payroll period .... 1a $ _____
- 1b Enter the number of pay periods you have per year (see Table 6) .... 1b _____
- 1c Enter the amount from Step 4(a) of the employee's Form W-4 .... 1c $ _____
- 1d Divide line 1c by the number on line 1b .... 1d $ _____
- 1e Add lines 1a and 1d .... 1e $ _____
- 1f Enter the amount from Step 4(b) of the employee's Form W-4 .... 1f $ _____
- 1g Divide line 1f by the number on line 1b .... 1g $ _____
- 1h Subtract line 1g from line 1e. If zero or less, enter -0-. This is the **Adjusted Wage Amount** ...... 1h $ _____

Step 2. **Figure the Tentative Withholding Amount**

based on your pay frequency, the employee's Adjusted Wage Amount, filing status (Step 1(c) of Form W-4), and whether the box in Step 2 of Form W-4 is checked.

- 2a Find the row in the STANDARD Withholding Rate Schedules (if the box in Step 2 of Form W-4 is NOT checked) or the Form W-4, Step 2, Checkbox, Withholding Rate Schedules (if it HAS been checked) of the Percentage Method tables in this section in which the amount on line 1h is at least the amount in column A but less than the amount in column B, and then enter here the amount from column A of that row .... 2a $ _____
- 2b Enter the amount from column C of that row .... 2b $ _____
- 2c Enter the percentage from column D of that row .... 2c _____ %
- 2d Subtract line 2a from line 1h .... 2d $ _____
- 2e Multiply the amount on line 2d by the percentage on line 2c .... 2e $ _____
- 2f Add lines 2b and 2e. This is the **Tentative Withholding Amount** .... 2f $ _____

Step 3. Account for tax credits
- 3a Enter the amount from Step 3 of the employee's Form W-4 .... 3a $ _____
- 3b Divide the amount on line 3a by the number of pay periods on line 1b .... 3b $ _____
- 3c Subtract line 3b from line 2f. If zero or less, enter -0- .... 3c $ _____

Step 4. Figure the final amount to withhold
- 4a Enter the additional amount to withhold from Step 4(c) of the employee's Form W-4 .... 4a $ _____
- 4b Add lines 3c and 4a. **This is the amount to withhold from the employee's wages this pay period** .... 4b $ _____

2023 Percentage Method Tables for Manual Payroll Systems With Forms W-4 from 2020 or Later
WEEKLY Payroll Period

STANDARD Withholding Rate Schedules (Use these if the box in Step 2 of Form W-4 is **NOT** checked)					Form W-4, Step 2, Checkbox, Withholding Rate Schedules (Use these if the box in Step 2 of Form W-4 **IS** checked)				
If the Adjusted Wage Amount (line 1h) is:		The tentative amount to withhold is:	Plus this percentage—	of the amount that the Adjusted Wage exceeds—	If the Adjusted Wage Amount (line 1h) is:		The tentative amount to withhold is:	Plus this percentage—	of the amount that the Adjusted Wage exceeds—
At least—	But less than—				At least—	But less than—			
A	B	C	D	E	A	B	C	D	E
Married Filing Jointly					**Married Filing Jointly**				
$0	$533	$0.00	0%	$0	$0	$266	$0.00	0%	$0
$533	$956	$0.00	10%	$533	$266	$478	$0.00	10%	$266
$956	$2,253	$42.30	12%	$956	$478	$1,126	$21.20	12%	$478
$2,253	$4,201	$197.94	22%	$2,253	$1,126	$2,100	$98.96	22%	$1,126
$4,201	$7,537	$626.50	24%	$4,201	$2,100	$3,768	$313.24	24%	$2,100
$7,537	$9,427	$1,427.14	32%	$7,537	$3,768	$4,713	$713.56	32%	$3,768
$9,427	$13,874	$2,031.94	35%	$9,427	$4,713	$6,937	$1,015.96	35%	$4,713
$13,874		$3,588.39	37%	$13,874	$6,937		$1,794.36	37%	$6,937
Single or Married Filing Separately					**Single or Married Filing Separately**				
$0	$266	$0.00	0%	$0	$0	$133	$0.00	0%	$0
$266	$478	$0.00	10%	$266	$133	$239	$0.00	10%	$133
$478	$1,126	$21.20	12%	$478	$239	$563	$10.60	12%	$239
$1,126	$2,100	$98.96	22%	$1,126	$563	$1,050	$49.48	22%	$563
$2,100	$3,768	$313.24	24%	$2,100	$1,050	$1,884	$156.62	24%	$1,050
$3,768	$4,713	$713.56	32%	$3,768	$1,884	$2,357	$356.78	32%	$1,884
$4,713	$11,384	$1,015.96	35%	$4,713	$2,357	$5,692	$508.14	35%	$2,357
$11,384		$3,350.81	37%	$11,384	$5,692		$1,675.39	37%	$5,692
Head of Household					**Head of Household**				
$0	$400	$0.00	0%	$0	$0	$200	$0.00	0%	$0
$400	$702	$0.00	10%	$400	$200	$351	$0.00	10%	$200
$702	$1,551	$30.20	12%	$702	$351	$775	$15.10	12%	$351
$1,551	$2,234	$132.08	22%	$1,551	$775	$1,117	$65.98	22%	$775
$2,234	$3,902	$282.34	24%	$2,234	$1,117	$1,951	$141.22	24%	$1,117
$3,902	$4,847	$682.66	32%	$3,902	$1,951	$2,424	$341.38	32%	$1,951
$4,847	$11,517	$985.06	35%	$4,847	$2,424	$5,759	$492.74	35%	$2,424
$11,517		$3,319.56	37%	$11,517	$5,759		$1,659.99	37%	$5,759

(Source: Internal Revenue Service)

2023 Percentage Method Tables for Manual Payroll Systems With Forms W-4 from 2020 or Later

DAILY Payroll Period

STANDARD Withholding Rate Schedules (Use these if the box in Step 2 of Form W-4 is **NOT** checked)					Form W-4, Step 2, Checkbox, Withholding Rate Schedules (Use these if the box in Step 2 of Form W-4 **IS** checked)				
If the Adjusted Wage Amount (line 1h) is:		The tentative amount to withhold is:	Plus this percentage—	of the amount that the Adjusted Wage exceeds—	If the Adjusted Wage Amount (line 1h) is:		The tentative amount to withhold is:	Plus this percentage—	of the amount that the Adjusted Wage exceeds—
At least—	But less than—				At least—	But less than—			
A	B	C	D	E	A	B	C	D	E
Married Filing Jointly					**Married Filing Jointly**				
$0.00	$106.50	$0.00	0%	$0.00	$0.00	$53.30	$0.00	0%	$0.00
$106.50	$191.20	$0.00	10%	$106.50	$53.30	$95.60	$0.00	10%	$53.30
$191.20	$450.60	$8.47	12%	$191.20	$95.60	$225.30	$4.23	12%	$95.60
$450.60	$840.20	$39.60	22%	$450.60	$225.30	$420.10	$19.79	22%	$225.30
$840.20	$1,507.30	$125.31	24%	$840.20	$420.10	$753.70	$62.65	24%	$420.10
$1,507.30	$1,885.40	$285.41	32%	$1,507.30	$753.70	$942.70	$142.71	32%	$753.70
$1,885.40	$2,774.80	$406.41	35%	$1,885.40	$942.70	$1,387.40	$203.19	35%	$942.70
$2,774.80		$717.70	37%	$2,774.80	$1,387.40		$358.84	37%	$1,387.40
Single or Married Filing Separately					**Single or Married Filing Separately**				
$0.00	$53.30	$0.00	0%	$0.00	$0.00	$26.60	$0.00	0%	$0.00
$53.30	$95.60	$0.00	10%	$53.30	$26.60	$47.80	$0.00	10%	$26.60
$95.60	$225.30	$4.23	12%	$95.60	$47.80	$112.60	$2.12	12%	$47.80
$225.30	$420.10	$19.79	22%	$225.30	$112.60	$210.00	$9.90	22%	$112.60
$420.10	$753.70	$62.65	24%	$420.10	$210.00	$376.80	$31.32	24%	$210.00
$753.70	$942.70	$142.71	32%	$753.70	$376.80	$471.30	$71.36	32%	$376.80
$942.70	$2,276.80	$203.19	35%	$942.70	$471.30	$1,138.40	$101.60	35%	$471.30
$2,276.80		$670.13	37%	$2,276.80	$1,138.40		$335.08	37%	$1,138.40
Head of Household					**Head of Household**				
$0.00	$80.00	$0.00	0%	$0.00	$0.00	$40.00	$0.00	0%	$0.00
$80.00	$140.40	$0.00	10%	$80.00	$40.00	$70.20	$0.00	10%	$40.00
$140.40	$310.20	$6.04	12%	$140.40	$70.20	$155.10	$3.02	12%	$70.20
$310.20	$446.70	$26.42	22%	$310.20	$155.10	$223.40	$13.21	22%	$155.10
$446.70	$780.40	$56.45	24%	$446.70	$223.40	$390.20	$28.23	24%	$223.40
$780.40	$969.40	$136.53	32%	$780.40	$390.20	$484.70	$68.27	32%	$390.20
$969.40	$2,303.50	$197.01	35%	$969.40	$484.70	$1,151.70	$98.51	35%	$484.70
$2,303.50		$663.95	37%	$2,303.50	$1,151.70		$331.96	37%	$1,151.70

2023 Percentage Method Tables for Manual Payroll Systems With Forms W-4 from 2020 or Later
BIWEEKLY Payroll Period

STANDARD Withholding Rate Schedules (Use these if the box in Step 2 of Form W-4 is **NOT** checked)					Form W-4, Step 2, Checkbox, Withholding Rate Schedules (Use these if the box in Step 2 of Form W-4 **IS** checked)				
If the Adjusted Wage Amount (line 1h) is:		The tentative amount to withhold is:	Plus this percentage—	of the amount that the Adjusted Wage exceeds—	If the Adjusted Wage Amount (line 1h) is:		The tentative amount to withhold is:	Plus this percentage—	of the amount that the Adjusted Wage exceeds—
At least—	But less than—				At least—	But less than—			
A	B	C	D	E	A	B	C	D	E
Married Filing Jointly					**Married Filing Jointly**				
$0	$1,065	$0.00	0%	$0	$0	$533	$0.00	0%	$0
$1,065	$1,912	$0.00	10%	$1,065	$533	$956	$0.00	10%	$533
$1,912	$4,506	$84.70	12%	$1,912	$956	$2,253	$42.30	12%	$956
$4,506	$8,402	$395.98	22%	$4,506	$2,253	$4,201	$197.94	22%	$2,253
$8,402	$15,073	$1,253.10	24%	$8,402	$4,201	$7,537	$626.50	24%	$4,201
$15,073	$18,854	$2,854.14	32%	$15,073	$7,537	$9,427	$1,427.14	32%	$7,537
$18,854	$27,748	$4,064.06	35%	$18,854	$9,427	$13,874	$2,031.94	35%	$9,427
$27,748		$7,176.96	37%	$27,748	$13,874		$3,588.39	37%	$13,874
Single or Married Filing Separately					**Single or Married Filing Separately**				
$0	$533	$0.00	0%	$0	$0	$266	$0.00	0%	$0
$533	$956	$0.00	10%	$533	$266	$478	$0.00	10%	$266
$956	$2,253	$42.30	12%	$956	$478	$1,126	$21.20	12%	$478
$2,253	$4,201	$197.94	22%	$2,253	$1,126	$2,100	$98.96	22%	$1,126
$4,201	$7,537	$626.50	24%	$4,201	$2,100	$3,768	$313.24	24%	$2,100
$7,537	$9,427	$1,427.14	32%	$7,537	$3,768	$4,713	$713.56	32%	$3,768
$9,427	$22,768	$2,031.94	35%	$9,427	$4,713	$11,384	$1,015.96	35%	$4,713
$22,768		$6,701.29	37%	$22,768	$11,384		$3,350.81	37%	$11,384
Head of Household					**Head of Household**				
$0	$800	$0.00	0%	$0	$0	$400	$0.00	0%	$0
$800	$1,404	$0.00	10%	$800	$400	$702	$0.00	10%	$400
$1,404	$3,102	$60.40	12%	$1,404	$702	$1,551	$30.20	12%	$702
$3,102	$4,467	$264.16	22%	$3,102	$1,551	$2,234	$132.08	22%	$1,551
$4,467	$7,804	$564.46	24%	$4,467	$2,234	$3,902	$282.34	24%	$2,234
$7,804	$9,694	$1,365.34	32%	$7,804	$3,902	$4,847	$682.66	32%	$3,902
$9,694	$23,035	$1,970.14	35%	$9,694	$4,847	$11,517	$985.06	35%	$4,847
$23,035		$6,639.49	37%	$23,035	$11,517		$3,319.56	37%	$11,517

2023 Percentage Method Tables for Manual Payroll Systems With Forms W-4 from 2020 or Later
SEMIMONTHLY Payroll Period

STANDARD Withholding Rate Schedules (Use these if the box in Step 2 of Form W-4 is **NOT** checked)					Form W-4, Step 2, Checkbox, Withholding Rate Schedules (Use these if the box in Step 2 of Form W-4 **IS** checked)				
If the Adjusted Wage Amount (line 1h) is:		The tentative amount to withhold is:	Plus this percentage—	of the amount that the Adjusted Wage exceeds—	If the Adjusted Wage Amount (line 1h) is:		The tentative amount to withhold is:	Plus this percentage—	of the amount that the Adjusted Wage exceeds—
At least—	But less than—				At least—	But less than—			
A	B	C	D	E	A	B	C	D	E
Married Filing Jointly					**Married Filing Jointly**				
$0	$1,154	$0.00	0%	$0	$0	$577	$0.00	0%	$0
$1,154	$2,071	$0.00	10%	$1,154	$577	$1,035	$0.00	10%	$577
$2,071	$4,881	$91.70	12%	$2,071	$1,035	$2,441	$45.80	12%	$1,035
$4,881	$9,102	$428.90	22%	$4,881	$2,441	$4,551	$214.52	22%	$2,441
$9,102	$16,329	$1,357.52	24%	$9,102	$4,551	$8,165	$678.72	24%	$4,551
$16,329	$20,425	$3,092.00	32%	$16,329	$8,165	$10,213	$1,546.08	32%	$8,165
$20,425	$30,060	$4,402.72	35%	$20,425	$10,213	$15,030	$2,201.44	35%	$10,213
$30,060		$7,774.97	37%	$30,060	$15,030		$3,887.39	37%	$15,030
Single or Married Filing Separately					**Single or Married Filing Separately**				
$0	$577	$0.00	0%	$0	$0	$289	$0.00	0%	$0
$577	$1,035	$0.00	10%	$577	$289	$518	$0.00	10%	$289
$1,035	$2,441	$45.80	12%	$1,035	$518	$1,220	$22.90	12%	$518
$2,441	$4,551	$214.52	22%	$2,441	$1,220	$2,276	$107.14	22%	$1,220
$4,551	$8,165	$678.72	24%	$4,551	$2,276	$4,082	$339.46	24%	$2,276
$8,165	$10,213	$1,546.08	32%	$8,165	$4,082	$5,106	$772.90	32%	$4,082
$10,213	$24,666	$2,201.44	35%	$10,213	$5,106	$12,333	$1,100.58	35%	$5,106
$24,666		$7,259.99	37%	$24,666	$12,333		$3,630.03	37%	$12,333
Head of Household					**Head of Household**				
$0	$867	$0.00	0%	$0	$0	$433	$0.00	0%	$0
$867	$1,521	$0.00	10%	$867	$433	$760	$0.00	10%	$433
$1,521	$3,360	$65.40	12%	$1,521	$760	$1,680	$32.70	12%	$760
$3,360	$4,840	$286.08	22%	$3,360	$1,680	$2,420	$143.10	22%	$1,680
$4,840	$8,454	$611.68	24%	$4,840	$2,420	$4,227	$305.90	24%	$2,420
$8,454	$10,502	$1,479.04	32%	$8,454	$4,227	$5,251	$739.58	32%	$4,227
$10,502	$24,954	$2,134.40	35%	$10,502	$5,251	$12,477	$1,067.26	35%	$5,251
$24,954		$7,192.60	37%	$24,954	$12,477		$3,596.36	37%	$12,477

2023 Percentage Method Tables for Manual Payroll Systems With Forms W-4 from 2020 or Later

MONTHLY Payroll Period

STANDARD Withholding Rate Schedules (Use these if the box in Step 2 of Form W-4 is **NOT** checked)					Form W-4, Step 2, Checkbox, Withholding Rate Schedules (Use these if the box in Step 2 of Form W-4 **IS** checked)				
If the Adjusted Wage Amount (line 1h) is:		The tentative amount to withhold is:	Plus this percentage—	of the amount that the Adjusted Wage exceeds—	If the Adjusted Wage Amount (line 1h) is:		The tentative amount to withhold is:	Plus this percentage—	of the amount that the Adjusted Wage exceeds—
At least—	But less than—				At least—	But less than—			
A	B	C	D	E	A	B	C	D	E
Married Filing Jointly					**Married Filing Jointly**				
$0	$2,308	$0.00	0%	$0	$0	$1,154	$0.00	0%	$0
$2,308	$4,142	$0.00	10%	$2,308	$1,154	$2,071	$0.00	10%	$1,154
$4,142	$9,763	$183.40	12%	$4,142	$2,071	$4,881	$91.70	12%	$2,071
$9,763	$18,204	$857.92	22%	$9,763	$4,881	$9,102	$428.90	22%	$4,881
$18,204	$32,658	$2,714.94	24%	$18,204	$9,102	$16,329	$1,357.52	24%	$9,102
$32,658	$40,850	$6,183.90	32%	$32,658	$16,329	$20,425	$3,092.00	32%	$16,329
$40,850	$60,121	$8,805.34	35%	$40,850	$20,425	$30,060	$4,402.72	35%	$20,425
$60,121		$15,550.19	37%	$60,121	$30,060		$7,774.97	37%	$30,060
Single or Married Filing Separately					**Single or Married Filing Separately**				
$0	$1,154	$0.00	0%	$0	$0	$577	$0.00	0%	$0
$1,154	$2,071	$0.00	10%	$1,154	$577	$1,035	$0.00	10%	$577
$2,071	$4,881	$91.70	12%	$2,071	$1,035	$2,441	$45.80	12%	$1,035
$4,881	$9,102	$428.90	22%	$4,881	$2,441	$4,551	$214.52	22%	$2,441
$9,102	$16,329	$1,357.52	24%	$9,102	$4,551	$8,165	$678.72	24%	$4,551
$16,329	$20,425	$3,092.00	32%	$16,329	$8,165	$10,213	$1,546.08	32%	$8,165
$20,425	$49,331	$4,402.72	35%	$20,425	$10,213	$24,666	$2,201.44	35%	$10,213
$49,331		$14,519.82	37%	$49,331	$24,666		$7,259.99	37%	$24,666
Head of Household					**Head of Household**				
$0	$1,733	$0.00	0%	$0	$0	$867	$0.00	0%	$0
$1,733	$3,042	$0.00	10%	$1,733	$867	$1,521	$0.00	10%	$867
$3,042	$6,721	$130.90	12%	$3,042	$1,521	$3,360	$65.40	12%	$1,521
$6,721	$9,679	$572.38	22%	$6,721	$3,360	$4,840	$286.08	22%	$3,360
$9,679	$16,908	$1,223.14	24%	$9,679	$4,840	$8,454	$611.68	24%	$4,840
$16,908	$21,004	$2,958.10	32%	$16,908	$8,454	$10,502	$1,479.04	32%	$8,454
$21,004	$49,908	$4,268.82	35%	$21,004	$10,502	$24,954	$2,134.40	35%	$10,502
$49,908		$14,385.22	37%	$49,908	$24,954		$7,192.60	37%	$24,954

2. Wage Bracket Method Tables for Manual Payroll Systems With Forms W-4 From 2020 or Later

If you compute payroll manually, your employee has submitted a Form W-4 for 2020 or later, and you prefer to use the Wage Bracket Method, use the worksheet below and the Wage Bracket Method tables that follow to figure federal income tax withholding.

These Wage Bracket Method tables cover a limited amount of annual wages (generally, less than $100,000). If you can't use the Wage Bracket Method tables because taxable wages exceed the amount from the last bracket of the table (based on filing status and pay period), use the Percentage Method tables in section 4.

Worksheet 2. Employer's Withholding Worksheet for Wage Bracket Method Tables for Manual Payroll Systems With Forms W-4 From 2020 or Later

Keep for Your Records

Table 5	Monthly	Semimonthly	Biweekly	Weekly	Daily
	12	24	26	52	260

Step 1. Adjust the employee's wage amount

- 1a Enter the employee's total taxable wages this payroll period .... 1a $ _____
- 1b Enter the number of pay periods you have per year (see Table 5) .... 1b _____
- 1c Enter the amount from Step 4(a) of the employee's Form W-4 .... 1c $ _____
- 1d Divide the amount on line 1c by the number of pay periods on line 1b .... 1d $ _____
- 1e Add lines 1a and 1d .... 1e $ _____
- 1f Enter the amount from Step 4(b) of the employee's Form W-4 .... 1f $ _____
- 1g Divide the amount on line 1f by the number of pay periods on line 1b .... 1g $ _____
- 1h Subtract line 1g from line 1e. If zero or less, enter -0-. This is the **Adjusted Wage Amount** ...... 1h $ _____

Step 2. Figure the Tentative Withholding Amount

- 2a Use the amount on line 1h to look up the tentative amount to withhold in the appropriate Wage Bracket Method table in this section for your pay frequency, given the employee's filing status and whether the employee has checked the box in Step 2 of Form W-4. This is the **Tentative Withholding Amount** .... 2a $ _____

Step 3. Account for tax credits

- 3a Enter the amount from Step 3 of the employee's Form W-4 .... 3a $ _____
- 3b Divide the amount on line 3a by the number of pay periods on line 1b .... 3b $ _____
- 3c Subtract line 3b from line 2a. If zero or less, enter -0- .... 3c $ _____

Step 4. Figure the final amount to withhold

- 4a Enter the additional amount to withhold from Step 4(c) of the employee's Form W-4 ..... 4a $ _____
- 4b Add lines 3c and 4a. **This is the amount to withhold from the employee's wages this pay period** .... 4b $ _____

Appendix C   Federal Income Tax Tables   463

2023 Wage Bracket Method Tables for Manual Payroll Systems with Forms W-4 From 2020 or Later
WEEKLY Payroll Period

If the Adjusted Wage Amount (line 1h) is		Married Filing Jointly		Head of Household		Single or Married Filing Separately	
At least	But less than	Standard withholding	Form W-4, Step 2, Checkbox withholding	Standard withholding	Form W-4, Step 2, Checkbox withholding	Standard withholding	Form W-4, Step 2, Checkbox withholding
				The Tentative Withholding Amount is:			
$0	$135	$0	$0	$0	$0	$0	$0
$135	$145	$0	$0	$0	$0	$0	$1
$145	$155	$0	$0	$0	$0	$0	$2
$155	$165	$0	$0	$0	$0	$0	$3
$165	$175	$0	$0	$0	$0	$0	$4
$175	$185	$0	$0	$0	$0	$0	$5
$185	$195	$0	$0	$0	$0	$0	$6
$195	$205	$0	$0	$0	$0	$0	$7
$205	$215	$0	$0	$0	$1	$0	$8
$215	$225	$0	$0	$0	$2	$0	$9
$225	$235	$0	$0	$0	$3	$0	$10
$235	$245	$0	$0	$0	$4	$0	$11
$245	$255	$0	$0	$0	$5	$0	$12
$255	$265	$0	$0	$0	$6	$0	$13
$265	$275	$0	$0	$0	$7	$0	$14
$275	$285	$0	$1	$0	$8	$1	$16
$285	$295	$0	$2	$0	$9	$2	$17
$295	$305	$0	$3	$0	$10	$3	$18
$305	$315	$0	$4	$0	$11	$4	$19
$315	$325	$0	$5	$0	$12	$5	$20
$325	$335	$0	$6	$0	$13	$6	$22
$335	$345	$0	$7	$0	$14	$7	$23
$345	$355	$0	$8	$0	$15	$8	$24
$355	$365	$0	$9	$0	$16	$9	$25
$365	$375	$0	$10	$0	$17	$10	$26
$375	$385	$0	$11	$0	$19	$11	$28
$385	$395	$0	$12	$0	$20	$12	$29
$395	$405	$0	$13	$0	$21	$13	$30
$405	$415	$0	$14	$1	$22	$14	$31
$415	$425	$0	$15	$2	$23	$15	$32
$425	$435	$0	$16	$3	$25	$16	$34
$435	$445	$0	$17	$4	$26	$17	$35
$445	$455	$0	$18	$5	$27	$18	$36
$455	$465	$0	$19	$6	$28	$19	$37
$465	$475	$0	$20	$7	$29	$20	$38
$475	$485	$0	$21	$8	$31	$21	$40
$485	$495	$0	$23	$9	$32	$23	$41
$495	$505	$0	$24	$10	$33	$24	$42
$505	$515	$0	$25	$11	$34	$25	$43
$515	$525	$0	$26	$12	$35	$26	$44
$525	$535	$0	$27	$13	$37	$27	$46
$535	$545	$1	$29	$14	$38	$29	$47
$545	$555	$2	$30	$15	$39	$30	$48
$555	$565	$3	$31	$16	$40	$31	$49
$565	$575	$4	$32	$17	$41	$32	$51
$575	$585	$5	$33	$18	$43	$33	$53
$585	$595	$6	$35	$19	$44	$35	$55
$595	$605	$7	$36	$20	$45	$36	$58
$605	$615	$8	$37	$21	$46	$37	$60
$615	$625	$9	$38	$22	$47	$38	$62
$625	$635	$10	$39	$23	$49	$39	$64
$635	$645	$11	$41	$24	$50	$41	$66
$645	$655	$12	$42	$25	$51	$42	$69
$655	$665	$13	$43	$26	$52	$43	$71
$665	$675	$14	$44	$27	$53	$44	$73
$675	$685	$15	$45	$28	$55	$45	$75
$685	$695	$16	$47	$29	$56	$47	$77
$695	$705	$17	$48	$30	$57	$48	$80
$705	$715	$18	$49	$31	$58	$49	$82
$715	$725	$19	$50	$32	$59	$50	$84
$725	$735	$20	$51	$34	$61	$51	$86
$735	$745	$21	$53	$35	$62	$53	$88
$745	$755	$22	$54	$36	$63	$54	$91
$755	$765	$23	$55	$37	$64	$55	$93

2023 Wage Bracket Method Tables for Manual Payroll Systems with Forms W-4 From 2020 or Later
WEEKLY Payroll Period

If the Adjusted Wage Amount (line 1h) is		Married Filing Jointly		Head of Household		Single or Married Filing Separately	
At least	But less than	Standard withholding	Form W-4, Step 2, Checkbox withholding	Standard withholding	Form W-4, Step 2, Checkbox withholding	Standard withholding	Form W-4, Step 2, Checkbox withholding
				The Tentative Withholding Amount is:			
$765	$775	$24	$56	$38	$65	$56	$95
$775	$785	$25	$57	$40	$67	$57	$97
$785	$795	$26	$59	$41	$69	$59	$99
$795	$805	$27	$60	$42	$71	$60	$102
$805	$815	$28	$61	$43	$74	$61	$104
$815	$825	$29	$62	$44	$76	$62	$106
$825	$835	$30	$63	$46	$78	$63	$108
$835	$845	$31	$65	$47	$80	$65	$110
$845	$855	$32	$66	$48	$82	$66	$113
$855	$865	$33	$67	$49	$85	$67	$115
$865	$875	$34	$68	$50	$87	$68	$117
$875	$885	$35	$69	$52	$89	$69	$119
$885	$895	$36	$71	$53	$91	$71	$121
$895	$905	$37	$72	$54	$93	$72	$124
$905	$915	$38	$73	$55	$96	$73	$126
$915	$925	$39	$74	$56	$98	$74	$128
$925	$935	$40	$75	$58	$100	$75	$130
$935	$945	$41	$77	$59	$102	$77	$132
$945	$955	$42	$78	$60	$104	$78	$135
$955	$965	$43	$79	$61	$107	$79	$137
$965	$975	$44	$80	$62	$109	$80	$139
$975	$985	$45	$81	$64	$111	$81	$141
$985	$995	$46	$83	$65	$113	$83	$143
$995	$1,005	$48	$84	$66	$115	$84	$146
$1,005	$1,015	$49	$85	$67	$118	$85	$148
$1,015	$1,025	$50	$86	$68	$120	$86	$150
$1,025	$1,035	$51	$87	$70	$122	$87	$152
$1,035	$1,045	$52	$89	$71	$124	$89	$154
$1,045	$1,055	$54	$90	$72	$126	$90	$157
$1,055	$1,065	$55	$91	$73	$129	$91	$159
$1,065	$1,075	$56	$92	$74	$131	$92	$161
$1,075	$1,085	$57	$93	$76	$133	$93	$164
$1,085	$1,095	$58	$95	$77	$135	$95	$166
$1,095	$1,105	$60	$96	$78	$137	$96	$169
$1,105	$1,115	$61	$97	$79	$140	$97	$171
$1,115	$1,125	$62	$98	$80	$142	$98	$173
$1,125	$1,135	$63	$100	$82	$144	$100	$176
$1,135	$1,145	$64	$102	$83	$147	$102	$178
$1,145	$1,155	$66	$104	$84	$149	$104	$181
$1,155	$1,165	$67	$106	$85	$151	$106	$183
$1,165	$1,175	$68	$109	$86	$154	$109	$185
$1,175	$1,185	$69	$111	$88	$156	$111	$188
$1,185	$1,195	$70	$113	$89	$159	$113	$190
$1,195	$1,205	$72	$115	$90	$161	$115	$193
$1,205	$1,215	$73	$117	$91	$163	$117	$195
$1,215	$1,225	$74	$120	$92	$166	$120	$197
$1,225	$1,235	$75	$122	$94	$168	$122	$200
$1,235	$1,245	$76	$124	$95	$171	$124	$202
$1,245	$1,255	$78	$126	$96	$173	$126	$205
$1,255	$1,265	$79	$128	$97	$175	$128	$207
$1,265	$1,275	$80	$131	$98	$178	$131	$209
$1,275	$1,285	$81	$133	$100	$180	$133	$212
$1,285	$1,295	$82	$135	$101	$183	$135	$214
$1,295	$1,305	$84	$137	$102	$185	$137	$217
$1,305	$1,315	$85	$139	$103	$187	$139	$219
$1,315	$1,325	$86	$142	$104	$190	$142	$221
$1,325	$1,335	$87	$144	$106	$192	$144	$224
$1,335	$1,345	$88	$146	$107	$195	$146	$226
$1,345	$1,355	$90	$148	$108	$197	$148	$229
$1,355	$1,365	$91	$150	$109	$199	$150	$231
$1,365	$1,375	$92	$153	$110	$202	$153	$233
$1,375	$1,385	$93	$155	$112	$204	$155	$236
$1,385	$1,395	$94	$157	$113	$207	$157	$238
$1,395	$1,405	$96	$159	$114	$209	$159	$241
$1,405	$1,415	$97	$161	$115	$211	$161	$243

2023 Wage Bracket Method Tables for Manual Payroll Systems with Forms W-4 From 2020 or Later
WEEKLY Payroll Period

If the Adjusted Wage Amount (line 1h) is		Married Filing Jointly		Head of Household		Single or Married Filing Separately	
At least	But less than	Standard withholding	Form W-4, Step 2, Checkbox withholding	Standard withholding	Form W-4, Step 2, Checkbox withholding	Standard withholding	Form W-4, Step 2, Checkbox withholding
				The Tentative Withholding Amount is:			
$1,415	$1,425	$98	$164	$116	$214	$164	$245
$1,425	$1,435	$99	$166	$118	$216	$166	$248
$1,435	$1,445	$100	$168	$119	$219	$168	$250
$1,445	$1,455	$102	$170	$120	$221	$170	$253
$1,455	$1,465	$103	$172	$121	$223	$172	$255
$1,465	$1,475	$104	$175	$122	$226	$175	$257
$1,475	$1,485	$105	$177	$124	$228	$177	$260
$1,485	$1,495	$106	$179	$125	$231	$179	$262
$1,495	$1,505	$108	$181	$126	$233	$181	$265
$1,505	$1,515	$109	$183	$127	$235	$183	$267
$1,515	$1,525	$110	$186	$128	$238	$186	$269
$1,525	$1,535	$111	$188	$130	$240	$188	$272
$1,535	$1,545	$112	$190	$131	$243	$190	$274
$1,545	$1,555	$114	$192	$132	$245	$192	$277
$1,555	$1,565	$115	$194	$134	$247	$194	$279
$1,565	$1,575	$116	$197	$136	$250	$197	$281
$1,575	$1,585	$117	$199	$138	$252	$199	$284
$1,585	$1,595	$118	$201	$141	$255	$201	$286
$1,595	$1,605	$120	$203	$143	$257	$203	$289
$1,605	$1,615	$121	$205	$145	$259	$205	$291
$1,615	$1,625	$122	$208	$147	$262	$208	$293
$1,625	$1,635	$123	$210	$149	$264	$210	$296
$1,635	$1,645	$124	$212	$152	$267	$212	$298
$1,645	$1,655	$126	$214	$154	$269	$214	$301
$1,655	$1,665	$127	$216	$156	$271	$216	$303
$1,665	$1,675	$128	$219	$158	$274	$219	$305
$1,675	$1,685	$129	$221	$160	$276	$221	$308
$1,685	$1,695	$130	$223	$163	$279	$223	$310
$1,695	$1,705	$132	$225	$165	$281	$225	$313
$1,705	$1,715	$133	$227	$167	$283	$227	$315
$1,715	$1,725	$134	$230	$169	$286	$230	$317
$1,725	$1,735	$135	$232	$171	$288	$232	$320
$1,735	$1,745	$136	$234	$174	$291	$234	$322
$1,745	$1,755	$138	$236	$176	$293	$236	$325
$1,755	$1,765	$139	$238	$178	$295	$238	$327
$1,765	$1,775	$140	$241	$180	$298	$241	$329
$1,775	$1,785	$141	$243	$182	$300	$243	$332
$1,785	$1,795	$142	$245	$185	$303	$245	$334
$1,795	$1,805	$144	$247	$187	$305	$247	$337
$1,805	$1,815	$145	$249	$189	$307	$249	$339
$1,815	$1,825	$146	$252	$191	$310	$252	$341
$1,825	$1,835	$147	$254	$193	$312	$254	$344
$1,835	$1,845	$148	$256	$196	$315	$256	$346
$1,845	$1,855	$150	$258	$198	$317	$258	$349
$1,855	$1,865	$151	$260	$200	$319	$260	$351
$1,865	$1,875	$152	$263	$202	$322	$263	$353
$1,875	$1,885	$153	$265	$204	$324	$265	$356
$1,885	$1,895	$154	$267	$207	$327	$267	$359
$1,895	$1,905	$156	$269	$209	$329	$269	$362
$1,905	$1,915	$157	$271	$211	$331	$271	$365
$1,915	$1,925	$158	$274	$213	$334	$274	$368

466 Appendix C *Federal Income Tax Tables*

2023 Wage Bracket Method Tables for Manual Payroll Systems with Forms W-4 From 2020 or Later
BIWEEKLY Payroll Period

If the Adjusted Wage Amount (line 1h) is		Married Filing Jointly		Head of Household		Single or Married Filing Separately	
At least	But less than	Standard withholding	Form W-4, Step 2, Checkbox withholding	Standard withholding	Form W-4, Step 2, Checkbox withholding	Standard withholding	Form W-4, Step 2, Checkbox withholding
				The Tentative Withholding Amount is:			
$0	$270	$0	$0	$0	$0	$0	$0
$270	$280	$0	$0	$0	$0	$0	$1
$280	$290	$0	$0	$0	$0	$0	$2
$290	$300	$0	$0	$0	$0	$0	$3
$300	$310	$0	$0	$0	$0	$0	$4
$310	$320	$0	$0	$0	$0	$0	$5
$320	$330	$0	$0	$0	$0	$0	$6
$330	$340	$0	$0	$0	$0	$0	$7
$340	$350	$0	$0	$0	$0	$0	$8
$350	$360	$0	$0	$0	$0	$0	$9
$360	$370	$0	$0	$0	$0	$0	$10
$370	$380	$0	$0	$0	$0	$0	$11
$380	$390	$0	$0	$0	$0	$0	$12
$390	$400	$0	$0	$0	$0	$0	$13
$400	$410	$0	$0	$0	$1	$0	$14
$410	$420	$0	$0	$0	$2	$0	$15
$420	$430	$0	$0	$0	$3	$0	$16
$430	$440	$0	$0	$0	$4	$0	$17
$440	$450	$0	$0	$0	$5	$0	$18
$450	$460	$0	$0	$0	$6	$0	$19
$460	$470	$0	$0	$0	$7	$0	$20
$470	$480	$0	$0	$0	$8	$0	$21
$480	$495	$0	$0	$0	$9	$0	$22
$495	$510	$0	$0	$0	$10	$0	$24
$510	$525	$0	$0	$0	$12	$0	$26
$525	$540	$0	$0	$0	$13	$0	$28
$540	$555	$0	$1	$0	$15	$1	$30
$555	$570	$0	$3	$0	$16	$3	$31
$570	$585	$0	$4	$0	$18	$4	$33
$585	$600	$0	$6	$0	$19	$6	$35
$600	$615	$0	$7	$0	$21	$7	$37
$615	$630	$0	$9	$0	$22	$9	$39
$630	$645	$0	$10	$0	$24	$10	$40
$645	$660	$0	$12	$0	$25	$12	$42
$660	$675	$0	$13	$0	$27	$13	$44
$675	$690	$0	$15	$0	$28	$15	$46
$690	$705	$0	$16	$0	$30	$16	$48
$705	$720	$0	$18	$0	$31	$18	$49
$720	$735	$0	$19	$0	$33	$19	$51
$735	$750	$0	$21	$0	$35	$21	$53
$750	$765	$0	$22	$0	$37	$22	$55
$765	$780	$0	$24	$0	$39	$24	$57
$780	$795	$0	$25	$0	$40	$25	$58
$795	$810	$0	$27	$0	$42	$27	$60
$810	$825	$0	$28	$2	$44	$28	$62
$825	$840	$0	$30	$3	$46	$30	$64
$840	$855	$0	$31	$5	$48	$31	$66
$855	$870	$0	$33	$6	$49	$33	$67
$870	$885	$0	$34	$8	$51	$34	$69
$885	$900	$0	$36	$9	$53	$36	$71
$900	$915	$0	$37	$11	$55	$37	$73
$915	$930	$0	$39	$12	$57	$39	$75
$930	$945	$0	$40	$14	$58	$40	$76
$945	$960	$0	$42	$15	$60	$42	$78
$960	$975	$0	$44	$17	$62	$44	$80
$975	$990	$0	$46	$18	$64	$46	$82
$990	$1,005	$0	$47	$20	$66	$47	$84
$1,005	$1,020	$0	$49	$21	$67	$49	$85
$1,020	$1,035	$0	$51	$23	$69	$51	$87
$1,035	$1,050	$0	$53	$24	$71	$53	$89
$1,050	$1,065	$0	$55	$26	$73	$55	$91
$1,065	$1,080	$1	$56	$27	$75	$56	$93
$1,080	$1,095	$2	$58	$29	$76	$58	$94
$1,095	$1,110	$4	$60	$30	$78	$60	$96

2023 Wage Bracket Method Tables for Manual Payroll Systems with Forms W-4 From 2020 or Later
BIWEEKLY Payroll Period

If the **Adjusted Wage Amount** (line 1h) is		Married Filing Jointly		Head of Household		Single or Married Filing Separately	
At least	But less than	Standard withholding	Form W-4, Step 2, Checkbox withholding	Standard withholding	Form W-4, Step 2, Checkbox withholding	Standard withholding	Form W-4, Step 2, Checkbox withholding
				The Tentative Withholding Amount is:			
$1,110	$1,125	$5	$62	$32	$80	$62	$98
$1,125	$1,140	$7	$64	$33	$82	$64	$100
$1,140	$1,160	$8	$66	$35	$84	$66	$104
$1,160	$1,180	$10	$68	$37	$86	$68	$109
$1,180	$1,200	$12	$70	$39	$89	$70	$113
$1,200	$1,220	$14	$73	$41	$91	$73	$117
$1,220	$1,240	$16	$75	$43	$94	$75	$122
$1,240	$1,260	$18	$78	$45	$96	$78	$126
$1,260	$1,280	$20	$80	$47	$98	$80	$131
$1,280	$1,300	$22	$82	$49	$101	$82	$135
$1,300	$1,320	$24	$85	$51	$103	$85	$139
$1,320	$1,340	$26	$87	$53	$106	$87	$144
$1,340	$1,360	$28	$90	$55	$108	$90	$148
$1,360	$1,380	$30	$92	$57	$110	$92	$153
$1,380	$1,400	$32	$94	$59	$113	$94	$157
$1,400	$1,420	$34	$97	$61	$115	$97	$161
$1,420	$1,440	$36	$99	$64	$118	$99	$166
$1,440	$1,460	$38	$102	$66	$120	$102	$170
$1,460	$1,480	$40	$104	$68	$122	$104	$175
$1,480	$1,500	$42	$106	$71	$125	$106	$179
$1,500	$1,520	$44	$109	$73	$127	$109	$183
$1,520	$1,540	$46	$111	$76	$130	$111	$188
$1,540	$1,560	$48	$114	$78	$132	$114	$192
$1,560	$1,580	$50	$116	$80	$136	$116	$197
$1,580	$1,600	$52	$118	$83	$141	$118	$201
$1,600	$1,620	$54	$121	$85	$145	$121	$205
$1,620	$1,640	$56	$123	$88	$149	$123	$210
$1,640	$1,660	$58	$126	$90	$154	$126	$214
$1,660	$1,680	$60	$128	$92	$158	$128	$219
$1,680	$1,700	$62	$130	$95	$163	$130	$223
$1,700	$1,720	$64	$133	$97	$167	$133	$227
$1,720	$1,740	$66	$135	$100	$171	$135	$232
$1,740	$1,760	$68	$138	$102	$176	$138	$236
$1,760	$1,780	$70	$140	$104	$180	$140	$241
$1,780	$1,800	$72	$142	$107	$185	$142	$245
$1,800	$1,820	$74	$145	$109	$189	$145	$249
$1,820	$1,840	$76	$147	$112	$193	$147	$254
$1,840	$1,860	$78	$150	$114	$198	$150	$258
$1,860	$1,880	$80	$152	$116	$202	$152	$263
$1,880	$1,900	$82	$154	$119	$207	$154	$267
$1,900	$1,920	$84	$157	$121	$211	$157	$271
$1,920	$1,940	$87	$159	$124	$215	$159	$276
$1,940	$1,960	$89	$162	$126	$220	$162	$280
$1,960	$1,980	$92	$164	$128	$224	$164	$285
$1,980	$2,000	$94	$166	$131	$229	$166	$289
$2,000	$2,020	$96	$169	$133	$233	$169	$293
$2,020	$2,040	$99	$171	$136	$237	$171	$298
$2,040	$2,060	$101	$174	$138	$242	$174	$302
$2,060	$2,080	$104	$176	$140	$246	$176	$307
$2,080	$2,100	$106	$178	$143	$251	$178	$311
$2,100	$2,130	$109	$181	$146	$256	$181	$317
$2,130	$2,160	$113	$185	$149	$263	$185	$324
$2,160	$2,190	$116	$189	$153	$269	$189	$331
$2,190	$2,220	$120	$192	$157	$276	$192	$338
$2,220	$2,250	$123	$196	$160	$283	$196	$346
$2,250	$2,280	$127	$201	$164	$290	$201	$353
$2,280	$2,310	$131	$207	$167	$297	$207	$360
$2,310	$2,340	$134	$214	$171	$304	$214	$367
$2,340	$2,370	$138	$220	$175	$311	$220	$374
$2,370	$2,400	$141	$227	$178	$319	$227	$382
$2,400	$2,430	$145	$234	$182	$326	$234	$389
$2,430	$2,460	$149	$240	$185	$333	$240	$396
$2,460	$2,490	$152	$247	$189	$340	$247	$403
$2,490	$2,520	$156	$253	$193	$347	$253	$410
$2,520	$2,550	$159	$260	$196	$355	$260	$418

2023 Wage Bracket Method Tables for Manual Payroll Systems with Forms W-4 From 2020 or Later
BIWEEKLY Payroll Period

If the Adjusted Wage Amount (line 1h) is		Married Filing Jointly		Head of Household		Single or Married Filing Separately	
At least	But less than	Standard withholding	Form W-4, Step 2, Checkbox withholding	Standard withholding	Form W-4, Step 2, Checkbox withholding	Standard withholding	Form W-4, Step 2, Checkbox withholding
				The Tentative Withholding Amount is:			
$2,550	$2,580	$163	$267	$200	$362	$267	$425
$2,580	$2,610	$167	$273	$203	$369	$273	$432
$2,610	$2,640	$170	$280	$207	$376	$280	$439
$2,640	$2,670	$174	$286	$211	$383	$286	$446
$2,670	$2,700	$177	$293	$214	$391	$293	$454
$2,700	$2,730	$181	$300	$218	$398	$300	$461
$2,730	$2,760	$185	$306	$221	$405	$306	$468
$2,760	$2,790	$188	$313	$225	$412	$313	$475
$2,790	$2,820	$192	$319	$229	$419	$319	$482
$2,820	$2,850	$195	$326	$232	$427	$326	$490
$2,850	$2,880	$199	$333	$236	$434	$333	$497
$2,880	$2,910	$203	$339	$239	$441	$339	$504
$2,910	$2,940	$206	$346	$243	$448	$346	$511
$2,940	$2,970	$210	$352	$247	$455	$352	$518
$2,970	$3,000	$213	$359	$250	$463	$359	$526
$3,000	$3,030	$217	$366	$254	$470	$366	$533
$3,030	$3,060	$221	$372	$257	$477	$372	$540
$3,060	$3,090	$224	$379	$261	$484	$379	$547
$3,090	$3,120	$228	$385	$265	$491	$385	$554
$3,120	$3,150	$231	$392	$271	$499	$392	$562
$3,150	$3,180	$235	$399	$278	$506	$399	$569
$3,180	$3,210	$239	$405	$285	$513	$405	$576
$3,210	$3,240	$242	$412	$291	$520	$412	$583
$3,240	$3,270	$246	$418	$298	$527	$418	$590
$3,270	$3,300	$249	$425	$304	$535	$425	$598
$3,300	$3,330	$253	$432	$311	$542	$432	$605
$3,330	$3,360	$257	$438	$318	$549	$438	$612
$3,360	$3,390	$260	$445	$324	$556	$445	$619
$3,390	$3,420	$264	$451	$331	$563	$451	$626
$3,420	$3,450	$267	$458	$337	$571	$458	$634
$3,450	$3,480	$271	$465	$344	$578	$465	$641
$3,480	$3,510	$275	$471	$351	$585	$471	$648
$3,510	$3,540	$278	$478	$357	$592	$478	$655
$3,540	$3,570	$282	$484	$364	$599	$484	$662
$3,570	$3,600	$285	$491	$370	$607	$491	$670
$3,600	$3,630	$289	$498	$377	$614	$498	$677
$3,630	$3,660	$293	$504	$384	$621	$504	$684
$3,660	$3,690	$296	$511	$390	$628	$511	$691
$3,690	$3,720	$300	$517	$397	$635	$517	$698
$3,720	$3,750	$303	$524	$403	$643	$524	$706
$3,750	$3,780	$307	$531	$410	$650	$531	$713
$3,780	$3,810	$311	$537	$417	$657	$537	$722
$3,810	$3,840	$314	$544	$423	$664	$544	$732
$3,840	$3,870	$318	$550	$430	$671	$550	$741

2023 Wage Bracket Method Tables for Manual Payroll Systems with Forms W-4 From 2020 or Later
SEMIMONTHLY Payroll Period

If the Adjusted Wage Amount (line 1h) is		Married Filing Jointly		Head of Household		Single or Married Filing Separately	
At least	But less than	Standard withholding	Form W-4, Step 2, Checkbox withholding	Standard withholding	Form W-4, Step 2, Checkbox withholding	Standard withholding	Form W-4, Step 2, Checkbox withholding
				The Tentative Withholding Amount is:			
$0	$290	$0	$0	$0	$0	$0	$0
$290	$300	$0	$0	$0	$0	$0	$1
$300	$310	$0	$0	$0	$0	$0	$2
$310	$320	$0	$0	$0	$0	$0	$3
$320	$330	$0	$0	$0	$0	$0	$4
$330	$340	$0	$0	$0	$0	$0	$5
$340	$350	$0	$0	$0	$0	$0	$6
$350	$360	$0	$0	$0	$0	$0	$7
$360	$370	$0	$0	$0	$0	$0	$8
$370	$380	$0	$0	$0	$0	$0	$9
$380	$390	$0	$0	$0	$0	$0	$10
$390	$400	$0	$0	$0	$0	$0	$11
$400	$410	$0	$0	$0	$0	$0	$12
$410	$420	$0	$0	$0	$0	$0	$13
$420	$430	$0	$0	$0	$0	$0	$14
$430	$440	$0	$0	$0	$0	$0	$15
$440	$450	$0	$0	$0	$1	$0	$16
$450	$460	$0	$0	$0	$2	$0	$17
$460	$470	$0	$0	$0	$3	$0	$18
$470	$480	$0	$0	$0	$4	$0	$19
$480	$490	$0	$0	$0	$5	$0	$20
$490	$500	$0	$0	$0	$6	$0	$21
$500	$510	$0	$0	$0	$7	$0	$22
$510	$520	$0	$0	$0	$8	$0	$23
$520	$535	$0	$0	$0	$9	$0	$24
$535	$550	$0	$0	$0	$11	$0	$26
$550	$565	$0	$0	$0	$12	$0	$28
$565	$580	$0	$0	$0	$14	$0	$29
$580	$595	$0	$1	$0	$15	$1	$31
$595	$610	$0	$3	$0	$17	$3	$33
$610	$625	$0	$4	$0	$18	$4	$35
$625	$640	$0	$6	$0	$20	$6	$37
$640	$655	$0	$7	$0	$21	$7	$38
$655	$670	$0	$9	$0	$23	$9	$40
$670	$685	$0	$10	$0	$24	$10	$42
$685	$700	$0	$12	$0	$26	$12	$44
$700	$715	$0	$13	$0	$27	$13	$46
$715	$730	$0	$15	$0	$29	$15	$47
$730	$745	$0	$16	$0	$30	$16	$49
$745	$760	$0	$18	$0	$32	$18	$51
$760	$775	$0	$19	$0	$34	$19	$53
$775	$790	$0	$21	$0	$35	$21	$55
$790	$805	$0	$22	$0	$37	$22	$56
$805	$820	$0	$24	$0	$39	$24	$58
$820	$835	$0	$25	$0	$41	$25	$60
$835	$850	$0	$27	$0	$43	$27	$62
$850	$865	$0	$28	$0	$44	$28	$64
$865	$880	$0	$30	$1	$46	$30	$65
$880	$895	$0	$31	$2	$48	$31	$67
$895	$910	$0	$33	$4	$50	$33	$69
$910	$925	$0	$34	$5	$52	$34	$71
$925	$940	$0	$36	$7	$53	$36	$73
$940	$955	$0	$37	$8	$55	$37	$74
$955	$970	$0	$39	$10	$57	$39	$76
$970	$985	$0	$40	$11	$59	$40	$78
$985	$1,000	$0	$42	$13	$61	$42	$80
$1,000	$1,015	$0	$43	$14	$62	$43	$82
$1,015	$1,030	$0	$45	$16	$64	$45	$83
$1,030	$1,045	$0	$46	$17	$66	$46	$85
$1,045	$1,060	$0	$48	$19	$68	$48	$87
$1,060	$1,075	$0	$50	$20	$70	$50	$89
$1,075	$1,090	$0	$51	$22	$71	$51	$91
$1,090	$1,105	$0	$53	$23	$73	$53	$92
$1,105	$1,120	$0	$55	$25	$75	$55	$94

2023 Wage Bracket Method Tables for Manual Payroll Systems with Forms W-4 From 2020 or Later
SEMIMONTHLY Payroll Period

If the **Adjusted Wage Amount** (line 1h) is		Married Filing Jointly		Head of Household		Single or Married Filing Separately	
At least	But less than	Standard withholding	Form W-4, Step 2, Checkbox withholding	Standard withholding	Form W-4, Step 2, Checkbox withholding	Standard withholding	Form W-4, Step 2, Checkbox withholding
				The Tentative Withholding Amount is:			
$1,120	$1,135	$0	$57	$26	$77	$57	$96
$1,135	$1,150	$0	$59	$28	$79	$59	$98
$1,150	$1,165	$0	$60	$29	$80	$60	$100
$1,165	$1,180	$2	$62	$31	$82	$62	$101
$1,180	$1,195	$3	$64	$32	$84	$64	$103
$1,195	$1,210	$5	$66	$34	$86	$66	$105
$1,210	$1,225	$6	$68	$35	$88	$68	$107
$1,225	$1,245	$8	$70	$37	$90	$70	$110
$1,245	$1,265	$10	$72	$39	$92	$72	$115
$1,265	$1,285	$12	$75	$41	$94	$75	$119
$1,285	$1,305	$14	$77	$43	$97	$77	$124
$1,305	$1,325	$16	$79	$45	$99	$79	$128
$1,325	$1,345	$18	$82	$47	$102	$82	$132
$1,345	$1,365	$20	$84	$49	$104	$84	$137
$1,365	$1,385	$22	$87	$51	$106	$87	$141
$1,385	$1,405	$24	$89	$53	$109	$89	$146
$1,405	$1,425	$26	$91	$55	$111	$91	$150
$1,425	$1,445	$28	$94	$57	$114	$94	$154
$1,445	$1,465	$30	$96	$59	$116	$96	$159
$1,465	$1,485	$32	$99	$61	$118	$99	$163
$1,485	$1,505	$34	$101	$63	$121	$101	$168
$1,505	$1,525	$36	$103	$65	$123	$103	$172
$1,525	$1,545	$38	$106	$67	$126	$106	$176
$1,545	$1,565	$40	$108	$70	$128	$108	$181
$1,565	$1,585	$42	$111	$72	$130	$111	$185
$1,585	$1,605	$44	$113	$74	$133	$113	$190
$1,605	$1,625	$46	$115	$77	$135	$115	$194
$1,625	$1,645	$48	$118	$79	$138	$118	$198
$1,645	$1,665	$50	$120	$82	$140	$120	$203
$1,665	$1,685	$52	$123	$84	$142	$123	$207
$1,685	$1,705	$54	$125	$86	$146	$125	$212
$1,705	$1,725	$56	$127	$89	$151	$127	$216
$1,725	$1,745	$58	$130	$91	$155	$130	$220
$1,745	$1,765	$60	$132	$94	$160	$132	$225
$1,765	$1,785	$62	$135	$96	$164	$135	$229
$1,785	$1,805	$64	$137	$98	$168	$137	$234
$1,805	$1,825	$66	$139	$101	$173	$139	$238
$1,825	$1,845	$68	$142	$103	$177	$142	$242
$1,845	$1,865	$70	$144	$106	$182	$144	$247
$1,865	$1,885	$72	$147	$108	$186	$147	$251
$1,885	$1,905	$74	$149	$110	$190	$149	$256
$1,905	$1,925	$76	$151	$113	$195	$151	$260
$1,925	$1,945	$78	$154	$115	$199	$154	$264
$1,945	$1,965	$80	$156	$118	$204	$156	$269
$1,965	$1,985	$82	$159	$120	$208	$159	$273
$1,985	$2,005	$84	$161	$122	$212	$161	$278
$2,005	$2,025	$86	$163	$125	$217	$163	$282
$2,025	$2,045	$88	$166	$127	$221	$166	$286
$2,045	$2,065	$90	$168	$130	$226	$168	$291
$2,065	$2,085	$92	$171	$132	$230	$171	$295
$2,085	$2,105	$95	$173	$134	$234	$173	$300
$2,105	$2,125	$97	$175	$137	$239	$175	$304
$2,125	$2,145	$99	$178	$139	$243	$178	$308
$2,145	$2,165	$102	$180	$142	$248	$180	$313
$2,165	$2,185	$104	$183	$144	$252	$183	$317
$2,185	$2,205	$107	$185	$146	$256	$185	$322
$2,205	$2,225	$109	$187	$149	$261	$187	$326
$2,225	$2,245	$111	$190	$151	$265	$190	$330
$2,245	$2,265	$114	$192	$154	$270	$192	$335
$2,265	$2,285	$116	$195	$156	$274	$195	$339
$2,285	$2,320	$119	$198	$159	$280	$198	$346
$2,320	$2,355	$124	$202	$163	$288	$202	$354
$2,355	$2,390	$128	$206	$168	$295	$206	$363
$2,390	$2,425	$132	$210	$172	$303	$210	$371
$2,425	$2,460	$136	$215	$176	$311	$215	$379

2023 Wage Bracket Method Tables for Manual Payroll Systems with Forms W-4 From 2020 or Later
SEMIMONTHLY Payroll Period

If the Adjusted Wage Amount (line 1h) is		Married Filing Jointly		Head of Household		Single or Married Filing Separately	
At least	But less than	Standard withholding	Form W-4, Step 2, Checkbox withholding	Standard withholding	Form W-4, Step 2, Checkbox withholding	Standard withholding	Form W-4, Step 2, Checkbox withholding
		\multicolumn{6}{c}{The Tentative Withholding Amount is:}					
$2,460	$2,495	$140	$223	$180	$320	$223	$388
$2,495	$2,530	$145	$230	$184	$328	$230	$396
$2,530	$2,565	$149	$238	$189	$336	$238	$405
$2,565	$2,600	$153	$246	$193	$345	$246	$413
$2,600	$2,635	$157	$253	$197	$353	$253	$421
$2,635	$2,670	$161	$261	$201	$362	$261	$430
$2,670	$2,705	$166	$269	$205	$370	$269	$438
$2,705	$2,740	$170	$276	$210	$378	$276	$447
$2,740	$2,775	$174	$284	$214	$387	$284	$455
$2,775	$2,810	$178	$292	$218	$395	$292	$463
$2,810	$2,845	$182	$300	$222	$404	$300	$472
$2,845	$2,880	$187	$307	$226	$412	$307	$480
$2,880	$2,915	$191	$315	$231	$420	$315	$489
$2,915	$2,950	$195	$323	$235	$429	$323	$497
$2,950	$2,985	$199	$330	$239	$437	$330	$505
$2,985	$3,020	$203	$338	$243	$446	$338	$514
$3,020	$3,055	$208	$346	$247	$454	$346	$522
$3,055	$3,090	$212	$353	$252	$462	$353	$531
$3,090	$3,125	$216	$361	$256	$471	$361	$539
$3,125	$3,160	$220	$369	$260	$479	$369	$547
$3,160	$3,195	$224	$377	$264	$488	$377	$556
$3,195	$3,230	$229	$384	$268	$496	$384	$564
$3,230	$3,265	$233	$392	$273	$504	$392	$573
$3,265	$3,300	$237	$400	$277	$513	$400	$581
$3,300	$3,335	$241	$407	$281	$521	$407	$589
$3,335	$3,370	$245	$415	$285	$530	$415	$598
$3,370	$3,405	$250	$423	$292	$538	$423	$606
$3,405	$3,440	$254	$430	$300	$546	$430	$615
$3,440	$3,475	$258	$438	$308	$555	$438	$623
$3,475	$3,510	$262	$446	$315	$563	$446	$631
$3,510	$3,545	$266	$454	$323	$572	$454	$640
$3,545	$3,580	$271	$461	$331	$580	$461	$648
$3,580	$3,615	$275	$469	$338	$588	$469	$657
$3,615	$3,650	$279	$477	$346	$597	$477	$665
$3,650	$3,685	$283	$484	$354	$605	$484	$673
$3,685	$3,720	$287	$492	$361	$614	$492	$682
$3,720	$3,755	$292	$500	$369	$622	$500	$690
$3,755	$3,790	$296	$507	$377	$630	$507	$699
$3,790	$3,825	$300	$515	$385	$639	$515	$707
$3,825	$3,860	$304	$523	$392	$647	$523	$715
$3,860	$3,895	$308	$531	$400	$656	$531	$724
$3,895	$3,930	$313	$538	$408	$664	$538	$732
$3,930	$3,965	$317	$546	$415	$672	$546	$741
$3,965	$4,000	$321	$554	$423	$681	$554	$749
$4,000	$4,035	$325	$561	$431	$689	$561	$757
$4,035	$4,070	$329	$569	$438	$698	$569	$766
$4,070	$4,105	$334	$577	$446	$706	$577	$775
$4,105	$4,140	$338	$584	$454	$714	$584	$786
$4,140	$4,175	$342	$592	$462	$723	$592	$797

2023 Wage Bracket Method Tables for Manual Payroll Systems with Forms W-4 From 2020 or Later
MONTHLY Payroll Period

If the Adjusted Wage Amount (line 1h) is		Married Filing Jointly		Head of Household		Single or Married Filing Separately	
At least	But less than	Standard withholding	Form W-4, Step 2, Checkbox withholding	Standard withholding	Form W-4, Step 2, Checkbox withholding	Standard withholding	Form W-4, Step 2, Checkbox withholding
				The Tentative Withholding Amount is:			
$0	$580	$0	$0	$0	$0	$0	$0
$580	$600	$0	$0	$0	$0	$0	$1
$600	$620	$0	$0	$0	$0	$0	$3
$620	$640	$0	$0	$0	$0	$0	$5
$640	$660	$0	$0	$0	$0	$0	$7
$660	$680	$0	$0	$0	$0	$0	$9
$680	$700	$0	$0	$0	$0	$0	$11
$700	$720	$0	$0	$0	$0	$0	$13
$720	$740	$0	$0	$0	$0	$0	$15
$740	$760	$0	$0	$0	$0	$0	$17
$760	$780	$0	$0	$0	$0	$0	$19
$780	$800	$0	$0	$0	$0	$0	$21
$800	$820	$0	$0	$0	$0	$0	$23
$820	$840	$0	$0	$0	$0	$0	$25
$840	$860	$0	$0	$0	$0	$0	$27
$860	$880	$0	$0	$0	$0	$0	$29
$880	$900	$0	$0	$0	$2	$0	$31
$900	$920	$0	$0	$0	$4	$0	$33
$920	$940	$0	$0	$0	$6	$0	$35
$940	$960	$0	$0	$0	$8	$0	$37
$960	$980	$0	$0	$0	$10	$0	$39
$980	$1,000	$0	$0	$0	$12	$0	$41
$1,000	$1,020	$0	$0	$0	$14	$0	$43
$1,020	$1,040	$0	$0	$0	$16	$0	$45
$1,040	$1,070	$0	$0	$0	$19	$0	$48
$1,070	$1,100	$0	$0	$0	$22	$0	$52
$1,100	$1,130	$0	$0	$0	$25	$0	$55
$1,130	$1,160	$0	$0	$0	$28	$0	$59
$1,160	$1,190	$0	$2	$0	$31	$2	$63
$1,190	$1,220	$0	$5	$0	$34	$5	$66
$1,220	$1,250	$0	$8	$0	$37	$8	$70
$1,250	$1,280	$0	$11	$0	$40	$11	$73
$1,280	$1,310	$0	$14	$0	$43	$14	$77
$1,310	$1,340	$0	$17	$0	$46	$17	$81
$1,340	$1,370	$0	$20	$0	$49	$20	$84
$1,370	$1,400	$0	$23	$0	$52	$23	$88
$1,400	$1,430	$0	$26	$0	$55	$26	$91
$1,430	$1,460	$0	$29	$0	$58	$29	$95
$1,460	$1,490	$0	$32	$0	$61	$32	$99
$1,490	$1,520	$0	$35	$0	$64	$35	$102
$1,520	$1,550	$0	$38	$0	$67	$38	$106
$1,550	$1,580	$0	$41	$0	$71	$41	$109
$1,580	$1,610	$0	$44	$0	$74	$44	$113
$1,610	$1,640	$0	$47	$0	$78	$47	$117
$1,640	$1,670	$0	$50	$0	$82	$50	$120
$1,670	$1,700	$0	$53	$0	$85	$53	$124
$1,700	$1,730	$0	$56	$0	$89	$56	$127
$1,730	$1,760	$0	$59	$1	$92	$59	$131
$1,760	$1,790	$0	$62	$4	$96	$62	$135
$1,790	$1,820	$0	$65	$7	$100	$65	$138
$1,820	$1,850	$0	$68	$10	$103	$68	$142
$1,850	$1,880	$0	$71	$13	$107	$71	$145
$1,880	$1,910	$0	$74	$16	$110	$74	$149
$1,910	$1,940	$0	$77	$19	$114	$77	$153
$1,940	$1,970	$0	$80	$22	$118	$80	$156
$1,970	$2,000	$0	$83	$25	$121	$83	$160
$2,000	$2,030	$0	$86	$28	$125	$86	$163
$2,030	$2,060	$0	$89	$31	$128	$89	$167
$2,060	$2,090	$0	$92	$34	$132	$92	$171
$2,090	$2,120	$0	$96	$37	$136	$96	$174
$2,120	$2,150	$0	$99	$40	$139	$99	$178
$2,150	$2,180	$0	$103	$43	$143	$103	$181
$2,180	$2,210	$0	$107	$46	$146	$107	$185
$2,210	$2,240	$0	$110	$49	$150	$110	$189

(Source: Internal Revenue Service)

2023 Wage Bracket Method Tables for Manual Payroll Systems with Forms W-4 From 2020 or Later
MONTHLY Payroll Period

If the Adjusted Wage Amount (line 1h) is		Married Filing Jointly		Head of Household		Single or Married Filing Separately	
At least	But less than	Standard withholding	Form W-4, Step 2, Checkbox withholding	Standard withholding	Form W-4, Step 2, Checkbox withholding	Standard withholding	Form W-4, Step 2, Checkbox withholding
			The Tentative Withholding Amount is:				
$2,240	$2,270	$0	$114	$52	$154	$114	$192
$2,270	$2,300	$0	$117	$55	$157	$117	$196
$2,300	$2,330	$1	$121	$58	$161	$121	$199
$2,330	$2,360	$4	$125	$61	$164	$125	$203
$2,360	$2,390	$7	$128	$64	$168	$128	$207
$2,390	$2,420	$10	$132	$67	$172	$132	$210
$2,420	$2,450	$13	$135	$70	$175	$135	$214
$2,450	$2,490	$16	$140	$74	$179	$140	$221
$2,490	$2,530	$20	$144	$78	$184	$144	$230
$2,530	$2,570	$24	$149	$82	$189	$149	$239
$2,570	$2,610	$28	$154	$86	$194	$154	$247
$2,610	$2,650	$32	$159	$90	$199	$159	$256
$2,650	$2,690	$36	$164	$94	$203	$164	$265
$2,690	$2,730	$40	$168	$98	$208	$168	$274
$2,730	$2,770	$44	$173	$102	$213	$173	$283
$2,770	$2,810	$48	$178	$106	$218	$178	$291
$2,810	$2,850	$52	$183	$110	$223	$183	$300
$2,850	$2,890	$56	$188	$114	$227	$188	$309
$2,890	$2,930	$60	$192	$118	$232	$192	$318
$2,930	$2,970	$64	$197	$122	$237	$197	$327
$2,970	$3,010	$68	$202	$126	$242	$202	$335
$3,010	$3,050	$72	$207	$130	$247	$207	$344
$3,050	$3,090	$76	$212	$134	$251	$212	$353
$3,090	$3,130	$80	$216	$139	$256	$216	$362
$3,130	$3,170	$84	$221	$144	$261	$221	$371
$3,170	$3,210	$88	$226	$149	$266	$226	$379
$3,210	$3,250	$92	$231	$153	$271	$231	$388
$3,250	$3,290	$96	$236	$158	$275	$236	$397
$3,290	$3,330	$100	$240	$163	$280	$240	$406
$3,330	$3,370	$104	$245	$168	$285	$245	$415
$3,370	$3,410	$108	$250	$173	$293	$250	$423
$3,410	$3,450	$112	$255	$177	$301	$255	$432
$3,450	$3,490	$116	$260	$182	$310	$260	$441
$3,490	$3,530	$120	$264	$187	$319	$264	$450
$3,530	$3,570	$124	$269	$192	$328	$269	$459
$3,570	$3,610	$128	$274	$197	$337	$274	$467
$3,610	$3,650	$132	$279	$201	$345	$279	$476
$3,650	$3,690	$136	$284	$206	$354	$284	$485
$3,690	$3,730	$140	$288	$211	$363	$288	$494
$3,730	$3,770	$144	$293	$216	$372	$293	$503
$3,770	$3,810	$148	$298	$221	$381	$298	$511
$3,810	$3,850	$152	$303	$225	$389	$303	$520
$3,850	$3,890	$156	$308	$230	$398	$308	$529
$3,890	$3,930	$160	$312	$235	$407	$312	$538
$3,930	$3,970	$164	$317	$240	$416	$317	$547
$3,970	$4,010	$168	$322	$245	$425	$322	$555
$4,010	$4,050	$172	$327	$249	$433	$327	$564
$4,050	$4,090	$176	$332	$254	$442	$332	$573
$4,090	$4,130	$180	$336	$259	$451	$336	$582
$4,130	$4,170	$184	$341	$264	$460	$341	$591
$4,170	$4,210	$189	$346	$269	$469	$346	$599
$4,210	$4,250	$194	$351	$273	$477	$351	$608
$4,250	$4,290	$199	$356	$278	$486	$356	$617
$4,290	$4,330	$204	$360	$283	$495	$360	$626
$4,330	$4,370	$208	$365	$288	$504	$365	$635
$4,370	$4,410	$213	$370	$293	$513	$370	$643
$4,410	$4,450	$218	$375	$297	$521	$375	$652
$4,450	$4,490	$223	$380	$302	$530	$380	$661
$4,490	$4,530	$228	$384	$307	$539	$384	$670
$4,530	$4,570	$232	$389	$312	$548	$389	$679
$4,570	$4,640	$239	$396	$318	$560	$396	$692
$4,640	$4,710	$247	$404	$327	$575	$404	$709
$4,710	$4,780	$256	$413	$335	$591	$413	$725
$4,780	$4,850	$264	$421	$344	$606	$421	$742
$4,850	$4,920	$273	$430	$352	$622	$430	$759

2023 Wage Bracket Method Tables for Manual Payroll Systems with Forms W-4 From 2020 or Later
MONTHLY Payroll Period

If the Adjusted Wage Amount (line 1h) is		Married Filing Jointly		Head of Household		Single or Married Filing Separately	
At least	But less than	Standard withholding	Form W-4, Step 2, Checkbox withholding	Standard withholding	Form W-4, Step 2, Checkbox withholding	Standard withholding	Form W-4, Step 2, Checkbox withholding
				The Tentative Withholding Amount is:			
$4,920	$4,990	$281	$445	$360	$639	$445	$776
$4,990	$5,060	$289	$461	$369	$656	$461	$793
$5,060	$5,130	$298	$476	$377	$673	$476	$809
$5,130	$5,200	$306	$491	$386	$690	$491	$826
$5,200	$5,270	$315	$507	$394	$706	$507	$843
$5,270	$5,340	$323	$522	$402	$723	$522	$860
$5,340	$5,410	$331	$538	$411	$740	$538	$877
$5,410	$5,480	$340	$553	$419	$757	$553	$893
$5,480	$5,550	$348	$568	$428	$774	$568	$910
$5,550	$5,620	$357	$584	$436	$790	$584	$927
$5,620	$5,690	$365	$599	$444	$807	$599	$944
$5,690	$5,760	$373	$615	$453	$824	$615	$961
$5,760	$5,830	$382	$630	$461	$841	$630	$977
$5,830	$5,900	$390	$645	$470	$858	$645	$994
$5,900	$5,970	$399	$661	$478	$874	$661	$1,011
$5,970	$6,040	$407	$676	$486	$891	$676	$1,028
$6,040	$6,110	$415	$692	$495	$908	$692	$1,045
$6,110	$6,180	$424	$707	$503	$925	$707	$1,061
$6,180	$6,250	$432	$722	$512	$942	$722	$1,078
$6,250	$6,320	$441	$738	$520	$958	$738	$1,095
$6,320	$6,390	$449	$753	$528	$975	$753	$1,112
$6,390	$6,460	$457	$769	$537	$992	$769	$1,129
$6,460	$6,530	$466	$784	$545	$1,009	$784	$1,145
$6,530	$6,600	$474	$799	$554	$1,026	$799	$1,162
$6,600	$6,670	$483	$815	$562	$1,042	$815	$1,179
$6,670	$6,740	$491	$830	$570	$1,059	$830	$1,196
$6,740	$6,810	$499	$846	$584	$1,076	$846	$1,213
$6,810	$6,880	$508	$861	$600	$1,093	$861	$1,229
$6,880	$6,950	$516	$876	$615	$1,110	$876	$1,246
$6,950	$7,020	$525	$892	$630	$1,126	$892	$1,263
$7,020	$7,090	$533	$907	$646	$1,143	$907	$1,280
$7,090	$7,160	$541	$923	$661	$1,160	$923	$1,297
$7,160	$7,230	$550	$938	$677	$1,177	$938	$1,313
$7,230	$7,300	$558	$953	$692	$1,194	$953	$1,330
$7,300	$7,370	$567	$969	$707	$1,210	$969	$1,347
$7,370	$7,440	$575	$984	$723	$1,227	$984	$1,364
$7,440	$7,510	$583	$1,000	$738	$1,244	$1,000	$1,381
$7,510	$7,580	$592	$1,015	$754	$1,261	$1,015	$1,397
$7,580	$7,650	$600	$1,030	$769	$1,278	$1,030	$1,414
$7,650	$7,720	$609	$1,046	$784	$1,294	$1,046	$1,431
$7,720	$7,790	$617	$1,061	$800	$1,311	$1,061	$1,448
$7,790	$7,860	$625	$1,077	$815	$1,328	$1,077	$1,465
$7,860	$7,930	$634	$1,092	$831	$1,345	$1,092	$1,481
$7,930	$8,000	$642	$1,107	$846	$1,362	$1,107	$1,498
$8,000	$8,070	$651	$1,123	$861	$1,378	$1,123	$1,515
$8,070	$8,140	$659	$1,138	$877	$1,395	$1,138	$1,532
$8,140	$8,210	$667	$1,154	$892	$1,412	$1,154	$1,549
$8,210	$8,280	$676	$1,169	$908	$1,429	$1,169	$1,572
$8,280	$8,350	$684	$1,184	$923	$1,446	$1,184	$1,594

2023 Wage Bracket Method Tables for Manual Payroll Systems with Forms W-4 From 2020 or Later
DAILY Payroll Period

If the Adjusted Wage Amount (line 1h) is		Married Filing Jointly		Head of Household		Single or Married Filing Separately	
At least	But less than	Standard withholding	Form W-4, Step 2, Checkbox withholding	Standard withholding	Form W-4, Step 2, Checkbox withholding	Standard withholding	Form W-4, Step 2, Checkbox withholding
				The Tentative Withholding Amount is:			
$0	$30	$0.00	$0.00	$0.00	$0.00	$0.00	$0.00
$30	$35	$0.00	$0.00	$0.00	$0.00	$0.00	$0.60
$35	$40	$0.00	$0.00	$0.00	$0.00	$0.00	$1.10
$40	$45	$0.00	$0.00	$0.00	$0.30	$0.00	$1.60
$45	$50	$0.00	$0.00	$0.00	$0.80	$0.00	$2.10
$50	$55	$0.00	$0.00	$0.00	$1.30	$0.00	$2.70
$55	$60	$0.00	$0.40	$0.00	$1.80	$0.40	$3.30
$60	$65	$0.00	$0.90	$0.00	$2.30	$0.90	$3.90
$65	$70	$0.00	$1.40	$0.00	$2.80	$1.40	$4.50
$70	$75	$0.00	$1.90	$0.00	$3.30	$1.90	$5.10
$75	$80	$0.00	$2.40	$0.00	$3.90	$2.40	$5.70
$80	$85	$0.00	$2.90	$0.30	$4.50	$2.90	$6.30
$85	$90	$0.00	$3.40	$0.80	$5.10	$3.40	$6.90
$90	$95	$0.00	$3.90	$1.30	$5.70	$3.90	$7.50
$95	$100	$0.00	$4.50	$1.80	$6.30	$4.50	$8.10
$100	$105	$0.00	$5.10	$2.30	$6.90	$5.10	$8.70
$105	$110	$0.10	$5.70	$2.80	$7.50	$5.70	$9.30
$110	$115	$0.60	$6.30	$3.30	$8.10	$6.30	$9.90
$115	$120	$1.10	$6.90	$3.80	$8.70	$6.90	$11.00
$120	$125	$1.60	$7.50	$4.30	$9.30	$7.50	$12.10
$125	$130	$2.10	$8.10	$4.80	$9.90	$8.10	$13.20
$130	$135	$2.60	$8.70	$5.30	$10.50	$8.70	$14.30
$135	$140	$3.10	$9.30	$5.80	$11.10	$9.30	$15.40
$140	$145	$3.60	$9.90	$6.30	$11.70	$9.90	$16.50
$145	$150	$4.10	$10.50	$6.90	$12.30	$10.50	$17.60
$150	$155	$4.60	$11.10	$7.50	$12.90	$11.10	$18.70
$155	$160	$5.10	$11.70	$8.10	$13.70	$11.70	$19.80
$160	$165	$5.60	$12.30	$8.70	$14.80	$12.30	$20.90
$165	$170	$6.10	$12.90	$9.30	$15.90	$12.90	$22.00
$170	$175	$6.60	$13.50	$9.90	$17.00	$13.50	$23.10
$175	$180	$7.10	$14.10	$10.50	$18.10	$14.10	$24.20
$180	$185	$7.60	$14.70	$11.10	$19.20	$14.70	$25.30
$185	$190	$8.10	$15.30	$11.70	$20.30	$15.30	$26.40
$190	$195	$8.60	$15.90	$12.30	$21.40	$15.90	$27.50
$195	$200	$9.20	$16.50	$12.90	$22.50	$16.50	$28.60
$200	$205	$9.80	$17.10	$13.50	$23.60	$17.10	$29.70
$205	$210	$10.40	$17.70	$14.10	$24.70	$17.70	$30.80
$210	$215	$11.00	$18.30	$14.70	$25.80	$18.30	$31.90
$215	$220	$11.60	$18.90	$15.30	$26.90	$18.90	$33.10
$220	$225	$12.20	$19.50	$15.90	$28.00	$19.50	$34.30
$225	$230	$12.80	$20.30	$16.50	$29.20	$20.30	$35.50
$230	$235	$13.40	$21.40	$17.10	$30.40	$21.40	$36.70
$235	$240	$14.00	$22.50	$17.70	$31.60	$22.50	$37.90
$240	$245	$14.60	$23.60	$18.30	$32.80	$23.60	$39.10
$245	$250	$15.20	$24.70	$18.90	$34.00	$24.70	$40.30
$250	$255	$15.80	$25.80	$19.50	$35.20	$25.80	$41.50
$255	$260	$16.40	$26.90	$20.10	$36.40	$26.90	$42.70
$260	$265	$17.00	$28.00	$20.70	$37.60	$28.00	$43.90
$265	$270	$17.60	$29.10	$21.30	$38.80	$29.10	$45.10
$270	$275	$18.20	$30.20	$21.90	$40.00	$30.20	$46.30
$275	$280	$18.80	$31.30	$22.50	$41.20	$31.30	$47.50
$280	$285	$19.40	$32.40	$23.10	$42.40	$32.40	$48.70
$285	$290	$20.00	$33.50	$23.70	$43.60	$33.50	$49.90
$290	$295	$20.60	$34.60	$24.30	$44.80	$34.60	$51.10
$295	$300	$21.20	$35.70	$24.90	$46.00	$35.70	$52.30
$300	$305	$21.80	$36.80	$25.50	$47.20	$36.80	$53.50
$305	$310	$22.40	$37.90	$26.10	$48.40	$37.90	$54.70
$310	$315	$23.00	$39.00	$26.90	$49.60	$39.00	$55.90
$315	$320	$23.60	$40.10	$28.00	$50.80	$40.10	$57.10
$320	$325	$24.20	$41.20	$29.10	$52.00	$41.20	$58.30
$325	$330	$24.80	$42.30	$30.20	$53.20	$42.30	$59.50
$330	$335	$25.40	$43.40	$31.30	$54.40	$43.40	$60.70
$335	$340	$26.00	$44.50	$32.40	$55.60	$44.50	$61.90
$340	$345	$26.60	$45.60	$33.50	$56.80	$45.60	$63.10

2023 Wage Bracket Method Tables for Manual Payroll Systems with Forms W-4 From 2020 or Later
DAILY Payroll Period

If the Adjusted Wage Amount (line 1h) is		Married Filing Jointly		Head of Household		Single or Married Filing Separately	
At least	But less than	Standard withholding	Form W-4, Step 2, Checkbox withholding	Standard withholding	Form W-4, Step 2, Checkbox withholding	Standard withholding	Form W-4, Step 2, Checkbox withholding
		The Tentative Withholding Amount is:					
$345	$350	$27.20	$46.70	$34.60	$58.00	$46.70	$64.30
$350	$355	$27.80	$47.80	$35.70	$59.20	$47.80	$65.50
$355	$360	$28.40	$48.90	$36.80	$60.40	$48.90	$66.70
$360	$365	$29.00	$50.00	$37.90	$61.60	$50.00	$67.90
$365	$370	$29.60	$51.10	$39.00	$62.80	$51.10	$69.10
$370	$375	$30.20	$52.20	$40.10	$64.00	$52.20	$70.30
$375	$380	$30.80	$53.30	$41.20	$65.20	$53.30	$71.60
$380	$385	$31.40	$54.40	$42.30	$66.40	$54.40	$73.20
$385	$390	$32.00	$55.50	$43.40	$67.60	$55.50	$74.80
$390	$395	$32.60	$56.60	$44.50	$69.00	$56.60	$76.40

5. Percentage Method Tables for Manual Payroll Systems With Forms W-4 From 2019 or Earlier

If you compute payroll manually and your employee **has not** submitted a Form W-4 for 2020 or later, and you prefer to use the Percentage Method or you can't use the Wage Bracket Method tables because the employee's annual wages exceed the amount from the last bracket of the table (based on marital status and pay period) or the employee claimed more than 10 allowances, use the worksheet below and the Percentage Method tables that follow to figure federal income tax withholding. This method works for any number of withholding allowances claimed and any amount of wages.

Periodic payments of pensions or annuities with a 2021 or earlier Form W-4P. In lieu of Worksheet 1B and the Percentage Method tables in section 1, you may use Worksheet 5 and the Percentage Method tables in this section to figure federal income tax withholding on periodic payments of pensions or annuities with a 2021 or earlier Form W-4P. As an alternative, if you prefer to use the Wage Bracket Method of withholding, you may use Worksheet 3 and the Wage Bracket Method tables in section 3 to figure federal income tax withholding on periodic payments of pensions or annuities with a 2021 or earlier Form W-4P.

Worksheet 5. Employer's Withholding Worksheet for Percentage Method Tables for Manual Payroll Systems With Forms W-4 From 2019 or Earlier

Keep for Your Records

Table 7	Annually	Semiannually	Quarterly	Monthly	Semimonthly	Biweekly	Weekly	Daily
	$4,300	$2,150	$1,075	$358	$179	$165	$83	$17

Step 1. Adjust the employee's wage amount

1a Enter the employee's total taxable wages this payroll period .... 1a $ _____

1b Enter the number of allowances claimed on the employee's most recent Form W-4 .... 1b _____

1c Multiply line 1b by the amount in Table 7 for your pay frequency .... 1c $ _____

1d Subtract line 1c from line 1a. If zero or less, enter -0-. This is the **Adjusted Wage Amount** .... 1d $ _____

Step 2. Figure the Tentative Withholding Amount

based on your pay frequency, the employee's Adjusted Wage Amount, and marital status (line 3 of Form W-4).

2a Find the row in the Percentage Method table in this section in which the amount on line 1d is at least the amount in column A but less than the amount in column B, and then enter here the amount from column A of that row .... 2a $ _____

2b Enter the amount from column C of that row .... 2b $ _____

2c Enter the percentage from column D of that row .... 2c _____ %

2d Subtract line 2a from line 1d .... 2d $ _____

2e Multiply the amount on line 2d by the percentage on line 2c .... 2e $ _____

2f Add lines 2b and 2e. This is the **Tentative Withholding Amount** .... 2f $ _____

Step 3. Figure the final amount to withhold

3a Enter the additional amount to withhold from line 6 of the employee's Form W-4 .... 3a $ _____

3b Add lines 2f and 3a. **This is the amount to withhold from the employee's wages this pay period** ...... 3b $ _____

2023 Percentage Method Tables for Manual Payroll Systems With Forms W-4 From 2019 or Earlier

WEEKLY Payroll Period

MARRIED Persons					SINGLE Persons				
If the Adjusted Wage Amount (line 1d) is		The tentative amount to withhold is...	Plus this percentage ...	of the amount that the wage exceeds...	If the Adjusted Wage Amount (line 1d) is		The tentative amount to withhold is...	Plus this percentage ...	of the amount that the wage exceeds...
at least...	But less than...				at least...	But less than...			
A	B	C	D	E	A	B	C	D	E
$0	$285	$0.00	0%	$0	$0	$101	$0.00	0%	$0
$285	$708	$0.00	10%	$285	$101	$313	$0.00	10%	$101
$708	$2,005	$42.30	12%	$708	$313	$961	$21.20	12%	$313
$2,005	$3,953	$197.94	22%	$2,005	$961	$1,935	$98.96	22%	$961
$3,953	$7,288	$626.50	24%	$3,953	$1,935	$3,603	$313.24	24%	$1,935
$7,288	$9,179	$1,426.90	32%	$7,288	$3,603	$4,548	$713.56	32%	$3,603
$9,179	$13,626	$2,032.02	35%	$9,179	$4,548	$11,219	$1,015.96	35%	$4,548
$13,626		$3,588.47	37%	$13,626	$11,219		$3,350.81	37%	$11,219

BIWEEKLY Payroll Period

MARRIED Persons					SINGLE Persons				
If the Adjusted Wage Amount (line 1d) is		The tentative amount to withhold is...	Plus this percentage ...	of the amount that the wage exceeds...	If the Adjusted Wage Amount (line 1d) is		The tentative amount to withhold is...	Plus this percentage ...	of the amount that the wage exceeds...
at least...	But less than...				at least...	But less than...			
A	B	C	D	E	A	B	C	D	E
$0	$569	$0.00	0%	$0	$0	$202	$0.00	0%	$0
$569	$1,415	$0.00	10%	$569	$202	$625	$0.00	10%	$202
$1,415	$4,010	$84.60	12%	$1,415	$625	$1,922	$42.30	12%	$625
$4,010	$7,906	$396.00	22%	$4,010	$1,922	$3,870	$197.94	22%	$1,922
$7,906	$14,577	$1,253.12	24%	$7,906	$3,870	$7,206	$626.50	24%	$3,870
$14,577	$18,358	$2,854.16	32%	$14,577	$7,206	$9,096	$1,427.14	32%	$7,206
$18,358	$27,252	$4,064.08	35%	$18,358	$9,096	$22,438	$2,031.94	35%	$9,096
$27,252		$7,176.98	37%	$27,252	$22,438		$6,701.64	37%	$22,438

SEMIMONTHLY Payroll Period

MARRIED Persons					SINGLE Persons				
If the Adjusted Wage Amount (line 1d) is		The tentative amount to withhold is...	Plus this percentage ...	of the amount that the wage exceeds...	If the Adjusted Wage Amount (line 1d) is		The tentative amount to withhold is...	Plus this percentage ...	of the amount that the wage exceeds...
at least...	But less than...				at least...	But less than...			
A	B	C	D	E	A	B	C	D	E
$0	$617	$0.00	0%	$0	$0	$219	$0.00	0%	$0
$617	$1,533	$0.00	10%	$617	$219	$677	$0.00	10%	$219
$1,533	$4,344	$91.60	12%	$1,533	$677	$2,082	$45.80	12%	$677
$4,344	$8,565	$428.92	22%	$4,344	$2,082	$4,193	$214.40	22%	$2,082
$8,565	$15,792	$1,357.54	24%	$8,565	$4,193	$7,806	$678.82	24%	$4,193
$15,792	$19,888	$3,092.02	32%	$15,792	$7,806	$9,854	$1,545.94	32%	$7,806
$19,888	$29,523	$4,402.74	35%	$19,888	$9,854	$24,307	$2,201.30	35%	$9,854
$29,523		$7,774.99	37%	$29,523	$24,307		$7,259.85	37%	$24,307

MONTHLY Payroll Period

MARRIED Persons					SINGLE Persons				
If the Adjusted Wage Amount (line 1d) is		The tentative amount to withhold is...	Plus this percentage ...	of the amount that the wage exceeds...	If the Adjusted Wage Amount (line 1d) is		The tentative amount to withhold is...	Plus this percentage ...	of the amount that the wage exceeds...
at least...	But less than...				at least...	But less than...			
A	B	C	D	E	A	B	C	D	E
$0	$1,233	$0.00	0%	$0	$0	$438	$0.00	0%	$0
$1,233	$3,067	$0.00	10%	$1,233	$438	$1,354	$0.00	10%	$438
$3,067	$8,688	$183.40	12%	$3,067	$1,354	$4,165	$91.60	12%	$1,354
$8,688	$17,129	$857.92	22%	$8,688	$4,165	$8,385	$428.92	22%	$4,165
$17,129	$31,583	$2,714.94	24%	$17,129	$8,385	$15,613	$1,357.32	24%	$8,385
$31,583	$39,775	$6,183.90	32%	$31,583	$15,613	$19,708	$3,092.04	32%	$15,613
$39,775	$59,046	$8,805.34	35%	$39,775	$19,708	$48,615	$4,402.44	35%	$19,708
$59,046		$15,550.19	37%	$59,046	$48,615		$14,519.89	37%	$48,615

2023 Percentage Method Tables for Manual Payroll Systems With Forms W-4 From 2019 or Earlier

QUARTERLY Payroll Period

MARRIED Persons					SINGLE Persons				
If the Adjusted Wage Amount (line 1d) is		The tentative amount to withhold is...	Plus this percentage ...	of the amount that the wage exceeds...	If the Adjusted Wage Amount (line 1d) is		The tentative amount to withhold is...	Plus this percentage ...	of the amount that the wage exceeds...
at least...	But less than...				at least...	But less than...			
A	B	C	D	E	A	B	C	D	E
$0	$3,700	$0.00	0%	$0	$0	$1,313	$0.00	0%	$0
$3,700	$9,200	$0.00	10%	$3,700	$1,313	$4,063	$0.00	10%	$1,313
$9,200	$26,063	$550.00	12%	$9,200	$4,063	$12,494	$275.00	12%	$4,063
$26,063	$51,388	$2,573.56	22%	$26,063	$12,494	$25,156	$1,286.72	22%	$12,494
$51,388	$94,750	$8,145.06	24%	$51,388	$25,156	$46,838	$4,072.36	24%	$25,156
$94,750	$119,325	$18,551.94	32%	$94,750	$46,838	$59,125	$9,276.04	32%	$46,838
$119,325	$177,138	$26,415.94	35%	$119,325	$59,125	$145,844	$13,207.88	35%	$59,125
$177,138		$46,650.49	37%	$177,138	$145,844		$43,559.53	37%	$145,844

SEMIANNUAL Payroll Period

MARRIED Persons					SINGLE Persons				
If the Adjusted Wage Amount (line 1d) is		The tentative amount to withhold is...	Plus this percentage ...	of the amount that the wage exceeds...	If the Adjusted Wage Amount (line 1d) is		The tentative amount to withhold is...	Plus this percentage ...	of the amount that the wage exceeds...
at least...	But less than...				at least...	But less than...			
A	B	C	D	E	A	B	C	D	E
$0	$7,400	$0.00	0%	$0	$0	$2,625	$0.00	0%	$0
$7,400	$18,400	$0.00	10%	$7,400	$2,625	$8,125	$0.00	10%	$2,625
$18,400	$52,125	$1,100.00	12%	$18,400	$8,125	$24,988	$550.00	12%	$8,125
$52,125	$102,775	$5,147.00	22%	$52,125	$24,988	$50,313	$2,573.56	22%	$24,988
$102,775	$189,500	$16,290.00	24%	$102,775	$50,313	$93,675	$8,145.06	24%	$50,313
$189,500	$238,650	$37,104.00	32%	$189,500	$93,675	$118,250	$18,551.94	32%	$93,675
$238,650	$354,275	$52,832.00	35%	$238,650	$118,250	$291,688	$26,415.94	35%	$118,250
$354,275		$93,300.75	37%	$354,275	$291,688		$87,119.24	37%	$291,688

ANNUAL Payroll Period

MARRIED Persons					SINGLE Persons				
If the Adjusted Wage Amount (line 1d) is		The tentative amount to withhold is...	Plus this percentage ...	of the amount that the wage exceeds...	If the Adjusted Wage Amount (line 1d) is		The tentative amount to withhold is...	Plus this percentage ...	of the amount that the wage exceeds...
at least...	But less than...				at least...	But less than...			
A	B	C	D	E	A	B	C	D	E
$0	$14,800	$0.00	0%	$0	$0	$5,250	$0.00	0%	$0
$14,800	$36,800	$0.00	10%	$14,800	$5,250	$16,250	$0.00	10%	$5,250
$36,800	$104,250	$2,200.00	12%	$36,800	$16,250	$49,975	$1,100.00	12%	$16,250
$104,250	$205,550	$10,294.00	22%	$104,250	$49,975	$100,625	$5,147.00	22%	$49,975
$205,550	$379,000	$32,580.00	24%	$205,550	$100,625	$187,350	$16,290.00	24%	$100,625
$379,000	$477,300	$74,208.00	32%	$379,000	$187,350	$236,500	$37,104.00	32%	$187,350
$477,300	$708,550	$105,664.00	35%	$477,300	$236,500	$583,375	$52,832.00	35%	$236,500
$708,550		$186,601.50	37%	$708,550	$583,375		$174,238.25	37%	$583,375

DAILY Payroll Period

MARRIED Persons					SINGLE Persons				
If the Adjusted Wage Amount (line 1d) is		The tentative amount to withhold is...	Plus this percentage ...	of the amount that the wage exceeds...	If the Adjusted Wage Amount (line 1d) is		The tentative amount to withhold is...	Plus this percentage ...	of the amount that the wage exceeds...
at least...	But less than...				at least...	But less than...			
A	B	C	D	E	A	B	C	D	E
$0.00	$56.90	$0.00	0%	$0.00	$0.00	$20.20	$0.00	0%	$0.00
$56.90	$141.50	$0.00	10%	$56.90	$20.20	$62.50	$0.00	10%	$20.20
$141.50	$401.00	$8.46	12%	$141.50	$62.50	$192.20	$4.23	12%	$62.50
$401.00	$790.60	$39.60	22%	$401.00	$192.20	$387.00	$19.79	22%	$192.20
$790.60	$1,457.70	$125.31	24%	$790.60	$387.00	$720.60	$62.65	24%	$387.00
$1,457.70	$1,835.80	$285.42	32%	$1,457.70	$720.60	$909.60	$142.71	32%	$720.60
$1,835.80	$2,725.20	$406.41	35%	$1,835.80	$909.60	$2,243.80	$203.19	35%	$909.60
$2,725.20		$717.70	37%	$2,725.20	$2,243.80		$670.16	37%	$2,243.80

3. Wage Bracket Method Tables for Manual Payroll Systems With Forms W-4 From 2019 or Earlier

If you compute payroll manually and your employee **has not** submitted a Form W-4 for 2020 or later, use the worksheet below and the Wage Bracket Method tables that follow to figure federal income tax withholding.

These Wage Bracket Method tables cover a limited amount of annual wages (generally, less than $100,000) and up to 10 allowances. If you can't use the Wage Bracket Method tables because taxable wages exceed the amount from the last bracket of the table (based on marital status and pay period) or the employee claimed more than 10 allowances, use the Percentage Method tables in section 5.

Periodic payments of pensions or annuities with a 2021 or earlier Form W-4P. In lieu of Worksheet 1B and the Percentage Method tables in section 1, you may use Worksheet 3 and the Wage Bracket Method tables in this section to figure federal income tax withholding on periodic payments of pensions or annuities with a 2021 or earlier Form W-4P. As an alternative, if you prefer to use the Percentage Method of withholding, you may use Worksheet 5 and the Percentage Method tables in section 5 to figure federal income tax withholding on periodic payments of pensions or annuities with a 2021 or earlier Form W-4P.

Worksheet 3. Employer's Withholding Worksheet for Wage Bracket Method Tables for Manual Payroll Systems With Forms W-4 From 2019 or Earlier

Keep for Your Records

Step 1.	Figure the tentative withholding amount		
	1a Enter the employee's total taxable wages this payroll period	1a	$
	1b Use the amount on line 1a to look up the tentative amount to withhold in the appropriate Wage Bracket Method table in this section for your pay frequency, given the employee's marital status (line 3 of Form W-4) and number of allowances claimed. This is the **Tentative Withholding Amount**	1b	$
Step 2.	Figure the final amount to withhold		
	2a Enter the additional amount to withhold from line 6 of the employee's Form W-4	2a	$
	2b Add lines 1b and 2a. **This is the amount to withhold from the employee's wages this pay period**	2b	$

2023 Wage Bracket Method Tables for Manual Payroll Systems With Forms W-4 From 2019 or Earlier

WEEKLY Payroll Period

MARRIED Persons

If the Wage Amount (line 1a) is		And the number of allowances is:										
At least	But less than	0	1	2	3	4	5	6	7	8	9	10
		The Tentative Withholding Amount is:										
$0	$285	$0	$0	$0	$0	$0	$0	$0	$0	$0	$0	$0
$285	$295	$1	$0	$0	$0	$0	$0	$0	$0	$0	$0	$0
$295	$305	$2	$0	$0	$0	$0	$0	$0	$0	$0	$0	$0
$305	$315	$3	$0	$0	$0	$0	$0	$0	$0	$0	$0	$0
$315	$325	$4	$0	$0	$0	$0	$0	$0	$0	$0	$0	$0
$325	$335	$5	$0	$0	$0	$0	$0	$0	$0	$0	$0	$0
$335	$345	$6	$0	$0	$0	$0	$0	$0	$0	$0	$0	$0
$345	$355	$7	$0	$0	$0	$0	$0	$0	$0	$0	$0	$0
$355	$365	$8	$0	$0	$0	$0	$0	$0	$0	$0	$0	$0
$365	$375	$9	$0	$0	$0	$0	$0	$0	$0	$0	$0	$0
$375	$385	$10	$1	$0	$0	$0	$0	$0	$0	$0	$0	$0
$385	$395	$11	$2	$0	$0	$0	$0	$0	$0	$0	$0	$0
$395	$405	$12	$3	$0	$0	$0	$0	$0	$0	$0	$0	$0
$405	$415	$13	$4	$0	$0	$0	$0	$0	$0	$0	$0	$0
$415	$425	$14	$5	$0	$0	$0	$0	$0	$0	$0	$0	$0
$425	$435	$15	$6	$0	$0	$0	$0	$0	$0	$0	$0	$0
$435	$445	$16	$7	$0	$0	$0	$0	$0	$0	$0	$0	$0
$445	$455	$17	$8	$0	$0	$0	$0	$0	$0	$0	$0	$0
$455	$465	$18	$9	$1	$0	$0	$0	$0	$0	$0	$0	$0
$465	$475	$19	$10	$2	$0	$0	$0	$0	$0	$0	$0	$0
$475	$485	$20	$11	$3	$0	$0	$0	$0	$0	$0	$0	$0
$485	$495	$21	$12	$4	$0	$0	$0	$0	$0	$0	$0	$0
$495	$505	$22	$13	$5	$0	$0	$0	$0	$0	$0	$0	$0
$505	$515	$23	$14	$6	$0	$0	$0	$0	$0	$0	$0	$0
$515	$525	$24	$15	$7	$0	$0	$0	$0	$0	$0	$0	$0
$525	$535	$25	$16	$8	$0	$0	$0	$0	$0	$0	$0	$0
$535	$545	$26	$17	$9	$1	$0	$0	$0	$0	$0	$0	$0
$545	$555	$27	$18	$10	$2	$0	$0	$0	$0	$0	$0	$0
$555	$565	$28	$19	$11	$3	$0	$0	$0	$0	$0	$0	$0
$565	$575	$29	$20	$12	$4	$0	$0	$0	$0	$0	$0	$0
$575	$585	$30	$21	$13	$5	$0	$0	$0	$0	$0	$0	$0
$585	$595	$31	$22	$14	$6	$0	$0	$0	$0	$0	$0	$0
$595	$605	$32	$23	$15	$7	$0	$0	$0	$0	$0	$0	$0
$605	$615	$33	$24	$16	$8	$0	$0	$0	$0	$0	$0	$0
$615	$625	$34	$25	$17	$9	$0	$0	$0	$0	$0	$0	$0
$625	$635	$35	$26	$18	$10	$1	$0	$0	$0	$0	$0	$0
$635	$645	$36	$27	$19	$11	$2	$0	$0	$0	$0	$0	$0
$645	$655	$37	$28	$20	$12	$3	$0	$0	$0	$0	$0	$0
$655	$665	$38	$29	$21	$13	$4	$0	$0	$0	$0	$0	$0
$665	$675	$39	$30	$22	$14	$5	$0	$0	$0	$0	$0	$0
$675	$685	$40	$31	$23	$15	$6	$0	$0	$0	$0	$0	$0
$685	$695	$41	$32	$24	$16	$7	$0	$0	$0	$0	$0	$0
$695	$705	$42	$33	$25	$17	$8	$0	$0	$0	$0	$0	$0
$705	$715	$43	$34	$26	$18	$9	$1	$0	$0	$0	$0	$0
$715	$730	$44	$36	$27	$19	$11	$2	$0	$0	$0	$0	$0
$730	$745	$46	$37	$29	$20	$12	$4	$0	$0	$0	$0	$0
$745	$760	$48	$39	$30	$22	$14	$5	$0	$0	$0	$0	$0
$760	$775	$49	$40	$32	$23	$15	$7	$0	$0	$0	$0	$0
$775	$790	$51	$42	$33	$25	$17	$8	$0	$0	$0	$0	$0
$790	$805	$53	$43	$35	$26	$18	$10	$2	$0	$0	$0	$0
$805	$820	$55	$45	$36	$28	$20	$11	$3	$0	$0	$0	$0

2023 Wage Bracket Method Tables for Manual Payroll Systems With Forms W-4 From 2019 or Earlier
WEEKLY Payroll Period

If the Wage Amount (line 1a) is		MARRIED Persons										
		And the number of allowances is:										
At least	But less than	0	1	2	3	4	5	6	7	8	9	10
		The Tentative Withholding Amount is:										
$820	$835	$57	$47	$38	$29	$21	$13	$5	$0	$0	$0	$0
$835	$850	$58	$49	$39	$31	$23	$14	$6	$0	$0	$0	$0
$850	$865	$60	$50	$41	$32	$24	$16	$8	$0	$0	$0	$0
$865	$880	$62	$52	$42	$34	$26	$17	$9	$1	$0	$0	$0
$880	$895	$64	$54	$44	$35	$27	$19	$11	$2	$0	$0	$0
$895	$910	$66	$56	$46	$37	$29	$20	$12	$4	$0	$0	$0
$910	$925	$67	$58	$48	$38	$30	$22	$14	$5	$0	$0	$0
$925	$940	$69	$59	$49	$40	$32	$23	$15	$7	$0	$0	$0
$940	$955	$71	$61	$51	$41	$33	$25	$17	$8	$0	$0	$0
$955	$970	$73	$63	$53	$43	$35	$26	$18	$10	$2	$0	$0
$970	$985	$75	$65	$55	$45	$36	$28	$20	$11	$3	$0	$0
$985	$1,000	$76	$67	$57	$47	$38	$29	$21	$13	$5	$0	$0
$1,000	$1,015	$78	$68	$58	$49	$39	$31	$23	$14	$6	$0	$0
$1,015	$1,030	$80	$70	$60	$50	$41	$32	$24	$16	$8	$0	$0
$1,030	$1,045	$82	$72	$62	$52	$42	$34	$26	$17	$9	$1	$0
$1,045	$1,060	$84	$74	$64	$54	$44	$35	$27	$19	$11	$2	$0
$1,060	$1,075	$85	$76	$66	$56	$46	$37	$29	$20	$12	$4	$0
$1,075	$1,090	$87	$77	$67	$58	$48	$38	$30	$22	$14	$5	$0
$1,090	$1,105	$89	$79	$69	$59	$49	$40	$32	$23	$15	$7	$0
$1,105	$1,120	$91	$81	$71	$61	$51	$41	$33	$25	$17	$8	$0
$1,120	$1,135	$93	$83	$73	$63	$53	$43	$35	$26	$18	$10	$2
$1,135	$1,150	$94	$85	$75	$65	$55	$45	$36	$28	$20	$11	$3
$1,150	$1,165	$96	$86	$76	$67	$57	$47	$38	$29	$21	$13	$5
$1,165	$1,180	$98	$88	$78	$68	$58	$48	$39	$31	$23	$14	$6
$1,180	$1,195	$100	$90	$80	$70	$60	$50	$41	$32	$24	$16	$8
$1,195	$1,210	$102	$92	$82	$72	$62	$52	$42	$34	$26	$17	$9
$1,210	$1,225	$103	$94	$84	$74	$64	$54	$44	$35	$27	$19	$11
$1,225	$1,240	$105	$95	$85	$76	$66	$56	$46	$37	$29	$20	$12
$1,240	$1,255	$107	$97	$87	$77	$67	$57	$48	$38	$30	$22	$14
$1,255	$1,270	$109	$99	$89	$79	$69	$59	$49	$40	$32	$23	$15
$1,270	$1,285	$111	$101	$91	$81	$71	$61	$51	$41	$33	$25	$17
$1,285	$1,300	$112	$103	$93	$83	$73	$63	$53	$43	$35	$26	$18
$1,300	$1,315	$114	$104	$94	$85	$75	$65	$55	$45	$36	$28	$20
$1,315	$1,330	$116	$106	$96	$86	$76	$66	$57	$47	$38	$29	$21
$1,330	$1,345	$118	$108	$98	$88	$78	$68	$58	$48	$39	$31	$23
$1,345	$1,360	$120	$110	$100	$90	$80	$70	$60	$50	$41	$32	$24
$1,360	$1,375	$121	$112	$102	$92	$82	$72	$62	$52	$42	$34	$26
$1,375	$1,390	$123	$113	$103	$94	$84	$74	$64	$54	$44	$35	$27
$1,390	$1,405	$125	$115	$105	$95	$85	$75	$66	$56	$46	$37	$29
$1,405	$1,420	$127	$117	$107	$97	$87	$77	$67	$57	$48	$38	$30
$1,420	$1,435	$129	$119	$109	$99	$89	$79	$69	$59	$49	$40	$32
$1,435	$1,450	$130	$121	$111	$101	$91	$81	$71	$61	$51	$41	$33
$1,450	$1,465	$132	$122	$112	$103	$93	$83	$73	$63	$53	$43	$35
$1,465	$1,480	$134	$124	$114	$104	$94	$84	$75	$65	$55	$45	$36
$1,480	$1,495	$136	$126	$116	$106	$96	$86	$76	$66	$57	$47	$38
$1,495	$1,510	$138	$128	$118	$108	$98	$88	$78	$68	$58	$48	$39
$1,510	$1,525	$139	$130	$120	$110	$100	$90	$80	$70	$60	$50	$41
$1,525	$1,540	$141	$131	$121	$112	$102	$92	$82	$72	$62	$52	$42
$1,540	$1,555	$143	$133	$123	$113	$103	$93	$84	$74	$64	$54	$44
$1,555	$1,570	$145	$135	$125	$115	$105	$95	$85	$75	$66	$56	$46
$1,570	$1,585	$147	$137	$127	$117	$107	$97	$87	$77	$67	$57	$47

2023 Wage Bracket Method Tables for Manual Payroll Systems With Forms W-4 From 2019 or Earlier
WEEKLY Payroll Period

If the Wage Amount (line 1a) is		MARRIED Persons									
		And the number of allowances is:									
At least	But less than	0	1	2	3	4	5	6	7	8	9	10
		The Tentative Withholding Amount is:										
$1,585	$1,600	$148	$139	$129	$119	$109	$99	$89	$79	$69	$59	$49
$1,600	$1,615	$150	$140	$130	$121	$111	$101	$91	$81	$71	$61	$51
$1,615	$1,630	$152	$142	$132	$122	$112	$102	$93	$83	$73	$63	$53
$1,630	$1,645	$154	$144	$134	$124	$114	$104	$94	$84	$75	$65	$55
$1,645	$1,660	$156	$146	$136	$126	$116	$106	$96	$86	$76	$66	$56
$1,660	$1,675	$157	$148	$138	$128	$118	$108	$98	$88	$78	$68	$58
$1,675	$1,690	$159	$149	$139	$130	$120	$110	$100	$90	$80	$70	$60
$1,690	$1,705	$161	$151	$141	$131	$121	$111	$102	$92	$82	$72	$62
$1,705	$1,720	$163	$153	$143	$133	$123	$113	$103	$93	$84	$74	$64
$1,720	$1,735	$165	$155	$145	$135	$125	$115	$105	$95	$85	$75	$65
$1,735	$1,750	$166	$157	$147	$137	$127	$117	$107	$97	$87	$77	$67
$1,750	$1,765	$168	$158	$148	$139	$129	$119	$109	$99	$89	$79	$69
$1,765	$1,780	$170	$160	$150	$140	$130	$120	$111	$101	$91	$81	$71
$1,780	$1,795	$172	$162	$152	$142	$132	$122	$112	$102	$93	$83	$73
$1,795	$1,810	$174	$164	$154	$144	$134	$124	$114	$104	$94	$84	$74
$1,810	$1,825	$175	$166	$156	$146	$136	$126	$116	$106	$96	$86	$76
$1,825	$1,840	$177	$167	$157	$148	$138	$128	$118	$108	$98	$88	$78
$1,840	$1,855	$179	$169	$159	$149	$139	$129	$120	$110	$100	$90	$80
$1,855	$1,870	$181	$171	$161	$151	$141	$131	$121	$111	$102	$92	$82
$1,870	$1,885	$183	$173	$163	$153	$143	$133	$123	$113	$103	$93	$83
$1,885	$1,900	$184	$175	$165	$155	$145	$135	$125	$115	$105	$95	$85
$1,900	$1,915	$186	$176	$166	$157	$147	$137	$127	$117	$107	$97	$87
$1,915	$1,930	$188	$178	$168	$158	$148	$138	$129	$119	$109	$99	$89

2023 Wage Bracket Method Tables for Manual Payroll Systems With Forms W-4 From 2019 or Earlier
WEEKLY Payroll Period

If the Wage Amount (line 1a) is		SINGLE Persons										
		And the number of allowances is:										
At least	But less than	0	1	2	3	4	5	6	7	8	9	10
		The Tentative Withholding Amount is:										
$0	$105	$0	$0	$0	$0	$0	$0	$0	$0	$0	$0	$0
$105	$115	$1	$0	$0	$0	$0	$0	$0	$0	$0	$0	$0
$115	$125	$2	$0	$0	$0	$0	$0	$0	$0	$0	$0	$0
$125	$135	$3	$0	$0	$0	$0	$0	$0	$0	$0	$0	$0
$135	$145	$4	$0	$0	$0	$0	$0	$0	$0	$0	$0	$0
$145	$155	$5	$0	$0	$0	$0	$0	$0	$0	$0	$0	$0
$155	$165	$6	$0	$0	$0	$0	$0	$0	$0	$0	$0	$0
$165	$175	$7	$0	$0	$0	$0	$0	$0	$0	$0	$0	$0
$175	$185	$8	$0	$0	$0	$0	$0	$0	$0	$0	$0	$0
$185	$195	$9	$1	$0	$0	$0	$0	$0	$0	$0	$0	$0
$195	$205	$10	$2	$0	$0	$0	$0	$0	$0	$0	$0	$0
$205	$215	$11	$3	$0	$0	$0	$0	$0	$0	$0	$0	$0
$215	$225	$12	$4	$0	$0	$0	$0	$0	$0	$0	$0	$0
$225	$235	$13	$5	$0	$0	$0	$0	$0	$0	$0	$0	$0
$235	$245	$14	$6	$0	$0	$0	$0	$0	$0	$0	$0	$0
$245	$255	$15	$7	$0	$0	$0	$0	$0	$0	$0	$0	$0
$255	$265	$16	$8	$0	$0	$0	$0	$0	$0	$0	$0	$0
$265	$275	$17	$9	$0	$0	$0	$0	$0	$0	$0	$0	$0
$275	$285	$18	$10	$1	$0	$0	$0	$0	$0	$0	$0	$0
$285	$295	$19	$11	$2	$0	$0	$0	$0	$0	$0	$0	$0
$295	$305	$20	$12	$3	$0	$0	$0	$0	$0	$0	$0	$0
$305	$315	$21	$13	$4	$0	$0	$0	$0	$0	$0	$0	$0
$315	$330	$22	$14	$6	$0	$0	$0	$0	$0	$0	$0	$0
$330	$345	$24	$15	$7	$0	$0	$0	$0	$0	$0	$0	$0
$345	$360	$26	$17	$9	$0	$0	$0	$0	$0	$0	$0	$0
$360	$375	$28	$18	$10	$2	$0	$0	$0	$0	$0	$0	$0
$375	$390	$30	$20	$12	$3	$0	$0	$0	$0	$0	$0	$0
$390	$405	$31	$21	$13	$5	$0	$0	$0	$0	$0	$0	$0
$405	$420	$33	$23	$15	$6	$0	$0	$0	$0	$0	$0	$0
$420	$435	$35	$25	$16	$8	$0	$0	$0	$0	$0	$0	$0
$435	$450	$37	$27	$18	$9	$1	$0	$0	$0	$0	$0	$0
$450	$465	$39	$29	$19	$11	$3	$0	$0	$0	$0	$0	$0
$465	$480	$40	$30	$21	$12	$4	$0	$0	$0	$0	$0	$0
$480	$495	$42	$32	$22	$14	$6	$0	$0	$0	$0	$0	$0
$495	$510	$44	$34	$24	$15	$7	$0	$0	$0	$0	$0	$0
$510	$525	$46	$36	$26	$17	$9	$0	$0	$0	$0	$0	$0
$525	$540	$48	$38	$28	$18	$10	$2	$0	$0	$0	$0	$0
$540	$555	$49	$39	$30	$20	$12	$3	$0	$0	$0	$0	$0
$555	$570	$51	$41	$31	$21	$13	$5	$0	$0	$0	$0	$0
$570	$585	$53	$43	$33	$23	$15	$6	$0	$0	$0	$0	$0
$585	$600	$55	$45	$35	$25	$16	$8	$0	$0	$0	$0	$0
$600	$615	$57	$47	$37	$27	$18	$9	$1	$0	$0	$0	$0
$615	$630	$58	$48	$39	$29	$19	$11	$3	$0	$0	$0	$0
$630	$645	$60	$50	$40	$30	$21	$12	$4	$0	$0	$0	$0
$645	$660	$62	$52	$42	$32	$22	$14	$6	$0	$0	$0	$0
$660	$675	$64	$54	$44	$34	$24	$15	$7	$0	$0	$0	$0
$675	$690	$66	$56	$46	$36	$26	$17	$9	$0	$0	$0	$0
$690	$705	$67	$57	$48	$38	$28	$18	$10	$2	$0	$0	$0
$705	$720	$69	$59	$49	$39	$29	$20	$12	$3	$0	$0	$0
$720	$735	$71	$61	$51	$41	$31	$21	$13	$5	$0	$0	$0
$735	$750	$73	$63	$53	$43	$33	$23	$15	$6	$0	$0	$0

2023 Wage Bracket Method Tables for Manual Payroll Systems With Forms W-4 From 2019 or Earlier
WEEKLY Payroll Period

If the Wage Amount (line 1a) is		SINGLE Persons — And the number of allowances is:										
At least	But less than	0	1	2	3	4	5	6	7	8	9	10
		The Tentative Withholding Amount is:										
$750	$765	$75	$65	$55	$45	$35	$25	$16	$8	$0	$0	$0
$765	$780	$76	$66	$57	$47	$37	$27	$18	$9	$1	$0	$0
$780	$795	$78	$68	$58	$48	$38	$29	$19	$11	$3	$0	$0
$795	$810	$80	$70	$60	$50	$40	$30	$21	$12	$4	$0	$0
$810	$825	$82	$72	$62	$52	$42	$32	$22	$14	$6	$0	$0
$825	$840	$84	$74	$64	$54	$44	$34	$24	$15	$7	$0	$0
$840	$855	$85	$75	$66	$56	$46	$36	$26	$17	$9	$0	$0
$855	$870	$87	$77	$67	$57	$47	$38	$28	$18	$10	$2	$0
$870	$885	$89	$79	$69	$59	$49	$39	$29	$20	$12	$3	$0
$885	$900	$91	$81	$71	$61	$51	$41	$31	$21	$13	$5	$0
$900	$915	$93	$83	$73	$63	$53	$43	$33	$23	$15	$6	$0
$915	$930	$94	$84	$75	$65	$55	$45	$35	$25	$16	$8	$0
$930	$945	$96	$86	$76	$66	$56	$47	$37	$27	$18	$9	$1
$945	$960	$98	$88	$78	$68	$58	$48	$38	$28	$19	$11	$2
$960	$975	$100	$90	$80	$70	$60	$50	$40	$30	$21	$12	$4
$975	$990	$104	$92	$82	$72	$62	$52	$42	$32	$22	$14	$5
$990	$1,005	$107	$93	$84	$74	$64	$54	$44	$34	$24	$15	$7
$1,005	$1,020	$110	$95	$85	$75	$65	$56	$46	$36	$26	$17	$8
$1,020	$1,035	$114	$97	$87	$77	$67	$57	$47	$37	$28	$18	$10
$1,035	$1,050	$117	$99	$89	$79	$69	$59	$49	$39	$29	$20	$11
$1,050	$1,065	$120	$102	$91	$81	$71	$61	$51	$41	$31	$21	$13
$1,065	$1,080	$123	$105	$93	$83	$73	$63	$53	$43	$33	$23	$14
$1,080	$1,095	$127	$109	$94	$84	$74	$65	$55	$45	$35	$25	$16
$1,095	$1,110	$130	$112	$96	$86	$76	$66	$56	$46	$37	$27	$17
$1,110	$1,125	$133	$115	$98	$88	$78	$68	$58	$48	$38	$28	$19
$1,125	$1,140	$137	$119	$100	$90	$80	$70	$60	$50	$40	$30	$20
$1,140	$1,155	$140	$122	$104	$92	$82	$72	$62	$52	$42	$32	$22
$1,155	$1,170	$143	$125	$107	$93	$83	$74	$64	$54	$44	$34	$24
$1,170	$1,185	$147	$128	$110	$95	$85	$75	$65	$55	$46	$36	$26
$1,185	$1,200	$150	$132	$114	$97	$87	$77	$67	$57	$47	$37	$28
$1,200	$1,215	$153	$135	$117	$99	$89	$79	$69	$59	$49	$39	$29
$1,215	$1,230	$156	$138	$120	$102	$91	$81	$71	$61	$51	$41	$31
$1,230	$1,245	$160	$142	$123	$105	$92	$83	$73	$63	$53	$43	$33
$1,245	$1,260	$163	$145	$127	$109	$94	$84	$74	$64	$55	$45	$35
$1,260	$1,275	$166	$148	$130	$112	$96	$86	$76	$66	$56	$46	$37
$1,275	$1,290	$170	$152	$133	$115	$98	$88	$78	$68	$58	$48	$38
$1,290	$1,305	$173	$155	$137	$118	$100	$90	$80	$70	$60	$50	$40
$1,305	$1,320	$176	$158	$140	$122	$104	$92	$82	$72	$62	$52	$42
$1,320	$1,335	$180	$161	$143	$125	$107	$93	$83	$73	$64	$54	$44
$1,335	$1,350	$183	$165	$147	$128	$110	$95	$85	$75	$65	$55	$46
$1,350	$1,365	$186	$168	$150	$132	$113	$97	$87	$77	$67	$57	$47
$1,365	$1,380	$189	$171	$153	$135	$117	$99	$89	$79	$69	$59	$49
$1,380	$1,395	$193	$175	$156	$138	$120	$102	$91	$81	$71	$61	$51
$1,395	$1,410	$196	$178	$160	$142	$123	$105	$92	$82	$73	$63	$53
$1,410	$1,425	$199	$181	$163	$145	$127	$108	$94	$84	$74	$64	$55
$1,425	$1,440	$203	$185	$166	$148	$130	$112	$96	$86	$76	$66	$56
$1,440	$1,455	$206	$188	$170	$151	$133	$115	$98	$88	$78	$68	$58
$1,455	$1,470	$209	$191	$173	$155	$137	$118	$100	$90	$80	$70	$60
$1,470	$1,485	$213	$194	$176	$158	$140	$122	$103	$91	$82	$72	$62
$1,485	$1,500	$216	$198	$180	$161	$143	$125	$107	$93	$83	$73	$64
$1,500	$1,515	$219	$201	$183	$165	$146	$128	$110	$95	$85	$75	$65

2023 Wage Bracket Method Tables for Manual Payroll Systems With Forms W-4 From 2019 or Earlier
WEEKLY Payroll Period

If the Wage Amount (line 1a) is		SINGLE Persons										
		And the number of allowances is:										
At least	But less than	0	1	2	3	4	5	6	7	8	9	10
		The Tentative Withholding Amount is:										
$1,515	$1,530	$222	$204	$186	$168	$150	$132	$113	$97	$87	$77	$67
$1,530	$1,545	$226	$208	$189	$171	$153	$135	$117	$99	$89	$79	$69
$1,545	$1,560	$229	$211	$193	$175	$156	$138	$120	$102	$91	$81	$71
$1,560	$1,575	$232	$214	$196	$178	$160	$141	$123	$105	$92	$82	$73
$1,575	$1,590	$236	$218	$199	$181	$163	$145	$127	$108	$94	$84	$74
$1,590	$1,605	$239	$221	$203	$184	$166	$148	$130	$112	$96	$86	$76
$1,605	$1,620	$242	$224	$206	$188	$170	$151	$133	$115	$98	$88	$78
$1,620	$1,635	$246	$227	$209	$191	$173	$155	$136	$118	$100	$90	$80
$1,635	$1,650	$249	$231	$213	$194	$176	$158	$140	$122	$103	$91	$82
$1,650	$1,665	$252	$234	$216	$198	$179	$161	$143	$125	$107	$93	$83
$1,665	$1,680	$255	$237	$219	$201	$183	$165	$146	$128	$110	$95	$85
$1,680	$1,695	$259	$241	$222	$204	$186	$168	$150	$131	$113	$97	$87
$1,695	$1,710	$262	$244	$226	$208	$189	$171	$153	$135	$117	$99	$89
$1,710	$1,725	$265	$247	$229	$211	$193	$174	$156	$138	$120	$102	$91
$1,725	$1,740	$269	$251	$232	$214	$196	$178	$160	$141	$123	$105	$92
$1,740	$1,755	$272	$254	$236	$217	$199	$181	$163	$145	$126	$108	$94
$1,755	$1,770	$275	$257	$239	$221	$203	$184	$166	$148	$130	$112	$96
$1,770	$1,785	$279	$260	$242	$224	$206	$188	$169	$151	$133	$115	$98
$1,785	$1,800	$282	$264	$246	$227	$209	$191	$173	$155	$136	$118	$100
$1,800	$1,815	$285	$267	$249	$231	$212	$194	$176	$158	$140	$121	$103
$1,815	$1,830	$288	$270	$252	$234	$216	$198	$179	$161	$143	$125	$107
$1,830	$1,845	$292	$274	$255	$237	$219	$201	$183	$164	$146	$128	$110
$1,845	$1,860	$295	$277	$259	$241	$222	$204	$186	$168	$150	$131	$113
$1,860	$1,875	$298	$280	$262	$244	$226	$207	$189	$171	$153	$135	$116
$1,875	$1,890	$302	$284	$265	$247	$229	$211	$193	$174	$156	$138	$120
$1,890	$1,905	$305	$287	$269	$250	$232	$214	$196	$178	$159	$141	$123
$1,905	$1,920	$308	$290	$272	$254	$236	$217	$199	$181	$163	$145	$126
$1,920	$1,935	$312	$293	$275	$257	$239	$221	$202	$184	$166	$148	$130

2023 Wage Bracket Method Tables for Manual Payroll Systems With Forms W-4 From 2019 or Earlier
BIWEEKLY Payroll Period

If the Wage Amount (line 1a) is		MARRIED Persons										
		And the number of allowances is:										
At least	But less than	0	1	2	3	4	5	6	7	8	9	10
		The Tentative Withholding Amount is:										
$0	$570	$0	$0	$0	$0	$0	$0	$0	$0	$0	$0	$0
$570	$580	$1	$0	$0	$0	$0	$0	$0	$0	$0	$0	$0
$580	$590	$2	$0	$0	$0	$0	$0	$0	$0	$0	$0	$0
$590	$600	$3	$0	$0	$0	$0	$0	$0	$0	$0	$0	$0
$600	$610	$4	$0	$0	$0	$0	$0	$0	$0	$0	$0	$0
$610	$620	$5	$0	$0	$0	$0	$0	$0	$0	$0	$0	$0
$620	$630	$6	$0	$0	$0	$0	$0	$0	$0	$0	$0	$0
$630	$640	$7	$0	$0	$0	$0	$0	$0	$0	$0	$0	$0
$640	$650	$8	$0	$0	$0	$0	$0	$0	$0	$0	$0	$0
$650	$660	$9	$0	$0	$0	$0	$0	$0	$0	$0	$0	$0
$660	$670	$10	$0	$0	$0	$0	$0	$0	$0	$0	$0	$0
$670	$680	$11	$0	$0	$0	$0	$0	$0	$0	$0	$0	$0
$680	$690	$12	$0	$0	$0	$0	$0	$0	$0	$0	$0	$0
$690	$700	$13	$0	$0	$0	$0	$0	$0	$0	$0	$0	$0
$700	$710	$14	$0	$0	$0	$0	$0	$0	$0	$0	$0	$0
$710	$720	$15	$0	$0	$0	$0	$0	$0	$0	$0	$0	$0
$720	$730	$16	$0	$0	$0	$0	$0	$0	$0	$0	$0	$0
$730	$740	$17	$0	$0	$0	$0	$0	$0	$0	$0	$0	$0
$740	$750	$18	$1	$0	$0	$0	$0	$0	$0	$0	$0	$0
$750	$760	$19	$2	$0	$0	$0	$0	$0	$0	$0	$0	$0
$760	$770	$20	$3	$0	$0	$0	$0	$0	$0	$0	$0	$0
$770	$780	$21	$4	$0	$0	$0	$0	$0	$0	$0	$0	$0
$780	$790	$22	$5	$0	$0	$0	$0	$0	$0	$0	$0	$0
$790	$800	$23	$6	$0	$0	$0	$0	$0	$0	$0	$0	$0
$800	$810	$24	$7	$0	$0	$0	$0	$0	$0	$0	$0	$0
$810	$820	$25	$8	$0	$0	$0	$0	$0	$0	$0	$0	$0
$820	$830	$26	$9	$0	$0	$0	$0	$0	$0	$0	$0	$0
$830	$840	$27	$10	$0	$0	$0	$0	$0	$0	$0	$0	$0
$840	$850	$28	$11	$0	$0	$0	$0	$0	$0	$0	$0	$0
$850	$860	$29	$12	$0	$0	$0	$0	$0	$0	$0	$0	$0
$860	$870	$30	$13	$0	$0	$0	$0	$0	$0	$0	$0	$0
$870	$880	$31	$14	$0	$0	$0	$0	$0	$0	$0	$0	$0
$880	$890	$32	$15	$0	$0	$0	$0	$0	$0	$0	$0	$0
$890	$900	$33	$16	$0	$0	$0	$0	$0	$0	$0	$0	$0
$900	$910	$34	$17	$1	$0	$0	$0	$0	$0	$0	$0	$0
$910	$920	$35	$18	$2	$0	$0	$0	$0	$0	$0	$0	$0
$920	$930	$36	$19	$3	$0	$0	$0	$0	$0	$0	$0	$0
$930	$940	$37	$20	$4	$0	$0	$0	$0	$0	$0	$0	$0
$940	$950	$38	$21	$5	$0	$0	$0	$0	$0	$0	$0	$0
$950	$960	$39	$22	$6	$0	$0	$0	$0	$0	$0	$0	$0
$960	$970	$40	$23	$7	$0	$0	$0	$0	$0	$0	$0	$0
$970	$980	$41	$24	$8	$0	$0	$0	$0	$0	$0	$0	$0
$980	$990	$42	$25	$9	$0	$0	$0	$0	$0	$0	$0	$0
$990	$1,000	$43	$26	$10	$0	$0	$0	$0	$0	$0	$0	$0
$1,000	$1,010	$44	$27	$11	$0	$0	$0	$0	$0	$0	$0	$0
$1,010	$1,020	$45	$28	$12	$0	$0	$0	$0	$0	$0	$0	$0
$1,020	$1,030	$46	$29	$13	$0	$0	$0	$0	$0	$0	$0	$0
$1,030	$1,040	$47	$30	$14	$0	$0	$0	$0	$0	$0	$0	$0
$1,040	$1,050	$48	$31	$15	$0	$0	$0	$0	$0	$0	$0	$0
$1,050	$1,060	$49	$32	$16	$0	$0	$0	$0	$0	$0	$0	$0
$1,060	$1,070	$50	$33	$17	$0	$0	$0	$0	$0	$0	$0	$0

2023 Wage Bracket Method Tables for Manual Payroll Systems With Forms W-4 From 2019 or Earlier
BIWEEKLY Payroll Period
MARRIED Persons

If the Wage Amount (line 1a) is At least	But less than	0	1	2	3	4	5	6	7	8	9	10
		\multicolumn{11}{c}{The Tentative Withholding Amount is:}										
$1,070	$1,080	$51	$34	$18	$1	$0	$0	$0	$0	$0	$0	$0
$1,080	$1,090	$52	$35	$19	$2	$0	$0	$0	$0	$0	$0	$0
$1,090	$1,100	$53	$36	$20	$3	$0	$0	$0	$0	$0	$0	$0
$1,100	$1,110	$54	$37	$21	$4	$0	$0	$0	$0	$0	$0	$0
$1,110	$1,120	$55	$38	$22	$5	$0	$0	$0	$0	$0	$0	$0
$1,120	$1,130	$56	$39	$23	$6	$0	$0	$0	$0	$0	$0	$0
$1,130	$1,140	$57	$40	$24	$7	$0	$0	$0	$0	$0	$0	$0
$1,140	$1,150	$58	$41	$25	$8	$0	$0	$0	$0	$0	$0	$0
$1,150	$1,160	$59	$42	$26	$9	$0	$0	$0	$0	$0	$0	$0
$1,160	$1,170	$60	$43	$27	$10	$0	$0	$0	$0	$0	$0	$0
$1,170	$1,180	$61	$44	$28	$11	$0	$0	$0	$0	$0	$0	$0
$1,180	$1,190	$62	$45	$29	$12	$0	$0	$0	$0	$0	$0	$0
$1,190	$1,200	$63	$46	$30	$13	$0	$0	$0	$0	$0	$0	$0
$1,200	$1,210	$64	$47	$31	$14	$0	$0	$0	$0	$0	$0	$0
$1,210	$1,220	$65	$48	$32	$15	$0	$0	$0	$0	$0	$0	$0
$1,220	$1,230	$66	$49	$33	$16	$0	$0	$0	$0	$0	$0	$0
$1,230	$1,240	$67	$50	$34	$17	$0	$0	$0	$0	$0	$0	$0
$1,240	$1,250	$68	$51	$35	$18	$1	$0	$0	$0	$0	$0	$0
$1,250	$1,260	$69	$52	$36	$19	$2	$0	$0	$0	$0	$0	$0
$1,260	$1,270	$70	$53	$37	$20	$3	$0	$0	$0	$0	$0	$0
$1,270	$1,280	$71	$54	$38	$21	$4	$0	$0	$0	$0	$0	$0
$1,280	$1,290	$72	$55	$39	$22	$5	$0	$0	$0	$0	$0	$0
$1,290	$1,300	$73	$56	$40	$23	$6	$0	$0	$0	$0	$0	$0
$1,300	$1,310	$74	$57	$41	$24	$7	$0	$0	$0	$0	$0	$0
$1,310	$1,320	$75	$58	$42	$25	$8	$0	$0	$0	$0	$0	$0
$1,320	$1,330	$76	$59	$43	$26	$9	$0	$0	$0	$0	$0	$0
$1,330	$1,340	$77	$60	$44	$27	$10	$0	$0	$0	$0	$0	$0
$1,340	$1,350	$78	$61	$45	$28	$11	$0	$0	$0	$0	$0	$0
$1,350	$1,360	$79	$62	$46	$29	$12	$0	$0	$0	$0	$0	$0
$1,360	$1,370	$80	$63	$47	$30	$13	$0	$0	$0	$0	$0	$0
$1,370	$1,380	$81	$64	$48	$31	$14	$0	$0	$0	$0	$0	$0
$1,380	$1,390	$82	$65	$49	$32	$15	$0	$0	$0	$0	$0	$0
$1,390	$1,400	$83	$66	$50	$33	$16	$0	$0	$0	$0	$0	$0
$1,400	$1,410	$84	$67	$51	$34	$17	$1	$0	$0	$0	$0	$0
$1,410	$1,420	$85	$68	$52	$35	$18	$2	$0	$0	$0	$0	$0
$1,420	$1,470	$88	$71	$55	$38	$21	$5	$0	$0	$0	$0	$0
$1,470	$1,520	$94	$76	$60	$43	$26	$10	$0	$0	$0	$0	$0
$1,520	$1,570	$100	$81	$65	$48	$31	$15	$0	$0	$0	$0	$0
$1,570	$1,620	$106	$86	$70	$53	$36	$20	$3	$0	$0	$0	$0
$1,620	$1,670	$112	$92	$75	$58	$41	$25	$8	$0	$0	$0	$0
$1,670	$1,720	$118	$98	$80	$63	$46	$30	$13	$0	$0	$0	$0
$1,720	$1,770	$124	$104	$85	$68	$51	$35	$18	$2	$0	$0	$0
$1,770	$1,820	$130	$110	$90	$73	$56	$40	$23	$7	$0	$0	$0
$1,820	$1,870	$136	$116	$96	$78	$61	$45	$28	$12	$0	$0	$0
$1,870	$1,920	$142	$122	$102	$83	$66	$50	$33	$17	$0	$0	$0
$1,920	$1,970	$148	$128	$108	$89	$71	$55	$38	$22	$5	$0	$0
$1,970	$2,020	$154	$134	$114	$95	$76	$60	$43	$27	$10	$0	$0
$2,020	$2,070	$160	$140	$120	$101	$81	$65	$48	$32	$15	$0	$0
$2,070	$2,120	$166	$146	$126	$107	$87	$70	$53	$37	$20	$4	$0
$2,120	$2,170	$172	$152	$132	$113	$93	$75	$58	$42	$25	$9	$0
$2,170	$2,220	$178	$158	$138	$119	$99	$80	$63	$47	$30	$14	$0

2023 Wage Bracket Method Tables for Manual Payroll Systems With Forms W-4 From 2019 or Earlier
BIWEEKLY Payroll Period

If the Wage Amount (line 1a) is		MARRIED Persons And the number of allowances is:										
At least	But less than	0	1	2	3	4	5	6	7	8	9	10
		The Tentative Withholding Amount is:										
$2,220	$2,270	$184	$164	$144	$125	$105	$85	$68	$52	$35	$19	$2
$2,270	$2,320	$190	$170	$150	$131	$111	$91	$73	$57	$40	$24	$7
$2,320	$2,370	$196	$176	$156	$137	$117	$97	$78	$62	$45	$29	$12
$2,370	$2,420	$202	$182	$162	$143	$123	$103	$83	$67	$50	$34	$17
$2,420	$2,470	$208	$188	$168	$149	$129	$109	$89	$72	$55	$39	$22
$2,470	$2,520	$214	$194	$174	$155	$135	$115	$95	$77	$60	$44	$27
$2,520	$2,570	$220	$200	$180	$161	$141	$121	$101	$82	$65	$49	$32
$2,570	$2,620	$226	$206	$186	$167	$147	$127	$107	$87	$70	$54	$37
$2,620	$2,670	$232	$212	$192	$173	$153	$133	$113	$93	$75	$59	$42
$2,670	$2,720	$238	$218	$198	$179	$159	$139	$119	$99	$80	$64	$47
$2,720	$2,770	$244	$224	$204	$185	$165	$145	$125	$105	$85	$69	$52
$2,770	$2,820	$250	$230	$210	$191	$171	$151	$131	$111	$91	$74	$57
$2,820	$2,870	$256	$236	$216	$197	$177	$157	$137	$117	$97	$79	$62
$2,870	$2,920	$262	$242	$222	$203	$183	$163	$143	$123	$103	$84	$67
$2,920	$2,970	$268	$248	$228	$209	$189	$169	$149	$129	$109	$90	$72
$2,970	$3,020	$274	$254	$234	$215	$195	$175	$155	$135	$115	$96	$77
$3,020	$3,070	$280	$260	$240	$221	$201	$181	$161	$141	$121	$102	$82
$3,070	$3,120	$286	$266	$246	$227	$207	$187	$167	$147	$127	$108	$88
$3,120	$3,170	$292	$272	$252	$233	$213	$193	$173	$153	$133	$114	$94
$3,170	$3,220	$298	$278	$258	$239	$219	$199	$179	$159	$139	$120	$100
$3,220	$3,270	$304	$284	$264	$245	$225	$205	$185	$165	$145	$126	$106
$3,270	$3,320	$310	$290	$270	$251	$231	$211	$191	$171	$151	$132	$112
$3,320	$3,370	$316	$296	$276	$257	$237	$217	$197	$177	$157	$138	$118
$3,370	$3,420	$322	$302	$282	$263	$243	$223	$203	$183	$163	$144	$124
$3,420	$3,470	$328	$308	$288	$269	$249	$229	$209	$189	$169	$150	$130
$3,470	$3,520	$334	$314	$294	$275	$255	$235	$215	$195	$175	$156	$136
$3,520	$3,570	$340	$320	$300	$281	$261	$241	$221	$201	$181	$162	$142
$3,570	$3,620	$346	$326	$306	$287	$267	$247	$227	$207	$187	$168	$148
$3,620	$3,670	$352	$332	$312	$293	$273	$253	$233	$213	$193	$174	$154
$3,670	$3,720	$358	$338	$318	$299	$279	$259	$239	$219	$199	$180	$160
$3,720	$3,770	$364	$344	$324	$305	$285	$265	$245	$225	$205	$186	$166
$3,770	$3,820	$370	$350	$330	$311	$291	$271	$251	$231	$211	$192	$172
$3,820	$3,870	$376	$356	$336	$317	$297	$277	$257	$237	$217	$198	$178

2023 Wage Bracket Method Tables for Manual Payroll Systems With Forms W-4 From 2019 or Earlier
BIWEEKLY Payroll Period

If the Wage Amount (line 1a) is		SINGLE Persons										
		And the number of allowances is:										
At least	But less than	0	1	2	3	4	5	6	7	8	9	10
		The Tentative Withholding Amount is:										
$0	$205	$0	$0	$0	$0	$0	$0	$0	$0	$0	$0	$0
$205	$215	$1	$0	$0	$0	$0	$0	$0	$0	$0	$0	$0
$215	$225	$2	$0	$0	$0	$0	$0	$0	$0	$0	$0	$0
$225	$235	$3	$0	$0	$0	$0	$0	$0	$0	$0	$0	$0
$235	$245	$4	$0	$0	$0	$0	$0	$0	$0	$0	$0	$0
$245	$255	$5	$0	$0	$0	$0	$0	$0	$0	$0	$0	$0
$255	$265	$6	$0	$0	$0	$0	$0	$0	$0	$0	$0	$0
$265	$275	$7	$0	$0	$0	$0	$0	$0	$0	$0	$0	$0
$275	$285	$8	$0	$0	$0	$0	$0	$0	$0	$0	$0	$0
$285	$295	$9	$0	$0	$0	$0	$0	$0	$0	$0	$0	$0
$295	$305	$10	$0	$0	$0	$0	$0	$0	$0	$0	$0	$0
$305	$315	$11	$0	$0	$0	$0	$0	$0	$0	$0	$0	$0
$315	$325	$12	$0	$0	$0	$0	$0	$0	$0	$0	$0	$0
$325	$335	$13	$0	$0	$0	$0	$0	$0	$0	$0	$0	$0
$335	$345	$14	$0	$0	$0	$0	$0	$0	$0	$0	$0	$0
$345	$355	$15	$0	$0	$0	$0	$0	$0	$0	$0	$0	$0
$355	$365	$16	$0	$0	$0	$0	$0	$0	$0	$0	$0	$0
$365	$375	$17	$0	$0	$0	$0	$0	$0	$0	$0	$0	$0
$375	$385	$18	$1	$0	$0	$0	$0	$0	$0	$0	$0	$0
$385	$395	$19	$2	$0	$0	$0	$0	$0	$0	$0	$0	$0
$395	$405	$20	$3	$0	$0	$0	$0	$0	$0	$0	$0	$0
$405	$415	$21	$4	$0	$0	$0	$0	$0	$0	$0	$0	$0
$415	$425	$22	$5	$0	$0	$0	$0	$0	$0	$0	$0	$0
$425	$435	$23	$6	$0	$0	$0	$0	$0	$0	$0	$0	$0
$435	$445	$24	$7	$0	$0	$0	$0	$0	$0	$0	$0	$0
$445	$455	$25	$8	$0	$0	$0	$0	$0	$0	$0	$0	$0
$455	$465	$26	$9	$0	$0	$0	$0	$0	$0	$0	$0	$0
$465	$475	$27	$10	$0	$0	$0	$0	$0	$0	$0	$0	$0
$475	$485	$28	$11	$0	$0	$0	$0	$0	$0	$0	$0	$0
$485	$495	$29	$12	$0	$0	$0	$0	$0	$0	$0	$0	$0
$495	$505	$30	$13	$0	$0	$0	$0	$0	$0	$0	$0	$0
$505	$515	$31	$14	$0	$0	$0	$0	$0	$0	$0	$0	$0
$515	$525	$32	$15	$0	$0	$0	$0	$0	$0	$0	$0	$0
$525	$535	$33	$16	$0	$0	$0	$0	$0	$0	$0	$0	$0
$535	$545	$34	$17	$1	$0	$0	$0	$0	$0	$0	$0	$0
$545	$555	$35	$18	$2	$0	$0	$0	$0	$0	$0	$0	$0
$555	$565	$36	$19	$3	$0	$0	$0	$0	$0	$0	$0	$0
$565	$575	$37	$20	$4	$0	$0	$0	$0	$0	$0	$0	$0
$575	$585	$38	$21	$5	$0	$0	$0	$0	$0	$0	$0	$0
$585	$595	$39	$22	$6	$0	$0	$0	$0	$0	$0	$0	$0
$595	$605	$40	$23	$7	$0	$0	$0	$0	$0	$0	$0	$0
$605	$615	$41	$24	$8	$0	$0	$0	$0	$0	$0	$0	$0
$615	$625	$42	$25	$9	$0	$0	$0	$0	$0	$0	$0	$0
$625	$635	$43	$26	$10	$0	$0	$0	$0	$0	$0	$0	$0
$635	$665	$45	$28	$12	$0	$0	$0	$0	$0	$0	$0	$0
$665	$695	$49	$31	$15	$0	$0	$0	$0	$0	$0	$0	$0
$695	$725	$53	$34	$18	$1	$0	$0	$0	$0	$0	$0	$0
$725	$755	$56	$37	$21	$4	$0	$0	$0	$0	$0	$0	$0
$755	$785	$60	$40	$24	$7	$0	$0	$0	$0	$0	$0	$0
$785	$815	$63	$43	$27	$10	$0	$0	$0	$0	$0	$0	$0
$815	$845	$67	$47	$30	$13	$0	$0	$0	$0	$0	$0	$0

2023 Wage Bracket Method Tables for Manual Payroll Systems With Forms W-4 From 2019 or Earlier
BIWEEKLY Payroll Period

If the Wage Amount (line 1a) is		SINGLE Persons										
		And the number of allowances is:										
At least	But less than	0	1	2	3	4	5	6	7	8	9	10
		The Tentative Withholding Amount is:										
$845	$875	$71	$51	$33	$16	$0	$0	$0	$0	$0	$0	$0
$875	$905	$74	$54	$36	$19	$3	$0	$0	$0	$0	$0	$0
$905	$935	$78	$58	$39	$22	$6	$0	$0	$0	$0	$0	$0
$935	$965	$81	$61	$42	$25	$9	$0	$0	$0	$0	$0	$0
$965	$995	$85	$65	$45	$28	$12	$0	$0	$0	$0	$0	$0
$995	$1,025	$89	$69	$49	$31	$15	$0	$0	$0	$0	$0	$0
$1,025	$1,055	$92	$72	$52	$34	$18	$1	$0	$0	$0	$0	$0
$1,055	$1,085	$96	$76	$56	$37	$21	$4	$0	$0	$0	$0	$0
$1,085	$1,115	$99	$79	$60	$40	$24	$7	$0	$0	$0	$0	$0
$1,115	$1,145	$103	$83	$63	$43	$27	$10	$0	$0	$0	$0	$0
$1,145	$1,175	$107	$87	$67	$47	$30	$13	$0	$0	$0	$0	$0
$1,175	$1,205	$110	$90	$70	$51	$33	$16	$0	$0	$0	$0	$0
$1,205	$1,235	$114	$94	$74	$54	$36	$19	$3	$0	$0	$0	$0
$1,235	$1,265	$117	$97	$78	$58	$39	$22	$6	$0	$0	$0	$0
$1,265	$1,295	$121	$101	$81	$61	$42	$25	$9	$0	$0	$0	$0
$1,295	$1,325	$125	$105	$85	$65	$45	$28	$12	$0	$0	$0	$0
$1,325	$1,355	$128	$108	$88	$69	$49	$31	$15	$0	$0	$0	$0
$1,355	$1,385	$132	$112	$92	$72	$52	$34	$18	$1	$0	$0	$0
$1,385	$1,415	$135	$115	$96	$76	$56	$37	$21	$4	$0	$0	$0
$1,415	$1,445	$139	$119	$99	$79	$60	$40	$24	$7	$0	$0	$0
$1,445	$1,475	$143	$123	$103	$83	$63	$43	$27	$10	$0	$0	$0
$1,475	$1,505	$146	$126	$106	$87	$67	$47	$30	$13	$0	$0	$0
$1,505	$1,535	$150	$130	$110	$90	$70	$50	$33	$16	$0	$0	$0
$1,535	$1,565	$153	$133	$114	$94	$74	$54	$36	$19	$3	$0	$0
$1,565	$1,595	$157	$137	$117	$97	$78	$58	$39	$22	$6	$0	$0
$1,595	$1,625	$161	$141	$121	$101	$81	$61	$42	$25	$9	$0	$0
$1,625	$1,655	$164	$144	$124	$105	$85	$65	$45	$28	$12	$0	$0
$1,655	$1,685	$168	$148	$128	$108	$88	$68	$49	$31	$15	$0	$0
$1,685	$1,715	$171	$151	$132	$112	$92	$72	$52	$34	$18	$1	$0
$1,715	$1,745	$175	$155	$135	$115	$96	$76	$56	$37	$21	$4	$0
$1,745	$1,775	$179	$159	$139	$119	$99	$79	$59	$40	$24	$7	$0
$1,775	$1,805	$182	$162	$142	$123	$103	$83	$63	$43	$27	$10	$0
$1,805	$1,835	$186	$166	$146	$126	$106	$86	$67	$47	$30	$13	$0
$1,835	$1,865	$189	$169	$150	$130	$110	$90	$70	$50	$33	$16	$0
$1,865	$1,895	$193	$173	$153	$133	$114	$94	$74	$54	$36	$19	$2
$1,895	$1,925	$197	$177	$157	$137	$117	$97	$77	$58	$39	$22	$5
$1,925	$1,975	$204	$181	$162	$142	$122	$102	$82	$62	$43	$26	$9
$1,975	$2,025	$215	$187	$168	$148	$128	$108	$88	$68	$49	$31	$14
$2,025	$2,075	$226	$193	$174	$154	$134	$114	$94	$74	$55	$36	$19
$2,075	$2,125	$237	$201	$180	$160	$140	$120	$100	$80	$61	$41	$24
$2,125	$2,175	$248	$212	$186	$166	$146	$126	$106	$86	$67	$47	$29
$2,175	$2,225	$259	$223	$192	$172	$152	$132	$112	$92	$73	$53	$34
$2,225	$2,275	$270	$234	$198	$178	$158	$138	$118	$98	$79	$59	$39
$2,275	$2,325	$281	$245	$208	$184	$164	$144	$124	$104	$85	$65	$45
$2,325	$2,375	$292	$256	$219	$190	$170	$150	$130	$110	$91	$71	$51
$2,375	$2,425	$303	$267	$230	$196	$176	$156	$136	$116	$97	$77	$57
$2,425	$2,475	$314	$278	$241	$205	$182	$162	$142	$122	$103	$83	$63
$2,475	$2,525	$325	$289	$252	$216	$188	$168	$148	$128	$109	$89	$69
$2,525	$2,575	$336	$300	$263	$227	$194	$174	$154	$134	$115	$95	$75
$2,575	$2,625	$347	$311	$274	$238	$202	$180	$160	$140	$121	$101	$81
$2,625	$2,675	$358	$322	$285	$249	$213	$186	$166	$146	$127	$107	$87

2023 Wage Bracket Method Tables for Manual Payroll Systems With Forms W-4 From 2019 or Earlier
BIWEEKLY Payroll Period

If the **Wage Amount** (line 1a) is		**SINGLE** Persons										
		And the number of allowances is:										
At least	But less than	0	1	2	3	4	5	6	7	8	9	10
		The Tentative Withholding Amount is:										
$2,675	$2,725	$369	$333	$296	$260	$224	$192	$172	$152	$133	$113	$93
$2,725	$2,775	$380	$344	$307	$271	$235	$198	$178	$158	$139	$119	$99
$2,775	$2,825	$391	$355	$318	$282	$246	$209	$184	$164	$145	$125	$105
$2,825	$2,875	$402	$366	$329	$293	$257	$220	$190	$170	$151	$131	$111
$2,875	$2,925	$413	$377	$340	$304	$268	$231	$196	$176	$157	$137	$117
$2,925	$2,975	$424	$388	$351	$315	$279	$242	$206	$182	$163	$143	$123
$2,975	$3,025	$435	$399	$362	$326	$290	$253	$217	$188	$169	$149	$129
$3,025	$3,075	$446	$410	$373	$337	$301	$264	$228	$194	$175	$155	$135
$3,075	$3,125	$457	$421	$384	$348	$312	$275	$239	$202	$181	$161	$141
$3,125	$3,175	$468	$432	$395	$359	$323	$286	$250	$213	$187	$167	$147
$3,175	$3,225	$479	$443	$406	$370	$334	$297	$261	$224	$193	$173	$153
$3,225	$3,275	$490	$454	$417	$381	$345	$308	$272	$235	$199	$179	$159
$3,275	$3,325	$501	$465	$428	$392	$356	$319	$283	$246	$210	$185	$165
$3,325	$3,375	$512	$476	$439	$403	$367	$330	$294	$257	$221	$191	$171
$3,375	$3,425	$523	$487	$450	$414	$378	$341	$305	$268	$232	$197	$177
$3,425	$3,475	$534	$498	$461	$425	$389	$352	$316	$279	$243	$207	$183
$3,475	$3,525	$545	$509	$472	$436	$400	$363	$327	$290	$254	$218	$189
$3,525	$3,575	$556	$520	$483	$447	$411	$374	$338	$301	$265	$229	$195
$3,575	$3,625	$567	$531	$494	$458	$422	$385	$349	$312	$276	$240	$203
$3,625	$3,675	$578	$542	$505	$469	$433	$396	$360	$323	$287	$251	$214
$3,675	$3,725	$589	$553	$516	$480	$444	$407	$371	$334	$298	$262	$225
$3,725	$3,775	$600	$564	$527	$491	$455	$418	$382	$345	$309	$273	$236
$3,775	$3,825	$611	$575	$538	$502	$466	$429	$393	$356	$320	$284	$247
$3,825	$3,875	$622	$586	$549	$513	$477	$440	$404	$367	$331	$295	$258

2023 Wage Bracket Method Tables for Manual Payroll Systems With Forms W-4 From 2019 or Earlier
SEMIMONTHLY Payroll Period

If the Wage Amount (line 1a) is		MARRIED Persons									
		And the number of allowances is:									
At least	But less than	0	1	2	3	4	5	6	7	8	9	10
		The Tentative Withholding Amount is:									
$0	$620	$0	$0	$0	$0	$0	$0	$0	$0	$0	$0	$0
$620	$630	$1	$0	$0	$0	$0	$0	$0	$0	$0	$0	$0
$630	$640	$2	$0	$0	$0	$0	$0	$0	$0	$0	$0	$0
$640	$650	$3	$0	$0	$0	$0	$0	$0	$0	$0	$0	$0
$650	$660	$4	$0	$0	$0	$0	$0	$0	$0	$0	$0	$0
$660	$670	$5	$0	$0	$0	$0	$0	$0	$0	$0	$0	$0
$670	$680	$6	$0	$0	$0	$0	$0	$0	$0	$0	$0	$0
$680	$690	$7	$0	$0	$0	$0	$0	$0	$0	$0	$0	$0
$690	$700	$8	$0	$0	$0	$0	$0	$0	$0	$0	$0	$0
$700	$710	$9	$0	$0	$0	$0	$0	$0	$0	$0	$0	$0
$710	$720	$10	$0	$0	$0	$0	$0	$0	$0	$0	$0	$0
$720	$730	$11	$0	$0	$0	$0	$0	$0	$0	$0	$0	$0
$730	$740	$12	$0	$0	$0	$0	$0	$0	$0	$0	$0	$0
$740	$750	$13	$0	$0	$0	$0	$0	$0	$0	$0	$0	$0
$750	$760	$14	$0	$0	$0	$0	$0	$0	$0	$0	$0	$0
$760	$770	$15	$0	$0	$0	$0	$0	$0	$0	$0	$0	$0
$770	$780	$16	$0	$0	$0	$0	$0	$0	$0	$0	$0	$0
$780	$790	$17	$0	$0	$0	$0	$0	$0	$0	$0	$0	$0
$790	$800	$18	$0	$0	$0	$0	$0	$0	$0	$0	$0	$0
$800	$810	$19	$1	$0	$0	$0	$0	$0	$0	$0	$0	$0
$810	$820	$20	$2	$0	$0	$0	$0	$0	$0	$0	$0	$0
$820	$830	$21	$3	$0	$0	$0	$0	$0	$0	$0	$0	$0
$830	$840	$22	$4	$0	$0	$0	$0	$0	$0	$0	$0	$0
$840	$850	$23	$5	$0	$0	$0	$0	$0	$0	$0	$0	$0
$850	$860	$24	$6	$0	$0	$0	$0	$0	$0	$0	$0	$0
$860	$870	$25	$7	$0	$0	$0	$0	$0	$0	$0	$0	$0
$870	$880	$26	$8	$0	$0	$0	$0	$0	$0	$0	$0	$0
$880	$890	$27	$9	$0	$0	$0	$0	$0	$0	$0	$0	$0
$890	$900	$28	$10	$0	$0	$0	$0	$0	$0	$0	$0	$0
$900	$910	$29	$11	$0	$0	$0	$0	$0	$0	$0	$0	$0
$910	$920	$30	$12	$0	$0	$0	$0	$0	$0	$0	$0	$0
$920	$930	$31	$13	$0	$0	$0	$0	$0	$0	$0	$0	$0
$930	$940	$32	$14	$0	$0	$0	$0	$0	$0	$0	$0	$0
$940	$950	$33	$15	$0	$0	$0	$0	$0	$0	$0	$0	$0
$950	$960	$34	$16	$0	$0	$0	$0	$0	$0	$0	$0	$0
$960	$970	$35	$17	$0	$0	$0	$0	$0	$0	$0	$0	$0
$970	$980	$36	$18	$0	$0	$0	$0	$0	$0	$0	$0	$0
$980	$990	$37	$19	$1	$0	$0	$0	$0	$0	$0	$0	$0
$990	$1,000	$38	$20	$2	$0	$0	$0	$0	$0	$0	$0	$0
$1,000	$1,010	$39	$21	$3	$0	$0	$0	$0	$0	$0	$0	$0
$1,010	$1,020	$40	$22	$4	$0	$0	$0	$0	$0	$0	$0	$0
$1,020	$1,030	$41	$23	$5	$0	$0	$0	$0	$0	$0	$0	$0
$1,030	$1,040	$42	$24	$6	$0	$0	$0	$0	$0	$0	$0	$0
$1,040	$1,050	$43	$25	$7	$0	$0	$0	$0	$0	$0	$0	$0
$1,050	$1,060	$44	$26	$8	$0	$0	$0	$0	$0	$0	$0	$0
$1,060	$1,070	$45	$27	$9	$0	$0	$0	$0	$0	$0	$0	$0
$1,070	$1,080	$46	$28	$10	$0	$0	$0	$0	$0	$0	$0	$0
$1,080	$1,090	$47	$29	$11	$0	$0	$0	$0	$0	$0	$0	$0
$1,090	$1,100	$48	$30	$12	$0	$0	$0	$0	$0	$0	$0	$0
$1,100	$1,110	$49	$31	$13	$0	$0	$0	$0	$0	$0	$0	$0
$1,110	$1,120	$50	$32	$14	$0	$0	$0	$0	$0	$0	$0	$0

2023 Wage Bracket Method Tables for Manual Payroll Systems With Forms W-4 From 2019 or Earlier

SEMIMONTHLY Payroll Period

If the Wage Amount (line 1a) is		MARRIED Persons										
		And the number of allowances is:										
At least	But less than	0	1	2	3	4	5	6	7	8	9	10
		The Tentative Withholding Amount is:										
$1,120	$1,130	$51	$33	$15	$0	$0	$0	$0	$0	$0	$0	$0
$1,130	$1,140	$52	$34	$16	$0	$0	$0	$0	$0	$0	$0	$0
$1,140	$1,150	$53	$35	$17	$0	$0	$0	$0	$0	$0	$0	$0
$1,150	$1,160	$54	$36	$18	$0	$0	$0	$0	$0	$0	$0	$0
$1,160	$1,170	$55	$37	$19	$1	$0	$0	$0	$0	$0	$0	$0
$1,170	$1,180	$56	$38	$20	$2	$0	$0	$0	$0	$0	$0	$0
$1,180	$1,190	$57	$39	$21	$3	$0	$0	$0	$0	$0	$0	$0
$1,190	$1,200	$58	$40	$22	$4	$0	$0	$0	$0	$0	$0	$0
$1,200	$1,210	$59	$41	$23	$5	$0	$0	$0	$0	$0	$0	$0
$1,210	$1,220	$60	$42	$24	$6	$0	$0	$0	$0	$0	$0	$0
$1,220	$1,230	$61	$43	$25	$7	$0	$0	$0	$0	$0	$0	$0
$1,230	$1,240	$62	$44	$26	$8	$0	$0	$0	$0	$0	$0	$0
$1,240	$1,250	$63	$45	$27	$9	$0	$0	$0	$0	$0	$0	$0
$1,250	$1,260	$64	$46	$28	$10	$0	$0	$0	$0	$0	$0	$0
$1,260	$1,270	$65	$47	$29	$11	$0	$0	$0	$0	$0	$0	$0
$1,270	$1,280	$66	$48	$30	$12	$0	$0	$0	$0	$0	$0	$0
$1,280	$1,290	$67	$49	$31	$13	$0	$0	$0	$0	$0	$0	$0
$1,290	$1,300	$68	$50	$32	$14	$0	$0	$0	$0	$0	$0	$0
$1,300	$1,310	$69	$51	$33	$15	$0	$0	$0	$0	$0	$0	$0
$1,310	$1,320	$70	$52	$34	$16	$0	$0	$0	$0	$0	$0	$0
$1,320	$1,330	$71	$53	$35	$17	$0	$0	$0	$0	$0	$0	$0
$1,330	$1,340	$72	$54	$36	$18	$0	$0	$0	$0	$0	$0	$0
$1,340	$1,350	$73	$55	$37	$19	$1	$0	$0	$0	$0	$0	$0
$1,350	$1,360	$74	$56	$38	$20	$2	$0	$0	$0	$0	$0	$0
$1,360	$1,370	$75	$57	$39	$21	$3	$0	$0	$0	$0	$0	$0
$1,370	$1,380	$76	$58	$40	$22	$4	$0	$0	$0	$0	$0	$0
$1,380	$1,390	$77	$59	$41	$23	$5	$0	$0	$0	$0	$0	$0
$1,390	$1,400	$78	$60	$42	$24	$6	$0	$0	$0	$0	$0	$0
$1,400	$1,410	$79	$61	$43	$25	$7	$0	$0	$0	$0	$0	$0
$1,410	$1,420	$80	$62	$44	$26	$8	$0	$0	$0	$0	$0	$0
$1,420	$1,430	$81	$63	$45	$27	$9	$0	$0	$0	$0	$0	$0
$1,430	$1,440	$82	$64	$46	$28	$10	$0	$0	$0	$0	$0	$0
$1,440	$1,450	$83	$65	$47	$29	$11	$0	$0	$0	$0	$0	$0
$1,450	$1,460	$84	$66	$48	$30	$12	$0	$0	$0	$0	$0	$0
$1,460	$1,470	$85	$67	$49	$31	$13	$0	$0	$0	$0	$0	$0
$1,470	$1,480	$86	$68	$50	$32	$14	$0	$0	$0	$0	$0	$0
$1,480	$1,490	$87	$69	$51	$33	$15	$0	$0	$0	$0	$0	$0
$1,490	$1,500	$88	$70	$52	$34	$16	$0	$0	$0	$0	$0	$0
$1,500	$1,510	$89	$71	$53	$35	$17	$0	$0	$0	$0	$0	$0
$1,510	$1,520	$90	$72	$54	$36	$18	$0	$0	$0	$0	$0	$0
$1,520	$1,530	$91	$73	$55	$37	$19	$1	$0	$0	$0	$0	$0
$1,530	$1,580	$94	$76	$58	$40	$22	$4	$0	$0	$0	$0	$0
$1,580	$1,630	$100	$81	$63	$45	$27	$9	$0	$0	$0	$0	$0
$1,630	$1,680	$106	$86	$68	$50	$32	$14	$0	$0	$0	$0	$0
$1,680	$1,730	$112	$91	$73	$55	$37	$19	$1	$0	$0	$0	$0
$1,730	$1,780	$118	$97	$78	$60	$42	$24	$6	$0	$0	$0	$0
$1,780	$1,830	$124	$103	$83	$65	$47	$29	$11	$0	$0	$0	$0
$1,830	$1,880	$130	$109	$88	$70	$52	$34	$16	$0	$0	$0	$0
$1,880	$1,930	$136	$115	$93	$75	$57	$39	$21	$3	$0	$0	$0
$1,930	$1,980	$142	$121	$99	$80	$62	$44	$26	$8	$0	$0	$0
$1,980	$2,030	$148	$127	$105	$85	$67	$49	$31	$13	$0	$0	$0

2023 Wage Bracket Method Tables for Manual Payroll Systems With Forms W-4 From 2019 or Earlier
SEMIMONTHLY Payroll Period

If the Wage Amount (line 1a) is		MARRIED Persons									
		And the number of allowances is:									
At least	But less than	0	1	2	3	4	5	6	7	8	9	10
		The Tentative Withholding Amount is:									
$2,030	$2,080	$154	$133	$111	$90	$72	$54	$36	$18	$1	$0	$0
$2,080	$2,130	$160	$139	$117	$96	$77	$59	$41	$23	$6	$0	$0
$2,130	$2,180	$166	$145	$123	$102	$82	$64	$46	$28	$11	$0	$0
$2,180	$2,230	$172	$151	$129	$108	$87	$69	$51	$33	$16	$0	$0
$2,230	$2,280	$178	$157	$135	$114	$92	$74	$56	$38	$21	$3	$0
$2,280	$2,330	$184	$163	$141	$120	$98	$79	$61	$43	$26	$8	$0
$2,330	$2,380	$190	$169	$147	$126	$104	$84	$66	$48	$31	$13	$0
$2,380	$2,430	$196	$175	$153	$132	$110	$89	$71	$53	$36	$18	$0
$2,430	$2,480	$202	$181	$159	$138	$116	$95	$76	$58	$41	$23	$5
$2,480	$2,530	$208	$187	$165	$144	$122	$101	$81	$63	$46	$28	$10
$2,530	$2,580	$214	$193	$171	$150	$128	$107	$86	$68	$51	$33	$15
$2,580	$2,630	$220	$199	$177	$156	$134	$113	$91	$73	$56	$38	$20
$2,630	$2,680	$226	$205	$183	$162	$140	$119	$97	$78	$61	$43	$25
$2,680	$2,730	$232	$211	$189	$168	$146	$125	$103	$83	$66	$48	$30
$2,730	$2,780	$238	$217	$195	$174	$152	$131	$109	$88	$71	$53	$35
$2,780	$2,830	$244	$223	$201	$180	$158	$137	$115	$94	$76	$58	$40
$2,830	$2,880	$250	$229	$207	$186	$164	$143	$121	$100	$81	$63	$45
$2,880	$2,930	$256	$235	$213	$192	$170	$149	$127	$106	$86	$68	$50
$2,930	$2,980	$262	$241	$219	$198	$176	$155	$133	$112	$91	$73	$55
$2,980	$3,030	$268	$247	$225	$204	$182	$161	$139	$118	$96	$78	$60
$3,030	$3,080	$274	$253	$231	$210	$188	$167	$145	$124	$102	$83	$65
$3,080	$3,130	$280	$259	$237	$216	$194	$173	$151	$130	$108	$88	$70
$3,130	$3,180	$286	$265	$243	$222	$200	$179	$157	$136	$114	$93	$75
$3,180	$3,230	$292	$271	$249	$228	$206	$185	$163	$142	$120	$99	$80
$3,230	$3,280	$298	$277	$255	$234	$212	$191	$169	$148	$126	$105	$85
$3,280	$3,330	$304	$283	$261	$240	$218	$197	$175	$154	$132	$111	$90
$3,330	$3,380	$310	$289	$267	$246	$224	$203	$181	$160	$138	$117	$95
$3,380	$3,430	$316	$295	$273	$252	$230	$209	$187	$166	$144	$123	$101
$3,430	$3,480	$322	$301	$279	$258	$236	$215	$193	$172	$150	$129	$107
$3,480	$3,530	$328	$307	$285	$264	$242	$221	$199	$178	$156	$135	$113
$3,530	$3,580	$334	$313	$291	$270	$248	$227	$205	$184	$162	$141	$119
$3,580	$3,630	$340	$319	$297	$276	$254	$233	$211	$190	$168	$147	$125
$3,630	$3,680	$346	$325	$303	$282	$260	$239	$217	$196	$174	$153	$131
$3,680	$3,730	$352	$331	$309	$288	$266	$245	$223	$202	$180	$159	$137
$3,730	$3,780	$358	$337	$315	$294	$272	$251	$229	$208	$186	$165	$143
$3,780	$3,830	$364	$343	$321	$300	$278	$257	$235	$214	$192	$171	$149
$3,830	$3,880	$370	$349	$327	$306	$284	$263	$241	$220	$198	$177	$155
$3,880	$3,930	$376	$355	$333	$312	$290	$269	$247	$226	$204	$183	$161
$3,930	$3,980	$382	$361	$339	$318	$296	$275	$253	$232	$210	$189	$167
$3,980	$4,030	$388	$367	$345	$324	$302	$281	$259	$238	$216	$195	$173
$4,030	$4,080	$394	$373	$351	$330	$308	$287	$265	$244	$222	$201	$179
$4,080	$4,130	$400	$379	$357	$336	$314	$293	$271	$250	$228	$207	$185
$4,130	$4,180	$406	$385	$363	$342	$320	$299	$277	$256	$234	$213	$191

2023 Wage Bracket Method Tables for Manual Payroll Systems With Forms W-4 From 2019 or Earlier
SEMIMONTHLY Payroll Period

If the Wage Amount (line 1a) is		SINGLE Persons										
		And the number of allowances is:										
At least	But less than	0	1	2	3	4	5	6	7	8	9	10
		The Tentative Withholding Amount is:										
$0	$220	$0	$0	$0	$0	$0	$0	$0	$0	$0	$0	$0
$220	$230	$1	$0	$0	$0	$0	$0	$0	$0	$0	$0	$0
$230	$240	$2	$0	$0	$0	$0	$0	$0	$0	$0	$0	$0
$240	$250	$3	$0	$0	$0	$0	$0	$0	$0	$0	$0	$0
$250	$260	$4	$0	$0	$0	$0	$0	$0	$0	$0	$0	$0
$260	$270	$5	$0	$0	$0	$0	$0	$0	$0	$0	$0	$0
$270	$280	$6	$0	$0	$0	$0	$0	$0	$0	$0	$0	$0
$280	$290	$7	$0	$0	$0	$0	$0	$0	$0	$0	$0	$0
$290	$300	$8	$0	$0	$0	$0	$0	$0	$0	$0	$0	$0
$300	$310	$9	$0	$0	$0	$0	$0	$0	$0	$0	$0	$0
$310	$320	$10	$0	$0	$0	$0	$0	$0	$0	$0	$0	$0
$320	$330	$11	$0	$0	$0	$0	$0	$0	$0	$0	$0	$0
$330	$340	$12	$0	$0	$0	$0	$0	$0	$0	$0	$0	$0
$340	$350	$13	$0	$0	$0	$0	$0	$0	$0	$0	$0	$0
$350	$360	$14	$0	$0	$0	$0	$0	$0	$0	$0	$0	$0
$360	$370	$15	$0	$0	$0	$0	$0	$0	$0	$0	$0	$0
$370	$380	$16	$0	$0	$0	$0	$0	$0	$0	$0	$0	$0
$380	$390	$17	$0	$0	$0	$0	$0	$0	$0	$0	$0	$0
$390	$400	$18	$0	$0	$0	$0	$0	$0	$0	$0	$0	$0
$400	$410	$19	$1	$0	$0	$0	$0	$0	$0	$0	$0	$0
$410	$420	$20	$2	$0	$0	$0	$0	$0	$0	$0	$0	$0
$420	$430	$21	$3	$0	$0	$0	$0	$0	$0	$0	$0	$0
$430	$440	$22	$4	$0	$0	$0	$0	$0	$0	$0	$0	$0
$440	$450	$23	$5	$0	$0	$0	$0	$0	$0	$0	$0	$0
$450	$460	$24	$6	$0	$0	$0	$0	$0	$0	$0	$0	$0
$460	$470	$25	$7	$0	$0	$0	$0	$0	$0	$0	$0	$0
$470	$480	$26	$8	$0	$0	$0	$0	$0	$0	$0	$0	$0
$480	$490	$27	$9	$0	$0	$0	$0	$0	$0	$0	$0	$0
$490	$500	$28	$10	$0	$0	$0	$0	$0	$0	$0	$0	$0
$500	$510	$29	$11	$0	$0	$0	$0	$0	$0	$0	$0	$0
$510	$520	$30	$12	$0	$0	$0	$0	$0	$0	$0	$0	$0
$520	$530	$31	$13	$0	$0	$0	$0	$0	$0	$0	$0	$0
$530	$540	$32	$14	$0	$0	$0	$0	$0	$0	$0	$0	$0
$540	$550	$33	$15	$0	$0	$0	$0	$0	$0	$0	$0	$0
$550	$560	$34	$16	$0	$0	$0	$0	$0	$0	$0	$0	$0
$560	$570	$35	$17	$0	$0	$0	$0	$0	$0	$0	$0	$0
$570	$580	$36	$18	$0	$0	$0	$0	$0	$0	$0	$0	$0
$580	$590	$37	$19	$1	$0	$0	$0	$0	$0	$0	$0	$0
$590	$600	$38	$20	$2	$0	$0	$0	$0	$0	$0	$0	$0
$600	$610	$39	$21	$3	$0	$0	$0	$0	$0	$0	$0	$0
$610	$620	$40	$22	$4	$0	$0	$0	$0	$0	$0	$0	$0
$620	$630	$41	$23	$5	$0	$0	$0	$0	$0	$0	$0	$0
$630	$640	$42	$24	$6	$0	$0	$0	$0	$0	$0	$0	$0
$640	$650	$43	$25	$7	$0	$0	$0	$0	$0	$0	$0	$0
$650	$660	$44	$26	$8	$0	$0	$0	$0	$0	$0	$0	$0
$660	$670	$45	$27	$9	$0	$0	$0	$0	$0	$0	$0	$0
$670	$680	$46	$28	$10	$0	$0	$0	$0	$0	$0	$0	$0
$680	$730	$49	$31	$13	$0	$0	$0	$0	$0	$0	$0	$0
$730	$780	$55	$36	$18	$0	$0	$0	$0	$0	$0	$0	$0
$780	$830	$61	$41	$23	$5	$0	$0	$0	$0	$0	$0	$0
$830	$880	$67	$46	$28	$10	$0	$0	$0	$0	$0	$0	$0

2023 Wage Bracket Method Tables for Manual Payroll Systems With Forms W-4 From 2019 or Earlier
SEMIMONTHLY Payroll Period

SINGLE Persons

If the Wage Amount (line 1a) is At least	But less than	0	1	2	3	4	5	6	7	8	9	10
		\multicolumn{11}{c}{The Tentative Withholding Amount is:}										
$880	$930	$73	$52	$33	$15	$0	$0	$0	$0	$0	$0	$0
$930	$980	$79	$58	$38	$20	$2	$0	$0	$0	$0	$0	$0
$980	$1,030	$85	$64	$43	$25	$7	$0	$0	$0	$0	$0	$0
$1,030	$1,080	$91	$70	$48	$30	$12	$0	$0	$0	$0	$0	$0
$1,080	$1,130	$97	$76	$54	$35	$17	$0	$0	$0	$0	$0	$0
$1,130	$1,180	$103	$82	$60	$40	$22	$4	$0	$0	$0	$0	$0
$1,180	$1,230	$109	$88	$66	$45	$27	$9	$0	$0	$0	$0	$0
$1,230	$1,280	$115	$94	$72	$51	$32	$14	$0	$0	$0	$0	$0
$1,280	$1,330	$121	$100	$78	$57	$37	$19	$1	$0	$0	$0	$0
$1,330	$1,380	$127	$106	$84	$63	$42	$24	$6	$0	$0	$0	$0
$1,380	$1,430	$133	$112	$90	$69	$47	$29	$11	$0	$0	$0	$0
$1,430	$1,480	$139	$118	$96	$75	$53	$34	$16	$0	$0	$0	$0
$1,480	$1,530	$145	$124	$102	$81	$59	$39	$21	$3	$0	$0	$0
$1,530	$1,580	$151	$130	$108	$87	$65	$44	$26	$8	$0	$0	$0
$1,580	$1,630	$157	$136	$114	$93	$71	$50	$31	$13	$0	$0	$0
$1,630	$1,680	$163	$142	$120	$99	$77	$56	$36	$18	$0	$0	$0
$1,680	$1,730	$169	$148	$126	$105	$83	$62	$41	$23	$5	$0	$0
$1,730	$1,780	$175	$154	$132	$111	$89	$68	$46	$28	$10	$0	$0
$1,780	$1,830	$181	$160	$138	$117	$95	$74	$52	$33	$15	$0	$0
$1,830	$1,880	$187	$166	$144	$123	$101	$80	$58	$38	$20	$2	$0
$1,880	$1,930	$193	$172	$150	$129	$107	$86	$64	$43	$25	$7	$0
$1,930	$1,980	$199	$178	$156	$135	$113	$92	$70	$49	$30	$12	$0
$1,980	$2,030	$205	$184	$162	$141	$119	$98	$76	$55	$35	$17	$0
$2,030	$2,080	$211	$190	$168	$147	$125	$104	$82	$61	$40	$22	$4
$2,080	$2,120	$218	$195	$174	$152	$131	$109	$88	$66	$45	$27	$9
$2,120	$2,160	$227	$200	$178	$157	$135	$114	$92	$71	$49	$31	$13
$2,160	$2,200	$236	$205	$183	$162	$140	$119	$97	$76	$54	$35	$17
$2,200	$2,240	$245	$209	$188	$166	$145	$123	$102	$80	$59	$39	$21
$2,240	$2,280	$254	$214	$193	$171	$150	$128	$107	$85	$64	$43	$25
$2,280	$2,320	$262	$223	$198	$176	$155	$133	$112	$90	$69	$47	$29
$2,320	$2,360	$271	$232	$202	$181	$159	$138	$116	$95	$73	$52	$33
$2,360	$2,400	$280	$241	$207	$186	$164	$143	$121	$100	$78	$57	$37
$2,400	$2,440	$289	$249	$212	$190	$169	$147	$126	$104	$83	$61	$41
$2,440	$2,480	$298	$258	$219	$195	$174	$152	$131	$109	$88	$66	$45
$2,480	$2,520	$306	$267	$228	$200	$179	$157	$136	$114	$93	$71	$50
$2,520	$2,560	$315	$276	$236	$205	$183	$162	$140	$119	$97	$76	$54
$2,560	$2,600	$324	$285	$245	$210	$188	$167	$145	$124	$102	$81	$59
$2,600	$2,640	$333	$293	$254	$215	$193	$171	$150	$128	$107	$85	$64
$2,640	$2,680	$342	$302	$263	$223	$198	$176	$155	$133	$112	$90	$69
$2,680	$2,720	$350	$311	$272	$232	$203	$181	$160	$138	$117	$95	$74
$2,720	$2,760	$359	$320	$280	$241	$207	$186	$164	$143	$121	$100	$78
$2,760	$2,800	$368	$329	$289	$250	$212	$191	$169	$148	$126	$105	$83
$2,800	$2,840	$377	$337	$298	$259	$219	$195	$174	$152	$131	$109	$88
$2,840	$2,880	$386	$346	$307	$267	$228	$200	$179	$157	$136	$114	$93
$2,880	$2,920	$394	$355	$316	$276	$237	$205	$184	$162	$141	$119	$98
$2,920	$2,960	$403	$364	$324	$285	$245	$210	$188	$167	$145	$124	$102
$2,960	$3,000	$412	$373	$333	$294	$254	$215	$193	$172	$150	$129	$107
$3,000	$3,040	$421	$381	$342	$303	$263	$224	$198	$176	$155	$133	$112
$3,040	$3,080	$430	$390	$351	$311	$272	$232	$203	$181	$160	$138	$117
$3,080	$3,120	$438	$399	$360	$320	$281	$241	$208	$186	$165	$143	$122
$3,120	$3,160	$447	$408	$368	$329	$289	$250	$212	$191	$169	$148	$126

2023 Wage Bracket Method Tables for Manual Payroll Systems With Forms W-4 From 2019 or Earlier
SEMIMONTHLY Payroll Period

If the Wage Amount (line 1a) is		SINGLE Persons										
		And the number of allowances is:										
At least	But less than	0	1	2	3	4	5	6	7	8	9	10
		The Tentative Withholding Amount is:										
$3,160	$3,200	$456	$417	$377	$338	$298	$259	$219	$196	$174	$153	$131
$3,200	$3,240	$465	$425	$386	$347	$307	$268	$228	$200	$179	$157	$136
$3,240	$3,280	$474	$434	$395	$355	$316	$276	$237	$205	$184	$162	$141
$3,280	$3,320	$482	$443	$404	$364	$325	$285	$246	$210	$189	$167	$146
$3,320	$3,360	$491	$452	$412	$373	$333	$294	$255	$215	$193	$172	$150
$3,360	$3,400	$500	$461	$421	$382	$342	$303	$263	$224	$198	$177	$155
$3,400	$3,440	$509	$469	$430	$391	$351	$312	$272	$233	$203	$181	$160
$3,440	$3,480	$518	$478	$439	$399	$360	$320	$281	$242	$208	$186	$165
$3,480	$3,520	$526	$487	$448	$408	$369	$329	$290	$250	$213	$191	$170
$3,520	$3,560	$535	$496	$456	$417	$377	$338	$299	$259	$220	$196	$174
$3,560	$3,600	$544	$505	$465	$426	$386	$347	$307	$268	$229	$201	$179
$3,600	$3,640	$553	$513	$474	$435	$395	$356	$316	$277	$237	$205	$184
$3,640	$3,680	$562	$522	$483	$443	$404	$364	$325	$286	$246	$210	$189
$3,680	$3,720	$570	$531	$492	$452	$413	$373	$334	$294	$255	$216	$194
$3,720	$3,760	$579	$540	$500	$461	$421	$382	$343	$303	$264	$224	$198
$3,760	$3,800	$588	$549	$509	$470	$430	$391	$351	$312	$273	$233	$203
$3,800	$3,840	$597	$557	$518	$479	$439	$400	$360	$321	$281	$242	$208
$3,840	$3,880	$606	$566	$527	$487	$448	$408	$369	$330	$290	$251	$213
$3,880	$3,920	$614	$575	$536	$496	$457	$417	$378	$338	$299	$260	$220
$3,920	$3,960	$623	$584	$544	$505	$465	$426	$387	$347	$308	$268	$229
$3,960	$4,000	$632	$593	$553	$514	$474	$435	$395	$356	$317	$277	$238
$4,000	$4,040	$641	$601	$562	$523	$483	$444	$404	$365	$325	$286	$247
$4,040	$4,080	$650	$610	$571	$531	$492	$452	$413	$374	$334	$295	$255
$4,080	$4,120	$658	$619	$580	$540	$501	$461	$422	$382	$343	$304	$264
$4,120	$4,160	$667	$628	$588	$549	$509	$470	$431	$391	$352	$312	$273
$4,160	$4,200	$676	$637	$597	$558	$518	$479	$439	$400	$361	$321	$282

2023 Wage Bracket Method Tables for Manual Payroll Systems With Forms W-4 From 2019 or Earlier
MONTHLY Payroll Period

If the Wage Amount (line 1a) is		MARRIED Persons										
		And the number of allowances is:										
At least	But less than	0	1	2	3	4	5	6	7	8	9	10
		The Tentative Withholding Amount is:										
$0	$1,235	$0	$0	$0	$0	$0	$0	$0	$0	$0	$0	$0
$1,235	$1,275	$2	$0	$0	$0	$0	$0	$0	$0	$0	$0	$0
$1,275	$1,315	$6	$0	$0	$0	$0	$0	$0	$0	$0	$0	$0
$1,315	$1,355	$10	$0	$0	$0	$0	$0	$0	$0	$0	$0	$0
$1,355	$1,395	$14	$0	$0	$0	$0	$0	$0	$0	$0	$0	$0
$1,395	$1,435	$18	$0	$0	$0	$0	$0	$0	$0	$0	$0	$0
$1,435	$1,475	$22	$0	$0	$0	$0	$0	$0	$0	$0	$0	$0
$1,475	$1,515	$26	$0	$0	$0	$0	$0	$0	$0	$0	$0	$0
$1,515	$1,555	$30	$0	$0	$0	$0	$0	$0	$0	$0	$0	$0
$1,555	$1,595	$34	$0	$0	$0	$0	$0	$0	$0	$0	$0	$0
$1,595	$1,635	$38	$2	$0	$0	$0	$0	$0	$0	$0	$0	$0
$1,635	$1,675	$42	$6	$0	$0	$0	$0	$0	$0	$0	$0	$0
$1,675	$1,715	$46	$10	$0	$0	$0	$0	$0	$0	$0	$0	$0
$1,715	$1,755	$50	$14	$0	$0	$0	$0	$0	$0	$0	$0	$0
$1,755	$1,795	$54	$18	$0	$0	$0	$0	$0	$0	$0	$0	$0
$1,795	$1,835	$58	$22	$0	$0	$0	$0	$0	$0	$0	$0	$0
$1,835	$1,875	$62	$26	$0	$0	$0	$0	$0	$0	$0	$0	$0
$1,875	$1,915	$66	$30	$0	$0	$0	$0	$0	$0	$0	$0	$0
$1,915	$1,955	$70	$34	$0	$0	$0	$0	$0	$0	$0	$0	$0
$1,955	$1,995	$74	$38	$3	$0	$0	$0	$0	$0	$0	$0	$0
$1,995	$2,035	$78	$42	$7	$0	$0	$0	$0	$0	$0	$0	$0
$2,035	$2,075	$82	$46	$11	$0	$0	$0	$0	$0	$0	$0	$0
$2,075	$2,115	$86	$50	$15	$0	$0	$0	$0	$0	$0	$0	$0
$2,115	$2,155	$90	$54	$19	$0	$0	$0	$0	$0	$0	$0	$0
$2,155	$2,195	$94	$58	$23	$0	$0	$0	$0	$0	$0	$0	$0
$2,195	$2,235	$98	$62	$27	$0	$0	$0	$0	$0	$0	$0	$0
$2,235	$2,275	$102	$66	$31	$0	$0	$0	$0	$0	$0	$0	$0
$2,275	$2,315	$106	$70	$35	$0	$0	$0	$0	$0	$0	$0	$0
$2,315	$2,355	$110	$74	$39	$3	$0	$0	$0	$0	$0	$0	$0
$2,355	$2,395	$114	$78	$43	$7	$0	$0	$0	$0	$0	$0	$0
$2,395	$2,435	$118	$82	$47	$11	$0	$0	$0	$0	$0	$0	$0
$2,435	$2,475	$122	$86	$51	$15	$0	$0	$0	$0	$0	$0	$0
$2,475	$2,515	$126	$90	$55	$19	$0	$0	$0	$0	$0	$0	$0
$2,515	$2,555	$130	$94	$59	$23	$0	$0	$0	$0	$0	$0	$0
$2,555	$2,595	$134	$98	$63	$27	$0	$0	$0	$0	$0	$0	$0
$2,595	$2,635	$138	$102	$67	$31	$0	$0	$0	$0	$0	$0	$0
$2,635	$2,675	$142	$106	$71	$35	$0	$0	$0	$0	$0	$0	$0
$2,675	$2,715	$146	$110	$75	$39	$3	$0	$0	$0	$0	$0	$0
$2,715	$2,755	$150	$114	$79	$43	$7	$0	$0	$0	$0	$0	$0
$2,755	$2,795	$154	$118	$83	$47	$11	$0	$0	$0	$0	$0	$0
$2,795	$2,835	$158	$122	$87	$51	$15	$0	$0	$0	$0	$0	$0
$2,835	$2,875	$162	$126	$91	$55	$19	$0	$0	$0	$0	$0	$0
$2,875	$2,915	$166	$130	$95	$59	$23	$0	$0	$0	$0	$0	$0
$2,915	$2,955	$170	$134	$99	$63	$27	$0	$0	$0	$0	$0	$0
$2,955	$2,995	$174	$138	$103	$67	$31	$0	$0	$0	$0	$0	$0
$2,995	$3,035	$178	$142	$107	$71	$35	$0	$0	$0	$0	$0	$0
$3,035	$3,075	$182	$146	$111	$75	$39	$3	$0	$0	$0	$0	$0
$3,075	$3,135	$188	$151	$116	$80	$44	$8	$0	$0	$0	$0	$0
$3,135	$3,195	$195	$157	$122	$86	$50	$14	$0	$0	$0	$0	$0
$3,195	$3,255	$202	$163	$128	$92	$56	$20	$0	$0	$0	$0	$0
$3,255	$3,315	$210	$169	$134	$98	$62	$26	$0	$0	$0	$0	$0

2023 Wage Bracket Method Tables for Manual Payroll Systems With Forms W-4 From 2019 or Earlier
MONTHLY Payroll Period

If the Wage Amount (line 1a) is		MARRIED Persons										
		And the number of allowances is:										
At least	But less than	0	1	2	3	4	5	6	7	8	9	10
		The Tentative Withholding Amount is:										
$3,315	$3,375	$217	$175	$140	$104	$68	$32	$0	$0	$0	$0	$0
$3,375	$3,435	$224	$181	$146	$110	$74	$38	$2	$0	$0	$0	$0
$3,435	$3,495	$231	$188	$152	$116	$80	$44	$8	$0	$0	$0	$0
$3,495	$3,555	$238	$195	$158	$122	$86	$50	$14	$0	$0	$0	$0
$3,555	$3,615	$246	$203	$164	$128	$92	$56	$20	$0	$0	$0	$0
$3,615	$3,675	$253	$210	$170	$134	$98	$62	$26	$0	$0	$0	$0
$3,675	$3,735	$260	$217	$176	$140	$104	$68	$32	$0	$0	$0	$0
$3,735	$3,795	$267	$224	$182	$146	$110	$74	$38	$2	$0	$0	$0
$3,795	$3,855	$274	$231	$188	$152	$116	$80	$44	$8	$0	$0	$0
$3,855	$3,915	$282	$239	$196	$158	$122	$86	$50	$14	$0	$0	$0
$3,915	$3,975	$289	$246	$203	$164	$128	$92	$56	$20	$0	$0	$0
$3,975	$4,035	$296	$253	$210	$170	$134	$98	$62	$26	$0	$0	$0
$4,035	$4,095	$303	$260	$217	$176	$140	$104	$68	$32	$0	$0	$0
$4,095	$4,155	$310	$267	$224	$182	$146	$110	$74	$38	$3	$0	$0
$4,155	$4,215	$318	$275	$232	$189	$152	$116	$80	$44	$9	$0	$0
$4,215	$4,275	$325	$282	$239	$196	$158	$122	$86	$50	$15	$0	$0
$4,275	$4,335	$332	$289	$246	$203	$164	$128	$92	$56	$21	$0	$0
$4,335	$4,395	$339	$296	$253	$210	$170	$134	$98	$62	$27	$0	$0
$4,395	$4,455	$346	$303	$260	$217	$176	$140	$104	$68	$33	$0	$0
$4,455	$4,515	$354	$311	$268	$225	$182	$146	$110	$74	$39	$3	$0
$4,515	$4,575	$361	$318	$275	$232	$189	$152	$116	$80	$45	$9	$0
$4,575	$4,635	$368	$325	$282	$239	$196	$158	$122	$86	$51	$15	$0
$4,635	$4,695	$375	$332	$289	$246	$203	$164	$128	$92	$57	$21	$0
$4,695	$4,755	$382	$339	$296	$253	$210	$170	$134	$98	$63	$27	$0
$4,755	$4,815	$390	$347	$304	$261	$218	$176	$140	$104	$69	$33	$0
$4,815	$4,875	$397	$354	$311	$268	$225	$182	$146	$110	$75	$39	$3
$4,875	$4,935	$404	$361	$318	$275	$232	$189	$152	$116	$81	$45	$9
$4,935	$4,995	$411	$368	$325	$282	$239	$196	$158	$122	$87	$51	$15
$4,995	$5,055	$418	$375	$332	$289	$246	$203	$164	$128	$93	$57	$21
$5,055	$5,115	$426	$383	$340	$297	$254	$211	$170	$134	$99	$63	$27
$5,115	$5,175	$433	$390	$347	$304	$261	$218	$176	$140	$105	$69	$33
$5,175	$5,235	$440	$397	$354	$311	$268	$225	$182	$146	$111	$75	$39
$5,235	$5,295	$447	$404	$361	$318	$275	$232	$189	$152	$117	$81	$45
$5,295	$5,355	$454	$411	$368	$325	$282	$239	$196	$158	$123	$87	$51
$5,355	$5,415	$462	$419	$376	$333	$290	$247	$204	$164	$129	$93	$57
$5,415	$5,475	$469	$426	$383	$340	$297	$254	$211	$170	$135	$99	$63
$5,475	$5,535	$476	$433	$390	$347	$304	$261	$218	$176	$141	$105	$69
$5,535	$5,595	$483	$440	$397	$354	$311	$268	$225	$182	$147	$111	$75
$5,595	$5,655	$490	$447	$404	$361	$318	$275	$232	$189	$153	$117	$81
$5,655	$5,715	$498	$455	$412	$369	$326	$283	$240	$197	$159	$123	$87
$5,715	$5,775	$505	$462	$419	$376	$333	$290	$247	$204	$165	$129	$93
$5,775	$5,835	$512	$469	$426	$383	$340	$297	$254	$211	$171	$135	$99
$5,835	$5,895	$519	$476	$433	$390	$347	$304	$261	$218	$177	$141	$105
$5,895	$5,955	$526	$483	$440	$397	$354	$311	$268	$225	$183	$147	$111
$5,955	$6,015	$534	$491	$448	$405	$362	$319	$276	$233	$190	$153	$117
$6,015	$6,075	$541	$498	$455	$412	$369	$326	$283	$240	$197	$159	$123
$6,075	$6,135	$548	$505	$462	$419	$376	$333	$290	$247	$204	$165	$129
$6,135	$6,195	$555	$512	$469	$426	$383	$340	$297	$254	$211	$171	$135
$6,195	$6,255	$562	$519	$476	$433	$390	$347	$304	$261	$218	$177	$141
$6,255	$6,315	$570	$527	$484	$441	$398	$355	$312	$269	$226	$183	$147
$6,315	$6,375	$577	$534	$491	$448	$405	$362	$319	$276	$233	$190	$153

2023 Wage Bracket Method Tables for Manual Payroll Systems With Forms W-4 From 2019 or Earlier
MONTHLY Payroll Period

If the Wage Amount (line 1a) is		MARRIED Persons										
		And the number of allowances is:										
At least	But less than	0	1	2	3	4	5	6	7	8	9	10
		The Tentative Withholding Amount is:										
$6,375	$6,435	$584	$541	$498	$455	$412	$369	$326	$283	$240	$197	$159
$6,435	$6,495	$591	$548	$505	$462	$419	$376	$333	$290	$247	$204	$165
$6,495	$6,555	$598	$555	$512	$469	$426	$383	$340	$297	$254	$211	$171
$6,555	$6,615	$606	$563	$520	$477	$434	$391	$348	$305	$262	$219	$177
$6,615	$6,675	$613	$570	$527	$484	$441	$398	$355	$312	$269	$226	$183
$6,675	$6,735	$620	$577	$534	$491	$448	$405	$362	$319	$276	$233	$190
$6,735	$6,795	$627	$584	$541	$498	$455	$412	$369	$326	$283	$240	$197
$6,795	$6,855	$634	$591	$548	$505	$462	$419	$376	$333	$290	$247	$204
$6,855	$6,915	$642	$599	$556	$513	$470	$427	$384	$341	$298	$255	$212
$6,915	$6,975	$649	$606	$563	$520	$477	$434	$391	$348	$305	$262	$219
$6,975	$7,035	$656	$613	$570	$527	$484	$441	$398	$355	$312	$269	$226
$7,035	$7,095	$663	$620	$577	$534	$491	$448	$405	$362	$319	$276	$233
$7,095	$7,155	$670	$627	$584	$541	$498	$455	$412	$369	$326	$283	$240
$7,155	$7,215	$678	$635	$592	$549	$506	$463	$420	$377	$334	$291	$248
$7,215	$7,275	$685	$642	$599	$556	$513	$470	$427	$384	$341	$298	$255
$7,275	$7,335	$692	$649	$606	$563	$520	$477	$434	$391	$348	$305	$262
$7,335	$7,395	$699	$656	$613	$570	$527	$484	$441	$398	$355	$312	$269
$7,395	$7,455	$706	$663	$620	$577	$534	$491	$448	$405	$362	$319	$276
$7,455	$7,515	$714	$671	$628	$585	$542	$499	$456	$413	$370	$327	$284
$7,515	$7,575	$721	$678	$635	$592	$549	$506	$463	$420	$377	$334	$291
$7,575	$7,635	$728	$685	$642	$599	$556	$513	$470	$427	$384	$341	$298
$7,635	$7,695	$735	$692	$649	$606	$563	$520	$477	$434	$391	$348	$305
$7,695	$7,755	$742	$699	$656	$613	$570	$527	$484	$441	$398	$355	$312
$7,755	$7,815	$750	$707	$664	$621	$578	$535	$492	$449	$406	$363	$320
$7,815	$7,875	$757	$714	$671	$628	$585	$542	$499	$456	$413	$370	$327
$7,875	$7,935	$764	$721	$678	$635	$592	$549	$506	$463	$420	$377	$334
$7,935	$7,995	$771	$728	$685	$642	$599	$556	$513	$470	$427	$384	$341
$7,995	$8,055	$778	$735	$692	$649	$606	$563	$520	$477	$434	$391	$348
$8,055	$8,115	$786	$743	$700	$657	$614	$571	$528	$485	$442	$399	$356
$8,115	$8,175	$793	$750	$707	$664	$621	$578	$535	$492	$449	$406	$363
$8,175	$8,235	$800	$757	$714	$671	$628	$585	$542	$499	$456	$413	$370
$8,235	$8,295	$807	$764	$721	$678	$635	$592	$549	$506	$463	$420	$377
$8,295	$8,355	$814	$771	$728	$685	$642	$599	$556	$513	$470	$427	$384

(Source: Internal Revenue Service)

2023 Wage Bracket Method Tables for Manual Payroll Systems With Forms W-4 From 2019 or Earlier
MONTHLY Payroll Period

If the Wage Amount (line 1a) is		SINGLE Persons										
		And the number of allowances is:										
At least	But less than	0	1	2	3	4	5	6	7	8	9	10
		The Tentative Withholding Amount is:										
$0	$440	$0	$0	$0	$0	$0	$0	$0	$0	$0	$0	$0
$440	$470	$2	$0	$0	$0	$0	$0	$0	$0	$0	$0	$0
$470	$500	$5	$0	$0	$0	$0	$0	$0	$0	$0	$0	$0
$500	$530	$8	$0	$0	$0	$0	$0	$0	$0	$0	$0	$0
$530	$560	$11	$0	$0	$0	$0	$0	$0	$0	$0	$0	$0
$560	$590	$14	$0	$0	$0	$0	$0	$0	$0	$0	$0	$0
$590	$620	$17	$0	$0	$0	$0	$0	$0	$0	$0	$0	$0
$620	$650	$20	$0	$0	$0	$0	$0	$0	$0	$0	$0	$0
$650	$680	$23	$0	$0	$0	$0	$0	$0	$0	$0	$0	$0
$680	$710	$26	$0	$0	$0	$0	$0	$0	$0	$0	$0	$0
$710	$740	$29	$0	$0	$0	$0	$0	$0	$0	$0	$0	$0
$740	$770	$32	$0	$0	$0	$0	$0	$0	$0	$0	$0	$0
$770	$800	$35	$0	$0	$0	$0	$0	$0	$0	$0	$0	$0
$800	$830	$38	$2	$0	$0	$0	$0	$0	$0	$0	$0	$0
$830	$860	$41	$5	$0	$0	$0	$0	$0	$0	$0	$0	$0
$860	$890	$44	$8	$0	$0	$0	$0	$0	$0	$0	$0	$0
$890	$920	$47	$11	$0	$0	$0	$0	$0	$0	$0	$0	$0
$920	$950	$50	$14	$0	$0	$0	$0	$0	$0	$0	$0	$0
$950	$980	$53	$17	$0	$0	$0	$0	$0	$0	$0	$0	$0
$980	$1,010	$56	$20	$0	$0	$0	$0	$0	$0	$0	$0	$0
$1,010	$1,040	$59	$23	$0	$0	$0	$0	$0	$0	$0	$0	$0
$1,040	$1,070	$62	$26	$0	$0	$0	$0	$0	$0	$0	$0	$0
$1,070	$1,100	$65	$29	$0	$0	$0	$0	$0	$0	$0	$0	$0
$1,100	$1,130	$68	$32	$0	$0	$0	$0	$0	$0	$0	$0	$0
$1,130	$1,160	$71	$35	$0	$0	$0	$0	$0	$0	$0	$0	$0
$1,160	$1,190	$74	$38	$2	$0	$0	$0	$0	$0	$0	$0	$0
$1,190	$1,220	$77	$41	$5	$0	$0	$0	$0	$0	$0	$0	$0
$1,220	$1,250	$80	$44	$8	$0	$0	$0	$0	$0	$0	$0	$0
$1,250	$1,280	$83	$47	$11	$0	$0	$0	$0	$0	$0	$0	$0
$1,280	$1,310	$86	$50	$14	$0	$0	$0	$0	$0	$0	$0	$0
$1,310	$1,340	$89	$53	$17	$0	$0	$0	$0	$0	$0	$0	$0
$1,340	$1,370	$92	$56	$20	$0	$0	$0	$0	$0	$0	$0	$0
$1,370	$1,430	$97	$60	$25	$0	$0	$0	$0	$0	$0	$0	$0
$1,430	$1,490	$104	$66	$31	$0	$0	$0	$0	$0	$0	$0	$0
$1,490	$1,550	$112	$72	$37	$1	$0	$0	$0	$0	$0	$0	$0
$1,550	$1,610	$119	$78	$43	$7	$0	$0	$0	$0	$0	$0	$0
$1,610	$1,670	$126	$84	$49	$13	$0	$0	$0	$0	$0	$0	$0
$1,670	$1,730	$133	$90	$55	$19	$0	$0	$0	$0	$0	$0	$0
$1,730	$1,790	$140	$97	$61	$25	$0	$0	$0	$0	$0	$0	$0
$1,790	$1,850	$148	$105	$67	$31	$0	$0	$0	$0	$0	$0	$0
$1,850	$1,910	$155	$112	$73	$37	$1	$0	$0	$0	$0	$0	$0
$1,910	$1,970	$162	$119	$79	$43	$7	$0	$0	$0	$0	$0	$0
$1,970	$2,030	$169	$126	$85	$49	$13	$0	$0	$0	$0	$0	$0
$2,030	$2,090	$176	$133	$91	$55	$19	$0	$0	$0	$0	$0	$0
$2,090	$2,150	$184	$141	$98	$61	$25	$0	$0	$0	$0	$0	$0
$2,150	$2,210	$191	$148	$105	$67	$31	$0	$0	$0	$0	$0	$0
$2,210	$2,270	$198	$155	$112	$73	$37	$1	$0	$0	$0	$0	$0
$2,270	$2,330	$205	$162	$119	$79	$43	$7	$0	$0	$0	$0	$0
$2,330	$2,390	$212	$169	$126	$85	$49	$13	$0	$0	$0	$0	$0
$2,390	$2,450	$220	$177	$134	$91	$55	$19	$0	$0	$0	$0	$0
$2,450	$2,510	$227	$184	$141	$98	$61	$25	$0	$0	$0	$0	$0

Appendix C Federal Income Tax Tables 503

2023 Wage Bracket Method Tables for Manual Payroll Systems With Forms W-4 From 2019 or Earlier
MONTHLY Payroll Period

If the Wage Amount (line 1a) is		SINGLE Persons — And the number of allowances is:										
At least	But less than	0	1	2	3	4	5	6	7	8	9	10
		The Tentative Withholding Amount is:										
$2,510	$2,570	$234	$191	$148	$105	$67	$31	$0	$0	$0	$0	$0
$2,570	$2,630	$241	$198	$155	$112	$73	$37	$1	$0	$0	$0	$0
$2,630	$2,690	$248	$205	$162	$119	$79	$43	$7	$0	$0	$0	$0
$2,690	$2,750	$256	$213	$170	$127	$85	$49	$13	$0	$0	$0	$0
$2,750	$2,810	$263	$220	$177	$134	$91	$55	$19	$0	$0	$0	$0
$2,810	$2,870	$270	$227	$184	$141	$98	$61	$25	$0	$0	$0	$0
$2,870	$2,930	$277	$234	$191	$148	$105	$67	$31	$0	$0	$0	$0
$2,930	$2,990	$284	$241	$198	$155	$112	$73	$37	$1	$0	$0	$0
$2,990	$3,050	$292	$249	$206	$163	$120	$79	$43	$7	$0	$0	$0
$3,050	$3,110	$299	$256	$213	$170	$127	$85	$49	$13	$0	$0	$0
$3,110	$3,170	$306	$263	$220	$177	$134	$91	$55	$19	$0	$0	$0
$3,170	$3,230	$313	$270	$227	$184	$141	$98	$61	$25	$0	$0	$0
$3,230	$3,290	$320	$277	$234	$191	$148	$105	$67	$31	$0	$0	$0
$3,290	$3,350	$328	$285	$242	$199	$156	$113	$73	$37	$2	$0	$0
$3,350	$3,410	$335	$292	$249	$206	$163	$120	$79	$43	$8	$0	$0
$3,410	$3,470	$342	$299	$256	$213	$170	$127	$85	$49	$14	$0	$0
$3,470	$3,530	$349	$306	$263	$220	$177	$134	$91	$55	$20	$0	$0
$3,530	$3,590	$356	$313	$270	$227	$184	$141	$98	$61	$26	$0	$0
$3,590	$3,650	$364	$321	$278	$235	$192	$149	$106	$67	$32	$0	$0
$3,650	$3,710	$371	$328	$285	$242	$199	$156	$113	$73	$38	$2	$0
$3,710	$3,770	$378	$335	$292	$249	$206	$163	$120	$79	$44	$8	$0
$3,770	$3,830	$385	$342	$299	$256	$213	$170	$127	$85	$50	$14	$0
$3,830	$3,890	$392	$349	$306	$263	$220	$177	$134	$91	$56	$20	$0
$3,890	$3,950	$400	$357	$314	$271	$228	$185	$142	$99	$62	$26	$0
$3,950	$4,010	$407	$364	$321	$278	$235	$192	$149	$106	$68	$32	$0
$4,010	$4,070	$414	$371	$328	$285	$242	$199	$156	$113	$74	$38	$2
$4,070	$4,130	$421	$378	$335	$292	$249	$206	$163	$120	$80	$44	$8
$4,130	$4,190	$428	$385	$342	$299	$256	$213	$170	$127	$86	$50	$14
$4,190	$4,270	$443	$394	$351	$308	$265	$222	$179	$136	$93	$57	$21
$4,270	$4,350	$461	$403	$360	$317	$274	$231	$188	$145	$102	$65	$29
$4,350	$4,430	$479	$413	$370	$327	$284	$241	$198	$155	$112	$73	$37
$4,430	$4,510	$496	$423	$380	$337	$294	$251	$208	$165	$122	$81	$45
$4,510	$4,590	$514	$435	$389	$346	$303	$260	$217	$174	$131	$89	$53
$4,590	$4,670	$531	$452	$399	$356	$313	$270	$227	$184	$141	$98	$61
$4,670	$4,750	$549	$470	$408	$365	$322	$279	$236	$193	$150	$107	$69
$4,750	$4,830	$567	$488	$418	$375	$332	$289	$246	$203	$160	$117	$77
$4,830	$4,910	$584	$505	$428	$385	$342	$299	$256	$213	$170	$127	$85
$4,910	$4,990	$602	$523	$444	$394	$351	$308	$265	$222	$179	$136	$93
$4,990	$5,070	$619	$540	$462	$404	$361	$318	$275	$232	$189	$146	$103
$5,070	$5,150	$637	$558	$479	$413	$370	$327	$284	$241	$198	$155	$112
$5,150	$5,230	$655	$576	$497	$423	$380	$337	$294	$251	$208	$165	$122
$5,230	$5,310	$672	$593	$514	$436	$390	$347	$304	$261	$218	$175	$132
$5,310	$5,390	$690	$611	$532	$453	$399	$356	$313	$270	$227	$184	$141
$5,390	$5,470	$707	$628	$550	$471	$409	$366	$323	$280	$237	$194	$151
$5,470	$5,550	$725	$646	$567	$488	$418	$375	$332	$289	$246	$203	$160
$5,550	$5,630	$743	$664	$585	$506	$428	$385	$342	$299	$256	$213	$170
$5,630	$5,710	$760	$681	$602	$524	$445	$395	$352	$309	$266	$223	$180
$5,710	$5,790	$778	$699	$620	$541	$462	$404	$361	$318	$275	$232	$189
$5,790	$5,870	$795	$716	$638	$559	$480	$414	$371	$328	$285	$242	$199
$5,870	$5,950	$813	$734	$655	$576	$498	$423	$380	$337	$294	$251	$208
$5,950	$6,030	$831	$752	$673	$594	$515	$436	$390	$347	$304	$261	$218

2023 Wage Bracket Method Tables for Manual Payroll Systems With Forms W-4 From 2019 or Earlier
MONTHLY Payroll Period

If the Wage Amount (line 1a) is		SINGLE Persons										
		And the number of allowances is:										
At least	But less than	0	1	2	3	4	5	6	7	8	9	10
		The Tentative Withholding Amount is:										
$6,030	$6,110	$848	$769	$690	$612	$533	$454	$400	$357	$314	$271	$228
$6,110	$6,190	$866	$787	$708	$629	$550	$472	$409	$366	$323	$280	$237
$6,190	$6,270	$883	$804	$726	$647	$568	$489	$419	$376	$333	$290	$247
$6,270	$6,350	$901	$822	$743	$664	$586	$507	$428	$385	$342	$299	$256
$6,350	$6,430	$919	$840	$761	$682	$603	$524	$446	$395	$352	$309	$266
$6,430	$6,510	$936	$857	$778	$700	$621	$542	$463	$405	$362	$319	$276
$6,510	$6,590	$954	$875	$796	$717	$638	$560	$481	$414	$371	$328	$285
$6,590	$6,670	$971	$892	$814	$735	$656	$577	$498	$424	$381	$338	$295
$6,670	$6,750	$989	$910	$831	$752	$674	$595	$516	$437	$390	$347	$304
$6,750	$6,830	$1,007	$928	$849	$770	$691	$612	$534	$455	$400	$357	$314
$6,830	$6,910	$1,024	$945	$866	$788	$709	$630	$551	$472	$410	$367	$324
$6,910	$6,990	$1,042	$963	$884	$805	$726	$648	$569	$490	$419	$376	$333
$6,990	$7,070	$1,059	$980	$902	$823	$744	$665	$586	$507	$429	$386	$343
$7,070	$7,150	$1,077	$998	$919	$840	$762	$683	$604	$525	$446	$395	$352
$7,150	$7,230	$1,095	$1,016	$937	$858	$779	$700	$622	$543	$464	$405	$362
$7,230	$7,310	$1,112	$1,033	$954	$876	$797	$718	$639	$560	$481	$415	$372
$7,310	$7,390	$1,130	$1,051	$972	$893	$814	$736	$657	$578	$499	$424	$381
$7,390	$7,470	$1,147	$1,068	$990	$911	$832	$753	$674	$595	$517	$438	$391
$7,470	$7,550	$1,165	$1,086	$1,007	$928	$850	$771	$692	$613	$534	$455	$400
$7,550	$7,630	$1,183	$1,104	$1,025	$946	$867	$788	$710	$631	$552	$473	$410
$7,630	$7,710	$1,200	$1,121	$1,042	$964	$885	$806	$727	$648	$569	$491	$420
$7,710	$7,790	$1,218	$1,139	$1,060	$981	$902	$824	$745	$666	$587	$508	$429
$7,790	$7,870	$1,235	$1,156	$1,078	$999	$920	$841	$762	$683	$605	$526	$447
$7,870	$7,950	$1,253	$1,174	$1,095	$1,016	$938	$859	$780	$701	$622	$543	$465
$7,950	$8,030	$1,271	$1,192	$1,113	$1,034	$955	$876	$798	$719	$640	$561	$482
$8,030	$8,110	$1,288	$1,209	$1,130	$1,052	$973	$894	$815	$736	$657	$579	$500
$8,110	$8,190	$1,306	$1,227	$1,148	$1,069	$990	$912	$833	$754	$675	$596	$517
$8,190	$8,270	$1,323	$1,244	$1,166	$1,087	$1,008	$929	$850	$771	$693	$614	$535
$8,270	$8,350	$1,341	$1,262	$1,183	$1,104	$1,026	$947	$868	$789	$710	$631	$553

2023 Wage Bracket Method Tables for Manual Payroll Systems With Forms W-4 From 2019 or Earlier
DAILY Payroll Period

If the Wage Amount (line 1a) is		MARRIED Persons									
		And the number of allowances is:									
At least	But less than	0	1	2	3	4	5	6	7	8	9	10
		The Tentative Withholding Amount is:									
$0	$60	$0.00	$0.00	$0.00	$0.00	$0.00	$0.00	$0.00	$0.00	$0.00	$0.00	$0.00
$60	$65	$0.60	$0.00	$0.00	$0.00	$0.00	$0.00	$0.00	$0.00	$0.00	$0.00	$0.00
$65	$70	$1.10	$0.00	$0.00	$0.00	$0.00	$0.00	$0.00	$0.00	$0.00	$0.00	$0.00
$70	$75	$1.60	$0.00	$0.00	$0.00	$0.00	$0.00	$0.00	$0.00	$0.00	$0.00	$0.00
$75	$80	$2.10	$0.40	$0.00	$0.00	$0.00	$0.00	$0.00	$0.00	$0.00	$0.00	$0.00
$80	$85	$2.60	$0.90	$0.00	$0.00	$0.00	$0.00	$0.00	$0.00	$0.00	$0.00	$0.00
$85	$90	$3.10	$1.40	$0.00	$0.00	$0.00	$0.00	$0.00	$0.00	$0.00	$0.00	$0.00
$90	$95	$3.60	$1.90	$0.30	$0.00	$0.00	$0.00	$0.00	$0.00	$0.00	$0.00	$0.00
$95	$100	$4.10	$2.40	$0.80	$0.00	$0.00	$0.00	$0.00	$0.00	$0.00	$0.00	$0.00
$100	$105	$4.60	$2.90	$1.30	$0.00	$0.00	$0.00	$0.00	$0.00	$0.00	$0.00	$0.00
$105	$110	$5.10	$3.40	$1.80	$0.10	$0.00	$0.00	$0.00	$0.00	$0.00	$0.00	$0.00
$110	$115	$5.60	$3.90	$2.30	$0.60	$0.00	$0.00	$0.00	$0.00	$0.00	$0.00	$0.00
$115	$120	$6.10	$4.40	$2.80	$1.10	$0.00	$0.00	$0.00	$0.00	$0.00	$0.00	$0.00
$120	$125	$6.60	$4.90	$3.30	$1.60	$0.00	$0.00	$0.00	$0.00	$0.00	$0.00	$0.00
$125	$130	$7.10	$5.40	$3.80	$2.10	$0.40	$0.00	$0.00	$0.00	$0.00	$0.00	$0.00
$130	$135	$7.60	$5.90	$4.30	$2.60	$0.90	$0.00	$0.00	$0.00	$0.00	$0.00	$0.00
$135	$140	$8.10	$6.40	$4.80	$3.10	$1.40	$0.00	$0.00	$0.00	$0.00	$0.00	$0.00
$140	$145	$8.60	$6.90	$5.30	$3.60	$1.90	$0.30	$0.00	$0.00	$0.00	$0.00	$0.00
$145	$150	$9.20	$7.40	$5.80	$4.10	$2.40	$0.80	$0.00	$0.00	$0.00	$0.00	$0.00
$150	$155	$9.80	$7.90	$6.30	$4.60	$2.90	$1.30	$0.00	$0.00	$0.00	$0.00	$0.00
$155	$160	$10.40	$8.40	$6.80	$5.10	$3.40	$1.80	$0.10	$0.00	$0.00	$0.00	$0.00
$160	$165	$11.00	$9.00	$7.30	$5.60	$3.90	$2.30	$0.60	$0.00	$0.00	$0.00	$0.00
$165	$170	$11.60	$9.60	$7.80	$6.10	$4.40	$2.80	$1.10	$0.00	$0.00	$0.00	$0.00
$170	$175	$12.20	$10.20	$8.30	$6.60	$4.90	$3.30	$1.60	$0.00	$0.00	$0.00	$0.00
$175	$180	$12.80	$10.80	$8.80	$7.10	$5.40	$3.80	$2.10	$0.50	$0.00	$0.00	$0.00
$180	$185	$13.40	$11.40	$9.40	$7.60	$5.90	$4.30	$2.60	$1.00	$0.00	$0.00	$0.00
$185	$190	$14.00	$12.00	$10.00	$8.10	$6.40	$4.80	$3.10	$1.50	$0.00	$0.00	$0.00
$190	$195	$14.60	$12.60	$10.60	$8.60	$6.90	$5.30	$3.60	$2.00	$0.30	$0.00	$0.00
$195	$200	$15.20	$13.20	$11.20	$9.20	$7.40	$5.80	$4.10	$2.50	$0.80	$0.00	$0.00
$200	$205	$15.80	$13.80	$11.80	$9.80	$7.90	$6.30	$4.60	$3.00	$1.30	$0.00	$0.00
$205	$210	$16.40	$14.40	$12.40	$10.40	$8.40	$6.80	$5.10	$3.50	$1.80	$0.20	$0.00
$210	$215	$17.00	$15.00	$13.00	$11.00	$9.00	$7.30	$5.60	$4.00	$2.30	$0.70	$0.00
$215	$220	$17.60	$15.60	$13.60	$11.60	$9.60	$7.80	$6.10	$4.50	$2.80	$1.20	$0.00
$220	$225	$18.20	$16.20	$14.20	$12.20	$10.20	$8.30	$6.60	$5.00	$3.30	$1.70	$0.00
$225	$230	$18.80	$16.80	$14.80	$12.80	$10.80	$8.90	$7.10	$5.50	$3.80	$2.20	$0.50
$230	$235	$19.40	$17.40	$15.40	$13.40	$11.40	$9.50	$7.60	$6.00	$4.30	$2.70	$1.00
$235	$240	$20.00	$18.00	$16.00	$14.00	$12.00	$10.10	$8.10	$6.50	$4.80	$3.20	$1.50
$240	$245	$20.60	$18.60	$16.60	$14.60	$12.60	$10.70	$8.70	$7.00	$5.30	$3.70	$2.00
$245	$250	$21.20	$19.20	$17.20	$15.20	$13.20	$11.30	$9.30	$7.50	$5.80	$4.20	$2.50
$250	$255	$21.80	$19.80	$17.80	$15.80	$13.80	$11.90	$9.90	$8.00	$6.30	$4.70	$3.00
$255	$260	$22.40	$20.40	$18.40	$16.40	$14.40	$12.50	$10.50	$8.50	$6.80	$5.20	$3.50
$260	$265	$23.00	$21.00	$19.00	$17.00	$15.00	$13.10	$11.10	$9.10	$7.30	$5.70	$4.00
$265	$270	$23.60	$21.60	$19.60	$17.60	$15.60	$13.70	$11.70	$9.70	$7.80	$6.20	$4.50
$270	$275	$24.20	$22.20	$20.20	$18.20	$16.20	$14.30	$12.30	$10.30	$8.30	$6.70	$5.00
$275	$280	$24.80	$22.80	$20.80	$18.80	$16.80	$14.90	$12.90	$10.90	$8.90	$7.20	$5.50
$280	$285	$25.40	$23.40	$21.40	$19.40	$17.40	$15.50	$13.50	$11.50	$9.50	$7.70	$6.00
$285	$290	$26.00	$24.00	$22.00	$20.00	$18.00	$16.10	$14.10	$12.10	$10.10	$8.20	$6.50
$290	$295	$26.60	$24.60	$22.60	$20.60	$18.60	$16.70	$14.70	$12.70	$10.70	$8.70	$7.00
$295	$300	$27.20	$25.20	$23.20	$21.20	$19.20	$17.30	$15.30	$13.30	$11.30	$9.30	$7.50
$300	$305	$27.80	$25.80	$23.80	$21.80	$19.80	$17.90	$15.90	$13.90	$11.90	$9.90	$8.00
$305	$310	$28.40	$26.40	$24.40	$22.40	$20.40	$18.50	$16.50	$14.50	$12.50	$10.50	$8.50

2023 Wage Bracket Method Tables for Manual Payroll Systems With Forms W-4 From 2019 or Earlier
DAILY Payroll Period

If the Wage Amount (line 1a) is		MARRIED Persons										
		And the number of allowances is:										
At least	But less than	0	1	2	3	4	5	6	7	8	9	10
		The Tentative Withholding Amount is:										
$310	$315	$29.00	$27.00	$25.00	$23.00	$21.00	$19.10	$17.10	$15.10	$13.10	$11.10	$9.10
$315	$320	$29.60	$27.60	$25.60	$23.60	$21.60	$19.70	$17.70	$15.70	$13.70	$11.70	$9.70
$320	$325	$30.20	$28.20	$26.20	$24.20	$22.20	$20.30	$18.30	$16.30	$14.30	$12.30	$10.30
$325	$330	$30.80	$28.80	$26.80	$24.80	$22.80	$20.90	$18.90	$16.90	$14.90	$12.90	$10.90
$330	$335	$31.40	$29.40	$27.40	$25.40	$23.40	$21.50	$19.50	$17.50	$15.50	$13.50	$11.50
$335	$340	$32.00	$30.00	$28.00	$26.00	$24.00	$22.10	$20.10	$18.10	$16.10	$14.10	$12.10
$340	$345	$32.60	$30.60	$28.60	$26.60	$24.60	$22.70	$20.70	$18.70	$16.70	$14.70	$12.70
$345	$350	$33.20	$31.20	$29.20	$27.20	$25.20	$23.30	$21.30	$19.30	$17.30	$15.30	$13.30
$350	$355	$33.80	$31.80	$29.80	$27.80	$25.80	$23.90	$21.90	$19.90	$17.90	$15.90	$13.90
$355	$360	$34.40	$32.40	$30.40	$28.40	$26.40	$24.50	$22.50	$20.50	$18.50	$16.50	$14.50
$360	$365	$35.00	$33.00	$31.00	$29.00	$27.00	$25.10	$23.10	$21.10	$19.10	$17.10	$15.10
$365	$370	$35.60	$33.60	$31.60	$29.60	$27.60	$25.70	$23.70	$21.70	$19.70	$17.70	$15.70
$370	$375	$36.20	$34.20	$32.20	$30.20	$28.20	$26.30	$24.30	$22.30	$20.30	$18.30	$16.30
$375	$380	$36.80	$34.80	$32.80	$30.80	$28.80	$26.90	$24.90	$22.90	$20.90	$18.90	$16.90
$380	$385	$37.40	$35.40	$33.40	$31.40	$29.40	$27.50	$25.50	$23.50	$21.50	$19.50	$17.50
$385	$390	$38.00	$36.00	$34.00	$32.00	$30.00	$28.10	$26.10	$24.10	$22.10	$20.10	$18.10
$390	$395	$38.60	$36.60	$34.60	$32.60	$30.60	$28.70	$26.70	$24.70	$22.70	$20.70	$18.70
$395	$400	$39.20	$37.20	$35.20	$33.20	$31.20	$29.30	$27.30	$25.30	$23.30	$21.30	$19.30
$400	$405	$39.90	$37.80	$35.80	$33.80	$31.80	$29.90	$27.90	$25.90	$23.90	$21.90	$19.90
$405	$410	$41.00	$38.40	$36.40	$34.40	$32.40	$30.50	$28.50	$26.50	$24.50	$22.50	$20.50
$410	$415	$42.10	$39.00	$37.00	$35.00	$33.00	$31.10	$29.10	$27.10	$25.10	$23.10	$21.10
$415	$420	$43.20	$39.60	$37.60	$35.60	$33.60	$31.70	$29.70	$27.70	$25.70	$23.70	$21.70
$420	$425	$44.30	$40.70	$38.20	$36.20	$34.20	$32.30	$30.30	$28.30	$26.30	$24.30	$22.30

2023 Wage Bracket Method Tables for Manual Payroll Systems With Forms W-4 From 2019 or Earlier
DAILY Payroll Period

If the Wage Amount (line 1a) is		SINGLE Persons									
		And the number of allowances is:									
At least	But less than	0	1	2	3	4	5	6	7	8	9	10
		The Tentative Withholding Amount is:									
$0	$25	$0.00	$0.00	$0.00	$0.00	$0.00	$0.00	$0.00	$0.00	$0.00	$0.00	$0.00
$25	$30	$0.70	$0.00	$0.00	$0.00	$0.00	$0.00	$0.00	$0.00	$0.00	$0.00	$0.00
$30	$35	$1.20	$0.00	$0.00	$0.00	$0.00	$0.00	$0.00	$0.00	$0.00	$0.00	$0.00
$35	$40	$1.70	$0.10	$0.00	$0.00	$0.00	$0.00	$0.00	$0.00	$0.00	$0.00	$0.00
$40	$45	$2.20	$0.60	$0.00	$0.00	$0.00	$0.00	$0.00	$0.00	$0.00	$0.00	$0.00
$45	$50	$2.70	$1.10	$0.00	$0.00	$0.00	$0.00	$0.00	$0.00	$0.00	$0.00	$0.00
$50	$55	$3.20	$1.60	$0.00	$0.00	$0.00	$0.00	$0.00	$0.00	$0.00	$0.00	$0.00
$55	$60	$3.70	$2.10	$0.40	$0.00	$0.00	$0.00	$0.00	$0.00	$0.00	$0.00	$0.00
$60	$65	$4.20	$2.60	$0.90	$0.00	$0.00	$0.00	$0.00	$0.00	$0.00	$0.00	$0.00
$65	$70	$4.80	$3.10	$1.40	$0.00	$0.00	$0.00	$0.00	$0.00	$0.00	$0.00	$0.00
$70	$75	$5.40	$3.60	$1.90	$0.30	$0.00	$0.00	$0.00	$0.00	$0.00	$0.00	$0.00
$75	$80	$6.00	$4.10	$2.40	$0.80	$0.00	$0.00	$0.00	$0.00	$0.00	$0.00	$0.00
$80	$85	$6.60	$4.60	$2.90	$1.30	$0.00	$0.00	$0.00	$0.00	$0.00	$0.00	$0.00
$85	$90	$7.20	$5.20	$3.40	$1.80	$0.10	$0.00	$0.00	$0.00	$0.00	$0.00	$0.00
$90	$95	$7.80	$5.80	$3.90	$2.30	$0.60	$0.00	$0.00	$0.00	$0.00	$0.00	$0.00
$95	$100	$8.40	$6.40	$4.50	$2.80	$1.10	$0.00	$0.00	$0.00	$0.00	$0.00	$0.00
$100	$105	$9.00	$7.00	$5.10	$3.30	$1.60	$0.00	$0.00	$0.00	$0.00	$0.00	$0.00
$105	$110	$9.60	$7.60	$5.70	$3.80	$2.10	$0.50	$0.00	$0.00	$0.00	$0.00	$0.00
$110	$115	$10.20	$8.20	$6.30	$4.30	$2.60	$1.00	$0.00	$0.00	$0.00	$0.00	$0.00
$115	$120	$10.80	$8.80	$6.90	$4.90	$3.10	$1.50	$0.00	$0.00	$0.00	$0.00	$0.00
$120	$125	$11.40	$9.40	$7.50	$5.50	$3.60	$2.00	$0.30	$0.00	$0.00	$0.00	$0.00
$125	$130	$12.00	$10.00	$8.10	$6.10	$4.10	$2.50	$0.80	$0.00	$0.00	$0.00	$0.00
$130	$135	$12.60	$10.60	$8.70	$6.70	$4.70	$3.00	$1.30	$0.00	$0.00	$0.00	$0.00
$135	$140	$13.20	$11.20	$9.30	$7.30	$5.30	$3.50	$1.80	$0.20	$0.00	$0.00	$0.00
$140	$145	$13.80	$11.80	$9.90	$7.90	$5.90	$4.00	$2.30	$0.70	$0.00	$0.00	$0.00
$145	$150	$14.40	$12.40	$10.50	$8.50	$6.50	$4.50	$2.80	$1.20	$0.00	$0.00	$0.00
$150	$155	$15.00	$13.00	$11.10	$9.10	$7.10	$5.10	$3.30	$1.70	$0.00	$0.00	$0.00
$155	$160	$15.60	$13.60	$11.70	$9.70	$7.70	$5.70	$3.80	$2.20	$0.50	$0.00	$0.00
$160	$165	$16.20	$14.20	$12.30	$10.30	$8.30	$6.30	$4.30	$2.70	$1.00	$0.00	$0.00
$165	$170	$16.80	$14.80	$12.90	$10.90	$8.90	$6.90	$4.90	$3.20	$1.50	$0.00	$0.00
$170	$175	$17.40	$15.40	$13.50	$11.50	$9.50	$7.50	$5.50	$3.70	$2.00	$0.30	$0.00
$175	$180	$18.00	$16.00	$14.10	$12.10	$10.10	$8.10	$6.10	$4.20	$2.50	$0.80	$0.00
$180	$185	$18.60	$16.60	$14.70	$12.70	$10.70	$8.70	$6.70	$4.70	$3.00	$1.30	$0.00
$185	$190	$19.20	$17.20	$15.30	$13.30	$11.30	$9.30	$7.30	$5.30	$3.50	$1.80	$0.20
$190	$195	$19.90	$17.80	$15.90	$13.90	$11.90	$9.90	$7.90	$5.90	$4.00	$2.30	$0.70
$195	$200	$21.00	$18.40	$16.50	$14.50	$12.50	$10.50	$8.50	$6.50	$4.60	$2.80	$1.20
$200	$205	$22.10	$19.00	$17.10	$15.10	$13.10	$11.10	$9.10	$7.10	$5.20	$3.30	$1.70
$205	$210	$23.20	$19.60	$17.70	$15.70	$13.70	$11.70	$9.70	$7.70	$5.80	$3.80	$2.20
$210	$215	$24.30	$20.60	$18.30	$16.30	$14.30	$12.30	$10.30	$8.30	$6.40	$4.40	$2.70
$215	$220	$25.40	$21.70	$18.90	$16.90	$14.90	$12.90	$10.90	$8.90	$7.00	$5.00	$3.20
$220	$225	$26.50	$22.80	$19.50	$17.50	$15.50	$13.50	$11.50	$9.50	$7.60	$5.60	$3.70
$225	$230	$27.60	$23.90	$20.30	$18.10	$16.10	$14.10	$12.10	$10.10	$8.20	$6.20	$4.20
$230	$235	$28.70	$25.00	$21.40	$18.70	$16.70	$14.70	$12.70	$10.70	$8.80	$6.80	$4.80
$235	$240	$29.80	$26.10	$22.50	$19.30	$17.30	$15.30	$13.30	$11.30	$9.40	$7.40	$5.40
$240	$245	$30.90	$27.20	$23.60	$19.90	$17.90	$15.90	$13.90	$11.90	$10.00	$8.00	$6.00
$245	$250	$32.00	$28.30	$24.70	$21.00	$18.50	$16.50	$14.50	$12.50	$10.60	$8.60	$6.60
$250	$255	$33.10	$29.40	$25.80	$22.10	$19.10	$17.10	$15.10	$13.10	$11.20	$9.20	$7.20
$255	$260	$34.20	$30.50	$26.90	$23.20	$19.70	$17.70	$15.70	$13.70	$11.80	$9.80	$7.80
$260	$265	$35.30	$31.60	$28.00	$24.30	$20.70	$18.30	$16.30	$14.30	$12.40	$10.40	$8.40
$265	$270	$36.40	$32.70	$29.10	$25.40	$21.80	$18.90	$16.90	$14.90	$13.00	$11.00	$9.00
$270	$275	$37.50	$33.80	$30.20	$26.50	$22.90	$19.50	$17.50	$15.50	$13.60	$11.60	$9.60

(Source: Internal Revenue Service)

2023 Wage Bracket Method Tables for Manual Payroll Systems With Forms W-4 From 2019 or Earlier
DAILY Payroll Period

If the **Wage Amount** (line 1a) is		SINGLE Persons									
		And the number of allowances is:									
At least	But less than	0	1	2	3	4	5	6	7	8	9	10
		The Tentative Withholding Amount is:										
$275	$280	$38.60	$34.90	$31.30	$27.60	$24.00	$20.40	$18.10	$16.10	$14.20	$12.20	$10.20
$280	$285	$39.70	$36.00	$32.40	$28.70	$25.10	$21.50	$18.70	$16.70	$14.80	$12.80	$10.80
$285	$290	$40.80	$37.10	$33.50	$29.80	$26.20	$22.60	$19.30	$17.30	$15.40	$13.40	$11.40
$290	$295	$41.90	$38.20	$34.60	$30.90	$27.30	$23.70	$20.00	$17.90	$16.00	$14.00	$12.00
$295	$300	$43.00	$39.30	$35.70	$32.00	$28.40	$24.80	$21.10	$18.50	$16.60	$14.60	$12.60
$300	$305	$44.10	$40.40	$36.80	$33.10	$29.50	$25.90	$22.20	$19.10	$17.20	$15.20	$13.20
$305	$310	$45.20	$41.50	$37.90	$34.20	$30.60	$27.00	$23.30	$19.70	$17.80	$15.80	$13.80
$310	$315	$46.30	$42.60	$39.00	$35.30	$31.70	$28.10	$24.40	$20.80	$18.40	$16.40	$14.40
$315	$320	$47.40	$43.70	$40.10	$36.40	$32.80	$29.20	$25.50	$21.90	$19.00	$17.00	$15.00
$320	$325	$48.50	$44.80	$41.20	$37.50	$33.90	$30.30	$26.60	$23.00	$19.60	$17.60	$15.60
$325	$330	$49.60	$45.90	$42.30	$38.60	$35.00	$31.40	$27.70	$24.10	$20.50	$18.20	$16.20
$330	$335	$50.70	$47.00	$43.40	$39.70	$36.10	$32.50	$28.80	$25.20	$21.60	$18.80	$16.80
$335	$340	$51.80	$48.10	$44.50	$40.80	$37.20	$33.60	$29.90	$26.30	$22.70	$19.40	$17.40
$340	$345	$52.90	$49.20	$45.60	$41.90	$38.30	$34.70	$31.00	$27.40	$23.80	$20.10	$18.00
$345	$350	$54.00	$50.30	$46.70	$43.00	$39.40	$35.80	$32.10	$28.50	$24.90	$21.20	$18.60
$350	$355	$55.10	$51.40	$47.80	$44.10	$40.50	$36.90	$33.20	$29.60	$26.00	$22.30	$19.20
$355	$360	$56.20	$52.50	$48.90	$45.20	$41.60	$38.00	$34.30	$30.70	$27.10	$23.40	$19.80
$360	$365	$57.30	$53.60	$50.00	$46.30	$42.70	$39.10	$35.40	$31.80	$28.20	$24.50	$20.90
$365	$370	$58.40	$54.70	$51.10	$47.40	$43.80	$40.20	$36.50	$32.90	$29.30	$25.60	$22.00
$370	$375	$59.50	$55.80	$52.20	$48.50	$44.90	$41.30	$37.60	$34.00	$30.40	$26.70	$23.10
$375	$380	$60.60	$56.90	$53.30	$49.60	$46.00	$42.40	$38.70	$35.10	$31.50	$27.80	$24.20
$380	$385	$61.70	$58.00	$54.40	$50.70	$47.10	$43.50	$39.80	$36.20	$32.60	$28.90	$25.30
$385	$390	$62.80	$59.10	$55.50	$51.80	$48.20	$44.60	$40.90	$37.30	$33.70	$30.00	$26.40
$390	$395	$64.00	$60.20	$56.60	$52.90	$49.30	$45.70	$42.00	$38.40	$34.80	$31.10	$27.50
$395	$400	$65.20	$61.30	$57.70	$54.00	$50.40	$46.80	$43.10	$39.50	$35.90	$32.20	$28.60

If the tax required to be withheld under the annual percentage is—	The annual tax withheld under your method may not differ by more than—
Less than $10.00	$9.99
$10 or more but under $100	$10 plus 10% of the excess over $10
$100 or more but under $1,000	$19 plus 3% of the excess over $100
$1,000 or more	$46 plus 1% of the excess over $1,000

7. Tables for Withholding on Distributions of Indian Gaming Profits to Tribal Members

If you make certain payments to members of Indian tribes from gaming profits, you must withhold federal income tax. You must withhold if (a) the total payment to a member for the year is over $13,850, and (b) the payment is from the net revenues of class II or class III gaming activities (classified by the Indian Gaming Regulatory Act) conducted or licensed by the tribes.

A class I gaming activity isn't subject to this withholding requirement. Class I activities are social games solely for prizes of minimal value or traditional forms of Indian gaming engaged in as part of tribal ceremonies or celebrations.

Class II. Class II includes (a) bingo and similar games, such as pull tabs, punch boards, tip jars, lotto, and instant bingo; and (b) card games that are authorized by the state or that aren't explicitly prohibited by the state and played at a location within the state.

Class III. A class III gaming activity is any gaming that isn't class I or class II. Class III includes horse racing, dog racing, jai alai, casino gaming, and slot machines.

Withholding Tables

To figure the amount of tax to withhold each time you make a payment, use the table on the next page for the period for which you make payments. For example, if you make payments weekly, use Table 1; if you make payments monthly, use Table 4. If the total payments to an individual for the year are $13,850 or less, no withholding is required.

Example. A tribal member is paid monthly. The monthly payment is $5,000. Use Table 4, Monthly Distribution Period, to figure the withholding. Subtract $4,881 from the $5,000 payment for a remainder of $119. Multiply this amount by 22% for a total of $26.18. Add $428.92 for total withholding of $455.10.

Depositing and reporting withholding. Combine the Indian gaming withholding with all other nonpayroll withholding (for example, backup withholding and withholding on gambling winnings). Generally, you must deposit the amounts withheld using electronic funds transfer. See *Depositing Taxes* in Pub. 15 for a detailed discussion of the deposit requirements.

Report Indian gaming withholding on Form 945. Also, report the payments and withholding to tribal members and to the IRS on Form 1099-MISC.

Tables for Withholding on Distributions of Indian Casino Profits to Tribal Members

Tables for All Individuals
(For Payments Made in 2023)

Table 1—WEEKLY DISTRIBUTION PERIOD

If the amount of the payment is:		The amount of income tax to withhold is:		
Not over	$266	$0		
Over—	But not over—			of excess over—
$266	$478	10%		$266
$478	$1,126	$21.20 plus 12%		$478
$1,126	$2,100	$98.96 plus 22%		$1,126
$2,100	------	$313.24 plus 24%		$2,100

Table 2—BIWEEKLY DISTRIBUTION PERIOD

If the amount of the payment is:		The amount of income tax to withhold is:		
Not over	$533	$0		
Over—	But not over—			of excess over—
$533	$956	10%		$533
$956	$2,253	$42.31 plus 12%		$956
$2,253	$4,201	$197.96 plus 22%		$2,253
$4,201	------	$626.54 plus 24%		$4,201

Table 3—SEMIMONTHLY DISTRIBUTION PERIOD

If the amount of the payment is:		The amount of income tax to withhold is:		
Not over	$577	$0		
Over—	But not over—			of excess over—
$577	$1,035	10%		$577
$1,035	$2,441	$45.80 plus 12%		$1,035
$2,441	$4,551	$214.52 plus 22%		$2,441
$4,551	------	$678.72 plus 24%		$4,551

Table 4—MONTHLY DISTRIBUTION PERIOD

If the amount of the payment is:		The amount of income tax to withhold is:		
Not over	$1,154	$0		
Over—	But not over—			of excess over—
$1,154	$2,071	10%		$1,154
$2,071	$4,881	$91.66 plus 12%		$2,071
$4,881	$9,102	$428.92 plus 22%		$4,881
$9,102	------	$1,357.50 plus 24%		$9,102

Table 5—QUARTERLY DISTRIBUTION PERIOD

If the amount of the payment is:		The amount of income tax to withhold is:		
Not over	$3,463	$0		
Over—	But not over—			of excess over—
$3,463	$6,213	10%		$3,463
$6,213	$14,644	$275.00 plus 12%		$6,213
$14,644	$27,306	$1,286.72 plus 22%		$14,644
$27,306	------	$4,072.36 plus 24%		$27,306

Table 6—SEMIANNUAL DISTRIBUTION PERIOD

If the amount of the payment is:		The amount of income tax to withhold is:		
Not over	$6,925	$0		
Over—	But not over—			of excess over—
$6,925	$12,425	10%		$6,925
$12,425	$29,288	$550.00 plus 12%		$12,425
$29,288	$54,613	$2,573.50 plus 22%		$29,288
$54,613	------	$8,145.00 plus 24%		$54,613

Table 7—ANNUAL DISTRIBUTION PERIOD

If the amount of the payment is:		The amount of income tax to withhold is:		
Not over	$13,850	$0		
Over—	But not over—			of excess over—
$13,850	$24,850	10%		$13,850
$24,850	$58,575	$1,100.00 plus 12%		$24,850
$58,575	$109,225	$5,147.00 plus 22%		$58,575
$109,225	------	$16,290.00 plus 24%		$109,225

Table 8—DAILY or MISCELLANEOUS DISTRIBUTION PERIOD

If the amount of the payment is:		The amount of income tax to withhold is:		
Not over	$53.30	$0		
Over—	But not over—			of excess over—
$53.30	$95.60	10%		$53.30
$95.60	$225.30	$4.23 plus 12%		$95.60
$225.30	$420.10	$19.79 plus 22%		$225.30
$420.10	------	$62.65 plus 24%		$420.10

How To Get Tax Help

If you have questions about a tax issue; need help preparing your tax return; or want to download free publications, forms, or instructions, go to *IRS.gov* to find resources that can help you right away.

Preparing and filing your tax return. Go to *IRS.gov/EmploymentEfile* for more information on filing your employment tax returns electronically.

Getting answers to your tax questions. On IRS.gov, you can get up-to-date information on current events and changes in tax law.

- *IRS.gov/Help*: A variety of tools to help you get answers to some of the most common tax questions.
- *IRS.gov/Forms*: Find forms, instructions, and publications. You will find details on the most recent tax changes and interactive links to help you find answers to your questions.
- You may also be able to access tax law information in your electronic filing software.

Need someone to prepare your tax return? There are various types of tax return preparers, including enrolled agents, certified public accountants (CPAs), attorneys, and many others who don't have professional credentials. If you choose to have someone prepare your tax return, choose that preparer wisely. A paid tax preparer is:

- Primarily responsible for the overall substantive accuracy of your return,
- Required to sign the return, and
- Required to include their preparer tax identification number (PTIN).

Although the tax preparer always signs the return, you're ultimately responsible for providing all the information required for the preparer to accurately prepare your return. Anyone paid to prepare tax returns for others should have a thorough understanding of tax matters. For more information on how to choose a tax preparer, go to *Tips for Choosing a Tax Preparer* on IRS.gov.

Coronavirus. Go to *IRS.gov/Coronavirus* for links to information on the impact of the coronavirus, as well as tax relief available for individuals and families, small and large businesses, and tax-exempt organizations.

Employers can register to use Business Services Online. The Social Security Administration (SSA) offers online service at *SSA.gov/employer* for fast, free, and secure online W-2 filing options to CPAs, accountants, enrolled agents, and individuals who process Form W-2, Wage and Tax Statement, and Form W-2c, Corrected Wage and Tax Statement.

IRS social media. Go to *IRS.gov/SocialMedia* to see the various social media tools the IRS uses to share the latest information on tax changes, scam alerts, initiatives, products, and services. At the IRS, privacy and security are our highest priority. We use these tools to share public information with you. **Don't** post your social security number (SSN) or other confidential information on social media sites. Always protect your identity when using any social networking site.

The following IRS YouTube channels provide short, informative videos on various tax-related topics in English, Spanish, and ASL.

- *Youtube.com/irsvideos*.
- *Youtube.com/irsvideosmultilingua*.
- *Youtube.com/irsvideosASL*.

Watching IRS videos. The IRS Video portal (*IRSVideos.gov*) contains video and audio presentations for individuals, small businesses, and tax professionals.

Online tax information in other languages. You can find information on *IRS.gov/MyLanguage* if English isn't your native language.

Free Over-the-Phone Interpreter (OPI) Service. The IRS is committed to serving our multilingual customers by offering OPI services. The OPI Service is a federally funded program and is available at Taxpayer Assistance Centers (TACs), other IRS offices, and every VITA/TCE return site. The OPI Service is accessible in more than 350 languages.

Accessibility Helpline available for taxpayers with disabilities. Taxpayers who need information about accessibility services can call 833-690-0598. The Accessibility Helpline can answer questions related to current and future accessibility products and services available in alternative media formats (for example, braille, large print, audio, etc.). The Accessibility Helpline doesn't have access to your IRS account. For help with tax law, refunds, or account-related issues, go to *IRS.gov/LetUsHelp*.

Disasters. Go to *Disaster Assistance and Emergency Relief for Individuals and Businesses* to review the available disaster tax relief.

Getting tax forms and publications. Go to *IRS.gov/Forms* to view, download, or print most of the forms, instructions, and publications you may need. Or, you can go to *IRS.gov/OrderForms* to place an order.

Getting tax publications and instructions in eBook format. You can also download and view popular tax publications and instructions (including Pub. 15-T) on mobile devices as eBooks at *IRS.gov/eBooks*.

Note. IRS eBooks have been tested using Apple's iBooks for iPad. Our eBooks haven't been tested on other dedicated eBook readers, and eBook functionality may not operate as intended.

Getting a transcript of your return. You can get a copy of your tax transcript or a copy of your return by calling 800-829-4933 or by mailing Form 4506-T (transcript request) or Form 4506 (copy of return) to the IRS.

Reporting and resolving your tax-related identity theft issues.

- Tax-related identity theft happens when someone steals your personal information to commit tax fraud. Your taxes can be affected if your EIN is used to file a fraudulent return or to claim a refund or credit.
- The IRS doesn't initiate contact with taxpayers by email, text messages (including shortened links), telephone calls, or social media channels to request or verify personal or financial information. This includes

requests for personal identification numbers (PINs), passwords, or similar information for credit cards, banks, or other financial accounts.

- Go to *IRS.gov/IdentityTheft*, the IRS Identity Theft Central webpage, for information on identity theft and data security protection for taxpayers, tax professionals, and businesses. If your EIN has been lost or stolen or you suspect you're a victim of tax-related identity theft, you can learn what steps you should take.

Making a tax payment. Go to *IRS.gov/Payments* for information on how to make a payment using any of the following options.

- *Debit or Credit Card*: Choose an approved payment processor to pay online or by phone.
- *Electronic Funds Withdrawal*: Schedule a payment when filing your federal taxes using tax return preparation software or through a tax professional.
- *Electronic Federal Tax Payment System*: Best option for businesses. Enrollment is required.
- *Check or Money Order*: Mail your payment to the address listed on the notice or instructions.
- *Cash*: You may be able to pay your taxes with cash at a participating retail store.
- *Same-Day Wire*: You may be able to do same-day wire from your financial institution. Contact your financial institution for availability, cost, and time frames.

Note. The IRS uses the latest encryption technology to ensure that the electronic payments you make online, by phone, or from a mobile device using the IRS2Go app are safe and secure. Paying electronically is quick, easy, and faster than mailing in a check or money order.

What if I can't pay now? Go to *IRS.gov/Payments* for more information about your options.

- Apply for an *online payment agreement* (*IRS.gov/OPA*) to meet your tax obligation in monthly installments if you can't pay your taxes in full today. Once you complete the online process, you will receive immediate notification of whether your agreement has been approved.
- Use the *Offer in Compromise Pre-Qualifier* to see if you can settle your tax debt for less than the full amount you owe. For more information on the Offer in Compromise program, go to *IRS.gov/OIC*.

Understanding an IRS notice or letter you've received. Go to *IRS.gov/Notices* to find additional information about responding to an IRS notice or letter.

Contacting your local IRS office. Keep in mind, many questions can be answered on IRS.gov without visiting an IRS TAC. Go to *IRS.gov/LetUsHelp* for the topics people ask about most. If you still need help, IRS TACs provide tax help when a tax issue can't be handled online or by phone. All TACs now provide service by appointment, so you'll know in advance that you can get the service you need without long wait times. Before you visit, go to *IRS.gov/TACLocator* to find the nearest TAC and to check hours, available services, and appointment options. Or, on the IRS2Go app, under the Stay Connected tab, choose the Contact Us option and click on "Local Offices."

The Taxpayer Advocate Service (TAS) Is Here To Help You

What Is TAS?

TAS is an *independent* organization within the IRS that helps taxpayers and protects taxpayer rights. Their job is to ensure that every taxpayer is treated fairly and that you know and understand your rights under the *Taxpayer Bill of Rights*.

How Can You Learn About Your Taxpayer Rights?

The Taxpayer Bill of Rights describes 10 basic rights that all taxpayers have when dealing with the IRS. Go to *TaxpayerAdvocate.IRS.gov* to help you understand what these rights mean to you and how they apply. These are *your* rights. Know them. Use them.

What Can TAS Do for You?

TAS can help you resolve problems that you can't resolve with the IRS. And their service is free. If you qualify for their assistance, you will be assigned to one advocate who will work with you throughout the process and will do everything possible to resolve your issue. TAS can help you if:

- Your problem is causing financial difficulty for you, your family, or your business;
- You face (or your business is facing) an immediate threat of adverse action; or
- You've tried repeatedly to contact the IRS but no one has responded, or the IRS hasn't responded by the date promised.

How Can You Reach TAS?

TAS has offices *in every state, the District of Columbia, and Puerto Rico*. Your local advocate's number is in your local directory and at *TaxpayerAdvocate.IRS.gov/Contact-Us*. You can also call them at 877-777-4778.

How Else Does TAS Help Taxpayers?

TAS works to resolve large-scale problems that affect many taxpayers. If you know of one of these broad issues, report it to them at *IRS.gov/SAMS*.

TAS for Tax Professionals

TAS can provide a variety of information for tax professionals, including tax law updates and guidance, TAS programs, and ways to let TAS know about systemic problems you've seen in your practice.

Appendix D

State Income Tax Information

The employee income tax rates for each state for 2023 are presented below. *Tax Bracket* refers to the year-to-date earnings of the individual. *Marginal Tax Rate* refers to the amount of tax actually collected on each dollar the employee earns and is subject to change as the employee's earnings increase during the year. Note that the tax bracket, although generally pertaining to payroll-related income, also applies to other sources of personal revenue such as interest and dividends. With the exception of states with no income tax, each state's revenue tables were the sources for this table.

State	Tax Bracket (Single)	Tax Bracket (Married)	Marginal Tax Rate
Alabama	$0+	$0+	2.0%
	$500+	$1,000+	4.0%
	$3,000+	$6,000+	5.0%
Alaska	$0+	$0+	0%
Arizona	$0+	$0+	2.5%
Arkansas	$0+	$0+	0.0%
	$4,800+	$4,800+	2.0%
	$9,500+	$9,500+	3.0%
	$14,300+	$14,300+	3.4%
	$23,600+	$23,600+	5.0%
	$39,700+	$39,700+	5.9%
California	$0+	$0+	1.1%
	$10,099+	$20,198+	2.2%
	$23,942+	$47,884+	4.4%
	$37,788+	$75,576+	6.6%
	$52,455+	$104,910+	8.8%
	$66,295+	$132,590+	10.23%
	$338,639+	$677,278+	11.33%
	$406,364+	$812,728+	12.43%
	$677,275+	$1,000,000+	13.53%
	$1,000,000+	$1,354,550+	14.63%
Colorado	$0+	$0+	4.40%

(continued)

State	Tax Bracket (Single)	Tax Bracket (Married)	Marginal Tax Rate
Connecticut	$0+	$0+	3.0%
	$10,000+	$20,000+	5.0%
	$50,000+	$100,000+	5.50%
	$100,000+	$200,000+	6.0%
	$200,000+	$400,000+	6.50%
	$250,000+	$500,000+	6.90%
	$500,000+	$1,000,000+	6.99%
Delaware	$2,000+	$2,000+	2.20%
	$5,000+	$5,000+	3.90%
	$10,001+	$10,001+	4.80%
	$20,000+	$20,000+	5.20%
	$25,000+	$25,000+	5.50%
	$60,000+	$60,000+	5.95%
District of Columbia	$0+	$0+	4.0%
	$10,000+	$10,000+	6.0%
	$40,000+	$40,000+	6.50%
	$60,000+	$60,000+	8.50%
	$250,000+	$250,000+	9.25%
	$500,000+	$500,000+	9.75%
	$1,000,000+	$1,000,000+	10.75%
Florida	$0+	$0+	0%
Georgia	$0	$0+	1.0%
	$750+	$1,000+	2.0%
	$2,250+	$3,000+	3.0%
	$3,750+	$5,000+	4.0%
	$5,250+	$7,000+	5.0%
	$7,000+	$10,000+	5.75%
Hawaii	$0+	$0+	1.40%
	$2,400+	$4,800+	3.20%
	$4,800+	$9,600+	5.50%
	$9,600+	$19,200+	6.40%
	$14,400+	$28,800+	6.80%
	$19,200+	$38,400+	7.20%
	$24,000+	$48,000+	7.60%
	$36,000+	$72,000+	7.90%
	$48,000+	$96,000+	8.25%
	$150,000+	$300,000+	9.00%
	$175,000+	$350,000+	10.00%
	$200,000+	$400,000+	11.00%
Idaho	$0+	$0+	1.0%
	$1,588	$3,176	3.0%
	$4,763+	$9,526+	4.5%
	$7,939+	$15,878+	6.625%
Illinois	$0+	$0+	4.95%
Indiana	$0+	$0+	3.15%

State	Tax Bracket (Single)	Tax Bracket (Married)	Marginal Tax Rate
Iowa	$0+	$0+	4.4%
	$6,001+	$12,001+	4.82%
	$30,001+	$60,001+	5.7%
	$75,0001+	$150,001+	6.0%
Kansas	$0+	$0+	3.10%
	$15,000+	$30,000+	5.25%
	$30,000+	$60,000+	5.70%
Kentucky	$0+	$0+	4.5%
Louisiana	$0+	$0+	1.85%
	$12,500+	$25,000+	3.50%
	$50,000+	$100,000+	4.25%
Maine	$0+	$0+	5.80%
	$24,500+	$49,050+	6.75%
	$58,850+	$116,100+	7.15%
Maryland	$0+	$0+	2.00%
	$1,000+	$1,000+	3.00%
	$2,000+	$2,000+	4.00%
	$3,000+	$3,000+	4.75%
	$100,000+	$150,000+	5.00%
	$125,000+	$175,000+	5.25%
	$150,000+	$225,000+	5.50%
	$250,000+	$300,000+	5.75%
Massachusetts	$0+	$0+	5.0%
Michigan	$0+	$0+	4.05%
Minnesota	$0+	$0+	5.35%
	$30,070+	$43,950+	6.80%
	$98,760+	$174,610+	7.85%
	$183,340+	$304,970+	9.85%
Mississippi	$0+	$0+	0%
	$4,000+	$4,000+	3.0%
	$5,000+	$5,000+	4.0%
	$10,000+	$10,000+	5.0%
Missouri	$0+	$0+	0%
	$1,207+	$1,207+	2.0%
	$2,414+	$2,414+	2.5%
	$3,621+	$3,621+	3.0%
	$4,828+	$4,828+	3.5%
	$6,035+	$6,035+	4.0%
	$7,242+	$7,242+	4.5%
	$8,449+	$8,440+	4.95%
Montana	$0+	$0+	1.8%
	$7,630+	$7,630+	4.4%
	$16,350+	$16,350+	6.0%
	$130,790+	$130,790+	6.6%

(continued)

State	Tax Bracket (Single)	Tax Bracket (Married)	Marginal Tax Rate
Nebraska	$0+	$0+	0%
	$3,660+	$7,530+	2.26%
	$5,990+	$11,610+	3.22%
	$19,470+	$28,910+	4.91%
	$28,210+	$44,980+	6.20%
	$35,820+	$55,810+	6.39%
	$33,635	$74,010+	6.75%
Nevada	$0+	$0+	0%
New Hampshire	$0+	$0+	0%
New Jersey	$0+	$0+	1.40%
	$20,000+	$20,000+	1.75%
	$35,000+	$50,000+	3.50%s*/2.45%m**
	$40,000+	$70,000+	5.525%s/3.50%m
	$75,000+	$80,000+	6.37%s/5.525%m
	$500,000+	$150,000+	8.97%s/6.37%m
	$1,000,000+	$500,000+	10.75%s/8.97%m
		$1,000,000+	10.75%
New Mexico	$0+	$0+	0%
	$6,925+	$13,850+	1.70%
	$12,425+	$21,850+	3.20%
	$17,925+	$29,850+	4.70%
	$22,925+	$37,850+	4.90%
	$216,925+	$328,850+	5.90%
New York (See New York Income tax booklet)		$0+	4.00%
	$0+	$8,500+	4.50%
	$8,500+	$11,700+	5.25%
	$11,700+	$13,900+	5.50%
	$13,900+	$80,650+	6.00%
	$80,650+	$96,800+	7.14%s/6.67%m
	$96,800+	$107,650+	7.64%s/7.17%m
	$107,650+	$157,650+	6.50%s/8.11%m
	$157,650+	$211,550+	11.01%s/6.50%m
	$215,400+	$323,200+	6.50%s/12.84%m
	$265,400+	$373,200+	7.35%m
		$1,077,550+	10.45%s/7.65%m
	$1,077,550+	$2,155,350	10.45%m
	$5,000,000+	$5,000,000	11.10%
	$25,000,000+	$5,000,000	11.70%
North Carolina	$0+	$0+	4.75%
North Dakota	$0+	$0+	0%
	$6,950+	$13,850+	1.10%
	$51,650+	$51,225+	2.04%
	$98,100+	$104,125+	2.27%
	$115,250+	$151,400+	2.64%
	$498,275+	$259,525+	2.90%

State	Tax Bracket (Single)	Tax Bracket (Married)	Marginal Tax Rate
Ohio	$26,050+	$26,050+	2.765%
	$46,100+	$46,100+	3.226%
	$92,150+	$92,150+	3.688%
	$115,300+	$115,300+	3.990%
Oklahoma	$0+	$0+	0.25%
	$6,350+	$12,700+	0.75%
	$7,350+	$14,700+	1.75%
	$8,850+	$17,700+	2.75%
	$11,250+	$22,500+	3.75%
	$13,550+	$24,900+	4.75%
Oregon	$0+	$0+	4.75%
	$4,050+	$8,100+	6.75%
	$10,200+	$20,400+	8.75%
	$125,000+	$250,000+	9.90%
Pennsylvania	$0+	$0+	3.07%
Rhode Island	$0+	$0+	3.75%
	$73,450+	$73,450+	4.75%
	$166,950+	$166,950+	5.99%
South Carolina	$0+	$0+	0%
	$3,300+	$3,300+	3.0%
	$16,880+	$16,880+	6.5%
South Dakota	$0+	$0+	0%
Tennessee	$0+	$0+	0%
Texas	$0+	$0+	0%
Utah	$0+	$0+	4.85%
Vermont	$0+	$0+	0%
	$3,500+	$10,538+	3.35%
	$48,900+	$86,388+	6.60%
	$113,550+	$193,938+	7.60%
	$233,050+	$289,988+	8.75%
Virginia	$0+	$0+	2.0%
	$3,000+	$3,000+	3.0%
	$5,000+	$5,000+	5.0%
	$17,000+	$17,000+	5.75%
Washington	$0+	$0+	0%
West Virginia	$0+	$0+	3.0%
	$10,000+	$6,000+	4.0%
	$25,000+	$15,000+	4.5%
	$40,000+	$24,000+	6.0%
	$60,000+	$36,000+	6.5%
Wisconsin	$0+	$0+	3.54%
	$12,760+	$17,010+	4.65%
	$25,520+	$34,030+	5.30%
	$280,950+	$374,600+	7.65%
Wyoming	$0+	$0+	0%

*s = single
**m = married

Appendix E

State Revenue Department or Labor Information

The following are state revenue or labor offices. Where possible, the email address is included. Many states have an Internet email submission form or live chat availability to answer questions.

Alabama

Department of Revenue
50 North Ripley Street
P.O. Box 303500
Montgomery, AL 36130
334-242-1170
www.revenue.alabama.gov

Alaska

Department of Revenue
P.O. Box 110400
Juneau, AK 99811-0400
907-465-2300
www.dor.alaska.gov

Arizona

Department of Revenue
1600 West Monroe Street
Phoenix, AZ 85007
602-255-3381
www.azdor.gov

Arkansas

Department of Finance and Administration
1900 W 7th, Ste 2047
Little Rock, AR 72201
501-682-7025
www.dfa.arkansas.gov

California

Employment Development Department
3321 Power Inn Road, Suite 220
Sacramento, CA 95826
888-745-3886
www.edd.ca.gov

Colorado

Department of Revenue
1881 Pierce Street, Entrance B
Lakewood, CO 80214
303-238-7378
cdor.colorado.gov/

Connecticut
Department of Labor
200 Folly Brook Blvd.
Wethersfield, CT 06109
860-263-6000
www.portal.ct.gov/DRS

Delaware
Division of Revenue - Wilmington Office
820 N. French Street
Wilmington, DE 19801
302-577-8200
www.revenue.delaware.gov

District of Columbia
Office of Tax and Revenue
1101 4th Street, SW Suite 270
West, Washington, DC 20024
202-727-4829
https://otr.cfo.dc.gov/

Florida
Department of Revenue
5050 West Tennessee Street
Tallahassee, FL 32399
850-717-6570
www.floridarevenue.com

Georgia
Department of Revenue
1800 Century Boulevard, NE, Suite 12000
Atlanta, GA 30345
877-423-6711
www.dor.georgia.gov

Hawaii
Department of Taxation
830 Punchbowl Street
Honolulu, HI 96813
808-587-1418
www.tax.hawaii.gov

Idaho
State Tax Commission
11321 W. Chinden Blvd.
Boise, ID 83714
208-334-7660
www.tax.idaho.gov

Illinois
Department of Revenue
555 West Monroe, Suite 1100
Chicago, IL 60661
800-732-8866
www.illinois.gov/agencies/agency.idor.html

Indiana
Department of Revenue
100 N Senate Avenue, IGCN, Room N105
Indianapolis, IN 46204
317-232-2240
www.in.gov/dor

Iowa
Department of Revenue
Hoover State Office Building - 1st Floor
1305 E. Walnut
Des Moines, IA 50319
515-281-3114
www.tax.iowa.gov

Kansas
Department of Revenue
P.O. Box 3506
Topeka, KS 66625-3506
785-368-8222
www.ksrevenue.gov

Kentucky
Department of Revenue
501 High Street
Frankfort, KY 40601
502-564-4581
www.revenue.ky.gov

Louisiana
617 North Third Street
Baton Rouge, LA 70802
855-307-3893
www.revenue.louisiana.gov

Maine
Department of Revenue Services
51 Commerce Drive
Augusta, ME 04330
207-626-8475, option 4
www.maine.gov/revenue

Maryland
Comptroller of Maryland
301 W. Preston Street, Room 206
Baltimore, MD 21201-2384
410-767-1306
www.marylandtaxes.gov

Massachusetts
Department of Revenue
100 Cambridge Street, 2nd Floor
Boston, MA 02114
617-626-2700
www.mass.gov/orgs/massachusetts-department-of-revenue

Michigan
Department of Treasury
P.O. Box 30059
Lansing, MI 48909
517-636-6925
www.michigan.gov/treasury

Minnesota
Department of Revenue
600 North Robert St.
St. Paul, MN 55146
651-282-9999
www.revenue.state.mn.us

Mississippi
Department of Revenue
500 Clinton Center Drive
Clinton, MS 39056
601-923-7300
www.dor.ms.gov

Missouri
Department of Revenue
PO Box 3375
Jefferson City, MO 65105-3375
573-522-0967
www.dor.mo.gov

Montana
Department of Revenue
P.O. Box 5835
Helena, MT 59604
406-444-6900
www.mtrevenue.gov

Nebraska
Department of Revenue
P.O. Box 94818
Lincoln, NE 68509
402-471-5729
www.revenue.nebraska.gov

Nevada
Department of Taxation
1550 College Parkway, Suite 115
Carson City, NV 89706
775-684-2000
tax.nv.gov

New Hampshire
Department of Revenue Administration
109 Pleasant Street (Medical & Surgical Building)
Concord, NH 03301
603-230-5000
www.revenue.nh.gov

New Jersey
Division of Taxation
P.O. Box 281
Trenton, NJ 08695
609-292-6400
www.state.nj.us/treasury/taxation

New Mexico
Taxation and Revenue Department
1200 South St. Francis Drive
Santa Fe, NM 87505
866-285-2996
www.tax.newmexico.gov

New York
Department of Taxation and Finance
State Office Campus, Building 12, Room 266B
Albany, NY 12240
518-485-6654
www.tax.ny.gov

North Carolina
Department of Revenue
4701 Atlantic Avenue, Suite 118
Raleigh, NC 27604
919-707-0880
www.ncdor.gov

North Dakota
Office of State Tax Commissioner
600 E. Boulevard Ave., Dept. 127
Bismarck, ND 58505-0599
701-328-7088
www.nd.gov/tax

Ohio
Department of Taxation
Attn: Compliance Business Tax Division
P.O. Box 1090
Columbus, OH 43216-21090
888-405-4039
www.tax.ohio.gov

Oklahoma
Tax Commission
2501 N Lincoln Blvd
Oklahoma City, OK 73194
405-521-3160
www.oklahoma.gov/tax

Oregon
Department of Revenue
955 Center St. NE
Salem, OR 97301-2555
503-945-8091
www.oregon.gov/DOR

Pennsylvania
Department of Revenue
P.O. Box 280904
Harrisburg, PA 17128-0904
717-787-1064
www.revenue.pa.gov

Rhode Island
Division of Taxation
One Capitol Hill
Providence, RI 02908
401-574-8829
www.tax.ri.gov

South Carolina
Department of Revenue
300A Outlet Pointe Boulevard
Columbia, SC 29210
844-898-8542
www.dor.sc.gov

South Dakota
Department of Revenue
445 East Capitol Ave.
Pierre, SD 57501-3185
605-773-3311
dor.sd.gov

Tennessee
Department of Revenue
500 Deaderick Street
Nashville, TN 37242
615-253-0600
www.tn.gov/revenue

Texas
Comptroller of Public Accounts
Lyndon B. Johnson State Office Building
111 East 17th Street
Austin, Texas 78774
800-252-5555
www.comptroller.texas.gov

Utah
State Tax Commission
210 North 1950 West
Salt Lake City, UT 84134
801-297-2200
www.tax.utah.gov

Vermont
Department of Taxes
133 State Street, First Floor
Montpelier, VT 05633
802-828-2551
www.tax.vermont.gov

Virginia
Virginia Tax
Office of Customer Services
P.O. Box 1115
Richmond, VA 23218-1115
804-367-8037
www.tax.virginia.gov

Washington
Department of Revenue
2101 4th Ave Suite 1400
Seattle, WA 98121
360-705-6705
www.dor.wa.gov

West Virginia
Department of Revenue
1001 Lee Street East
Charleston, WV 25301
304-558-3333
www.revenue.wv.gov

Wisconsin
Department of Revenue
2135 Rimrock Road
Madison, WI 53713
608-266-2772
www.revenue.wi.gov

Wyoming
Department of Revenue
122 West 25th Street, Suite E301
Herschler Building East
Cheyenne, WY 82002
307-777-5275
revenue.wyo.gov

Appendix F

Payroll Certification Information

Payroll certification examinations are available to document mastery of payroll accounting topics. The National Association of Certified Professional Bookkeepers (NACPB), the American Institute of Professional Bookkeepers (AIPB), and the American Payroll Association (APA) each offer certification exams. Contact details for each examination are at the end of this appendix.

Correlation of Certification Exam Topics and Specific Learning Objectives

The following table contains information about the topics covered by each payroll certification and the location of that information in this text.

Payroll Certification Exam Topics	Learning Objective
401(k) plans	4-2, 4-5
Account classification	7-2, 7-3
Accounting terminology	7-2
Additional Medicare tax—highly compensated employees	1-2, 5-3
Advances and overpayments	5-5
Affordable Care Act Form 1095	1-2
Benefits costs and benchmarking	6-6, 7-6
Bonuses and commissions	3-2, 3-6
Cafeteria (Section 125) plans	4-2
Calculation of FICA taxes (Social Security and Medicare): Employee	5-3
Calculation of FICA taxes (Social Security and Medicare): Employer	6-1, 6-3
Calculation of involuntary (mandated) deductions	4-5, 5-5
Communication with IRS and SSA	2-2, 4-6
Cybersecurity	2-5
Data privacy	1-4
Data retention	2-5
De minimis fringe benefits	4-1, 4-3
Deceased employee pay	3-7
Deferred compensation	3-6
Docking exempt employee pay	3-2
Employee benefits	4-1, 4-2

Payroll Certification Exam Topics	Learning Objective
Employee classification	1-6
Employee vs. independent contractor	1-2, 1-6, 2-2
Employer-provided benefits: Cafeteria plan, awards, personal use of company vehicle, group-term life insurance	4-2, 4-3, 4-4
Employment forms	2-2
Enterprise test	3-1
Exempt vs. nonexempt	1-6
Expatriate taxation	2-2
Fair Labor Standards Act	1-2
Federal forms	1-4, 6-3
Federal income tax calculation: Taxable wages, tax computation	5-2
Fiduciary responsibility	7-5
FLSA provisions	1-2
Form W-4: Additional withholding, employee changes	2-2
Form 843 treatment	6-3
Fringe benefits	4-1, 4-3, 4-4
FUTA, including credit reduction states	5-3
General Journal entries	7-3
General Ledger entries	7-4
Global payroll	2-2
Gross pay calculation	3-2, 3-3, 3-4, 3-5, 3-6
Gross-up of compensation	5-1
Identifying payroll job requirements	3-2, 3-4, 6-1, 6-2, 7-2
Internal controls	2-4
IRS regulations	5-2, 6-1, 6-2
Jury duty	3-7
Leased employees	2-3
Legislation affecting payroll, contract acts	1-1, 1-2
Multiple worksite reporting	1-4, 1-5, 2-2
Net pay calculations	5-1, 5-2, 5-3, 5-4, 5-5
New hire documentation	2-2
Nonproductive time	3-7
Nonqualified deferred compensation	3-7
Nonqualified plans	4-2, 4-3
Nontaxable benefits	4-3
On-premises benefits: Athletic facilities, child care, etc.	4-3
Overtime premium calculation: FLSA, weighted average, commission, salary, piece-rate	3-4
Pay calculation: Regular, tipped, time worked, other pay situations	3-2, 3-3, 3-5, 3-6
Payment methods: Cash, check, direct deposit, paycard	5-6
Payroll account reconciliation	7-4, 7-6
Payroll audit	2-5, 7-6
Payroll in the United States: Employee documentation	2-2
Payroll practices, confidentiality	1-4, 1-5, 2-3
Payroll systems	1-4, 1-5, 7-5
Payroll: Process and challenges	1-4, 1-5, 7-5, 7-6
Payroll technology	1-4, 1-5, 5-6
Payroll trending	7-6
Penalties	6-4
Pension payments and withholding	4-1, 4-6
Planning and organizing payroll operations	1-4, 1-5, 2-1
Qualified employee discounts	4-3, 4-4
Qualified moving expenses	4-3, 4-4
Reconciling wages and taxes	6-3
Recording accruals and reversals	7-4, 7-5
Recordkeeping requirements, including retention	2-3, 2-4, 2-5

Payroll Certification Exam Topics	Learning Objective
Repaying employer loans	5-5
Resident nonalien	2-2
Retirement plans: Qualified	4-2
Retroactive pay	3-7
State wage and hour laws	3-1
State withholding certificates	2-2
Stock compensation	3-2, 3-6
Tax deposits: Requirements, lookback period, deposits	6-2, 6-3
Taxable tips	3-1, 6-3
Temporary employees	2-3
Time management	1-4, 1-5
Trends: Technology	1-4, 1-5
Unemployment and disability taxes	6-1, 6-3
Voluntary deductions/other deductions calculations computation	4-5, 4-6
Withholding taxes, FICA taxes	5-2, 5-3, 5-4

Contact Information for Payroll Certifications

National Association of Certified Professional Bookkeepers

844-249-3551

info@certifiedpublicbookkeeper.org

National Association of Certified Public Bookkeepers (NACPB), LLC 1838 N 1075 W, Suite 300

Farmington, UT 84025

https://nacpb.org/bookkeeping-school/licenses/certified-public-bookkeeper/

Requirement

- Successful completion of the NACPB Payroll Certification Exam.

American Institute of Professional Bookkeepers

800-622-0121

info@aipb.org

AIPBSuite 5006001 Montrose Road

Rockville, MD 20852

https://aipb.org/certification-program/

Requirements

- A minimum of two years of professional full-time (or part-time equivalent) experience may be obtained before or after the exam.
- Successful completion of a two-part exam.
- Signed acknowledgment of the AIPB's Code of Ethics.

American Payroll Association

(210) 224-6406
American Payroll Association
660 North Main Avenue, Suite 100
San Antonio, Texas, 78205
http://www.americanpayroll.org/certification

Two levels of payroll certification are available from the American Payroll Association: Certified Payroll Professional (CPP) and Fundamental Payroll Certification (FPC). The following are the criteria for eligibility for each certification available from the APA.

Certified Payroll Professional

The Certification Board of the American Payroll Association (APA) requires that payroll professionals fulfill **ONE** of the following criteria before they take the Certified Payroll Professional Examination.

Criteria 1

The payroll professional has been practicing a total of three (3) years out of the five (5) years preceding the date of the examination. The practice of payroll is defined as direct or related involvement in at least one of the following:

- Payroll production, payroll reporting, and payroll accounting.
- Payroll systems and payroll taxation.
- Payroll administration.
- Payroll education/consulting.

Criteria 2

Before a candidate takes the examination, the payroll professional has been employed in the practice of payroll as defined in Criteria 1 for at least the past 24 months *and* has completed within the last 24 months ALL of the following courses within **ONE** of the following three options offered by the APA:

Option 1

- Payroll Practice Essentials (three-day course: live or virtual) and
- Intermediate Payroll Concepts (two-day course: live or virtual) and
- Advanced Payroll Concepts (two-day course: live or virtual) and
- Strategic Payroll Practices (two-day course: live or virtual)

Option 2

- Payroll 101: Foundations of Payroll Certificate Program and
- Payroll 201: The Payroll Administration Certificate Program

Option 3

Certified Payroll Professional Boot Camp

Criteria 3

Before a candidate takes the examination, the payroll professional has been employed in the practice of payroll as defined in Criteria 1 for at least the past 18 months, has **obtained** the **Fundamental Payroll Certification (FPC)**, *and* has completed within the past 18 months ALL of the following courses within **ONE** of the following two options offered by the APA:

Option 1

- Intermediate Payroll Concepts (two-day course: live or virtual) and
- Advanced Payroll Concepts (two-day course: live or virtual) and
- Strategic Payroll Practices (two-day course: live or virtual)

Option 2

Payroll 201: The Payroll Administration Certificate Program

Fundamental Payroll Certification (FPC)

The Fundamental Payroll Certification (FPC) is open to all those who wish to demonstrate a baseline of payroll competency. The FPC is designed for all of the following:

- Entry-level payroll professionals.
- Sales professionals/consultants serving the payroll industry.
- Systems analysts/engineers writing payroll programs.
- Payroll Service Bureau client representatives.

APA membership and payroll experience are not required to take the FPC examination.

Glossary

401(k) A defined contribution plan in which employees may contribute either a specific amount or a percentage of their gross pay on a pre-tax or post-tax basis through payroll deductions.

403(b) A retirement plan designed for employees of certain nonprofit organizations.

457 A retirement plan offered by governmental and certain nongovernmental employers in which contributions are deducted on a pre-tax basis.

A

Accrual An accounting method in which revenues and expenses are recorded when they occur, not necessarily when any cash is exchanged.

Additional Medicare tax An additional 0.9 percent Medicare tax levied upon employees who earn in excess of a certain amount per year, as mandated by the Affordable Care Act.

Adjusting entries Journal entries created at the end of an accounting period to allocate income and expenses to the proper accounts.

Affordable Care Act (ACA) Mandated health care coverage for all Americans regardless of employment status.

Age Discrimination in Employment Act (ADEA) The Age Discrimination in Employment Act of 1967 protects workers over age 40 from age-based discrimination.

Allocation The storing of costs in one account and then dividing the costs based on a quantifiable activity.

American Recovery Plan Act (ARPA) Legislation designed to stimulate the economy by creating jobs and prescribing transparency by employers.

American Rescue Plan Act (ARPA) of 2021 Extended employee retention credits, family and sick related leave for COVID-19–related items.

American Rescue Plan Act of 2021 Extended employee retention credits, family and sick related leave for COVID-19–related items.

American Taxpayer Relief Act of 2012 (ATRA) Legislation that prevented the expirations of tax cuts that would have affected employees.

Americans with Disabilities Act Amendments Act (ADAAA) Legislation that extended the definition of disabilities to protect workers from discrimination in the workplace.

Americans with Disabilities Act of 1990 (ADA) Legislation protecting the antidiscrimination rights of American workers with disabilities as an extension of the Civil Rights Act of 1964.

Annual depositor Employers who have an annual payroll tax liability of less than $1,000 during the lookback period and are notified in writing by the IRS that they submit Form 944 and remit taxes on an annual basis.

Annual total compensation report A list of all compensation that an employee earns per year, including (but not limited to) salary, commissions, bonuses, and all fringe benefits; examples include health insurance, employer contributions to the employee's retirement plan, life insurance, and tuition reimbursement.

Asset An item of value that a business uses in the course of its operations and from which it expects future economic benefit.

Automated Clearing House (ACH) The electronic network of financial institutions in the United States through which monetary transactions are transmitted in batches.

B

Balance sheet A financial statement that lists the totals in the assets, liabilities, and owners' equity accounts of a firm for a specific date.

Benefit analysis A calculation of the costs and benefits of a company, department, project, or employee.

Biweekly payroll A pay frequency in which employees are paid 26 times per year.

Blockchain A digital means of transferring electronic currency using small amounts of data transmitted via multiple computers.

C

Cafeteria plan A benefit plan pursuant to Section 125 of the Internal Revenue Code that allows employees to designate specific amounts to be deducted from their payroll to pay for health and child care expenses on a pre-tax basis.

Cents-per-mile rule A method used to determine the value of a company car fringe benefit based on a fixed amount times the number of miles driven for personal purposes.

Certified payroll A report mandated for certain federal government contracts that verifies the accuracy of labor expenses incurred during completion of contract-related activities.

Charitable contribution A payroll deduction in which an employee designates a specific amount of gross pay to be paid to community, religious, educational, or another IRS-designated charitable organization.

Circular E See *Publication 15*.

Civil Rights Act of 1964 Federal legislation that protects employees from discrimination based on race, color, religion, sex, or national origin.

Civil Rights Act of 1991 Federal law that instituted monetary penalties for companies found guilty of discrimination as described under the Civil Rights Act of 1964.

Combination pay Employee compensation that reflects two or more discrete pay bases during the same pay period.

Commission Employee compensation paid upon completion of a task, often pertaining to sales-based activities.

Commuting rule A valuation method used to determine the value of personal use of a company vehicle based on the number of miles driven for commuting to and from work.

Compensation The total amount of cash and noncash salary/wages and benefits that an employee receives in return for working for a company.

Compensatory (comp) time Paid time off granted to employees instead of paid overtime.

Consolidated Appropriations Act of 2018 Signed into law in March 2018, this act increased the funding for the E-Verify program, which is an Internet-based system that offers employers instant verification of an employee's eligibility to work in the United States. It is important to note that the E-Verify program does not replace the need for the completion of Form I-9 upon employee hire because it is a voluntary service.

Consolidated Omnibus Budget Reformation Act of 1985 (COBRA) Provided continuance of employee medical benefits after separation from the company.

Consumer Credit Protection Act (CCPA) Federal law that pertains to the percentage of wage garnishment that may be withheld from employee pay to satisfy legal obligations.

Copeland Anti-Kickback Act Federal legislation enacted in 1934 that prohibits a federal contractor or subcontractor from inducing an employee to forgo a portion of the wages guaranteed by the contract.

Coronavirus Aid, Relief and Economic Stimulus (CARES) Act of 2020 Provided economic support and payroll tax relief during the SARS COV-2 (COVID-19) pandemic to encourage employers to retain their employees and tax relief for businesses.

Credit The right side of the T-account.

Cryptocurrency A form of currency that is digitally encrypted and transmitted.

Current Tax Payment Act (CTPA) of 1943 Federal law enacted in 1943 that required employers to submit a timely remittance to the government of any taxes withheld from employee pay.

D

Daily payroll A pay frequency in which employees are paid each business day.

Davis–Bacon Act of 1931 Federal legislation enacted in 1931 that requires federal contractors to pay employees an amount commensurate with the prevailing local wage.

De minimis A benefit with a very small monetary value that is deemed impractical in terms of tracking using an accounting system.

Debit The left side of the T-account.

Defense of Marriage Act of 1996 (DOMA) Legislation, which was repealed in 2013, that prevented same-sex marriages and related employment benefits.

Defined benefit A company-sponsored pension plan that uses the employee's salary and length of service to compute the amount of the benefit.

Defined contribution A retirement plan to which the employee, and sometimes the employer, makes a regular contribution.

Departmental classification The division of payroll-related costs by employee function or organizational department.

Direct deposit The electronic transmission of employee wages from the employer to the employee's account at a financial institution.

Disposable income The amount of employee wages remaining after withholding federal, state, and local taxes.

Document destruction The act of destroying documents that contain sensitive payroll and employee information.

Draw A loan against future earnings that employees will repay from commissions.

Due care The caution that a reasonable person would exercise to avoid being charged with negligence.

E

E-Verify An Internet-based system that allows employers to verify an employee's legal eligibility to work inside the United States by checking Social Security and Department of Homeland Security databases electronically. It does not replace the legal requirement to file the I-9.

Eight and Eighty (8 and 80) A two-week, 80-hour pay period used to determine overtime for employees who work for hospitals and emergency providers.

Electronic Federal Tax Payment System (EFTPS) The Electronic Federal Tax Payment System, a free tax payment service provided for use for employers in the United States.

Employee Retirement Income Security Act (ERISA) Legislation provided protection for employees' retirement savings, preventing employers from using employee savings to satisfy business expenses.

Employer Identification Number (EIN) A number assigned to employers by the IRS for tax reporting.

Enterprise coverage Firms explicitly covered under FLSA.

Equal Employment Opportunity Commission (EEOC) An entity of the federal government created as part of the Civil Rights Act of 1984, the EEOC enforces civil rights provisions in the workplace.

Equal Pay Act of 1963 Federal legislation mandating that males and females receive equal compensation for comparable work.

Escheatment The transfer of personal property to the employee's state of residence when no legal owner claims the property.

ESOP Employee Stock Ownership Plan.

Ethics An individual's definition of right and wrong.

Exempt An employee who is not subject to the overtime provisions of the Fair Labor Standards Act.

Expense The cost of doing business, which may contain both cash and noncash amounts.

F

Fair Labor Standards Act (FLSA) The law established the idea of minimum hourly wage and maximum weekly hours for hourly employees, among other employee-centered items.

Fair market value (FMV) The amount of money that a person would spend to obtain a good or service in an arm's-length transaction.

Family and Medical Leave Act of 1993 (FMLA) Legislation provided protection for employees to take unpaid leave with employer-provided benefits and still retain their original job or a similar one with the same pay rate upon return to work.

Federal income tax A tax levied by the federal government on individuals.

Federal Insurance Contributions Act (FICA) Legislation that provided funding for social welfare benefits including Social Security and Medicare.

Federal Unemployment Tax Act (FUTA) Legislation that pays for the federal administration of unemployment laws, which are managed by each state.

FICA (Federal Insurance Contribution Act) tax The collective term for the combination of Social Security and Medicare taxes.

Fiduciary A relationship, specifically financial, built on trust between a trustee and a beneficiary.

File maintenance The application of all transactions, including any necessary modifications, to an employee's file.

File security The protection of sensitive payroll information by restricting access and securely storing files.

Flexible spending arrangement (FSA) A tax-advantaged employee spending account as designated by the Internal Revenue Code.

Foreign Account Tax Compliance Act (FATCA) Federal law that regulates the income tax withholdings of foreign employees.

Form 940 The employer's annual federal unemployment tax return.

Form 941 The employer's quarterly federal tax return.

Form 944 The employer's annual federal tax return.

Form SS-8 The form used by the IRS to determine if a worker is an employee or an independent contractor.

Form W-2 Wage and tax statement.

Form W-3 Transmittal of wage and tax statements.

Fringe benefit A company-sponsored benefit that supplements an employee's salary, usually on a noncash basis.

FTE FTE is a calculation tool whereby the number of hours that an employee works is divided by the number of standard hours for the employer.

G

Garnishment A legal procedure for the collection of money owed to a plaintiff through payroll deductions.

General Journal A chronological record of a firm's financial transactions.

General Ledger A record of a firm's financial transactions, grouped by account.

General Valuation Rule (GVR) The method used to determine the value of most fringe benefits using fair market value.

Generally Accepted Accounting Principles (GAAP) A framework relating to accounting practice including rules, procedures, and standards defined by industry professionals and used by U.S. companies.

Gross pay The amount of wages paid to an employee based on work performed, prior to any mandatory or voluntary deductions.

H

H-1B visa A program that allows employers to temporarily hire foreign workers who possess specialized expertise and have earned a bachelor's degree or higher.

Health Insurance Portability and Accountability Act of 1996 (HIPAA) Legislation that protects confidential personal medical records.

Health savings account (HSA) A savings account that provides tax advantages for individuals with health plans that have high deductions via pre-tax payroll deductions.

High-deductible health plan (HDHP) A health care plan with an annual deductible that is at least $1,500 for self-coverage and $3,000 for family coverage; annual out-of-pocket limits are $7,500 for self-coverage and $15,000 for family coverage.

Hiring packet A package of forms that a firm issues to new employees; examples are Form W-4, Form I-9, and health insurance enrollment.

Hourly Wage determination based on the number of complete and partial hours during which an employee performs work-related tasks.

Hundredth-hour system The division of an hour into 100 increments used to compute employee wages as accurately as possible.

I

I-9 The Employment Eligibility Verification form issued by U.S. Citizenship and Immigration Services.

Immigration Reform and Control Act of 1986 (IRCA) Legislation requiring employers to verify the employee's eligibility to work in the United States or to sponsor their ability to work.

Incentive stock option (ISO) A type of employee compensation in which the employee receives a firm's stock on a tax-advantaged basis.

Income statement A financial report used to determine a firm's net income by computing the difference between revenues and expenses for a period; also known as the profit and loss statement.

Independence The ability of an accountant to act professionally without external pressures that would cause a third party to question the integrity of actions and decisions.

Independent contractor An individual who contracts to do work for a firm using his or her own tools and processes without being subject to direction by a firm's management.

Individual coverage FLSA coverage for employees whose firms do not meet the requirements for enterprise coverage.

Integrity Possessing honesty and high moral principles.

Internal control A firm's process of maintaining efficiency and effectiveness, work quality, accurate and reliable financial reports, and legal compliance.

IRA Individual Retirement Account.

L

Labor distribution The classification of a firm's labor by internally designated classifications.

Labor usage Report that contains details about the number of hours worked and the wages paid to employees.

Lease-value rule A method of determining the value of a company car as a fringe benefit using the fair market value and the annual lease as the basis.

Leased employee A person who provides services for a company subject to the provisions of IRS code section 414(n).

Liability A financial obligation of the firm arising from revenues received in advance of services or sales or expenses incurred but not paid.

Lilly Ledbetter Fair Pay Act of 2009 Federal law that removed the 180-day statute of limitations in allegations of unfair pay practices.

Living wage The minimum amount that a family would need to live comfortably for a normal standard of living.

Local income taxes Payroll taxes levied by a city or county government.

Lookback period The time frame used by the IRS to determine the payroll tax deposit schedule for a firm.

M

Mandated deduction Post-tax payroll deduction ordered by a court of law or otherwise nonvoluntary in nature.

Mandatory deduction Payroll deduction over which the employee has no control; examples include taxes, garnishments, and certain retirement contributions.

Marketplace A service provided through the Affordable Care Act of 2010 in which people may shop for and select health care plans.

Medicare tax A payroll tax mandated to be paid by all employees of a firm to fund the Medicare and Medicaid programs.

Minimum wage The minimum hourly amount that employers may legally pay to employees.

Monthly depositor A firm that must deposit its federal income tax and FICA payroll withholdings and contributions on a monthly basis, based on the lookback period.

Monthly payroll A pay frequency in which employees are paid 12 times per year.

N

Net pay An employee's wages or salary less all mandatory and voluntary deductions.

New-hire reporting A process by which a firm notifies governmental authorities of any new hires shortly after the hire date.

Next business day depositor A semiweekly schedule depositor whose payroll tax liabilities exceed $100,000 for any pay period.

Nonexempt An employee who is subject to all overtime provisions of the Fair Labor Standards Act; generally, an hourly employee.

O

Objectivity Making decisions that are free from bias or subjectivity.

Occupational Safety and Health Act of 1970 (OSHA) The legislation that provided guidance for safe workplace conditions.

Old-Age, Survivors, and Disability Insurance (OASDI) Synonymous with Social Security, this is the original name for the social welfare structure.

On-call time The nonwork time that an employee is expected to be available for workplace-related emergencies.

Outsourced vendor A party external to a firm that provides goods or services.

Overtime Time that an employee works beyond his or her normal working hours.

Owners' equity The financial investment and any accumulated profits or losses of the owner of a firm.

P

Pay advice A document detailing employee pay and deductions that either accompanies the paycheck or notifies the employee of the direct deposit of net pay.

Pay period The recurring period during which a firm collects employee labor data and pays employees in accordance with wage or salary agreements.

Paycard A debit card, issued to employees, that contains electronically transmitted wages.

Payroll audit An examination of a firm's payroll records to determine legal compliance.

Payroll register The payroll accountant's internal tool that helps ensure the accuracy of employee compensation and includes each employee's earnings information for a pay period.

Payroll review Verification of payroll accuracy for a period.

Payroll tax report Report offering details of the period's tax liability that an employer must file with governmental authorities.

Percentage method A method used to compute an employee's income tax liability that involves computations based on the employee's wages, marital status, pay frequency, and number of withholdings claimed on Form W-4.

Personal Responsibility and Work Opportunity Reconciliation Act of 1996 (PRWOR) Legislation that provided social welfare relief for a limited time.

Personal Responsibility, Work and Family Promotion Act of 2002 Act that reauthorized PRWOR when it expired.

Piece rate Employee compensation based on production of units or completion of an action during a specified time period.

Post-tax deduction Amount deducted from employee pay after all income and FICA taxes have been deducted; amounts may be voluntary or court mandated.

Posting Transferring the details of General Journal entries to the General Ledger accounts.

Glossary 531

Premium-only plan (POP) A form of cafeteria plan in which employee portions of employer-provided insurance plans may be deducted on a pre-tax basis.

Privacy Act of 1974 Protecting employees by removing personal identifiers from payroll records and restricting access to personnel records.

Professional competence The continuing capability to perform professional duties with an agreed-upon standard of quality.

Professionalism A process reflecting the transparency and public accountability of accounting records.

Protecting Americans from Tax Hikes (PATH) Act An act to prevent tax fraud that extended the Work Opportunity Tax Credit.

Prove Ensuring that the sum of the rows of the payroll register equals the sum of the columns.

Publication 15 The Employer's Tax Guide published by the Internal Revenue Service; also known as *Circular E*.

Publication 15-B The IRS Employer's Guide to Fringe Benefits.

Publication 15-T The Federal Income Tax Withholding Methods.

Q

Qualified plan A written plan for the issuance of employee achievement awards that does not favor highly compensated employees.

Quarter-hour system The division of an hour into 15-minute increments as a means of computing hourly work.

Quarterly depositor A monthly schedule depositor who has a payroll tax liability of less than $2,500 during the preceding or current quarter may remit the payroll tax liability when filing Form 941.

R

Regulation E Federal legislation protecting consumers who use electronic funds transfer to access their net pay.

Remit To send money in payment of an obligation.

Resignation Voluntary termination of employment, usually initiated by the employee.

Respect for Marriage Act of 2022 Legalized all marriages, including same-sex and interracial, at the federal level.

Reversal A general journal entry recorded at the start of the following month to undo the accruals recorded in the prior month.

Review process Examination and analysis of accounting records to ensure accuracy and completeness.

Rule The accounting practice in which the final totals of financial reports are double-underlined.

S

Salary A fixed amount paid to an employee on a regular basis, often expressed in annual terms.

Sarbanes–Oxley Act of 2002 (SOX) Public Law 107-204 concerning publicly owned companies and auditing firms; requires appropriate internal controls and the integrity of financial statements.

Schedule B The report of tax liability for semiweekly depositors.

SECURE 2.0 Act An act passed as part of the Consolidated Appropriations Act of 2022 that expanded the SECURE Act of 2019 by improving employee retirement savings and offering employer incentives.

Semimonthly payroll The payroll frequency in which employees are paid 24 times per year.

Semiweekly depositor A firm that must deposit its federal income tax and FICA payroll withholdings and contributions within three days of the pay date, based on the lookback period.

SEP A Simplified Employee Pension individual retirement account.

Separation of duties An internal control method in which payroll duties are spread among two or more employees.

Setting Every Community Up for Retirement Enhancement (SECURE) Act Act that incentivizes small employers to offer retirement plans, either alone or collectively with other small employers, to improve retirement security for U.S. workers.

SIMPLE The Savings Incentive Match Plan for Employees.

SIMPLE 401(k) A retirement plan for employees of companies that employ 100 or fewer workers. An annual investment limit of $11,500 exists for this type of retirement plan.

Sixteenth Amendment to the U.S. Constitution Allowed the U.S. government to levy and collect income taxes on individuals.

Sleep time Employees who are required to be on duty for 24 hours or more may be allowed up to 5 hours of sleep without a reduction in pay.

Social Security Act (SSA) An act that was passed to promote social welfare for old-age workers and surviving families of workers who had been disabled or deceased in the course of their employment.

Social Security tax A tax paid by both employers and employees that is used to fund the Social Security program.

SOX The Sarbanes–Oxley Act of 2002. Public law 107-204, concerning publicly owned companies and auditing firms to ensure appropriate internal controls and the integrity of financial statements.

Special accounting rule Employers may elect to treat employee amounts for noncash fringe benefits used during November and December as not being paid until January of the following year; employees must be notified in writing by January 31 of the following year if the special accounting rule was used.

State income taxes Income taxes levied by a state government on employee payroll.

State Unemployment Tax Act (SUTA) Employment tax requiring employers to provide monetary benefits for workers who are displaced through no fault of their own.

Statutory deductions Payroll deductions mandated by law.

Statutory employee A special class of employees who run their own business but must be treated as employees for tax reasons.

T

Tax Cuts and Jobs Act An act to provide a budget resolution that represented changes to individual and business tax rates.

Tax remittance The payment of a firm's payroll tax liability.

Taxpayer Certainty and Disaster Tax Relief Act (TCDRA) of 2020 Modifications to the CARES Act of 2020 that extended the employee retention credits (ERC) through June 30, 2021; increased qualified ERC amount per employee to $14,000; changed definition of qualified wages for both over and under 500 employees.

Temporary employee A worker who is employed by a temporary staffing agency and works under the direction of the agency on a temporary basis for different companies.

Termination Cessation of employment with a firm initiated by the employer.

Time card A record of the time worked during a period for an individual employee.

Tip credit The difference between the tipped employee minimum wage and the federal minimum wage.

Tipped employee An employee who engages in an occupation in which he or she customarily and regularly receives more than $30 per month in tips.

Tipped wage The base wage paid to employees who earn the majority of their income through customer tips.

Total Computing the sum of each row and each column of the payroll register.

Travel time Time that an employee spends traveling for the employer's benefit.

Trend Report A report showing the increases and decreases of expenses or revenues within a business over time.

Trial balance An internal accounting statement in which the accountant determines that the debits equal the credits for the amounts in the General Ledger.

U

Uniformed Services Employment and Reemployment Rights Act of 1994 (USERRA) Legislation protecting the job rights of employees called to full-time service by the U.S. military.

Union dues Amounts paid on a regular basis by employees who are required to be part of a union as a condition of their employment.

V

Virtual private network (VPN) A method to provide employees with secured Internet connections when working from remote locations.

Voluntary deduction Amount that an employee elects to have deducted from his or her paycheck and remitted to a third party; examples include charitable contributions, savings bond purchases, and health club fees.

W

W-4 The Employee Withholding Allowance Certificate.

Wage base The maximum annual salary that is subject to tax liability, commonly used for Social Security, FUTA, and SUTA taxes.

Wage-bracket method The use of tax tables located in federal and state publications that facilitate the determination of employee income tax deductions for payroll.

Wait time The time that an employee is paid to wait on the employer's premises for the benefit of the employer.

Walsh–Healey Public Contracts Act Legislation enacted in 1936 that required employers working on federal contracts in excess of $10,000 to pay employees the federal minimum wage and follow the overtime provisions of the Fair Labor Standards Act.

Weekly payroll The payroll frequency in which employees are paid 52 times per year.

Workers' compensation A mandatory insurance policy paid by employers that provides wage replacement and medical benefits to employees who are injured in the course of their employment.

Index

A

AARP. *See* American Association for Retired Persons (AARP)
AB 1513, 133
ACA of 2010. *See* Affordable Care Act (ACA) of 2010
Accountants. *See also* Payroll accountants
   certification, 523–526
   confidentiality, 20
   integrity, 20
   professionalism, 20
   responsibilities of, 376
Accountant shortage, 361
Accounting
   ethical guidelines for, 19–21
   human resources and, 178
   trends in, 381
   types of, 4
Accounting data software, 81
Accounting entries, 360
Accounting equation, 364
Accounting reports, payroll entries in, 377–380
Accounting software programs, 145, 366
Accrual, in payroll, 369–370
ACH (Automated Clearing House), 290
Achievement awards, 187
ADA. *See* Americans with Disabilities Act of 1990 (ADA)
ADAAA. *See* Americans with Disabilities Act Amendments Act (ADAAA)
Additional Medicare tax, 235
ADEA. *See* Age Discrimination in Employment Act of 1967 (ADEA)
Adequate payroll system design, 88
Adjusting entries, 369
Administrative exemption, 65
ADP, 23
Affordable Care Act (ACA) of 2010, 16, 194, 235
   employer contributions to, on Form W-2, 307
   required reporting by employers, 307
Age discrimination, 5
Age Discrimination in Employment Act of 1967 (ADEA), 5
Agricultural workers, 283
AICPA. *See* American Institute of Certified Public Accountants (AICPA)
AICPA Code of Ethics Section 17, 21
Alabama, state revenue department information, 518
Alaska, state revenue department information, 518
Aliens, resident and nonresident, 283, 448
Allocations, overhead, 379
Alphabet, 28
American Accounting Association (AAA), 361
American Association for Retired Persons (AARP), 5
American Civil Liberties Union (ACLU), 197
American Institute of Certified Professional Accountants (AICPA), 361
American Institute of Certified Public Accountants (AICPA), 19
   Code of Ethics guidelines of, 19, 20
American Institute of Professional Bookkeepers, 525
American Payroll Association, 81, 245, 249, 525–526
American Recovery and Reinvestment Act of 2009 (ARRA), 10
American Rescue Plan Act (ARPA), 18, 293
Americans with Disabilities Act Amendments Act (ADAAA), 7
Americans with Disabilities Act of 1990 (ADA), 7
American Taxpayer Relief Act of 2012 (ATRA), 10
Annual schedule depositors, 291, 292
Annual total compensation report, 321–323
Appendix E, 85
Apple, 28
Arizona, state revenue department information, 518
Arkansas, state revenue department information, 518
Arms-length transaction, 179
ARPA. *See* American Rescue Plan Act (ARPA)
ARRA. *See* American Recovery and Reinvestment Act of 2009 (ARRA)
Assets, in financial accounting, 364–365
Assets = Liabilities + Owners' Equity, 364
ATRA. *See* American Taxpayer Relief Act of 2012 (ATRA)
Audit, 25
   example of, 363
   of payroll records, 363
Auditors, 81
Audit payroll records, 83
Automated Clearing House (ACH), 290
Automated systems, 72
Awards, 187

B

Balance sheet, 377, 378
Behavioral control, 52

Benefit analysis, as function of payroll, 320–323
Benefit analysis report, 320–321
Benefit reports rules, 200–201
Benefits
  importance of analysis report, 321
  second largest expense to employers, 320
Bermudez Vaquero v. Stoneledge Furniture LLC, 150
Biden, Joe, 251
Billable *vs.* nonbillable report, 379
BitPay, 251–252
Biweekly payroll, 49
Blockchain technology, 251
Bureau of Labor Statistics (BLS), 66
Businesses
  large, 28–29
  payroll processing for, 28–35
Business expenses
  payroll in context of, 315–318
  pay-roll related entries and, 375–376

C

Cafeteria plans, 182–186
  benefit of, 184
  definition, 182
  federal tax withholding and, 448
CalculateHours, 72
California
  Employment Training Tax (ETT) in, 288, 295
  quarterly contribution return and report of wages, 300
  State Disability Insurance (SDI) in, 295
  state revenue department information, 518
California Labor Code 226.2, 133
Capital One 360, 23
CAPTCHA programs, 28
CARES Act of 2020. *See* Coronavirus Aid, Relief, and Economic Stimulus (CARES) Act of 2020
Cash, 246–247
Cash award, 187
CCPA. *See* Consumer Credit Protection Act (CCPA)
CCPA disposable income, 245
Cents-per-mile rule, 190, 191
Certification information, 523–526
Certified payroll, 33–34
Certified payroll professional (CPP), 526
CFAA of 1986. *See* Computer Fraud and Abuse Act (CFAA) of 1986
Charitable contributions, 196, 241–242
  net pay with, 196–197
Checks, 247–249
Chipotle Mexican Grill Inc. (CMG), 22
Circular E, 32, 216
Civil Rights Act of 1964, 5
  prohibited discrimination, 5
Civil Rights Act of 1991, 8
Class-action lawsuit, 23
ClockShark, 72
Cloud-based accounting system, 30
Cloud-based computing, 33
CMG. *See* Chipotle Mexican Grill Inc. (CMG)
COBRA. *See* Consolidated Omnibus Budget Reformation Act of 1985 (COBRA)
Code of Ethics
  American Institute of Certified Public Accountants (AICPA), 19, 20
  basic guidelines for, 19
Code section 414(n), 67
Colorado, state revenue department information, 518
Combination pay, 149
Combination pay methods, 149–152
  base salary plus commission, 149–150
  different, 150
  incentive stock options (ISOs), 152
  payroll draw, 150
  salary plus commission and draw, 151
Commission-based compensation, 131
Commission-based employees, 132–133
Commissions, 71, 118
  base salary plus, 149–150
  employee ineligible for, 151
  salary plus, 151
  tracking sheet, 132
  work, gross pay, 131–133
Common-Law Privacy Act, 25
Commuting rule, 190, 191
Company culture, 177
Company framework, employees and, 318
Company policy, 154
Company profitability, labor expenses and, 318–320
Compensation, 178
Compensation laws, 153
Compensation method, 247
Compensatory (comp) time, 153
Computation method, 232
Computer-based accounting systems, 30–31
Computer Fraud and Abuse Act (CFAA) of 1986, 25
Computer glitches, 375
Computerized systems, 75
Confidential business documents, 85
Confidentiality, payroll accountant, 20
Confidential records, 26

Connecticut, state revenue department information, 519
Consolidated Appropriations Act of 2018, 6, 18
Consolidated Omnibus Budget Reformation Act of 1985 (COBRA), 6–7
Consumer credit, 244–245
Consumer Credit Protection Act (CCPA), 197
Consumer Financial Protection Bureau (CFPB), 77
Contemporary payroll practices, 22–26
Contribution-based fund, 13
Copeland Anti-Kickback Act of 1934, 24
Coronavirus Aid, Relief, and Economic Stimulus (CARES) Act of 2020, 18
Cottage industry, 450
Court-mandated deductions, 193
Court-ordered garnishments, 197
COVID-19 pandemic, 3, 7, 119, 130, 142, 184, 239, 281, 283, 291, 320
  ARPA of 2021, 18
  benefit plans, 178, 179
  federal student loan garnishment, 242
  Form 941, 293
  HIPAA, 9
  OSHA, 5–6
  payroll accountants, 361
  payroll system, 25
  SUTA, 14
  underpayment issue, 246
  workers' compensation, 16
CPP. *See* Certified payroll professional (CPP)
Credit
  in financial accounting, 365
  on T-account, 365
Credit reduction, FUTA and, 285
Cross-training, 78
Cryptocurrency, 251–252
  advantage, 251
  definition, 251
  disadvantage, 251
Current Tax Payment Act (CTPA) of 1943, 15, 376
Cyberattacks, 78
Cybersecurity, 77–78

D

Daily payroll, 49
Data adjusting entries, 369, 370
Data privacy, 77
Davis-Bacon Act, 12, 24, 33
Debit
  in financial accounting, 365
  on T-account, 365

Deceased employees, wages for, 448
Deductions. *See also* Post-tax deductions; Pre-tax deductions
  statutory, 280
Defense of Marriage Act (DOMA)
  of 1996, 10
  in 2013, 7
Defined benefit plan, 195
Defined contribution plan, 195
Delaware, state revenue department information, 519
De minimis fringe benefits, 179, 180, 188, 202
Denver, Colorado, head tax (Occupational Privilege Tax [OPT]), 295, 324
Departmental classification, 319
Department of Defense Data Wipe Method, 87
Department of Health and Human Services, 14
Department of Homeland Security, 58
Department of Labor, 279
Department Supervisor, 120
Dependent care assistance programs, 449
Deposit frequencies, 291–292
Depositing rules, 199–200
Diane B. Allen Equal Pay Act, 20
Digital copies, 68
Digitization, of payroll functions, 68
Digitized employee records, 68
Direct deposit, 249–250
Disability, definitions of, 7
Disability plan premiums, 194–195
Disabled worker, 157
  wages, 449
Discrimination
  based on age, 5
  Civil Rights Act of 1964 prohibited, 5
  Diane B. Allen Equal Pay Act, 20
Dismissal pay, 453
Disney, layoff at, 279
Disposable income, 197
District of Columbia, 519
Documentation. *See also* Employee documentation
  internal controls and record retention, 73–84
  laws and types of, 83
  pay records and employee file maintenance, 68–73
  retention requirements, 81–83
  types of, 68
Documentation controls, 75
Document destruction, 85–87
  best practice in, 87
  defined, 85
  procedures, 84–87

Dodd-Frank Act, 10
DoD 5220.22-M, 87
DOMA. *See* Defense of Marriage Act (DOMA)
Domestic service workers, 451
Draw
   definition, 150
   payroll, 150
   salary plus commission and, 151
Due care, 21
Duties, alternating, 78

E

EAD. *See* Employment authorization document (EAD)
EEOC. *See* Equal Employment Opportunity Commission (EEOC)
eFileCabinet, 68
EFTPS. *See* Electronic Federal Tax Payment System (EFTPS)
Eight and Eighty (8 and 80) overtime, 142
EINs. *See* Employer Identification Numbers (EINs)
Electronic accounting records, 87
Electronic Federal Tax Payment System (EFTPS), 290, 293
Electronic Fund Transfer Act of 1978, 77
Electronic records, 79–80, 85
   and remote workers, 88
Ellis v. Google, LLC, 5
Employee(s). *See also entries for specific types of employees*
   advances and overpayments, 245–246
   American Civil Liberties Union (ACLU), 197
   business expense reimbursement, 449
   class, 118
   commission-based, 132–133
   company framework and, 318
   compensated, 236–238
   compensation using payroll register, 147–148
   cross-training, 78
   deceased, wages for, 448
   disabled, 449
   earnings record, 235
   family, 449
   federal income tax, 221, 222
   file maintenance, practices involved in, 79
   Form W-4, 235
   gross pay, 118, 128, 218
   hospital, 451
   hourly rate, 147
   income tax rates, 513
   vs. independent contractors, 51–54, 64
   ineligible for commission, 151
   methods of separation, 84
   net pay. *See* Net pay
   overtime hospitals and residential care facilities, 141–142
   part-time, 295
   pay methods. *See* Pay methods
   payroll, 71
   payroll register for multiple, 148
   pay transparency puts pressure on, 119
   personal information, 88
   piece-rate, 118
   primary classifications, 120
   resident alien, 283, 448
   salaried nonexempt worker, 144
   specific payroll information, 145
   supervisor, 76
   termination, 84–85
   tipped, 310
   with two different pay rates for different functions, 144–145
   wages for deceased, 159
   W-2 year-end tax statement, 194
Employee Benefits Security Administration (Department of Labor), 376
Employee business expense reimbursement, 449
Employee compensation plans, 152
Employee 401(K) contributions, 200
Employee demands, 3
Employee documentation, 51–65. *See also* Documentation
   employee database information, 64
   employees *vs.* independent contractors, 51–54
   foreign workers, 59–63
   hiring packets, 58–59
   new-hire reporting, 59, 60
   statutory employees, 63–64
   U.S. workers in foreign subsidiaries, 63
   withhold additional, 58
Employee earnings records
   defined, 363
   example of, 363
   explanation of, 362–364
   on Form 941, 363
   function of, 362–363
   General Journal and, 365–366
   payroll register and, 362–364
   periodic tax reports and, 363
   summary of, 381
   uses of, 363
   Wayland Custom Woodworking, 412–426
Employee file maintenance, 68–73, 79
Employee Information Form, 48

Employee-paid taxes, 280
Employee pay, 118
Employee pay-related General Journal entries, 368
Employee payroll tax requirements, 290–292
Employee retention credits (ERC), 18
Employee retirement funds, 6
Employee Retirement Income Security Act of 1974 (ERISA), 6, 376
Employee safety programs, 5
Employee Stock Ownership Plan (ESOP), 195
Employee's Withholding Certificate (Form W-4), 18
Employee termination, dismissal pay for, 453
Employee wages, 66
Employer Identification Numbers (EINs), 26, 48
Employer obligation, 15
Employer-paid taxes, 280
Employer payroll-related General Journal entries, 368–369
Employer payroll tax responsibilities
    benefit analysis, as a function of payroll, 320–323
    Disney's layoffs, 279
    federal unemployment taxes and, 282–285
    labor expenses and company profitability, 318–320
    local employer-only payroll taxes and, 288
    mid-year and year-end tax reporting and deposits, 293–315
    overview of, 278, 280
    payroll as business expense and, 315–318
    reporting periods and requirements for tax deposits and, 290–292
    Social Security and Medicare taxes and, 280–282
    state unemployment taxes and, 282, 285–288
    summary of, 324
    trends in, 324
    workers' compensation insurance and, 288–289
Employer-provided snacks and meals, 188–189
Employers
    and employee. *See* Employee(s)
    fiduciary responsibility to remit withholdings from employee pay, 376
    payroll-related General Journal entries and, 368
    remittance, 15
    tax deposits by, 290–292
Employer's Annual Federal Unemployment (FUTA) Tax Return (Form 940), 290, 305–307, 313, 440–444
Employer-sponsored healthcare coverage, reporting, 307
Employer tax reporting and deposits, mid-year and year-end
    explanation of, 293
    Form 940 (Employer's Annual Federal Employment [FUTA] Tax Return, 305–309, 313
    Form 941 (Employer's Quarterly Federal Tax Return), 293, 294, 296–299, 313
    Form 944 (Employer's Annual Federal Tax Return), 295, 302–304
    matching final annual pay to Form W-2, 307, 310–312
    Schedule B, 293, 295, 299
    state tax remittance, 295, 300, 301
    unemployment tax reporting, 295, 305–307
Employment authorization document (EAD), 47
Employment, growing level of, 379
Employment legislation, 4
Employment Standards Administration Wage, 13
Employment tax revenue remittances, 278
Employment termination, 84–87
Employment Training Tax (ETT; California), 288, 295
Enterprise Resource Planning (ERP), 31
Equal Employment Opportunity Commission (EEOC), 5, 24, 49
Equal Pay Act of 1963, 4, 5
ERISA. *See* Employee Retirement Income Security Act of 1974 (ERISA)
ERP. *See* Enterprise Resource Planning (ERP)
Errors, 80
Escheatment, 248
ESOP. *See* Employee Stock Ownership Plan (ESOP)
Ethical principles, 20
Ethics, 19
Ethisphere, 20
E-Verify program, 7, 18, 58
ExakTime, 28
Excluded fringe benefits, 187–189
    employer-provided snacks and meals, 188–189
    gift cards, 188
    gym memberships, 187–188
    personal use of company vehicle, 188
    prizes and awards, 187
Executive exemption, 65
Executive Order 11478, 5
Executive Order 13765, 16
Executive Order 14026, 12
Executive Order 14067, 251
Exempt workers, 15, 65, 118, 120, 127
    leased and temporary employees, 67
    and nonexempt workers, 65–67
    U.S. Department of Labor guidelines for, 120
Expense accounts, 367
Expenses, 369
External payroll management, 32–33

F

Fact Sheet #13, 52
Failure to deposit penalty, 316–317
Failure to file penalty, 316–317

Fair Labor Standards Act (FLSA) of 1938, 4, 14, 48, 71
   exempt employees, 127
   guidelines, 14
   hourly employees, 130
   legal protections under, 15
   methods, 158–159
   minimum wage poster, 50
   minimum wage standards, 133
   modified in 1974, 120
   overtime calculator, 145
   payroll records, 82
   piece-rate workers, 135
   provisions of, 120
   public-sector employees, 153
   regulation, 15
   salaried employees, 118
   salaried nonexempt worker for, 129
   Section 13(a)(1), 127
   Section 14(c), 157
   section 7(j) applies, 141
   Section 13(a)(17) of, 127
   Section 14(a) of, 157
   3(s)(1)(c) of, 153
   U.S. Department of Labor, 129
   wage and hour provisions, 131
Fair market value (FMV), 189
Fair v. Communications Unlimited Inc., 15
Family and Medical Leave Act of 1993 (FMLA), 8
Family employees, 449
Family leave legislation, 8
FATCA. *See* Foreign Account Tax Compliance Act (FATCA)
FCC. *See* Federal Communications Commission (FCC)
FDIC. *See* Federal Deposit Insurance Corporation (FDIC)
Federal Communications Commission (FCC), 250
Federal Deposit Insurance Corporation (FDIC), 250
Federal Employment Compensation Act, 288
Federal income tax, 11, 12, 220–221
   computation, 237–238
   definition, 220
   employer deposits for, 290–292
   percentage method for wages paid in 2020, 404
   special classes of withholding, 448–454
   withholding amounts, 220–233
Federal income tax tables, 455–512
   married persons-biweekly payroll period, 487–489
   married persons-daily payroll period, 505–506
   married persons-monthly payroll period, 499–501
   married persons-semimonthly payroll period, 493–495
   married persons-weekly payroll period, 481–483
   percentage method (2019 or earlier), 477–479
   percentage method (2020 or later), 456–461
   single persons-biweekly payroll period, 490–492
   single persons-daily payroll period, 507–508
   single persons-monthly payroll period, 502–504
   single persons-semimonthly payroll period, 496–498
   single persons-weekly payroll period, 484–486
   wage-bracket method (2019 or earlier), 480–509
   wage-bracket method (2020 or later), 462–476
   withholding on distributions, 509
Federal Insurance Contributions Act (FICA) taxes, 13, 234, 236, 238, 280–281. *See also* Medicare taxes; Social Security tax
Federal laws, 29
Federally mandated payroll laws, 11
Federal minimum wage, 120, 123
   tipped employee minimum wage and, 123
Federal privacy laws, 85
Federal tax withholding, special classes of, 448–454
Federal unemployment tax, 218
Federal Unemployment Tax Act (FUTA), 13
   credit reduction and, 285
   employer responsibility for, 282–285
   examples of, 284
   explanation of, 282
   full 2023 rate, 283
   professions exempt from, 283
   U.S. citizens only, 283
Federal wage, 121
Federal withholding, 179
Fellowship grants, 453
FICA. *See* Federal Insurance Contributions Act (FICA) taxes
Fiduciary responsibility, of employers, 376
Fiedziuszko, Slawomir, 64
File maintenance
   defined, 79
   practices involved in, 79
File security, 76–77
Final rule, 123
Financial accounting concepts
   categories of, 364
   debits and credits, 365
   example, 364, 365
   explanation of, 364–365
   General Journal, 365–366
   General Ledger, 366
Financial business transactions, 364, 365
Financial control, 52
Fixed amount *vs.* percentage deduction, 221
Flexible pay, 217
Flexible spending arrangement (FSA), 183–185
   cafeteria plan-based, 183
   definition, 183

effect on annual gross salary, 184
   vs. health savings account, 185
   pre-tax *vs.* post-tax with, 184
Florida, state revenue department information, 519
FLSA of 1938. *See* Fair Labor Standards Act (FLSA) of 1938
Fluctuating workweek, 71
FMLA. *See* Family and Medical Leave Act of 1993
FMV. *See* Fair market value (FMV)
Foreign Account Tax Compliance Act (FATCA), 63
Foreign governments and international organizations, treatment under employment taxes, 449
Foreign service by U.S. citizens, 449
Foreign subsidiaries, U.S. workers in, 63
Foreign workers, 59–63
Form 673, 63
Form 940 (Employer's Annual Federal Employment [FUTA] Tax Return), 290, 305–309, 440–444
Form 941 (Employer's Quarterly Federal Tax Return), 290, 293–299, 313, 438–441
Form 944 (Employer's Annual Federal Tax Return), 295, 302–304
Form 1095-A (IRS), 16
Form 1095-B (IRS), 16
Form 1095-C (IRS), 16
Form I-9 (Employee Eligibility Verification Form), 7, 54, 56–58
   by Department of Homeland Security, 58
   E-Verify program, 7, 18, 58
   payroll accountant, 58
   Wayland Custom Woodworking, 427–428
Form SS-4, 26, 27
Form SS-8, 15, 51, 53
Form W-2 (wage and tax statement), 26, 31, 58, 181, 200, 446
Form W-3 (Transmittal of Wage and Tax Statements), 58, 313–315, 447
Form W-4 (Employee Withholding Allowance Certificate), 54, 55, 58, 218, 220–222, 231, 430–432
   payroll tax computation using, 222–224
Form WH-347 certified payroll, 33
401(k) retirement plans, 195
   number of participants and dollar contributions in, 376
403(b) retirement plans, 195
414(n) code section, 67
457 retirement plans, 195
FPC. *See* Fundamental Payroll Certification (FPC)
Fraudulent activity, 81, 82
Fringe benefits
   within context of payroll, 178–182
   definition, 176
   de minimis, 188

   excluded from cafeteria plans, 305
   excluded, not subject to FUTA taxes, 305
   exclusion rules, 187–189
   flexible spending arrangement (FSA), 183–185
   hallmarks, 178
   health savings account (HSA), 185–186
   interpret cafeteria plan types, 182–186
   noncash, 202
   in pay, 179
   and payroll taxes, 179–181
   post-tax deductions, 196–198
   premium-only plan (POP), 182–183
   pre-tax deductions, 193–196
   purpose, 178–179
   rules for withholding, depositing, and reporting benefits, 198–201
   summary, 202
   treatment under employment taxes, 450
   types, 181
   valuation rules, 189–192
   voluntary, 181
FSA. *See* Flexible spending arrangement (FSA)
Full-time equivalent (FTE), 16
Full-time student wage, 157–158
Fundamental accounting equation, 364
Fundamental Payroll Certification (FPC), 526
Fund protection, 77
FUTA. *See* Federal Unemployment Tax Act (FUTA)

G

Garnishment rules, 196
Garnishments, 196, 242–243
   court-ordered, 197
GDPR. *See* General Data Protection Regulation (GDPR)
GE. *See* General Electric (GE)
General Accounting Office, 26
General Data Protection Regulation (GDPR), 63
General Electric (GE), 28
General Journal
   accounting conventions in, 366
   completing payroll-related entries in, 367–371
   defined, 365
   employee pay-related entries in, 368
   employer payroll-related entries in, 368
   explanation of, 365–366
   payroll accruals and reversals in, 369–371
   payroll period, sample, 367
   payroll register and, 367
   payroll-related entries in, 368
   transaction in, example, 365
   Wayland Custom Woodworking, 412–426

General Ledger
  example of, 372–373
  explanation of, 366, 371
  payroll entries in, 372–373
  posting example of, 366
  posting practices for, 374
Generally Accepted Accounting Principles (GAAP), 360, 379
General valuation rule (GVR), 189–191
Georgia, state revenue department information, 519
Gift cards, 188
Gig economy, 53, 381
Google Authenticator app, 78
Government employment, treatment under employment taxes, 450
Graziadio v. Culinary Institute of America (2016), 84
Great Depression (1929), 120
Great Depression (1930), 12, 284
Gross pay. *See also* Minimum wage
  calculation of hours and fractions of hours, 136–140
  for commission-based employees, 132–133
  commission work, 131–133
  compensatory time, 153
  definition, 118, 193
  for different pay bases, 127–135
  employee, 128, 218
  full-time student wage, 157–158
  for hourly workers, 130
  for hourly workers in more than one job classification, 130
  jury duty, 155
  and net pay, 118
  nonqualified deferred compensation, 158
  on-call time, 153–154
  payroll register, 145–149
  pension payments, 158
  piece-rate work, 133–135
  retroactive pay, 158–159
  for salaried workers, 127–130
  sleep time, 154–155
  special pay situations, 153–159
  subminimum wage situations, 156
  summary, 160
  travel time, 154–155
  vacation and holiday hours, 155–156
  wait time, 154–155
Group insurance coverage, 183
Gusto, 30
Gym memberships, 187–188

H

Hawaii, state revenue department information, 519
H-1B visas, 47, 59, 63
HDHP. *See* High-deductible health plan (HDHP)
Head tax (Denver), 240, 295, 324
Health and disability insurance, 194–195
Healthcare costs, 184
Health insurance coverage, 16
Health Insurance Portability and Accountability Act of 1996 (HIPAA), 9
Health insurance premium, pre-tax deduction of, 183
Health savings account (HSA), 185–186
Healthy work-life policies, 3–11
High-deductible health plan (HDHP), 185, 186
Highly compensated employees
  Medicare taxes and, 282
  Social Security taxes and, 281
HIPAA. *See* Health Insurance Portability and Accountability Act of 1996 (HIPAA)
Hiring packets, 58–59
Holiday hours, 155–156
Holiday time pay, 137, 320
Homeworkers, 450
Hospital employees, 451
Hosted payroll accounting software, 29
Hourly calculations of pay, 137
Hourly employees. *See also* Tipped employees
  calculating pay for, 136–140
  defined, 118
  hourly pay with different rates, 131
  in more than one job classification, 130
  overtime pay and, 140
  pay with different rates, 131
  salary translation to hourly rates, 128–129
Hourly nonexempt employees, 66
Hourly rate
  computations, 128
  salary translation to, 128–129
Hourly workers, 130
  in more than one job classification, 130
Household employees, 120, 451
HSA. *See* Health savings account (HSA)
Human resources information system, 68, 178
Hundred, 318
Hundredth-hour system, 138–139

I

IC. *See* Independent contractor (IC)
Idaho, state revenue department information, 519

IFAC. *See* International Federation of Accountants (IFAC)
I-9 Form. *See* Form I-9 (Employee Eligibility Verification Form)
Illinois, state revenue department information, 519
IMA. *See* Institute of Management Accountants (IMA)
Immigrant labor, 47
Immigration Reform and Control Act of 1986 (IRCA), 7, 59
Incentive stock options (ISOs), 152
   executive salary with, 152
Income statement, 377
Income Tax Regulation §31.3301-1, 283
Independence, 21
Independent contractor (IC), 15, 52
   employees *vs.*, 51–54, 64
   payment records for, 52
Independent Contractor Status, 53
Indiana, state revenue department information, 519
Individual membership, 189
Individual Retirement Account (IRA), 195
Industrial Revolution, 11
Industrial workers, 450
In-house employees, 120
Institute of Management Accountants (IMA), 19, 361
Insurance, 193
   for employees, treatment under employment taxes, 449
   federal income, 221
   health and disability, 194–195
   types of, 183
Insurance agents or solicitors, 451
Integrated software packages, 22
Integrity, 20
Interest loans with below-market interest rates, 451
Internal controls, 73–84
   alternating duties and, 78
   authorized signers, 74
   critical issue for, 74
   cross-training and, 78
   cybersecurity and payroll, 77–78
   definition, 73
   documentation controls and, 75
   document retention requirements, 81–83
   electronic records and, 79–80
   employee file maintenance, 79
   file security, 76–77
   leave of absence, 76
   overtime approval and, 75–76
   overview, 73–75
   payroll as a non-solo effort, 80–81
   review of time collected and, 75
   unpaid time off, 76
Internal errors, 4
Internal Revenue Code, 182
Internal Revenue Service (IRS), 4, 6, 10, 18, 26
   on classification as American company, 283
   code section 414(n), 67
   common-law tests, 52
   employer payroll tax deposit schedule, 290–292
   Form 843, 314
   Form SS-8, 51, 53
   Form W-4, 54
   income tax withholding assistant, 224–225
   on payroll deposit frequencies, 291
   Procedure 98-25, 1998-1 CB 689, 77, 79
   Publication 15 (Circular E), 216
   Publication 502, 183
   Publication 535, 187
   Publication 1494, 196
   Publication 1779, 53
   Publication 15-B, 179, 181, 195
   Publication 15-T, 227
   Section 409(a), 158
   Section 125 of, 182
   §6672, 317
   special accounting rule, 199
   statutory employees, 63
   26 CFR 1.6001, 79, 81, 82
   waiving of penalties for failure to deposit and file, 316
International Federation of Accountants (IFAC), 19
Internet, 26
Internet-based accounting software, 31
Internet-based systems, 31–32
Internet-connected devices, 22
Interpret cafeteria plan types, 182–186
Intuit Payroll, 30
Investigative information, 87
Iowa, state revenue department information, 519
IRA. *See* Individual Retirement Account (IRA)
IRCA. *See* Immigration Reform and Control Act of 1986 (IRCA)
Iron Mountain, 85
IRS. *See* Internal Revenue Service (IRS)
IRS Code 6056, 194
IRS Fact Sheet 23, 72
IRS Foreign Earned Income Exclusion, 63
IRS Form 4070
   for tipped employees, 123
ISOs. *See* Incentive stock options (ISOs)
iTookOff, 72

J

Jessie Chavez v. PVH Corporation (2013), 77
Job leveling, 127
Jury duty, 155

K

Kansas, state revenue department information, 519
Kentucky, state revenue department information, 519
Knowledge-based employment, 153
Kronos company payroll processing, 33

L

Labor costs, layoffs at Disney, 279
Labor distribution, 319–320
Labor distribution report, 319–320
Labor expenses, company profits and, 318–320
Labor reports, 379
Labor trends, 379
Labor usage report, 379
Leased employees, 67
Lease-value rule, 190
Leave-sharing plans, 451
Ledbetter, Lilly, 5
Legal framework, 11
    governmental contracts and, 12
    minimum wage and, 12
    to payroll accounting, 11–18
    social welfare system, 12
    timeline of, 12
Liabilities
    in financial accounting, 364
    payroll-related, 376
Liability accounts, 368
Lilly Ledbetter Fair Pay Act of 2009, 4, 5, 82
Limited liability companies (LLCs), 186
Living wage, 14
Local employer-only payroll taxes, 288
Local income taxes, 240–241
Long-term disability insurance, 194
Lookback period, 290–291
Louisiana, state revenue department information, 520
Lump-sum distributions, 245

M

Maine
    employer-paid Competitive Skills Scholarship Program tax, 288
    state revenue department information, 520
Maintenance, 88
    of employee files, 79
Mandated deductions, 196, 216
Mandatory deductions, 181, 220
Manual payroll accountants, 32
Manual payroll systems, 29, 32, 233
Manual systems, federal income tax in, 221
Marginal tax rate, 513
Marketplace, 7
Maryland, state revenue department information, 520
Massachusetts, state revenue department information, 520
Material contribution, 52
McDonald's Corporation, 25
McElrath v. Uber Technologies, 152
Meat-packing plants, 15
Medical expenses, 183
Medicare, 13
Medicare and Medicaid Act of 1965, 13
Medicare taxes, 235–236
    employee and employer responsibilities, 280–282
    special classes of federal tax withholding and, 448–454
Michigan, state revenue department information, 520
Microsoft, 3, 28
Microsoft Dynamics 365 GP, 30, 31
Mid-year employer tax reporting and deposits, 293–315
"Mini-COBRA" plans, 7
Minimum wage, 14, 118, 120–123
    definition, 120
    Fair Labor Standards Act, 129
    federal, 120, 123
    hourly rates by state, 122
    inside sales representative, 132
    no state, 122
    outside sales representative, 132
    overtime for, 130
    pay for nonexempt workers, 120–126
    piece-rate pay, 134
    salaried wage compared to, 129–130
    salaried workers compared to, 129–130
    state, 123
    for tipped employees, 121, 123–126
Minimum wage rates, 69
Minnesota, state revenue department information, 520
Mississippi, state revenue department information, 520
Missouri, state revenue department information, 520
Montana, state revenue department information, 520
Monthly payroll, 49
Monthly schedule depositors, 291
Multifactor authentication, 78
Multistate employer registration form, 61–63

MyPayrollHR, 75
myPay Solutions, 23, 29

N

Nebraska, state revenue department information, 520
Net pay, 118
   with charitable contribution, 196–197
   computation, 218–220, 236
   federal income tax withholding amounts, 220–233
   grossed-up pay, 219
   local income taxes, 240–241
   Medicare taxes, 235–236
   percentage method, 227–233
   post-tax deductions, 241–246
   Social Security and Medicare, 233–238
   with state income tax, 239–240
   state-specific taxes, 239–240
   summary, 253
   wage-bracket method, 225–227
Nevada, state revenue department information, 520
New employees, reporting, 54–64
New Hampshire, state revenue department information, 520
New-hire reporting, 48, 59, 60
New Jersey
   Diane B. Allen Equal Pay Act, 20
   state revenue department information, 521
New Mexico, state revenue department information, 521
Newspaper carriers and vendors, 452
New York, state revenue department information, 521
Next business day schedule depositors, 291, 292
Nintendo, 3
Noncash award, 187
Noncash compensation, 187
Noncash fringe benefits, 202
Noncash payments, treatment under employment taxes, 452
Nonexempt employees, 71, 72, 118, 120, 127, 129
   overtime, 140
Nonexempt salaried workers
   minimum wage pay for, 120–126
   salaried, 127
Nonexempt workers, 15, 65
   exempt *vs.*, 65–67
Nonproductive time, 133
Nonprofit organizations, 452
Nonqualified deferred compensation, 158–159
Nonresident aliens, 448
Non-solo effort, payroll as, 80–81
Nontaxable achievement award, 187
Normal business hours, 72

North Carolina, state revenue department information, 521
North Dakota, state revenue department information, 521

O

OASDI. *See* Old-Age, Survivors, and Disability Insurance (OASDI)
Obergefell v. Hodges (2015), 10
Objectivity, 21
Occupational Privilege Tax (OPT; head tax; Denver), 240, 295, 324
Occupational Safety and Health Act of 1970 (OSHA), 5, 289
Office of Child Support Enforcement (OSCE), 9
Office of Management and Budget (OMB), 59
Off-site gym membership, 188
Ohio, state revenue department information, 521
Oklahoma
   state revenue department information, 521
   tipped employees in, 126
Old-Age, Survivors, and Disability Insurance (OASDI), 13, 234
OMB. *See* Office of Management and Budget (OMB)
On-call time, 153–154
Online accounting software, 23
Online banks, 23
OnPay, 30
OPT. *See* Occupational Privilege Tax (OPT)
Oregon, state revenue department information, 521
OSCE. *See* Office of Child Support Enforcement (OSCE)
OSHA. *See* Occupational Safety and Health Act of 1970 (OSHA)
Outsourced payroll systems, 32–33, 316
Outsourced vendor, 30
Outsourcing payroll activities, 29
Overhead allocations, 379
Overpayments, 245–246
Overtime, 118, 130
   nonexempt employee, 140
   wage payment with, 147–148
Overtime Earnings columns, 148
Overtime hours, 137
Overtime pay
   for employees of hospitals and residential care facilities, 141–142
   for employees who work in two or more separate functions, 144–145
   piece-rate employee, 143
   salaried nonexempt worker, 144
   standard, 140–141
   for tipped employees, 142–143

Overtime reports, 379
Owners' equity, in financial accounting, 364

P

Paid time off, 320
Paper-based payroll data, 76
Paper checks, 247, 249
Partners, 452
Part-time employees, 295
PATH Act. *See* Protecting Americans from Tax Hikes (PATH) Act
Pay advice, 179, 180, 249
Pay calculations
    hundredth-hour system for, 138–139
    for piece-rate employees, 134, 135
    quarter-hour system for, 137–138
    of weekly regular time and overtime, 72
Paycards, 31, 77, 250–251
Paychex, 23, 30, 33, 320
Paychex Flex, 28, 76
Pay cycles, 48–51
Pay employment taxes, 178
Pay methods
    cash, 246–247
    checks, 247–249
    cryptocurrency, 251–252
    direct deposit, 249–250
    paycards, 250–251
    summary, 253
Pay periods, 48, 51
    computation, 69
Pay rate, 69–71
Pay records, 68–73
    calculations of weekly regular time and overtime in, 72
    documentation, 68
    entering hours in, 71–72
    pay rate and, 69–71
    technological advances and, 69
Payroll, 77–78
    benefit analysis as function of, 320–323
    as business expense, 315–318
    cybersecurity and, 77–78
    department, 48
    documentation regulations, 48
    economic effects of, 381
    employee, 71
    fraud, 81
    fringe benefits within context of, 178–182
    as non-solo effort, 80–81
    record-keeping and maintenance, 88
    steps to ensure accurate, 74
    time-tracking applications, 72
Payroll accountants, 19, 26, 46, 72, 136, 189
    certification, 523–526
    certified payroll, 33–34
    computer-based systems, 30–31
    confidentiality, 20
    Form I-9 (Employee Eligibility Verification Form), 58
    integrity, 20
    internal tool, 145
    Internet-based systems, 31–32
    large businesses, 28–29
    local income tax, 240
    manual payroll systems, 32
    Medicare tax, 236
    objectivity and independence, 21
    outsourced payroll systems, 32–33
    payroll preparation method, 23
    professional competence and due care, 21
    professionalism, 20
    quarter-hour system for, 137
    small businesses, 29–30
Payroll accounting, 85
    in COVID-19 pandemic, 361
    due care, 21
    ethical guidelines for, 19–21
    by Internal Revenue Code, 80
    legal framework to, 11–18
    reconciliation, 374–375
Payroll apps, 68
Payroll audit, 81, 363
Payroll audit process, 74
Payroll certification information, 523–526
Payroll checks, 81
Payroll cycles, 50
Payroll data, 76
Payroll disbursement, 77
Payroll documentation regulations, 48
Payroll draw, 150
Payroll effects, on the accounting system, 375–376
Payroll entries, in accounting reports, 377–380
Payroll errors, 4, 24
Payroll fraud, 21
Payroll functions, digitization of, 68
Payroll information
    confidentiality, 73
Payroll outsourcing companies, 145
Payroll practices. *See also* Payroll accounting; Payroll processing
    healthy work-life policies, 3–11

identify contemporary, 22–26
integrated software packages, 22
in large businesses, 28–29
modern tools, 22
preparation options and, 23–25
privacy protection and, 25–26
in small businesses, 29–30
and system fundamentals, 35
Payroll preparation methods, 23–25
Payroll procedures, 46
    document destruction procedures, 84–87
    employee documentation and, 51–65
    employee file maintenance, 68–73
    employment termination, 84–87
    establishment, 88
    exempt and nonexempt workers, 65–67
    internal controls and record retention for, 73–84
    and pay cycles, 48–51
    pay periods, 51
    pay records, 68–73
    payroll cycles, 50
    reporting new employees, 54–64
    summary, 88
Payroll process flowchart, 380
Payroll processing
    certified payroll, 33–34
    computer-based systems, 30–31
    for different businesses, 28–35
    Internet-based systems, 31–32
    large businesses, 28–29
    manual payroll systems, 32
    outsourced payroll systems, 32–33
    small businesses, 29–30
    trend in, 31
Payroll professionals, cross-training of, 78
Payroll records, 76
    audit, 83
    maintenance, 79
Payroll record security, 77
Payroll register, 82, 145–149
    with annotations, 146
    data, 145–147
    data for, 284
    employee earnings records and, 362–364
    explanation of, 362–364
    function of, 377
    to General Journal entries, 367
    method to complete, 367–371
    for multiple employees, 148
    purpose, 146
    summary of, 381
    track employee compensation using, 147–148
Payroll-related business expenses, 375–376
Payroll-related liabilities, 376
Payroll review process, 74
Payroll specialist, 21
Payroll systems, 2, 68
    basic elements of, 28
    computerized, 30
    employers', 4
    internal controls and record retention for, 73–84
    manual, 29, 32
    outsourced, 32–33
    responsibilities within, 24
    security, 26
Payroll taxes, 179–181
    computation using Form W-4, 222–224
    public transportation, 239
Payroll tax reports, 322
Pay transparency laws, 18
PCAOB. *See* Public Company Accounting Oversight Board (PCAOB)
Penalties for failure to deposit and failure to file, 316–317
Pennsylvania, state revenue department information, 521
Pension payments, 158
Pension plans, 453
PEOs. *See* Professional Employer Organizations (PEOs)
Percentage method, 227–233
    for manual payrolls with Forms W-4, 404
    manual payroll system, 456–461
    vs. wage-bracket method, 232–233
Periodic tax reports, 363
Period totals, 363
Personal protective equipment, 5
Personal Responsibility and Work Opportunity Reconciliation Act of 1996 (PRWOR), 9
Personal Responsibility, Work and Family Promotion Act of 2002, 9
Personal service, 245
Piece rate, 71
Piece rate compensation, 71
Piece-rate employees, 118, 135
    overtime, 143
Piece-rate workers, 133–135
    overtime rates for, 135
Pizza Fridays, 189
Point-of-sale (POS) purchases, 250
POP. *See* Premium-only plan (POP)
Post-closing trial balance, 377, 378
Posting practices, for General Ledger, 371, 374

Post-tax deductions, 196–198, 216, 241–246
    charitable contributions, 241–242
    consumer credit, 244–245
    definition, 193
    employee advances and overpayments, 245–246
    garnishments, 242–243
    pre-tax deductions *vs.* See Pre-tax deductions
    supplemental health and disability insurance, 194–195
    union dues, 245
Preferred destruction methods, 85
Premium-only plan (POP), 182–183
Pre-tax deductions, 193–196, 216, 221, 234, 236
    federal income, 221–225
    post-tax deductions *vs.* See Post-tax deductions
    provisions, 183
    Social Security and Medicare taxes with, 236
    tax effect, 236
Pre-tax medical premium, 193–194
Pre-tax *vs.* post-tax, with FSA, 184
Privacy Act 09-40-0006, 25
Privacy Act of 1974, 24, 25
Privacy acts, 25
Privacy protection, 25–26
Private personnel information, 87
Private sector employees, 153
Privilege taxes, 295, 301, 324
Prizes, 187
Professional competence, 21
Professional Employer Organizations (PEOs), 67
Professional ethics, 19
Professional exemption, 65–66
Professionalism, 20
ProShred, 85
Protecting Americans from Tax Hikes (PATH) Act, 11
Prove, 147
PRWOR. *See* Personal Responsibility and Work Opportunity Reconciliation Act of 1996 (PRWOR)
Publication 15, 32, 216, 220
Publication 502, 183
Publication 1779, 53
Publication 15-B, 179, 181, 187, 189, 190, 195
Publication 15-T, 32, 455
Public Company Accounting Oversight Board (PCAOB), 21
Public-sector employees, 153
    compensatory time, 153
Public transportation payroll tax, 239

Q

Qualified insurance benefits, 182
Qualified plan, 187
Qualified wages, 18

Quarter-hour system, 137–138
Quarterly schedule depositors, 291
QuickBooks, 22, 23, 30, 31, 247, 250
Qui tam rewards, 10

R

Railroad Retirement Act, 452
Record-keeping, 88
Record retention, 73–84
Refugees, 47
Regular Earnings column, 147
Regular hours, 137
Regulation E, 77, 250
Regulation Z, 77
Relationship of the parties, 52
Religious exemptions, 452
Remits, 369
Reporting new employees, 54–64
Reporting periods, employer, 290–292
Resident aliens, 283, 448
Resignation, 84
Resilient payroll system design, 35
Respect for Marriage Act in 2022, 5, 7, 10
Retention period, 82
Retirement plans, 195–196
    employee contribution, 196
    employer contributions to, 305
    treatment under employment taxes, 453
Retroactive pay, 158–159
Reversal, of General Journal entries, 370–371
Review process, 74
Rhode Island, state revenue department information, 521
Right-to-work laws, 11
Rounding, 404
Rule, 147

S

Sage 100, 22, 23, 30, 31, 247
Salaried employees, 118, 151
Salaried exempt employee, 118, 148, 149
Salaried nonexempt employee, 118, 127, 129–130, 133
Salaried nonexempt overtime, 144
Salaried workers
    gross pay for, 127–130
    hourly wage computation, 137
    and minimum wage comparisons, 129–130
    salary translation to hourly rates, 128
    unpaid leave, 129
Salary
    definition of, 118
    to hourly rate computations, 128

payment, 148
   translation to hourly rates, 128–129
Salespersons, 452, 453
Same-sex spouses, 7
Sarbanes-Oxley Act of 2002 (SOX), 10, 19, 24, 78
Savings Incentive Match Plan for Employees (SIMPLE), 195
Schedule B, for Form 941, 293, 295, 299
Schedule deposit frequencies, 291–292
Scholars, 454
Scholarships, 453
S corporation, 451
SEC regulations. *See* Securities and Exchanges Commission (SEC) regulations
Section 14(a), 157
Section 125 plans, 182, 183, 448
Section 409(a), 158
SECURE Act. *See* Setting Every Community Up for Retirement Enhancement (SECURE) Act
SECURE 2.0 Act, 6
Secure sockets layer (SSL) encryption, 28
Securities and Exchanges Commission (SEC) regulations, 14
Semimonthly payroll, 49
Semiweekly schedule depositors, 291, 292
SEP. *See* Simplified Employee Pension (SEP)
Separation of duties, 81
SEP plans, 195
Setting Every Community Up for Retirement Enhancement (SECURE) Act, 6
7(j) section applies, 141
Severance pay, 453
Shareholders, 452
Shavertown, Pennsylvania, 352
Sick pay, 454
Sick time, 85, 137
SIMPLE. *See* Savings Incentive Match Plan for Employees (SIMPLE)
SIMPLE plans, 195
SIMPLE 401(k) plans, 195
Simplified Employee Pension (SEP), 195, 453
Sixteenth Amendment to the U.S. Constitution, 11
Sleep time, 154–155
Small and medium-sized employers, 119
Small businesses, 29–30
Social and financial distress, 13
Social obligations, 21
Social Security Act (SSA), 13, 233
Social Security and Medicare, 233–238
   taxes with pre-tax deductions, 236
Social Security and Medicare taxes, 195

Social Security fund, 13
Social Security Number, 26
Social Security tax, 13, 234–235
   deposit schedules for, 291–292
   employee and employer responsibilities, 280–282
   highly compensated employees and, 282
   special classes of federal tax withholding and, 448–454
Social Security wage base, 18
Social welfare legislation, 13
"Soft" benefits, 177
Software
   for accounting, 360, 366
   artificial intelligence (AI), 366
   increase in use of, 366
Sophisticated payroll systems, 25
South Carolina, state revenue department information, 521
South Dakota, state revenue department information, 521
SOX. *See* Sarbanes-Oxley Act of 2002 (SOX)
Special accounting rule, 199
Spreadsheet program, 145
Square Payroll, 68
SSA. *See* Social Security Act (SSA)
SSL encryption. *See* Secure sockets layer (SSL) encryption
Stakeholders, 379
State-based minimum wage, 140
State Disability Insurance (SDI; California), 295
State income taxes, 218
State income tax information, 513–517
State income tax, net pay with, 239–240
State laws, 179
State payday requirements, 70
State revenue department or labor information, 518–522
State-specific taxes, 239–240
State's privacy law, 25
States' termination and resignation pay guidelines, 86
State tax remittance, 295, 300, 301
State Unemployment Tax Act (SUTA), 13, 14
   examples of, 287
   explanation of, 282, 285, 287
   purpose of, 282
   requirements of, 284
   state variations in, 282, 285–287
   tips to minimize taxes, 287–288
   wage base and rates of (2023), 285–286
   wage base of, 284–285
Statutory deductions, 280
Statutory employees, 63–64
Straight-time compensation, 127
Strategic planning, 73
Students, treatment under employment taxes, 454

Subminimum wage situations, 156
Supplemental health and disability insurance, 194–195
Supplemental health insurance deduction, 195
Supplemental Unemployment Compensation Plan Benefits, 454
SurePayroll, 30
SUTA. *See* State Unemployment Tax Act (SUTA)

T

T-accounts, 365
Taxable benefit withholdings, 199
Tax bracket, 513
Tax credit, 18
Tax Cuts and Jobs Act (TCJA), 8–9, 18, 67, 218
Tax deposits, employer
   deposit frequencies, 291–292
   lookback period, 290–291
Taxes, 216
   employee-and employer-paid, 280
Taxes and other deductions remittance, 315–316
Tax guide (Publication 15-T), 18
Taxpayer Certainty and Disaster Tax Relief Act (TCDRA) of 2020, 18, 184
Tax penalties, 316–317
Tax remittance, 83, 295
Tax reports, periodic, 363
Taylor, Frederick, 133
TCDRA of 2020. *See* Taxpayer Certainty and Disaster Tax Relief Act (TCDRA) of 2020
Teachers, 454
Technology
   artificial intelligence (AI), 366
   changes due to, 381
   documentation, 87
   for tracking employee attendance and calculating pay, 72
   vulnerability of company data caused by, 74
Temporary employees, 67
Tennessee, state revenue department information, 521
Termination, 82, 84
Texas, state revenue department information, 522
3(s)(1)(c), 153
Time-and-a-half, 75
Time cards, 129
Time-collection systems, 28, 75
TimeDock, 72
Timekeeping system, 140
Time off, 320
TimeStation, 72
Time theft, 138

Tip credit, 123, 124
Tipped employees, 121, 123–126
   Form W-2 for, 310
   IRS Form 4070 for, 123
   minimum hourly wages for, 124–125
   minimum wage, 123
   in Oklahoma, 126
   overtime pay for, 142–143
   Rhode Island, 126
Tipped wages, 123
Tips, 454
Title III, 197
Total, 147
Total compensation report, 200, 321–323
Tracking, of employee payroll expenses, 318
Trainees, 454
Transaction analysis, using T-accounts, 365
Transparency, 379
Travel time, 154–155
Trend reports, 379
Trial balance, 377–379
TriNet, 68
12 CFR Part 205, 250
26 IRC Section 3306, 305
29 CFR 525.12(h)(2)(ii), 135
29 CFR 785, 155
29 CFR 790.6, 155
29 CFR 778.111, 143
29 CFR 778.113(a), 129
29 CFR 778.114, 127
29 CFR 2510, 376
26 CFR 1.6001, 79, 81, 82

U

UKG, 28
Ultimate Kronos Group, 78
Unemployment tax reporting, 295, 305–307
Uniformed Services Employment and Reemployment Rights Act of 1994 (USERRA), 9
Union dues, 196, 197, 245
United Furniture Industries Inc., 85
United States
   ethical and legal conflicts in, 20
   workers in foreign subsidiaries, 63
Unpaid leave, 129
U.S. Bank, 23
U.S. Bureau of Labor Statistics
   accounting jobs, 4
U.S. Central Bank Digital Currency, 251
U.S. Citizenship and Immigration Services, 59
U.S. Department of Labor, 12, 52, 58, 144

Employee Benefits Security Administration, 376
for exempt employees, 120
Fair Labor Standards Act (FLSA), 129
USERRA. *See* Uniformed Services Employment and Reemployment Rights Act of 1994 (USERRA)
U.S. v. Windsor, 10
Utah, state revenue department information, 522

V

Vacation, 85
   and holiday hours, 155–156
Valuation rules, 189–192
   general valuation rule, 189–191
   other transportation benefits, 192
   unsafe conditions, 191–192
Vanderbilt University, 320
Vermont, state revenue department information, 522
Virginia, state revenue department information, 522
Virtual private network (VPN), 28
Vocational education program, 157–158
Voluntary deductions, 193, 216, 406, 408
   pre-tax *vs.* post-tax deductions, 193–198
   summary, 202
Voluntary fringe benefits, 181
Voluntary post-tax deduction, 196
VPN. *See* Virtual private network (VPN)

W

Wage and Hour Division, 53
Wage base, 234, 235
Wage-bracket method, 225–227, 232
   percentage method *vs.,* 232–233
Wage payment, 147–148
Wages
   in cash, 246–247
   for deceased employees, 159
Wait time, 154–155
Walsh-Healey Public Contracts Act, 12–13
Walt Disney Corporation, 279
Warehouse Manager, 120
Washington, state revenue department information, 522
Wave, 31
Wayland Custom Woodworking (continuing payroll project)
   forms used for, 427–447
   general information about, 404–412
   General Journal entries, 412–426
Web-based applications, 72
Web-based portals, 28
Web-based services, 76
Weekly payroll, 49
Well-designed payroll system, 2
Wells Fargo, 23
West Virginia, state revenue department information, 522
W-4 Form. *See* Form W-4 (Employee Withholding Allowance Certificate)
WhenIWork, 28
Wilkes-Barre Bookkeeping LLC, 352
Wire transfers, 290
Wisconsin, state revenue department information, 522
Withheld tax, 220
Withholding amounts, federal income tax, 220–233
Withholding rules, 198–199
Work direction, 52
Workers' compensation (workers' comp), 15, 16, 454
   categories of injuries for, 289
   employer requirements for, 288–290
   laws by state, 17
   premium computation for, 289
Work Opportunity Tax Credit, 11
W-2 Wage and Tax Form
   example of, 312
   explanation of, 310, 311
   matching final annual pay to, 307
   retirement plan checkbox decision chart, 311
   Social Security and Medicare wages on, 310
   for tipped employees, 310
Wyoming, state revenue department information, 522

Y

Year-end employer tax reporting and deposits, 293–315

Z

Zeller Law Group, 82
Zenefits, 76